Business Marketing Management: B2B

Business Marketing Management: B2B

11e

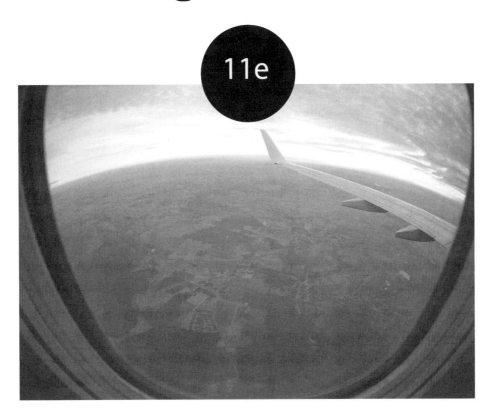

MICHAEL D. HUTT

Arizona State University

•

THOMAS W. SPEH

Miami University

SOUTH-WESTERN
CENGAGE Learning

Australia • Brazil • Japan • Korea • Mexico • Singapore • Spain • United Kingdom • United States

SOUTH-WESTERN
CENGAGE Learning

Business Marketing Management: B2B, Eleventh International Edition
Michael D. Hutt and Thomas W. Speh

Vice President of Editorial, Business: Jack W. Calhoun

Editor-in-Chief: Erin Joyner

Acquisitions Editor: Michael Roche

Developmental Editor: Ted Knight

Editorial Assistant: Megan Fischer

Media Editor: John Rich

Marketing Manager: Gretchen Swann

Marketing Coordinator: Leigh Smith

Senior Marketing Communications Manager: Jim Overly

Art Direction, Production Management, and Composition: PreMediaGlobal

Manufacturing Planner: Ron Montgomery

Rights Acquisitions Specialist, Image: Deanna Ettinger

Rights Acquisitions Specialist, Text: Amber Hosea

Senior Art Director: Stacy Shirley

Cover Designer: Patti Hudepohl

Cover Photo Credits:
  B/W Image: Getty Images/
  Hisham Ibrahim
  Color Image: Shutterstock Images/
  Franz Pfluegl

ExamView® is a registered trademark of eInstruction Corp. Windows is a registered trademark of the Microsoft Corporation used herein under license. Macintosh and Power Macintosh are registered trademarks of Apple Computer, Inc. used herein under license. © 2008 Cengage Learning. All Rights Reserved.

Library of Congress Control Number: 2011944035

International Edition:

ISBN-13: 978-1-133-18957-2

ISBN-10: 1-133-18957-1

Cengage Learning International Offices

Asia
www.cengageasia.com
tel: (65) 6410 1200

Australia/New Zealand
www.cengage.com.au
tel: (61) 3 9685 4111

Brazil
www.cengage.com.br
tel: (55) 11 3665 9900

India
www.cengage.co.in
tel: (91) 11 4364 1111

Latin America
www.cengage.com.mx
tel: (52) 55 1500 6000

UK/Europe/Middle East/Africa
www.cengage.co.uk
tel: (44) 0 1264 332 424

Represented in Canada by Nelson Education, Ltd.
www.nelson.com
tel: (416) 752 9100/(800) 668 0671

Cengage Learning is a leading provider of customized learning solutions with office locations around the globe, including Singapore, the United Kingdom, Australia, Mexico, Brazil, and Japan. Locate your local office at: **www.cengage.com/global**

For product information: **www.cengage.com/international**

Visit your local office: **www.cengage.com/global**

Visit our corporate website: **www.cengage.com**

To Rita and to Sara, and in memory of Michele

PREFACE

Special challenges and opportunities confront the marketer who serves the needs of organizations rather than households. Business-to-business customers represent a lucrative and complex market worthy of separate analysis. A growing number of collegiate schools of business in the United States, Canada, and Europe have added industrial or business marketing to their curricula. In addition, a large and growing network of scholars in the United States and Europe is actively engaged in research to advance theory and practice in the business marketing field. Both the breadth and quality of this research has increased markedly during the past decade.

The rising importance of the field can be demonstrated by several factors. First, because more than half of all business school graduates enter firms that compete in business markets, a comprehensive treatment of business marketing management appears to be particularly appropriate. The business marketing course provides an ideal platform to deepen a student's knowledge of the competitive realities of the global marketplace, customer relationship management, cross-functional decision-making processes, supply chain management, e-commerce, and related areas. Such core content areas strike a responsive chord with corporate recruiters and squarely address key educational priorities established by the American Assembly of Collegiate Schools of Business (AACSB).

Second, the business marketing course provides a perfect vehicle for examining the special features of high-technology markets and for isolating the unique challenges that confront the marketing strategist in this arena. High-tech markets represent a rapidly growing and dynamic sector of the world economy and a fiercely competitive global battleground but often receive only modest attention in the traditional marketing curriculum. Electronic (e) commerce also falls squarely into the domain of the business market. In fact, the opportunity for e-commerce in the business-to-business market is estimated to be several times larger than the opportunity that exists in the business-to-consumer market.

Third, the Institute for the Study of Business Markets (ISBM) at Pennsylvania State University has provided an important impetus to research in the area. ISBM has become a major information resource for researchers and practitioners and has assumed an active role in stimulating and supporting research on substantive business marketing issues. In turn, the number of research studies centered on the business-to-business domain has significantly expanded in recent years, and specialized journals in the area attract a steady stream of submissions. The hard work, multiyear commitments, and leadership of the editors of these journals are worthy of note: *Journal of Business-to-Business Marketing*, J. David Lichtenthal, Baruch College; *Journal of Business and Industrial Marketing*, Wesley J. Johnston, Georgia State University; and *Industrial Marketing Management*, Peter LaPlaca, University of Connecticut.

Three objectives guided the development of this edition:

1. To highlight the similarities between consumer-goods and business-to-business marketing and to explore in depth the points of departure. Particular attention is given to market analysis, organizational buying behavior, customer relationship management, supply chain management,

and the ensuing adjustments required in the marketing strategy elements used to reach organizational customers.

2. To present a managerial rather than a descriptive treatment of business marketing. Whereas some descriptive material is required to convey the dynamic nature of the business marketing environment, the relevance of the material is linked to marketing strategy decision making.

3. To integrate the growing body of literature into a strategic treatment of business marketing. In this text, relevant work is drawn from organizational buying behavior, procurement, organizational behavior, supply chain management, strategic management, and the behavioral sciences, as well as from specialized studies of business marketing strategy components.

The book is structured to provide a complete and timely treatment of business marketing while minimizing the degree of overlap with other courses in the marketing curriculum. A basic marketing principles course (or relevant managerial experience) provides the needed background for this text.

New to This Edition

Although the basic objectives, approach, and style of earlier editions have been maintained, several changes and additions have been made that reflect both the growing body of literature and the emerging trends in business marketing practice. Specifically, the following themes and distinctive features are incorporated into the eleventh edition:

- **Customer Relationship Strategies**: Expanded treatment of the drivers of relationship marketing effectiveness and the financial impact of marketing investments.

- **Sustainability**: A timely and richly illustrated discussion of the distinctive competitive advantages that can be secured by a focus on environmental priorities.

- **Global Marketing Strategies**: A fresh approach for developing strategies for a two-speed economy—low-growth developed markets and high-growth emerging economies.

- **Social Media**: A timely treatment of how the evolving social media landscape is impacting business-to-business communications.

- **Characteristics of High-Performing Salespeople**: A fresh treatment of the characteristics and processes that set top-performing salespersons apart from their peers, particularly in high-opportunity customer engagements.

- **Other New Topics of Interest**: The new edition includes expanded treatment of building strong B2B brands, sales force deployment, and marketing performance metrics.

- **Streamlined Coverage**: Content from two chapters—Business Market Sectors and E-Commerce—has been streamlined and integrated into the discussion to provide a more engaging and actionable treatment in 15 compact chapters.

Organization of the Eleventh Edition

The needs and interests of the reader provided the focus in the development of this volume. The authors' goal is to present a clear, timely, and engaging examination of business marketing management. To this end, each chapter provides an overview, highlights key concepts, and includes several carefully chosen examples of contemporary business marketing practice, as well as a cogent summary and a set of provocative discussion questions. Contemporary business marketing strategies and challenges are illustrated with three types of vignettes: "B2B Top Performers," "Inside Business Marketing," and "Ethical Business Marketing."

The book is divided into five parts with a total of 15 chapters. Part I introduces the distinguishing features of the business marketing environment. Careful examination is given to each of the major types of customers, the nature of the procurement function, and key trends that are reshaping buyer–seller relationships. Relationship management establishes the theme of Part II, in which chapter-length attention is given to organizational buying behavior and customer relationship management. By thoroughly updating and illustrating the core content, this section provides a timely and comprehensive treatment of customer profitability analysis and relationship management strategies for business markets. After this important background is established, Part III centers on the techniques that can be applied in assessing market opportunities: market segmentation and demand analysis, including sales forecasting.

Part IV centers on the planning process and on designing marketing strategy for business markets. Recent work drawn from the strategic management and strategic marketing areas provides the foundation for this section. This edition provides an expanded and integrated treatment of marketing strategy development using the balanced scorecard, enriched by strategy mapping. Special emphasis is given to defining characteristics of successful business-to-business firms and to the interfacing of marketing with other key functional areas such as manufacturing, research and development, and customer service. This functionally integrated planning perspective serves as a focal point in the analysis of the strategy development process. Here at the core of the volume, a separate chapter provides an integrated treatment of strategy formulation for the global market arena, giving particular attention to the new forms of competitive advantage that rapidly developing economies present (for example, China).

Next, each component of the marketing mix is examined from a business marketing perspective. The product chapter gives special attention to the brand-building process, to sustainability, and to the strategic importance of providing competitively superior value to customers. Adding further depth to this core section are the chapters on managing product innovation and managing services for business markets. In turn, special attention is given to supply chain strategies for business markets. Building on the treatment of customer relationship marketing provided in Part II, the personal selling chapter explores methods for organizing the sales force and serving key accounts, the skills and characteristics of high-performing salespersons, and managerial tools to support sales force deployment decisions.

Marketing performance measurement provides the central focus for Part V. It provides a compact treatment of marketing control systems and uses the balanced scorecard as an organizing framework for marketing profitability analysis. Special attention is given to identifying the drivers of marketing strategy performance and to the critical area of strategy implementation in the business marketing firm.

Chapter Cases

A short case, isolating core concepts, is included for each chapter. Two-thirds of the chapter cases are new to this edition and uncover opportunities and challenges confronting firms such as Sealed Air, IBM, Intuit, International Flavors and Fragrances, Danaher, and GE. These cases provide a valuable tool for sparking class discussion and bringing strategy issues to life. The Chapter Cases can be found at the end of your textbook. Based on requests from adopters, we also include a comprehensive list of cases available through the Harvard Business School, the Richard Ivey School of Business at The University of Western Ontario, INSEAD, and other outlets that might be selected for use in the course. The case candidates are keyed to the chapters, allowing instructors to tailor the course to their teaching style and their course objectives.

Instructor's Manual   The Instructor's Manual for the eleventh edition of *Business Marketing Management: B2B* provides a variety of creative suggestions designed to help the instructor incorporate all the materials available to create a dynamic learning environment. A few of the key features available in the Instructor's Manual for this edition include:

- Course design suggestions
- Chapter overviews and supporting materials
- Suggested readings listed by chapter
- Analysis suggestions for chapter cases

Engagement Exercises

An important new addition to the Instructor's Manual for this edition is a set of carefully-designed engagement exercises for each chapter that promote collaborative learning and student comprehension of key concepts. Based on the teaching style of the instructor, these engagement exercises can be employed to achieve the desired balance of lecture-based class time versus collaborative learning. The exercises contain caselets, activities, Internet exercises, readings, and discussion points relevant to each chapter. Each engagement exercise provides options or in-class strategies that instructors can use to match the activities with their teaching style and preferences. Supported by teaching notes, the exercises center on three levels of student engagement: conceptual, critical thinking, and intellectual innovation. We are indebted to Debbie M. Coleman, Miami University, for developing the engagement exercises and for class-testing many of them in her Business Marketing class.

The Instructor's Manual files are available for download at this text's companion site, which can be reached through www.cengagebrain.com. The revised and updated Test Bank includes over 1500 multiple-choice and true/false questions, emphasizing the important concepts presented in each chapter, along with an average of five essay questions per chapter. The Test Bank questions vary in levels of difficulty so that each instructor can tailor the testing to meet specific needs. Each question is tagged to AACSB standards, discipline guidelines, and Rubin/Dierdorff standards. The Test Bank files are available on the companion website.

ExamView (Computerized) Test Bank The Test Bank is also available on the companion web site in computerized format (ExamView), allowing instructors to select problems at random by level of difficulty or type, customize or add test questions, and scramble questions to create up to 99 versions of the same test. This software is available in Mac or Windows formats.

PowerPoint Presentation Slides The PowerPoint presentation slides bring classroom lectures and discussions to life with the Microsoft PowerPoint presentation tool. These presentations are organized by chapter, helping to create an easy-to-follow lecture, and are extremely professor friendly and easy to read. There are two PowerPoint versions for this edition: the GOLD version includes varying slide background and animation; the SILVER version provides simpler design for professors who would like to add their own material. The PowerPoint presentation slides are available on the companion web site. We express our gratitude to Ray DeCormier, Central Connecticut State University, for developing the PowerPoint files and for contributing his expertise to this project.

Web Site

Visit the text's Web companion site www.cengagebrain.com to find instructor's support materials as well as study resources that will help students practice and apply the concepts they have learned in class.

Videos

A new video package has been prepared to provide a relevant and interesting visual teaching tool for the classroom. Each video segment applies text materials to the real world, demonstrating how everyday companies effectively deal with business marketing management issues.

Student Resources

Online quizzes for each chapter are available on the Web site for those students who would like additional study materials. After each quiz is submitted, automatic feedback tells the students how they scored and what the correct answers are to the questions they missed. Students are then able to e-mail their results directly to their instructor, if desired.

Acknowledgments

The development of a textbook draws upon the contributions of many individuals. First, we would like to thank our students and former students at Arizona State University, Miami University, the University of Alabama, and the University of

Vermont. They provided important input and feedback when selected concepts or chapters were originally class tested. We would also like to thank our colleagues at each of these institutions for their assistance and support.

Second, we express our gratitude to several distinguished colleagues who carefully reviewed a recent volume and provided incisive comments and valuable suggestions that improved the eleventh edition. They include Blaine Branchik, Quinnipiac University; Brian Brown, University of Massachusetts, Amherst; Abbie Griffin, University of Utah; Peter A. Reday, Youngstown State University; Larry P. Schramm, Oakland University; Judy Wagner, East Carolina University; and Jianfeng Wang, Mansfield University of Pennsylvania.

We would also like to express our continuing appreciation to others who provided important suggestions that helped shape earlier editions: Kenneth Anselmi, East Carolina University; Joseph A. Bellizzi, Arizona State University; Paul D. Boughton, Saint Louis University; Michael R. Czinkota, Georgetown University; S. Altan Erdem, University of Houston–Clear Lake; Troy Festervand, Middle Tennessee State University; Srinath Gopalakrishna, University of Missouri, Columbia; Paris A. Gunther, University of Cincinnati; Jon M. Hawes, University of Akron; Jonathan Hibbard, Boston University; Lee Hibbert, Freed-Hardeman University; George John, University of Minnesota; Joe H. Kim, Rider University; Kenneth M. Lampert, Metropolitan State University, Minnesota; Jay L. Laughlin, Kansas State University; J. David Lichtenthal, Baruch College; Gary L. Lilien, Pennsylvania State University; Lindsay N. Meredith, Simon Fraser University; K. C. Pang, University of Alabama at Birmingham; Richard E. Plank, University of South Florida; Constantine Polytechroniou, University of Cincinnati; Bernard A. Rausch, Illinois Institute of Technology; Paul A. Roobol, Western Michigan University; Beth A. Walker, Arizona State University; Elizabeth Wilson, Suffolk University; James F. Wolter, Grand Valley State University; Ugut Yucelt, Pennsylvania State University at Harrisburg; and John M. Zerio, American Graduate School of International Management.

We are especially indebted to four members of the Board of Advisors for Arizona State University's Center for Services Leadership. Each served as a senior executive sponsor for a funded research study, provided access to the organizations, and contributed valuable insights to the research. Collectively, these studies sharpened the strategy content of the volume. Included here are Michael Daniels, Senior Vice President, Global Technology Services, IBM Global Services; Greg Reid, Chief Marketing Officer, YRC Worldwide Inc.; Adrian Paull, Vice President, Customer Product Support, Honeywell Aerospace; and Merrill Tutton, President, AT&T UK, Emeritus. We would like to thank Jim Ryan, President and Chief Executive Officer, W. W. Grainger, for his insights and contributions to this edition. We would also like to thank Mohan Kuruvilla, Adjunct Professor, Indian Institute of Management Kozhikode, for his keen insights and recommendations.

The talented staff of South-Western/Cengage Learning displayed a high level of enthusiasm and deserves special praise for their contributions in shaping this edition. In particular, Mike Roche provided valuable advice and keen insights for this edition. We express our gratitude to Diane A. Davis, Arizona State University, for once again lending her superb administrative skills and creative talent to the project and for delivering under pressure.

Finally, but most importantly, our overriding debt is to our wives, Rita and Sara, whose encouragement, understanding, and direct support were vital to the completion of this edition. Their involvement and dedication are deeply appreciated.

Michael D. Hutt
Thomas W. Speh

ABOUT THE AUTHORS

Michael D. Hutt (PhD, Michigan State University) is the Ford Motor Company Distinguished Professor of Marketing at the W. P. Carey School of Business, Arizona State University. He has also held faculty positions at Miami University (Ohio) and the University of Vermont.

Dr. Hutt's teaching and research interests are concentrated in the areas of business-to-business marketing and strategic marketing. His current research centers on the marketing–finance interface, particularly the application of financial portfolio theory to customer management. Dr. Hutt's research has been published in the *Journal of Marketing, Journal of Marketing Research, MIT Sloan Management Review, Journal of Retailing, Journal of the Academy of Marketing Science,* and other scholarly journals. He is also the co-author of *Macro Marketing* (John Wiley & Sons) and contributing author of *Marketing: Best Practices* (South-Western).

Assuming a variety of leadership roles for American Marketing Association programs, Dr. Hutt co-chaired the Faculty Consortium on Strategic Marketing Management. He is a member of the editorial review boards of the *Journal of Business-to-Business Marketing, Journal of Business and Industrial Marketing, Industrial Marketing Management, Journal of the Academy of Marketing Science,* and *Journal of Strategic Marketing.* For his 2000 contribution to *MIT Sloan Management Review,* he received the Richard Beckhard Prize and in 2007, he was named the Outstanding Professor for Doctoral Programs by the W. P. Carey School of Business. Dr. Hutt has consulted on marketing strategy issues for firms such as IBM, Motorola, Honeywell, AT&T, Arvin Industries, ADT, and Black-Clawson, and for the food industry's Public Policy Subcommittee on the Universal Product Code.

Thomas W. Speh, PhD, is Professor of Marketing Emeritus and Associate Director of MBA Programs at the Farmer School of Business, Miami University (Ohio). Dr. Speh earned his PhD from Michigan State University. Prior to his tenure at Miami, Dr. Speh taught at the University of Alabama.

Dr. Speh has been a regular participant in professional marketing and logistics meetings and has published articles in a number of academic and professional journals, including the *Journal of Marketing, Sloan Management Review, Harvard Business Review, Journal of the Academy of Marketing Sciences, Journal of Business Logistics, Journal of Retailing, Journal of Purchasing and Materials Management,* and *Industrial Marketing Management.* He was the recipient of the Beta Gamma Sigma Distinguished Faculty award for excellence in teaching at Miami University's School of Business and of the Miami University Alumni Association's Effective Educator award.

Dr. Speh has been active in both the Warehousing Education and Research Council (WERC) and the Council of Logistics Management (CLM). He has served as president of WERC and as president of the CLM. Dr. Speh has been a consultant on strategy issues to such organizations as Xerox, Procter & Gamble, Burlington Northern Railroad, Sara Lee, J. M. Smucker Co., and Millenium Petrochemicals, Inc.

CONTENTS IN BRIEF

CONTENTS

PART V   EVALUATING BUSINESS MARKETING STRATEGY AND PERFORMANCE   361

Chapter 15   Marketing Performance Measurement   363

Chapter Cases

Business Marketing Management: B2B

PART

I

THE ENVIRONMENT OF BUSINESS MARKETING

A Business Marketing Perspective

The business market poses special challenges and significant opportunities for the marketing manager. This chapter introduces the complex forces that are unique to the business marketing environment. After reading this chapter, you will understand:

1. The dynamic nature of the business marketing environment and the basic similarities and differences between consumer-goods and business marketing

2. The types of customers in this important market

3. The underlying factors that influence the demand for industrial goods

4. The nature of buyer-seller relationships in a product's supply chain

5. The basic characteristics of industrial products and services

Business Marketing

Business marketers serve the largest market of all: The dollar volume of transactions in the industrial or business market significantly exceeds that of the ultimate consumer market. In the business market, a single customer can account for an enormous level of purchasing activity. For example, the corporate procurement department at IBM spends more than $40 billion annually on industrial products and services.[1] Others, such as Procter & Gamble, Apple, Merck, Dell, and Kimberly Clark, each spend more than half of their annual sales revenue on purchased goods and services.[2] Indeed, all formal organizations—large or small, public or private, for-profit or not-for-profit—participate in the exchange of industrial products and services, thus constituting the business market.

Business markets are "markets for products and services, local to international, bought by businesses, government bodies, and institutions (such as hospitals) for incorporation (for example, ingredient materials or components), for consumption (for example, process materials, office supplies, consulting services), for use (for example, installations or equipment), or for resale.... The only markets not of direct interest are those dealing with products or services which are principally directed at personal use or consumption such as packaged grocery products, home appliances, or consumer banking."[3] The factors that distinguish business marketing from consumer marketing are the nature of the customer and how that customer uses the product. In business marketing, the customers are organizations (businesses, governments, and institutions).

Business firms buy industrial goods to form or facilitate the production process or use as components for other goods and services. Government agencies and private institutions buy industrial goods to maintain and deliver services to their own market: the public. Industrial or business marketing (the terms can be used interchangeably) accounts for more than half the economic activity in the United States, Canada, and most other nations. More than 50 percent of all business school graduates join firms that compete directly in the business market. The heightened interest in high-technology markets—and the sheer size of the business market—has spawned an increased emphasis on business marketing management in universities and corporate executive training programs.[4]

This book explores the business market's special opportunities and challenges and identifies the new requirements for managing the marketing function in this vital sector of the global economy. The following questions establish the theme of this first chapter: What are the similarities and differences between consumer-goods

---

[1]Tim Ferguson, "IBM Shifts Procurement HQ to China," ZDNet News: October 13, 2006, accessed at http://www.zdnet.com/news on June 1, 2008.

[2]Chip W. Hardt, Nicolas Reinecke, and Peter Spiller, "Inventing the 21st Century Purchasing Organization," *The McKinsey Quarterly* (4, 2007): pp. 115–117.

[3]Prospectus for the Institute for the Study of Business Markets, College of Business Administration, the Pennsylvania State University and J. David Lichtenthal, Venkatapparao Mummaleni, and David T. Wilson, "The Essence of Business Marketing Theory, Research, and Tactics: Contributions from the Journal of Business-to-Business Marketing," *Journal of Business-to-Business Marketing* 15 (2, 2008): pp. 91–123.

[4]J. David Lichtenthal, "Business-to-Business Marketing in the 21st Century," *Journal of Business-to-Business Marketing* 12 (1, 2, 1998): pp. 1–5; J. Lichtenthal, "Advocating Business Marketing Education: Relevance and Rigor—Uttered as One," *Journal of Business-to-Business Marketing* 14 (1, 2007): pp. 1–12; and Michael D. Hutt and Thomas W. Speh, "Business Marketing Education: A Distinctive Role in the Undergraduate Curriculum," *Journal of Business-to-Business Marketing* 12 (1, 2, 1998): pp. 103–126.

TABLE 1.1 | TYPES OF BUSINESS MARKET CUSTOMERS

Commercial Customers	Institutional Customers	Governmental Customers
Manufacturers	Schools, colleges, universities	Federal government
Construction companies	Health-care organizations	• Non-defense
Service firms	Libraries	• Defense
Transportation companies	Foundations	State government
Selected professional groups	Art galleries	Local government
Wholesalers	Clinics	• Counties
Retailers		• Townships

© Cengage Learning 2013

marketing and business marketing? What customers constitute the business market? How can the multitude of industrial goods be classified into manageable categories? What forces influence the behavior of business market demand?

Business Market Customers

Cisco Systems, Inc., provides the networking solutions that are the foundation of the Internet and of most corporate, education, and government networks on a global scale. Rather than serving individuals or household consumers, Cisco is a leading-edge business-to-business firm that markets its products and services to *organizations*: commercial enterprises (for example, corporations and telecommunications firms), governmental units, and institutions (for example, universities and health-care organizations). Marketing managers at Cisco give special attention to transforming complex technology products and services into concrete solutions to meet customer requirements. For example, when Pep Boys, the leading automotive aftermarket and service chain in the United States wanted to connect its 593 retail store locations across 36 states, Cisco provided the network solution.[5] Likewise, the new, multipurpose Cowboys Stadium in Dallas incorporates advanced video technologies from Cisco to improve the fan experience and maximize the value of the venue. Using Cisco StadiumVision, fans remain engaged anywhere in the stadium with 3000 TV displays featuring customized HD video game footage and real-time, relevant information (for example, breaking news).[6]

Each of the three business market sectors—commercial firms, institutions, and governments—has identifiable and unique characteristics that business marketers must understand if marketers wish to grow their client bases (see Table 1.1). A significant first step in creating successful marketing strategy is to isolate the unique dimensions of each major business market sector. How much market potential does each sector represent? Who makes the purchasing decisions? The answers provide a foundation on which managers can formulate marketing programs that respond to the specific needs and characteristics of each business market sector.

---

[5]Customer Success Story: "Cisco Helps Pep Boys Improve Point-of-Sale Applications, Security Posture, and Future Flexibility," http://www.cisco.com, accessed June 6, 2008, pp. 1–4.

[6]"Cowboys to Deploy Cisco Connected Sports Solutions in State-of-the-Art Venue," June 17, 2009; accessed on May 12, 2011 at http://www.cisco.com, pp. 1–2.

Commercial Enterprises as Customers

Commercial enterprises include manufacturers, construction companies, service firms (for example, hotels), transportation companies, selected professional groups (for example, dentists), and resellers (wholesalers and retailers purchasing equipment and supplies to use in their operations). Manufacturers are the most important commercial customers: The 100 largest ones purchase more than $1 trillion of goods and services annually.[7]

A Concentration of Customers

A startling fact about the study of manufacturers is that so few of them remain. Available evidence suggests that there are approximately 325,000 manufacturing firms in the United States.[8] And although only 30,000 manufacturing firms (fewer than 10 percent) employ more than 100 workers each, this handful of firms ships more than 75 percent of all U.S. manufactured products. Because manufacturing operations are so concentrated in the United States, the business marketer normally serves *far fewer but far larger* customers than does a consumer-products marketer. For example, Intel sells microprocessors to a few large manufacturers, such as Dell and Hewlett-Packard, which, in turn, target millions of potential computer buyers. Clearly, large buyers are generally vitally important to business marketers.

In addition to concentration by size, business markets are also concentrated geographically. More than half of all U.S. manufacturers are located in only eight states: California, New York, Ohio, Illinois, Michigan, Texas, Pennsylvania, and New Jersey. Most large metropolitan areas are lucrative business markets. Geographical concentration of industry, however, means only that a large potential volume exists in a given area; each buyer's requirements may still vary significantly.

Smaller manufacturing firms also constitute an important business market segment. In fact, more than two-thirds of all U.S. manufacturers employ fewer than 20 people.[9] In addition to small manufacturers, more than 5 million small businesses in the United States employ fewer than six people each. Based on sheer numbers, small businesses represent a dominant category of business market customers—but a market that is often difficult to serve.[10] Because the organizational buyer in smaller firms has different needs—and often a very different orientation—astute marketers adjust their marketing programs to this market segment's particular needs. To illustrate, FedEx wanted to increase its share of the small shipper market but recognized that picking up packages at many small businesses is more expensive than picking them up at one larger location.[11] To cost-effectively reach these customers, FedEx encourages small shippers to bring their packages to conveniently located FedEx drop-off points. The strategy has been successful.

---

[7]Anne Millen Porter, "Containing Total Spend," *Purchasing* 132 (November 6, 2008): pp. 18–25.

[8]U.S. Department of Commerce, Bureau of the Census, 2008 County Business Patterns, accessed at www.census.gov, May 12, 2011.

[9]Ibid.

[10]Arun Sharma, R. Krishnan, and Dhruv Grewal, "Value Creation in Business Markets," *Industrial Marketing Management* 30 (June 2001): pp. 391–402.

[11]Thomas H. Davenport, Jeanne G. Harris, and Ajay K. Kohli, "How Do They Know Their Customers So Well?" *MIT Sloan Management Review* 42 (Winter 2001): p. 65.

Government Units as Customers

Federal (1), state (50), and local (89,000) **government** units generate the greatest volume of purchases of any customer category in the United States. Collectively, these units spend more than $2.1 trillion on goods and services each year—the federal government accounts for $875 billion, and states and local government account for the rest.[12] Government units purchase from virtually every category of goods and services—office supplies, notebook computers, food, health care, military equipment. As customers become more adept at shopping online, Internet-savvy customers expect the same level of service from the government when renewing drivers' licenses, purchasing permits, or accessing information from public agencies. For business marketing firms, large and small, that sell information technology products and services, these e-government initiatives are sparking a large market opportunity.

Government Buying   The government uses two general purchasing strategies: formal advertising (also known as open bid) or negotiated contract. With *formal advertising*, the government solicits bids from appropriate suppliers. This strategy is followed when the product is standardized and the specifications are straightforward (for example, 20-pound bond paper or a personal computer with certain defined characteristics). Contracts are generally awarded to the lowest bidder; however, the government agency may select the next-to-lowest bidder if it can document that the lowest bidder would not fulfill the contract responsibly.

In contrast, the government uses a *negotiated contract* to purchase goods and services that cannot be differentiated on the basis of price alone (such as complex scientific equipment of R&D projects) or when there are few potential suppliers. There may be some competition because the contracting office can conduct negotiations with competing suppliers simultaneously. The purchasing decision for the government is much like that for a large corporation. Which is the best possible product at the lowest price, and will the product meet performance expectations?

Institutions as Customers

Institutional customers comprise the third sector of the business market (see Table 1.1). They make up a sizable market—total expenditures on public elementary and secondary schools alone exceed $500 billion, and national health expenditures exceed $2.5 trillion.[13] Schools and health-care organizations make up a sizable component of the institutional market, which also includes colleges and universities, libraries, foundations, art galleries, and clinics. On the one hand, institutional purchasers are similar to governments in that the purchasing process is often constrained by political considerations and dictated by law. In fact, many institutions are administered by government units—schools, for example. On the other hand, other institutions are privately operated and managed like corporations; they may even have a broader range of purchase

---

[12]U.S. Census Bureau, *The 2011 Statistical Abstract of the United States*, accessed at http://www.census.gov on May 12, 2011.

[13]Ibid.

requirements than their large corporate counterparts. Like the commercial enterprise, institutions are adopting sophisticated approaches to purchasing.

Institutional Buying   Many institutions are staffed with professionals, including doctors, professors, and researchers. Depending on its size, the institution may employ a purchasing agent and, in large institutions, a sizable purchasing department. Business marketing and sales personnel, in formulating their marketing and personal selling approaches, must understand the needs of the full range of participants in the buying process. Often, the salesperson must carefully cultivate the professional staff in terms of product benefits, while developing a delivery timetable, maintenance contract, and price schedule to satisfy the purchasing department. Leading business marketers also use the Internet to provide added value to their customers. For example, Cardinal Health, Inc., has embraced the Internet as the centerpiece of its marketing strategy and provides an online catalog, daily Internet specials, and a host of services for its customers—purchasing managers at hospitals and health-care facilities worldwide.

An important factor in institutional buying is group purchasing. Hospitals, schools, and universities may join cooperative purchasing associations to secure purchasing efficiencies. Group buying allows institutions to enjoy lower prices, improved quality (through improved testing and supplier selection), reduced administrative costs, and greater competition. In addition to responding to the needs of individual institutions, the business marketer must be prepared to meet the special requirements of cooperative purchasing groups and large hospital chains.

Business Marketing Management

Many large firms that produce goods such as steel, production equipment, or computer-memory chips cater exclusively to business market customers and never directly interact with their ultimate consumers. Other firms participate in both the consumer-goods and the business markets. The introduction of laser printers and personal computers brought Hewlett-Packard, historically a business-to-business marketer, into the consumer market. Conversely, the strength of Apple's brand extends to the business market where, for example, the iPad enjoyed immediate success and sparked demand for other Apple products, including Mac computers. Over 75 percent of *Fortune* 500 companies were using or testing the iPad just months after it was introduced. J. P. Morgan Chase, Cardinal Health, and Tellabs, Inc., are among the corporate customers using the iPad for product demonstrations, approving shipping orders, and calling up finance options.[14] To serve such corporate customers, some fundamental adjustments in marketing strategy are required.

Products such as smart phones, office furniture, personal computers, and software are purchased in both the consumer and the business markets. What distinguishes business marketing from consumer-goods marketing is the *intended use of the product* and the *intended consumer*. Sometimes the products are identical, but a

---

[14]Ian King, "IBM Earnings, Apple iPad Sales Point to Spending Boom," *Bloomberg News*, January 19, 2011, accessed at http://bloomberg.com on January 22, 2011.

B2B TOP PERFORMERS

Jim Ryan, Chairman, President and Chief Executive Officer, W. W. Grainger, Inc.

W. W. Grainger, Inc. (NYSE: GWW), with sales of $7.3 billion, is the leading broad line supplier of facilities maintenance products serving businesses and institutions throughout North America with an expanding presence in Europe, Asia and Latin America. Through its network of more than 600 branches, 24 distribution centers, an iconic catalog, and multiple Web sites, Grainger helps customers save time and money by providing them with the right products to keep their facilities running.

Jim Ryan was named Chairman in April 2009 and President and Chief Executive Officer in June 2008. He has been President of Grainger since 2006; in February 2007 he was named Chief Operating Officer and appointed to the Board of Directors. Ryan's career at Grainger is testimony to his philosophy that "you prepare to be a leader by deliberately taking on unfamiliar and difficult assignments—those that many shy away from. Challenging assignments are the training ground that provides the highest level of learning, preparing you for leadership at the top levels of large companies." Jim's rise through the ranks of Grainger includes senior assignments in IT, Grainger Parts, Marketing, Sales & Service, and the company's eBusiness. While in IT, Ryan oversaw the implementation of the SAP system and achieved corporate Y2K compliance. Both of these accomplishments reflect Ryan's focus on seeking out challenging undertakings.

Grainger's success is focused on helping its customers reduce the overall acquisition costs for maintenance, repair, and operating (MRO) items. Grainger encourages customers to reduce their inventories of MRO items and rely on Grainger's responsive distribution systems and expertise to

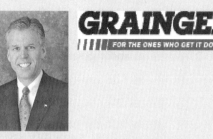

provide these items just when they are needed, decreasing the acquisition costs of these indirect materials. Grainger's philosophy is to be "customer intimate," where a customer's and a supplier's (Grainger) processes are fully integrated so that the customer becomes more efficient. Essentially, Grainger seeks to reduce the customer's total costs of acquiring MRO products.

Ryan believes that students preparing to be future leaders of B2B companies can best prepare for that role by developing four skills during their college education: (1) discipline and a strong work ethic; (2) cultivating "people skills"; (3) building analytical skills; and (4) organizational skills. He advises young people to focus on the strong work ethic early in their careers and to accept tough jobs other managers are not interested in tackling. Echoing his own tactics, Ryan advises students that "you learn the critical management skills when you take on those assignments that are unfamiliar and complicated." His accomplishments as a leader of a successful company are testimony to the wisdom of his approach.

SOURCE: Reprinted by permission of Grainger.

fundamentally different marketing approach is needed to reach the organizational buyer. Interestingly, some of the most valuable brands in the world belong to business marketers: Cisco, Google, BlackBerry, Caterpillar, IBM, FedEx, GE, DuPont, Intel, Hewlett-Packard, and 3M.[15]

---

[15]Frederick E. Webster Jr. and Kevin Lane Keller, "A Roadmap for Branding in Industrial Markets," *Journal of Brand Management* 11 (May 2004): pp. 388–402; and Matthew Schwartz, "B to B's Best: Brands," *B to B*, Special Issue (2007), accessed at http://www.btobonline.com on May 15, 2008.

Business Markets versus Consumer-Goods Markets

The basic task of management cuts across both consumer-goods and business marketing. Marketers serving both sectors can benefit by rooting their organizational plan in a *market orientation*, which requires superior proficiency in understanding and satisfying customers.[16] Such market-driven firms demonstrate:

- A set of values and beliefs that places the customers' interests first[17];

- The ability to generate, disseminate, and productively use superior information about customers and competitors[18]; and

- The coordinated use of interfunctional resources (for example, research and development, manufacturing).[19]

Distinctive Capabilities   A close examination of a market-driven firm reveals two particularly important capabilities: market sensing and customer linking.[20] First, the **market-sensing capability** concerns how well the organization is equipped to continuously sense changes in its market and anticipate customer responses to marketing programs. Market-driven firms spot market changes and react well in advance of their competitors (for example, Coca-Cola in the consumer-goods market and 3M in the business market). Second, the **customer-linking capability** comprises the particular skills, abilities, and processes an organization has developed to create and manage close customer relationships.

Consumer-goods firms, such as Procter & Gamble (P&G), demonstrate these capabilities in working with powerful retailers like Wal-Mart. Here, multifunctional teams in both organizations work together by sharing delivery and product-movement information and by jointly planning promotional activity and product changes. Although evident in manufacturer–reseller relations in the consumer-goods market, strong customer-linking capabilities are crucial in the business market, where close buyer–seller relationships prevail. Leading business-to-business firms like IBM and Hewlett-Packard demonstrate distinctive customer-linking skills, and Cisco has propelled its legendary record of growth by forging close working relationships with customers and channel partners alike.

Managing Customers as Assets   Marketing expenditures that were once viewed as short-term expenses are now being considered as customer assets that

---

[16]George S. Day, "The Capabilities of Market-Driven Organizations," *Journal of Marketing* 58 (October 1994): pp. 37–52; and Gary F. Gebhardt, Gregory S. Carpenter, and John F. Sherry Jr., "Creating a Market Orientation: A Longitudinal, Multifirm, Grounded Analysis of Cultural Transformation," *Journal of Marketing* 70 (October 2006): pp. 37–55.

[17]Rohit Deshpande, John U. Farley, and Frederick E. Webster Jr., "Corporate Culture, Customer Orientation, and Innovativeness in Japanese Firms: A Quadrad Analysis," *Journal of Marketing* 57 (January 1993): pp. 23–37.

[18]Ajay K. Kohli and Bernard J. Jaworski, "Market Orientation: The Construct, Research Propositions, and Managerial Implications," *Journal of Marketing* 54 (April 1990): pp. 1–18.

[19]John C. Narver and Stanley F. Slater, "The Effect of a Market Orientation on Business Profitability," *Journal of Marketing* 54 (October 1990): pp. 20–35.

[20]Day, "Capabilities of Market-Driven Organizations," pp. 37–52; and Girish Ramani and V. Kumar, "Interaction Orientation and Firm Performance," *Journal of Marketing* 72 (January 2008): pp. 27–45.

deliver value for the firm and its shareholders.[21] As global competition intensifies, marketing managers are under increasing pressure to demonstrate the return on investment from marketing spending, deliver strong financial performance, and be more accountable to shareholders.[22] To meet these performance standards, firms must develop and nurture **customer relationship management capabilities**, which include all the skills required to identify, initiate, develop, and maintain profitable customer relationships.

Emphasizing a Profit Focus   Developing a firm grasp on the profit impact of marketing strategy actions is fundamental to the job of a business marketing manager. Included here is the need to isolate the forces that drive customer profitability, aligning resources spent on customers to the revenues and profit that will be secured. To this end, Robert S. Kaplan and David P. Norton assert:

> A company that forgets, or never realizes, that it has unprofitable products and customers in the current period will almost surely continue to incur losses in unprofitable products and customers in future periods. Having a clear picture about where the company is making money and losing money should be a vital input to any strategy review.[23]

Partnering for Increased Value   A business marketer becomes a preferred supplier to major customers such as Apple, Texas Instruments, or Procter & Gamble by working closely as a partner, developing an intimate knowledge of the customer's operations, and contributing unique value to that customer's business. Business marketing programs increasingly involve a customized blend of tangible products, service support, and ongoing information services both before and after the sale. Market-driven firms place a high priority on customer-linking capabilities and closely align product decisions—as well as delivery, handling, service, and other supply chain activities—with the customer's operations. For firms like Intel or Boeing to deliver maximum value to their customers, each must receive maximum value from its suppliers. For instance, Intel could not have achieved its commanding global market share without the cost, quality, technology, and other advances its suppliers contribute.[24]

What Makes a Marketing Leader?[25]

Jeff Immelt, CEO at General Electric, recently issued a mandate that marketing must become a vital operating function across the firm and an engine for organic growth.

---

[21]V. Kumar and Werner Reinartz, *Customer Relationship Management* (John Wiley & Sons, 2006). See also Crina O. Tarasi, Ruth N. Bolton, Michael D. Hutt, and Beth A. Walker, "Balancing Risk and Return in a Customer Portfolio," *Journal of Marketing* 75 (May 2011): pp. 1–17.

[22]Frederick E. Webster Jr., Alan J. Malter, and Shankar Ganesan, "The Decline and Dispersion of Marketing Competence," *MIT Sloan Management Review* 46 (Summer 2005): pp. 35–43.

[23]Robert S. Kaplan and David P. Norton, *The Execution Premium: Linking Strategy to Operations for Competitive Advantage* (Harvard Business Press, 2008), p. 258.

[24]Gina Roos, "Intel Corporation: It Takes Quality to Be Preferred by World's Biggest Chipmaker," *Purchasing* 131 (November 15, 2001): pp. 21–22.

[25]Beth Comstock, Ranjay Gulati, and Stephen Liguori, "Unleashing the Power of Marketing," *Harvard Business Review* 88 (October 2010): pp. 90–98.

In response, the firm doubled the size of the marketing function, from 2500 several years ago to more than 5000 managers today, and created chief marketing officer (CMO) positions at all GE businesses and at the corporate level. Likewise, the firm convened its best marketers to define the specific capabilities that a world-class business marketing function needed to master (for example, market knowledge, segmentation, and branding). Once the capabilities were defined, senior GE executives observed that some managers are better equipped at translating capabilities into actionable results, so they studied the characteristics of the firm's top-performing marketing managers. They have found that leaders transform marketing into a strategic function by performing four fundamental roles. They call them a marketer's DNA. These are:

- *The Instigator.* Marketing leaders need to capitalize on their close connection to customers, think strategically, and challenge the status quo in order to define opportunities that may not be apparent to others in the business. This role involves scanning the entire business landscape for marketing ideas as opposed to thinking exclusively about current products and markets.

- *The Innovator.* Marketing leaders need to take an active role in shaping the company's innovation agenda. In performing this role, the leader needs to expand beyond product features to consider new business models or fresh approaches to pricing, delivery, and customer engagement. To pursue a new strategic path, a leader must demonstrate courage and persistence, plus the political skills to overcome objections.

- *The Integrator.* The integrator builds bridges across multiple functions to unite organizational members on a clear strategy path. Marketing leaders are adept at making unique customer insights relevant and meaningful to those inside the organization.

- *The Implementer.* To translate plans into actionable strategies, marketing executives must mobilize diverse organizational members across the firm, many of whom report to others. So marketing leaders are skilled at building coalitions and persuading others by using functional expertise, customer insights, and teamwork rather than by exercising authority.

Creating the Customer Value Proposition[26]

Business marketing strategy must be based on an assessment of the company, the competitor, and the customer. A successful strategy focuses on identifying those opportunities in which the firm can deliver superior value to customers based on its distinctive competencies. From this perspective, marketing can be best understood as the process of defining, developing, and delivering value.

Market-driven firms attempt to match their resources, skills, and capabilities with particular customer needs that are not being adequately served. By understanding

---

[26]James C. Anderson, James A. Narus, and Wouter van Rossum, "Customer Value Propositions in Business Markets," *Harvard Business Review* 84 (March 2006): pp. 91–99.

customer needs, marketing managers can define value from the customer's perspective and convert that information into requirements for creating satisfied customers. In turn, a firm's capabilities and skills determine the degree to which the company can meet these requirements and provide greater value than its competitors.

A business marketing firm's offering includes many technical, economic, service, or social benefits that provide value to customers—but so do the offerings of competitors. So, customers compare the value elements of a firm's offering with those offered by the next best alternative.[27] A **customer value proposition** captures the particular set of benefits that a supplier offers to advance the performance of the customer organization. Rather than merely attempting to list more benefits than competitors, "best practice suppliers base their value proposition on the few elements that matter most to target customers, demonstrate the value of this superior performance, and communicate it in a way that conveys a sophisticated understanding of the customer's business priorities."[28] The building blocks of a successful value proposition include:

- Points of parity—the value elements with essentially the same performance characteristics as the next best alternative.

- Points of difference—the value elements that render the supplier's offering either superior or inferior to the next best alternative.

Value Proposition Illustrated   Sonoco, a global packaging supplier headquartered in South Carolina, approached a large European customer, a producer of consumer goods, about redesigning the packaging for one of its successful product lines. Although the redesigned packaging provided several favorable points of difference relative to the next best alternative, Sonoco executives decided to place special emphasis on one point of parity and two points of difference in the customer value proposition: The redesigned packaging will deliver significantly greater manufacturing efficiency in the customer's fill lines, through higher-speed closing, and provide a distinctive look that customers will find more appealing—all for the same price as the present packaging.

What Matters Most?   A point of parity was included in the value proposition because **key buying influentials** (those who have power in the buying process) within the customer organization would not even consider a packaging redesign if the price increased. The first point of difference in the value proposition (increased efficiency) delivered cost savings, allowing the customer to dramatically streamline its production schedule. The second point of difference (more distinctive customer packaging) enhanced the firm's market position and appeal to its customers, allowing it to realize meaningful growth in its revenues and profit. While the other favorable points of difference were certainly mentioned in discussions with the customer organization, Sonoco executives chose to emphasize those points that mattered most to the customer.

---

[27]Wolfgang Ulaga and Andreas Eggert, "Value-Based Differentiation in Business Relationships: Gaining and Sustaining Key Supplier Status," *Journal of Marketing* 70 (January 2006): pp. 119–136.

[28]Anderson, Narus, and van Rossum, "Customer Value Propositions," p. 93.

Characteristics of Business Markets

Business marketing and consumer-goods marketing are different. A common body of knowledge, principles, and theory applies to both consumer and business marketing, but because their buyers and markets function quite differently, they merit separate attention.[29] Consumer and business marketing differ in the nature of markets, market demand, buyer behavior, buyer–seller relationships, environmental influences (economic, political, legal), and market strategy. Yet, the potential payoffs are high for the firm that can successfully penetrate the business market. The nature of the demand for industrial products poses unique challenges—and opportunities—for the marketing manager.

Derived Demand **Derived demand** refers to the direct link between the demand for an industrial product and the demand for consumer products: *The demand for industrial products is derived from the ultimate demand for consumer products.* Consider the materials and components used in a Harley-Davidson motorcycle. Harley-Davidson manufactures some of the components, but the finished product reflects the efforts of more than 200 suppliers or business marketers who deal directly with the firm. In purchasing a Harley-Davidson motorcycle, the customer is stimulating the demand for a diverse array of products manufactured by business marketing firms—such as tires, electrical components, coil springs, aluminum castings, and other items.

Fluctuating Demand Because demand is derived, the business marketer must carefully monitor demand patterns and changing buying preferences in the household consumer market, often on a worldwide basis. For example, a decline in mortgage rates can spark an increase in new home construction and a corresponding increase in appliance sales. Retailers generally respond by increasing their stock of inventory. As appliance producers like Whirlpool increase the rate of production to meet the demand, business marketers that supply these manufacturers with items such as motors, timers, or paint experience a surge in sales. A downturn in the economy creates the opposite result. This explains why the demand for many industrial products tends to *fluctuate* more than the demand for consumer products.

Stimulating Demand Some business marketers must not only monitor final consumer markets but also develop a marketing program that reaches the ultimate consumer directly. Aluminum producers use television and magazine ads to point out the convenience and recycling opportunities that aluminum containers offer to the consumer—the ultimate consumer influences aluminum demand by purchasing soft drinks in aluminum, rather than plastic, containers. More than 4 billion pounds of aluminum are used annually in the production of beverage containers. Similarly, Boeing promotes the convenience of air travel in a media campaign targeted to the consumer market to create a favorable environment for longer-term demand for its planes; DuPont advertises to ultimate consumers to stimulate the sales of carpeting, which incorporates their product.

---

[29]David J. Lichtenthal and Venkatapparao Mummalaneni, "Commentary: Relative Presence of Business-to-Business Research in the Marketing Literature: Review and Future Directions," *Journal of Business-to-Business Marketing* 16 (1, 2009): pp. 40–54.

Price Sensitivity   **Demand elasticity** refers to the responsiveness of the quantity demanded to a change in price. Demand is elastic when a given percentage change in price brings about an even larger percentage change in the quantity demanded. Inelasticity results when demand is insensitive to price—that is, when the percentage change in demand is less than the percentage change in price. Consider the demand for electronic components that is stimulated by companies making electronic games. As long as final consumers continue to purchase and upgrade these games and are generally insensitive to price, manufacturers of the equipment are relatively insensitive to the price of electronic components. At the opposite end of the spectrum, if consumers are price sensitive when purchasing soup and other canned grocery products, manufacturers of soup will be price sensitive when purchasing metal cans. Thus, the derived demand indicates that the demand for metal cans is price elastic.

Final consumer demand has a pervasive impact on the demand for products in the business market. By being sensitive to trends in the consumer market, the business marketer can often identify both impending problems and opportunities for growth and diversification.

A Global Market Perspective   A complete picture of the business market must include a horizon that stretches beyond the boundaries of the United States. The demand for many industrial goods and services is growing more rapidly in many foreign countries than in the United States. Countries like Germany, Japan, Korea, and Brazil offer large and growing markets for many business marketers. In turn, China and India represent economies with exploding levels of growth. Countless small firms and many large ones—such as GE, 3M, Intel, Boeing, Dow Chemical, and Caterpillar[30]—derive a significant portion of their sales and profits from international markets. For example, China plans to invest more than $300 billion over the next few years in the country's infrastructure, representing an enormous market opportunity for all of GE's industrial businesses, including power generation, health care, and infrastructure (for example, water purification).

Business and Consumer Marketing: A Contrast

Many consumer-goods companies with a strong reputation in the consumer market decide to capitalize on opportunities they perceive in the business market. The move is often prompted by a maturing product line, a desire to diversify operations, or the strategic opportunity to profitably apply R&D or production strength in a rapidly growing business market. P&G, departing from its packaged consumer-goods tradition, is using its expertise in oils, fats, and pulps to diversify into fast-growing industries.

The J. M. Smucker Company operates successfully in both the consumer and the business markets. Smucker, drawing on its consumer product base (jellies and preserves), produces filling mixes used by manufacturers of yogurt and dessert items. Marketing strawberry preserves to ultimate consumers differs significantly from

---

[30]Harold L. Sirkin, James W. Hemerling, and Arindam K. Bhattacharya, *Globality: Competing with Everyone from Everywhere for Everything* (Business Plus, 2008), pp. 23–24.

marketing a strawberry filling to a yogurt manufacturer. Key differences are highlighted in the following illustration.

Smucker: A Consumer and Business Marketer

Smucker reaches the consumer market with a line of products sold through retail outlets. New products are carefully developed, tested, targeted, priced, and promoted for particular market segments. To secure distribution, the firm employs food brokers who call on both wholesale- and retail-buying units. The company's own sales force reaches selected larger accounts. Achieving a desired degree of market exposure and shelf space in key retail food outlets is essential to any marketer of consumer food products. Promotional plans for the line include media advertising, coupons, special offers, and incentives for retailers. Pricing decisions must reflect the nature of demand, costs, and the behavior of competitors. In sum, the marketer must manage each component of the marketing mix: product, price, promotion, and distribution.

The marketing mix takes on a different form in the business market. Attention centers on manufacturers that potentially could use Smucker products to produce other goods; the Smucker product will lose its identity as it is blended into yogurt, cakes, or cookies. Once Smucker has listed all the potential users of its product (for example, large food processors, bakeries, yogurt producers), the business marketing manager attempts to identify meaningful market segments that Smucker can profitably serve. A specific marketing strategy is developed for each market segment.

When a potential organizational consumer is identified, the company's sales force calls directly on the account. The salesperson may begin by contacting a company president but, at first, generally spends a great deal of time with the R&D director or the product-development group leader. The salesperson is thus challenged to identify the **key buying influentials**—those who have power in the buying process. Senior-level Smucker executives may also assist in the selling process.

Armed with product specifications (for example, desired taste, color, calories), the salesperson returns to the Smucker R&D department to develop samples. Several months may pass before a mixture is finally approved. Next, attention turns to price, and the salesperson's contact point shifts to the purchasing department. Because large quantities (truckloads or drums rather than jars) are involved, a few cents per pound can be significant to both parties. Quality and service are also vitally important.

Once a transaction is culminated, the product is shipped directly from the Smucker warehouse to the manufacturer's plant. The salesperson follows up frequently with the purchasing agent, the plant manager, and other executives. Product movement and delivery information is openly shared, and close working relationships develop between managers at Smucker and key decision makers in the buying organization. How much business can Smucker expect from this account? The performance of the new consumer product in the marketplace determines this: The demand for industrial goods is, as noted, derived from ultimate consumer demand. Note also the importance of: (1) developing a close and continuing working relationship with business market customers and (2) understanding the requirements of the total range of buying influentials in the target company.

Distinguishing Characteristics

The Smucker illustration spotlights some of the features that differentiate business marketing strategy from consumer-goods marketing strategy. The business marketer emphasizes personal selling rather than advertising (TV, newspaper) to reach potential buyers. Only a small portion of the business marketer's promotional budget is likely to be invested in advertising, most commonly through trade journals or direct mail. This advertising, however, often establishes the foundation for a successful sales call. The industrial salesperson must understand the technical aspects of the organization's requirements and how those requirements can be satisfied, as well as know who influences the buying decision and why.

The business marketer's product also includes an important service component. The organizational consumer evaluates the quality of both the physical product and the attached services. Attention centers on the total package of benefits the consumer receives. Price negotiation is frequently an important part of the industrial buying/selling process. Products made to particular quality or design specifications must be individually priced. Business marketers generally find that direct distribution to larger customers strengthens relationships between buyer and seller. Smaller accounts can be profitably served through intermediaries—manufacturers' representatives or industrial distributors.

As the Smucker example illustrates, business marketing strategies differ from consumer-goods marketing strategies in the relative emphasis given to certain elements of the marketing mix. It is important to note that the example also highlights fundamental differences between the buyers in each market. In an organization, a variety of individuals influence the purchase decision. Several major questions confront Smucker's business marketing manager: Who are the key participants in the purchasing process? What is their relative importance? What criteria does each participant apply to the decision? Thus, the business marketer must understand the process an organization follows in purchasing a product and identify which organizational members have roles in this process. Depending on the complexity of the purchase, this process may span many weeks or months and may involve the participation of several organization members. The business marketer who becomes involved in the purchase process early may have the greatest chance for success.

A Relationship Emphasis

Relationships in the business market are often close and enduring. Rather than constituting the end result, a sale signals the beginning of a relationship. By convincing a large food processor such as General Foods to use its product, Smucker initiates a potential long-term business relationship. More than ringing up a sale, Smucker creates a customer! To maintain that relationship, the business marketer must develop an intimate knowledge of the customer's operations and contribute unique value to its business. **Relationship marketing** centers on all marketing activities directed toward establishing, developing, and maintaining successful exchanges with customers.[31] Building one-to-one relationships with customers is the heart of business marketing. Figure 1.1 provides a recap of key characteristics of business market customers.

---

[31]Robert M. Morgan and Shelby D. Hunt, "The Commitment-Trust Theory of Relationship Marketing," *Journal of Marketing* 58 (July 1994): pp. 20–38.

FIGURE 1.1 | **CHARACTERISTICS OF BUSINESS MARKET CUSTOMERS**

Characteristic	Example
• Business market customers are comprised of commercial enterprises, institutions, and governments.	• Among Dell's customers are Boeing, Arizona State University, and numerous state and local government units.
• A single purchase by a business customer is far larger than that of an individual consumer.	• An individual may buy one unit of a software package upgrade from Microsoft while Citigroup purchases 10,000.
• The demand for industrial products is derived from the ultimate demand for consumer products.	• New home purchases stimulate the demand for carpeting, appliances, cabinets, lumber, and a wealth of other products.
• Buyer-seller relationships tend to be close and enduring	• IBM's relationship with some key customers spans decades.
• Buying decisions by business customers often involve multiple buying influences, rather than a single decision maker.	• A cross-functional team at Procter & Gamble (P&G) evaluates alternative laptop personal computers and selects Hewlett-Packard.
• While serving different types of customers, business marketers and consumer-goods marketers share the same job titles.	• Job titles include marketing manager, product manager, sales manager, account manager.

© Cengage Learning 2013

The Supply Chain

Figure 1.2 further illuminates the importance of a relationship perspective in business marketing by considering the chain of suppliers involved in the creation of an automobile. Consider Honda Motor Company. At its Marysville, Ohio, auto assembly plant, Honda introduced many new concepts to the U.S. auto industry, including just-in-time parts delivery and a high level of flexible model construction. For instance, the Ohio plant can readily shift from the Acura TL luxury sedan to the Accord, based on customer demand.[32] A new small-car plant in Indiana gives Honda further capacity to make Civic- and Accord-size vehicles—fuel-efficient models particularly coveted by auto buyers as gas prices increase. Across its seven plants in North America, Honda annually purchases more than $17 billion of parts and materials from U.S. suppliers.[33]

The relationships between the auto producers and their suppliers fall squarely into the business marketing domain. Similarly, business marketers such as TRW rely on a whole host of others farther back on the supply chain for raw materials, components, and other support. Each organization in this chain is involved in the creation of a product, marketing processes (including delivery), and support and

---

[32]Tom Krisher, "Honda Grows While U.S. Auto Industry Falters," accessed at http://biz.yahoo.com on July 2, 2008.

[33]"Honda's First U.S. Auto Plant Celebrates 25 Years of Production," November 1, 2007, accessed at http://www.world.honda.com on July 2, 2008.

FIGURE 1.2 | **THE SUPPLY CHAIN**

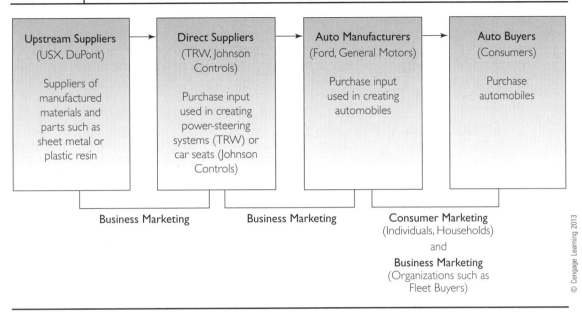

service after the sale. In performing these value-creating activities, each also affects the quality level of the Honda product. Michael Porter and Victor Millar observe that "to gain competitive advantage over its rivals, a company must either perform these activities at a lower cost or perform them in a way that leads to differentiation and a premium price (more value)."[34]

Supply Chain Management

Supply chain management is a technique for linking a manufacturer's operations with those of all of its strategic suppliers and its key intermediaries and customers to enhance efficiency and effectiveness. The Internet allows members of the supply chain all over the world to share timely information, exchange engineering drawings during new product development, and synchronize production and delivery schedules. The goal of supply chain strategy is to improve the speed, precision, and efficiency of manufacturing through strong supplier relationships. This goal is achieved through information sharing, joint planning, shared technology, and shared benefits. If the business marketer can become a valued partner in a customer's supply chain, the rewards are substantial: The focus shifts from price to value and from products to solutions.[35] To achieve these results, the business marketing firm must demonstrate the ability to meet the customer's precise quality, delivery, service, and information requirements.

---

[34]Michael E. Porter and Victor E. Millar, "How Information Gives You Competitive Advantage," *Harvard Business Review* 63 (July–August 1985): pp. 149–160; see also Michael E. Porter, *Competitive Advantage* (The Free Press, 1985).

[35]Marc Bourde, Charlie Hawker, and Theo Theocharides, "Taking Center Stage: The 2005 Chief Procurement Officer Survey" (IBM Global Services, 2005), pp. 1–13, accessed at http://www.ibm.com on July 15, 2005.

Managing Relationships in the Supply Chain

Customers in the business market place a premium on the business marketer's supply chain management capabilities. IBM spends 85 percent of its purchasing dollars with 50 suppliers.[36] Of particular importance to IBM is the quality of engineering support it receives from suppliers. IBM actively seeks supplier partners that will contribute fresh ideas, responsive service, and leading-edge technology to attract buyers of future IBM products.

To effectively initiate and sustain a profitable relationship with a customer like IBM, Honda, or Procter & Gamble, the marketing manager must carefully coordinate the multiple linkages that define the relationships. Given these new marketing requirements, Frank V. Cespedes emphasizes the importance of "concurrent marketing" among the groups that are most central to customer contact efforts: product, sales, and service units.[37] In his view, recent market developments place more emphasis on the firm's ability to:

- Generate timely market knowledge by segment and by individual account;

- Customize product service packages for diverse customer groups, and

- Capitalize on local field knowledge from sales and service units to inform product strategy in real time.

Developing and nurturing close, long-term relationships is an important goal for the business marketer. Built on trust and demonstrated performance, such strategic partnerships require open lines of communication between multiple layers of the buying and selling organizations. Given the rising importance of long-term, strategic relationships with both customers and suppliers, organizations are increasingly emphasizing relationship management skills. Because these skills reside in people rather than in organizational structures, roles, or tasks, marketing personnel with these skills become valuable assets to the organization.[38]

Commercial Enterprises as Consumers

Business market customers, as noted at the outset of the chapter, can be broadly classified into three categories: (1) commercial enterprises, (2) governmental organizations, and (3) institutions. However, the supply chain concept provides a solid foundation for classifying the commercial customers that constitute the business market. Commercial enterprises can be divided into three categories: (1) users, (2) original equipment manufacturers (OEMs), and (3) dealers and distributors.

Users   Users purchase industrial products or services to produce other goods or services that are, in turn, sold in the business or consumer markets. User customers purchase goods—such as computers, photocopiers, or automated manufacturing

---

[36]James Carbone, "Reinventing Purchasing Wins Medal for Big Blue," *Purchasing* 129 (September 16, 1999): pp. 45–46.

[37]Frank V. Cespedes, *Concurrent Marketing: Integrating Products, Sales, and Service* (Harvard Business School Press, 1995), chap. 2.

[38]Frederick E. Webster Jr., "The Changing Role of Marketing in the Corporation," *Journal of Marketing* 56 (October 1992): p. 14. See also, Joseph P. Cannon and William D. Perreault Jr., "Buyer-Seller Relationships in Business Markets," *Journal of Marketing Research* 36 (November 1999): pp. 439–460.

systems—to set up or support the manufacturing process. When purchasing machine tools, Ford is a user. These machine tools do not become part of the automobile but instead help to produce it.

Original Equipment Manufacturers (OEMs)   The OEM purchases industrial goods to incorporate into other products it sells in the business or ultimate consumer market. For example, Intel Corporation produces the microprocessors that constitute the heart of Dell's personal computer. In purchasing these microprocessors, Dell is an OEM. Similarly, Apple is an OEM in purchasing a touch-screen controller from Broadcom Corp.—about $4 to $5 of content in every iPhone.[39]

Dealers and Distributors   Dealers and distributors include commercial enterprises that purchase industrial goods for resale (in basically the same form) to users and OEMs. The distributor accumulates, stores, and sells a large assortment of goods to industrial users, assuming title to the goods it purchases. Handling billions of dollars worth of transactions each year, industrial distributors are growing in size and sophistication. The strategic role assumed by distributors in the business market is examined in detail in Chapter 10 (Channels).

Overlap of Categories   The three categories of commercial enterprises are not mutually exclusive. Their classification is based on the intended purpose the product serves for the customer. Ford is a user when purchasing a machine tool for the manufacturing process, but the same company is an OEM when purchasing radios to be installed in the ultimate consumer product.

A marketer must have a good understanding of the diverse organizational consumers that make up the business market. Properly classifying commercial customers as users, OEMs, or dealers or distributors is an important first step to a sharpened understanding of the buying criteria that a particular commercial customer uses in evaluating an industrial product.

Understanding Buying Motivations   Consider the different types of commercial customers that purchase a particular industrial product such as electrical timing mechanisms. Each class of customer views the product differently because each purchases the product for a different reason.

A food-processing firm such as Pillsbury buys electrical timers for use in a high-speed canning system. For this customer, quality, reliability, and prompt and predictable delivery are critical. Whirlpool, an OEM that incorporates the industrial product directly into consumer appliances, is concerned with the effect of the timers on the quality and dependability of the final consumer product. Because the timers are needed in large quantities, the appliance manufacturer is also concerned about the producer's production capacity and delivery reliability. Finally, an industrial distributor is most interested in matching the capability of the timing mechanisms to the needs of customers (users and OEMs) in a specific geographical market.

---

[39]Eric J. Savitz, "Battle for Smartphone Market Share Pressures Margins," *Barron's*, June 30, 2008, p. 37.

Classifying Goods for the Business Market[40]

Having classified business market customers, we must now ask what type of goods they require, and how each type is marketed. One useful method of classifying industrial goods is to ask the following questions: How does the industrial good or service enter the production process, and how does it enter the cost structure of the firm? The answer enables the marketer to identify those who are influential in the organizational buying process and to understand how to design an effective business marketing strategy. In general, industrial goods can be divided into three broad categories: entering goods, foundation goods, and facilitating goods (Figure 1.3).

Entering Goods

Entering goods become part of the finished product. This category of goods consists of raw materials and manufactured materials and parts. Their cost is an expense item assigned to the manufacturing process.

Raw Materials   Observe in Figure 1.3 that **raw materials** include both farm products and natural products. Raw materials are processed only to the level required for economical handling and transport; they basically enter the buying organization's production process in their natural state. Fueled by the massive growth in the Chinese economy, Freeport-McMoRan Copper & Gold, Inc., the copper producer, has seen demand surge. McDonald's uses more than 700 million pounds of potatoes each year and dictates the fortunes of many farmers in that agricultural segment. In fact, when attempting to introduce a raspberry sorbet, McDonald's found, to its surprise, that not enough raspberries were being grown![41]

Manufactured Materials and Parts   In contrast to raw materials, **manufactured materials and parts** undergo more initial processing. Component materials such as textiles or sheet steel have been processed before reaching a clothing manufacturer or automaker but must be processed further before becoming part of the finished consumer product. Both Ford and GE spend more than $900 million annually on steel. Component parts, on the other hand, include small motors, motorcycle tires, and automobile batteries; they can be installed directly into another product with little or no additional processing. For example, Black & Decker spends $100 million each year on plastic parts, and Hewlett-Packard and Dell spend hundreds of millions on displays, monitors, and the microprocessors that power personal computers.

Foundation Goods

The distinguishing characteristic of foundation goods is that they are capital items. As capital goods are used up or worn out, a portion of their original cost is assigned

---

[40]Data on the dollar purchases of particular products by selected customers are drawn from Anne Millen Porter and Elena Epatko Murphy, "Hey Big Spender … The 100 Largest Industrial Buyers," *Purchasing* (November 9, 1995): pp. 31–42.

[41]James Brian Quinn, *Intelligent Enterprise: A Knowledge and Service Based Paradigm for Industry* (The Free Press, 1992), p. 20.

FIGURE 1.3 | CLASSIFYING GOODS FOR THE BUSINESS MARKET

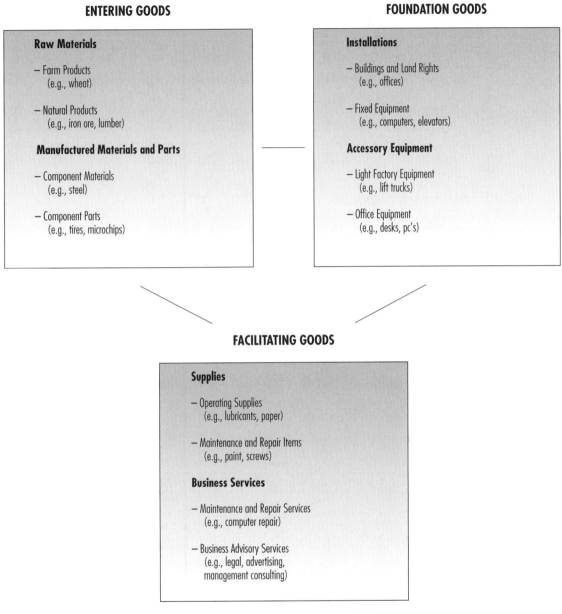

ENTERING GOODS

Raw Materials

— Farm Products
 (e.g., wheat)

— Natural Products
 (e.g., iron ore, lumber)

Manufactured Materials and Parts

— Component Materials
 (e.g., steel)

— Component Parts
 (e.g., tires, microchips)

FOUNDATION GOODS

Installations

— Buildings and Land Rights
 (e.g., offices)

— Fixed Equipment
 (e.g., computers, elevators)

Accessory Equipment

— Light Factory Equipment
 (e.g., lift trucks)

— Office Equipment
 (e.g., desks, pc's)

FACILITATING GOODS

Supplies

— Operating Supplies
 (e.g., lubricants, paper)

— Maintenance and Repair Items
 (e.g., paint, screws)

Business Services

— Maintenance and Repair Services
 (e.g., computer repair)

— Business Advisory Services
 (e.g., legal, advertising,
 management consulting)

SOURCE: KOTLER, PHIL, *Marketing Management: Analysis, Planning & Control*, 4th Edition, © 1980, p. 172. Adapted by permission of Pearson Education, Inc., Upper Saddle River, NJ.

to the production process as a depreciation expense. Foundation goods include installations and accessory equipment.

Installations   **Installations** include the major long-term investment items that underlie the manufacturing process, such as buildings, land rights, and fixed equipment. Large computers and machine tools are examples of fixed equipment. The demand for installations is shaped by the economic climate (for example, favorable interest rates) but is driven by the market outlook for a firm's products. In the face of strong worldwide demand for its microprocessors, Intel is building new plants, expanding existing ones, and making significant investments in capital equipment. A typical semiconductor chip plant costs at least $5 billion to build, including the land, building, and installed manufacturing equipment.[42]

Accessory Equipment   **Accessory equipment** is generally less expensive and is short-lived compared with installations, and it is not considered part of the fixed plant. This equipment can be found in the plant as well as in the office. Portable drills, personal computers, and photocopying machines illustrate this category.

Facilitating Goods

Facilitating goods are the supplies and services (see Figure 1.3) that support organizational operations. Because these goods do not enter the production process or become part of the finished product, their costs are handled as expense items.

Supplies   Virtually every organization requires operating supplies, such as printer cartridges, paper, or business forms, and maintenance and repair items, such as paint and cleaning materials. These items generally reach a broad cross section of industrial users. In fact, they are very similar to the kinds of supplies that consumers might purchase at a hardware or discount store.

For example, along with products specifically designed for commercial use, Procter & Gamble (P&G) sells adaptations of its well-known consumer products in its professional division.[43] Targeting the business market, customers here include hotels, fast-food restaurants, retailers, and health-care organizations. P&G senses a huge market opportunity—the U.S. market for janitorial and housekeeping cleaning products exceeds $3.2 billion annually.

Services   Says analyst James Brian Quinn, "As the service sector has grown to embrace 80 percent of all U.S. employment, specialized service firms have become very large and sophisticated relative to the scale and expertise that individual staff and service groups have within integrated companies."[44] To capture the skills of these specialists and to direct attention to what they do best, many firms are shifting or "outsourcing" selected service functions to outside suppliers. This opens up opportunities for firms that provide such services as computer support, payroll processing, logistics, food operations, and equipment maintenance. These specialists possess a level of expertise or efficiency that organizations can

---

[42]Ryan Randazzo, Edythe Jensen, and Mary Jo Pitzl, "New $5B Intel Facility Planned for Chandler, *The Arizona Republic*, February 19, 2011, p. B-1.

[43]Ellen Byron, "Aiming to Clean Up, P&G Courts Business Customers," *The Wall Street Journal*, January 26, 2007, pp. B1–B2.

[44]James Brian Quinn, "Strategic Outsourcing: Leveraging Knowledge Capabilities," *Sloan Management Review* 40 (Summer 1999): p. 9; see also Mark Gottfredson, Rudy Puryear, and Stephen Phillips, "Strategic Sourcing: From Periphery to Core," *Harvard Business Review* 83 (February 2005): pp. 132–139.

profitably tap. For example, Cisco Systems turned to FedEx to coordinate the movement of parts through its supply chain and on to the customer. By merging the parts shipments in transit for a single customer, the desired product can be assembled at the customer's location, never spending a moment in a Cisco warehouse.[45] Business services include **maintenance and repair support** (for example, machine repair) and **advisory support** (for example, management consulting or information management). Like supplies, services are considered expense items.

Moreover, the explosive growth of the Internet has increased the demand for a range of electronic commerce services, from Web site design to the complete hosting of an e-commerce site. The Internet also provides a powerful new channel for delivering technical support, customer training, and advertising. For example, Intel is shifting over half of its advertising budget to online media and is asking its partners in the "Intel Inside" cooperative ad campaign, like Sony, to increase spending on online media.[46] In turn, the Internet provides the opportunity to manage a particular activity or function from a remote, or even offshore, location. To illustrate, IBM manages the procurement functions for United Technologies Corporation via the Web.[47]

Business Marketing Strategy

Marketing pattern differences reveal the significance of a goods classification system. A marketing strategy appropriate for one category of goods may be entirely unsuitable for another. Often, entirely different promotional, pricing, and distribution strategies are required. The physical nature of the industrial good and its intended use by the organizational customer dictate to an important degree the marketing program's requirements. Some strategy highlights follow.

Illustration: Manufactured Materials and Parts

Recall that manufactured materials and parts enter the buying organization's own product. Whether a part is standardized or customized often dictates the nature of marketing strategy. For custom-made parts, personal selling and customer relationship management activities assume an important role in marketing strategy. The value proposition centers on providing a product that advances the customer's competitive position. The business marketer must also demonstrate strong supply chain capabilities. Standardized parts are typically purchased in larger quantities on a contractual basis, and the marketing strategy centers on providing a competitive price, reliable delivery, and supporting services. Frequently, industrial distributors are used to provide responsive delivery service to smaller accounts.

---

[45]Douglas A. Blackman, "Overnight, Everything Changed for FedEx: Can It Reinvent Itself?" *The Wall Street Journal*, November 4, 1999, pp. A1, A16.

[46]Stuart Elliot, "As Customers Flock to the Web, Intel Gives Chase with Its Ad Budget," *The New York Times*, October 10, 2007, p. C9.

[47]"United Technologies: Outsourcing Procurement Yields High Efficiency and Tight Spending Controls," IBM Corporation, June 5, 2005, accessed at http://www.ibm.com on April 10, 2010.

For manufactured materials and parts, the marketer's challenge is to locate and accurately define the unique needs of diverse customers, uncover key buying influentials, and create solutions to serve these customers profitably.

Illustration: Installations

Installations such as fixed equipment were classified earlier as foundation goods because they are capital assets that affect the buyer's scale of operations. Here the product or technology itself, along with the service capabilities of the firm, are the central factors in marketing strategy, and direct manufacturer-to-user channels of distribution are the norm. Less costly, more standardized installations such as a drill press may be sold through marketing intermediaries.

Once again, personal selling or account management is the dominant promotional tool. The salesperson or account team works closely with prospective organizational buyers. Negotiations can span several months and involve the top executives in the buying organization, especially for buildings or custom-made equipment. Customer buying motives center on economic factors (such as the projected performance of the capital asset) and emotional factors (such as industry leadership). A buyer may be quite willing to select a higher-priced installation if the projected return on investment supports the decision. The focal points for the marketing of installations include a strong customer relationship management effort, effective engineering and product design support, and the ability to offer a product or technology solution that provides a higher return on investment than its competition. Initial price, distribution, and advertising play lesser roles.

Illustration: Supplies

The final illustration centers on a facilitating good: supplies. Again we find different marketing patterns. Most supply items reach a broad market of business customers from many different industries. Although some large users are serviced directly, a wide variety of channel partners are required to cover this broad and diverse market adequately.

The goal of the business marketer is to secure a place on the purchasing function's list of preferred or preapproved suppliers. Importantly, many firms are adopting e-procurement systems to dramatically streamline the process employees follow in buying supplies and other operating resources. From the desktop, an employee simply logs on to the system, selects the needed items from an electronic catalog of suppliers the purchasing function has preapproved, and sends the order directly to the supplier.

For supplies, the marketer's promotional mix includes catalog listings, advertising, and, to a lesser extent, personal selling. Advertising is directed to resellers (industrial distributors) and final users. Personal selling is less important for supplies than it is for other categories of goods with a high unit value, such as installations. Thus, personal selling efforts may be confined to resellers and large users of supplies. Price may be critical in the marketing strategy because many supply items are undifferentiated. However, customized service strategies might be designed to differentiate a firm's offerings from those of competitors. By providing the right product assortment, timely and reliable delivery, and customized services, the business marketer may be able to provide distinctive value to the customer and develop a long-term, profitable relationship.

A Look Ahead

Figure 1.4 shows the chief components of the business marketing management process. Business marketing strategy is formulated within the boundaries established by the corporate mission and objectives. A corporation determining its mission must define its business and purpose, assess environmental trends, and evaluate its strengths and weaknesses. Building e-commerce capabilities and transforming these capabilities into offerings that provide superior customer value constitute vital corporate objectives at leading organizations like GE. Corporate objectives provide guidelines for forming specific marketing objectives. Business marketing planning must be coordinated and synchronized with corresponding planning efforts in R&D, procurement, finance, production, customer service, and other areas. Clearly, strategic plans emerge out of a bargaining process among functional areas. Managing conflict, promoting cooperation, and developing

---

FIGURE 1.4 | A FRAMEWORK FOR BUSINESS MARKETING MANAGEMENT

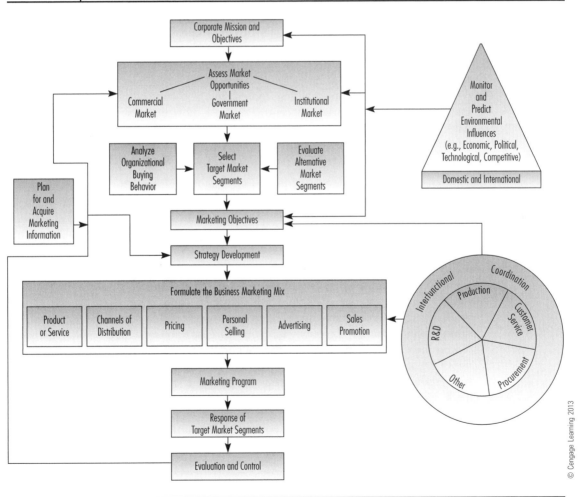

© Cengage Learning 2013

coordinated strategies are all fundamental to the business marketer's interdisciplinary role.

The business marketing management framework (see Figure 1.4) provides an overview of the five major parts of the text. This chapter introduced some of the features that distinguish industrial from consumer-goods marketing and explored the major types of customers that make up the business market: commercial enterprises, governmental units, and institutions. Each sector represents a sizable market opportunity, presents special characteristics and needs, and requires a unique marketing strategy response.

Part II examines the organizational buying process and the myriad forces that affect the organizational decision maker. Occupying a central position in Part II is customer relationship management—a managerial process that leading firms in business-to-business marketing have mastered. Here special attention is given to the specific strategies that business marketers can follow in developing profitable relationships with customers. Part III turns to the selection of target segments and specific techniques for measuring the response of these segments. Part IV centers on designing market-driven strategies. Each component of the marketing mix is treated from the business marketing perspective. Special attention is given to creating and managing offerings and managing connections, including treatment of supply chain strategies. Particular emphasis is also given to defining value from the customer's perspective and developing responsive pricing, advertising, and personal selling strategies to deliver that value proposition to target segments.

The processes of implementing, monitoring, and controlling the marketing program are analyzed in Part V. A central theme is how business marketing managers can enhance profitability by maximizing the return on marketing strategy expenditures.

Summary

The business market offers significant opportunities and special challenges for the marketing manager. In business-to-business marketing, the customers are organizations. More specifically, the business market can be divided into three major sectors: commercial enterprises; governments (federal, state, and local); and institutions. Commercial enterprises include manufacturers, construction companies, service firms, transportation companies, selected professional groups, and resellers. Of these, manufacturers account for the largest dollar volume of purchases. Governmental units also make substantial purchases of products. Government buyers use two general purchasing strategies: the formal advertising approach for standardized products and negotiated contracts for unique requirements. Institutional customers, such as health-care organizations and universities, comprise the third sector of the business market. Across business market sectors, purchasing managers are using the Internet to identify potential suppliers, communicate with suppliers, and conduct business.

Market-driven firms in the business market demonstrate superior skill for understanding and satisfying customers. They also possess strong market-sensing and customer-linking capabilities. To deliver strong financial performance, business-to-business firms must also demonstrate customer relationship management skills, which include all the skills required to identify, initiate, develop, and monitor profitable customer relationships. Best-practice marketing strategists base their value propositions on the points of difference that matter the most to target customers, responding clearly and directly to the customer's business priorities. Although a common body of knowledge and theory spans all of marketing, important differences exist between consumer and business marketing, among them the nature of markets, demand patterns, buyer behavior, and buyer–seller relationships.

The dramatic worldwide rise in competition requires a global perspective on markets. To secure a competitive advantage in this challenging environment, business market customers are developing closer, more collaborative ties with fewer suppliers than they have used in the past. They are using the Internet to promote efficiency and real-time communication across the supply chain and demanding quality and speed from their suppliers to an unprecedented degree. These important trends in procurement place a premium on the supply chain management capabilities of the business marketer. Business marketing programs increasingly involve a customized blend of tangible products, service support, and ongoing information services both before and after the sale. Customer relationship management constitutes the heart of business marketing.

The diverse organizations that make up the business market can be broadly divided into: (1) commercial enterprises, (2) governmental organizations, and (3) institutions. Because purchases these organizational consumers make are linked to goods and services they generate in turn, derived demand is an important and often volatile force in the business market. Industrial goods can be classified into three categories, based on how the product enters the buying organization's cost structure and the production process: (1) entering goods, (2) foundation goods, and (3) facilitating goods. Specific categories of goods may require unique marketing programs.

Discussion Questions

1. Describe the key elements of a customer value proposition. Next, explain how a compelling value proposition might include points of parity as well as *points of difference.*

2. Explain how a company such as GE might be classified by some business marketers as a user customer but by others as an OEM customer.

3. Consumer products are frequently classified as convenience, shopping, or specialty goods. This classification system is based on how consumers shop for particular products. Would this classification scheme apply equally well in the business marketing environment?

4. Honda of America relies on 400 suppliers in North America to provide more than 60 percent of the parts and materials for the Accord. What strategies could a business marketer follow in becoming a new supplier to Honda? What criteria would Honda consider in evaluating suppliers?

5. Evaluate this statement: "The ways that leading companies manage time in the supply chain—in new-product development, in production,

in sales and distribution—are the most powerful new sources of competitive advantage."

6. What are the chief differences between consumer-goods marketing and business marketing? Use the following matrix as a guide in organizing your response:

	Consumer-Goods Marketing	Business Marketing
Customers	_____	_____
Buying Behavior	_____	_____
Buyer–Seller Relationship	_____	_____
Product	_____	_____
Price	_____	_____
Promotion	_____	_____
Channels	_____	_____

7. Evaluate this statement: "The demand for major equipment (a foundation good) is likely to be less responsive to shifts in price than that for materials, supplies, and components." Do you agree or disagree? Support your position.

8. DuPont, one of the largest industrial producers of chemicals and synthetic fibers, spends millions of dollars annually on advertising its products to final consumers. For example, DuPont invested more than $1 million in a TV advertising blitz that emphasized the comfort of jeans made of DuPont's stretch polyester–cotton blend. DuPont does not produce jeans or market them to final consumers, so why were large expenditures made on consumer advertising?

9. Many firms are shifting selected service functions to outside suppliers. For example, Harley-Davidson recently outsourced its transportation department function to UPS Supply Chain Solutions. What factors would prompt such a decision, and what criteria would a customer like Harley-Davidson emphasize in choosing a supplier?

10. Home Depot is quite busy each morning because local contractors, home remodelers, and other small-business customers are buying the products they require for the day's projects. Such small-business customers represent a huge market opportunity for Home Depot or Lowe's. Describe particular strategies these retailers could follow to target and serve these customers.

Internet Exercises

1. Many firms, large and small, have outsourced key functions, like payroll processing to ADP. Go to http://www.adp.com and (1) identify the range of services that ADP offers; (2) describe the types of customers the firm serves.

2. BASF "doesn't make the products you buy, but makes them better." Go to http://www.basf.com and (1) outline the markets that BASF serves and (2) the products it sells.

PART

II

MANAGING RELATIONSHIPS IN BUSINESS MARKETING

CHAPTER

2

Organizational Buying Behavior

A wide array of forces inside and outside the organization influence the organizational buyer. Knowledge of these forces provides the marketer with a foundation for responsive business marketing strategies. After reading this chapter, you will understand:

1. The decision process organizational buyers apply as they confront differing buying situations and the resulting strategy implications for the business marketer

2. The individual, group, organizational, and environmental variables that influence organizational buying decisions

3. A model of organizational buying behavior that integrates these important influences

4. How a knowledge of organizational buying characteristics enables the marketer to make more informed decisions about product design, pricing, and promotion strategies

Want to win the support of buying influentials? *Enhance their customers' experie*[...] Market-driven business firms continuously sense and act on trends in their m[...] kets. Consider Johnson Controls, Inc., a diverse, multi-industry company that i[...] leading supplier of auto interiors (including seats, electronics, headliners, a[...] instrument panels) to manufacturers.[1] The striking success of the firm rests [...] the close relationships that its sales reps and marketing managers have form[...] with design engineers and purchasing executives in the auto industry. To illustra[...] some of Johnson Controls' salespersons work on-site with design teams at Fo[...] GM, or Honda. To provide added value to the new-product-design process, [...] firm emphasizes environment-friendly materials and also invests annually in mar[...] research on the needs and preferences of auto buyers—the customer's custom[...] Moreover, to enhance the customer experience, technicians at Johnson Contro[...] research lab test seating and interior components for comfort, safety, ease-of-reach, usability, and function. Using a simulator that generates the bumps, dips, and turns of an open-road drive, scientists can record the passengers' experiences and capture valuable information for developing components that improve comfort and safety as well as customer satisfaction. By staying close to the needs of auto buyers, Johnson Controls became the preferred supplier to design engineers who are continually seeking innovative ways to make auto interiors more distinctive and inviting.

Understanding the dynamics of organizational buying behavior is crucial for identifying profitable market segments, locating buying influences within these segments, and reaching organizational buyers efficiently and effectively with an offering that responds to their needs. Each decision the business marketer makes is based on organizational buyers' probable response. This chapter explores the key stages of the organizational buying process and isolates the salient characteristics of different purchasing situations. Next, attention turns to the myriad forces that influence organizational buying behavior. Knowledge of how organizational buying decisions are made provides the business marketer with a solid foundation for building responsive marketing strategies.

The Organizational Buying Process

Organizational buying behavior is a process, not an isolated act or event. Tracing the history of a procurement decision uncovers critical decision points and evolving information requirements. In fact, organizational buying involves several stages, each of which yields a decision. Figure 2.1 lists the major stages in the organizational buying process.[2]

The purchasing process begins when someone in the organization recognizes a problem that can be solved or an opportunity that can be captured by acquiring a specific product. Problem recognition can be triggered by internal or external forces.

---

[1]"Product Solutions: Smarter Seats," accessed at http://www.johnsoncontrols.com on April 8, 2011

[2]The discussion in this section is based on Patrick J. Robinson, Charles W. Faris, and Yoram Wind, *Industrial Buying and Creative Marketing* (Boston: Allyn and Bacon, 1967), pp. 12–18; see also Jeffrey E. Lewin and Naveen Donthu, "The Influence of Purchase Situations on Buying Center Structure and Investment: A Select Meta-Analysis of Organizational Buying Behavior Research," *Journal of Business Research* 58 (October 2005): pp. 1381–1390; and Morry Ghingold and David T. Wilson, "Buying Center Research and Business Marketing Practice: Meeting the Challenge of Dynamic Marketing," *Journal of Business and Industrial Marketing* 13 (2, 1998): pp. 96–108.

FIGURE 2.1 | Mᴀᴊᴏʀ Sᴛᴀɢᴇs ᴏf ᴛʜᴇ Oʀɢᴀɴɪᴢᴀᴛɪᴏɴᴀʟ Bᴜʏɪɴɢ Pʀᴏᴄᴇss

Stage	Description
1. Problem Recognition	Managers at P&G need new high-speed packaging equipment to support a new product launch.
2. General Description of Need	Production managers work with a purchasing manager to determine the characteristics needed in the new packaging system.
3. Product Specifications	An experienced production manager assists a purchasing manager in developing a detailed and precise description of the needed equipment.
4. Supplier Search	After conferring with production managers, a purchasing manager identifies a set of alternative suppliers that could satisfy P&G's requirements.
5. Acquisition and Analysis of Proposals	Alternative proposals are evaluated by a purchasing manager and a number of members of the production department.
6. Supplier Selection	Negotiations with the two finalists are conducted, and a supplier is chosen.
7. Selection of Order Routine	A delivery date is established for the production equipment.
8. Performance Review	After equipment is installed, purchasing and production managers evaluate the performance of the equipment and the service support provided by the supplier.

Internally, a firm like P&G may need new high-speed production equipment to support a new product launch. Or a purchasing manager may be unhappy with the price or service of an equipment supplier. Externally, a salesperson can precipitate the need for a product by demonstrating opportunities for improving the organization's performance. Likewise, business marketers also use advertising to alert customers to problems and demonstrate how a particular product may solve them.

During the organizational buying process, many small or incremental decisions are made that ultimately translate into a supplier's final choice. To illustrate, a production manager might unknowingly establish specifications for a new production system that only one supplier can meet (Stages 2 and 3). This type of decision early in the buying process dramatically influences the favorable evaluation and ultimate selection of that supplier.

The Search Process

Once the organization has defined the product that meets its requirements, attention turns to this question: Which of the many possible suppliers are promising candidates? The organization invests more time and energy in the supplier search when the proposed product has a strong bearing on organizational performance. When the information needs of the buying organization are low, Stages 4 and 5 occur simultaneously, especially for standardized items. In this case, a purchasing manager may merely check a catalog or secure an updated price from the Internet. Stage 5 emerges as a distinct category only when the information needs of the organization are high. Here, the process of acquiring and analyzing proposals may involve purchasing managers, engineers, users, and other organizational members.

Supplier Selection and Performance Review   After being selected as a chosen supplier (Stage 6) and agreeing to purchasing guidelines (Stage 7), such as required quantities and expected time of delivery, a marketer faces further tests. A performance review is the final stage in the purchasing process. The performance review may lead the purchasing manager to continue, modify, or cancel the agreement. A review critical of the chosen supplier and supportive of rejected alternatives can lead members of the decision-making unit to reexamine their position. If the product fails to meet the needs of the using department, decision makers may give further consideration to vendors screened earlier in the procurement process. To keep a new customer, the marketer must ensure that the buying organization's needs have been completely satisfied. Failure to follow through at this critical stage leaves the marketer vulnerable.

The stages in this model of the procurement process may not progress sequentially and may vary with the complexity of the purchasing situation. For example, some of the stages are compressed or bypassed when organizations make routine buying decisions. However, the model provides important insights into the organizational buying process. Certain stages may be completed concurrently; the process may be discontinued by a change in the external environment or in upper-management thinking. The organizational buying process is shaped by a host of internal and external forces, such as changes in economic or competitive conditions or a basic shift in organizational priorities.

Organizations with significant experience in purchasing a particular product approach the decision quite differently from first-time buyers. Therefore, attention must center on buying situations rather than on products. Three types of buying situations have been delineated: (1) new task, (2) modified rebuy, and (3) straight rebuy.[3]

New Task

In the **new-task buying situation**, organization decision makers perceive the problem or need as totally different from previous experiences; therefore, they need a significant amount of information to explore alternative ways of solving the problem and searching for alternative suppliers.

When confronting a new-task buying situation, organizational buyers operate in a stage of decision making referred to as **extensive problem solving**.[4] The buying influentials and decision makers lack well-defined criteria for comparing alternative products and suppliers, but they also lack strong predispositions toward a particular solution. In the consumer market, this is the same type of problem solving an individual or household might follow when buying a first home.

---

[3]Robinson, Faris, and Wind, *Industrial Buying and Creative Marketing*, chap. 1; see also Erin Anderson, Wujin Chu, and Barton Weitz, "Industrial Purchasing: An Empirical Exploration of the Buyclass Framework," *Journal of Marketing* 51 (July 1987): pp. 71–86; and Morry Ghingold, "Testing the 'Buygrid' Buying Process Model," *Journal of Purchasing and Materials Management* 22 (Winter 1986): pp. 30–36.

[4]The levels of decision making discussed in this section are drawn from John A. Howard and Jagdish N. Sheth, *The Theory of Buyer Behavior* (New York: John Wiley and Sons, 1969), chap. 2.

Buying-Decision Approaches[5]   Two distinct buying-decision approaches are used: judgmental new task and strategic new task. The greatest level of uncertainty confronts firms in judgmental new-task situations because the product may be technically complex, evaluating alternatives is difficult, and dealing with a new supplier has unpredictable aspects. Consider purchasers of a special type of production equipment who are uncertain about the model or brand to choose, the suitable level of quality, and the appropriate price to pay. For such purchases, buying activities include a moderate amount of information search and a moderate use of formal tools in evaluating key aspects of the buying decision.

Even more effort is invested in **strategic new-task decisions.** These purchasing decisions are of extreme importance to the firm strategically and financially. If the buyer perceives that a rapid pace of technological change surrounds the decision, search effort is increased but concentrated in a shorter time period.[6] Long-range planning drives the decision process. To illustrate, a large health insurance company placed a $600,000 order for workstation furniture. The long-term effect on the work environment shaped the six-month decision process and involved the active participation of personnel from several departments.

Strategy Guidelines   The business marketer confronting a new-task buying situation can gain a differential advantage by participating actively in the initial stages of the procurement process. The marketer should gather information on the problems facing the buying organization, isolate specific requirements, and offer proposals to meet the requirements. Ideas that lead to new products often originate not with the marketer but with the customer.

Marketers who are presently supplying other items to the organization ("in" suppliers) have an edge over other firms: They can see problems unfolding and are familiar with the "personality" and behavior patterns of the organization. The successful business marketer carefully monitors the changing needs of organizations and is prepared to assist new-task buyers.

Straight Rebuy

When there is a continuing or recurring requirement, buyers have substantial experience in dealing with the need and require little or no new information. Evaluation of new alternative solutions is unnecessary and unlikely to yield appreciable improvements. Thus, a **straight rebuy** approach is appropriate.

Routine problem solving is the decision process organizational buyers employ in the straight rebuy. Organizational buyers apply well-developed choice criteria to the purchase decision. The criteria have been refined over time as the buyers have developed predispositions toward the offerings of one or a few carefully screened suppliers. In the consumer market, this is the same type of problem solving that a shopper might use in selecting 30 items in 20 minutes during a weekly trip to the

---

[5]The discussion of buying decision approaches in this section is drawn from Michele D. Bunn, "Taxonomy of Buying Decision Approaches," *Journal of Marketing* 57 (January 1993): pp. 38–56; see also, Michele D. Bunn, Gul T. Butaney, and Nicole P. Huffman, "An Empirical Model of Professional Buyers' Search Effort," *Journal of Business-to-Business Marketing* 8 (4, 2001): pp. 55–81.

[6]Allen M. Weiss and Jan B. Heide, "The Nature of Organizational Search in High Technology Markets," *Journal of Marketing Research* 30 (May 1993): pp. 230–233. See also Christian Homburg and Sabine Kuester, "Towards an Improved Understanding of Industrial Buying Behavior: Determinants of the Number of Suppliers," *Journal of Business-to-Business Marketing* 8 (2, 2001): pp. 5–29.

supermarket. Indeed, many organizational buying decisions made each day are routine. For example, organizations of all types are continually buying **operating resources**—the goods and services needed to run the business, such as computer and office supplies, maintenance and repair items, and travel services. Procter & Gamble alone spends more than $5 billion annually on operating resources.[7]

Buying Decision Approaches   Research suggests that organizational buyers employ two buying-decision approaches: causal and routine low priority. Causal purchases involve no information search or analysis, and the product or service is of minor importance. The focus is simply on transmitting the order. In contrast, routine low-priority decisions are somewhat more important to the firm and involve a moderate amount of analysis. Describing the purchase of $5000 worth of cable to be used as component material, a buyer aptly describes this decision-process approach:

> On repeat buys, we may look at other sources or alternate methods of manufacturing, etc., to make sure no new technical advancements are available in the marketplace. But, generally, a repeat buy is repurchased from the supplier originally selected, especially for low dollar items.

Strategy Guidelines   The purchasing department handles straight rebuy situations by routinely selecting a supplier from a list of approved vendors and then placing an order. As organizations shift to e-procurement systems, purchasing managers retain control of the process for these routine purchases while allowing individual employees to directly buy online from approved suppliers.[8] Employees use a simple point-and-click interface to navigate through a customized catalog detailing the offerings of approved suppliers, and then order required items. Individual employees like the self-service convenience, and purchasing managers can direct attention to more critical strategic issues. Marketing communications should be designed to reach not only purchasing managers but also individual employees who are now empowered to exercise their product preferences.

The marketing task appropriate for the straight rebuy situation depends on whether the marketer is an "in" supplier (on the list) or an "out" supplier (not among the chosen few). An "in" supplier must reinforce the buyer–seller relationship, meet the buying organization's expectations, and be alert and responsive to the changing needs of the organization.

The "out" supplier faces a number of obstacles and must convince the organization that it can derive significant benefits from breaking the routine. This can be difficult because organizational buyers perceive risk in shifting from the known to the unknown. The organizational spotlight shines directly on them if an untested supplier falters. Buyers may view testing, evaluations, and approvals as costly, time consuming, and unnecessary.

The marketing effort of the "out" supplier rests on an understanding of the basic buying needs of the organization: Information gathering is essential. The marketer must convince organizational buyers that their purchasing requirements have

---

[7]Doug Smock, "Strategic Sourcing: P&G Boosts Leverage," *Purchasing* 133 (November 4, 2004): pp. 40–43.

[8]Talai Osmonbekov, Daniel C. Bello, and David I. Gillilard, "Adoption of Electronic Commerce Tools in Business Procurement: Enhanced Buying Center Structure and Processes," *Journal of Business and Industrial Marketing* 17 (2/3, 2002): pp. 151–166.

changed or that the requirements should be interpreted differently. The objective is to persuade decision makers to reexamine alternative solutions and revise the preferred list to include the new supplier.

Modified Rebuy

In the **modified rebuy** situation, organizational decision makers feel they can derive significant benefits by reevaluating alternatives. The buyers have experience in satisfying the continuing or recurring requirement, but they believe it is worthwhile to seek additional information and perhaps to consider alternative solutions.

Several factors may trigger such a reassessment. Internal forces include the search for quality improvements or cost reductions. A marketer offering cost, quality, or service improvements can be an external precipitating force. The modified rebuy situation is most likely to occur when the firm is displeased with the performance of present suppliers (for example, poor delivery service).

Limited problem solving best describes the decision-making process for the modified rebuy. Decision makers have well-defined criteria but are uncertain about which suppliers can best fit their needs. In the consumer market, college students buying their second computer might follow a limited problem-solving approach.

Buying-Decision Approaches   Two buying-decision approaches typify this buying-class category. Both strongly emphasize the firm's strategic objectives and long-term needs. The simple modified rebuy involves a narrow set of choice alternatives and a moderate amount of both information search and analysis. Buyers concentrate on the long-term-relationship potential of suppliers.

The **complex modified rebuy** involves a large set of choice alternatives and poses little uncertainty. The range of choice enhances the buyer's negotiating strength. The importance of the decision motivates buyers to actively search for information, apply sophisticated analysis techniques, and carefully consider long-term needs. This decision situation is particularly well suited to a competitive bidding process.

Strategy Guidelines   In a modified rebuy, the direction of the marketing effort depends on whether the marketer is an "in" or an "out" supplier. An "in" supplier should make every effort to understand and satisfy the procurement need and to move decision makers into a straight rebuy. The buying organization perceives potential payoffs by reexamining alternatives. The "in" supplier should ask why and act immediately to remedy any customer problems. The marketer may be out of touch with the buying organization's requirements.

The goal of the "out" supplier should be to hold the organization in modified rebuy status long enough for the buyer to evaluate an alternative offering. Knowing the factors that led decision makers to reexamine alternatives could be pivotal. A particularly effective strategy for an "out" supplier is to offer performance guarantees as part of the proposal.[9] To illustrate, the following guarantee prompted International Circuit Technology, a manufacturer of printed circuit boards, to change to a new supplier for plating chemicals: "Your plating costs will be no more than x cents per

---

[9]Mary Siegfried Dozbaba, "Critical Supplier Relationships: Converting Higher Performance," *Purchasing Today* (February 1999): pp. 22–29.

FIGURE 2.2 | **FORCES INFLUENCING ORGANIZATIONAL BUYING BEHAVIOR**

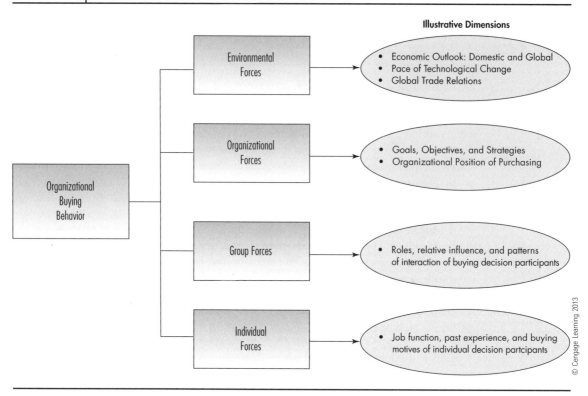

square foot or we will make up the difference."[10] Given the nature of the production process, plating costs can be easily monitored by comparing the square footage of circuit boards moving down the plating line with the cost of plating chemicals for the period. Pleased with the performance, International Circuit Technology now routinely reorders from this new supplier.

The eight-stage model of the organizational buying process provides the foundation for exploring the myriad forces that influence a buying decision by an organization. Observe in Figure 2.2 how organizational buying behavior is influenced by environmental forces (for example, the growth rate of the economy); organizational forces (for example, the size of the buying organization); group forces (for example, patterns of influence in buying decisions); and individual forces (for example, personal preferences).

Environmental Forces

A projected change in business conditions, a technological development, or a new piece of legislation can drastically alter organizational buying plans. Among the environmental forces that shape organizational buying behavior are economic, political,

---

[10]Somerby Dowst, "CEO Report: Wanted: Suppliers Adept at Turning Corners," *Purchasing* 101 (January 29, 1987): pp. 71–72.

legal, and technological influences. Collectively, such environmental influences define the boundaries within which buyer–seller relationships develop. Particular attention is given to selected economic and technological forces that influence buying decisions.

Economic Influences

Because of the derived nature of industrial demand, the marketer must be sensitive to the strength of demand in the ultimate consumer market. The demand for many industrial products fluctuates more widely than the general economy. Firms that operate on a global scale must be sensitive to the economic conditions that prevail across regions. To complicate matters, a "two-speed world is emerging, characterized by slower growth in the developed economies of the United States, Europe, and Japan and more rapid growth in Southeast Asia and the BRIC countries (Brazil, Russia, India, and China)."[11] The number of North American companies purchasing goods and services from China, eastern Europe, and India has increased sharply in recent years and will continue to rise.[12]

According to strategists at the Boston Consulting Group, however, "the days of reducing costs simply by sourcing from China are probably over. In the future, companies will rely on a more diversified base of low-cost suppliers across multiple regions."[13] This shifts the focus from low-cost country sourcing to "best cost" country sourcing, an approach that evaluates a range of factors beyond labor costs, such as trade barriers and the inherent risks of longer supply chains. Since the earthquake in Japan exposed vulnerabilities and disrupted the operations of many firms, risk management rises to the top of the agenda as companies seek ways to make their supply chains more flexible and agile in the face of such unpredictable shocks.

The economic environment influences an organization's ability and, to a degree, its willingness to buy. However, shifts in general economic conditions do not affect all sectors of the market evenly. For example, a rise in interest rates may damage the housing industry (including lumber, cement, and insulation) but may have minimal effects on industries such as paper, hospital supplies, office products, and soft drinks. Marketers that serve broad sectors of the business market must be particularly sensitive to the differential effect of selective economic shifts on buying behavior.

Technological Influences

The rate of technological change in an industry influences the composition of the decision-making unit in the buying organization. As the pace of technological change increases, the importance of the purchasing manager in the buying process declines. Technical and engineering personnel tend to be more important when the rate of technological change is great. Recent research also suggests that buyers who perceive

---

[11]Jesús de Juan, Victor Du, David Lee, Sachin Nandgaon Kar, and Kevin Waddell, "Global Sourcing in the Postdownturn Era," September 2010, The Boston Consulting Group, Inc., accessed at http://www.bcg.com on April 12, 2011, p. 4.

[12]"Global Procurement Study Finds Companies Unprepared to Manage Increased Sourcing from China and India Effectively," accessed at http://www.atkearney.com on May 18, 2005.

[13]de Juan et al., "Global Sourcing in the Postdownturn Era," p. 9.

the pace of technological change to be more rapid: (1) conduct more intense search efforts and (2) spend less time on their overall search processes.[14] Why? "In cost-benefit terms, a fast pace of change implies that distinct benefits are associated with search effort, yet costs are associated with prolonging the process" because the acquired information is "time sensitive."[15]

Organizational Forces

An understanding of the buying organization is based on its strategic priorities, the role of procurement and supply chain management in the executive hierarchy, and the firm's competitive challenges.

Growing Influence of Purchasing

As a rule, the influence of procurement and supply chain management functions is growing. Why? Globalization is upsetting traditional patterns of competition, and companies are feeling the squeeze from rising material costs and stiff customer resistance to price increases. Meanwhile, to enhance efficiency and effectiveness, many firms are outsourcing some functions that were traditionally performed within the organization. As a result, at companies around the world, CEOs are counting on the procurement function to keep their businesses strongly positioned in today's intensively competitive marketplace.[16]

So the scope of a chief procurement officer's (CPO's) role has expanded beyond the traditional core values of cost savings, quality, and supply continuity to include more strategic responsibilities. CPOs remain responsible for delivering cost savings, improving asset utilization, and preserving supplier viability but now must achieve these goals in a way that increases the attractiveness and competitiveness of the firm's end products and services.[17] CPOs are also responsible for procuring materials in a socially and environmentally responsible way that might even include monitoring the carbon footprints or labor practices of suppliers.

Strategic Priorities in Procurement

As the influence of purchasing grows, chief procurement officers feel the heat of the spotlight, so they are pursuing an ambitious set of strategic priorities (Figure 2.3). Here attention centers on corporate goals and how procurement can help their internal customers (that is, other business functions) achieve these goals. For example, Rick Hughes, CPO at Procter & Gamble, works closely with P&G's chief marketing officer (CMO) and has helped improve the return on the $7.5 billion in annual

---

[14]Weiss and Heide, "The Nature of Organizational Search," pp. 220–233; see also Jan B. Heide and Allen M. Weiss, "Vendor Consideration and Switching Behavior for Buyers in High-Technology Markets," *Journal of Marketing* 59 (July 1995): pp. 30–43.

[15]Weiss and Heide, "The Nature of Organizational Search," p. 221.

[16]John LaPorta, "Assessing and Accelerating the Skills of Your Procurement Staff," *Supply and Demand Chain Executive*, January 12, 2011, pp. 1–4, accessed at http://www.sdcexec.com on April 10, 2011.

[17]Robert M. Monczka, "Value Focused Supply: Linking Supply to Competitive Business Strategies" (Tempe AZ: Institute for Supply Management and W. P. Carey School of Business at Arizona State University, 2010), pp. 2–22, accessed at http://www.capsresearch.org on April 10, 2011.

FIGURE 2.3 | **STRATEGIC PRIORITIES IN PROCUREMENT**

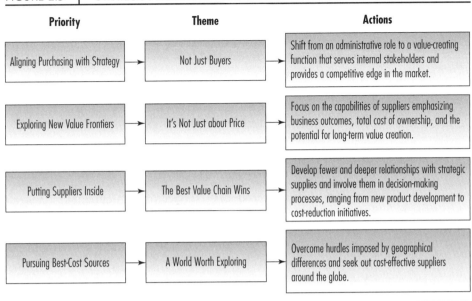

Priority	Theme	Actions
Aligning Purchasing with Strategy	Not Just Buyers	Shift from an administrative role to a value-creating function that serves internal stakeholders and provides a competitive edge in the market.
Exploring New Value Frontiers	It's Not Just about Price	Focus on the capabilities of suppliers emphasizing business outcomes, total cost of ownership, and the potential for long-term value creation.
Putting Suppliers Inside	The Best Value Chain Wins	Develop fewer and deeper relationships with strategic supplies and involve them in decision-making processes, ranging from new product development to cost-reduction initiatives.
Pursuing Best-Cost Sources	A World Worth Exploring	Overcome hurdles imposed by geographical differences and seek out cost-effective suppliers around the globe.

SOURCE: Adapted from Marc Bourde, Charlie Hawker, and Theo Theocharides, "Taking Center Stage: The 2005 Chief Procurement Officer Survey," (Somers, NY: IBM Global Services, May 2005), pp. 1–14. Accessed at http://www.ibm.com/bcs on July 1, 2005; and Chip W. Hardt, Nicholas Reinecke, and Peter Spiller, "Inventing the 21st Century Purchasing Organization," *The McKinsey Quarterly* 2007, No. 4, pp. 115–124.

marketing and advertising investments that the firm makes.[18] As direct participants in the strategy process, procurement managers are also giving increased emphasis to suppliers' *capabilities*, exploring new areas where a strategic supplier can add value to the firm's product or service offerings. Apple Inc.'s elite status as a premier product innovator is reinforced by its position as a recognized leader in supply chain management. In designing the iPad, Apple drew on some of the same skilled suppliers that it had used in developing the popular iPhone and iPod Touch.[19]

Leading-edge purchasing organizations have also learned that the "best value chain wins," so they are building closer relationships with a carefully chosen set of strategic suppliers and aligning the activities of the supply chain with customers' needs.[20] For example, Honda of America reduced the cost of the Accord's purchased content by setting cost targets for each component—engine, chassis, and so on.[21] Then, purchasing managers worked with global suppliers to understand the cost structure of each component, observe how it is manufactured, and identify ways to reduce costs, add value, or do both.

---

[18]Brett Booen, "The Best Chief Procurement Officers (CPOs) in the World," *Supply Chain Digital*, January 3, 2011, pp. 2–3, accessed at http://www.supplychaindigital.com on April 10, 2011.

[19]Don Clark, "IPad Taps Familiar Apple Suppliers," *The Wall Street Journal*, April 5, 2010, p. 1, accessed at http://www.online.wsj.com on April 10, 2011.

[20]Mark Gottfredson, Rudy Puryear, and Stephen Phillips, "Strategic Sourcing: From Periphery to the Core," *Harvard Business Review* 83 (February 2005): pp. 132–139.

[21]Timothy M. Laseter, *Balanced Sourcing: Cooperation and Competition in Supplier Relationships* (San Francisco: Jossey-Bass, 1998), pp. 5–18.

Procurement Manager's Toolkit

Let's examine three tools that procurement managers use and the corresponding implications that each presents for business marketing strategy. Included here are the three approaches that procurement managers apply in: (1) calculating the total cost of ownership of an acquired good or service, (2) segmenting purchase categories to isolate those that have the greatest impact on firm performance, and (3) deploying e-procurement processes.

Total Cost of Ownership (TCO)

When purchasing a product or service, the procurement manager always considers a host of costs above and beyond the actual purchase price. **TCO** considers the full range of costs associated with the purchase and use of a product or service over its complete life cycle. For example, a firm can justify buying a higher-quality product and paying a premium price because the initial purchase cost will be offset by fewer manufacturing defects, lower inventory requirements, and lower administrative costs.

Observe in Table 2.1 that an organizational customer considers three different types of costs in a total cost-in-use calculation:

1. **Acquisition costs** include not only the selling price and transportation costs but also the administrative costs of evaluating suppliers, expediting orders, and correcting errors in shipments or delivery.

2. **Possession costs** include financing, storage, inspection, taxes, insurance, and other internal handling costs.

3. **Usage costs** are those associated with ongoing use of the purchased product such as installation, employee training, user labor, and field repair, as well as product replacement and disposal costs.

INSIDE BUSINESS MARKETING

Use TCO to Inform Next Car Purchase

Edmunds, Inc. applies the TCO philosophy to its True Cost to Own® pricing system that allows a car shopper to calculate the ownership costs of alternative makes and models. Included here are the costs associated with buying, owning, and operating a car over a five-year period. As you may expect, two cars that are offered for the same purchase price represent striking differences in the total cost to own over the five-year period. To view the True Cost to Own® any vehicle, go to http://www.edmunds.com/tco.html.

SOURCE: Philip Reed, "True Cost to Own (TCO): Revealing the Hidden Costs of Car Ownership," April 30, 2009, accessed at http://www.edmunds.com on April 15, 2011.

TABLE 2.1 | CUSTOMERS' TOTAL COST OF OWNERSHIP

Acquisition Costs	+	Possession Costs	+	Usage Costs	=	Total Cost in Use
Price		Interest cost		Installation costs		
Paperwork cost		Storage cost		Training cost		
Transportation costs		Quality control		User labor cost		
Expediting cost		Taxes and insurance		Product longevity		
Cost of mistakes in order		Shrinkage and obsolescence		Replacement costs		
Prepurchase product evaluation costs		General internal handling costs		Disposal costs		

SOURCE: Adapted from Frank V. Cespedes, "Industrial Marketing: Managing New Requirements," *Sloan Management Review* 35 (Spring 1994), p. 46.

Strategy Response: Develop Value-Based Sales Tools

Astute business marketers can pursue value-based strategies that provide customers with a lower cost-in-use solution.[22] For example, the logistical expenses of health-care supplies typically account for 10 to 15 percent of a hospital's operating costs. Medical products firms, like Becton, Dickinson and Company (BD), develop innovative product/service packages that respond to each component of the cost-in-use equation. Such firms can reduce a hospital's acquisition costs by offering an electronic ordering system, possession costs by emphasizing just-in-time service, and usage costs by creating an efficient system for disposing of medical supplies after use. Sales teams at BD document those savings for their hospital customers and draw on those rich case histories to illustrate the lower total cost-in-use of their offerings in proposals to new customer prospects. Value-based strategies seek to move the selling proposition from one that centers on current prices and individual transactions to a longer-term relationship built on value and lower total cost-in-use.

Segmenting Purchase Categories[23]

Each firm purchases a unique portfolio of products and services. Leaders in procurement are giving increased attention to segmenting total purchases into distinct categories and sharpening their focus on those purchases that have the greatest effect on revenue generation or present the greatest risk to corporate performance. From Figure 2.4, observe that various categories of purchases are segmented on the basis of procurement complexity and the nature of the effect on corporate performance (that is, revenue impact/business risk).

Which Purchases Affect Performance? Procurement complexity considers factors such as the technical complexity, the scope of supply chain coordination required, and the degree to which life cycle costs are relevant. The revenue impact/ business risk dimension considers the degree to which a purchase category can

[22]Frank V. Cespedes, "Industrial Marketing: Managing New Requirements," *Sloan Management Review* 35 (Spring 1994): pp. 45–60.

[23]This section is based on Matthew G. Anderson and Paul B. Katz, "Strategic Sourcing," *International Journal of Logistics Management* 9 (1, 1998): pp. 1–13.

FIGURE 2.4 | SEGMENTING THE BUY

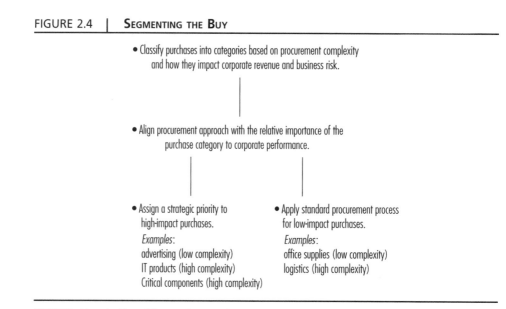

SOURCE: Adapted with modifications from Matthew G. Anderson and Paul B. Katz, "Strategic Sourcing." *International Journal of Logistics Management 9* (1, 1998), p. 7.

influence customers' perceptions of value. For example, purchasing managers at Ford decided that some components are important to brand identity, such as steering wheels, road wheels, and other highly visual parts.

Purchasing managers can use a segmentation approach to isolate those purchase categories that have the greatest effect on corporate revenues. For example, advertising services could have tremendous risk implications relative to customer perceptions of value, whereas office supplies remain a cost issue. Or, in the high-tech arena, the procurement of a new generation of semiconductor technology may essentially be a bet on the company's future.[24]

Strategy Implications   Business marketers should assess where their offerings are positioned in the portfolio of purchases a particular organization makes. This varies by firm and by industry. The revenue and profit potential for the business marketer is greatest in those purchasing organizations that view the purchase as strategic—high revenue impact and high customer-value impact. For example, in the auto industry, electronic braking systems, audio and navigation systems, as well as turbochargers, fit into this category and represent about one-quarter of a passenger vehicle's cost.[25] Here the marketer can contribute offerings directly tied to the customer organization's strategy, enjoying an attractive profit margin. If the business marketer can become a central component of the customer's supply chain, the effect is even more significant: a valuable, long-term relationship in which the customer views the supplier as an extension of its organization. For categories of goods that purchasing organizations view as less strategic (for example, office supplies), the

---

[24]Ibid., p. 7.

[25]Srikant Inampudi, Aurobind Satpathy, and Anant Singh, "Can North American Auto Suppliers Create Value?" *The McKinsey Quarterly*, June 2008, accessed at http://www.mckinsey.com on June 8, 2008.

appropriate marketing strategy centers on providing a complete product assortment, competitive pricing, timely service support, and simplified ordering. By understanding how customers segment their purchases, business marketers are better equipped to target profitable customer groups and develop customized strategies.

E-Procurement

Like consumers who are shopping at Amazon (http://www.amazon.com), purchasing managers use the Internet to find new suppliers, communicate with current suppliers, or place an order. Why are purchasing organizations embracing online purchasing technologies? Because they "deliver measurable benefits in the form of material cost savings, process efficiencies, and performance enhancements" according to Tim Minahan, a supply chain consultant at the Aberdeen Group.[26] Studying procurement processes at 60 companies, including American Express, Motorola, and Alcoa, Aberdeen found that e-procurement cut purchasing cycle time in half, reduced material costs by 14 percent and purchasing administrative costs by 60 percent, and enhanced the ability of procurement units to identify new suppliers on a global scale.

Reverse Auctions

One online procurement tool that sparks debate in the business market is the reverse auction. Rather than one seller and many buyers, a **reverse auction** involves one buyer who invites bids from several prequalified suppliers who face off in a dynamic, real-time, competitive bidding process. Reverse auctions are most widely used in the automobile, electronics, aerospace, and pharmaceutical industries. Proponents claim that reverse auctions can lower the cost of procuring products and services by 20 percent or more. Critics counter that reverse auctions can inflict real damage on supplier relationships and that the realized savings are often overstated.[27] For example, during the recent economic downturn, many firms used reverse auctions as a tactical weapon to drive supplier prices down but often found that the winning bidder delivered less value—lower quality and poorer service than existing suppliers.

Reverse auctions are best suited for commodity-type items such as purchasing materials, diesel fuel, metal parts, chemicals, and many raw materials. On the other hand, reverse auctions are generally *not* appropriate for strategic relationships, where suppliers have specialized capabilities and few suppliers can meet quality and performance standards. Rob Harlan, senior director of information technology for Motorola, aptly states: "We pride ourselves on strong supplier relationships. We are not going to jeopardize these for short-term gains with online auctions."[28]

A Strategic Approach to Reverse Auctions[29] Pricing experts suggest that customers use reverse auctions for two purposes: (1) to purchase commodity products at the lowest possible price and (2) to tempt suppliers of differentiated products to

---

[26]Tim A. Minahan, "Best Practices in E-Sourcing: Optimizing and Sustaining Supply Savings," September 2004, p. 3, research report by Aberdeen Group, Inc., Boston, Massachusetts; accessed at http://www.ariba.com on June 15, 2005.

[27]Mohanbir Sawhney, "Forward Thinking about Reverse Auctions," June 1, 2003 issue of CIO Magazine, accessed at http://www.cio.com on June 20, 2005, pp. 1–6.

[28]Minahan, "Best Practices in E-Sourcing," p. 52.

[29]This discussion is based on John Bloomer, Joe Zale, and John E. Hogan, "Battling Powerful Procurement Groups: How to Profitably Participate in Reverse Auctions," *SPG Insights* (Fall 2004): pp. 1–3; accessed at http://www.imakenews.com/strategicpricing on August 1, 2008.

sacrifice their profit margins in the heat of bidding. If a firm's offering is not highly differentiated from competition, participating in an auction may represent the only choice. However, to minimize the risk of winning an unprofitable bid, a careful estimate should be made of the true incremental cost of supplying the customer, including the costs associated with special terms and conditions as well as unique technical, marketing, and sales support. This analysis will provide the business marketing strategist with a "walk-away" price.

In contrast, if a firm's offering provides significant value to customers relative to competition, John Bloomer, Joe Zale, and John Hogan, consultants at the Strategic Pricing Group, recommend the following decisive tactics:

1. "Preempt the auction: convince the buyer not to go forward with the auction because you have a unique value proposition and are not inclined to participate.

2. Manage the process: influence bid specifications and vendor qualification criteria.

3. Walk away: simply refuse to participate..."[30]

A strategic approach to reverse auctions, then, defines success as winning only those bids that are profitable and that do not undermine pricing for other products or for other customers.

Organizational Positioning of Purchasing

As purchasing moves from a transaction-based support role and assumes a more prominent strategic spot at the executive level, many leading firms are centralizing the procurement function. An organization that centralizes procurement decisions approaches purchasing differently than a company in which purchasing decisions are made at individual user locations. When purchasing is centralized, a separate organizational unit has authority for purchases at a regional, divisional, or headquarters level. For example, by centralizing procurement, American Express realized nearly $600 million in purchasing savings in the first three years.[31] IBM, Sara Lee, 3M, Walt Disney, Wendy's International, and Citicorp are among other corporations that emphasize centralized procurement. A marketer who is sensitive to organizational influences can more accurately map the decision-making process, isolate buying influentials, identify salient buying criteria, and target marketing strategy for centralized buyers.

Strategy Response: Key Account Management

The organization of the marketer's selling strategy should parallel the organization of the purchasing function of key accounts. To avoid disjointed selling activities and internal conflict in the sales organization, and to serve the special needs of important

---

[30]Ibid., p. 2.

[31]Susan Avery, "American Express Changes Ahead," *Purchasing* 133 (November 4, 2004): pp. 34–38.

customers, many business marketers have developed key account management programs to establish a close working relationship that, according to Benson Shapiro and Rowland Moriarty, "cuts across multiple levels, functions, and operating units in both the buying and selling organizations."[32] For example, IBM assigns a dedicated account team to work with large customers, like Boeing or State Farm Insurance.

> Key account management can best be described as an enterprise-wide initiative (involving not just the sales force) to develop strategic relationships (not transactional relationships) with a limited number of customers in order to achieve long-term, sustained, significant, and measurable business value for both the customer and the provider.[33]

For large, multinational organizations that have the structure, processes, and information systems to centrally coordinate purchases on a global scale, the customer might be considered for global account management status. A **global account management program** treats a customer's worldwide operations as one integrated account, with coherent terms for pricing, service, and product specifications.[34] For example, Xerox and Hewlett-Packard each have over 100 corporate clients who are given global account status.

ETHICAL BUSINESS MARKETING

Gift Giving: "Buy Me These Boots and You'll Get My Business"

Greg Davies, director of sales for Action Printing in Fond du Lac, Wisconsin, encountered this awkward situation. Leaving a restaurant after taking a potential customer to lunch, the prospective client stopped to examine the window display of a country-and-western store located nearby. That's when Davies's prospect turned to him and said very slowly: "I have always wanted a pair of boots like this." "There was no mistaking it: He expected me to buy him the boots," recalls Davies, who simply smiled and began walking again. He declined because company policy, as well as his personal value system, forbids the exchange of expensive personal gifts for business. As you would imagine, from that day forward, Greg felt awkward around the prospect.

Sales experts suggest that Greg made the right business decision, as well as the right moral decision. He stood behind a well-conceived company policy. In turn, Jacques Werth, a sales consultant, agreed with the decision to walk away. "If your relationship is based on extravagant gifts, entertainment, and other perks, you're likely to lose the business when a bigger bribe comes along, anyway."

SOURCE: Melinda Ligos, "Gimme, Gimme, Gimme!" *Sales & Marketing Management* (March 2001), pp. 33–40.

---

[32]Benson P. Shapiro and Rowland T. Moriarty, *National Account Management: Emerging Insights* (Cambridge, MA: Marketing Science Institute, 1982), p. 8.

[33]Mark Lubkeman and Vikas Taneja, "Creating Value in Key Accounts," The Boston Consulting Group, Inc., 2011, p. 2, accessed at http://www.bcg.com on April 13, 2011.

[34]George S. Yip and Audrey J. M. Bink, "Managing Global Accounts," *Harvard Business Review* 85 (September 2007): pp. 103–111.

Group Forces

Multiple buying influences and group forces are critical in organizational buying decisions. The organizational buying process typically involves a complex set of smaller decisions made or influenced by several individuals. The group members' degree of involvement varies from routine rebuys, in which the purchasing agent simply takes into account the preferences of others, to complex new-task buying situations, in which a group plays an active role.

The industrial salesperson must address three questions.

- Which organizational members take part in the buying process?

- What is each member's relative influence in the decision?

- What criteria are important to each member in evaluating prospective suppliers?

The salesperson who can correctly answer these questions is ideally prepared to meet the needs of a buying organization and has a high probability of becoming the chosen supplier.

The Buying Center

The concept of the buying center provides rich insights into the role of group forces in organizational buying behavior.[35] The buying center consists of individuals who participate in the purchasing decision and share the goals and risks arising from the decision. The size of the buying center varies, but an average buying center includes more than four persons per purchase; the number of people involved in all stages of one purchase may be as many as 20.[36]

The composition of the buying center may change from one purchasing situation to another and is not prescribed by the organizational chart. A buying group evolves during the purchasing process in response to the information requirements of the specific situation. Because organizational buying is a process rather than an isolated act, different individuals are important to the process at different times.[37] A design engineer may exert significant influence early in the process when product specifications are being established; others may assume a more dominant role in later phases. A salesperson must define the buying situation and the information requirements from the organization's perspective in order to anticipate the size and composition of the buying center. Again, the composition of the buying center evolves during the purchasing process, differs from firm to firm, and varies from one purchasing situation to another.

---

[35]For a comprehensive review of buying center research, see Wesley J. Johnston and Jeffrey E. Lewin, "Organizational Buying Behavior: Toward an Integrative Framework," *Journal of Business Research* 35 (January 1996): pp. 1–15; and J. David Lichtenthal, "Group Decision Making in Organizational Buying: A Role Structure Approach," in *Advances in Business Marketing*, vol. 3, ed. Arch G. Woodside (Greenwich, CT: JAI Press, 1988), pp. 119–157.

[36]For example, see Robert D. McWilliams, Earl Naumann, and Stan Scott, "Determining Buying Center Size," *Industrial Marketing Management* 21 (February 1992): pp. 43–49.

[37]Ghingold and Wilson, "Buying Center Research and Business Marketing Practice," pp. 96–108; see also Gary L. Lilien and M. Anthony Wong, "Exploratory Investigation of the Structure of the Buying Center in the Metalworking Industry," *Journal of Marketing Research* 21 (February 1984): pp. 1–11.

TABLE 2.2	THE INVOLVEMENT OF BUYING CENTER PARTICIPANTS AT DIFFERENT STAGES OF THE PROCUREMENT PROCESS

Stages of Procurement Process for a Medical Supplier

Buying Center Participants	Identification of Need	Establishment of Objectives	Identification and Evaluation of Buying Alternatives	Selection of Suppliers
Physicians	High	High	High	High
Nursing	Low	High	High	Low
Administration	Moderate	Moderate	Moderate	High
Engineering	Low	Moderate	Moderate	Low
Purchasing	Low	Low	Low	Moderate

SOURCE: Adapted by permission. Reprinted from *Industrial Marketing Management, 8*(1), Gene R. Laczniak, "An Empirical Study of Hospital Buying," p. 61, copyright © 1979, with permission of Elsevier.

Isolating the Buying Situation   Defining the buying situation and determining whether the firm is in the early or later stages of the procurement decision-making process are important first steps in defining the buying center. The buying center for a new-task buying situation in the not-for-profit market is presented in Table 2.2. The product, intensive-care monitoring systems, is complex and costly. Buying center members are drawn from five functional areas, each participating to varying degrees in the process. A marketer who concentrated exclusively on the purchasing function would be overlooking key buying influentials.

Erin Anderson and her colleagues queried a large sample of sales managers about the patterns of organizational buying behavior their salespeople confront daily. Sales forces that frequently encounter new-task buying situations generally observe that:

> The buying center is large, slow to decide, uncertain about its needs and the appropriateness of the possible solutions, more concerned about finding a good solution than getting a low price or assured supply, more willing to entertain proposals from "out" suppliers and less willing to favor "in" suppliers, more influenced by technical personnel, [and] less influenced by purchasing agents.[38]

By contrast, Anderson and her colleagues found that sales forces facing more routine purchase situations (that is, straight and modified rebuys) frequently observe buying centers that are "small, quick to decide, confident in their appraisals of the problem and possible solutions, concerned about price and supply, satisfied with 'in' suppliers, and more influenced by purchasing agents."[39]

Predicting Composition   A marketer can also predict the composition of the buying center by projecting the effect of the industrial product on various functional areas in the organization. If the procurement decision will affect the marketability of

---

[38]Anderson , Chu, and Weitz, "Industrial Purchasing," p. 82.

[39]Ibid.

INSIDE BUSINESS MARKETING

Innovate and Win with BMW

Leading procurement organizations expect their suppliers to innovate, and they reward them when they do. At firms such as P&G, Coca-Cola, and BMW, purchasing executives use "potential to innovate" as a key criterion for selecting suppliers and evaluate contributions to innovation as part of the supplier development process.

Business marketers who contribute innovative ideas to the new-product-development process at such firms win the support of purchasing managers, marketing executives, design engineers, and other members of the buying center. For example, a salesperson for a top supplier to BMW proposed adding optic-fiber-enabled light rings to headlights to add a distinguishing

feature to the brand. "Drivers on the German autobahn or elsewhere would see the distinctive lights of a high-performance BMW approaching from behind and know to move aside and let it pass. BMW and the supplier jointly developed the idea—and the contract ensures exclusive rights for the automaker." As a result of this collaboration, BMW gained access to new technology that adds value to its brand and the supplier won a lucrative, long-term contract.

SOURCE: A. T. Kearney, "Creating Value through Strategic Supply Management: 2004 Assessment of Excellence in Procurement," (February 2005). Accessed at http://www.atkearney.com on June 25, 2005.

a firm's product (for example, product design, price), the marketing department will be active in the process. Engineering will be influential in decisions about new capital equipment, materials, and components; setting specifications; defining product performance requirements; and qualifying potential vendors. Manufacturing executives will be included for procurement decisions that affect the production mechanism (for example, materials or parts used in production). When procurement decisions involve a substantial economic commitment or impinge on strategic or policy matters, top management will have considerable influence.

Buying Center Influence

Members of the buying center assume different roles throughout the procurement process. Frederick Webster Jr. and Yoram Wind have given the following labels to each of these roles: users, gatekeepers, influencers, deciders, and buyers.[40]

As the role name implies, **users** are the personnel who use the product in question. Users may have anywhere from inconsequential to extremely important influence on the purchase decision. In some cases, the users initiate the purchase action by requesting the product. They may even develop the product specifications.

Gatekeepers control information to be reviewed by other members of the buying center. They may do so by disseminating printed information, such as advertisements, or by controlling which salesperson speaks to which individuals in the buying center. To illustrate, the purchasing agent might perform this screening role by opening the gate to the buying center for some sales personnel and closing it to others.

---

[40]Frederick E. Webster Jr. and Yoram Wind, *Organizational Buying Behavior* (Englewood Cliffs, NJ: Prentice-Hall, 1972), p. 77. For a review of buying role research, see Lichtenthal, "Group Decision Making in Organizational Buying," pp. 119–157.

Influencers affect the purchasing decision by supplying information for the evaluation of alternatives or by setting buying specifications. Typically, those in technical departments, such as engineering, quality control, and R&D, have significant influence on the purchase decision. Sometimes, outside individuals can assume this role. For high-tech purchases, technical consultants often assume an influential role in the decision process and broaden the set of alternatives being considered.[41]

Deciders actually make the buying decision, whether or not they have the formal authority to do so. The identity of the decider is the most difficult role to determine: Buyers may have formal authority to buy, but the president of the firm may actually make the decision. A decider could be a design engineer who develops a set of specifications that only one vendor can meet.

The **buyer** has formal authority to select a supplier and implement all procedures connected with securing the product. More powerful members of the organization often usurp the power of the buyer. The buyer's role is often assumed by the purchasing agent, who executes the administrative functions associated with a purchase order.

One person could assume all roles, or separate individuals could assume different buying roles. To illustrate, as users, personnel from marketing, accounting, purchasing, and production may all have a stake in which information technology system is selected. Thus, the buying center can be a very complex organizational phenomenon.

Identifying Patterns of Influence   Key influencers are frequently located outside the purchasing department. To illustrate, the typical capital equipment purchase involves an average of four departments, three levels of the management hierarchy (for example, manager, regional manager, vice president), and seven different individuals.[42] In purchasing component parts, personnel from production and engineering are often most influential in the decision. It is interesting to note that a comparative study of organizational buying behavior found striking similarities across four countries (the United States, the United Kingdom, Australia, and Canada) in the involvement of various departments in the procurement process.[43]

Past research provides some valuable clues for identifying powerful buying center members (Table 2.3).[44] To illustrate, individuals who have an important personal stake in the decision possess, expert knowledge concerning the choice, and/or are

---

[41]Paul G. Patterson and Phillip L. Dawes, "The Determinants of Choice Set Structure in High-Technology Markets," *Industrial Marketing Management* 28 (July 1999): pp. 395–411; and Philip L. Dawes, Don Y. Lee, and David Midgley, "Organizational Learning in High-Technology Purchase Situations: The Antecedents and Consequences of the Participation of External IT Consultants," *Industrial Marketing Management* 36 (April 2007): pp. 285–299.

[42]Wesley J. Johnston and Thomas V. Bonoma, "The Buying Center: Structure and Interaction Patterns," *Journal of Marketing* 45 (Summer 1981): pp. 143–156; see also Gary L. Lilien and M. Anthony Wong, "An Exploratory Investigation of the Structure of the Buying Center in the Metalworking Industry," *Journal of Marketing Research* 21 (February 1984): pp. 1–11; and Arch G. Woodside, Timo Liakko, and Risto Vuori, "Organizational Buying of Capital Equipment Involving Persons across Several Authority Levels," *Journal of Business and Industrial Marketing* 14 (1, 1999): pp. 30–48.

[43]Peter Banting, David Ford, Andrew Gross, and George Holmes, "Similarities in Industrial Procurement across Four Countries," *Industrial Marketing Management* 14 (May 1985): pp. 133–144.

[44]John R. Ronchetto, Michael D. Hutt, and Peter H. Reingen, "Embedded Influence Patterns in Organizational Buying Systems," *Journal of Marketing* 53 (October 1989): pp. 51–62; see also Ajay Kohli, "Determinants of Influence in Organizational Buying: A Contingency Approach," *Journal of Marketing* 53 (July 1989): pp. 50–65; Daniel H. McQuiston and Peter R. Dickson, "The Effect of Perceived Personal Consequences on Participation and Influence in Organizational Buying," *Journal of Business Research* 23 (September 1991): pp. 159–177; and Jerome M. Katrichis, "Exploring Departmental Level Interaction Patterns in Organizational Purchasing Decisions," *Industrial Marketing Management* 27 (March 1998): pp. 135–146.

TABLE 2.3 | CLUES FOR IDENTIFYING POWERFUL BUYING CENTER MEMBERS

- *Isolate the personal stakeholders.* Those individuals who have an important personal stake in the decision will exert more influence than other members of the buying center. For example, the selection of production equipment for a new plant will spawn the active involvement of manufacturing executives.
- *Follow the information flow.* Influential members of the buying center are central to the information flow that surrounds the buying decision. Other organizational members will direct information to them.
- *Identify the experts.* Expert power is an important determinant of influence in the buying center. Those buying center members who possess the most knowledge—and ask the most probing questions of the salesperson—are often influential.
- *Trace the connections to the top.* Powerful buying center members often have direct access to the top-management team. This direct link to valuable information and resources enhances the status and influence of the buying center members.
- *Understand purchasing's role.* Purchasing is dominant in repetitive buying situations by virtue of technical expertise, knowledge of the dynamics of the supplying industry, and close working relationships with individual suppliers.

SOURCE: Adapted from John R. Ronchetto, Michael D. Hutt, and Peter H. Reingen, "Embedded Influence Patterns in Organizational Buying Systems," Journal of Marketing 53 (October 1989): pp. 51–62.

central to the flow of decision-related information tend to assume an active and influential role in the buying center. Purchasing managers assume a dominant role in repetitive buying situations.

Based on their buying center research, Donald W. Jackson Jr. and his colleagues provide these strategy recommendations:

> Marketing efforts will depend upon which individuals of the buying center are more influential for a given decision. Because engineering and manufacturing are more influential in product selection decisions, they may have to be sold on product characteristics. On the other hand, because purchasing is most influential in supplier selection decisions, they may have to be sold on company characteristics.[45]

Individual Forces

Individuals, not organizations, make buying decisions. Each member of the buying center has a unique personality, a particular set of learned experiences, a specified organizational function, and a perception of how best to achieve both personal and organizational goals. Importantly, research confirms that organizational members who perceive that they have an important personal stake in the buying decision participate more forcefully in the decision process than their colleagues.[46] To understand the organizational buyer, the marketer should be aware of individual perceptions of the buying situation.

---

[45]Donald W. Jackson, Jr., Janet E. Keith, and Richard K. Burdick, "Purchasing Agents' Perceptions of Industrial Buying Center Influence," *Journal of Marketing* 48 (Fall 1984): pp. 75–83.

[46]McQuiston and Dickson, "The Effect of Perceived Personal Consequences on Participation and Influence in Organizational Buying," pp. 159–177.

Differing Evaluative Criteria

Evaluative criteria are specifications that organizational buyers use to compare alternative industrial products and services; however, these criteria may conflict. Industrial product users generally value prompt delivery and efficient servicing; engineering values product quality, standardization, and testing; and purchasing assigns the most importance to maximum price advantage and economy in shipping and forwarding.[47]

Product perceptions and evaluative criteria differ among organizational decision makers as a result of differences in their educational backgrounds, their exposure to different types of information from different sources, the way they interpret and retain relevant information (perceptual distortion), and their level of satisfaction with past purchases.[48] Engineers have an educational background different from that of plant managers or purchasing agents: They are exposed to different journals, attend different conferences, and possess different professional goals and values. A sales presentation that is effective with purchasing may be entirely off the mark with engineering.

Responsive Marketing Strategy   A marketer who is sensitive to differences in the product perceptions and evaluative criteria of individual buying center members is well equipped to prepare a responsive marketing strategy. To illustrate, a research study examined the industrial adoption of solar air-conditioning systems and identified the criteria important to key decision makers.[49] Buying center participants for this purchase typically include production engineers, heating and air-conditioning (HVAC) consultants, and top managers. The study revealed that marketing communications directed at production engineers should center on operating costs and energy savings; HVAC consultants should be addressed concerning noise level and initial cost of the system; and top managers are most interested in whether the technology is state-of-the-art. Knowing the criteria of key buying center participants has significant operational value to the marketer when designing new products and when developing and targeting advertising and personal selling presentations.

Information Processing

Volumes of information flow into every organization through direct-mail advertising, the Internet, journal advertising, trade news, word-of-mouth, and personal sales presentations. What an individual organizational buyer chooses to pay attention to, comprehend, and retain has an important bearing on procurement decisions.

Selective Processes   Information processing is generally encompassed in the broader term cognition, which U. Neisser defines as "all the processes by which the

---

[47]Jagdish N. Sheth, "A Model of Industrial Buyer Behavior," *Journal of Marketing* 37 (October 1973): p. 51; see also Sheth, "Organizational Buying Behavior: Past Performance and Future Expectations," *Journal of Business & Industrial Marketing* 11 (3/4, 1996): pp. 7–24.

[48]Sheth, "A Model of Industrial Buyer Behavior," pp. 52–54.

[49]Jean-Marie Choffray and Gary L. Lilien, "Assessing Response to Industrial Marketing Strategy," *Journal of Marketing* 42 (April 1978): pp. 20–31. For related research, see R. Venkatesh, Ajay K. Kohli, and Gerald Zaltman, "Influence Strategies in Buying Centers," *Journal of Marketing* 59 (October 1995): pp. 71–82; and Mark A. Farrell and Bill Schroder, "Influence Strategies in Organizational Buying Decisions," *Industrial Marketing Management* 25 (July 1996): pp. 293–303.

sensory input is transformed, reduced, elaborated, stored, recovered, and used."[50] Important to an individual's cognitive structure are the processes of selective exposure, attention, perception, and retention.

1. *Selective exposure.* Individuals tend to accept communication messages consistent with their existing attitudes and beliefs. For this reason, a purchasing agent chooses to talk to some salespersons and not to others.

2. *Selective attention.* Individuals filter or screen incoming stimuli to admit only certain ones to cognition. Thus, an organizational buyer is more likely to notice a trade advertisement that is consistent with his or her needs and values.

3. *Selective perception.* Individuals tend to interpret stimuli in terms of their existing attitudes and beliefs. This explains why organizational buyers may modify or distort a salesperson's message in order to make it more consistent with their predispositions toward the company.

4. *Selective retention.* Individuals tend to recall only information pertinent to their own needs and dispositions. An organizational buyer may retain information concerning a particular brand because it matches his or her criteria.

Each of these selective processes influences the way an individual decision maker responds to marketing stimuli. Because the procurement process often spans several months and because the marketer's contact with the buying organization is infrequent, marketing communications must be carefully designed and targeted.[51] Key decision makers "tune out" or immediately forget poorly conceived messages. They retain messages they deem important to achieving goals.

Risk-Reduction Strategies

Individuals are motivated by a strong desire to reduce risk in purchase decisions. Perceived risk includes two components: (1) uncertainty about the outcome of a decision and (2) the magnitude of consequences from making the wrong choice. Research highlights the importance of perceived risk and the purchase type in shaping the structure of the decision-making unit.[52] Individual decision making is likely to occur in organizational buying for straight rebuys and for modified rebuys when the perceived risk is low. In these situations, the purchasing agent may initiate action.[53] Modified rebuys of higher risk and new tasks seem to spawn a group structure.

[50]U. Neisser, *Cognitive Psychology* (New York: Appleton, 1966), p. 4.

[51]See, for example, Brent M. Wren and James T. Simpson, "A Dyadic Model of Relationships in Organizational Buying: A Synthesis of Research Results," *Journal of Business and Industrial Marketing* 11 (3/4, 1996): pp. 68–79.

[52]Elizabeth J. Wilson, Gary L. Lilien, and David T. Wilson, "Developing and Testing a Contingency Paradigm of Group Choice in Organizational Buying," *Journal of Marketing Research* 28 (November 1991): pp. 452–466.

[53]Sheth, "A Model of Industrial Buyer Behavior," p. 54; see also W. E. Patton III, Charles P. Puto, and Ronald H. King, "Which Buying Decisions Are Made by Individuals and Not by Groups?" *Industrial Marketing Management* 15 (May 1986): pp. 129–138.

In confronting "risky" purchase decisions, how do organizational buyers behave? As the risk associated with an organizational purchase decision increases, the following occur[54]:

- The buying center becomes larger and comprises members with high levels of organizational status and authority.

- The information search is active and a wide variety of information sources are consulted. As the decision process unfolds, personal information sources (for example, discussions with managers at other organizations that have made similar purchases) become more important.

- Buying center participants invest greater effort and deliberate more carefully throughout the purchase process.

- Sellers who have a proven track record with the firm are favored—the choice of a familiar supplier helps reduce perceived risk.

Rather than price, product quality and after-sale service are typically most important to organizational buyers when they confront risky decisions. When introducing new products, entering new markets, or approaching new customers, the marketing strategist should evaluate the effect of alternative strategies on perceived risk.

Summary

Knowledge of the process that organizational buyers follow in making purchasing decisions is fundamental to responsive marketing strategy. As a buying organization moves from the problem-recognition phase, in which a procurement need is defined, to later phases, in which suppliers are screened and ultimately chosen, the marketer can play an active role. In fact, the astute marketer often triggers initial awareness of the problem and helps the organization effectively solve that problem. Incremental decisions made throughout the buying process narrow the field of acceptable suppliers and dramatically influence the ultimate outcome.

The nature of the buying process depends on the organization's level of experience with similar procurement problems. It is thus crucial to know how the organization defines the buying situation: as a new task, a modified rebuy, or a straight rebuy. Each buying situation requires a unique problem-solving approach, involves unique buying influentials, and demands a unique marketing response.

Myriad forces—environmental, organizational, group, and individual—influence organizational buying behavior. First, environmental forces define the boundaries within which industrial buyers and sellers interact, such as general business conditions or the rate of technological change. Second, organizational forces dictate the

---

[54]Johnston and Lewin, "Organizational Buying Behavior: Toward an Integrative Framework," pp. 8–10. See also Charles P. Puto, W. E. Patton III, and Ronald H. King, "Risk Handling Strategies in Industrial Vendor Selection Decisions," *Journal of Marketing* 49 (Winter 1985), pp. 89–98.

link between buying activities and the strategic priorities of the firm and the position that the purchasing function occupies in the organizational structure. Rather than devoting exclusive attention to "buying for less," leading organizations tie procurement activities directly to corporate strategy and use online procurement tools to streamline processes and advance performance. Procurement managers emphasize the total cost of ownership in evaluating alternative offerings and adopt a segmentation approach to isolate those purchase categories that have the greatest impact on corporate performance.

Third, the relevant unit of analysis for the marketing strategist is the buying center. The composition of this group evolves during the buying process, varies from firm to firm, and changes from one purchasing situation to another. Fourth, the marketer must ultimately concentrate attention on individual members of the buying center. Each brings a particular set of experiences and a unique personal and organizational frame of reference to the buying decision. The marketer who is sensitive to individual differences is best equipped to develop responsive marketing communications that the organizational buyer will remember.

Unraveling the complex forces that encircle the organizational buying process is indeed difficult. This chapter offers a framework that enables the marketing manager to begin this task by asking the right questions. The answers provide the basis for effective and efficient business marketing strategy.

Discussion Questions

1. Segmentation is a tool that marketers use to identify target markets. Increasingly, purchasing managers are using the segmentation approach to determine which suppliers are most critical to the goals of the organization. Explain.

2. The levels of risk associated with organizational purchases range from low to high. Discuss how the buying process for a risky purchase differs from the process for a routine purchase.

3. Describe the total-cost-of-ownership orientation that purchasing managers use and illustrate how you could apply it to your next automobile purchase decision.

4. Organizations purchase millions of notebook computers each year. Identify several evaluative criteria that purchasing managers might use in choosing a particular brand. In your view, which criteria would be most decisive in the buying decision?

5. A small manufacturer developed a new high-speed packaging system that could be appealing to food-processing firms such as Pillsbury and General Mills. This new packaging system is far more efficient but must be priced 15 percent higher than competitors' products. Because purchasing managers evaluate the "total cost of ownership" of major purchases, what selling points should the business marketer emphasize to demonstrate the superiority of this new product?

6. Carol Brooks, purchasing manager for Apex Manufacturing Company, read the *Wall Street Journal* this morning and carefully studied, clipped, and saved a full-page ad by the Allen-Bradley Company. Ralph

Thornton, the production manager at Apex, read several articles from the same paper but could not recall seeing this particular ad or, for that matter, any ads. How could this occur?

7. Harley-Davidson, the U.S. motorcycle producer, recently purchased some sophisticated manufacturing equipment to enhance its position in a very competitive market. First, what environmental forces might have been important in spawning this capital investment? Second, which functional units were likely to have been represented in the buying center?

8. Explain how the composition of the buying center evolves during the purchasing process and how it varies from one firm to another, as well as from one purchasing situation to another. What steps can a salesperson take to identify the influential members of the buying center?

9. Jim Jackson, an industrial salesperson for Pittsburgh Machine Tool, will call on two accounts this afternoon. The first will be a buying organization Jim has been servicing for the past three years. The second call, however, poses more of a challenge. This buying organization has been dealing with a prime competitor of Pittsburgh Machine Tool for five years. Jim, who has good rapport with the purchasing and engineering departments, feels that the time may be right to penetrate this account. Recently, Jim learned that the purchasing manager was extremely unhappy with the existing supplier's poor delivery service. Define the buying situations confronting Jim and outline the appropriate strategy he should follow in each case.

10. The Kraus Toy Company recently decided to develop a new electronic game. Can an electrical parts supplier predict the likely composition of the buying center at Kraus Toy? What steps could an industrial salesperson take to influence the composition of the buying center?

Internet Exercises

1. GE Healthcare has developed an e-commerce initiative to support its marketing strategy, which targets health-care organizations on a worldwide basis. Go to http://www.gemedicalsystems.com and

   a. identify the products and services that the GE unit offers, and

   b. provide a critique of the Web site and consider the degree to which it provides access to the information that a potential buyer might want.

2. Ariba, Inc., is a leading provider of e-procurement software solutions. Go to http://www.ariba.com and

   a. describe the key products and services that the firm offers to its customers, and

   b. review a case history that describes a particular customer and how it has applied one of Ariba's procurement solutions.

Customer Relationship Management Strategies for Business Markets

A well-developed ability to create and sustain successful working relationships with customers gives business marketing firms a significant competitive advantage. After reading this chapter, you will understand:

1. The patterns of buyer–seller relationships in the business market

2. The factors that influence the profitability of individual customers

3. A procedure for designing effective customer relationship management programs

4. The critical determinants of relationship marketing effectiveness

Every night, John Chambers, CEO of Cisco Systems, receives a personal update on 15 to 20 major customers via voice mail. "E-mail would be more efficient but I want to hear the emotion, I want to hear the frustration; I want to hear the caller's level of comfort with the strategy we're employing," says Chambers. "I can't get that through e-mail."[1]

Leading business marketing firms like Cisco and General Electric succeed by providing superior value to customers, by satisfying the special needs of even the most demanding customers, and by understanding the factors that influence individual customer profitability.[2] Compared with the consumer packaged-goods sector, customer profitability is particularly important in business markets because marketing managers allocate a greater proportion of their marketing resources at the individual customer level.[3] The ability of an organization to create and maintain profitable relationships with these most valuable customers is a durable basis of competitive advantage. Building and maintaining lasting customer relationships requires paying careful attention to detail, meeting promises, and swiftly responding to new requirements.

The new era of business marketing is built upon effective relationship management.[4] Many business marketing firms create what might be called a **collaborative advantage** by demonstrating special skills in managing relationships with key customers or by jointly developing innovative strategies with alliance partners.[5] These firms have learned how to be good partners, and these superior relationship skills are a valuable asset. This chapter explores the types of relationships that characterize the business market. What market and situational factors are associated with different types of buyer–seller relationships? What factors influence customer profitability? What strategies can business marketers employ to build profitable relationships with customers? What are the critical drivers of relationship marketing effectiveness?

Relationship Marketing[6]

Relationship marketing centers on all activities directed toward establishing, developing, and maintaining successful exchanges with customers and other constituents.[7] Nurturing and managing customer relationships has emerged as an important strategic priority in most firms. Why? First, loyal customers are far more profitable than customers who are price sensitive and perceive few differences among alternative offerings. Second, a firm that is successful in developing strong relationships with customers secures important and durable advantages that are hard for competitors to understand, copy, or displace.

---

[1]Frederick E. Reichheld, "Lead for Loyalty," *Harvard Business Review* 79 (July–August 2001): p. 82.

[2]Beth Comstock, Ranjay Gulati, and Stephen Liguori, "Unleashing the Power of Marketing," *Harvard Business Review* 88 (October 2010): pp. 1800–1808.

[3]Douglas Bowman and Das Narayandas, "Linking Customer Management Effort to Customer Profitability in Business Markets," *Journal of Marketing Research* 41 (November 2004): pp. 433–447.

[4]For a comprehensive review, see Robert W. Palmatier, *Relationship Marketing* (Boston: Marketing Science Institute, 2008).

[5]Rosabeth Moss Kanter, "Collaborative Advantage," *Harvard Business Review* 72 (July–August 1994): pp. 96–108.

[6]This section is based on George S. Day, "Managing Market Relationships," *Journal of the Academy of Marketing Science* 28 (Winter 2000): pp. 24–30, except when others are cited.

[7]Robert M. Morgan and Shelby D. Hunt, "The Commitment-Trust Theory of Relationship Marketing," *Journal of Marketing* 58 (July 1994): pp. 20–38.

FIGURE 3.1 | **THE RELATIONSHIP SPECTRUM**

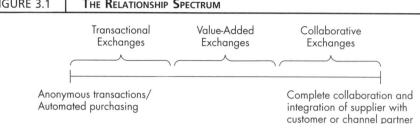

SOURCE: With kind permission from *Springer Science+Business Media: Journal of Academy of Marketing Science*, "Managing Market Relationships," 28, 2000, p. 25, by George S. Day. Copyright © 2000.

Types of Relationships

A business marketer may begin a relationship with GE as a supplier (one of many), move to a preferred supplier status (one of a few), and ultimately enter a collaborative relationship with GE (sole source for particular items). Observe in Figure 3.1 that buyer–seller relationships are positioned on a continuum, with transactional exchange and collaborative exchange serving as the endpoints. Central to every relationship is an exchange process where each side gives something in return for a payoff of greater value. **Transactional exchange** centers on the timely exchange of basic products for highly competitive market prices. George Day notes that such exchanges

> include the kind of autonomous encounters a visitor to a city has with the taxi or bus from the airport, as well as a series of ongoing transactions in a business-to-business market where the customer and supplier focus only on the timely exchange of standard products at competitive prices.[8]

Moving across the continuum, relationships become closer or more collaborative. The open exchange of information is a characteristic of collaborative (close) versus transactional (distant) exchange. Likewise, **operational linkages** reflect how much the systems, procedures, and routines of the buying and selling firms have been connected to facilitate operations.[9] These relationship connectors are a feature of a collaborative relationship. For example, such linkages provide the basis for order replenishment or just-in-time deliveries that Honda receives each day from suppliers at its Marysville, Ohio, production facility. **Collaborative exchange** features very close information, social, and operational linkages as well as mutual commitments made in expectation of long-run benefits. According to James Anderson and James Narus, collaborative exchange involves

> a process where a customer and supplier firm form strong and extensive social, economic, service, and technical ties over time, with the intent of lowering total costs and/or increasing value, thereby achieving mutual benefit.[10]

---

[8]Day, "Managing Market Relationships," p. 25.

[9]Joseph P. Cannon and William D. Perreault Jr., "Buyer-Seller Relationships in Business Markets," *Journal of Marketing Research* 36 (November 1999): pp. 439–460.

[10]James C. Anderson and James A. Narus, "Partnering as a Focused Market Strategy," *California Management Review* 33 (Spring 1991): p. 96. See also Ven Srivam, Robert Krapfel, and Robert Spekman, "Antecedents to Buyer-Seller Collaboration: An Analysis from the Buyer's Perspective," *Journal of Business Research* (December 1992): pp. 303–320.

Value-Adding Exchanges

Between the two extremes on the relationship continuum are value-adding exchanges, where the focus of the selling firm shifts from attracting customers to keeping customers. The marketer pursues this objective by developing a comprehensive understanding of a customer's needs and changing requirements, tailoring the firm's offerings to those needs, and providing continuing incentives for customers to concentrate most of their purchases with them. To illustrate, W. W. Grainger provides a customized Web page for each of its premier corporate customers that individual employees in the customer organization can use to track expenditures on maintenance and operating supplies against key performance benchmarks.

Nature of Relationships

Transactional exchange involves items like packaging materials or cleaning services where competitive bidding is often employed to secure the best terms. Such exchanges are purely contractual arrangements that involve little or no emotional commitment to sustaining the relationship in the future. By contrast, customized, high-technology products—like semiconductor test equipment—fit the collaborative exchange category. Whereas transactional exchange centers on negotiations and an arm's-length relationship, collaborative exchange emphasizes joint problem solving and multiple linkages that integrate the processes of the two parties. Trust and commitment provide the foundation for collaborative exchange.[11] **Relationship commitment** involves a partner's belief that an ongoing relationship is so important that it deserves maximum effort to maintain it. In turn, **trust** exists when one party has confidence in a partner's reliability and integrity. Recent research highlights the powerful role that contact personnel (for example, salespersons) assume in forging a long-term relationship. "Individuals who build trust in each other will transfer this bond to the firm level."[12]

Strategic Choices

Business marketers have some latitude in choosing where to participate along the relationship continuum. However, limits are imposed by the characteristics of the market and by the significance of the purchase to the buyer. A central challenge for the marketer is to overcome the gravitational pull toward the transaction end of the exchange spectrum. According to Day,

> Rivals are continually working to attract the best accounts away; customer requirements, expectations, and preferences keep changing, and the possibility of friction-free exploration of options in real time on the Web conspire to raise the rate of customer defections.[13]

---

[11]Morgan and Hunt, "The Commitment-Trust Theory," pp. 20–38. See also Patricia M. Doney and Joseph P. Cannon, "An Examination of the Nature of Trust in Buyer-Seller Relationships," *Journal of Marketing* 61 (April 1997): pp. 35–51.

[12]Das Narayandas and V. Kasturi Rangan, "Building and Sustaining Buyer-Seller Relationships in Mature Industrial Markets," *Journal of Marketing* 68 (July 2004): p. 74; and Robert W. Palmatier, Lisa K. Scheer, and Jan-Benedict E. M. Steenkamp, "Customer Loyalty to Whom? Managing the Benefits and Risks of Salesperson-Owned Loyalty," *Journal of Marketing Research* 44 (May 2007): pp. 185–199.

[13]Day, "Managing Market Relationships," p. 25.

FIGURE 3.2 | THE SPECTRUM OF BUYER-SELLER RELATIONSHIPS

	Transactional Exchange ←→	Collaborative Exchange
Availability of Alternatives	Many Alternatives	Few Alternatives
Supply Market Dynamism	Stable	Volatile
Importance of Purchase	Low	High
Complexity of Purchase	Low	High
Information Exchange	Low	High
Operational Linkages	Limited	Extensive

SOURCE: Adapted from Joseph P. Cannon and William D. Perreault Jr., "Buyer-Seller Relationships in Business Markets," *Journal of Marketing Research* 36 (November 1999): pp. 439–460.

Managing Buyer–Seller Relationships

Buyers and sellers craft different types of relationships in response to market conditions and the characteristics of the purchase situation. To develop specific relationship-marketing strategies for a particular customer, the business marketer must understand that some customers elect a collaborative relationship, whereas others prefer a more distant or transactional relationship. Figure 3.2 highlights the typical characteristics of relationships at the endpoints of the buyer–seller relationship spectrum.

Transactional Exchange

Customers are more likely to prefer a **transactional relationship** when a competitive supply market features many alternatives, the purchase decision is not complex, and the supply market is stable. This profile fits some buyers of office supplies, commodity chemicals, and shipping services. In turn, customers emphasize a transactional orientation when they view the purchase as less important to the organization's objectives. Such relationships are characterized by lower levels of information exchange and are less likely to involve operational linkages between the buying and selling firms.

Collaborative Exchange

Buying firms prefer a more **collaborative relationship** when alternatives are few, the market is dynamic (for example, rapidly changing technology), and the complexity of the purchase is high. In particular, buyers seek close relationships with suppliers when they deem the purchase important and strategically significant. This behavior fits some purchasers of manufacturing equipment, enterprise software, or critical component parts. Indeed, Cannon and Perreault state that "the closest partnerships ... arise both when the purchase is important and when there is a need—from the customer's perspective—to overcome procurement obstacles that result from fewer supply alternatives and more purchase uncertainty."[14]

Moreover, the relationships that arise for important purchases are more likely to involve operational linkages and high levels of information exchange. Switching costs are especially important to collaborative customers.

Switching Costs

In considering possible changes from one selling firm to another, organizational buyers consider two **switching costs**: investments and risk of exposure. First, organizational buyers invest in their relationships with suppliers in many ways. As Barbara Bund Jackson states:

> They invest money; they invest in *people*, as in training employees to run new equipment; they invest in *lasting assets*, such as equipment itself; and they invest in changing basic business *procedures* like inventory handling.[15]

Because of these past investments, buyers may hesitate to incur the disruptions and switching costs that result when they select new suppliers.

Risk of exposure provides a second major category of switching costs. Attention centers on the risks to buyers of making the wrong choice. Customers perceive more risk when they purchase products important to their operations, when they buy from less established suppliers, and when they buy technically complex products.

Strategy Guidelines

The business marketer manages a portfolio of relationships with customers—some of these customers view the purchase as important and desire a close, tightly connected buyer–seller relationship; other customers assign a lower level of importance to the purchase and prefer a looser relationship. Given the differing needs and orientations of customers, the business marketer's first step is to determine which type of relationship matches the purchasing situation and supply-market conditions for a particular customer. Second, a strategy must be designed that is appropriate for each strategy type.

Collaborative Customers   Relationship-building strategies, targeted on strong and lasting commitments, are especially appropriate for these customers. Business marketers can sensibly invest resources to secure commitments and directly assist customers with planning. Here sales and service personnel work not only with purchasing managers but also with a wide array of managers on strategy and coordination issues. Regular visits to the customer by executives and technical personnel can strengthen the relationship. Operational linkages and information-sharing mechanisms should be designed into the relationship to keep product

---

[14]Cannon and Perreault, "Buyer-Seller Relationships," p. 453.

[15]Barbara Bund Jackson, "Build Customer Relationships That Last," *Harvard Business Review* 63 (November–December 1985): p. 125.

and service offerings aligned with customer needs. Given the long time horizon and switching costs, customers are concerned both with the marketers' long-term capabilities and with their immediate performance. Because the customers perceive significant risk, they demand competence and commitment from sellers and are easily frightened by even a hint of supplier inadequacy.

Value Drivers in Collaborative Relationships   A recent study examined this intriguing question: What avenues of differentiation can suppliers of routinely purchased products use to create value in business-to-business relationships, thereby winning key supplier status?[16] The results suggest that relationship benefits display a much stronger potential for differentiation in key supplier relationships than cost considerations. Importantly, service support and personal interaction were identified as the core differentiators, followed by a supplier's know-how and its ability to improve a customer's time to market. Product quality and delivery performance, along with cost savings associated with the acquisition process and from operations, display a moderate potential to help a firm gain key supplier status. Finally, price displayed the weakest potential for differentiation. The researchers, Wolfgang Ulaga and Andreas Eggert, conclude: "Whereas cost factors serve as key criteria to get a supplier on the short list of those vendors considered for a relationship, relationship benefits dominate when deciding which supplier" should be awarded key supplier status.[17]

Transaction Customers   These customers display less loyalty or commitment to a particular supplier and can easily switch part or all of the purchases from one vendor to another. A business marketer who offers an immediate, attractive combination of product, price, technical support, and other benefits has a chance of winning business from a transactional customer. The salesperson centers primary attention on the purchasing staff and seldom has important ties to senior executives in the buying organization. M. Bensaou argues that it is unwise for marketers to make specialized investments in transactional relationships:

> Firms that invest in building trust through frequent visits, guest engineers, and cross-company teams when the product and market context calls for simple, impersonal control and data exchange mechanisms are overdesigning the relationship. This path is not only costly but also risky, given the specialized investments involved, in particular, the intangible ones (for example, people, information, or knowledge).[18]

Rather than adopting the approach of "one design fits all," the astute marketer matches the strategy to the product and market conditions that surround a particular customer relationship and understands the factors that influence profitability.

---

[16]Wolfgang Ulaga and Andreas Eggert, "Value-Based Differentiation in Business Relationships: Gaining and Sustaining Key Supplier Status," *Journal of Marketing* 70 (January 2006): pp. 119–136.

[17]Ibid., p. 131.

[18]M. Bensaou, "Portfolio of Buyer-Seller Relationships," *Sloan Management Review* 40 (Summer 1999): p. 43.

Measuring Customer Profitability[19]

To improve customer satisfaction and loyalty, many business-to-business firms have developed customized products and increased the specialized services they offer. Although customers embrace such actions, they often lead to declining profits, especially when the enhanced offerings are not accompanied by increases in prices or order volumes. For a differentiation strategy to succeed, "the value created by the differentiation—measured by higher margins and higher sales volumes—has to exceed the cost of creating and delivering customized features and services."[20] By understanding the drivers of customer profitability, the business marketing manager can more effectively allocate marketing resources and take action to convert unprofitable relationships into profitable ones.

Activity-Based Costing

Most studies of customer profitability yield a remarkable insight: "Only a minority of a typical company's customers is truly profitable."[21] Why? Many firms fail to examine how the costs of specialized products and services vary among individual customers. In other words, they focus on profitability at an aggregate level (for example, product or territory), fail to assign operating expenses to customers, and misjudge the profitability of individual customers. To capture customer-specific costs, many firms have adopted activity-based costing.

Activity-based costing (ABC) illuminates exactly what activities are associated with serving a particular customer and how these activities are linked to revenues and the consumption of resources.[22] The ABC system and associated software link customer transaction data from customer relationship management (CRM) systems with financial information. The ABC system provides marketing managers with a clear and accurate picture of the gross margins and cost-to-serve components that yield individual customer profitability.

Unlocking Customer Profitability

By accurately tracing costs to individual customers, managers are better equipped to diagnose problems and take appropriate action. For example, Kanthal, a heating wire manufacturer, learned to its surprise that one of its largest and most coveted accounts—General Electric's Appliance Division—was also one of its most unprofitable customers.[23] A customer order that normally would cost Kanthal $150 to process cost more than $600 from GE because of frequent order changes, expedited deliveries, and scheduling adjustments. A senior manager at Kanthal suggested to GE that the numerous change orders were costly not only to Kanthal but also to GE. After a quick internal review, GE managers agreed, corrected internal inefficiencies, and then awarded Kanthal with the largest contract in the firm's history.

---

[19]This section, unless otherwise noted, draws on Robert S. Kaplan and V. G. Narayanan, "Measuring and Managing Customer Profitability," *Journal of Cost Management* 15 (5, September–October 2001): pp. 5–15.

[20]Robert S. Kaplan, "Add a Customer Profitability Metric to Your Balanced Scorecard," *Balanced Scorecard Report*, July–August 2005 (Boston: Harvard Business School Publishing Corporation): p. 3.

[21]Kaplan and Narayanan, "Measuring and Managing Customer Profitability," p. 5.

[22]Ibid., p. 7. See also Robert S. Kaplan and Steven R. Anderson, "Time-Driven Activity-Based Costing," *Harvard Business Review* 82 (November 2004): pp. 131–138.

[23]Kaplan and Narayanan, "Measuring and Managing Customer Profitability," p. 11.

FIGURE 3.3 | **THE WHALE CURVE ILLUSTRATION: 20% OF CUSTOMERS GENERATE 175% OF CUMULATIVE PROFITS**

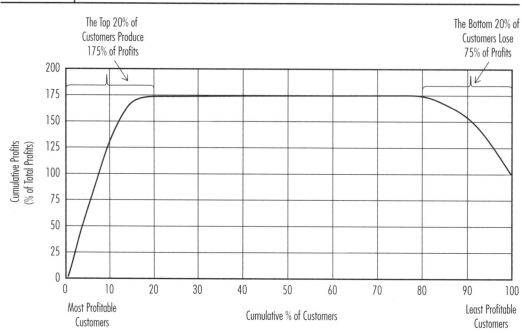

SOURCE: Adapted with modifications from Robert S. Kaplan and V.G. Narayanan, "Measuring and Managing Customer Profitability," *Journal of Cost Management* 15 (September/October 2001): p. 8.

The contract incorporated a surcharge for any change GE made to an existing order and established a minimum order size. By isolating the true cost of serving GE, Kanthal converted an unprofitable relationship into a profitable one and provided further value by helping a key customer reduce costs.

The Profitable Few

Once a firm implements an ABC approach and plots cumulative profitability against customers, a striking portrait emerges that is often referred to as the *whale curve* (Figure 3.3). Robert S. Kaplan, who is codeveloper of activity-based costing, and his colleague, V. G. Narayanan, describe the pattern that many companies find:

> Whereas cumulative sales usually follow the typical 20/80 rule (that is, 20 percent of the customers provide 80 percent of the sales), the whale curve for cumulative profitability usually reveals that the most profitable 20 percent of customers generate between 150 percent and 300 percent of total profits. The middle 70 percent of customers break even and the least profitable 10 percent of customers lose from 50 to 200 percent of total profits, leaving the company with its 100 percent of total profits.[24]

[24]Ibid., p. 7. See also Robert S. Kaplan and David P. Norton, *The Execution Premium* (Boston: Harvard Business Press, 2008): pp. 255–261.

TABLE 3.1 | THE CHARACTERISTICS OF HIGH- VERSUS LOW-COST-TO-SERVE CUSTOMERS

	High-Cost-to-Serve Customers	Low-Cost-to-Serve Customers
Presale Costs	Extensive presales support required (i.e., technical and sales resources)	Limited presales support (i.e., standard pricing and ordering)
Production Costs	Order custom products Small order quantities Unpredictable ordering pattern Manual processing	Order standard products Large order quantities Predictable ordering cycle Electronic processing
Delivery Costs	Fast delivery	Standard delivery
Post-sale Service Costs	Extensive post-sales support required (i.e., customer training, installation, technical support)	Limited post-sales support

SOURCE: Adapted, with modifications, from Robert S. Kaplan and V. G. Narayanan, "Measuring and Managing Customer Profitability," *Journal of Cost Management* 15 (September/October 2001): p. 8 and Benson P. Shapiro, V. Kasturi Rangan, Rowland Moriarty, Jr., and Elliot B. Ross, "Manage Customers for Profits (Not Just Sales)," *Harvard Business Review* 65 (September–October 1987): pp. 101–108.

As a rule, large customers tend to be included among the most profitable (see left side of Figure 3.3) or the least profitable (see right side of Figure 3.3)—they are seldom in the middle. Interestingly, some of the firm's largest customers often turn out to be among the most unprofitable. A firm does not generate enough sales volume with a small customer to incur large absolute losses. Only large buyers can be large-loss customers. In Figure 3.3, low-cost-to-serve customers appear on the profitable side of the whale curve and high-cost-to-serve customers end up on the unprofitable side unless they pay a premium price for the specialized support they require.

Managing High- and Low-Cost-to-Serve Customers

What causes some customers to be more expensive than others? Note from Table 3.1 that high-cost-to-serve customers, for example, desire customized products, frequently change orders, and require a significant amount of presales and post-sales support. By contrast, low-cost-to-serve customers purchase standard products, place orders and schedule deliveries on a predictable cycle, and require little or no presales or post-sales support.

Look Inside First   After reviewing the profitability of individual customers, the business marketer can consider possible strategies to retain the most valuable customers and to transform unprofitable customers into profitable ones. However, managers should first examine their company's own internal processes to ensure that it can accommodate customer preferences for reduced order sizes or special services at the lowest cost. For example, a large publisher of business directories reduced the cost of serving its customer base by assigning key account managers to its largest customers (that is, the 4 percent of customers who accounted for 45 percent of its sales) and serving the smallest customers over the Internet and by a telephone sales force.[25]

---

[25]George S. Day, "Creating a Superior Customer-Relating Capability," *MIT Sloan Management Review* 44 (Spring 2003): pp. 77–82.

FIGURE 3.4 | Cᴜsᴛᴏᴍᴇʀ Pʀᴏғɪᴛᴀʙɪʟɪᴛʏ

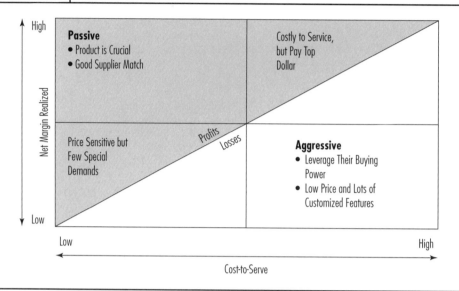

These actions not only cut costs dramatically but also gave each group of customers what they had wanted all along: Large customers wanted a central point of contact where they could secure services customized to their needs; small customers preferred minimal contact with a direct salesperson but wanted the assurance that they could receive advice and support if required.

A Sharper Profit Lens   Business marketing managers can view their customers through the lens of a simple 2×2 diagram (Figure 3.4). The vertical axis shows the net margin earned from sales to a particular customer. The **net margin** equals the net price, after all discounts, minus manufacturing costs. The horizontal axis shows the **costs of serving the customer**, including order-related costs plus the customer-specific marketing, technical, and administrative expenses.

Identifying Profitable Customers   Observe from Figure 3.4 that profitable customers can take different forms. To illustrate, a customer like Honda of America would be at the lower left corner of the diagram: demanding low prices, so net margins are low, but also working with its suppliers to streamline activities so that the cost-to-serve is also low. High-cost-to-serve customers who occupy the upper right corner of Figure 3.4 can also be profitable if the net margins earned on sales to them more than compensate the company for the cost of the resources used in serving them.

A company is indeed fortunate if several of its customers occupy the upper left-hand quadrant of the diagram: high margins *and* low cost-to-serve. Because these customers represent a valuable asset, marketing managers should forge close relationships with them, anticipate their changing needs, and have protective measures (for example, special services) in place in case competitors attempt to win them away.

INSIDE BUSINESS MARKETING

Loyalty and Customer Profitability

In examining the customer base of many firms, four distinct types of customers are present:

- *True friends* (high loyalty and high profitability) are the firm's most valuable customer assets. They are extremely satisfied with the firm's offerings, buy consistently over time, and offer the highest profit potential. They should be managed with special care.

- *Butterflies* (low loyalty and high profitability) are profitable but they enjoy flitting around to find the best prices and avoid building a stable relationship with any seller. To manage this type of customer, the firm should seek ways to lower the cost-to-serve and be willing to abandon the relationships.

- *Barnacles* (high loyalty and low profitability) are long-term customers but do not purchase

enough to generate a satisfactory return on investment. However, these customers can become profitable if properly managed. For example, if the customer is also buying the same or similar items from a competitor, specific up-selling and cross-selling can be done to boost profits. However, if cash flow is their problem, marketing resources should be diverted to Butterflies.

- *Strangers* (low loyalty and low profitability) represent a poor fit with the company's products and services. The key strategy is to identify these customers early and refrain from making marketing investments.

SOURCE: V. Kumar and Bharath Rajan, "Nurturing the Right Customers," *Strategic Finance*, September 2009, pp. 27–33.

Managing Unprofitable Customers[26]

The most challenging set of customers for marketing managers is found in the lower right-hand corner of Figure 3.4: low margins and high cost-to-serve. First, the marketing manager should explore possible ways to reduce the cost of activities associated with serving these customers. For example, perhaps post-sales support could be shifted to the Internet. Second, the manager should direct attention to the customer actions that contribute to higher selling costs. To illustrate, the high cost-to-serve may be caused by the customer's unpredictable ordering patterns or by the large demands it places on technical and sales personnel. By detailing the costs of these activities and openly sharing this information with the customer, the business marketing manager can encourage the customer to work with the company more efficiently. From the earlier example, recall that Kanthal used this approach not only to restore profitability but also to help one of its largest customers, General Electric's Appliance Division, refine its internal processes and reduce its costs.

Firing Customers

By improving processes and refining pricing strategies, business marketing managers can transform many, but not all, customers from unprofitable to profitable. What should we do with those unprofitable customers that remain in the high-cost-to-serve quadrant of Figure 3.4? To answer this question, we have to dig deeper into the

---

[26]This section is based on Robert S. Kaplan and Robin Cooper, *Cost and Effect: Using Integrated Cost Systems to Drive Profitability and Performance* (Boston: Harvard Business School Press, 1998), pp. 193–201.

customer relationship and assess the other benefits that certain customers may provide. Some customers are new, and the initial investment to attract them will ultimately be repaid in higher sales volume and profitability. Other customers provide an opportunity for learning. For example, some firms that serve Toyota or Honda incurred initial losses in serving these demanding customers but secured insights into management processes and technology they could effectively apply to all their customers.

Suppose, however, that a customer is unprofitable, not new, and offers little or no opportunity for learning. Furthermore, suppose that the customer resists all attempts to convert the unprofitable relationship into a profitable one. Under these conditions, Robert S. Kaplan and Robin Cooper observe that we might consider firing them, but a more subtle approach will do: "We can, perhaps, let the customer fire itself by refusing to grant discounts and reducing or eliminating marketing and technical support."[27] Customer divestment is a viable strategic option, but one that must be exercised sparingly and only after other options have been thoroughly examined.[28]

Customer Relationship Management

Customer retention has always been crucial to success in the business market, and it now provides the centerpiece of strategy discussions as firms embrace customer relationship management. **Customer relationship management** (CRM) is a cross-functional process for achieving:

- A continuing dialogue with customers

- Across all their contact and access points, with

- Personalized treatment of the most valuable customers,

- To ensure customer retention and the effectiveness of marketing initiatives.[29]

To meet these challenging requirements, business marketing firms, large and small, are making substantial investments in CRM systems—enterprise software applications that integrate sales, marketing, and customer service information. To improve service and retain customers, CRM systems synthesize information from all of a company's contact points or "touch points"—including e-mail, call centers, sales and service representatives—to support later customer interactions and to inform market forecasts, product design, and supply chain management.[30] Salespersons, call center personnel, Web managers, resellers, and customer service representatives all have the same real-time information on each customer.

For an investment in CRM software to yield positive returns, a firm needs a customer strategy. Strategy experts contend that many CRM initiatives fail because executives mistake CRM software for a marketing strategy. Darrell Rigby and his colleagues contend: "It isn't. CRM is the bundling of customer strategy and processes,

---

[27]Ibid., p. 200.

[28]Vikas Mittal, Matthew Sarkees, and Feisal Murshed, "The Right Way to Manage Unprofitable Customers," *Harvard Business Review* 86 (April 2008): pp. 95–102.

[29]George S. Day, "Capabilities for Forging Customer Relationships," Working Paper, Report No. 00-118, Marketing Science Institute, Cambridge, MA, 2000, p. 4.

[30]Larry Yu, "Successful Customer-Relationship Management," *MIT Sloan Management Review* 42 (Summer 2001): p. 18.

TABLE 3.2 | **CREATING A CUSTOMER RELATIONSHIP MANAGEMENT STRATEGY**

		CRM Priorities		
Acquiring the Right Customers	**Crafting the Right Value Proposition**	**Instituting the Best Processes**	**Motivating Employees**	**Learning to Retain Customers**
		Critical Tasks		
• Identify your most valuable customers. • Calculate your share of their purchases (wallet) for your goods and services.	• Determine the products or services your customers need today and will need tomorrow. • Assess the products or services that your competitors offer today and tomorrow. • Identify new products or services that you should be offering.	• Research the best way to deliver your products or services to customers. • Determine the service capabilities that must be developed and the technology investments that are required to implement customer strategy.	• Identify the tools your employees need to foster customer relationships. • Earn employee loyalty by investing in training and development and constructing appropriate career paths for employees.	• Understand why customers defect and how to win them back. • Identify the strategies your competitors are using to win your high-value customers.
		CRM Technology Can Help		
• Analyze customer revenue and cost data to identify current and future high-value customers. • Target marketing communications to high-value customers.	• Capture relevant product and service behavior data from customer transactions. • Create new distribution channels. • Develop new pricing models.	• Process transactions faster. • Provide better information to customer contact employees. • Manage logistics and the supply chain more efficiently.	• Align employee incentives and performance measures. • Distribute customer knowledge to employees throughout the organization.	• Track customer defection and retention levels. • Track customer service satisfaction levels.

SOURCE: Adapted from Darrell K. Rigby, Frederick F. Reichheld, and Phil Schefter, "Avoid the Four Perils of CRM," *Harvard Business Review* 80 (January–February 2002): p. 106.

supported by relevant software, for the purpose of improving customer loyalty and, eventually, corporate profitability."[31] CRM software can help, but only after a customer strategy has been designed and executed. To develop responsive and profitable customer strategies, special attention must be given to five areas: (1) acquiring the right customers, (2) crafting the right value proposition, (3) instituting the best processes, (4) motivating employees, and (5) learning to retain customers (Table 3.2). Observe how CRM technology from leading producers such as Oracle Corporation

---

[31]Darrell K. Rigby, Frederick F. Reichheld, and Phil Schefter, "Avoid the Four Perils of CRM," *Harvard Business Review* 80 (January–February 2002): p. 102.

can be used to capture critical customer data, transform it into valuable information, and distribute it throughout the organization to support the strategy process from customer acquisition to customer retention. Thus, a well-designed and executed customer strategy, supported by a CRM system, provides the financial payoff.

Acquiring the Right Customers

Customer relationship management directs attention to two critical assets of the business-to-business firm: its stock of current and potential customer relationships and its collective knowledge of how to select, initiate, develop, and maintain profitable relationships with these customers.[32] Customer portfolio management, then, is the process of creating value across a firm's customer relationships—from transactional to collaborative—with an emphasis on balancing the customer's desired level of relationship against the profitability of doing so.[33]

Account selection requires a clear understanding of customer needs, a tight grasp on the costs of serving different groups of customers, and an accurate forecast of potential profit opportunities. The choice of potential accounts to target is facilitated by an understanding of how different customers define value. **Value**, as defined by James Anderson and James Narus, refers to "the economic, technical, service, and social benefits received by a customer firm in exchange for the price paid for a product offering."[34] By gauging the value of their offerings to different groups of customers, business marketers are better equipped to target accounts and to determine how to provide enhanced value to particular customers.

The account selection process should also consider profit potential. Because the product is critical to their operations, some customers place a high value on supporting services (for example, technical advice and training) and are willing to pay a premium price for them. Other customers are most costly to serve, do not value service support, and are extremely price sensitive. Because customers have different needs and represent different levels of current and potential opportunities, a marketer should divide its customers into groups. The marketer wishes to develop a broader and deeper relationship with the most profitable ones and assign a low priority to the least profitable ones.[35] Frank Cespedes asserts that "account selection, therefore, must be explicit about which demands the seller can meet and leverage in dealings with other customers. Otherwise, the seller risks overserving unprofitable accounts and wasting resources that might be allocated to other customer groups."[36]

[32]Ruth N. Bolton, Katherine N. Lemon, and Peter Verhoof, "Expanding Business-to-Business Customer Relationships," *Journal of Marketing* 72 (January 2008): pp. 46–64.

[33]Michael D. Johnson and Fred Selnes, "Diversifying Your Customer Portfolio," *MIT Sloan Management Review* 46 (Spring 2005): pp. 11–14. See also Christian Homburg, Viviana V. Steiner, and Dirk Totzek, "Managing Dynamics in a Customer Portfolio," *Journal of Marketing* 73 (September 2009): pp. 70–89.

[34]Anderson and Narus, "Partnering as a Focused Market Strategy," p. 98. See also Ajay Menon, Christian Homburg, and Nikolas Beutin, "Understanding Customer Value in Business-to-Business Relationships," *Journal of Business-to-Business Marketing* 12 (2, 2005): pp. 1–33; and Ulaga and Eggert, "Value-Based Differentiation," pp. 119–136.

[35]Frederick F. Reichheld, "Lead for Loyalty," *Harvard Business Review* 79 (July–August 2001): pp. 76–84.

[36]Frank V. Cespedes, *Concurrent Marketing: Integrating Product, Sales, and Service* (Boston: Harvard Business School Press, 1995), p. 193. See also Don Peppers, Martha Rogers, and Bob Dorf, "Is Your Company Ready for One-to-One Marketing?" *Harvard Business Review* 77 (January–February 1999): pp. 151–160.

Crafting the Right Value Proposition

A **value proposition** represents the products, services, ideas, and solutions that a business marketer offers to advance the performance goals of the customer organization. Recall from Chapter 1 that the customer value proposition must address this essential question: How do the value elements (benefits) in a supplier's offering compare to those of the next-best alternative? A value proposition may include points of parity (certain value elements are the same as the next-best option) and points of difference (the value elements that make the supplier's offering either superior or inferior to the next-best alternative). For example, a supplier may offer improved technology (positive) at a higher price (negative) and fail to convince customers that the new technology justifies the price increase: "Best-practice suppliers base their value proposition on the few elements that matter most to target customers, demonstrate the value of this superior performance, and communicate it in a way that conveys a sophisticated understanding of the customer's business priorities."[37]

The Bandwidth of Strategies   To develop customer-specific product offerings, the business marketer should next examine the nature of buyer–seller relationships in the industry. The strategies competing firms in an industry pursue fall into a range referred to as the industry bandwidth of working relationships.[38] Business marketers either attempt to span the bandwidth with a portfolio of relationship-marketing strategies or concentrate on a single strategy, thereby having a narrower range of relationships than the industry bandwidth.

Observe in Figure 3.5 how two different industries (medical equipment and hospital supplies) are positioned on the relationship continuum. Because the underlying technology is complex and dynamic, collaborative relations characterize the medical equipment industry. Here, a range of services—technical support, installation, professional training, and maintenance agreements—can augment the core product. By contrast, collaborative relations in the hospital supply industry tend to be more focused and center on helping health-care organizations meet their operational needs (for example, efficient ordering processes and timely delivery).

By diagnosing the spectrum of relationship strategies competitors in an industry follow, a business marketer can tailor strategies that more closely respond both to customers who desire a collaborative emphasis and to those who seek a transaction emphasis. The strategy involves *flaring out* from the industry bandwidth in the collaborative as well as in the transactional direction (see Figure 3.5b).

Flaring Out by Unbundling   An unbundling strategy can reach customers who desire a greater transaction emphasis. Here, related services are unbundled to yield the core product (**a** in Figure 3.5b), which meets a customer's basic price, quality, and availability requirements. For each service that is unbundled, the price is lowered. Augmented services, such as technical assistance, consulting, and just-in-time delivery, are each offered, but in a menu fashion, on an incremental price basis. Importantly, the price increments for the entire set of unbundled services should be greater than the price premium sought for the collaborative offering. This reflects the efficiencies of

---

[37]James C. Anderson, James A. Narus, and Wouter van Rossum, "Customer Value Propositions in Business Markets," *Harvard Business Review* 84 (March 2006): p. 93.

[38]This discussion draws on Anderson and Narus, "Partnering as a Focused Market Strategy," pp. 95–113.

FIGURE 3.5 | **Transactional and Collaborative Working Relationships**

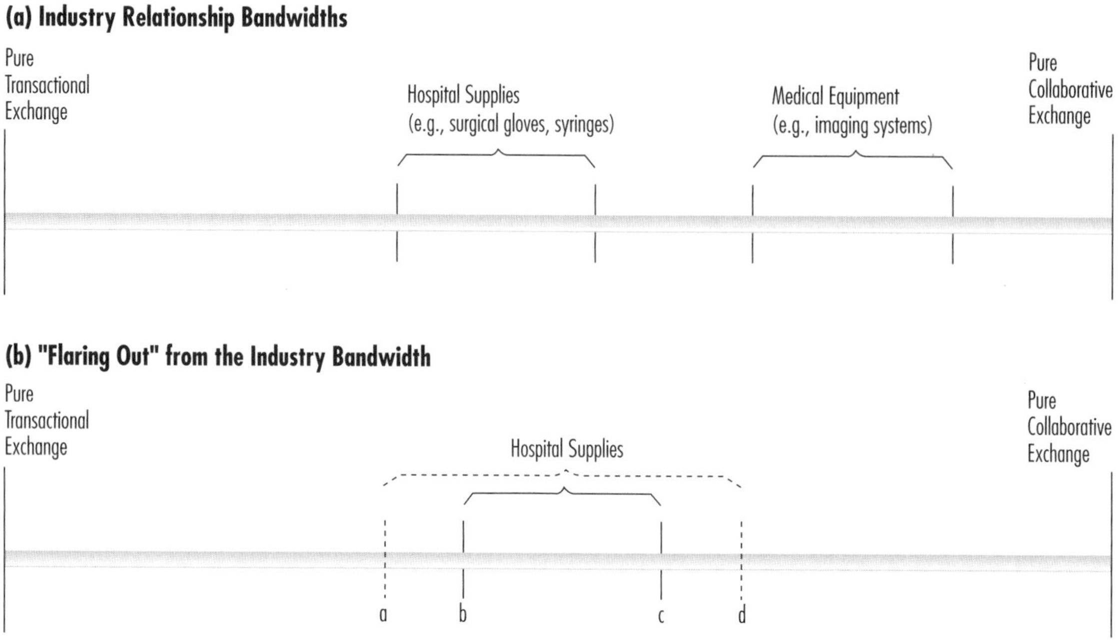

(a) Industry Relationship Bandwidths

Pure
Transactional
Exchange

Hospital Supplies
(e.g., surgical gloves, syringes)

Medical Equipment
(e.g., imaging systems)

Pure
Collaborative
Exchange

(b) "Flaring Out" from the Industry Bandwidth

Pure
Transactional
Exchange

Hospital Supplies

Pure
Collaborative
Exchange

a   b   c   d

SOURCE: Adapted from James C. Anderson and James A. Narus, "Partnering as a Focused Marketing Strategy," *California Management Review* 33 (Spring 1991): p. 97.

providing the complete bundle of services to a collaborative account. This pricing policy is market oriented in that it allows customer firms to choose the product and relationship offering that *they perceive* to provide the greatest value.

Flaring Out with Augmentation   At the other extreme, the collaborative offering (**d** in Figure 3.5b) becomes the augmented product enriched with features the customer values. Augmented features might include coordinated cost-reduction programs, technical assistance, delivery schedule guarantees, and cooperative advertising. Because collaborative efforts are designed to add value or reduce the costs of exchange between partnering firms, a price premium should be received for the collaborative offering.

Allegiance Healthcare Corporation has developed ways to improve hospital supply ordering, delivery, and billing that provide enhanced value to the customer.[39] Instead of miscellaneous supplies arriving in boxes sorted at the convenience of Allegiance's needs, they arrive on "client-friendly" pallets customized to meet the distribution needs of the individual hospital. Moreover, hospitals can secure a structural connection to Allegiance through its ValueLink ordering system for added value and convenience.

---

[39]Valarie A. Zeithaml, Roland T. Rust, and Katherine N. Lemon, "The Customer Pyramid: Creating and Serving Profitable Customers," *California Management Review* 43 (Summer 2001): p. 134.

Creating Flexible Service Offerings   Business marketers can gain a competitive edge by creating a portfolio of service offerings and then drawing on this portfolio to provide customized solutions for groups of customers or even individual customers.[40] First, an offering should be created that includes the bare-bones-minimum number of services valued by all customers in a particular market segment. Microsoft refers to these offerings as "naked solutions." Second, optional services are created that add value by reducing costs or improving the performance of a customer's operations. To meet the needs of particular customers, optional services can then be "custom wrapped" with the core offering to create added value.

Instituting the Best Processes

The sales force assumes a central relationship–management role in the business market. Technical service and customer service personnel also assume implementation roles that are important and visible in buying organizations. Successful relationship strategies are shaped by an effective organization and deployment of the personal selling effort and close coordination with supporting units, such as logistics and technical service. Some firms divide the sales organization into units that each serve a distinct relationship category such as transactional accounts or partnership accounts. Through a careful screening process, promising transaction accounts are periodically upgraded to partnerships.

Best Practices at IBM[41]   In serving a particular customer, a number of IBM employees come into contact with the customer organization. To ensure consistent strategy execution, IBM identifies three customer-contact roles for each of its accounts, specifies desired measurable actions for each role, and monitors the customer's degree of satisfaction with each role (Table 3.3). The IBM client representative assigned to the customer is the *relationship owner*, but the account team may include other specialists who complete a project for the customer (*project owner*) or solve a particular customer problem (*problem resolution owner*). Any IBM employee who works on the account can secure timely information from the CRM system to identify recent actions or issues to be addressed. Moreover, for each role, there is an in-process measure and a customer feedback measure.

Consider an IBM technical manager assigned responsibility for installing CRM software for a large bank. As a project owner, this manager's goal is to determine the customer's conditions of satisfaction and then exceed those expectations. When the work is completed, members of the customer organization are queried concerning their satisfaction and the project owner acts on the feedback to ensure that all promises have been kept. Clearly, a sound complaint management process is essential. Recent research found that if a complaint is ineffectively handled, the firm faces a high risk of losing *even* those customers who had previously been very satisfied.[42]

---

[40]James C. Anderson and James A. Narus, "Capturing the Value of Supplementary Services," *Harvard Business Review* 73 (January–February 1995): pp. 75–83. See also David Rickard, "The Joys of Bundling: Assessing the Benefits and Risks," The Boston Consulting Group, Inc., 2008, accessed at http://www.bcg.com on May 15, 2008.

[41]This discussion is based on Larry Schiff, "How Customer Satisfaction Improvement Works to Fuel Full Business Recovery at IBM," *Journal of Organizational Excellence* 20 (Spring 2001): pp. 3–18.

[42]Christian Homburg and Andreas Fürst, "How Organizational Complaint Handling Drives Customer Loyalty: An Analysis of the Mechanistic and the Organic Approach," *Journal of Marketing* 69 (July 2005): pp. 95–114.

TABLE 3.3 | ROLE-BASED STRATEGY EXECUTION AT IBM: MEASURED ACTIONS AND RESULTS

Role	Strategy Goal	Measured Actions	Measured Results (Customer)
Relationship Owner	Improve Customer Relationships	Meet with customer twice per year to identify customer's expectations and set action plan	IBM Customer Satisfaction Survey Results
Project Owner	Exceed Customer Expectations for Each Transaction	Collect conditions of satisfaction, get customer feedback	IBM Transaction Survey Results
Problem Resolution	Fix Customer Problems	Solve in seven days or meet action plan	Customer Satisfaction with Problem Resolution

SOURCE: Adapted from Larry Schiff, "How Customer Satisfaction Improvement Works to Fuel Business Recovery at IBM," *Journal of Organizational Excellence* (Spring 2001): pp. 12–14.

Research suggests that the performance attributes that influence the customer satisfaction of business buyers include:

- The responsiveness of the supplier in meeting the firm's needs
- Product quality
- A broad product line
- Delivery reliability
- Knowledgeable sales and service personnel[43]

Motivating Employees

Dedicated employees are the cornerstone of a successful customer relationship strategy. As Frederick F. Reichheld notes:

> Leaders who are dedicated to treating people right drive themselves to deliver superior value, which allows them to attract and retain the best employees. That's partly because higher profits result from customer retention, but more important, it's because providing excellent service and value generates pride and a sense of purpose among employees.[44]

Employee loyalty is earned by investing heavily in training and development, providing challenging career paths to facilitate professional development, and aligning employee incentives to performance measures.[45] For example, Square D, an Illinois-based producer of electrical and industrial equipment, altered its performance-measurement and incentive systems to fit the firm's new customer strategy. Consistent with the goal of attracting high-value customers, salesperson incentives are no longer based on the number of units sold but on the number of customers acquired and on profit margins.

---

[43]Bowman and Narayandas, "Linking Customer Management Effort," pp. 433–447.

[44]Reichheld, "Lead for Loyalty," p. 78.

[45]Rigby, Reichheld, and Schefter, "Avoid the Four Perils of CRM," p. 104.

Research clearly demonstrates the link between salespeople's job satisfaction and customer satisfaction in business markets. Christian Homburg and Ruth M. Stock report that the relationship between salespeople's job satisfaction is particularly strong when there is a high frequency of customer interaction, high intensity of customer integration into the value-creating process, and high product or service innovativeness.[46]

Learning to Retain Customers

Business marketers track customer loyalty and retention because the cost of serving a long-standing customer is often far less than the cost of acquiring a new customer.[47] Why? Established customers often buy more products and services from a trusted supplier, and, as they do, the cost of serving them declines. The firm learns how to serve them more efficiently and also spots opportunities for expanding the relationship. Thus, the profit from that customer tends to increase over the life of the relationship. To that end, a goal for IBM is to gain an increasing share of a customer's total information technology expenditures (that is, share of wallet). Rather than merely attempting to improve satisfaction ratings, IBM seeks to be recognized as providing superior value to its customers. Larry Schiff, an IBM strategist, notes: "If you delight your customers and are perceived to provide the best value in your market, you'll gain loyalty and market/wallet share."[48] Although loyal customers are likely to be satisfied, all satisfied customers do not remain loyal. Business marketers earn customer loyalty by providing superior value that ensures high satisfaction and by nurturing trust and mutual commitments.

Pursuing Growth from Existing Customers   Business marketers should identify a well-defined set of existing customers who demonstrate growth potential and selectively pursue a greater share of their business. Based on the cost-to-serve and projected profit margins, the question becomes: Which of our existing customers represent the best growth prospects? In targeting individual customers, particular attention should be given to: (1) estimating the current share of wallet the firm has attained; (2) pursuing opportunities to increase that share; and (3) carefully projecting the enhanced customer profitability that will result.[49]

Evaluating Relationships   Some relationship-building efforts fail because the expectations of the parties do not mesh—for example, when the business marketer follows a relationship approach and the customer responds in a transaction mode. By isolating customer needs and the costs of augmented service features, the marketer is better equipped to profitably match product offerings to the particular customer's needs.

The goal of a relationship is to enable the buyer and seller to maximize joint value. This points to the need for a formal evaluation of relationship outcomes. For example, sales executives at best-practice firms work closely with their partnership

---

[46]Christian Homburg and Ruth M. Stock, "The Link Between Salespeople's Job Satisfaction and Customer Satisfaction in a Business-to-Business Context: A Dyadic Analysis," *Journal of the Academy of Marketing Science* 32 (Spring 2004): pp. 144–158; and Christian Homburg and Ruth M. Stock, "Exploring the Conditions under Which Salesperson Work Satisfaction Can Lead to Customer Satisfaction," *Psychology and Marketing* 22 (5, 2005): pp. 393–420.

[47]Reichheld, "Lead for Loyalty," pp. 76–84.

[48]Schiff, "How Customer Satisfaction Improvement Works to Fuel Full Business Recovery at IBM," p. 8.

[49]James C. Anderson and James A. Narus, "Selectively Pursuing More of Your Customer's Business," *MIT Sloan Management Review* 44 (Spring 2003): pp. 42–49.

accounts to establish mutually defined goals. After an appropriate period, partnerships that do not meet these goals are downgraded and shifted from the strategic market sales force to the geographic sales force.

Business marketers should also continually update the value of their product and relationship offering. Attention here should center on particular new services that might be incorporated as well as on existing services that might be unbundled or curtailed. Working relationships with customer firms are among the most important marketing assets of the firm. They deserve delicate care and continual nurturing!

Relationship Marketing Success[50]

Assuming a central role in implementing the customer relationship marketing (RM) strategy for the business-to-business firm is the salesperson. Firm-to-firm relationships in the business market involve multiple interactions among individuals, forming a network of relationships. To ensure that customers are as satisfied as possible, business marketers must effectively manage the complex web of influences that intersect in buyer–seller relationships.[51]

Figure 3.6 provides a model of interfirm relationship marketing. **Relationship marketing activities** represent dedicated relationship marketing programs, developed and implemented to build strong relational bonds. These activities influence three important drivers of relationship marketing effectiveness—relationship quality, breadth, and composition—each capturing a different dimension of the relationship and exerting a positive influence on the seller's performance activity.

Drivers of Relationship Marketing Effectiveness

Some customer relationships are characterized by extensive interactions and close bonds among members of the buying and selling organizations. By contrast, other relationships might be confined to a few relational ties that the salesperson has developed with members of the purchasing staff. Drawing on insights from social network theory, the following drivers of relational marketing effectiveness have been identified.

Relationship Quality   **Relationship quality** represents a high-caliber relational bond with an exchange partner that captures a number of interaction characteristics such as commitment and trust. "Commitment represents a desire to maintain a valued relationship and, thus, an exchange partner's relationship motivation toward a partner. Trust involves the evaluation of a partner's reliability and integrity, which generates confidence in the partner's future actions that support cooperation."[52] Partners involved in high-quality, committed relationships are willing to disclose proprietary information, which enables sellers to identify the customer's unmet needs, cross-sell additional products more effectively, and price products properly, thereby enhancing profitability.

Relationship Breadth   A key objective of the business marketer is to develop a keen understanding of a customer's needs in order to develop a value proposition that

---

[50]Unless otherwise noted, this section is based on Palmatier, *Relationship Marketing*.

[51]Homburg and Stock, "The Link between Salespeople's Job Satisfaction and Customer Satisfaction in a Business-to-Business Context: A Dyadic Analysis," pp. 144–158.

[52]Robert W. Palmatier, "Interfirm Relational Drivers of Customer Value," *Journal of Marketing* 72 (July 2008): p. 77.

FIGURE 3.6 | **A MODEL OF INTERFIRM RELATIONSHIP MARKETING**

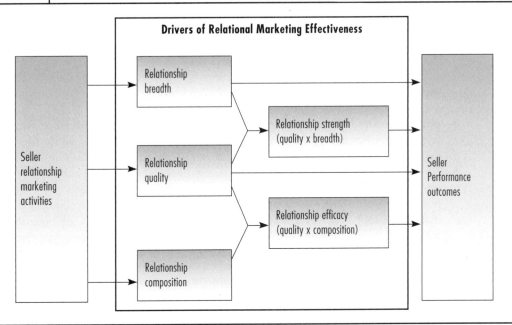

squarely addresses those needs. **Relationship breadth** represents the number of interpersonal ties that a firm has with an exchange partner. A seller that has forged more interpersonal ties with a customer can gain better access to information, identify profit-enhancing opportunities, and become more efficient in building and maintaining the relationship. Research indicates that multiple interfirm ties are particularly vital when serving customer organizations that have high employee turnover.[53]

Relationship Composition   **Relationship composition** centers on the decision-making capability of relational contacts at the customer firm; a contact portfolio that includes high-level decision makers increases a seller's ability to effect change in customer organizations. For example, greater authority in the contact portfolio allows a salesperson to access information, adapt offerings, and reach influential decision makers. A competitor who has access only to contacts with less authority faces difficult odds in winning the account. Research suggests that building relationships with key decision makers generates the highest returns among customer organizations that are the most difficult to access.[54]

Relationship Strength   A clear portrait of a buyer–seller relationship will consider both relationship quality and relationship breadth. (See Figure 3.6.) Therefore, **relationship strength** reflects the ability of a relationship to withstand

---

[53]Ibid., p. 86.

[54]Ibid., pp. 85–86.

stress and/or conflict, such that multiple, high-quality relational bonds result in strong, resilient relationships. A service failure, like equipment failure or poor delivery service, creates conflict in a buyer–seller relationship. A customer relationship characterized by many cursory contacts (greater breadth, low quality) will afford little protection to the seller during this period of stress. However, based on confidence (trust), multiple, high-quality relationship ties (greater breadth, high quality) will support the seller during the service recovery process.

Relationship Efficacy   Representing the interaction between relationship quality and relationship composition, **relationship efficacy** captures the ability of an interfirm relationship to achieve desired objectives. High-quality relationships with members of the customer organization, coupled with a well-structured and diverse contact portfolio, gives sellers the means to execute responsive strategy. Robert W. Palmatier observes that a "portfolio might encompass high-quality, broad relationships but it suffers if those contacts are restricted to one functional area with little decision-making (low composition) because the seller lacks access to divergent (nonredundant) information and cannot promote customer change."[55]

Relationship Marketing (RM) Programs

To strengthen relational ties with customers, three types of relationship marketing programs are employed.

- **Social RM programs** use social engagements (for example, meals and sporting events) or frequent, customized communication to personalize the relationship and highlight the customer's special status. The relational bonds that result from this specialized treatment are difficult for rivals to duplicate and may prompt customers to reciprocate in the form of repeat sales and positive recommendations of the seller to others.

- **Structural RM programs** are designed to increase productivity and/or efficiency for customers through targeted investments that customers would not likely make themselves. For example, the seller might provide an electronic order-processing interface of customized packaging for the customer. By offering unique benefits and, in the case of electronic ordering, a structural bond, these programs create competitive advantages and discourage customers from switching to competitors.

- **Financial RM programs** provide economic benefits, such as special discounts, free shipping, or extended payment terms, to increase customer loyalty. Because competitors can readily match the economic incentives, the advantages tend to be unsustainable.

Such relationship marketing investments generate customer feelings of gratitude, which lead to gratitude-based reciprocal behaviors, resulting in enhanced seller performance.[56]

---

[55]Palmatier, *Relationship Marketing*, p. 25.

[56]Robert W. Palmatier, Cheryl Burke Jarvis, Jennifer R. Bechkoff, and Frank R. Kardes, "The Role of Customer Gratitude in Relationship Marketing," *Journal of Marketing* 73 (September 2009): pp. 1–18.

Financial Impact of RM Programs[57]

Do RM programs pay off? A recent study measured the incremental profits generated by RM programs to isolate the return on investment (ROI).

Social In evaluating the short-term financial returns of the different RM strategies, the study found that social RM investments have a direct and significant (approximately 180 percent) impact on profit—far greater than the impact of structural or financial RM programs. For the customer, social programs create a feeling of interpersonal debt, stimulating a pressing need to reciprocate and thereby generating immediate returns. Yet, Robert Palmatier observes: "Social programs may cause customers to think highly of the salesperson rather than the selling firm, which increases the risk that the selling firm loses the customer if the salesperson leaves. Therefore, the selling firm should keep other avenues open for direct communication with customers."[58]

Structural The financial impact of structural RM programs (for example, providing a value-enhancing linkage) depends on the frequency of interaction a firm has with customers. While break-even returns are achieved for customers with average interaction frequency, the return on structural RM investment is approximately 120 percent for those customers who receive frequent contact from the seller. As a result, the business marketing strategist should target those customers for whom structural solutions offer the most value. Moreover, while merely breaking even in the short term, structural linkages like electronic order processing should increase long-term profits because customers are inclined to take advantage of the value provided.

Financial Since economic incentives often attract "deal-prone" customers and are easy for rivals to match, financial RM programs generally fail to generate positive economic returns. Of course, such programs (for example, special discounts) may represent a necessary response to a competitive threat that is needed to protect existing customer relationships. By contrast, social and structural RM programs are offensive weapons that provide greater financial returns and a more durable competitive advantage.

Targeting RM Programs[59]

Some customers are more receptive to relationship marketing initiatives than others. As purchasing managers emphasize cost-reducing and productivity-enhancing objectives, they carefully scrutinize the time and effort that can be invested in particular supplier relationships. **Relationship orientation** (RO) represents the customer's desire to engage in strong relationships with a current or potential supplier.

---

[57]This section is based on Robert W. Palmatier, Srinath Gopalakrishna, and Mark B. Houston, "Returns on Business-to-Business Relationship Marketing Investments: Strategies for Leveraging Profits," *Marketing Science* 25 (September–October 2006): pp. 477–493.

[58]Palmatier, *Relationship Marketing*, p. 64.

[59]This section is based on Robert W. Palmatier, Lisa K. Scheer, Kenneth R. Evans, and Todd J. Arnold, "Achieving Relationship Marketing Effectiveness in Business-to-Business Exchanges," *Journal of the Academy of Marketing Science* 36 (June 2008): pp. 174–190.

"Customers tend to be more … open to relationship building when they face some risk, uncertainty, or dependence in the exchange process or are very motivated about the product or service category. In these situations, customers find the expertise, added flexibility, and risk-reduction benefits of a relationship valuable and likely welcome the seller's relationship efforts."[60]

Allocating RM Resources   Research demonstrates that the returns on RM investments improve if business marketers are able to target customers on the basis of their RO rather than size. For example, salespeople report higher returns for their RM efforts directed toward buyers with the highest self-reported RO than for those with the lowest RO. Importantly, the study reveals a separate strategy that can be used effectively for customers who demonstrate a *low* RO. These customers would shift 21 percent of their business to another supplier of similar products if the transaction were completely automated (that is, if no salesperson was involved). This suggests that the business marketer could drastically lower costs and better serve some customers by accurately detecting those with a low RO and offering them the option of using an electronic ordering interface. By properly aligning RM resources to the needs of customers, the salesperson can direct attention to those customers who are most receptive to relationship-building efforts.

Summary

Relationships, rather than simple transactions, provide the central focus in business marketing. By demonstrating superior skills in managing relationships with key customers as well as with alliance partners, business marketing firms can create a collaborative advantage.

To develop profitable relationships with customers, business marketers must first understand the different forms that exchange relationships can take. Transactional exchange centers on the timely exchange of basic products and services for highly competitive market prices. By contrast, collaborative exchange involves very close personal, informational, and operational connections the parties develop to achieve long-term mutual goals. Across the relationship spectrum, different types of relationships feature different relationship connectors. For example, collaborative relationships for important purchases emphasize operational linkages that integrate the operations of the buying and selling organizations and involve high levels of information exchange.

Activity-based costing provides a solid foundation for measuring and managing the profitability of individual customers. When the full costs of serving customers are known, many companies find that 15 to 20 percent of the customers generate 100 percent (or much more) of the profits, a large group of customers break even, and 5 to 10 percent of the customers generate sizable losses. By measuring the cost-to-serve and the net profit from individual customers, business marketing managers can take actions to transform unprofitable relationships into profitable ones through process improvements, menu-based pricing, or relationship management.

---

[60]Palmatier, *Relationship Marketing*, p. 90.

Customer relationship management involves aligning customer strategy and business processes for the purpose of improving customer loyalty and, eventually, corporate profitability. To that end, a customer strategy encompasses: (1) acquiring the right customers, (2) crafting the right value proposition, (3) instituting the best processes, (4) motivating employees, and (5) learning to retain customers.

Relationship marketing (RM) activities represent dedicated relationship marketing programs, developed and implemented to build strong relational bonds with customers. These activities influence the three important drivers of RM effectiveness—relationship quality, breadth, and composition. To strengthen relational ties with customers, three types of RM programs are used: social, structural, and financial. Returns on RM investments improve when business marketers are able to target customers on the basis of their relationship orientation rather than size.

Discussion Questions

1. Evaluate this statement: Large customers tend to be either the most or least profitable in the customer base of a business-to-business firm.

2. Some customers are more open to relationship marketing initiatives than others. Under what conditions would customers tend to be more responsive to relationship-building efforts by the salesperson?

3. Describe how a firm might use menu-based pricing to restore profitability to a high-cost-to-serve customer who demands extensive service and customized support.

4. Describe how an office supply firm may have a core offering of products and services for a small manufacturer and an augmented offering for a university.

5. A marketing research company found that 6 percent of its clients generated 30 percent of sales and nearly all of its profits. At the other end of the continuum, 70 percent of its clients provided annual billings (revenue) that were below break-even levels, because these customers required an extensive amount of service from research employees. The company took immediate action to terminate relationships with clients who would not give them a higher share of their marketing research expenditures. Evaluate this decision and suggest a set of criteria that the firm might use to screen new clients.

6. As drivers of relationship marketing effectiveness, compare and contrast relationship breadth and relationship composition.

7. Sony develops "collaborative relationships" with some suppliers and "transactional relationships" with other suppliers. What criteria would purchasing executives use in segmenting suppliers into these two categories? Describe the steps a business marketer might take to move the relationship with Sony from a transactional relationship to a more collaborative one.

8. Why is the cost of serving a long-standing customer far less than the cost of acquiring a new customer?

9. Some consulting organizations persuasively argue that by properly incorporating suppliers into their product-development process, firms

can cut their bills for purchased parts and materials by as much as 30 percent. Explore how a buyer–seller partnership might create these cost savings.

10. Discuss the switching costs that Southwest Airlines would incur if it began to phase out its fleet of Boeing airliners with replacements from Airbus. What steps could Airbus take to reduce these switching costs? How might Boeing counter to strengthen its relationship with Southwest?

Internet Exercise

1. Oracle Corporation provides customer relationship management software solutions to all sectors of the business market. Go to http://oracle.com and review "success stories" and

   a. identify a particular Oracle customer from the government sector, and
   b. describe the benefits that this government customer received from the software solution.

PART

III

Assessing Market Opportunities

CHAPTER

4

Segmenting the Business Market and Estimating Segment Demand

The business marketing manager serves a market comprising many different types of organizational customers with varying needs. Only when this aggregate market is broken down into meaningful categories can the business marketing strategist readily and profitably respond to unique needs. Once the segments are determined, then the marketer must estimate demand for each segment. Accurate projections of future sales are one of the most significant and challenging dimensions of organizational demand analysis. After reading this chapter, you will understand:

1. The benefits of and requirements for segmenting the business market

2. The potential bases for segmenting the business market

3. A procedure for evaluating and selecting market segments

4. The role of market segmentation in the development of business marketing strategy

5. A process for estimating demand in each market segment

6. Specific techniques to effectively develop a forecast of demand

A strategist at Hewlett-Packard notes:

> Knowing customers' needs is not enough…. We need to know what new products, features, and services will surprise and delight them. We need to understand their world so well that we can bring new technology to problems that customers may not yet truly realize they have.[1]

High-growth companies, large and small, succeed by:

- Selecting a well-defined group of potentially profitable customers

- Developing a distinctive value proposition (product and/or service offering) that meets these customers' needs better than their competitors

- Focusing marketing resources on acquiring, developing, and retaining profitable customers[2]

The business market consists of three broad sectors—commercial enterprises, institutions, and government. Whether marketers elect to operate in one or all of these sectors, they encounter diverse organizations, purchasing structures, and decision-making styles. Each sector has many segments; each segment may have unique needs and require a unique marketing strategy. For example, some customers demonstrate attractive profit potential and are receptive to a relationship strategy, whereas others adopt a short-term, transaction focus, suggesting the need for a more streamlined strategy response.[3] The business marketer who recognizes the needs of the various market segments is best equipped to isolate profitable market opportunities and respond with an effective marketing program.

The goal of this chapter is to demonstrate how the manager can select and evaluate segments of the business market and then develop accurate estimates of demand. First, the chapter delineates the benefits of and the requirements for successful market segmentation. Second, it explores and evaluates specific bases for segmenting the business market. Third, the chapter provides a framework for evaluating and selecting market segments. Procedures for assessing the costs and benefits of entering alternative market segments and for implementing a segmentation strategy are emphasized. The final section of the chapter examines the demand forecasting process and explains the critical aspects of how business marketers create demand forecasts.

Business Market Segmentation Requirements and Benefits

A **market segment** represents "a group of present or potential customers with some common characteristic which is relevant in explaining (and predicting) their response to a supplier's marketing stimuli."[4] Effective segmentation of markets is the first step

---

[1]David E. Schnedler, "Use Strategic Market Models to Predict Customer Behavior," *Sloan Management Review* 37 (Spring 1996): p. 92; see also, Eric von Hippel, Stefan Thomke, and Mary Sonnack, "Creating Breakthroughs at 3M," *Harvard Business Review* 77 (September–October 1999): pp. 47–57.

[2]Dwight L. Gertz and João P. A. Baptista, *Grow to Be Great: Breaking the Downsizing Cycle* (New York: The Free Press, 1995), p. 54.

[3]Per Vagn Freytog and Ann Højbjerg Clarke, "Business to Business Market Segmentation," *Industrial Marketing Management* 30 (August 2001): pp. 473–486.

[4]Yoram Wind and Richard N. Cardozo, "Industrial Market Segmentation," *Industrial Marketing Management* 3 (March 1974): p. 155; see also Vincent-Wayne Mitchell and Dominic F. Wilson, "Balancing Theory and Practice: A Reappraisal of Business-to-Business Segmentation," *Industrial Marketing Management* 27 (September 1998): pp. 429–455.

in crafting a marketing strategy because the characteristics and needs of each segment will define the direction and focus of the marketing program. Segmentation that is done well provides the necessary information for understanding what elements of the marketing mix are going to be critical in satisfying the target customers in those segments.

Requirements

Potential customers in a market segment have common characteristics that define what things are important to them and how they will respond to various marketing stimuli. The question for the business marketer is: "what are the key criteria for determining which characteristics best define a unique market segment?" A business marketer has four criteria for evaluating the desirability of potential market segments:

1. *Measurability*—The degree to which information on the particular buyer characteristics exists or can be obtained.

2. *Accessibility*—The degree to which the firm can effectively focus its marketing efforts on chosen segments.

3. *Substantiality*—The degree to which the segments are large or profitable enough to be worth considering for separate marketing cultivation.

4. *Responsiveness*—The degree to which segments respond differently to different marketing mix elements, such as pricing or product features.

In summary, the art of market segmentation involves identifying groups of customers that are large and unique enough to justify a separate marketing strategy. The ultimate goal is to have the greatest amount of difference *between* groups (segments) and high similarities *within* them.[5]

Benefits

If the requirements for effective segmentation are met, several benefits accrue to the firm. First, the mere attempt to segment the business market forces the marketer to become more attuned to the unique needs of customer segments. Second, knowing the needs of particular market segments helps the business marketer focus product-development efforts, develop profitable pricing strategies, select appropriate channels of distribution, develop and target advertising messages, and train and deploy the sales force. Thus, market segmentation provides the foundation for efficient and effective business marketing strategies.

Third, market segmentation provides the business marketer with valuable guidelines for allocating marketing resources. Business-to-business firms often serve multiple market segments and must continually monitor their relative attractiveness and performance. Research by Mercer Management Consulting indicates that, for many companies, nearly one-third of their market segments generate no profit and that 30 to 50 percent of marketing and customer service costs are wasted on efforts to acquire and retain customers in these segments.[6] Ultimately, costs, revenues, and profits must be evaluated segment by segment—and even account by account.

---

[5]Jessica Tsai, "The Smallest Slice," *CRM Magazine* 12 (2, February 2008): p. 37.

[6]Gertz and Baptista, *Grow to Be Great*, p. 55.

INSIDE BUSINESS MARKETING

How to See What's Next

Strategists falter when they invest too much attention to "what is" and too little to "what could be." For example, by maintaining a strict focus on existing market segments and ignoring new ones, the business marketer may miss important signals of change that customers are sending.

To break this pattern and spot new market opportunities, business marketing strategists should examine three customer groups and the market signals they are sending:

- *Undershot customers*—the existing solutions fail to fully satisfy their needs. They eagerly buy new product versions at steady or increasing prices.

- *Overshot customers*—the existing solutions are too good (for example, exceed the technical performance required). These customers are reluctant to purchase new product versions.

- *Nonconsuming customers*—those who lack the skills, resources, or ability to benefit from existing solutions. These customers are forced to turn to others with greater skills or training for service.

Although most strategists center exclusive attention on undershot customers, "watching for innovations that have the potential to drive industry change actually requires paying careful attention to the least demanding, most overshot customers and non-consumers seemingly on the fringe of the market." For example, computing jobs that were processed by specialists in the corporate mainframe computer center are now routinely completed by millions of individuals, and corporate photocopying centers were disbanded as low-cost, self-service copiers became a common fixture in offices across organizations.

SOURCE: Clayton M. Christensen and Scott D. Anthony, "Are You Reading the Right Signals?" *Strategy & Innovation Newsletter* (Cambridge, MA.: Harvard Business School Publishing Corporation, September/October 2004), p. 5.

As market or competitive conditions change, corresponding adjustments may be required in the firm's market segmentation strategy. Thus, market segmentation provides a basic unit of analysis for marketing planning and control.

Marketers can gain valuable strategy insights by identifying the needs and requirements of different types of commercial enterprises or business customers. To illustrate, the **North American Industrial Classification System (NAICS)** organizes business activity into meaningful economic sectors and identifies groups of business firms that use similar production processes.[7] The NAICS is an outgrowth of the North American Free Trade Agreement (NAFTA); it provides for standard economic data reporting among Canada, Mexico, and the United States. Every plant or business establishment receives a code that reflects the primary product produced at that location. The new system, which includes traditional industries while incorporating new and emerging-technology industries, replaces the Standard Industrial Classification (SIC) system that was used for decades.

Figure 4.1 illustrates the building blocks of the system. Observe that the first two digits identify the economic sector and that as more digits are added, the classification becomes finer. For example, all business establishments that create, disseminate, or provide the means to distribute information are included in the Information sector: NAICS Code 51. Nineteen other economic sectors are included in the system. More specifically, U.S. establishments that produce paging equipment are assigned

---

[7]http://www.naics.com, "History of SIC/NAICS," accessed June 15, 2005.

FIGURE 4.1 | NORTH AMERICAN INDUSTRIAL CLASSIFICATION SYSTEM

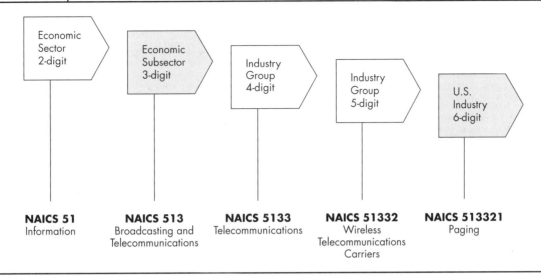

NAICS 51
Information

NAICS 513
Broadcasting and
Telecommunications

NAICS 5133
Telecommunications

NAICS 51332
Wireless
Telecommunications
Carriers

NAICS 513321
Paging

SOURCE: Reprinted from K. Douglas Hoffman et al., *Marketing: Best Practices* (Mason, Ohio: South-Western/Thomson Learning, 2003): p. 171.

an NAICS Code of 513321. Individual countries customize the six-digit codes for industry subdivisions, but at the five-digit level they are standardized across the three countries.

Using the NAICS If marketing managers understand the needs and requirements of a few firms within a classification category, they can project requirements for other firms that share that category. Each group should be relatively homogeneous in terms of raw materials required, component parts used, and manufacturing processes employed. The NAICS provides a valuable tool for identifying new customers and for targeting profitable segments of business buyers.

Bases for Segmenting Business Markets

Whereas the consumer-goods marketer is interested in securing meaningful profiles of individuals (demographics, lifestyle, benefits sought), the business marketer profiles organizations (size, end use) and organizational buyers (decision style, criteria). Thus, the business or organizational market can be segmented on several bases, broadly classified into two major categories: macrosegmentation and microsegmentation.

Macrosegmentation centers on the characteristics of the buying organization and the buying situation and thus divides the market by such organizational characteristics as size, geographic location, the North American Industrial Classification System (NAICS) category, and organizational structure. In contrast, **microsegmentation** requires a higher degree of market knowledge, focusing on the characteristics of decision-making units within each macrosegment—including buying decision criteria, perceived importance of the purchase, and attitudes toward vendors. Strategy experts

INSIDE BUSINESS MARKETING

Balancing Risk and Return in a Customer Portfolio

For an investor, financial portfolio theory demonstrates that optimal performance, for a given level of risk, can best be achieved by building a diversified mix of investment assets that includes the stocks of both large and small firms, drawn from diverse industry sectors and representing both U. S. and foreign companies. In building a customer portfolio, similar benefits can be realized by diversifying across different customer categories.

In choosing among customers to add to a portfolio, the less a customer's purchasing behavior promises to be like that of the current portfolio, the stronger its contribution to the stability and predictability of the portfolio; conversely, the more the behavior is like that of the existing portfolio, the weaker is its contribution. Therefore, the attractiveness of a customer hinges not only on the size and frequency of purchases but also on the degree to which the customer's pattern of purchases covaries with those of other customers in the portfolio. The declining cash flow from one customer may be offset by increased returns from another. For example, during a recession, a transportation company may experience a decline in revenue from discretionary retailers (e.g., Kohl's) that is offset by an increase from discount retailers (e.g., Walmart) or declining revenue from auto producers is partially offset by a growing revenue stream from after-market auto parts retailers (e.g., AutoZone).

SOURCE: Crina O. Tarasi, Ruth N. Bolton, Michael D. Hutt, and Beth A. Walker, "Balancing Risk and Return in a Customer Portfolio," *Journal of Marketing* 75 (May 2011): pp. 1–17.

recommend a two-stage approach to business market segmentation: (1) identify meaningful macrosegments, and then (2) divide the macrosegments into microsegments.[8]

In evaluating alternative bases for segmentation, the marketer is attempting to identify good predictors of differences in buyer behavior. Once such differences are recognized, the marketer can approach target segments with an appropriate marketing strategy. Secondary sources of information, coupled with data in a firm's information system, can be used to divide the market into macrolevel segments. The concentration of the business market allows some marketers to monitor the purchasing patterns of each customer. For example, a firm that sells component parts to the automobile industry is dealing with a relatively small set of potential customers even on a global scale; an auto manufacturer selling to the end market is dealing with millions of potential customers. Such market concentration, coupled with rapidly advancing customer relationship management systems, makes it easier for business marketers to monitor the buying patterns of individual customer organizations.

Macrolevel Bases

Table 4.1 presents selected macrolevel bases of segmentation. Recall that these are concerned with the general characteristics of the buying organization, the nature of the product application, and the characteristics of the buying situation.

Macrolevel Characteristics of Buying Organizations   A strategist may find it useful to partition the market by size of potential buying organization. Large buying organizations may possess unique requirements and respond to marketing stimuli

---

[8]Wind and Cardozo, "Industrial Market Segmentation," p. 155; see also Mitchell and Wilson, "Balancing Theory and Practice," pp. 429–455.

TABLE 4.1 | SELECTED MACROLEVEL BASES OF SEGMENTATION

Variables	Illustrative Breakdowns
Characteristics of Buying Organizations	
Size (the scale of operations of the organization)	Small, medium, large; based on sales or number of employees
Geographical location	USA, Asia Pacific, Europe, Middle East, and Africa
Usage rate	Nonuser, light user, moderate user, heavy user
Structure of procurement	Centralized, decentralized
Product/Service Application	
NAICS category	Varies by product or service
End market served	Varies by product or service
Value in use	High, low
Characteristics of Purchasing Situation	
Type of buying situation	New task, modified rebuy, straight rebuy
Stage in purchase decision process	Early stages, late stages

© Cengage Learning 2013

that are different from those responded to by smaller firms. The influence of presidents, vice presidents, and owners declines with an increase in corporate size; the influence of other participants, such as purchasing managers, increases.[9] Alternatively, the marketer may recognize regional variations and adopt geographical units as the basis for differentiating marketing strategies.

Usage rate constitutes another macrolevel variable. Buyers are classified on a continuum ranging from nonuser to heavy user. Heavy users may have needs different from moderate or light users. For example, heavy users may place more value on technical or delivery support services than their counterparts. Likewise, an opportunity may exist to convert moderate users into heavy users through adjustments in the product or service mix.

The structure of the procurement function constitutes a final macrolevel characteristic of buying organizations. Firms with a centralized purchasing function behave differently than do those with decentralized procurement. The structure of the purchasing function influences the degree of buyer specialization, the criteria emphasized, and the composition of the buying center. Centralized buyers place significant weight on long-term supply availability and the development of a healthy supplier complex. Decentralized buyers tend to emphasize short-term cost efficiency.[10] Thus the position of procurement in the organizational hierarchy provides a base for categorizing organizations and for isolating specific needs and marketing requirements. Many business marketers develop a key account team to meet the special requirements of large, centralized procurement units (see Chapter 2).

---

[9]Joseph A. Bellizzi, "Organizational Size and Buying Influences," *Industrial Marketing Management* 10 (February 1981): pp. 17–21; see also Arch G. Woodside, Timo Liukko and Risto Vuori, "Organizational Buying of Capital Equipment Involving Persons across Several Authority Levels," *Journal of Business and Industrial Marketing* 14 (1, 1999): pp. 30–48.

[10]Timothy M. Laseter, *Balanced Sourcing: Cooperation and Competition in Supplier Relationships* (San Francisco: Jossey-Bass, 1998), pp. 59–86.

Product/Service Application   Because a specific industrial good is often used in different ways, the marketer can divide the market on the basis of specific end-use applications. The NAICS system and related information sources are especially valuable for this purpose. To illustrate, the manufacturer of a component such as springs may reach industries incorporating the product into machine tools, bicycles, surgical devices, office equipment, telephones, and missile systems. Similarly, Intel's microchips are used in household appliances, retail terminals, toys, cell phones, and aircraft as well as in computers. By isolating the specialized needs of each user group as identified by the NAICS category, the firm is better equipped to differentiate customer requirements and to evaluate emerging opportunities.

At Apple's Web site (http://www.apple.com), Mac customers are segmented into these categories: creative pro (e.g., publishers), science (e.g., research labs), business (e.g., small-business owners), and education (e.g., teachers or students). A tailored set of applications is available to meet the unique requirements of each segment.

Value in Use   Strategic insights are also provided by exploring the value in use of various customer applications. **Value in use** is a product's economic value to the user relative to a specific alternative in a particular application. The economic value of an offering frequently varies by customer application. Milliken & Company, the textile manufacturer, has built one of its businesses by becoming a major supplier of towels to industrial laundries. These customers pay Milliken a 10 percent premium over equivalent towels offered by competitors.[11] Why? Milliken provides added value, such as a computerized routing program that improves the efficiency and effectiveness of the industrial laundries' pick-up and delivery function.

The segmentation strategy adopted by a manufacturer of precision motors further illuminates the value-in-use concept.[12] The firm found that its customers differed in the motor speed required in their applications and that a dominant competitor's new, low-priced machine wore out quickly in high- and medium-speed applications. The marketer concentrated on this vulnerable segment, demonstrating the superior life cycle cost advantages of the firm's products. The marketer also initiated a long-term program to develop a competitively priced product and service offering for customers in the low-speed segment.

Purchasing Situation   A final macrolevel base for segmenting the organizational market is the purchasing situation. First-time buyers have perceptions and information needs that differ from those of repeat buyers. Therefore, buying organizations are classified as being in the early or late stages of the procurement process, or, alternatively, as *new-task*, *straight rebuy*, or *modified rebuy* organizations (see Chapter 2). The position of the firm in the procurement decision process or its location on the buying situation continuum dictates marketing strategy.

These examples illustrate those macrolevel bases of segmentation that marketers can apply to the business market. Other macrolevel bases may more precisely fit a specific situation. A key benefit of segmentation is that it forces the manager to search for bases that explain similarities and differences among buying organizations.

---

[11]Philip Kotler, "Marketing's New Paradigm: What's Really Happening Out There," *Planning Review* 20 (September–October 1992): pp. 50–52.

[12]Robert A. Garda, "How to Carve Niches for Growth in Industrial Markets," *Management Review* 70 (August 1981): pp. 15–22.

TABLE 4.2 | SELECTED MICROLEVEL BASES OF SEGMENTATION

Variables	Illustrative Breakdowns
Key criteria	Quality, delivery, supplier reputation
Purchasing strategies	Single source … multiple sources
Structure of decision-making unit	Major decision participants (for example, purchasing manager and plant manager)
Importance of purchase	High importance … low importance
Organizational innovativeness	Innovator … follower
Personal characteristics	
Demographics	Age, educational background
Decision style	Normative, conservative, mixed mode
Risk	Risk taker, risk avoider
Confidence	High … low
Job responsibility	Purchasing, production, engineering

© Cengage Learning 2013

Microlevel Bases

Having identified macrosegments, the marketer often finds it useful to divide each macrosegment into smaller microsegments on the basis of the similarities and differences between decision-making units. Often, several microsegments—each with unique requirements and unique responses to marketing stimuli—are buried in macrosegments. To isolate them effectively, the marketer must move beyond secondary sources of information by soliciting input from the sales force or by conducting a special market segmentation study. Selected microbases of segmentation appear in Table 4.2.

Key Criteria   For some business products, the marketer can divide the market according to which criteria are the most important in the purchase decision.[13] Criteria include product quality, prompt and reliable delivery, technical support, price, and supply continuity. The strategist also might divide the market based on supplier profiles that decision makers appear to prefer (for example, high quality, prompt delivery, premium price versus standard quality, less prompt delivery, low price).

Illustration: Price versus Service[14]   Signode Corporation produces and markets a line of steel strapping used for packaging a range of products, including steel and many manufactured items. Facing stiff price competition and a declining market share, management wanted to move beyond traditional macrolevel

---

[13]Schnedler, "Use Strategic Market Models," pp. 85–92; and Kenneth E. Mast and Jon M. Hawes, "Perceptual Differences between Buyers and Engineers," *Journal of Purchasing and Materials Management* 22 (Spring 1986): pp. 2–6; Donald W. Jackson Jr., Richard K. Burdick, and Janet E. Keith, "Purchasing Agents' Perceived Importance of Marketing Mix Components in Different Industrial Purchase Situations," *Journal of Business Research* 13 (August 1985): pp. 361–373; and Donald R. Lehmann and John O'Shaughnessy, "Decision Criteria Used in Buying Different Categories of Products," *Journal of Purchasing and Materials Management* 18 (Spring 1982): pp. 9–14.

[14]V. Kasturi Rangan, Rowland T. Moriarty, and Gordon S. Swartz, "Segmenting Customers in Mature Industrial Markets," *Journal of Marketing* 56 (October 1992): pp. 72–82.

segmentation to understand how Signode's 174 national accounts viewed price versus service trade-offs. Four segments were uncovered:

1. **Programmed buyers** (sales = $6.6 million): Customers who were not particularly price or service sensitive and who made purchases in a routine fashion—product is not central to their operation.

2. **Relationship buyers** (sales = $31 million): Knowledgeable customers who valued partnership with Signode and did not push for price or service concessions—product is moderately important to the firm's operations.

3. **Transaction buyers** (sales = $24 million): Large and very knowledgeable customers who actively considered the price versus service trade-offs but often placed price over service—product is very important to their operations.

4. **Bargain hunters** (sales = $23 million): Large-volume buyers who were very sensitive to any changes in price or service—product is very important to their operations.

The study enabled Signode to sharpen its strategies in this mature business market and to understand more clearly the cost of serving the various segments. Particularly troubling to management was the bargain-hunter segment. These customers demanded the lowest prices and the highest levels of service and had the highest propensity to switch. Management decided to use price cuts only as a defense against competitors' cuts and directed attention instead at ways to add service value to this and other segments.

Value-Based Strategies   Many customers actively seek business marketing firms that can help them create new value to gain a competitive edge in their markets. Based on a comprehensive study of its customer base, Dow Corning identified three important customer segments and the value proposition that customers in each segment are seeking[15]:

innovation-focused customers who are committed to being first to the market with new technologies and who seek new-product-development expertise and innovative solutions that will attract new customers;

customers in fast-growing markets who are pressured by competitive battles over market growth and seek proven performance in technology, manufacturing, and supply chain management;

customers in highly competitive markets who produce mature products, center on process efficiency and effectiveness in manufacturing, and seek cost-effective solutions that keep overall costs down.

The marketer can benefit by examining the criteria decision-making units in various sectors of the business market—commercial, governmental, and institutional—use. As organizations in each sector undergo restructuring efforts, the buying criteria that key decision makers use also change. For example, the cost pressures and reform

---

[15]Eric W. Balinski, Philip Allen, and J. Nicholas DeBonis, *Value-Based Marketing for Bottom-Line Success* (New York: McGraw-Hill and the American Marketing Association, 2003), pp. 147–152.

efforts in the health-care industry are changing how hospitals buy medical equipment and pharmaceuticals. To reduce administrative costs and enhance bargaining power, hospitals are following the lead of commercial enterprises by streamlining their operations. Also, they are forming buying groups, centralizing the purchasing function, and insisting on lower prices and better service. Reform efforts are likewise moving government buyers to search for more efficient purchasing procedures and for better value from vendors. Marketers that respond in this challenging environment are rewarded.

Purchasing Strategies   Microsegments can be classified according to buying organizations' purchasing strategy. Some buyers seek to have several suppliers, giving each one a healthy share of their purchase volume; others are more interested in assured supply and concentrate their purchases with one or perhaps two suppliers. Raytheon, the manufacturer of small airplanes for the civilian and business aircraft market, decided on a strategy of concentration. It relies on one firm—Castle Metals—to supply all of its needs for the different metals used in an aircraft. The company may reassess its sole supplier every so often, but any "out-supplier" in this situation would have a very difficult time securing some of Raytheon's business. In another case, Honda looks for suppliers who are able to make suggestions for improving its business operations. Honda has realized that many of the innovations it has developed in its processes have come from its suppliers' suggestions. So a key strategy for Honda is to identify suppliers who are creative and invest in new technology for possibly improving Honda's business.

Structure of the Decision-Making Unit   The structure of the decision-making unit, or buying center, likewise provides a way to divide the business market into subsets of customers by isolating the patterns of involvement in the purchasing process of particular decision participants (for example, engineering versus top management). For the medical equipment market, DuPont initiated a formal positioning study among hospital administrators, radiology department administrators, and technical managers to identify the firm's relative standing and the specific needs (criteria) for each level of buying influence within each segment.[16] The growing importance of buying groups, multihospital chains, and nonhospital health-care delivery systems pointed to the need for a more refined segmentation approach.

The study indicates that the medical equipment market can be segmented on the basis of the type of institution and the responsibilities of the decision makers and decision influencers in those institutions. The structure of the decision-making unit and the decision criteria used vary across the following three segments:

- Groups that select a single supplier that all member hospitals must use, such as investor-owned hospital chains;

- Groups that select a small set of suppliers from which individual hospitals may select needed products;

- Private group practices and the nonhospital segment.

[16]Gary L. Coles and James D. Culley, "Not All Prospects Are Created Equal," *Business Marketing* 71 (May 1986): pp. 52–57.

Based on the study, DuPont's salespersons can tailor their presentations to the decision-making dynamics of each segment. In turn, advertising messages can be more precisely targeted. Such an analysis enables the marketer to identify meaningful microsegments and respond with finely tuned marketing communications.

Importance of Purchase   Classifying organizational customers on the basis of the perceived importance of a product is especially appropriate when various customers apply the product in various ways. Buyer perceptions differ according to the effect of the product on the total mission of the firm. A large commercial enterprise may consider the purchase of consulting services routine; the same purchase for a small manufacturing concern is "an event."

Organizational Innovativeness   Some organizations are more innovative and willing to purchase new industrial products than others. A study of the adoption of new medical equipment among hospitals found that psychographic variables can improve a marketer's ability to predict the adoption of new products.[17] These include such factors as an organization's level of change resistance or desire to excel. When psychographic variables are combined with organizational demographic variables (for example, size), accuracy in predicting organizational innovativeness increases.

Because products diffuse more rapidly in some segments than in others, microsegmentation based on organizational innovativeness enables the marketer to identify segments that should be targeted first when it introduces new products. The accuracy of new-product forecasting also improves when diffusion patterns are estimated segment by segment.[18]

Personal Characteristics   Some microsegmentation possibilities deal with the personal characteristics of decision makers: demographics (age, education), personality, decision style, risk preference or risk avoidance, confidence, job responsibilities, and so forth. Although some interesting studies have shown the usefulness of segmentation based on individual characteristics, further research is needed to explore its potential as a firm base for microsegmentation.

Illustration: Microsegmentation[19]

Philips Lighting Company, the North American division of Philips Electronics, found that purchasing managers emphasize two criteria in purchasing light bulbs: how much they cost and how long they last. Philips learned, however, that the price and life of bulbs did not account for the total cost of lighting. Because lamps contain environmentally toxic mercury, companies faced high disposal costs at the end of a lamp's useful life.

---

[17]Thomas S. Robertson and Yoram Wind, "Organizational Psychographics and Innovativeness," *Journal of Consumer Research* 7 (June 1980): pp. 24–31; see also Thomas S. Robertson and Hubert Gatignon, "Competitive Effects on Technology Diffusion," *Journal of Marketing* 50 (July 1986): pp. 1–12.

[18]Yoram Wind, Thomas S. Robertson, and Cynthia Fraser, "Industrial Product Diffusion by Market Segment," *Industrial Marketing Management* 11 (February 1982): pp. 1–8.

[19]W. Chan Kim and Renée Mauborgne, "Creating New Market Space," *Harvard Business Review* 77 (January–February 1999): pp. 88–89. For other segmentation studies, see Mark J. Bennion Jr., "Segmentation and Positioning in a Basic Industry," *Industrial Market Management* 16 (February 1987): pp. 9–18; Arch G. Woodside and Elizabeth J. Wilson, "Combining Macro and Micro Industrial Market Segmentation," in *Advances in Business Marketing*, ed. Arch G. Woodside (Greenwich, CT: JAI Press, 1986), pp. 241–257; and Peter Doyle and John Saunders, "Market Segmentation and Positioning in Specialized Industrial Markets," *Journal of Marketing* 49 (Spring 1985): pp. 24–32.

New-Product and Segmentation Strategy To capitalize on a perceived opportunity, Philips introduced the Alto, an environmentally friendly bulb that reduces customers' overall costs and in addition allows the buying organization to demonstrate environmental concern to the public. Rather than targeting purchasing managers, Philips's marketing strategists centered attention on chief financial officers (CFOs), who embraced the cost savings, and public relations executives, who saw the benefit of purchasing actions that protect the environment. By targeting different buying influentials, Philips created a new market opportunity. In fact, the Alto has already replaced more than 25 percent of traditional fluorescent lamps in U.S. stores, schools, and office buildings.

The Segmentation Process

Macrosegmentation centers on characteristics of buying *organizations* (for example, size), *product application* (for example, end market served), and the *purchasing situation* (for example, stage in the purchase decision process). Microsegmentation concentrates on characteristics of organizational decision-making units—for instance, choice criteria assigned the most importance in the purchase decision.

Choosing Market Segments

Business marketers begin the segmentation process at the macrolevel. If they find that the information about the macrosegments is sufficient to develop an effective marketing strategy, then it may not be necessary to go on to any further microsegmentation. However, if they cannot develop a distinct strategy based on the macrosegment, then it may be necessary to undertake research on microsegmentation variables within each macrosegment. A marketing research study is often needed to identify characteristics of decision-making units, as the Philips Lighting case illustrated. At this level, chosen macrosegments are divided into microsegments on the basis of similarities and differences between the decision-making units to identify small groups of buying organizations that each exhibit a distinct response to the firm's marketing strategy. As firms develop more segments with special requirements, it then becomes necessary to assess whether the cost of developing a unique strategy for a specific segment is worth the profit to be generated from that segment. The marketer must evaluate the potential profitability of alternative segments before investing in separate marketing strategies. As firms develop a clearer picture of the revenue and costs of serving particular segments and customers, they often find that a small group of customers subsidizes a large group of marginal and, in some cases, unprofitable customers.[20] (See Chapter 3.)

Innovate Through Segmentation! In some cases it may be more effective to examine existing customers in a new light. As A. G. Lafley and Lam Charam note, "segmentation itself can be an innovative act, if we identify a corner of our market that is rarely treated as a segment. Can we look at buyers through some other lens than typical tried and true variables such as company size and industry?

---

[20]Arun Sharma, R. Krishnan, and Dhruv Grewal, "Value Creation in Markets: A Critical Area of Focus for Business-to-Business Markets," *Industrial Marketing Management* 30 (June 2001): pp. 391–402.

Identifying an overlooked segment is less expensive than inventing a new technology and may sprout even more opportunities."[21]

Account-Based Marketing The rise of account-based marketing (ABM) represents the ultimate expression of the trend toward smaller and more precisely targeted marketing strategies. ABM is an approach that treats an individual account as a market in its own right. Done right, it ensures that marketing and sales are fully focused on a target client's most important business issues and that they work collaboratively to create value propositions that specifically address those issues. Far beyond the basics of personalized messaging and segmented offers, true ABM has the potential to deepen relationships with existing clients and build profitability by shortening the sales cycle and increasing win rates and sole-sourced contracts.[22]

ABM is the ultimate in segmentation, as one company is viewed as a separate segment. This approach may become more prevalent in the future as industry consolidation continues to grow. One could see the commercial aircraft industry as a good example of this ultimate level of segmentation—only two companies now produce large, commercial airliners: Boeing and Airbus S.A.S.

Isolating Market Segment Profitability

To improve on traditional market segmentation, many business marketing firms categorize customers into tiers that differ in current and/or future profitability to the firm. "By knowing the characteristics of profitable customers, companies can direct their marketing efforts to specific segments that are most likely to yield profitable customers."[23] This requires a process of evaluation that makes explicit the near-term potential and the longer-term resource commitments necessary to effectively serve customers in a segment. In particular, special attention is given to the individual drivers of customer profitability, namely, the cost to serve a particular group of customers and the revenues that result (see Chapter 3).

FedEx Corporation, for example, categorizes its business customers (for internal purposes) as the good, the bad, and the ugly—based on their profitability.[24] Rather than using the same strategy for all customers, the company assigns a priority to the good, tries to convert the bad to good, and discourages the ugly. Like many other firms, FedEx discovered that many customers are too costly to serve and demonstrate little potential to become profitable, even in the long term. By understanding the needs of customers at different tiers of profitability, service can be tailored to achieve even higher levels of profitability. For example, FedEx encourages small shippers to bring their packages to conveniently located drop-off points and offers a rapid-response pick-up service for large shippers. Once profitability tiers are identified, "highly profitable customers can be pampered appropriately, customers of average profitability can be cultivated to yield higher profitability, and unprofitable customers can be either made more profitable or weeded out."[25]

---

[21]A. G. Lafley and Ram Charan, "Making Inspiration Routine," *Inc* 30 (6, June 2008): pp. 98–101.

[22]Jeff Sands, "Account-Based Marketing," *B to B*, 91 (6, May 8, 2006): p. 11.

[23]Robert S. Kaplan and V. G. Narayanan, "Measuring and Managing Customer Profitability," *Journal of Cost Management* 15 (September–October 2001): p. 13.

[24]R. Brooks, "Alienating Customers Isn't Always a Bad Idea, Many Firms Discover," *The Wall Street Journal*, January 7, 1999, pp. A1 and A12, discussed in Valarie A. Zeithaml, Roland T. Rust, and Katherine N. Lemon, "The Customer Pyramid: Creating and Serving Profitable Customers," *California Management Review* 43 (Summer 2001): p. 118.

[25]Zeithaml, Rust, and Lemon, "The Customer Pyramid," p. 141.

Implementing a Segmentation Strategy

A well-developed segmentation plan will fail without careful attention to implementing the plan. Successful implementation requires attention to the following issues:

- How should the sales force be organized?

- What special technical or customer service requirements will organizations in the new segment have?

- Who will provide these services?

- Which media outlets can be used to target advertising at the new segment?

- Has a comprehensive online strategy been developed to provide continuous service support to customers in this segment?

- What adaptations will be needed to serve selected international market segments?

The astute business marketing strategist must plan, coordinate, and monitor implementation details. Frank Cespedes points out that "as a firm's offering becomes a product-service-information mix that must be customized for diverse segments, organizational interdependencies increase"[26] and marketing managers, in particular, are involved in more cross-functional tasks. Managing the critical points of contact with the customer is fundamental to the marketing manager's role.

Estimating Segment Demand

Looking back at the Internet boom, executives at telecommunications firms like Alcatel-Lucent and others now openly acknowledge that they did not see the steep drop in demand coming. Indeed, spending by phone companies on telecommunications gear nearly doubled from 1996 to 2000, to $47.5 billion; all forecasts indicated that this attractive growth path would continue.[27] During this period, telecom equipment makers were dramatically expanding production capacity and aggressively recruiting thousands of new employees. However, in 2001, the demand failed to materialize and the major telecom equipment makers reported significant financial losses. In turn, firms across the industry announced a series of massive job cuts. What happened? "Lousy" sales forecasts played an important role, according to Gregory Duncan, a telecom consultant at National Economic Research Associates.[28]

The Role of the Demand Estimation

Estimating demand within selected market segments is vital to marketing management. The forecast of demand reflects management's estimate of the probable level of company sales, taking into account both the potential opportunity and the

---

[26]Frank V. Cespedes, *Concurrent Marketing: Integrating Product, Sales, and Service* (Boston: Harvard Business School Press, 1995), p. 271. See also John Boejgaard and Chris Ellegaard, "Unfolding Implementation in Industrial Market Segmentation," *Industrial Marketing Management* 39 (November 2010): pp. 1291–1299.

[27]Dennis K. Berman, "'Lousy Sales Forecasts Helped Fuel the Telecom Mess," *The Wall Street Journal*, July 7, 2001, p. B1.

[28]Ibid.

level and type of marketing effort demanded. Virtually every decision made by the marketer is based on a forecast, formal or informal.

Laying the Foundation   Consider a company that wishes to introduce new telecommunications services to businesses. How large is the market opportunity? An estimate of demand provides the foundation for the planning process. Three broad groups of stakeholders require demand forecasts: engineering design and implementation teams; marketing and commercial development teams; and external entities, such as potential investors, government regulators, equipment and application suppliers, and distribution partners. In the marketing area, strategic questions that must be answered before launch of service and that depend on the estimate of demand include: Where should sales outlets be located? How many are required to cover the target market? What sales levels should be expected from each outlet? What performance targets should be established for each? Demand forecasts are needed to project the company's revenues, profits, and cash flow to assess business viability; to determine cash, equity, and borrowing requirements; and to set up appropriate pricing structures and levels.[29] In short, without knowledge of market demand, marketing executives cannot develop sound strategy and make effective decisions about the allocation of resources.

Setting the Course   A primary application of the estimate of demand is clearly in the planning and control of marketing strategy by market segment. Once demand is estimated for each segment, the manager can allocate expenditures on the basis of potential sales volume. Spending huge sums of money on advertising and personal selling has little benefit in segments where the market opportunity is low. Of course, expenditures would have to be based on both expected demand and the level of competition. Actual sales in each segment can also be compared with forecasted sales, taking into account the level of competition, in order to evaluate the effectiveness of the marketing program.

Consider the experience of a Cleveland manufacturer of quick-connective couplings for power transmission systems. For more than 20 years, one of its large distributors had been increasing its sales volume. In fact, this distributor was considered one of the firm's top producers. The manufacturer then analyzed the estimates of demand for each of its 31 distributors. The large distributor ranked thirty-first in terms of volume relative to potential business, achieving only 15.4 percent of estimated demand. A later evaluation revealed that the distributor's sales personnel did not know the most effective way to sell couplings to its large-customer accounts.

Estimates of probable demand should be developed *after* the firm has made decisions about its marketing strategy for a particular segment. Only after the marketing strategy is developed can expected sales be forecasted. Many firms are tempted to use the forecast as a tool for deciding the level of marketing expenditures. One study (which sampled 900 firms) found that slightly more than 25 percent of the respondent firms set their advertising budgets after the forecast of demand was developed.[30] Small companies whose budgeting and forecasting decisions were fragmented made

[29]Peter McBurney, Simon Parsons, and Jeremy Green, "Forecasting Market Demand for New Telecommunications Services: An Introduction," *Telematics and Information* 19 (2002): p. 233.

[30]Douglas C. West, "Advertising Budgeting and Sales Forecasting: The Timing Relationship," *International Journal of Advertising* 14 (1, 1995): pp. 65–77.

up the majority of the firms in this group. Clearly, marketing strategy is a determinant of the level of sales and not vice versa.

Supply Chain Links   Sales forecasts are critical to the smooth operation of the entire supply chain. When timely sales forecast information is readily available to all firms in the supply chain, plans can be tightly coordinated and all parties share in the benefits.[31] Sales forecast data is used to distribute inventory in the supply chain, manage stock levels at each link, and schedule resources for all the members of a supply chain that provide materials, components, and services to a manufacturer. Accurate forecasts go hand-in-hand with effective management practices in directing the entire supply chain process. Specific tools are available to develop accurate estimates of market potential; the business marketer must understand the purpose of each alternative technique as well as its strengths and limitations.

Methods of Forecasting Demand

Estimating demand may be highly mathematical or informally based on sales force estimates. Two primary approaches to demand forecasting are recognized: (1) qualitative and (2) quantitative, which includes time series and causal analysis.

Qualitative Techniques

Qualitative techniques, which are also referred to as **management judgment** or **subjective techniques,** rely on informed judgment and rating schemes. The sales force, top-level executives, or distributors may be called on to use their knowledge of the economy, the market, and the customers to create qualitative demand estimates. Techniques for qualitative analysis include the executive judgment method, the sales force composite method, and the Delphi method.

The effectiveness of qualitative approaches depends on the close relationships between customers and suppliers that are typical in the business-to-business market. Qualitative techniques work well for such items as heavy capital equipment or when the nature of the forecast does not lend itself to mathematical analysis. These techniques are also suitable for new-product or new-technology forecasts when historical data are scarce or nonexistent.[32] An important advantage of qualitative approaches is that it brings users of the forecast into the forecasting process. The effect is usually an increased understanding of the procedure and a higher level of commitment to the resultant forecast.

Executive Judgment   According to a large sample of business firms, the **executive judgment method** enjoys a high level of usage.[33] The judgment method, which combines and averages top executives' estimates of future sales, is popular because it is easy to apply and to understand. Typically, executives from various departments, such as sales, marketing, production, finance, and procurement, are

---

[31]John T. Mentzer and Mark A. Moon, "Understanding Demand," *Supply Chain Management Review* 8 (May–June 2004): p. 45.

[32]A. Michael Segalo, *The IBM/PC Guide to Sales Forecasting* (Wayne, PA: Banbury, 1985), p. 21.

[33]Nada Sanders, "Forecasting Practices in U.S. Corporations: Survey Results," *Interfaces* 24 (March–April 1994): pp. 92–100.

brought together to apply their collective expertise, experience, and opinions to the forecast.

The primary limitation of the approach is that it does not systematically analyze cause-and-effect relationships. Further, because there is no established formula for deriving estimates, new executives may have difficulty making reasonable forecasts. The resulting forecasts are only as good as the executives' opinions. The accuracy of the executive judgment approach is also difficult to assess in a way that allows meaningful comparison with alternative techniques.[34]

The executives' "ballpark" estimates for the intermediate and the long-run time frames are often used in conjunction with forecasts developed quantitatively. However, when historical data are limited or unavailable, the executive judgment approach may be the only alternative. Mark Moriarty and Arthur Adams suggest that executive judgment methods produce accurate forecasts when: (1) forecasts are made frequently and repetitively, (2) the environment is stable, and (3) the linkage between decision, action, and feedback is short.[35] Business marketers should examine their forecasting situation in light of these factors in order to assess the usefulness of the executive judgment technique.

Sales Force Composite   The rationale behind the **sales force composite** approach is that salespeople can effectively estimate future sales volume because they know the customers, the market, and the competition. In addition, participating in the forecasting process helps sales personnel understand how forecasts are derived and boosts their incentive to achieve the desired level of sales. The composite forecast is developed by combining the sales estimates from all salespeople. By providing the salesperson with a wealth of customer information that can be conveniently accessed and reviewed, customer relationship management (CRM) systems (see Chapter 3) enhance the efficiency and effectiveness of the sales force composite.[36] CRM systems also allow a salesperson to track progress in winning new business at key accounts.

Few companies rely solely on sales force estimates; rather, they usually adjust or combine the estimates with forecasts developed either by top management or by quantitative methods. The advantage of the sales force composite method is the ability to draw on sales force knowledge about markets and customers. This advantage is particularly important for a market in which buyer–seller relationships are close and enduring. The salesperson is often the best source of information about customer purchasing plans and inventory levels. The method can also be executed with relative ease at minimal cost. Research suggests that salespeople who: (a) are properly trained to gather and incorporate customer data into the forecast, (b) receive appropriate levels of feedback in the form of forecast accuracy measures on the effectiveness of their efforts, and (c) understand the impact of the forecast on resource allocations throughout the organization are more active contributors to the sales forecasting process.[37]

[34]Spyros Makridakis and Steven Wheelwright, "Forecasting: Issues and Challenges for Marketing Management," *Journal of Marketing* 41 (October 1977): p. 31.

[35]Mark M. Moriarty and Arthur J. Adams, "Management Judgment Forecasts, Composite Forecasting Models and Conditional Efficiency," *Journal of Marketing Research* 21 (August 1984): p. 248.

[36]Robert Mirani, Deanne Moore, and John A. Weber, "Emerging Technologies for Enhancing Supplier-Reseller Partnerships," *Industrial Marketing Management* 30 (February 2001): pp. 101–114.

[37]Teresa M. McCarthy Byrne, Mark A. Moon, and John T. Mentzer, "Motivating the Industrial Sales Force in the Sales Forecasting Process," *Industrial Marketing Management* 40 (January 2011): pp. 128–138.

The problems with sales force composites are similar to those of the executive judgment approach: They do not involve systematic analysis of cause and effect, and they rely on informed judgment and opinions. Some sales personnel may overestimate sales in order to look good or underestimate them in order to generate a lower quota. Management must carefully review all estimates. As a rule, sales force estimates are relatively accurate for short-run projections but less effective for long-term forecasts.

Delphi Method In the **Delphi approach to forecasting**, the opinions of a panel of experts on future sales are converted into an informed consensus through a highly structured feedback mechanism.[38] As in the executive judgment technique, management officials are used as the panel, but each estimator remains anonymous. On the first round, written opinions about the likelihood of some future event are sought (for example, sales volume, competitive reaction, or technological break-throughs). The responses to this first questionnaire are used to produce a second. The objective is to provide feedback to the group so that first-round estimates and information available to some of the experts are made available to the entire group.

After each round of questioning, the analyst who administers the process assembles, clarifies, and consolidates information for dissemination in the succeeding round. Throughout the process, panel members are asked to reevaluate their estimates based on the new information from the group. Opinions are kept anonymous, eliminating both "me-too" estimates and the need to defend a position. After continued reevaluation, the goal is to achieve a consensus. The number of experts varies from six to hundreds, depending on how the process is organized and its purpose. The number of rounds of questionnaires depends on how rapidly the group reaches consensus.

Generally, the Delphi technique is applied to long-term forecasting of demand, particularly for new products or situations not suited to quantitative analysis. This approach can provide some good ballpark estimates of demand when the products are new or unique and when there is no other data available. Like all qualitative approaches to estimating demand, it is difficult to measure the accuracy of the estimates.

Qualitative forecasting approaches are important in the process of assessing future product demand, and they are most valuable in situations where little data exists and where a broad estimate of demand is acceptable. New or unique products do not lend themselves to more quantitative approaches to forecasting, so the qualitative methods play a very important role in estimating demand for these items.

Quantitative Techniques

Quantitative demand forecasting, also referred to as systematic or objective forecasting, offers two primary methodologies: (1) time series and (2) regression or causal. **Time-series** techniques use historical data ordered chronologically to project the trend and growth rate of sales. The rationale behind time-series analysis is that the past pattern of sales will apply to the future. However, to discover the underlying pattern of sales, the analyst must first understand all of the possible patterns that may affect the sales series. Thus, a time series of sales may include trend, seasonal, cyclical, and irregular patterns. Once the effect of each has been isolated, the analyst can then project the expected future of each pattern. Time-series methods are well

---

[38]Raymond E. Willis, *A Guide to Forecasting for Planners and Managers* (Englewood Cliffs, NJ: Prentice-Hall, 1987), p. 343.

suited to short-range forecasting because the assumption that the future will be like the past is more reasonable over the short run than over the long run.[39]

Regression or **causal** analysis, on the other hand, uses an opposite approach, identifying factors that have affected past sales and implementing them in a mathematical model.[40] Demand is expressed mathematically as a function of the items that affect it. A forecast is derived by projecting values for each of the factors in the model, inserting these values into the regression equation, and solving for expected sales. Typically, causal models are more reliable for intermediate than for long-range forecasts because the magnitude of each factor affecting sales must first be estimated for some future time, which becomes difficult when estimating farther into the future.

The specifics of the quantitative approaches to estimating demand are beyond the scope of this chapter. However, the key aspects of these approaches for the business-to-business manager to keep in mind are as follows:

1. To develop an estimate of demand with time-series analysis, the analyst must determine each pattern (the trend, cycle, seasonal pattern) and then extrapolate them into the future. This requires a significant amount of historical sales information. Once a forecast of each pattern is developed, the demand forecast is assembled by combining the estimates for each pattern.

2. A critical aspect of regression analysis is to identify the economic variable(s) to which past sales are related. For forecasting purposes, the *Survey of Current Business* (see http://www.bea.gov/scb) is particularly helpful because it contains monthly, quarterly, and annual figures for hundreds of economic variables. The *Survey* is developed by the Bureau of Economic Analysis, U.S. Department of Commerce. The forecaster can test an array of economic variables from the *Survey* to find the variable(s) with the best relationship to past sales.

3. Although causal methods have measurable levels of accuracy, there are some important caveats and limitations. The fact that demand and some causal variables (independent variables) are correlated (associated) does not mean that the independent variable "caused" sales. The independent variable should be logically related to demand.

4. Regression methods require considerable historical data for equations to be valid and reliable, but the data may not be available. Caution must always be used in extrapolating relationships into the future. The equation relates what has happened; economic and industry factors may change in the future, making past relationships invalid.

5. A valuable study on forecasting methods suggests choosing a methodology based on the underlying behavior of the market rather than the time horizon of the forecast.[41] This research indicates that when markets are sensitive to changes in market and environmental variables, causal methods work best, whether the forecast is short or long range; time-series approaches are more effective when the market exhibits no sensitivity to market and/or environmental changes.

[39]Spyros Makridakis, "A Survey of Time Series," *International Statistics Review* 44 (1, 1976): p. 63.

[40]Segalo, *IMM-PC Guide to Sales Forecasting*, p. 27.

[41]Robert J. Thomas, "Method and Situational Factors in Sales Forecast Accuracy," *Journal of Forecasting* 12 (January 1993): p. 75.

CPFR: A New Collaborative Approach to Estimating Demand

CPFR, or Collaborative Planning Forecasting and Replenishment, is a unique approach to forecasting demand that involves the combined efforts of many functions within the firm as well as with partners in the supply chain. In this approach, one individual in the firm is given the responsibility for coordinating the forecasting process with functional managers across the firm. So sales, marketing, production, logistics, and procurement personnel will be called upon to jointly discuss their plans for the upcoming period. In this way, all the parties who may influence sales performance will participate directly in the demand estimation process.

Once the firm has a good grasp internally of each function's forthcoming strategies and plans, the "demand planner" from the firm will then reach out to customers, distributors, and manufacturers' representatives to assess what their marketing, promotion, and sales plans are for the product in question.

These plans are then shared with the company's functional managers, and demand estimates are adjusted accordingly. The demand planner then develops a final demand estimate for the coming period based on this wide array of input. As one might expect, the CPFR approach to estimating demand often results in a very accurate forecast of demand due to the intensive sharing of information among the firm's functional managers and key supply chain and channel partners.

The most practical approach for application of CPFR is for the trading parties to map their partners' forecasts into their own terms, understand where their partners' plans deviate significantly from their own, and then collaborate on the assumptions that may be leading to different estimates. Through this iterative process, intermediaries and manufacturers use collaborative feedback to synchronize their supply chains, while keeping their enterprise planning processes intact.[42]

Combining Several Forecasting Techniques

Recent research on forecasting techniques indicates that forecasting accuracy can be improved by combining the results of several forecasting methods.[43] The results of combined forecasts greatly surpass most individual projections, techniques, and analyses by experts. Mark Moriarty and Arthur Adams suggest that managers should use a composite forecasting model that includes both systematic (quantitative) and judgmental (qualitative) factors.[44] In fact, they suggest that a composite forecast be created to provide a standard of comparison in evaluating the results provided by any single forecasting approach. Each forecasting approach relies on varying data to derive sales estimates. By considering a broader range of factors that affect sales, the combined approach provides a more accurate forecast. Rather than searching for the single "best" forecasting technique, business marketers should direct increased attention to the composite forecasting approach.

---

[42]"Taking It One Step at a Time: Tapping into the Benefits of Collaborative Planning, Forecasting, and Replenishment (CPFR)," *An Oracle White Paper* (August 2005), http://www.oracle.com/applications/retail/library/white-papers/taking-it-one-step.pdf.

[43]J. Scott Armstrong, "The Forecasting Canon: Nine Generalizations to Improve Forecast Accuracy," *FORESIGHT: The International Journal of Applied Forecasting* 1 (1, June 2005): pp. 29–35.

[44]Moriarty and Adams, "Management Judgment Forecasts," p. 248.

Summary

The business market contains a complex mix of customers with diverse needs and objectives. The marketing strategist who analyzes the aggregate market and identifies neglected or inadequately served groups of buyers (segments) is ideally prepared for a market assault. Specific marketing strategy adjustments can be made to fit the unique needs of each target segment. Of course, such differentiated marketing strategies are feasible only when the target segments are measurable, accessible, responsive, and large enough to justify separate attention.

Procedurally, business market segmentation involves categorizing actual or potential buying organizations into mutually exclusive clusters (segments), each of which exhibits a relatively homogeneous response to marketing strategy variables. To accomplish this task, the business marketer can draw upon two types of segmentation bases: macrolevel and microlevel. Macrodimensions are the key characteristics of buying organizations and of the purchasing situation. The NAICS together with other secondary sources of information are valuable in macrolevel segmentation. Microlevel bases of segmentation center on key characteristics of the decision-making unit and require a higher level of market knowledge.

This chapter outlined a systematic approach for the business marketer to apply when identifying and selecting target segments. Before a final decision is made, the marketer must weigh the costs and benefits of a segmented marketing strategy. In developing a market segmentation plan, the business marketing manager isolates the costs and revenues associated with serving particular market segments. By directing its resources to its most profitable customers and segments, the business marketer is less vulnerable to focused competitors that may seek to "cherry-pick" the firm's most valuable customers.

The forecasting techniques available to the business marketer are: (1) qualitative and (2) quantitative. Qualitative techniques rely on informed judgments of future sales and include executive judgment, the sales force composite, and the Delphi methods. By contrast, quantitative techniques have more complex data requirements and include time-series and causal approaches. The time-series method uses chronological historical data to project the future trend and growth rate of sales. Causal methods, on the other hand, seek to identify factors that have affected past sales and to incorporate them into a mathematical model. The essence of sound demand forecasting is to combine effectively the forecasts provided by various methods.

Discussion Questions

1. Sara Lee Corporation derives more than $1.5 billion of sales each year from the institutional market (for example, hospitals, schools, restaurants). Explain how a firm such as Sara Lee or General Mills might apply the concept of market segmentation to the institutional market.

2. Some firms follow a single-stage segmentation approach using macrodimensions; others use both macrodimensions and microdimensions. As a business marketing manager, what factors would you consider in making a choice between the two methods?

3. Cogent is a rapidly growing company that makes software which identifies people using biometrics—fingerprints, faces, eyeballs, and other

personal characteristics. The firm is making terminals that allow customers to pay for products with their fingerprints. Assess the potential of the "pay by touch" system and suggest possible market segments that might be receptive to the new offering.

4. Automatic Data Processing, Inc. (ADP) handles payroll and tax-filing processing for more than 300,000 customers. In other words, firms outsource these functions to ADP. Suggest possible segmentation bases that ADP might employ in this service market. What criteria would be important to organizational buyers in making the decision to turn payroll processing over to an outside firm?

5. FedEx believes that its future growth will come from business-to-business e-commerce transactions where customers demand quick and reliable delivery service. Outline a segmentation plan that the firm might use to become the market leader in this rapidly expanding area.

6. What features of the business market support the use of qualitative forecasting approaches? What benefits does the business market analyst gain by combining these qualitative approaches with quantitative forecasting methods?

7. What limitations must be understood before applying and interpreting the demand forecasting results generated by causal methods?

8. Compare and contrast the sales force composite and the Delphi methods of developing a sales forecast.

9. Although qualitative forecasting techniques are important in the sales forecasting process in many industrial firms, the marketing manager must understand the limitations of these approaches. Outline these limitations.

10. As alternative methods for demand forecasting, what is the underlying logic of: (1) time- series and (2) regression or causal methods?

Internet Exercise

1. Xerox positions itself as "The Document Company" because the firm provides solutions to help customers manage documents—paper, electronic, online. Go to http://www.xerox.com, click on "Industry Solutions," and

   a. Describe the industry sectors that the firm seems to cover in its market segmentation plan.

   b. Identify the particular product and service that Xerox has developed for bank customers.

PART

IV

FORMULATING BUSINESS MARKETING STRATEGY

CHAPTER

5

Business Marketing Planning: Strategic Perspectives

To this point, you have developed an understanding of organizational buying behavior, customer relationship management, market segmentation, and a host of other tools managers use. All of this provides a fundamentally important perspective to the business marketing strategist. After reading this chapter, you will understand:

1. Marketing's strategic role in corporate strategy development

2. The multifunctional nature of business marketing decision making

3. The components of a business model that can be converted into superior positions of advantage in the business market

4. A valuable framework for detailing the processes and systems that drive strategy success

Consider GE's bold new initiative to recognize and reward marketing leaders who demonstrate special promise:

> We identify our top 50 up-and-coming marketers as rock stars and make their development a company priority. They receive additional coaching and career counseling, and GE includes them in planning the marketing function's future.[1]

To meet the challenges brought on by growing domestic and global competition, business-to-business firms are increasingly recognizing the vital role of the marketing function in developing and implementing successful business strategies. Effective business strategies share many common characteristics, but at a minimum they are responsive to market needs, they exploit the special competencies of the organization, and they use valid assumptions about environmental trends and competitive behavior. Above all, they must offer a realistic basis for securing and sustaining a competitive advantage.[2] This chapter examines the nature and critical importance of strategy development in the business marketing firm.

First, the chapter highlights the special role of the marketing function in corporate strategy development, with a functionally integrated perspective of business marketing planning. Next, it identifies the sources of competitive advantage by exploring the key components of a business model and how they can be managed to secure distinctive strategic positioning. Finally, a framework is offered for converting strategy goals into a tightly integrated customer strategy. This discussion provides a foundation for exploring business marketing strategy on a global scale—the theme of the next chapter.

Marketing's Strategic Role

Market-driven firms are centered on customers—they take an outside-in view of strategy and demonstrate an ability to sense market trends ahead of their competitors.[3] Many firms—like Johnson & Johnson, 3M, and Dow Chemical—have numerous divisions, product lines, products, and brands. Policies established at the corporate level provide the framework for strategy development in each business division to ensure survival and growth of the entire enterprise. In turn, corporate and divisional policies establish the boundaries within which individual product or market managers develop strategy.

The Hierarchy of Strategies

Three major levels of strategy dominate most large multiproduct organizations: (1) corporate strategy, (2) business-level strategy, and (3) functional strategy.[4]

---

[1]Beth Comstock, Ranjay Gulati, and Stephen Liquori, "Unleashing the Power of Marketing," *Harvard Business Review* 88 (October 2010): p. 98.

[2]Rajan Varadarajan, "Strategic Marketing and Marketing Strategy: Domain, Definition, Fundamental Issues and Foundational Promises," *Journal of the Academy of Marketing Science* 38 (January 2010): pp. 119–140.

[3]For a comprehensive review, see Ahmet H. Kirca, Satish Jayachandran, and William O. Bearden, "Market Orientation: A Meta Analytic Review of Its Antecedents and Impact on Performance," *Journal of Marketing* 69 (April 2005): pp. 24–41. See also Roland T. Rust, Christine Moorman, and Gaurav Bhalla, "Rethinking Marketing," *Harvard Business Review* 88 (January–February 2010): pp. 94–101.

[4]This discussion draws on Frederick E. Webster Jr., "The Changing Role of Marketing in the Corporation," *Journal of Marketing* 56 (October 1992): pp. 1–17.

Corporate strategy defines the businesses in which a company competes, preferably in a manner that uses resources to convert distinctive competence into competitive advantage. Essential questions at this level include: What are our core competencies? What businesses are we in? What businesses should we be in? How should we allocate resources across these businesses to achieve our overall organizational goals and objectives? At this level of strategy, the role of marketing is to: (1) assess market attractiveness and the competitive effectiveness of the firm, (2) promote a customer orientation to the various constituencies in management decision making, and (3) formulate the firm's overall value proposition (as a reflection of its distinctive competencies, in terms reflecting customer needs), articulating it to the market and to the organization at large. According to Frederick Webster Jr., "At the corporate level, marketing managers have a critical role to play as advocates, for the customer and for a set of values and beliefs that put the customer first in the firm's decision making."[5]

Business-level strategy centers on how a firm competes in a given industry and positions itself against its competitors. The focus of competition is not between corporations; rather, it is between their individual business units. A **strategic business unit (SBU)** is a single business or collection of businesses that has a distinct mission, a responsible manager, and its own competitors and that is relatively independent of other business units. The 3M Corporation has defined 40 strategic business units. Each develops a plan describing how it will manage its mix of products to secure a competitive advantage consistent with the level of investment and risk that management is willing to accept. An SBU could be one or more divisions of the industrial firm, a product line within one division, or, on occasion, a single product. Strategic business units may share resources such as a sales force with other business units to achieve economies of scale. An SBU may serve one or many product-market units.

For each business unit in the corporate portfolio, the following essential questions must be answered: How can we compete most effectively for the product market the business unit serves? What distinctive skills can give the business unit a competitive advantage? Similarly, the former CEO at GE, Jack Welch, would ask his operating executives to crisply answer the following questions[6]:

- Describe the global competitive environment in which you operate.

- In the last two years, what have your competitors done?

- In the same period, what have you done to them in the marketplace?

- How might they attack you in the future?

- What are your plans to leapfrog them?

The marketing function contributes to the planning process at this level by providing a detailed and complete analysis of customers and competitors and the firm's distinctive skills and resources for competing in particular market segments.

Functional strategy centers on how resources allocated to the various functional areas can be used most efficiently and effectively to support the business-level

---

[5]Webster, "The Changing Role of Marketing," p. 11. See also Peter Verhoef and Peter S. H. Leeflang, "Understanding the Marketing Department's Influence within the Firm," *Journal of Marketing* 73 (March 2009): pp. 14–37.

[6]Noel M. Tichy and Stratford Sherman, *Control Your Destiny or Someone Else Will* (New York: Doubleday, 1993), p. 26; see also Jack Welch and John A. Byrne, *Jack: Straight from the Gut* (New York: Warner Books, 2001).

strategy. The primary focus of marketing strategy at this level is to allocate and coordinate marketing resources and activities to achieve the firm's objective within a specific product market.

Strategy Formulation and the Hierarchy[7]

The interplay among the three levels of the strategy hierarchy can be illustrated by examining the collective action perspective of strategy formulation. This approach applies to strategic decisions that: (1) cut across functional areas, (2) involve issues related to the organization's long-term objectives, or (3) involve allocating resources across business units or product markets. Included here are decisions about the direction of corporate strategy, the application of a core technology, or the choice of an alliance partner.

Observe in Figure 5.1 that strategic decision processes often involve the active participation of several functional interest groups that hold markedly different beliefs about the appropriateness of particular strategies or corporate goals. Strategic decisions represent the outcome of a bargaining process among functional interest groups (including marketing), each of which may interpret the proposed strategy in an entirely different light.

Turf Issues and Thought-World Views Two forces contribute to the conflict that often divides participants in the strategy formulation process. First, different meanings assigned to a proposed strategy are often motivated by deeper differences in what might be called "organizational subcultures." Subcultures exist when one subunit shares different values, beliefs, and goals than another subunit, resulting in different **thought-worlds**.[8] For example, marketing managers are concerned with market opportunities and competitors, whereas R&D managers value technical sophistication and innovation. Second, functional managers are likely to resist strategic changes that threaten their turf. To the extent that the subunit defines the individual's identity and connotes prestige and power, the organizational member may be reluctant to see it altered by a strategic decision.

Negotiated Outcomes Collective decisions emerge from negotiation and compromise among partisan participants. The differences in goals, thought-worlds, and self-interests across participants lead to conflicts about actions that should be taken. Choices must be negotiated with each interest group attempting to achieve its own ends. The ultimate outcomes of collective decisions tend to unfold incrementally and depend more on the partisan values and influence of the various interest groups than on rational analysis. A study of a highly contested strategic decision in a *Fortune* 500 company illustrates the tension that may exist between marketing and R&D.

Two marketing executives describe how the decision was ultimately resolved.[9] According to the marketing manager:

> [Marketing] did an extremely effective job of stepping right in the middle of it and strangling it.... What has happened is by laying out the market unit

---

[7]Gary L. Frankwick, James C. Ward, Michael D. Hutt, and Peter H. Reingen, "Evolving Patterns of Organizational Beliefs in the Formation of Marketing Strategy," *Journal of Marketing* 58 (April 1994): pp. 96–110; see also Michael D. Hutt, Beth A. Walker, and Gary L. Frankwick, "Hurdle the Cross-Functional Barriers to Strategic Change," *Sloan Management Review* 36 (Spring 1995): pp. 22–30.

[8]See, for example, Christian Homburg, Ore Jensen, and Harley Krohmer, "Configurations of Marketing and Sales," *Journal of Marketing* 72 (March 2008): pp. 123–154; and Christian Homburg and Ore Jensen, "The Thought Worlds of Marketing and Sales: Which Differences Make a Difference?" *Journal of Marketing* 71 (July 2007): pp. 124–141.

[9]Frankwick , Ward, Hutt, and Reingen, "Evolving Patterns of Organizational Beliefs," pp. 107–108.

FIGURE 5.1 | A COLLECTIVE ACTION PERSPECTIVE OF THE STRATEGY FORMULATION PROCESS

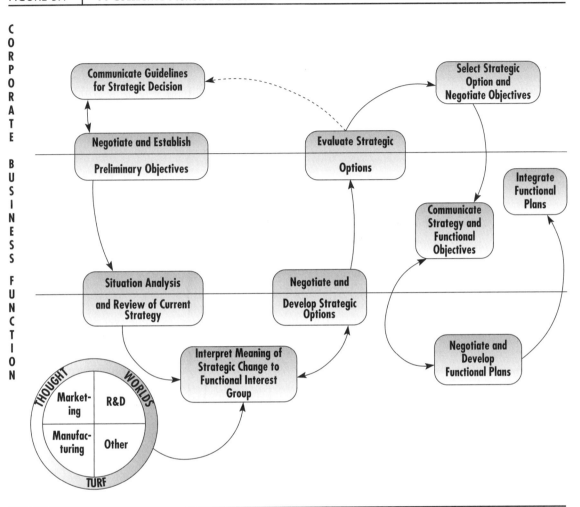

SOURCE: Gary L. Frankwick, James C. Ward, Michael D. Hutt, and Peter H. Reingen, "Evolving Patterns of Organizational Beliefs in the Formation of Strategy," *Journal of Marketing* 58 (April 1994): p. 98. Reprinted with permission by the American Marketing Association.

concerns and again, refocusing on the fact that we are market-based, basically what Marketing did was force the R&D team into submission where they no longer have the autonomy they once had to go about making decisions—they now get input. And whether it's formal or informal, they definitely get the buy-in of marketing before they move forward on what they're doing now.

According to the vice president of marketing:

Before I felt it was technology driving the process. Now I feel that technology is partnering with the marketplace. And the reason I feel that way is because we have [marketing people] in place that are working closely with how the technology develops.

Implications for Marketing Managers   In advocating a strategic course, marketing managers must be sensitive to the likely response it may arouse in other interest groups. To build pockets of commitment and trust, managers should develop and use a communication network that includes organizational members who have a major stake in the decision. Marketing managers can use these personal networks to understand the interests of other stakeholders, communicate their own interests clearly and sensitively, and thus diffuse the anxiety of others about threats to their turf.

Functionally Integrated Planning: The Marketing Strategy Center[10]

Rather than operating in isolation from other functional areas, the successful business marketing manager is an integrator—one who understands the capabilities of manufacturing, R&D, and customer service and who capitalizes on their strengths in developing marketing strategies that are responsive to customer needs. Marketing managers also assume a central role in strategy implementation.[11] Recent research indicates that in companies found to be strong on strategy execution, over 70 percent of employees affirm that they have a clear idea of the decisions and actions for which they are responsible; that figure drops to 32 percent in organizations weak on execution.[12]

Responsibility charting is an approach that can classify decision-making roles and highlight the multifunctional nature of business marketing decision making. The decision areas (rows) in the matrix might, for example, relate to a planned product-line expansion. The various functional areas that may assume particular roles in this decision process head the matrix columns. The following list defines the alternative roles that participants can assume in the decision-making process.[13]

1. *Responsible* (R): The manager takes the initiative for analyzing the situation, developing alternatives, and assuring consultation with others and then makes the initial recommendation. Upon approval of the decision, the role ends.

2. *Approve* (A): The manager accepts or vetoes a decision before it is implemented or chooses from alternatives developed by the participants assuming a "responsible" role.

3. *Consult* (C): The manager is consulted or asked for substantive input before the decision is approved but does not possess veto power.

4. *Implement* (M): The manager is accountable for implementing the decision, including notifying other relevant participants about the decision.

5. *Inform* (I): Although the manager is not necessarily consulted before the decision is approved, he or she is informed of the decision once it is made.

---

[10]Michael D. Hutt and Thomas W. Speh, "The Marketing Strategy Center: Diagnosing the Industrial Marketer's Interdisciplinary Role," *Journal of Marketing* 48 (Fall 1984): pp. 53–61; see also Jeen-Su Lim and David A. Reid, "Vital Cross- Functional Linkages with Marketing," *Industrial Marketing Management* 22 (February 1993): pp. 159–165.

[11]Charles H. Noble and Michael P. Mokwa, "Implementing Marketing Strategies: Developing and Testing a Managerial Theory," *Journal of Marketing* 63 (October 1999): pp. 57–73.

[12]Gary L. Neilson, Karla L. Martin, and Elizabeth Powers, "The Secrets to Successful Strategy Execution," *Harvard Business Review* 86 (June 2008): p. 63.

[13]Joseph E. McCann and Thomas N. Gilmore, "Diagnosing Organizational Decision Making through Responsibility Charting," *Sloan Management Review* 25 (Winter 1983): pp. 3–15.

B2B TOP PERFORMERS

Cross-Functional Relationships: Effective Managers Deliver on Promises

Ask an R&D manager to identify a colleague from marketing who is particularly effective at getting things done and he or she readily offers a name and a memorable episode to justify the selection. To explore the characteristics of high-performing cross-functional managers, detailed accounts of effective and ineffective interactions were gathered from managers at a *Fortune* 100 high-technology firm. Interestingly, the top-of-mind characteristics that colleagues emphasize when describing high performers are soft skills like openness rather than hard skills like technical proficiency or marketing savvy. Here is a profile:

- High-performing managers are revered by their colleagues for their *responsiveness*. Remembering effective cross-functional episodes, colleagues describe high performers as "timely," "prompt," and "responsive" (for example, "When I need critical information, I turn to him and he gets right back to me").

- Rather than a "functional mindset," high performers demonstrate *perspective-taking* skills—the ability to anticipate and understand the perspectives and priorities of managers from other units (for example, "He's a superb marketing strategist but he also recognizes the special technical issues that we've

been working through to get this product launched on schedule").

- When colleagues describe the *communication style* of their high-performing cross-functional counterparts, they focus on three consistent themes: openness, frequency, and quality. Interactions with high performers are described as "candid," "unencumbered," and characterized by a "free flow of thoughts and suggestions." Such high-quality interactions clarify goals and responsibilities.

By "delivering on their promises," effective managers develop a web of close relationships across functions. "He has really good personal relationships with a lot of people and he has a network—he really understands the mechanisms that you have to use to get things done."

SOURCE: Michael D. Hutt and Thomas W. Speh, "Undergraduate Education: The Implications of Cross-Functional Relationships in Business Marketing—the Skills of High-Performing Managers," *Journal of Business-to-Business Marketing* 14 (1, 2007); available online at http://www.tandf.co.uk/journals/haworth-journals.asp © 2007 by the Haworth Press, Inc. See also Edward U. Bond III, Beth A. Walker, Michael D. Hutt, and Peter H. Reingen, "Reputational Effectiveness in Cross-Functional Working Relationships," *Journal of Product Innovation Management* 21 (January 2004): pp. 44–60.

Representatives of a particular functional area may, of course, assume more than one role in the decision-making process. The technical service manager may be consulted during the new-product-development process and may also be held accountable for implementing service-support strategy. Likewise, the marketing manager may be responsible for and approve many of the decisions related to the product-line expansion. For other actions, several decision makers may participate. To illustrate, the business unit manager, after consulting R&D, may approve (or veto) a decision for which the marketing manager is responsible.

The members of the organization involved in the business marketing decision-making process constitute the **marketing strategy center**. The composition or functional area representation of the strategy center evolves during the marketing strategy development process, varies from firm to firm, and varies from one situation to another. Likewise, the composition of the marketing strategy center is not strictly prescribed by the organizational chart. The needs of a particular strategy situation, especially the information requirements, significantly influence the composition of the strategy center. Thus, the marketing strategy center shares certain parallels with the buying center (see Chapter 2).

Managing Strategic Interdependencies   A central challenge for the business marketer in the strategy center is to minimize interdepartmental conflict while fostering shared appreciation of the interdependencies with other functional units. Individual strategy center participants are motivated by both personal and organizational goals. They interpret company objectives in relation to their level in the hierarchy and the department they represent. Various functional units operate under unique reward systems and reflect unique orientations or thought-worlds. For example, marketing managers are evaluated on the basis of sales, profits, or market share, whereas production managers are assessed on the basis of manufacturing efficiency and cost-effectiveness. In turn, R&D managers may be oriented toward long-term objectives; customer service managers may emphasize more immediate ones. Strategic plans emerge out of a bargaining process among functional areas. Managing conflict, promoting cooperation, and developing coordinated strategies are all fundamental to the business marketer's interdisciplinary role. By understanding the concerns and orientations of personnel from other functional areas, the business marketing manager is better equipped to forge effective cross-unit working relationships.

The Components of a Business Model[14]

For a strategy to succeed, individuals must understand and share a common definition of a firm's existing business concept. For example, ask any employee at Dell and they will tell you about the "Dell model" that sets them apart from competitors. A **business concept** or model consists of four major components (Figure 5.2):

- Customer Interface
- Core Strategy
- Strategic Resources
- Value Network

The major components of the business concept are tied together by three important "bridge" elements: customer benefits, configuration, and company boundaries.

---

[14]Except where noted, this discussion is based on Gary Hamel, *Leading the Revolution* (Boston: Harvard Business School Press, 2000), pp. 70–94. See also Ramon Casadesus-Masanell and Joan E. Ricart, "How to Design a Winning Business Model," *Harvard Business Review* 89 (January–February 2011): pp. 100–107.

FIGURE 5.2 | **COMPONENTS OF A BUSINESS MODEL**

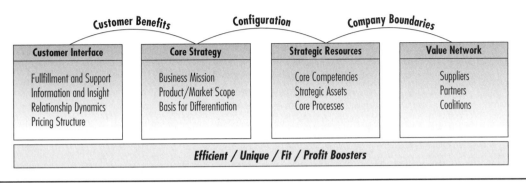

Customer Interface

Customer benefits provide the bridge between the core strategy and the customer interface. Customer benefits link the core strategy directly to the needs of customers. The customer interface includes four elements:

1. **Fulfillment and support** refers to the channels a business marketing firm uses to reach customers and the level of service support it provides.

2. **Information and insight** refers to the knowledge captured from customers and the degree to which this information is used to provide enhanced value to the customer.

3. **Relationship dynamics** refers to the nature of the interaction between the firm and its customers (for example, the proportion of relational versus transactional customers; see Chapter 3). Key question: What steps can be taken to raise the hurdle for competitors by exceeding customer expectations or strengthening the customer's sense of affiliation with the firm?

4. **Pricing structure.** A business concept may offer several pricing choices. For example, a firm can bundle products and services or price them on a menu basis. For example, when airlines buy a Boeing 777, which is equipped with jet engines produced by GE, they pay GE a fee for each flight hour in line with a fixed-priced maintenance agreement. So, rather than products, GE is selling "power by the hour."

Core Strategy

The **core strategy** determines how the firm chooses to compete. From Figure 5.2, observe that three elements are involved in setting a core strategy:

1. The **business mission** describes the overall objectives of the strategy, sets a course and direction, and defines a set of performance criteria that are used to measure progress. The business mission must be broad enough to allow

B2B TOP PERFORMERS

Winning with a New Business Model at Dow Corning

Dow Corning Corporation is the world's largest and most innovative producer of silicone-based products. Although the leader in this large and diverse market, smaller, regional competitors began to take market share away from Dow Corning by selling low-priced silicone products with little or no technical support. Rather than paying for a host of high-quality services such as new-product-development assistance that Dow Corning customarily provides, these customers eagerly sought the lowest price. To meet the challenge, Dow Corning conducted a market segmentation study, isolated the characteristics of this "low-cost" buyer, and created a no-frills Web-based business model to reach this customer segment. To avoid confusion with existing customers and the firm's premium product lines, a new brand was created—Xiameter (http://www.xiameter.com).

To clarify the brand premise and the company connection, the tag line—"The new measure of value from Dow Corning"—was added. By steering price-sensitive customers to the Internet—a low-cost sales channel—the branding strategy allows Dow Corning "to compete head-on with the low-price suppliers of mature product lines, without damaging its position as a value-added leader at the premium price end of the market." Customers, from the United States to high-growth potential countries like China, have responded positively to the Xiameter brand.

SOURCE: Bob Lamons, "Dow Targets Segment to Keep Market Share," *Marketing News*, June 15, 2005, p. 8. See also Randall S. Rozin and Liz Magnusson, "Processes and Methodologies for Creating a Global Business-to-Business Brand," *Journal of Brand Management* 10 (February 2003): pp. 185–207.

for business concept innovation, and it should be distinguished from the mission of competitors in the industry. For example, by focusing its mission on copiers and copying, Xerox allowed Hewlett-Packard to build a dominant lead in the printer business.

2. **Product/market scope** defines *where* the firm competes. The product markets that constitute the domain of a business can be defined by customer benefits, technologies, customer segments, and channels of distribution.[15] Strategists might consider this question: Are particular customer segments being overlooked by competitors or customers who might welcome a new product-service solution?

3. **Basis for differentiation** captures the essence of how a firm competes differently than its rivals. George Day and Robin Wensley explain:

A business is differentiated when some value-adding activities are performed in a way that leads to perceived superiority along dimensions that are valued by customers. For these activities to be profitable, the customer must be willing to pay a premium for the benefits and the premium must exceed the added costs of superior performance.[16]

[15]George S. Day, *Strategic Market Planning: The Pursuit of Competitive Advantage* (St. Paul, MN: West Publishing, 1984).

[16]George S. Day and Robin Wensley, "Assessing Advantage: A Framework for Diagnosing Competitive Superiority," *Journal of Marketing* 52 (April 1988): pp. 3–4. See also Douglas W. Vorhies and Neil A. Morgan, "Benchmarking Marketing Capabilities for Sustainable Competitive Advantage," *Journal of Marketing* 69 (January 2005): pp. 80–94.

There are many ways for a firm to differentiate products and services:

- Provide superior service or technical assistance competence through speed, responsiveness to complex orders, or ability to solve special customer problems.

- Provide superior quality that reduces customer costs or improves their performance.

- Offer innovative product features that use new technologies.

Strategic Resources

A business marketing firm gains a competitive advantage through its superior skills and resources. The firm's strategic resources include core competencies, strategic assets, and core processes.

1. **Core competencies** are the set of skills, systems, and technologies a company uses to create uniquely high value for customers.[17] For example, GE Healthcare drew on its competencies in sensing technologies to develop a new stand-alone business to provide home health monitoring innovations.[18] Concerning core competencies, the guiding questions for the strategist are: What important benefits do our competencies provide to customers? What do we know or do especially well that is valuable to customers and is transferable to new market opportunities?

2. **Strategic assets** are the more tangible requirements for advantage that enable a firm to exercise its capabilities. Included are brands, customer data, distribution coverage, patents, and other resources that are both rare and valuable. Attention centers on this question: Can we use these strategic assets in a different way to provide new levels of value to existing or prospective customers?

3. **Core processes** are the methodologies and routines companies use to transform competencies, assets, and other inputs into value for customers. For example, drug discovery is a core process at Merck, and delivery fulfillment is a core process at FedEx. Here the strategist considers these questions: Which processes are most competitively unique and create the most customer value? Could we use our process expertise effectively to enter other markets?

From Figure 5.2, note that a configuration component links strategic resources to the core strategy. "Configuration refers to the unique way in which competencies, assets, and processes are interrelated in support of a particular strategy."[19] For example, Honda manages key activities in the new-product-development process differently than its rivals.

The Value Network

The final component of a business concept is the **value network** that complements and further enriches the firm's research base. Included here are suppliers, strategic alliance partners, and coalitions. To illustrate, nimble competitors such as Cisco and

[17]James Brian Quinn, "Strategic Outsourcing: Leveraging Knowledge Capabilities," *Sloan Management Review* 40 (Summer 1999): pp. 9–21.

[18]Comstock , Gulati, and Liquori, "Unleashing the Power of Marketing," p. 95.

[19]Hamel, *Leading the Revolution*, p. 78.

FIGURE 5.3 | The Principles of Strategic Positioning

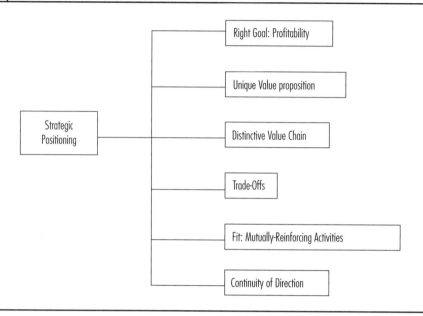

SOURCE: Adapted from Michael E. Porter, "What Is Strategy?" *Harvard Business Review* 74 (November–December 1996): pp. 61–78.

Apple demonstrate special skills in forging relationships with suppliers and alliance partners. Concerning the value network, the guiding question for the strategist is: What market opportunities might become available to us "if we could 'borrow' the assets and competencies of other companies and marry them with our own?"[20]

Strategic Positioning[21]

Competitive strategy, at the core, is about being different, choosing to compete in a distinctive way. A business model should reveal the way in which a firm is deliberately emphasizing a different set of activities in order to deliver a unique mix of customer value. Michael Porter asserts that six fundamental principles provide a company with the foundation for establishing and maintaining a distinctive strategic positioning (see Figure 5.3).

- Center on the *right goal*—superior long-term return on investment rather than performance goals defined in terms of sales volume or market share leadership.

- Deliver a *customer value proposition*, or set of benefits, that differs from those of rivals. (For example, Southwest Airlines delivers low-cost, convenient service to customers—particular benefits that full-service rivals cannot match.)

- Create a *distinctive value chain* by performing different activities than rivals or performing similar activities in different ways. (For example, by streamlining

---

[20]Ibid., p. 90.

[21]This section is based on Michael E. Porter, "What Is Strategy?" *Harvard Business Review* 74 (November–December 1996): pp. 61–78.

the passenger boarding process, Southwest achieves faster turnaround at the gate and can provide more frequent departures with fewer planes.)

- Accept *trade-offs* and recognize that a company must forgo some product features or services to remain truly distinctive in others. (For example, Continental Airlines introduced Continental Lite to compete directly against Southwest. By trying to be low cost on some routes and full service on others, Continental lost several hundred million dollars before grounding Continental Lite.)

- Emphasize the way in which all the elements of the strategy *fit* and reinforce one another. (For example, from its standardized fleet of Boeing 737 aircraft to its well-trained ground crews that speed flight turnaround, and its strict limits on the type and length of routes, Southwest's activities complement and reinforce one another, creating a whole system of competing that locks out imitators.)

- Build strong customer relationships and develop unique skills by defining a distinctive value proposition that provides *continuity of direction*. (For example, Southwest continues to pursue its disciplined strategic agenda.)

Michael Porter observes:

> Having a strategy is a matter of discipline. It requires a strong focus on profitability rather than just growth, an ability to define a unique value proposition, and a willingness to make tough trade-offs in choosing what not to do…. It involves the configuration of a tailored value chain—the series of activities required to produce and deliver a product or service—that enables a company to offer unique value.[22]

Let's examine how a business-to-business firm has used these principles to establish a business model and maintain a distinctive strategic positioning.

Strategic Positioning Illustrated[23]

Paccar operates in the fiercely competitive heavy-duty truck industry, designing and manufacturing trucks under the Kenworth and Peterbilt brand names. The firm, headquartered in Bellevue, Washington, commands 20 percent of the North American heavy truck market and derives approximately half of its revenues and profits from outside the United States.

A Unique Focus   Rather than centering on large-fleet buyers or large leasing companies, Paccar has chosen to focus on one group of customers—drivers who own their own trucks and contract directly with shippers or serve as contractors to larger trucking companies. Paccar provides an array of specialized services that specifically address the needs of owner-operators: luxurious sleeper cabins, noise-insulated cabins, and sleek interior and exterior options (numbering in the thousands)

---

[22]Michael E. Porter, "Strategy and the Internet," *Harvard Business Review* 79 (March 2001): p. 72.

[23]This illustration is based on Michael E. Porter, "The Five Competitive Forces that Shape Strategy," *Harvard Business Review* 86 (January 2008): p. 89.

that prospective buyers can select to put their personal signatures on their trucks. Paccar delivers its products and services to customers through an extensive dealer network of nearly 1800 locations worldwide.

Distinctive Value Proposition   Built to order, these customized trucks are delivered to customers in six to eight weeks and incorporate features and value-added services that are embraced by owner-operators. Paccar's trucks feature an aerodynamic design that reduces fuel consumption, and they maintain resale value better than the trucks offered by rivals. To reduce out-of-service time, Paccar offers a comprehensive roadside assistance program and an information-technology-supported system for expediting and delivering spare parts. According to Michael Porter, "Customers pay Paccar a 10 percent premium, and its Kenworth and Peterbilt brands are considered status symbols at truck stops."[24] Moreover, Paccar has received recognition for consistently leading the heavy-duty truck market in quality, innovation, and customer satisfaction.[25]

By configuring its activities on new-product development, manufacturing, and service support differently from rivals, and by tailoring these activities to its customer value proposition, Paccar has achieved an enviable record of financial performance: 68 straight years of profitability, averaging a long-run return on equity above 20 percent.

Building the Strategy Plan

By finding an intricate match between strategy and operations, strategic positioning depends on doing many things well—not just a few. But yet, the underperformance of most companies is caused by breakdowns between strategy and operations. Robert S. Kaplan and David P. Norton contend that execution of successful strategy involves two basic rules: "understand the management cycle that links strategy and operations, and know what tools to apply at each stage of the cycle."[26] To that end, they propose that companies develop a management system to plan, coordinate, and monitor the links between strategy and operations. This **management system** represents "the integrated set of processes and tools that a company uses to develop its strategy, translate it into operational actions, and monitor and improve the effectiveness of both."[27] (See Figure 5.4.)

Observe that the management system involves five stages, beginning with strategy development (Stage 1) and then moving on to the crucial stage of translating the strategy (Stage 2) into objectives and measures that can be clearly communicated to all functional areas and employees. We will give special attention to two tools: (1) the **balanced scorecard** that provides managers with a comprehensive system for converting a company's vision and strategy into a tightly connected set of performance measures; and (2) the **strategy map**—a tool for visualizing a firm's strategy as a chain of cause-and-effect relationships among strategic objectives. These tools and processes assume a central role in designing key processes (Stage 3), monitoring performance (Stage 4), and adapting the strategy (Stage 5).

---

[24]Ibid.

[25]"Kenworth Wins J.D. Power Awards," August 27, 2007, accessed at http://www.paccar.com/company/jdpower on July 11, 2008.

[26]Robert S. Kaplan and David P. Norton, "Mastering the Management System," *Harvard Business Review* 86 (January 2008): p. 63.

[27]Ibid., p. 64.

FIGURE 5.4 | THE MANAGEMENT SYSTEM: LINKING STRATEGY AND OPERATIONS

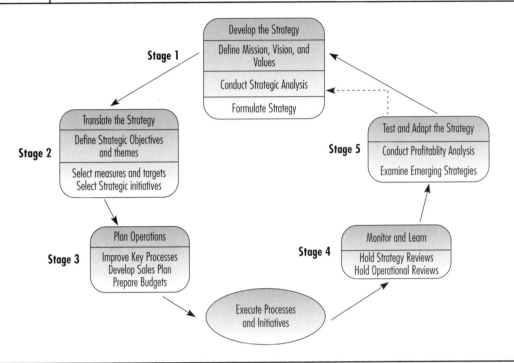

SOURCE: Adapted with modifications from Robert S. Kaplan and David P. Norton, "Mastering the Management System," *Harvard Business Review* 86 (January 2008): p. 65.

The Balanced Scorecard[28]

Measurement is a central element in the strategy process. The balanced scorecard combines financial measures of past performance with measures of the drivers of performance. Observe in Figure 5.5 that the scorecard examines the performance of a business unit from four perspectives: (1) financial, (2) customer, (3) internal business processes, and (4) learning and growth.

The architects of the approach, Robert Kaplan and David Norton, emphasize that "the scorecard should tell the story of the strategy, starting with the long-run financial objectives, and then linking them to the sequence of actions that must be taken with financial processes, customers, and finally employees and systems to deliver the desired long-run economic performance."[29]

Financial Perspective

Financial performance measures allow business marketing managers to monitor the degree to which the firm's strategy, implementation, and execution are increasing

---

[28]Except where noted, this discussion is based on Robert S. Kaplan and David P. Norton, *Strategy Maps: Converting Intangible Assets into Tangible Outcomes* (Boston: Harvard Business School Publishing Corporation, 2004). See also Robert S. Kaplan and David P. Norton, *The Balanced Scorecard: Translating Strategy into Action* (Boston: Harvard Business School Press, 1996), chaps. 1–3.

[29]Kaplan and Norton, *The Balanced Scorecard*, p. 47.

FIGURE 5.5 | **THE BALANCED SCORECARD: A FRAMEWORK TO TRANSLATE A STRATEGY INTO OPERATIONAL TERMS**

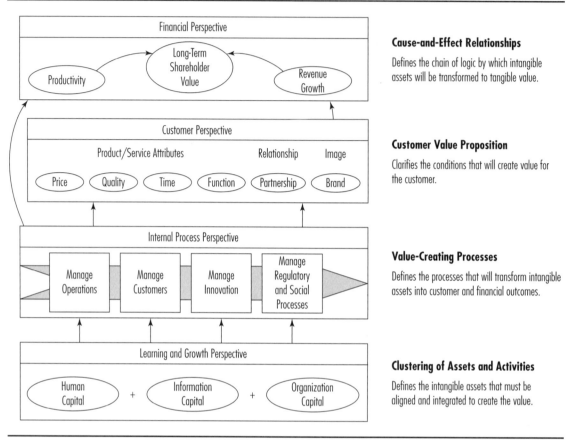

Cause-and-Effect Relationships

Defines the chain of logic by which intangible assets will be transformed to tangible value.

Customer Value Proposition

Clarifies the conditions that will create value for the customer.

Value-Creating Processes

Defines the processes that will transform intangible assets into customer and financial outcomes.

Clustering of Assets and Activities

Defines the intangible assets that must be aligned and integrated to create the value.

SOURCE: Reprinted by permission of *Harvard Business Review*. From "Balanced Scorecard Framework" by Robert S. Kaplan in Strategy Maps, p. 31. Copyright © 2004 by the Harvard Business School Publishing Corporation; all rights reserved.

profits. Measures such as return on investment, revenue growth, shareholder value, profitability, and cost per unit are among the performance measures that show whether the firm's strategy is succeeding or failing. Companies emphasize two basic levers in developing a financial strategy: revenue growth and productivity.[30] The revenue-growth strategy centers on securing sales from new markets and new products or strengthening and expanding relationships with existing customers. The productivity strategy can also take two forms: improve the company's cost structure by reducing expenses and/or use assets more efficiently by decreasing the working and fixed capital needed to support a given level of output.

Recent research confirms the wisdom of a balanced approach to strategy by isolating the strategy that winning firms follow to survive a recession and thrive when it ends.[31] These firms cut costs mainly by improving operational efficiency

---

[30]Robert S. Kaplan and David P. Norton, "Having Trouble with Your Strategy? Then Map It," *Harvard Business Review* 78 (September–October 2000): pp. 167–176.

[31]Ranjay Gulati, Nitin Nohria, and Franz Wohlgezogen, "Roaring Out of Recession," *Harvard Business Review* 88 (March 2010): pp. 62–69.

rather than by slashing the number of employees more than peers. However, the offensive moves of winning firms are comprehensive. "They develop new business opportunities by making significantly greater investments than their rivals do in R&D and marketing, and they invest in assets, such as plants and machinery."[32]

The balanced scorecard seeks to match financial objectives to a business unit's growth and life cycle stages. Three stages of a business are isolated and linked to appropriate financial objectives:

1. **Growth:** Business units that have products and services with significant growth potential and that must commit considerable resources (for example, production facilities and distribution networks) to capitalize on the market opportunity.

   Financial Objectives: Sales growth rate by segment; percentage of revenue from new product, services, and customers.

2. **Sustain:** Business units, likely representing the majority of businesses within a firm, that expect to maintain or to perhaps moderately increase market share from year to year.

   Financial Objectives: Share of target customers and accounts; customer and product-line profitability.

3. **Harvest:** Mature business units that warrant only enough investment to maintain production equipment and capabilities.

   Financial Objectives: Payback; customer and product-line profitability.

Customer Perspective

In the customer component of the balanced scorecard, the business unit identifies the market segments it will target (see Chapter 4). Those segments supply the revenue stream that support critical financial objectives. Marketing managers must also identify the value proposition—how the firm proposes to deliver competitively superior and sustainable value to the target customers and market segments. The central element of any business strategy is the value proposition that describes a company's unique product and service attributes, customer relationship management practices, and corporate reputation. Importantly, the value proposition should clearly communicate to targeted customers what the company expects to do better and differently than its competitors.

Key Value Propositions and Customer Strategies   Business-to-business firms typically choose among four forms of differentiation in developing a value proposition[33]:

- **Low total cost**—customers are offered attractive prices, excellent and consistent quality, ease of purchase, and responsive service (for example, Dell, Inc.).

- **Product innovation and leadership**—customers receive products that expand existing performance boundaries through new features and functions (for example, Intel and Sony).

---

[32]Ibid., p. 67.

[33]Kaplan and Norton, *Strategy Maps*, pp. 322–344.

TABLE 5.1 | THE CUSTOMER PERSPECTIVE—CORE MEASURES

Market Share	Represents the proportion of business in a given market (in terms of number of customers, dollars spent, or unit volume sold) that a business unit sells.
Customer Acquisition	Tracks, in absolute or relative terms, the rate at which a business unit attracts or wins new customers or business.
Customer Retention	Tracks, in absolute or relative terms, the rate at which a business unit retains customers.
Customer Satisfaction	Matches the satisfaction level of customers on specific performance criteria such as quality, service, or on-time delivery reliability.
Customer Profitability	Assesses the net profit of a customer, or segment, after deducting the unique expenses required to support that customer or segment.

SOURCE: Adapted from Robert S. Kaplan and David P. Norton, *The Balanced Scorecard: Translating Strategy into Action* (Boston: Harvard Business School Press, 1996): p. 68.

- **Complete customer solutions**—customers feel that the company understands them and can provide customized products and services tailored to their unique requirements (for example, IBM).

- **Lock-in**—customers purchase a widely used proprietary product or service from the firm and incur high switching costs (for example, Microsoft's operating system, Cisco's infrastructure products, or Google's search engine).

For the chosen strategy, Table 5.1 presents the core customer outcome measures used to monitor performance in each target segment. The customer perspective complements traditional market share analysis by tracking customer acquisition, customer retention, customer satisfaction, and customer profitability.

Internal Business Process Perspective

To develop the value proposition that will reach and satisfy targeted customer segments and to achieve the desired financial objectives, critical internal business processes must be developed and continually enriched. Internal business processes support two crucial elements of a company's strategy: (1) they create and deliver the value proposition for customers and (2) they improve processes and reduce costs, enriching the productivity component in the financial perspective. Among the processes vital to the creation of customer value are:

1. Operations Management Processes,

2. Customer Management Processes,

3. Innovation Management Processes.

Strategic Alignment Robert S. Kaplan and David P. Norton emphasize that "value is created through internal business processes."[34] Table 5.2 shows how key internal processes can be aligned to support the firm's customer strategy or differentiating-value proposition. First, observe that the relative emphasis (see shaded areas) given to a

---

[34]Ibid., p. 43.

TABLE 5.2 | ALIGNING INTERNAL BUSINESS PROCESSES TO THE CUSTOMER STRATEGY

Customer Strategy	The Focus of Internal Business Processes		
	Operations Management	**Customer Relationship Management**	**Innovation Management**
Low-Total-Cost Strategy	Highly Efficient Operating Processes Efficient, Timely Distribution	Ease of Access for Customers; Superb Post-sales Service	Seek Process Innovations Gain Scale Economies
Product Leadership Strategy	Flexible Manufacturing Processes Rapid Introduction of New Products	Capture Customer Ideas for New Offering Educate Customers about Complex New Products/ Services	Disciplined, High-Performance Product Development First-to-Market
Complete Customer Solutions Strategy	Deliver Broad Product/ Service Line Create Network of Suppliers for Extended Product/ Service Capabilities	Create Customized Solutions for Customers Build Strong Customer Relationships Develop Customer Knowledge	Identify New Opportunities to Serve Customers Anticipate Future Customer Needs
Lock-in Strategies	Provide Capacity for Proprietary Product/Service Reliable Access and Ease of Use	Create Awareness Influence Switching Costs of Existing and Potential Customers	Develop and Enhance Proprietary Product Increase Breadth/ Applications of Standard

SOURCE: Adapted from Robert S. Kaplan and David P. Norton, *Strategy Maps: Converting Intangible Assets into Tangible Outcomes* (Boston: Harvard Business School Publishing Corporation, 2004), pp. 322–344.

particular process varies by strategy. For example, a firm that actively pursues a product-leadership strategy highlights innovation-management processes, whereas a company adopting a low-total-cost strategy assigns priority to operations-management processes. Second, although the level of emphasis might vary, note how the various processes work together to reinforce the value proposition. For example, a low-total-cost strategy can be reinforced by an innovation-management process that uncovers process improvements and a customer relationship management process that delivers superb post-sales support.

From our discussion of strategic positioning, recall that it is much harder for a rival to match a set of interlocked processes than it is to replicate a single process. Michael Porter observes:

> Strategic fit among many activities is fundamental not only to competitive advantage but also to the sustainability of that advantage…. . Positions built on systems of activities are far more sustainable than those built on individual activities.[35]

Learning and Growth The fourth component of the balanced scorecard, **learning and growth**, highlights how the firm's intangible assets must be aligned to its strategy to achieve long-term goals. **Intangible assets** represent "the capabilities

[35]Porter, "What Is Strategy?" p. 73.

of the company's employees to satisfy customer needs."[36] The three principal drivers of organizational learning and growth are:

1. *Human capital*—the availability of employees who have the skills, talent, and know-how to perform activities required by the strategy;

2. *Information capital*—the availability of information systems, applications, and information-technology infrastructure to support the strategy;

3. *Organization capital*—the culture (for example, values), leadership, employee incentives, and teamwork to mobilize the organization and execute the strategy.

Strategic Alignment   To create value and advance performance, the intangible assets of the firm must be aligned with the strategy. For example, consider a company that plans to invest in staff training and has two choices—a training program on total quality management (TQM) or a training initiative on customer relationship management (CRM). A company like Dell, which pursues a low-total-cost strategy, might derive higher value from TQM training, whereas IBM's consulting unit, which pursues a total customer solution strategy, would benefit more from CRM training. Unfortunately, research suggests that two-thirds of organizations fail to create a strong alignment between their strategies and their human resources and information technology programs.[37]

Measuring Strategic Readiness   Senior management must ensure that the firm's human resources and information technology systems are aligned with the chosen strategy. To achieve desired performance goals in the other areas of the scorecard, key objectives must be achieved on measures of employee satisfaction, retention, and productivity. Likewise, front-line employees, such as sales or technical service representatives, must have ready access to timely and accurate information. However, skilled employees who are supported by a carefully designed information system will not contribute to organizational goals if they are not motivated or empowered to do so. Many firms, such as FedEx and 3M, have demonstrated the vital role of motivated and empowered employees in securing a strong customer franchise.

Now that each of the components of the balanced scorecard has been defined, let's explore a clever tool that can be used to communicate the desired strategy path to all employees while detailing the processes that will be used to implement the strategy.

Strategy Map

To provide a visual representation of the cause-and-effect relationships among the components of the balanced scorecard, Kaplan and Norton developed what they call a strategy map. They say that a strategy must provide a clear portrait that reveals how a firm will achieve its desired goals and deliver on its promises to employees, customers, and shareholders. "A strategy map enables an organization to describe and illustrate, in clear and general language, its objectives, initiatives, and targets; the measures used to assess performance (such as market share and customer surveys); and the linkages that are the foundation for strategic direction."[38]

---

[36]Thomas A. Stewart, *Intellectual Capital: The New Wealth of Organizations* (New York: Doubleday, 1998), p. 67, cited in Kaplan and Norton, *Strategy Maps*, pp. 202–203.

[37]Kaplan and Norton, *Strategy Maps*, p. 13.

[38]Kaplan and Norton, "Having Trouble with Your Strategy?" p. 170.

FIGURE 5.6 | **STRATEGY MAP TEMPLATE: PRODUCT LEADERSHIP**

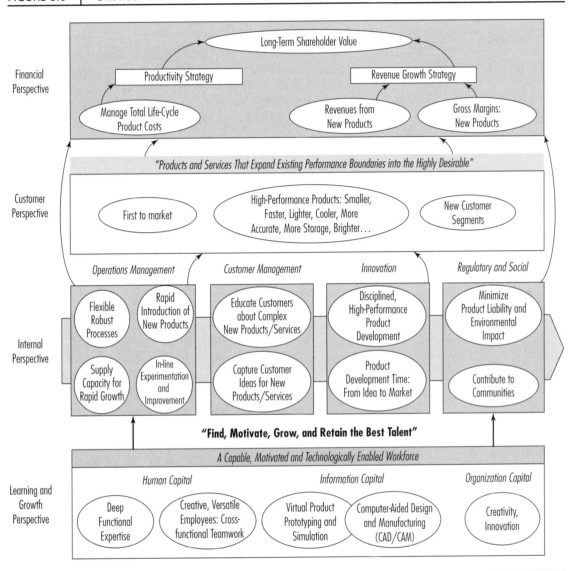

Key Strategy Principles Figure 5.6 shows the strategy map template for a firm pursuing a product-leadership strategy. We can use this illustration to review and reinforce the key principles that underlie a strategy map:

- *Companies emphasize two performance levels in developing a financial strategy—a productivity strategy and a revenue-growth strategy.*

- *Strategy involves choosing and developing a differentiated customer value proposition.* Note the value proposition for product leadership: "Products and services that expand existing performance boundaries into the highly desirable." Recall that the other value propositions and customer strategies include low total cost, complete customer solutions, and system lock-in.

- *Value is created through internal business processes.* The financial and customer perspectives in the balanced scorecard and strategy map describe the performance outcomes the firm seeks, such as increases in shareholder value through revenue growth and productivity improvements, as well as enhanced performance outcomes from customer acquisition, retention, loyalty, and growth.

- *Strategy involves identifying and aligning the critical few processes that are most important for creating and delivering the customer value proposition.* For a product-leadership strategy, observe how each of the internal business processes directly supports the customer value proposition—product leadership.

- *Value is enhanced when intangible assets (for example, human capital) are aligned with the customer strategy.* From Figure 5.6, note the strategic theme for learning and growth: "a capable, motivated, and technologically enabled workforce." When the three components of learning and growth—human, information, and organization capital—are aligned with the strategy, the firm is better able to mobilize action and execute that strategy.

To recap, the balanced scorecard provides a series of measures and objectives across four perspectives: financial, customer, internal business process, and learning and growth. By developing mutually reinforcing objectives across these four areas, a strategy map can be used to tell the story of a business unit's customer strategy and to highlight the internal business processes that drive performance.

Summary

Guided by a deep understanding of the needs of customers and the capabilities of competitors, market-driven organizations are committed to a set of processes, beliefs, and values that promote the achievement of superior performance by satisfying customers better than competitors do. Because many business-to-business firms have numerous divisions, product lines, and brands, three major levels of strategy exist in most large organizations: (1) corporate, (2) business level, and (3) functional. Moving down the strategy hierarchy, the focus shifts from strategy formulation to strategy implementation. Marketing is best viewed as the functional area that manages critical connections between the organization and customers. Business marketing planning must be coordinated and synchronized with corresponding planning efforts in other functional areas. Strategic plans emerge out of a bargaining process among functional areas. Managing conflict, promoting cooperation, and developing coordinated strategies are all fundamental to the business marketer's role.

A business model or concept consists of four major components: (1) a core strategy, (2) strategic resources, (3) the customer interface, and (4) the value network. The core strategy is the essence of how the firm competes, whereas strategic resources capture what the firm knows (core competencies), what the firm owns (strategic assets), and what employees actually do (core processes). Specifying the benefits to customers is a critical decision when designing a core strategy. The customer interface component refers to how customer relationship management strategies are designed and managed, whereas the value network component considers how partners and supply chain members can complement and strengthen the resource base of the firm. To establish and maintain a distinctive strategic positioning, a company should focus on profitability, rather than just revenue growth, deliver a unique value proposition, and configure activities—like new-product development or customer relationship management—differently from rivals and in a manner that supports its value proposition.

Successful execution involves linking strategy to operations, using tools and processes such as the balanced scorecard and strategy map. The balanced scorecard converts a strategy goal into concrete objectives, and measures are organized into four different perspectives: financial, customer, internal business process, and learning and growth. The approach involves identifying target customer segments, defining the differentiating customer value proposition, aligning the critical internal processes that deliver value to customers in these segments, and selecting the organizational capabilities necessary to achieve customer and financial objectives. Business marketers primarily emphasize one of the following value propositions or customer strategies: low total cost, product leadership, complete customer solutions, or system lock-in. A strategy map provides a visual representation of a firm's critical objectives and the cause-and-effect relationships among them that drive superior organizational performance.

Discussion Questions

1. Strategy experts argue that effective and aligned internal business processes determine how value is created in an organization. Provide an illustration to demonstrate the point.

2. "Trying to be all things to all customers almost guarantees a weak strategic position for a firm." Agree or disagree? Explain.

3. Describe how the primary focus of marketing managers at the corporate level differs from the focus marketing managers take at the business-unit or functional level.

4. A day in the life of a business marketing manager involves interactions with managers from other functions in the firm. First, identify the role of R&D, manufacturing, and logistics functions in creating and implementing marketing strategy. Next, describe some of the common sources of conflict that can emerge in cross-functional relationships.

5. Commenting on the decision-making process of his organization, a senior executive noted: "Sometimes the process is bloody, ugly, just like sausage meat being made. It's not pretty to watch but the end results are not too bad." Why do various functional interest groups often embrace conflicting positions during the strategic decision process? How are decisions ever made?

6. Describe how the learning and growth objectives in a balanced scorecard might differ for a firm pursuing a low-total-cost strategy versus one that emphasizes complete customer solutions.

7. Describe why a business-to-business firm that plans to enter a new market segment may have to realign its internal business processes to succeed in this segment.

8. The fourth component of the balanced scorecard, learning and growth, captures the intangible assets of the firm (for example, human, information, and organization capital). Describe the role these intangible assets might assume in executing strategy at FedEx or Google.

9. Select a firm such as FedEx, Apple, IBM, Boeing, GE, or Caterpillar and assess its business model. Develop a list of particular skills, resources, and strategies that are especially important to the selected firm's strategic position. Give particular attention to those skills, resources, or characteristics that competitors would have the most difficulty in matching.

10. Gary Hamel, a leading strategy consultant, contends that managers as well as Wall Street analysts like to talk about business models, but few of them could define "what a business model or business concept really is." Describe the major components of a business model and discuss how these components are linked to the benefits a firm provides to customers.

Internet Exercise

1. 3M is a large, diversified, technology company that has numerous business units and manufactures thousands of products. Go to http://www.3m.com and

   a. identify the major market or industry sectors that the firm serves;
   b. describe a new product that 3M has recently introduced for the health-care sector.

CHAPTER

6

Business Marketing Strategies for Global Markets

Business marketing firms that restrict their attention to the domestic market are overlooking enormous international market opportunities and a challenging field of competitors. After reading this chapter, you will understand:

1. How to capture the sources of global advantage in rapidly developing economies such as China and India

2. The spectrum of international market-entry options and the strategic significance of different forms of global market participation

3. The distinctive types of international strategy

4. The essential components of a global strategy

A recent *Business Week* article focused on the significant increase in global competition that large U.S. industrial corporations are facing. Huge but relatively unknown firms from emerging markets are challenging Western firms in almost every global setting.

> From India's Infosys Technologies (IT services) to B[illegible] Embraer (light jets), and from Taiwan's Acer (computers) to Mexico's [illegible] materials), a new class of formidable competitors is rising. [illegible] emerging multinationals today, and within 15 yea[illegible] of them. The biggest challenge posed by these [illegible] be in Western markets, but within developing na[illegible] est global growth—and home to 80 percent of t[illegible] hundreds of millions of whom have moved in[illegible] these new multinationals will force American [illegible] strategies for Third World product development, [illegible] local companies.[1]

Truly, business-to-business marketing is worldwide in scope, a[illegible] existence of many business marketing firms will hinge on their ability to a[illegible] sively, compete aggressively, and seize market opportunities in rapidly expandin[illegible] global economies. Numerous business marketing firms—such as GE, IBM, Intel, Boeing, and Caterpillar—currently derive much of their profit from global markets. They have realigned operations and developed a host of new strategies to strengthen market positions and compete effectively against the new breed of strong global rivals.

This chapter will examine the need for, and the formulation of, global business marketing strategies. The discussion is divided into four parts. First, attention centers on rapidly developing economies, like China, and the sources of global advantage they can represent for business marketing firms. Second, international market-entry options are isolated and described. Third, "multi-domestic" and "global" strategies are compared, and prescriptions are provided for where they are most effectively applied. Fourth, the critical requirements for a successful global strategy are explored.

Capturing Global Advantage[2]

Global companies face a radically altered business landscape following the recent financial crisis, most notably a slowdown in world economic growth. Moreover, a two-speed world economy is emerging, sharply defined by slower growth in the developed economies of the United States, Europe, and Japan and much faster growth in Southeast Asia and the BRIC countries (Brazil, Russia, India, and

[1] Jeffrey E. Garten, "A New Threat to America, Inc.," *Business Week*, July 25, 2005, p. 114. For a review of the top-100 international challengers, see Harold L. Sirkin, James W. Hemerling, and Arindam K. Bhattacharya, *Globality: Competing with Everyone from Everywhere for Everything* (New York: Business Plus, 2008).

[2] This section is based on Arindam Bhattacharya, Jim Hemerling, and Bernd Waltermann, "Competing for Advantage: How to Succeed in the New Global Reality," The Boston Consulting Group, Inc., January 2010, pp. 1–13, accessed at http://www.bcg.com.

China). For example, rapidly developing economies (RDEs) such as China, India, and Brazil enjoy high growth but low average household income. For these countries, the growth of the gross domestic product (GDP) ranges from 8 to 12 percent. By contrast, low-growth countries like the United States and western Europe experience annual GDP growth of 2 to 4 percent, but their households have higher salaries and more disposable income.

Competing successfully in this challenging business environment requires business-to-business companies to meet the needs of both low-growth and high-growth markets while differentiating their offerings from foreign and local competitors. Many formidable rivals from RDEs are capitalizing on their low-cost position in these fast-growing markets and assuming a leading role in some global markets from natural gas and iron ore to automotive forgings, micromotors, and regional jets. "These global trends—the shifting center of gravity from the West to the East, the rise of new global challengers from RDEs, and the growing volatility and complexity of the business environment ... call for new competitive models to win."[3]

In the past, the underlying philosophy guiding globalization strategies was "oneness"—replicating the home country business model and its key processes across markets. However, Arindam Bhattacharya and his colleagues at the Boston Consulting Group (BCG) assert that the new global reality requires a philosophy of "manyness"—many products and services drawing on many skills, ideas, and systems to compete in many markets. To that end, they offer the BCG Global Advantage Diamond to portray the key elements that must be developed and integrated to secure a strong position in global markets (see Figure 6.1).

FIGURE 6.1 | **THE BCG GLOBAL ADVANTAGE DIAMOND**

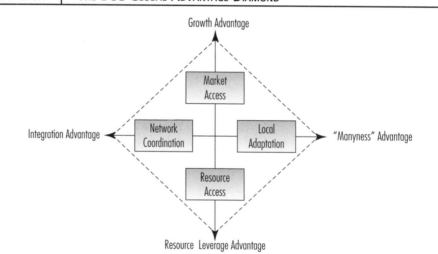

SOURCE: BCG analysis. Figure located in "Competing for Advantage: How to Succeed in the New Global Reality," January 2010, by Arindam Bhattacharya, Jim Hemerling, and Bernd Waltermann, The Boston Consulting Group. (http://www.bcg.com/documents/file37656.pdf).

---

[3]Ibid., p. 2.

Successful companies are able to adapt their business models to new groups of target customers in RDEs and develop new ways to integrate these different business models to achieve synergies and share best practices within the firm. To achieve global leadership, integrated strategies should incorporate the following elements:

- *Market access*: driving sales growth by reaching new markets and targeting new market segments;

- *Resource access*: leveraging valuable resources (for example, talent, assets, raw materials, and knowledge) in RDEs to achieve competitive advantage;

- *Local adaptation*: developing and adapting products and services to satisfy the unique needs of RDE customers;

- *Network coordination*: integrating operations to capitalize on the strength of the company's global network.

Market Access

Companies can expand market access in RDEs by: (1) increasing the number of countries served and/or (2) penetrating more deeply into new customer segments and new product categories in existing markets. Deeper market penetration often poses more difficult challenges for Western companies because their business models have traditionally targeted premium products for customers located on the top of the income pyramid. Based on cost advantages, this allows local competitors in RDEs to offer lower priced, simpler products and services to customers below the premium segment.

To capture the next wave of growth, multinational companies must go beyond the premium segments. "That means addressing the so-called midmarket, which has grown the fastest in many emerging markets and product categories, as well as the next *billion* consumers, who sit above the poorest of the poor in the income pyramid, often in difficult to reach locations."[4] While routinely ignored by multinational companies, the next billion purchase more than $1 trillion in goods and services per year. These consumers spend more than one-third of their household income on nonessentials. Products created for the developed world, however, do not meet their requirements or budgets.

Reverse Innovation at GE[5]   Rising to this challenge, General Electric has delivered on its promise to create health-care innovations that would substantially lower costs, increase access, and improve quality. Two products issuing from this strategic initiative include: (1) a portable, PC-based ultrasound machine that sells for as little as $15,000 compared to the $100,000 to $300,000 price range for conventional ultrasound equipment; and (2) a $1000 handheld electrocardiogram (ECG) device. Importantly, these products were originally developed for markets in RDEs (the ECG device for rural India and the ultrasound machine for rural China) and are now being widely adopted in the United States. This approach stands in sharp

---

[4]Ibid., p. 4.

[5]Jeffrey R. Immelt, Vijay Govindarajan, and Chris Trimble, "How GE Is Disrupting Itself," *Harvard Business Review* 87 (October 2009): pp. 56–65.

contrast to the typical innovation model in which products are developed for the home market and then adapted to local conditions in the RDE if possible. GE refers to this process as *reverse innovation*.

The portable ultrasound is being used by rural clinics in China that serve more than 90 percent of the population but lack the funds for sophisticated imaging equipment. Of course, the performance of the portable model does not match that of high-end ultrasound machines, but it fits the requirements and budgets of rural clinics where doctors use it for simple applications. In the United States, customers for the portable ultrasound include ambulance squads and emergency rooms. Portable ultrasounds now represent a rapidly growing global product line for GE and generate more than $275 million in revenue. GE's handheld ECG device not only enjoys success in emerging economies but is now being widely adopted by general practitioners in the United States.

Resource Access

Many leading-edge companies have shifted their focus from low-cost-country sourcing to "best-cost-country sourcing," an approach that considers a full range of factors beyond labor costs. Companies must weigh the trade-offs among factor costs, supply chain restraints, transportation costs, and relative strengths and weaknesses of RDEs. Longer lead times in a global supply chain add cost risk and variability to delivery schedules. Jesús de Juan, the lead author of a recent Boston Consulting Group study on sourcing, observes: "The days of reducing costs simply from sourcing from China are probably over. In the future, companies will rely on a more diversified base of low-cost suppliers across multiple regions."[6]

Expanding resource access can allow companies to create a diversified portfolio of supply sources in different regions and develop "best-cost" supply chains that provide competitive advantage in RDEs and on a global scale. Many companies like GE, Microsoft, and Apple are transferring steps in their value chain—like R&D or manufacturing—in order to attract talented personnel and to enhance design and manufacturing capabilities. Apart from enhancing global competitiveness, companies are leveraging their sourcing efforts in RDEs to secure access and penetration in local markets.

Following Key Customers to RDEs   Many small and mid-sized companies are following their customers to RDEs. For example, Phoenix Electric Manufacturing Company, a Chicago-based producer of electric motors for power tools, kitchen appliances, and other products, added a factory in China.[7] The move enabled Phoenix Electric to retain its largest customers—GE and Emerson Electric—which have shifted most of their consumer-electronics production to the area. Similarly, Hiwasse Manufacturing, an Arkansas-based manufacturer of steel products used in the control panels of refrigerators, ovens, and other appliances, added a facility in Mexico near a GE appliance manufacturing facility.[8]

---

[6]Jesús de Juan, Victor Du, David Lee, Sachin Nandgaonkar, and Kevin Waddell, "Global Sourcing in the Postdownturn Era," The Boston Consulting Group, Inc., September 2010, pp. 1–10, accessed at http://www.bcg.com.

[7]Dexter Roberts and Michael Arndt, "It's Getting Hotter in the East," *Business Week*, August 22–29, 2005, pp. 78–81.

[8]Louis Uchitelle, "If You Can Make It Here …," *New York Times*, September 4, 2005, p. B-5.

TABLE 6.1	DETERMINING WHICH PRODUCTS TO OUTSOURCE TO RAPIDLY DEVELOPING ECONOMIES (RDEs) AND WHICH TO KEEP AT HOME

Selected Criteria	Maintain Home-Based Manufacturing	Relocate to RDEs
Labor Contract	Low	High
Growth of Demand in Home Market	Low	High
Size of RDE Market	Low	High
Degree of Standardization	Low	High
Intellectual Property Content	High	Low
Logistical Requirements	High	Low

SOURCE: Adapted from Arindam Bhattacharya et al., "Capturing Global Advantage: How Leading Industrial Companies Are Transforming Their Industries by Sourcing and Selling in China, India, and Other Low-Cost Countries," *The Boston Consulting Group, Inc.*, April 2004, pp. 26–30, accessed at http://www.bcg.com.

A Twofold Strategy   As major industrial sectors relocate manufacturing operations to RDEs, business-to-business firms that supply these sectors must take decisive action. Jim Hemerling and his associates at the Boston Consulting Group provide this advice:

> Most companies need to develop a twofold strategic plan: to fill market gaps at home, and to follow selected customers to their new locations. In our experience, it is rarely feasible to pursue only one or the other.[9]

For example, gaps can be filled at home by pursuing new lines of business or new product or service opportunities where the home country advantage can be defended. In turn, when moving to a RDE, suppliers must adjust their operating models to fully capture the cost advantages.

The Outsourcing Decision[10]   The decision to relocate manufacturing, R&D, or customer service to RDEs is a strategic decision involving a host of economic, competitive, and environmental considerations. Clearly, some products and services are better candidates for outsourcing than others.

What Should Go?   The criteria that favor relocation to RDEs include products or services with high labor content, high growth potential, large RDE markets, and standardized manufacturing or service delivery processes (Table 6.1). These criteria reflect each of the sources of global advantage we have explored. For services, the processes most easily relocated are those that have well-defined process maps or those that are rule-based (for example, the established protocol that a customer service call center uses).

---

[9]Jim Hemerling, Dave Young, and Thomas Bradtke, "Navigating the Five Currents of Globalization: How Leading Companies Are Capturing Global Advantage" *BCG Focus* (April 2005), pp. 9–10, The Boston Consulting Group, Inc., accessed at http://www.bcg.com.

[10]Arindam Bhattacharya, Thomas Bradtke, Jim Hemerling, Jean Lebreton, Xavier Mosquet, Immo Rupf, Harold L. Sirkin, and Dave Young, "Capturing Global Advantage: How Leading Industrial Companies Are Transforming Their Industries by Sourcing and Selling in China, India, and Other Low-Cost Countries," The Boston Consulting Group, Inc., April 2004, accessed at http://www.bcg.com.

INSIDE BUSINESS MARKETING

How Offshore Outsourcing Affects Customer Satisfaction— and a Company's Stock Price!

Recent research suggests that sending customer service abroad negatively affects customer satisfaction. Jonathan Whitaker and his research colleagues analyzed the outsourcing activities of 150 North American companies and business units. As a group, those firms that outsourced saw a drop in their score on the American Consumer Satisfaction Index. Importantly, the declines in consumer satisfaction scores were roughly the same whether companies outsourced customer service domestically or overseas.

Customer satisfaction scores tend to move in the same direction as companies' stock prices. Based on this historical relationship, the average decline in consumer satisfaction found at companies outsourcing customer service is associated with a roughly 1 to 5 percent decline in a company's market capitalization, depending on the industry in which the company operates. That is a steep price! By the way, market capitalization is a measure of the value of a firm (that is, total outstanding shares × stock price).

To improve the quality of outsourced customer service, special attention should be given to ensuring that the provider has all the information required to help the customer and is fully empowered to do so. Interestingly, the researchers found that "back-office offshoring had no effect on overall customer satisfaction. So the savings a company garners this way are not offset by dissatisfaction among customers."

SOURCE: Jonathan Whitaker, M.S. Krishnan, and Claes Fornell, "Customer Service: How Offshore Outsourcing Affects Customer Satisfaction," *The Wall Street Journal*, July 7, 2008, p. R4.

What Should Not Go? Products and services that should remain at home include "those for which protection of intellectual property is critical, those with extreme logistical requirements, those with very high technology content or performance requirements, and those for which customers are highly sensitive to the location of production" (for example, certain military contracts).[11] Concerns about intellectual property (IP) theft is a major issue in most RDEs, particularly in China. Experts suggest that some multinational companies in China are losing the battle to protect their IP, largely because they emphasize legal tactics rather than including IP directly into their strategic and operational decisions. By carefully analyzing and selecting which products and technologies to sell in China, the best companies reduce the chance that competitors will steal their IP.

Local Adaptation

Reaching new customers in RDEs requires a different business model from the one used to reach a firm's high-priced, premium market segments. So, a differentiated approach that responds to local demands in RDEs is needed if market success is to be achieved. Established priorities and organizational rigidities in the global business present formidable barriers to change. To unlock the potential, GE created a local growth team (LGT) model to create new offerings for

---

[11]Ibid., p. 29.

customers in RDEs, such as China and India, and empowered them to develop their own strategies, organizations, and products.[12] The LGT model is based on five critical principles:

- Shift power to where the growth is.

- Build new offerings from the ground up.

- Build LGTs from the ground up, just like forming a new company.

- Customize objectives, targets, and metrics for the RDE environment.

- Provide senior executive support to the LGT, including a direct reporting link to senior management.

LGTs empower local executives to meet customer needs in RDEs. For example, maternal and infant care represents a large potential market in India with its infant mortality rate of 55 children for every 1000 born. GE's baby warmer, developed and built in India, is aimed at this market.[13] Eighty percent of Indian hospitals use baby warmers, which provide direct heat in open cradles. The appeal of GE's offering is its low price ($3000), simple design, and user-friendly display board. Ravi Kaushik, GE Marketing Director for Maternal Care, observes: "We're targeting the bottom of the pyramid ... I have the technology, and I need to get it to the lowest market."[14] The product is now sold in 62 countries, including Brazil, Russia, Egypt, and Italy.

Network Coordination

Even while adapting to local conditions, the best managed global firms leverage their global networks by sharing best practices, knowledge, technology, and systems. Economies of scale and scope can be advanced through process standardization, adoption of common technology, and rapid information sharing. For example, resource advantages developed in different markets can be shared and diffused to other operating units around the world. Likewise, network advantage is promoted by sharing successes around the world—taking innovations developed in RDEs back to developed markets (like the GE examples presented earlier).

While capturing a network advantage seems to clash with the concept of local adaptation, successful companies have been able to exploit "a diverse and distributed global network in order to simultaneously foster and leverage this diversity, rather than streamlining it."[15] For example, a global device manufacturer uses a highly standardized approach to assess a market, then uses it to generate differentiated strategies for each of its markets. A strong network of production bases around the world and a highly efficient global supply chain provide a strong platform to support these differentiated strategies.

---

[12]Immelt, Gavindarajan, and Trimble, "How GE Is Disrupting Itself," pp. 56–65.

[13]Megha Bahree, "GE Remodels Business in India," *The Wall Street Journal*, April 26, 2011, p. B8.

[14]Ibid., p. B8.

[15]Bhattacharya, Hemerling, and Waltermann, "Competing for Advantage," p. 6.

INSIDE BUSINESS MARKETING

Made in America—Again

A study released by the Boston Consulting Group (BCG) argues that the United States is well positioned for a "manufacturing renaissance" within the next five years as the wage gap with China shrinks and certain U.S. states become some of the cheapest locations for manufacturing in the developed world. Harold L. Sirkin, a senior partner at BCG, notes:

> All over China, wages are climbing at 15 to 20 percent a year because of the supply-and-demand imbalance for skilled labor. We expect net labor costs for manufacturing in China and the U.S. to converge by around 2015. As a result of the changing economies, you're going to see a lot more products "Made in the USA" in the next five years.

Wage rates in Chinese cities such as Shanghai and Tianjin are projected to be only 30 percent cheaper than rates in low-cost U.S. states such as South Carolina, Mississippi, and Alabama. Moreover, since wage rates account for 20 to 30 percent of a product's total cost, manufacturing will be only 10 to 15 percent cheaper than in the United States—even before transportation and inventory costs are included. When those costs are factored into the equation, the total cost advantage will drop to single digits or be erased entirely, according to the BCG report.

Indeed, some firms are already adjusting their production locations and supply chains. For example, NCR Corporation is bringing back the production of its ATMs to Columbus, Georgia, in order to lower operating costs, speed product development, and improve internal collaboration. Likewise, Caterpillar is expanding U.S. operations with the construction of a new 600,000-square-foot manufacturing facility in Victoria, Texas.

Even as companies reduce their investment in China to make goods targeted for the United States, China will continue to be a major manufacturing location, giving increased emphasis to serving its domestic market as well as western Europe.

SOURCE: "Made in the USA, Again: Manufacturing is Expected to Return to America as China's Rising Labor Costs Erase Most Savings from Offshoring," The Boston Consulting Group, Inc., May 5, 2011, accessed at http://www.bcg.com on June 15, 2011.

Global Market Entry Options[16]

To develop an effective global marketing strategy, managers must evaluate the alternative ways that a firm can participate in international markets. The particular mode of entry should consider the level of a firm's experience overseas and the stage in the evolution of its international involvement. Figure 6.2 illustrates a spectrum of options for participating in global markets. They range from low-commitment choices, such as exporting, to highly complex levels of participation, such as global strategies. Each is examined in this section.

Exporting

A company's first encounter with an overseas market usually involves **exporting** because it requires the least commitment and risk. Goods are produced at one or two home plants, and sales are made through distributors or importing agencies in

---

[16]The following discussion is based on Franklin R. Root, *Entry Strategy for International Markets* (Lexington, MA: D. C. Heath, 1987); and Michael R. Czinkota and Ilka A. Ronkainen, *International Marketing*, 2d ed. (Hinsdale, IL: Dryden Press, 1990).

FIGURE 6.2 | SPECTRUM OF INVOLVEMENT IN GLOBAL MARKETING

Low Commitment   **High Commitment**

Exporting	Contracting	Strategic Alliance	Joint Venture	Multi-domestic Strategy	Global Strategy

Low Complexity   **High Complexity**

each country. Exporting is a workable entry strategy when the firm lacks the resources to make a significant commitment to the market, wants to minimize political and economic risk, or is unfamiliar with the country's market requirements and cultural norms. Exporting is the most popular global market entry option among small and medium-sized firms.[17]

Many companies begin export activities haphazardly, without carefully screening markets or options for market entry. These companies may or may not have a measure of success, and they might overlook better export opportunities. If early export efforts are unsuccessful because of poor planning, the company may be misled into abandoning exporting altogether. Formulating an export strategy based on good information and proper assessment increases the chances that the best options will be chosen, that resources will be used effectively, and that efforts will consequently be carried through to success.

The Commercial Service of the U.S. Department of Commerce has developed and maintains a network of international trade specialists in the United States to help American companies export their products and conduct business abroad. Trade specialists operate offices known as Export Assistance Centers (EACs) located in almost 100 cities in the United States and Puerto Rico that assist small and medium-sized companies. EACs are known as "one-stop shops" because they combine the trade and marketing expertise and resources of the Commercial Service along with the finance expertise and resources of the Small Business Administration (SBA) and the Export-Import Bank. Thus they provide companies with a wide array of services in one location, and they also maximize resources by working closely with state and local government as well as with private partners to offer companies a full range of expertise in international trade, marketing, and finance.[18]

Although it preserves flexibility and reduces risk, exporting may limit the future prospects for growth in the country. First, exporting involves giving up direct control of the marketing program, which makes it difficult to coordinate activities, implement strategies, and resolve conflicts with customers and channel members. George Day explains why customers may sense a lack of exporter commitment:

In many global markets customers are loath to form long-run relationships with a company through its agents because they are unsure whether the

[17]Jery Whitelock and Damd Jobber, "An Evaluation of External Factors in the Decision of UK Industrial Firms to Enter a New Non-Domestic Market: An Exploratory Study," *European Journal of Marketing* 38 (11/12, 2004): p. 1440.

[18]*A Basic Guide to Exporting*, the U.S. Department of Commerce with the assistance of Unz & Co., Inc., http://www.export.gov/exportbasics/index.asp, accessed on July 18, 2008.

business will continue to service the market, or will withdraw at the first sign of adversity. This problem has bedeviled U.S. firms in many countries, and only now are they living down a reputation for opportunistically participating in many countries and then withdrawing abruptly to protect short-run profits.[19]

Contracting

A somewhat more involved and complex form of international market entry is **contracting**. Included among contractual entry modes are: (1) licensing and (2) management contracts.

Licensing Under a **licensing** agreement, one firm permits another to use its intellectual property in exchange for royalties or some other form of payment. The property might include trademarks, patents, technology, know-how, or company name. In short, licensing involves exporting intangible assets.

As an entry strategy, licensing requires neither capital investment nor marketing strength in foreign markets. This lets a firm test foreign markets without a major commitment of management time or capital. Because the licensee is typically a local company that can serve as a buffer against government action, licensing also reduces the risk of exposure to such action. With increasing host-country regulation, licensing may enable the business marketer to enter a foreign market that is closed to either imports or direct foreign investment.

Licensing agreements do pose some limitations. First, some companies are hesitant to enter into license agreements because the licensee may become an important competitor in the future. Second, licensing agreements typically include a time limit. Although terms may be extended once after the initial agreement, many foreign governments do not readily permit additional extensions. Third, a firm has less control over a licensee than over its own exporting or manufacturing abroad.

Management Contracts To expand their overseas operations, many firms have turned to management contracts. In a **management contract** the industrial firm assembles a package of skills that provide an integrated service to the client. When equity participation, either full ownership or a joint venture, is not feasible or is not permitted by a foreign government, a management contract provides a way to participate in a venture. Management contracts have been used effectively in the service sector in such areas as computer services, hotel management, and food services. Michael Czinkota and Ilka Ronkainen point out that management contracts can "provide organizational skills not available locally, expertise that is immediately available rather than built up, and management assistance in the form of support services that would be difficult and costly to replicate locally."[20]

One specialized form of a management contract is a turnkey operation. This arrangement permits a client to acquire a complete operational system, together with the skills needed to maintain and operate the system without assistance. Once the package agreement is online, the client owns, controls, and operates the system. Management contracts allow firms to commercialize their superior skills (know-how) by participating in the international market.

---

[19]George S. Day, *Market Driven Strategy: Processes for Creating Value* (New York: The Free Press, 1990), p. 272.

[20]Czinkota and Ronkainen, *International Marketing*, p. 493.

Other contractual modes of entry have grown in prominence in recent years. **Contract manufacturing** involves sourcing a product from a producer located in a foreign country for sale there or in other countries. Here assistance might be required to ensure that the product meets the desired quality standards. Contract manufacturing is most appropriate when the local market lacks sufficient potential to justify a direct investment, export entry is blocked, and a quality licensee is not available.

Strategic Global Alliances (SGA)

A **strategic global alliance** (SGA) is a business relationship established by two or more companies to cooperate out of mutual need and to share risk in achieving a common objective. This strategy works well for market entry or to shore up existing weaknesses and increase competitive strengths. A U.S. firm with a reliable supply base might partner with a Japanese importer that has the established distribution channels and customer base in Japan to form a strong entry into the Japanese market.[21] Alliances offer a number of benefits, such as access to markets or technology, economies of scale in manufacturing and marketing, and the sharing of risk among partners.

Although global strategic alliances offer potential, they pose a special management challenge. Among the stumbling blocks are these:[22]

- Partners are organized quite differently for making marketing and product-design decisions, creating *problems in coordination and trust.*

- Partners that combine the best set of skills in one country may be poorly equipped to support each other in other countries, leading to *problems in implementing alliances on a global scale.*

- The quick pace of technological change often guarantees that the most attractive partner today may not be the most attractive partner tomorrow, leading to *problems in maintaining alliances over time.*

Building a Dedicated Alliance Function   Although many firms generate positive results from strategic alliances, an elite group of firms has demonstrated the capability to generate superior alliance value as measured by the extent to which the alliance met its stated objectives, the degree to which the alliance enhanced the company's competitive position, stock market gains from alliance announcements, and related performance dimensions. Included among the top performers are firms such as Hewlett-Packard, Oracle, and Eli Lily & Company. How did they do it? By creating a dedicated strategic alliance function—headed by a vice president or director of strategic alliances with his or her own staff and budget, says Jeffrey H. Dyer and his research team.[23] The dedicated function coordinates all alliance-related activity within the organization and is charged with institutionalizing processes and systems

---

[21]Laura Delaney, "Expanding Your Business Globally," *MultiLingual*, 19 (April, 2008): pp. 10–11.

[22]Thomas J. Kosnik, "Stumbling Blocks to Global Strategic Alliances," *Systems Integration Age*, October 1988, pp. 31–39. See also Eric Rule and Shawn Keon, "Competencies of High-Performing Strategic Alliances," *Strategy and Leadership*, 27 (September–October 1998): pp. 36–37.

[23]Jeffrey Dyer, Prashant Kale, and Harbir Singh, "How to Make Strategic Alliances Work," *MIT Sloan Management Review* 42 (2001): pp. 37–43.

to teach, share, and leverage prior alliance management experience and know-how throughout the company.[24]

Integrating Points of Contact   Firms that are adept at managing strategic alliances use a flexible approach, letting their alliances evolve in form as conditions change over time. They invest adequate resources and management attention in these relationships, and they integrate the organizations so that the appropriate points of contact and communication are managed. Successful alliances achieve five levels of integration:[25]

1. *Strategic integration*, which entails continuing contact among senior executives to define broad goals or discuss changes in each company;

2. *Tactical integration*, which brings middle managers together to plan joint activities, to transfer knowledge, or to isolate organizational or system changes that will improve interfirm connections;

3. *Operational integration*, which provides the information, resources, or personnel that managers require to carry out the day-to-day work of the alliance;

4. *Interpersonal integration*, which builds a necessary foundation for personnel in both organizations to know one another personally, learn together, and create new value; and

5. *Cultural integration*, which requires managers involved in the alliance to have the communication skills and cultural awareness to bridge the differences.

Joint Ventures

In pursuing international entry options, a corporation confronts a wide variety of ownership choices, ranging from 100 percent ownership to a minority interest. Frequently, full ownership may be a desirable, but not essential, prerequisite for success. Thus a joint venture becomes feasible. The **joint venture** involves a joint-ownership arrangement (between, for example, a U.S. firm and one in the host country) to produce and/or market goods in a foreign market. In contrast to a strategic alliance, a joint venture creates a new firm. Some joint ventures are structured so that each partner holds an equal share; in others, one partner has a majority stake. The contributions of partners can also vary widely and may include financial resources, technology, sales organizations, know-how, or plant and equipment. Representing a successful relationship is the 50-50 joint venture between Xerox Corporation and Tokyo-based Fuji Photo Film Company. Through the joint venture, Xerox gained a presence in the Japanese market, learned valuable quality management skills that improved its products, and developed a keen understanding of important Japanese rivals such as Canon, Inc., and Ricoh Company. This joint venture has thrived for more than three decades.[26]

[24]Simon Hayes, "Getting Strategic Alliances Right," *Synnovation* 3 (May 2008), p. 72, accessed at www.eds.com/synnovation on July 5, 2008.

[25]Rosabeth Moss Kanter, "Collaborative Advantage," *Harvard Business Review* 72 (July–August 1994): pp. 96–108.

[26]David P. Hamilton, "United It Stands—Fuji Xerox Is a Rarity in World Business: A Joint Venture That Works," *The Wall Street Journal*, September 26, 1996, p. R19.

Advantages   Joint ventures offer a number of advantages. First, they may open up market opportunities that neither partner could pursue alone. Kenichi Ohmae explains the logic:

> If you run a pharmaceutical company with a good drug to distribute in Japan but have no sales force to do it, find someone in Japan who also has a good product but no sales force in your country. You get double the profit by putting two strong drugs through your fixed cost sales network, and so does your new ally. Why duplicate such high expenses all down the line? ... Why not join forces to maximize contribution to each other's fixed costs?[27]

Second, joint ventures may provide for better relationships with local organizations (for example, local authorities) and with customers. By being attuned to the host country's culture and environment, the local partner may enable the joint venture to respond to changing market needs, be more aware of cultural sensitivities, and be less vulnerable to political risk.

The Downside   Problems can arise in maintaining joint-venture relationships. A study suggests that perhaps more than 50 percent of joint ventures are disbanded or fall short of expectations.[28] The reasons involve problems with disclosing sensitive information, disagreements over how profits are to be shared, clashes over management style, and differing perceptions on strategy. Mihir Desai, Fritz Foley, and James Hines studied more than 3000 American global companies and report that joint ventures appear to be falling out of favor.[29] Why? Increasing forces of globalization such as fragmented production processes make the decision to not collaborate payoff. If a firm is considering a joint venture, Desai, Foley, and Hines suggest that they first isolate the reasons for considering a joint venture and make sure that "they can't buy the required services or that knowledge through an arms-length contract that doesn't require sharing ownership.... Second, explicitly lay out expectations for the partners in legal and informal documents prior to the creation of the entity so that it's clear what each party is providing. Third, try out partners without setting up a joint venture by conducting business with them in some way.... Finally, specify simple exit provisions at the onset and then don't be afraid to walk and go it alone."

Choosing a Mode of Entry

For an initial move into the global market, the full range of entry modes, presented earlier, may be considered—from exporting, licensing, and contract manufacturing to joint ventures and wholly owned subsidiaries. In high-risk markets, firms can reduce their equity exposure by adopting low-commitment modes such as licensing, contract manufacturing, or joint ventures with a minority share. Although non-equity modes of entry—such as licensing or contract manufacturing—involve minimal risk and commitment, they may not provide the desired level of control or financial performance. Joint ventures and wholly owned subsidiaries provide a greater degree of control over operations and greater potential returns.

---

[27]Kenichi Ohmae, "The Global Logic of Strategic Alliances," *Harvard Business Review* 67 (March–April 1989): p. 147.

[28]Arvind Parkhe, "Building Trust in International Alliances," *Journal of World Business* 33 (Winter 1998): pp. 417–437.

[29]Mihir A. Desai, C. Fritz Foley, and James Hines, "The Costs of Shared Ownership: Evidence From International Joint Ventures," *Journal of Financial Economics* 73 (2004): pp. 323–374.

Once operations are established in a number of foreign markets, the focus often shifts away from foreign opportunity assessment to local market development in each country. This shift might be prompted by the need to respond to local competitors or the desire to more effectively penetrate the local market. Planning and strategy assume a country-by-country focus.

Multi-domestic versus Global Strategies

Business marketing executives are under increasing pressure to develop globally integrated strategies to achieve efficiency and rationalization across their geographically dispersed subsidiaries. As such, the challenge of internationalizing the firm is not in providing a homogeneous offering across markets, but rather in finding the best balance between local adaptation (a multi-domestic strategy) and global optimization, where one integrated strategy is applied globally.[30] Multinational firms have traditionally managed operations outside their home country with **multi-domestic strategies** that permit individual subsidiaries to compete independently in their home-country markets. The multinational headquarters coordinates marketing policies and financial controls and may centralize R&D and some support activities. Each subsidiary, however, resembles a strategic business unit that is expected to contribute earnings and growth to the organization. The firm can manage its international activities like a portfolio. Examples of multi-domestic industries include most types of retailing, construction, metal fabrication, and many services.

In contrast, a **global strategy** seeks competitive advantage with strategic choices that are highly integrated across countries. For example, features of a global strategy might include a standardized core product that requires minimal local adaptation and that targets foreign-country markets chosen on the basis of their contribution to globalization benefits. Prominent examples of global industries are automobiles, commercial aircraft, consumer electronics, and many categories of industrial machinery. Major volume and market share advantages might be sought by directing attention to the United States, Europe, and Japan, as well as to the rapidly developing economies of China and India.

Source of Advantage: Multi-domestic versus Global

When downstream activities (those tied directly to the buyer, such as sales and customer service) are important to competitive advantage, a multi-domestic pattern of international competition is common. In **multi-domestic industries**, firms pursue separate strategies in each of their foreign markets—competition in each country is essentially independent of competition in other countries (for example, Alcoa in the aluminum industry, Honeywell in the controls industry).

Global competition is more common in industries in which upstream and support activities (such as technology development and operations) are vital to competitive advantage. A **global industry** is one in which a firm's competitive position in one country is significantly influenced by its position in other countries (for example, Intel in the semiconductor industry, Boeing in the commercial aircraft industry).

In his book, *Redefining Global Strategy: Crossing Borders in a World Where Differences Still Matter*, Pankaj Ghemawat suggests that most types of economic activity that can

---

[30]G. Tomas M. Hult, S. Tamer Cavusgil, Seyda Deligonul, Tunga Kiyak, and Katarina Lagerström, "What Drives Performance in Globally Focused Marketing Organizations? A Three-Country Study," *Journal of International Marketing* 15 (2007): pp. 58–85.

be conducted either within or across borders are still quite localized.[31] He argues that firms must be very careful in deciding between a multi-domestic or global strategy because the "internationalization of numerous key economic activities, including fixed capital investment, telephone and Internet traffic, tourism, patents, stock investments, etc., remains at around only 10 percent." In his view, national borders are still significant, and effective international strategies need to take into account both cross-border similarities and critical differences.[32] In the current global business environment where security is a major issue, intellectual property rights are in question, there are increased threats of economic protectionism, and a number of countries are reasserting national sovereignty, the decision to follow a purely global strategy must be carefully scrutinized.

Coordination and Configuration   Further insights into international strategy can be gained by examining two dimensions of competition in the global market: configuration and coordination. **Configuration** centers on where each activity is performed, including the number of locations. Options range from concentrated (for example, one production plant serving the world) to dispersed (for example, a plant in each country—each with a complete value chain from operations to marketing, sales, and customer service). By concentrating an activity such as production in a central location, firms can gain economies of scale or speed learning. Alternatively, dispersing activities to a number of locations may minimize transportation and storage costs, tailor activities to local market differences, or facilitate learning about market conditions in a country.

Coordination refers to how similar activities performed in various countries are coordinated or coupled with each other. If, for example, a firm has three plants—one in the United States, one in England, and one in China—how do the activities in these plants relate to one another? Numerous coordination options exist because of the many possible levels of coordination and the many ways an activity can be performed. For example, a firm operating three plants could, at one extreme, allow each plant to operate autonomously (unique production processes, unique products). At the other extreme, the three plants could be closely coordinated, utilizing a common information system and producing products with identical features. Dow Chemical, for example, uses an enterprise software system that allows it to shift purchasing, manufacturing, and distribution functions worldwide in response to changing patterns of supply and demand.[33]

Types of International Strategy

Figure 6.3 portrays some of the possible variations in international strategy. Observe that the purest global strategy concentrates as many activities as possible in one country, serves the world market from this home base, and closely coordinates activities that must be performed near the buyer (for example, service). Caterpillar, for example, views its battle with the formidable Japanese competitor Komatsu in global terms. As well as using advanced manufacturing systems that allow it to fully exploit

---

[31]Pankaj Ghemawat, *Redefining Global Strategy: Crossing Borders in a World Where Differences Still Matter* (Boston: Harvard Business School Press, 2007), pp. 9–32.

[32]Ibid., p. 22.

[33]Thomas H. Davenport, "Putting the Enterprise into the Enterprise System," *Harvard Business Review*, 76 (July–August 1998): pp. 121–131.

FIGURE 6.3 | **TYPES OF INTERNATIONAL STRATEGY**

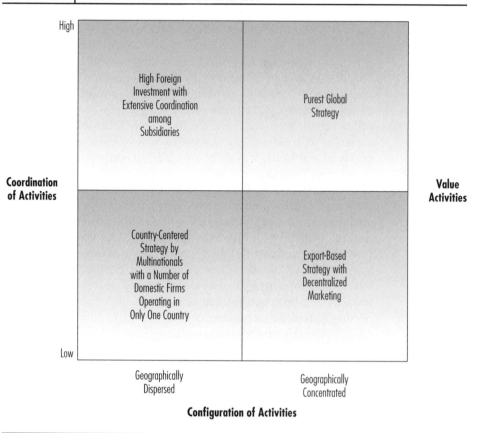

SOURCE: Figure: "Types of International Strategy," from Michael E. Porter, "Changing Patterns of International Competition," in California Management Review vol. 28, no. 2 (Winter 1986), pp. 9–40. © 1986 by the Regents of the University of California. Reprinted by permission of University of California Press.

the economies of scale from its worldwide sales volume, Caterpillar also carefully coordinates activities in its global dealer network. This integrated global strategy gives Caterpillar a competitive advantage in cost and effectiveness.[34] By serving the world market from its home base in the United States and by closely coordinating sales and service with customers around the world, Boeing also aptly illustrates a pure global strategy. Airbus—the European aerospace consortium—is a strong and clever rival that competes aggressively with Boeing for orders at airlines around the world.[35]

A Global Battle for the PC Market   Other interesting global face-offs involve Dell, Inc., versus Lenovo Group, Inc. Dell is now pursuing an integrated global strategy and challenging Lenovo, China's largest producer in its home market.[36]

---

[34]Donald V. Fites, "Make Your Dealers Your Partners," *Harvard Business Review* 74 (March–April 1996): pp. 84–95.

[35]Alex Taylor III, "Blue Skies for Airbus," *Fortune*, August 2, 1999, pp. 102–108.

[36]Evan Ramstad and Gary McWilliams, "For Dell, Success in China Tells Tale of Maturing Market," *The Wall Street Journal*, July 5, 2005, pp. A1, A8.

Meanwhile, Lenovo gained worldwide reach when it purchased IBM's PC division. In turn, Hewlett-Packard remains a formidable rival for both.

Other Paths   Figure 6.3 illustrates other international strategy patterns. Canon, for example, concentrates manufacturing and support activities in Japan but gives local marketing subsidiaries significant latitude in each region of the world. Thus, Canon pursues an export-based strategy. In contrast, Xerox concentrates some activities and disperses others. Coordination, however, is extremely high: The Xerox brand, marketing approach, and servicing strategy are standardized worldwide. Michael Porter notes:

> Global strategy has often been characterized as a choice between worldwide standardization and local tailoring, or as the tension between the economic imperative (large-scale efficient facilities) and the political imperative (local content, local production).... A firm's choice of international strategy involves a search for competitive advantage from configuration/coordination throughout the value chain.[37]

A Strategic Framework

Recall that companies may pursue multi-domestic strategies or global strategies. The need for a global strategy is determined by the nature of international competition in a particular industry. On the one hand, many industries are multi-domestic, and competition takes place on a country-by-country basis with few linkages across operating units (for example, construction and many service offerings). Multi-domestic industries do not need a global strategy because the focus should be on developing a series of distinct domestic strategies.

Multi-domestic Strategy[38]   Pankaj Ghemawat provocatively argues that the world is not flat but semi-globalized, and that borders still exist and they matter when it comes to designing strategy. However, instead of focusing exclusively on the physical boundaries, he suggests that managers look at differences between countries and regions in terms of a framework that includes the following dimensions:

1. Cultural
2. Administrative/Political
3. Geographic
4. Economic

By analyzing these dimensions, a strategist can illuminate country-to-country differences, understand the liability of "foreignness," identify and evaluate foreign competitors, and discount market sizes by distance. Following this assessment, the business-to-business manager is better equipped to develop a responsive strategy for each country.

---

[37]Michael E. Porter, "Changing Patterns of International Competition," *California Management Review* 28 (Winter 1986): p. 25.

[38]Ghemawat, *Redefining Global Strategy*, pp. 19–32.

Global Strategy   For truly global industries, a firm's position in one country significantly affects its position elsewhere, so it needs a global strategy. Competing across countries through an integrated global strategy requires a series of choices that are described below.

Global Strategy[39]

Build on a Unique Competitive Position

A business marketing firm should globalize first in those business and product lines where it has unique advantages. To achieve international competitive success, a firm must enjoy a meaningful advantage on either cost or differentiation. To this end, the firm must be able to perform activities at a lower cost than its rivals or perform activities in a unique way that creates customer value and supports a premium price. For example, Denmark's Novo-Nordisk Group (Novo) is the world's leading exporter of insulin and industrial enzymes. By pioneering high-purity insulins and advancing insulin delivery technology, Novo achieved a level of differentiation that gave it a strong competitive position in the health-care market in the United States, Europe, and Japan.

Emphasize a Consistent Positioning Strategy

Rather than modifying the firm's product and service offerings from country to country, "a global strategy requires a patient, long-term campaign to enter every significant foreign market while maintaining and leveraging the company's unique strategic positioning."[40] One of the greatest barriers to the success of firms in smaller countries is the perceived need to serve all customer segments and to offer an expanded product assortment to capture the limited market potential. However, by maintaining a consistent position, a firm reinforces its distinctive strategy and keeps its strategic attention focused on the much larger international opportunity.

Establish a Clear Home Base for Each Distinct Business

Although the location of corporate headquarters is less important and may reflect historical factors, a firm must develop a clear home base for competing in each of its strategically distinct businesses. "The **home base** for a business is the location where strategy is set, core product and process technology is created and maintained, and a critical mass of sophisticated production and service activities reside."[41] For example, Japan, Honda's home base for both motorcycles and automobiles, is where 95 percent of its R&D employees are located and all of its core engine research is conducted. For Hewlett-Packard (H-P), the United States hosts 77 percent of

---

[39]This section is based on Michael E. Porter, "Competing across Locations: Enhancing Competitive Advantage through a Global Strategy," in Michael E. Porter, ed., *On Competition* (Boston: Harvard Business School Press, 1998), pp. 309–350. See also Shaoming Zou and S. Tamer Cavusgil, "The GMS: A Broad Conceptualization of Global Marketing Strategy and Its Effect on Firm Performance," *Journal of Marketing* 66 (October 2002): pp. 40–56.

[40]Porter, "Competing across Locations," p. 331.

[41]Ibid., p. 332.

the physical space dedicated to manufacturing, R&D, and administration but only 43 percent of H-P's physical space dedicated to marketing. At H-P's home base, R&D managers with specialized expertise are designated worldwide experts; they transfer their knowledge either electronically or through periodic visits to subsidiaries around the world. Regional subsidiaries take responsibility for some process-oriented R&D activities and for local marketing.

The home base should be located in a country or region with the most favorable access to required resources (inputs) and supporting industries (for example, specialized suppliers). Such a location provides the best environment for capturing productivity and innovation benefits. Honda as well as H-P benefit from a strong supplier network that supports each of its principal businesses. The home base should also serve as the central integrating point for activities and have clear worldwide responsibility for the business unit.

Leverage Product-Line Home Bases at Different Locations

As a firm's product line broadens and diversifies, different countries may best provide the home bases for some product lines. Responsibility for leading a particular product line should be assigned to the country with the best locational advantages. Each subsidiary, then, specializes in products for which it has the most favorable advantages (for example, specialized suppliers) and serves customers worldwide. For example, H-P locates many product-line home bases outside the United States, such as its line of compact ink-jet printers, which is based in Singapore. In turn, Honda has begun to create a product-line home base for Accord station wagons in the United States. The model was conceived, designed, and developed through the joint efforts of Honda's California and Ohio R&D facilities.

Disperse Activities to Extend Home-Base Advantages

Although the home base is where core activities are concentrated, other activities can be dispersed to extend the firm's competitive position. Potential opportunities should be examined in three areas:

- *Capturing competitive advantages in purchasing.* Inputs that are not central to the innovation process, such as raw materials or general-purpose component parts, must be purchased from the most cost-effective location.

- *Securing or improving market access.* By locating selected activities near the market, a firm demonstrates commitment to foreign customers, responds to actual or threatened government mandates, and may be better equipped to tailor offerings to local preferences. For example, Honda has invested more than $2 billion in facilities in the United States. Likewise, a host of firms, like Honeywell, GE, and Intel, have made large investments in China and India.

- *Selectively tapping competitive advantages at other locations.* To improve capabilities in important skills or technologies at home, global competitors can locate selected activities in centers of innovation in other countries. The goal here is to supplement, but not replace, the home base. To illustrate, Honda gains exposure to California's styling expertise and Germany's high-performance design competencies through small, local, company-financed design centers that transfer knowledge back to the Japanese home base.

Coordinate and Integrate Dispersed Activities

Coordination across geographically dispersed locations raises formidable challenges, among them those of language and cultural differences and of aligning the reward systems for individual managers and subsidiaries with the goals of the global enterprise as a whole. However, successful global competitors achieve unified action by:

1. Establishing a clear global strategy that is understood by organizational members across countries;

2. Developing information and accounting systems that are consistent on a worldwide basis, thereby facilitating operational coordination;

3. Encouraging personal relationships and the transfer of learning among subsidiary managers across locations;

4. Relying on carefully designed incentive systems that weigh the overall contribution to the entire enterprise in addition to subsidiary performance.

Summary

Rapidly developing economies (RDEs) such as China and India present a host of opportunities and a special set of challenges for business-to-business firms. Companies that decisively and intelligently pursue integrated strategies can secure a sustainable advantage. Such strategies should center on: (1) expanding *market access* to reach new segments like the mid-market and consumers that reside at lower levels on the income pyramid; (2) leveraging *resource access* to create "best-cost" supply chains; (3) pursuing *local adaptation initiatives* to tailor products to the unique requirements and budgets of RDE consumers; and (4) emphasizing *network coordination* to capture the benefits of the company's global reach, including economies of scale and best-practices sharing. Top-performing companies are those that are able to adapt and localize their business models to target new market segments in RDEs. In turn, they are also adept at finding innovative ways to integrate these different business models into their mainstream operations to achieve synergies and share winning strategies across the global business.

Once a business marketing firm decides to sell its products in a particular country, it must select an entry strategy. The range of options includes exporting, contractual entry modes (for example, licensing), strategic alliances, and joint ventures. A more elaborate form of participation is represented by multinational firms that use multi-domestic strategies. Here a separate strategy might be pursued in each country served. The most advanced level of participation in international markets is provided by firms that use a global strategy. Such firms seek competitive advantage by pursuing strategies that are highly interdependent across countries. Global competition tends to be more common in industries in which primary activities, like R&D and manufacturing, are vital to competitive advantage.

A global strategy must begin with a unique competitive position that offers a clear competitive advantage. Providing the best odds of global competitive success are businesses and product lines where companies have the most unique advantages.

The home base for a business is the location where strategy is set, and the home base for some product lines may be best positioned in other countries. Although core activities are located at the home base, other activities can be dispersed to strengthen the company's competitive position. Successful global competitors demonstrate special capabilities in coordinating and integrating dispersed activities. Coordination ensures clear positioning and a well-understood concept of global strategy among subsidiary managers across countries. Successful global marketers understand the key risks associated with operating in the global environment, and they take steps to mitigate these risks through their strategic approach to different global markets. To create effective global strategies and capture important market opportunities, business-to-business firms must develop a deep understanding of local markets and the special competitive and environmental forces that will drive performance.

Discussion Questions

1. Western companies routinely ignore the mid-market, which has grown the fastest in many emerging markets, as well as the *next billion* consumers, who sit above the poorest of the poor in the income pyramid. Describe how the reverse innovation process can be used to develop new offerings for RDE market segments.

2. A small Michigan-based firm that produces and sells component parts to General Motors, Ford, and Chrysler Group LLC wishes to extend market coverage to Europe and Japan. What type of market entry strategy would provide the best fit?

3. Why would Hewlett-Packard assign product-line responsibility to a subsidiary located outside the United States?

4. A major U.S. electronics firm decides the best approach to a global business strategy is to employ a multi-domestic strategy. It will focus its efforts on China. Discuss some of the key threats the firm faces as it enters this market. How could it mitigate some of the risks associated with these threats?

5. A global strategy begins with a unique competitive position that offers a clear competitive advantage. What steps can a global competitor take to ensure that the strategy is implemented in a consistent way in countries around the world?

6. Describe the characteristics of products and services that would represent poor candidates for outsourcing.

7. Evaluate this statement: Many business-to-business firms need to fill market gaps at home with new products and services and also follow selected customers to their new locations in rapidly developing economies like India or China.

8. Cisco, which is based in California, has opened a second global headquarters—its Globalization Center East—in Bangalore, India. What strategic benefits would Cisco derive from this move?

9. A supplier of copper tubing and wire has adopted a multi-domestic strategy to enter the eastern European market. What factors should it

assess in these countries in order to formulate its marketing strategy in each one. Explain.

10. Evaluate this statement: Products that address developing countries' special needs cannot be sold in developed countries because they are not good enough to compete there.

Internet Exercise

1. General Electric (GE) sells over $5 billion worth of goods and services to Chinese customers in the business market. Go to http://www.ge.com and first identify the various GE divisions, like Healthcare, that contribute to sales volume and then identify a few products from each division that likely address important needs or priorities in China.

Managing Products for Business Markets

By providing a solution for customers, the product is the central force of business marketing strategy. The firm's ability to put together a line of products and services that provide superior value to customers is the heart of business marketing management. After reading this chapter, you will understand:

1. How to build a strong business-to-business brand

2. The way in which sustainability strategies are transforming the competitive landscape

3. The strategic importance of providing competitively superior value to customers

4. The various types of industrial product lines and the value of product positioning

5. A strategic approach for managing products across the stages of the technology adoption life cycle

A business marketer's marketplace identity is established through its brand and through the products and services it offers. Because brands constitute one of the most valuable intangible assets that firms possess, branding has emerged as a priority to marketing executives, CEOs, and the financial community.[1] Product management is directly linked to market analysis and market selection. Products are developed to fit the needs of the market and are modified as those needs change. Drawing on such tools of demand analysis as business market segmentation and market potential forecasting, the marketer evaluates opportunities and selects profitable market segments, thus determining the direction of product policy. Product policy cannot be separated from market selection decisions. In evaluating potential product/market fits, a firm must evaluate new market opportunities, determine the number and aggressiveness of competitors, and gauge its own strengths and weaknesses. The marketing function assumes a lead role in transforming an organization's distinctive skills and resources into products and services that enjoy positional advantages in the market.[2]

This chapter first explores the nature of the brand-building process and the way in which a strong brand can sharpen the focus and energize the performance of the firm. Second, it examines product quality, sustainability, and value from the customer's perspective and directly links them to business marketing strategy. Award-winning branding campaigns by leading business-to-business firms are profiled. Third, because industrial products can assume several forms, the chapter describes industrial product-line options, while offering an approach for positioning and managing products in high-technology markets.

Building a Strong B2B Brand

Although consumer packaged-goods companies like Procter & Gamble (P&G), Coca-Cola, and Nestle have excelled by developing a wealth of enduring and highly profitable brands, some of the most valuable and powerful brands belong to business-to-business firms: IBM, Microsoft, General Electric, Intel, Hewlett-Packard, Cisco, Google, Oracle, Canon, Siemens, Caterpillar, and a host of others. For most business marketers, the company name is the brand, so the key questions become: "What do you want your company name to stand for? What do you want it to mean in the mind of the customer?"[3]

David Aaker says, "**Brand equity** is a set of brand assets and liabilities linked to a brand, its name, and symbol that add to or subtract from the value provided by a product or service and/or to that firm's customers."[4] As we will explore, the assets and liabilities that impact brand equity include brand loyalty, name awareness, perceived quality and other brand associations, and proprietary brand assets (for example, patents). A **brand**, then, is a name, sign, symbol, or logo that identifies the products and services of one firm and differentiates them from competitors.

---

[1]Mark S. Glynn, "Primer in B2B Brand-building Strategies with a Reader Practicum," *Journal of Business Research* (2011), forthcoming.

[2]Rajan Varadarajan and Satish Jayachandran, "Marketing Strategy: An Assessment of the State of the Field and Outlook," *Journal of the Academy of Marketing Science* 27 (Spring 1999): pp. 120–143.

[3]Frederick E. Webster Jr. and Kevin Lane Keller, "A Roadmap for Branding in Industrial Markets," *Journal of Brand Management* 12 (May 2004): p. 389.

[4]David Aaker, *Managing Brand Equity* (New York: The Free Press, 1991), p. 15.

FIGURE 7.1 | CUSTOMER-BASED BRAND EQUITY PYRAMID

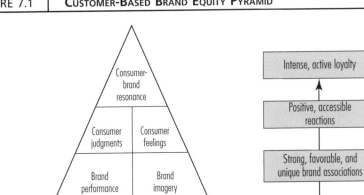

SOURCE: Reprinted with permission from Marketing Management, "Building Customer-Based Brand Equity," published by American Marketing Association, Kevin Lane Keller, Volume 10 (July/August 2001): p. 19.

Providing a rich and incisive perspective, Kevin Lane Keller defines **customer-based brand equity** (CBBE) as the differential effect that customers' brand knowledge has on their response to marketing activities and programs for that brand.[5] The basic premise of his CBBE model is that the power of a brand lies in "what consumers have learned, felt, seen, and heard about the brand over time."[6] So, the power of a brand is represented by all the thoughts, feelings, perceptions, images, and experiences that become linked to the brand in the minds of customers.

Brand-Building Steps[7]

The CBBE model lays out a series of four steps for building a strong brand (see Figure 7.1, right side): (1) develop deep brand awareness or a brand identity; (2) establish the meaning of the brand through unique brand associations (that is, points of difference); (3) elicit a positive brand response from customers through marketing programs; and (4) build brand relationships with customers, characterized by intense loyalty. Providing the foundation for successful brand management is the set of brand-building blocks (see Figure 7.1, left side) aligned with the branding ladder—salience, performance, imagery, judgments, feelings, and resonance.

Brand Identity   To achieve the right identity for a brand, the business marketer must create brand salience with customers. **Brand salience** is tied directly to brand awareness: How often is the brand evoked in different situations? What type of cues or reminders does a customer need to recognize a brand? **Brand awareness** refers to the customer's ability to recall or recognize a brand under different conditions. The goal here is to ensure that customers understand the particular product or service

---

[5]Kevin Lane Keller, *Strategic Brand Management* (3rd ed., Upper Saddle River, NJ: Prentice Hall, 2007).

[6]Webster and Keller, "A Roadmap for Branding," p. 15.

[7]This section is based on Kevin Lane Keller, "Building Customer-Based Brand Equity," *Marketing Management* 10 (July/August 2001): pp. 15–19.

category where the brand competes by creating clear connections to the specific products or services that are solely under the brand name.

Brand Meaning   **Brand positioning** involves establishing unique brand associations in the minds of customers to differentiate the brand and establish competitive superiority.[8] Although a multitude of different types of brand associations are possible, brand meaning can be captured by examining two broad categories: (1) **brand performance**—the way in which the product or service meets customers' more functional needs (for example, quality, price, styling, and service effectiveness) and (2) **brand imagery**—the ways in which the brand attempts to meet customers' more abstract psychological or social needs.

Brand positioning should incorporate both points of parity and points of difference in the customer value proposition (see Chapter 3). "Points of difference are strong, favorable, unique brand associations that drive customers' behavior; points of parity are those associations where the brand 'breaks even' with competitors and negates their intended points of difference."[9] Strong business-to-business brands such as Cisco, IBM, Google, and FedEx have clearly established strong, favorable (that is, valuable to customers), and unique brand associations with customers.

Brand Response   As a branding strategy is implemented, special attention should be directed to how customers react to the brand and the associated marketing activities. Four types of **customer judgments** are particularly vital to the creation of a strong brand (in ascending order of importance):

1. *Quality*—the customers' attitudes toward a brand's perceived quality as well as their perceptions of value and satisfaction;

2. *Credibility*—the extent to which the brand as a whole is perceived by customers as credible in terms of expertise, trustworthiness, and likeability;

3. *Consideration set*—the degree to which customers find the brand to be an appropriate option worthy of serious consideration;

4. *Superiority*—the extent to which customers believe that the brand offers unique advantages over competitors' brands.

Feelings relate to the customers' emotional reaction to the brand and include numerous types that have been tied to brand building, including warmth, fun, excitement, and security. For example, Apple's brand might elicit feelings of **excitement** (customers are energized by the brand and believe that the brand is cool); IBM or FedEx may evoke feelings of **security** (the brand produces a feeling of comfort or self-assurance); and Cisco's branding campaign, "Welcome to the Human Network," might elicit **warmth** (the brand makes customers feel peaceful). Cisco's vice president–corporate marketing, Marilyn Mersereau, says, "Instead of being a product player with the 'Powered by Cisco' campaign, we're trying to position Cisco to be a

---

[8]Kevin Lane Keller, Brian Sternthal, and Alice Tybout, "Three Questions You Need to Ask about Your Brand," *Harvard Business Review* 80 (September 2002): pp. 80–89.

[9]Webster and Keller, "A Roadmap for Branding," p. 390.

platform for your life experience," educating customers about the ways Cisco makes it easier for people to connect with one another via the Web.[10]

Forging Brand Relationships   An examination of the level of personal identification and the nature of the relationship a customer has formed with the brand is the final step in the brand-building process. **Brand resonance** represents the strength of the psychological bond that a customer has with a brand and the degree to which this connection translates into loyalty, attachment, and active engagement with the brand. Keller observes, "Brand resonance reflects a completely harmonious relationship between customers and the brand.... The strongest brands will be the ones to which those consumers become so attached that they, in effect, become evangelists and actively seek means to interact with the brand and share their experiences with others."[11]

Brand Strategy Guidelines

In building a strong brand, Kevin Lane Keller identifies some key guidelines that are particularly crucial in the business-to-business setting.[12] First, employees at all levels of the organization must understand the meaning and vision for the brand. A **brand mantra**—a short three- to five-word summary of the essence of the brand—can be powerful in communicating the core values of the brand to employees (e.g., McKinsey & Company—"hire the best minds in management consulting"; FedEx—"Overnight Delivery Guaranteed"; or DuPont—"The miracle of science"). Second, larger and more complex companies should develop a coherent branding strategy and then build on the reputation of that brand. This provides the opportunity to develop sub-brands with descriptive product modifiers that capitalize on the highly credible corporate brand name (e.g., Dow Water & Process Solutions, Dow Oil & Gas).

Third, a firm with a strong brand can command a price premium for its products or services. However, to sustain that premium, important points of differentiation must be clearly communicated to target customer segments in order to ensure that customers appreciate the unique value that the brand provides. An often overlooked means of differentiation is to link the brand to relevant non-product-related brand associations such as the company's customer list of leading-edge companies. Fourth, successful branding requires a well-conceived market segmentation plan. Since business customers are primarily interested in a solution to a problem, not just a product, different market segments value different sets of benefits. Likewise, within the same buying organization, senior executives employ different choice criteria and often seek different solutions (e.g., drive business performance) than those sought by middle managers (e.g., meet technical requirements). By recognizing such differences, a more sharply focused brand communication strategy can be developed.

---

[10]"B to B's Best Brands: Cisco," B to B's Best, 2007, accessed at http://www.btobonline.com on July 15, 2008.

[11]Keller, "Building Customer Brand-Based Equity," p. 19.

[12]Kevin Lane Keller, "Building a Strong Business-to-Business Brand," in Mark S. Glynn and Arch G. Woodside (eds.), *Business-to-Business Brand Management: Theory, Research and Executive Case Study Exercises* [Advances in Business Marketing and Purchasing, Volume 15], Bingley, UK: Emerald Group Publishing Limited, 2009, pp. 11–31.

Profiling a Strong Brand: IBM

The powerful differentiating benefits that a strong brand can convey are revealed in IBM's brand strategy. The company launched its "Smarter Planet" business strategy to build a clear perception concerning what IBM is all about. Rather than a hardware or mainframe computer manufacturer, IBM is the world's largest professional service organization based on its depth of industry knowledge and number of consultants. John Kennedy, VP of Integrated Communications at IBM, asserts:

> We're a company that builds smarter traffic systems ... makes utility grids smarter ... makes financial systems smarter ... makes healthcare systems smarter. And of course, we can help midsize companies tackle their biggest problems and become smarter, as well.[13]

To that end, IBM launched a communication program involving all marketing channels, promoting the way in which the firm's knowledge and capabilities are uniquely positioned to help corporations, government, transportation, energy, education, health care, and cities work smarter, contributing to a smarter planet. Such smarter-planet style projects require a collaborative partner that can tackle the integrating challenges involving computer hardware, sensor networks, specialized software, and hands-on work by industry experts. And IBM persuasively argues that it is best equipped to serve "as the digital general contractor on big projects."[14]

In a major speech to the Council on Foreign Relations, Samuel J. Palmisanno, IBM's CEO, provided a vision of how smart technology could improve the way in which the world works and described how IBM is devoting significant resources to make smarter systems a reality in every part of the world. The smarter-planet campaign appears to be resonating with senior-level decision makers and government officials, allowing IBM to: (1) stake out a leadership position on issues vital to business and government; (2) establish thought leadership in new areas such as smart grids and transportation systems in cities; and (3) position the company as a collaborative partner in driving new solutions.[15]

The smarter-planet strategy has also significantly expanded IBM's market potential. During the first year, the goal set by IBM's CEO was to create 300 smarter solutions in partnership with clients. Over 1200 solutions were developed across industry sectors, from smart supply chains to smart traffic congestion management systems. And the list continues to grow.[16] Based on creativity and demonstrated business performance against competing brands on multiple continents, the smarter-planet campaign has received numerous awards, including the Gold Global Effie in recognition of marketplace success.[17]

---

[13]Joel Makower, "A Closer Look at IBM's 'Smarter Planet' Campaign," GreenBiz.com, January 4, 2009, p. 6, accessed at http://www.greenbiz.com on June 4, 2011.

[14]Steve Lohr, "Big Blue's Smarter Marketing Playbook," January 12, 2010, p. 1, accessed at http://bits.blogs.nytimes.com on June 2, 2011.

[15]"IBM: Smarter Branding for a Smarter Planet," Public Relations Society of America, January 1, 2010, pp. 1–3, accessed at http://www.prsa.org on June 4, 2011.

[16]Speech by Samuel J. Palmisano, Chief Executive Officer, IBM, "A Smarter Planet," January 12, 2010, p. 2, London, England, accessed at http://www.ibm.com on June 2, 2011.

[17]"IBM Smarter Planet Campaign from Ogilvy & Mather Wins Golden Effie," June 9, 2010, p. 1, accessed at http://www.ogilvy.com on June 2, 2011.

How Financial Markets React   A host of business-to-business companies have launched brand-building initiatives, but do such investments generate positive returns? Some recent research on the brand attitude of buyers in evaluating computer-related firms provides some answers.[18] Brand attitude is a component and indicator of brand equity. **Brand attitude** is defined as the percentage of organizational buyers who have a positive image of a company minus those with a negative opinion. This study found that changes in brand attitude are associated with stock market performance and tend to lead accounting financial performance (that is, an increase in brand attitude will be reflected in improved financial performance three to six months later). In short, the research demonstrates that investments in building brand attitude for high-technology firms do indeed pay off and increase the firm's value.

In another intriguing study, Thomas J. Madden, Frank Fehle, and Susan Fournier provide empirical evidence of the link between branding and shareholder value creation.[19] They found that a portfolio of brands identified as strong by the Interbrand/*Business Week* valuation method displays significant performance advantages compared to the overall market. "Firms that have developed strong brands create value for their shareholders by yielding returns that are greater in magnitude than a relevant market benchmark, and perhaps more important, do so with less risk."[20]

Product Quality and Customer Value

Rising customer expectations make product quality and customer value important strategic priorities. On a global scale, many international companies insist that suppliers, as a prerequisite for negotiations, meet quality standards set out by the Geneva-based International Standards Organization (ISO). These quality requirements, referred to as **ISO-9000 standards**, were developed for the European Community but have gained a global following.[21] Certification requires a supplier to thoroughly document its quality-assurance program. The certification program is becoming a seal of approval to compete for business not only overseas but also in the United States. For instance, the Department of Defense employs ISO standards in its contract guidelines. Although Japanese firms continue to set the pace in the application of sophisticated quality-control procedures in manufacturing, companies such as Kodak, AT&T, Xerox, Ford, Hewlett-Packard, Intel, GE, and others have made significant strides.

The quest for improved product quality touches the entire supply chain as these and other companies demand improved product quality from their suppliers, large and small. For example, GE has an organization-wide goal of achieving Six Sigma quality, meaning that a product would have a defect level of no more than 3.4 parts per million. Using the Six Sigma approach, GE measures every process,

---

[18]David A. Aaker and Robert Jacobson, "The Value Relevance of Brand Attitude in High-Technology Markets," *Journal of Marketing Research* 38 (November 2001): pp. 485–493. See also Christian Homburg, Martin Klarmann, and Jens Schmitt, "Brand Awareness in Business Markets," *International Journal of Research in Marketing* 27 (3, 2010): pp. 201–212.

[19]Thomas J. Madden, Frank Fehle, and Susan Fournier, "Brands Matter: An Empirical Demonstration of the Creation of Shareholder Value through Branding," *Journal of the Academy of Marketing Science* 34 (2, 2006): pp. 224–235.

[20]Ibid., pp. 232–233.

[21]Wade Ferguson, "Impact of ISO 9000 Series Standards on Industrial Marketing," *Industrial Marketing Management* 25 (July 1996): pp. 325–310.

identifies the variables that lead to defects, and takes steps to eliminate them. GE also works directly to assist suppliers in using the approach. Overall, GE reports that Six Sigma has produced striking results—cost savings in the billions and fundamental improvements in product and service quality. Recently, GE has centered its Six Sigma efforts on functions that "teach customers," such as marketing and sales.[22]

Meaning of Quality

The quality movement has passed through several stages.[23] *Stage one* centered on conformance to standards or success in meeting specifications. But conformance quality or zero defects do not satisfy a customer if the product embodies the wrong features. *Stage two* emphasized that quality was more than a technical specialty and that pursuing it should drive the core processes of the entire business. Particular emphasis was given to total quality management and measuring customer satisfaction. However, customers choose a particular product over competing offerings because they perceive it as providing superior *value*—the product's price, performance, and service render it the most attractive alternative. *Stage three*, then, examines a firm's quality performance relative to that of competitors and examines customer perceptions of the value of competing products. The focus here is on market-perceived quality and value versus that of competitors. Moreover, attention shifts from zero defects in products to zero defections of customers (that is, *customer loyalty*). Merely satisfying customers who have the freedom to make choices is not enough to keep them loyal.[24]

Sustainability: Strategic Imperative

Mega-trends, like the quality movement, force companies to adapt or innovate, or be left behind. Sustainability is an emerging mega-trend that is transforming the competitive landscape, forcing companies to change the way they think about products, processes, and business models.[25] Fueling this mega-trend is the intensified global competition for natural resources (particularly oil) coupled with escalating public and governmental concern about climate change, industrial pollution, food safety, and natural resource depletion. Broadly defined, **sustainability** involves the integration of economic, environmental, and societal considerations into business decision making. For experienced business strategists, sustainability is an integral part of value creation.[26]

Rather than damaging the bottom line, research shows that, when properly conceived, "sustainability is a mother lode of organizational and technological

---

[22]Erin White, "Rethinking the Quality-Improvement Program," *The Wall Street Journal*, September 19, 2005, p. B3.

[23]Bradley T. Gale, *Managing Customer Value: Creating Quality and Service That Customers Can See* (New York: The Free Press, 1994), pp. 25–30.

[24]Thomas O. Jones and W. Earl Sasser, "Why Satisfied Customers Defect," *Harvard Business Review* 73 (November–December 1995): pp. 88–99; and Richard L. Oliver, "Whence Customer Loyalty," *Journal of Marketing* 63 (Special Issue 1999): pp. 33–44.

[25]David A. Lubin and Daniel C. Esty, "The Sustainability Imperative," *Harvard Business Review* 88 (May 2010): 42–50.

[26]Maurice Berns, Andrew Townend, Zayna Khayat, Balu Balagopal, Martin Reeves, Michael S. Hopkins, and Nina Kruschwitz, "Sustainability and Competitive Advantage," *MIT Sloan Management Review* 51 (Fall 2009): pp. 19–26.

FIGURE 7.2 | HOW SUSTAINABILITY AFFECTS VALUE CREATION

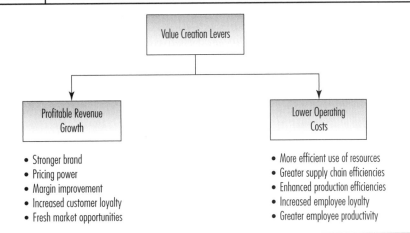

SOURCE: Adapted from Maurice Berns, Andrew Townend, Zayna Khayat, Balu Balagopal, Martin Reeves, Michael S. Hopkins, and Nina Kruschwitz, "Sustainability and Competitive Advantage," *MIT Sloan Management Review* 51 (Fall 2009): pp. 19–26.

innovations that yield both bottom-line and top-line returns. Becoming environmentally friendly lowers costs because companies end up reducing the inputs they use. In addition, the process generates additional revenue from better products ..." or from new businesses.[27]

Enthusiasm for sustainability is growing across industries, particularly in commodity, chemical, consumer product, industrial goods, machinery, and retail companies. A recent comprehensive global survey of firms across industries reveals that executives are virtually united in the view that sustainability will have a powerful impact on their processes and competitive strategies.[28] Some firms, however, are adopting sustainability practices faster than their peers. Two distinct segments emerge: cautious adopters and embracers. Cautious adopters view sustainability as a vehicle for cost cutting, resource efficiency, and risk management (e.g., complying with regulatory mandates). By contrast, embracer companies recognize that sustainability strategies provide a means for gaining competitive advantage through innovation, process improvements, brand building, and access to new markets. And, as it turned out in the study, embracers represent the highest-performing businesses in the study. In short, these firms view sustainability investments as an important driver of value creation for the firm, providing opportunities for enhanced profitability from margin improvement and revenue growth (see Figure 7.2). In addition to these tangible benefits, observe that sustainability efforts also confer intangible benefits such as an improved brand reputation and the enhanced ability to attract and retain talented employees.

Capturing Opportunities Companies that excel in sustainability do "old things in new ways" such as outperforming competition on regulatory compliance and

---

[27]Ram Nidumolu, C. K. Prahalad, and M. R. Rangaswami, "Why Sustainability Is Now the Driver of Innovation," *Harvard Business Review* 87 (September 2009): pp. 56–64.

[28]Knut Haanaes, Balu Balagopal, Ming Tech Kong, Ingrid Velken, David Arthur, Michael S. Hopkins, and Nina Kruschwitz, "New Sustainability Study: The 'Embracers' Seize Advantage," *MIT Sloan Management Review* 52 (Spring 2011): pp. 23–35.

environment-related cost management.[29] For example, 3M has reduced expenses related to energy usage, resources, and waste by over $200 million from 2005 to 2010. Leading performers also do "new things in new ways" such as redesigning products, processes, and whole systems to optimize natural resource efficiencies across their value chains.[30] Dow developed a solar roofing shingle that can be integrated into rooftops with standard asphalt shingle materials. As the vision expands for these top-performing companies, sustainability innovations transform core businesses and even lead to the creation of new businesses and new sources of differentiation.

GE's Ecomagination Marketing Campaign[31]

GE's "Ecomagination" initiative provides a rich illustration of the powerful growth opportunities that can be captured by listening to customers and designing sustainable products and services that capitalize on the particular capabilities of the firm. Launched in 2005 by CEO Jeffrey Immelt, the company set a widely publicized goal to double the revenue that the firm derives from clean energy products from $10B to $20B by 2010. In his words, "Ecomagination" is a business initiative to help meet customers' demand for more energy-efficient products and to drive reliable growth for GE—growth that delivers for investors long term."[32]

Across business units, GE increased its portfolio of Ecomagination products and armed its salespeople with value calculators that vividly define the energy savings that the new GE products deliver for business customers. The results were stunning. The Ecomagination product line exceeded revenue goals and positions GE as a leader in rapidly growing market segments such as energy infrastructure, water purification, jet engines, locomotives, and energy-efficient appliances. (Updates on the initiative are available at http://www.ge.ecomagination.com.)

In developing a sustainability initiative, a firm must select an area where customer and company interests intersect. These areas present an opportunity to create shared value—a meaningful benefit for customers and for society that is also valuable to the business. Companies that make the right strategy choices and build focused and integrated sustainability initiatives in concert with their core capabilities will increasingly distance themselves from competitors. Michael E. Porter and Mark R. Kramer aptly observe: "When a well-run business applies its vast resources, expertise, and management talent to problems that it understands and in which it has a stake, it can have a greater impact on social good than any other institution or philanthropic organization.[33]

Meaning of Customer Value

Delivering customer value is the heart of business marketing strategy. Strategy experts Dwight Gertz and João Baptista suggest that "a company's product or service is competitively superior if, at price equality with competing products, target

---

[29]Lubin and Esty, "The Sustainability Imperative," pp. 47–48.

[30]Ibid.

[31]This discussion is based on Dick Martin, *Secrets of the Marketing Masters* (New York: AMACOM, 2009), pp. 196–200.

[32]Ibid., p. 200.

[33]Michael E. Porter and Mark R. Kramer, "Strategy & Society: The Link between Competitive Advantage and Corporate Social Responsibility," *Harvard Business Review* 84 (December 2006): p. 92.

B2B TOP PERFORMERS

Green Is Green

In developing GE's "Ecomagination" marketing campaign, Beth Comstock, Chief Marketing Officer (CMO) at GE, initiated "discovery sessions" with some of the company's largest customers from industries such as energy, aviation, or public utilities to explore market and technology trends with senior GE executives, including CEO Jeffrey Immelt. In effect, they were asked to imagine life ten years ahead and project the products that they would need from GE. Thirty-five customers at a time attended these sessions. After a half dozen of these sessions were held, Beth Comstock and the senior team at GE received a clear message: *Tighter environmental regulations, growing customer expectations, and rising energy costs would translate into demand for cleaner technologies across all of the company's infrastructure businesses.*

In developing the Ecomagination campaign, Comstock moved slowly and began a yearlong process of securing feedback from employees, customers, activists, and public officials. Employees were the toughest audiences and, in many ways, the most important stakeholders in her view. "If employees don't buy in, customers won't either," she observes. "Marketing is all about culture—internally and externally. You can't create something that sticks unless you get it into the culture."

A critical turning point in winning support for the campaign internally and among other skeptical constituencies came when Jeffrey Immelt introduced the campaign with the slogan: "green is green." "Ecomagination" was about making money by drawing on GE's distinctive capabilities and giving customers what they need. It was not adopted because it was trendy or even the moral thing to do. It was adopted because GE found common ground where customer and company interests intersect.

SOURCE: Dick Martin, *Secrets of the Marketing Masters* (New York: AMACOM, 2009), pp. 194–201.

segments always choose it. Thus, value is defined in terms of consumer choice in a competitive context."[34] In turn, the value equation includes a vital service component. For the service component, business marketing strategists must "recognize that specifications aren't just set by a manufacturer who tells the customer what to expect; instead, consumers also may participate in setting specifications." Frontline sales and service personnel add value to the product offering and the consumption experience by meeting or, indeed, exceeding the customer's service expectations.[35] **Customer value,** then, represents a "business customer's overall assessment of a relationship with a supplier based on perceptions of benefits received and sacrifices made."[36]

---

[34]Dwight L. Gertz and João P. A. Baptista, *Grow to Be Great: Breaking the Downsizing Cycle* (New York: The Free Press, 1995), p. 128.

[35]C. K. Prahalad and M. S. Krishnan, "The New Meaning of Quality in the Information Age," *Harvard Business Review* 77 (September–October 1999): pp. 109–112. See also, C. K. Prahalad and Venkat Ramaswamy, *The Future of Competition: Co-Creating Unique Value with Customers* (Boston: Harvard Business School Press, 2004).

[36]Ajay Menon, Christian Homburg, and Nikolas Beutin, "Understanding Customer Value in Business-to-Business Relationships," *Journal of Business-to-Business Marketing* 12 (2, 2005): p. 5. See also Wolfgang Ulaga and Andreas Eggert, "Value-Based Differentiation in Business Relationships: Gaining and Sustaining Key Supplier Status," *Journal of Marketing* 70 (January 2006): pp. 119–136.

FIGURE 7.3 | **WHAT VALUE MEANS TO BUSINESS CUSTOMERS**

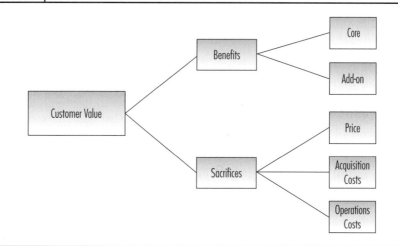

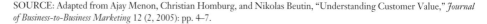

SOURCE: Adapted from Ajay Menon, Christian Homburg, and Nikolas Beutin, "Understanding Customer Value," *Journal of Business-to-Business Marketing* 12 (2, 2005): pp. 4–7.

Benefits   Customer benefits take two forms (Figure 7.3):

1. *Core benefits*—the core requirements (for example, specified product quality) for a relationship that suppliers must fully meet to be included in the customer's consideration set;

2. *Add-on benefits*—attributes that differentiate suppliers, go beyond the basic denominator provided by all qualified vendors, and create added value in a buyer–seller relationship (for example, value-added customer service).

Sacrifices   Consistent with the total cost perspective that business customers emphasize (Chapter 2), sacrifices include: (1) the purchase price, (2) acquisition costs (for example, ordering and delivery costs), and (3) operations costs (for example, defect-free incoming shipments of component parts reduces operations costs).

What Matters Most?   Based on a large study of nearly 1000 purchasing managers across a wide variety of product categories in the United States and Germany, Ajay Menon, Christian Homburg, and Nikolas Beutin uncovered some rich insights into customer value in business-to-business relationships.[37]

Add-on Benefits   First, the research demonstrates that add-on benefits more strongly influence customer value than do core benefits. Why? All qualified suppliers perform well on core benefits, so add-on benefits tend to be the differentiator for customer value as customers choose among competing offerings. Therefore, business marketers can use value-added services or joint working relationships that influence add-on benefits to strengthen customer relationships. For example, a leading manufacturer of tires for earth-moving equipment offers free consulting

---

[37]Menon, Homburg, and Beutin, "Understanding Customer Value," pp. 1–33.

services that help customers design maintenance procedures that yield significant cost savings.[38]

Trust   Second, the study reinforces the vital role of trust in a business relationship (see Chapter 3), demonstrating, in fact, that trust has a stronger impact on core benefits than product characteristics.

Reducing Customer's Costs   Third, the results highlight the importance of marketing strategies that are designed to assist the customer in reducing operations costs. The research team observes:

> Ensuring on-time delivery of components and raw materials, getting involved in the customer firm's manufacturing and R&D strategy-making processes, and deploying resources needed to ensure a smooth relationship with the customer will help reduce the customer's operations costs.[39]

By pursuing such initiatives, the business marketer does not have to rely solely on price to demonstrate and deliver value to the customer.

Product Support Strategy: The Service Connection

The marketing function must ensure that every part of the organization focuses on delivering superior value to customers. Business marketing programs involve a number of critical components that customers carefully evaluate: tangible products, service support, and ongoing information services both before and after the sale. To provide value and to successfully implement these programs, the business marketing firm must carefully coordinate activities among personnel in product management, sales, and service.[40] For example, to customize a product and delivery schedule for an important customer requires close coordination among product, logistics, and sales personnel. Moreover, some customer accounts might require special field-engineering, installation, or equipment support, thereby increasing the required coordination between sales and service units.

Post-purchase service is especially important to buyers in many industrial product categories ranging from computers and machine tools to custom-designed component parts. Responsibility for service support, however, is often diffused throughout various departments, such as applications engineering, customer relations, or service administration. Significant benefits accrue to the business marketer who carefully manages and coordinates product, sales, and service connections to maximize customer value.

Product Policy

Product policy involves the set of all decisions concerning the products and services that the company offers. Through product policy, a business marketing firm attempts to satisfy customer needs and to build a sustainable competitive advantage by capitalizing on its core competencies. This section explores the types of industrial product

[38]Das Narayandas, "Building Loyalty in Business Markets," *Harvard Business Review* 83 (September–October 2005): p. 134.

[39]Menon, Homburg, and Beutin, "Understanding Customer Value," p. 25.

[40]Frank V. Cespedes, *Concurrent Marketing: Integrating Product, Sales, and Service* (Boston: Harvard Business School Press, 1995), pp. 58–85.

lines and the importance of anchoring product-management decisions on an accurate definition of the product market. A framework is also provided for assessing product opportunities on a global scale.

Types of Product Lines Defined

Because product lines of industrial firms differ from those of consumer-packaged-goods firms, classification is useful. Industrial product lines can be categorized into four types[41]:

1. **Proprietary or catalog products.** These items are offered only in certain configurations and produced in anticipation of orders. Product-line decisions concern adding, deleting, or repositioning products in the line.

2. **Custom-built products.** These items are offered as a set of basic units, with numerous accessories and options. For example, NCR offers a line of retail workstations used by large customers like Wal-Mart and 7-Eleven stores as well as by smaller businesses. The basic workstation can be expanded to connect to scanners, check readers, electronic payment devices, and other accessories to meet a business's particular needs. The firm's wide array of products provides retailers with an end-to-end solution, from data warehousing to the point-of-service workstation at checkout. The marketer offers the organizational buyer a set of building blocks. Product-line decisions center on offering the proper mix of options and accessories.

3. **Custom-designed products.** These items are created to meet the needs of one or a small group of customers. Sometimes the product is a unique unit, such as a power plant or a specific machine tool. In addition, some items produced in relatively large quantities, such as an aircraft model, may fall into this category. The product line is described in terms of the company's capability, and the customer buys that capability. Ultimately, this capability is transformed into a finished good.

4. **Industrial services.** Rather than an actual product, the buyer is purchasing a company's capability in an area such as maintenance, technical service, or management consulting. (Special attention is given to services marketing in Chapter 9.)

All types of business marketing firms confront product policy decisions, whether they offer physical products, pure services (no physical product), or a product-service combination. Each product situation presents unique problems and opportunities for the business marketer; each draws on a unique capability. Product strategy rests on the intelligent use of the firm's distinctive capabilities.

Defining the Product Market

Accurately defining the product market is fundamental to sound product-policy decisions.[42] Careful attention must be given to the alternative ways to satisfy customer

---

[41]Benson P. Shapiro, *Industrial Product Policy: Managing the Existing Product Line* (Cambridge, MA: Marketing Science Institute, 1977), pp. 37–39.

[42]For a related discussion on competitive analysis, see Beth A. Walker, Dimitri Kapelianis, and Michael D. Hutt, "Competitive Cognition," *MIT Sloan Management Review* 46 (Summer 2005): pp. 10–12.

needs. For example, many different products could provide competition for personal computers. Application-specific products, such as enhanced pocket pagers and smart phones that send e-mail and connect to the Web, are potential competitors. A wide array of information appliances that provide easy access to the Internet also pose a threat. In such an environment, Regis McKenna maintains, managers "must look for opportunities in—and expect competition from—every possible direction. A company with a narrow product concept will move through the market with blinders on, and it is sure to run into trouble."[43] By excluding products and technology that compete for the same end-user needs, the product strategist can quickly become out of touch with the market. Both customer needs and the ways of satisfying those needs change.

Product Market   A **product market** establishes the distinct arena in which the business marketer competes. Four dimensions of a market definition are strategically relevant:

1. *Customer function dimension.* This involves the benefits that are provided to satisfy the needs of organizational buyers (for example, mobile messaging).

2. *Technological dimension.* There are alternative ways a particular function can be performed (for example, cell phone, pager, notebook computer).

3. *Customer segment dimension.* Customer groups have distinct needs that must be served (for example, sales representatives, physicians, international travelers).

4. *Value-added system dimension.* Competitors serving the market can operate along a sequence of stages.[44] The value-added system for smart phones includes equipment providers, such as Apple and Nokia, and service providers, like Verizon and AT&T. Analysis of the value-added system may indicate potential opportunities or threats from changes in the system (for example, potential alliances between equipment and service providers).

Planning for Today and Tomorrow   Competition to satisfy the customer's need exists at the technology level as well as at the supplier or brand level. By establishing accurate product-market boundaries, the product strategist is better equipped to identify customer needs, the benefits sought by the market segment, and the turbulent nature of competition at both the technology and supplier or brand levels. Derek Abell offers these valuable strategy insights:

- Planning for today requires a clear, precise *definition* of the business—a delineation of target customer segments, customer functions, and the business approach to be taken; planning for tomorrow is concerned with how the business should be *redefined* for the future.

- Planning for today focuses on *shaping up* the business to meet the needs of today's customers with excellence. It involves identifying factors that are critical

---

[43]Regis McKenna, *Relationship Marketing* (Reading MA: Addison-Wesley, 1991), p. 184.

[44]George S. Day, *Strategic Market Planning: The Pursuit of Competitive Advantage* (St. Paul, MN: West, 1984), p. 73.

B2B TOP PERFORMERS

BASF: Using Services to Build a Strong Brand

BASF AG, headquartered in Germany, is the world's largest chemical company, with global sales of over $33 billion and North American sales of $8 billion. Consistently ranked as one of Fortune's most admired global companies, the firm competes in what many would describe as a commodity business. Rather than pursue a low-total-cost strategy and compete on price, BASF decided to transform itself into an innovative service-oriented company. Services, like R&D support or on-site field services, are hard for rivals to duplicate and when well executed, provide the ultimate differentiation strategy. To communicate its value proposition to customers, the firm launched its advertising campaign with the familiar tag line:

"We don't make a lot of products you buy. We make a lot of the products you buy better."

A senior executive at BASF's ad agency, Tony Graetzer, describes the rationale for this campaign, which has been recognized with numerous awards: "Companies are frequently viewed as tied on the quality of their products, but they are never viewed as tied on the quality of their services." Winning companies provide superior service. By emphasizing how it helps make its customers' products better and delivering on its promises, the BASF brand has become synonymous with customer partnerships and technology leadership.

SOURCE: Bob Lamons, *The Case for B2B Branding* (Mason, Ohio: Thomson, 2005), pp. 91–94.

to success and smothering them with attention; planning for tomorrow can entail *reshaping* the business to compete more effectively in the future.[45]

Seeing What Is Next   Strategy experts also argue provocatively that many firms are overlooking three important customer groups that may present the greatest opportunity for explosive growth[46]:

- *Nonconsumers* who may lack the specialized skills, training, or resources to purchase the product or service;

- *Undershot customers* for whom existing products are not good enough;

- *Overshot customers* for whom existing products provide more performance than they can use.

Planning Industrial Product Strategy

Formulating a strategic marketing plan for an existing product line is the most vital part of a company's marketing planning efforts. Having identified a product market, attention now turns to planning product strategy. Product-positioning analysis provides a useful tool for charting the strategy course.

---

[45]Derek F. Abell, "Competing Today While Preparing for Tomorrow," *Sloan Management Review* 40 (Spring 1999): p. 74.

[46]Clayton M. Christensen, Scott D. Anthony, and Erik A. Roth, *Seeing What's Next* (Boston: Harvard Business School Press, 2004), p. 5.

FIGURE 7.4 | **Steps in the Product-Positioning Process**

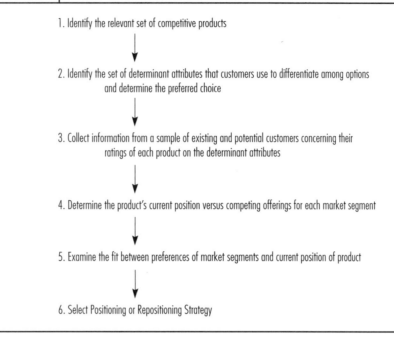

1. Identify the relevant set of competitive products

2. Identify the set of determinant attributes that customers use to differentiate among options and determine the preferred choice

3. Collect information from a sample of existing and potential customers concerning their ratings of each product on the determinant attributes

4. Determine the product's current position versus competing offerings for each market segment

5. Examine the fit between preferences of market segments and current position of product

6. Select Positioning or Repositioning Strategy

SOURCE: Adapted with modifications from Harper W. Boyd Jr., Orville C. Walker Jr., and Jean-Claude Larréché, *Marketing Management: A Strategic Approach with a Global Orientation* (Chicago: Irwin/McGraw-Hill, 1998), p. 197.

Product Positioning

Once the product market is defined, a strong competitive position for the product must be secured. **Product positioning** represents the place that a product occupies in a particular market; it is found by measuring organizational buyers' perceptions and preferences for a product in relation to its competitors. Because organizational buyers perceive products as bundles of attributes (for example, quality, service), the product strategist should examine the attributes that assume a central role in buying decisions.

The Process[47]

Observe from Figure 7.4 that the positioning process begins by identifying the relevant set of competing products (Step 1) and defining those attributes that are **determinant** (Step 2)—attributes that customers use to differentiate among the alternatives and that are important to them in determining which brand they prefer. In short, then, determinant attributes are choice criteria that are both important and differentiating. Of course, some attributes are important to organizational buyers, but they may not be differentiating. For example, safety might be an important attribute in the heavy-duty truck market, but business market customers may consider the competing products offered by Navistar, Volvo, and Mack Trucks as quite

[47]This section is based on Harper W. Boyd Jr., Orville C. Walker Jr., and Jean-Claude Larréché, *Marketing Management: A Strategic Approach with a Global Orientation* (Chicago: Irwin/McGraw-Hill, 1998), pp. 190–200.

comparable on this dimension. Durability, reliability, and fuel economy might constitute the determinant attributes.

Step 3 involves collecting information from a sample of existing and potential customers concerning how they perceive the various options on each of the determinant attributes. The sample should include buyers (particularly buying influentials) from organizations that represent the full array of market segments the product strategist wishes to serve. After examining the product's current position versus competing offerings (Step 4), the analyst can isolate: (1) the competitive strength of the product in different segments and (2) the opportunities for securing a differentiated position in a particular target segment (Step 5).

Isolating Strategy Opportunities

Step 6 involves the selection of the positioning or repositioning strategy. Here the product manager can evaluate particular strategy options. First, for some attributes, the product manager may wish to: (1) pursue a strategy to increase the importance of an attribute to customers and (2) increase the difference between the competition's and the firm's products. For example, the importance of an attribute such as customer training might be elevated through marketing communications emphasizing how the potential buyer can increase its efficiency and employee performance through the firm's training. If successful, such efforts might move customer training from an important attribute to a determinant attribute in the eyes of customers. Second, if the firm's performance on a determinant product attribute is truly higher than that of competitors—but the market perceives that other alternatives enjoy an edge—marketing communications can be developed to bring perceptions in line with reality. Third, the competitive standing of a product can be advanced by improving the firm's level of performance on determinant attributes that organizational buyers emphasize.

Product Positioning Illustrated[48]

This product-positioning approach was successfully applied to a capital equipment product at a major corporation. The product that provided the focus of the analysis is sold in three sizes to two market segments: end users and consulting engineers. Marketing research identified 15 attributes, including reliability, service support, company reputation, and ease of maintenance.

A New Strategy   The research found that the firm's brand enjoyed an outstanding rating on product reliability and service support. Both attributes were generally determinant for the company against most competitors. To reinforce the importance of both attributes, management decided to offer an enhanced warranty program. Both end users and consulting engineers view warranties as important but not a point of differentiation across competing brands. Management surmised, however, that by establishing a new warranty standard for the industry, the attribute could become determinant, adding to the brand's leverage over competitors. In addition, management felt that the new warranty program might also benefit the brand's reputation on other attributes such as reliability and company reputation.

---

[48]This section is based largely on Behram J. Hansotia, Muzaffar A. Shaikh, and Jagdish N. Sheth, "The Strategic Determinancy Approach to Brand Management," *Business Marketing* 70 (Fall 1985): pp. 66–69.

Better Targeting   The study also provided some surprises. Price was not nearly as important to organizational buyers as management had initially believed. This suggested that there were opportunities to increase revenue through product differentiation and service support. Likewise, the research found that the firm's brand dominated all competitors in the large- and medium-sized products, but not in the small-sized products. This particular product had an especially weak competitive position in the consulting engineer segment. Special service support strategies were developed to strengthen the product's standing in this segment. Clearly, product positioning provides a valuable tool for designing creative strategies for business markets.

The Technology Adoption Life Cycle

After decades of being content with letters, telegrams, and telephones, consumers have embraced voice-mail, e-mail, Internet browsers, and a range of information appliances. In each case, the conversion of the market came slowly. Once a particular threshold of consumer acceptance was achieved, there was a stampede. Geoffrey Moore defines **discontinuous innovations** as "new products or services that require the end-user and the marketplace to dramatically change their past behavior, with the promise of gaining equally dramatic new benefits."[49] During the past quarter century, discontinuous innovations have been common in the computer-electronics industry, creating massive new spending, fierce competition, and a whole host of firms that are redrawing the boundaries of the high-technology marketplace.

A popular tool employed by strategists at high-technology firms is the technology adoption life cycle—a framework developed by Geoffrey Moore, a leading consultant to Hewlett-Packard and a host of other Silicon Valley firms.

Types of Technology Customers

Fundamental to Moore's framework are five classes of customers who constitute the potential market for a discontinuous innovation (Table 7.1). Business marketers can benefit by putting innovative products in the hands of **technology enthusiasts**. They serve as gatekeepers to the rest of the technology life cycle, and their endorsement is needed for an innovation to get a fair hearing in the organization. Whereas technology enthusiasts possess influence, they do not have ready access to the resources needed to move an organization toward a large-scale commitment to the new technology. By contrast, **visionaries** have resource control and can often be influential in publicizing an innovation's benefits and giving it a boost during the early stages of market development. However, visionaries are difficult for a marketer to serve because each demands special and unique product modifications. Their demands can quickly tax a technology firm's R&D resources and stall the market penetration of the innovation.

The Chasm   Truly innovative products often enjoy a warm welcome from early technology enthusiasts and visionaries, but then sales falter and often even plummet.

---

[49]Geoffrey A. Moore, *Inside the Tornado: Marketing Strategies from Silicon Valley's Cutting Edge* (New York: HarperCollins, 1995), p. 13.

TABLE 7.1 | THE TECHNOLOGY ADOPTION LIFE CYCLE: CLASSES OF CUSTOMERS

Customer	Profile
Technology enthusiasts (*innovators*)	Interested in exploring the latest innovation, these consumers possess significant influence over how products are perceived by others in the organization but lack control over resource commitments.
Visionaries (*early adopters*)	Desiring to exploit the innovation for a competitive advantage, these consumers are the true revolutionaries in business and government who have access to organizational resources but frequently demand special modifications to the product that are difficult for the innovator to provide.
Pragmatists (*early majority*)	Making the bulk of technology purchases in organizations, these individuals believe in technology evolution, not revolution, and seek products from a market leader with a proven track record of providing useful productivity improvements.
Conservatives (*late majority*)	Pessimistic about their ability to derive any value from technology investments, these individuals represent a sizable group of customers who are price sensitive and reluctantly purchase high-tech products to avoid being left behind.
Skeptics (*laggards*)	Rather than potential customers, these individuals are ever-present critics of the hype surrounding high-technology products.

SOURCE: Adapted from Geoffrey A. Moore, *Inside the Tornado: Marketing Strategies from Silicon Valley's Cutting Edge* (New York: HarperCollins, 1995), pp. 14–18.

Frequently, a chasm develops between visionaries who are intuitive and support revolution and **pragmatists** who are analytical, support evolution, and provide the pathway to the mainstream market. The business marketer that can successfully guide a product across the chasm creates an opportunity to gain acceptance with the mainstream market of pragmatists and conservatives. As Table 7.1 relates, pragmatists make most technology purchases in organizations, and conservatives include a sizable group of customers who are hesitant to buy high-tech products but do so to avoid being left behind.

Strategies for the Technology Adoption Life Cycle

The fundamental strategy for crossing the chasm and moving from the early market to the mainstream market is to provide pragmatists with a 100 percent solution to their problems. Many high-technology firms err by attempting to provide something for everyone while never meeting the complete requirements of any particular market segment. Pragmatists seek the whole product—the minimum set of products and services that provide them with a compelling reason to buy. Geoffrey Moore notes that "the key to a winning strategy is to identify a simple beachhead of pragmatist customers in a mainstream market segment and to accelerate the formation of 100 percent of their whole product. The goal is to win a niche foothold in the mainstream as quickly as possible—that is what is meant by *crossing the chasm*."[50]

---

[50]Ibid., p. 22. For a related discussion, see Clayton M. Christensen and Michael E. Raynor, *The Innovator's Solution: Creating and Sustaining Successful Growth* (Boston: Harvard Business School Press, 2003), pp. 73–95.

INSIDE BUSINESS MARKETING

The Gorilla Advantage in High-Tech Markets

High-tech companies that can get their products designed into the very standards of the market have enormous influence over the future direction of that market. For example, all PC-based software has to be Microsoft- and Intel-compatible. All networking solutions must be compatible with Cisco Systems' standards; all printers must be Hewlett-Packard–compatible. This is the essence of gorilla power in high-tech markets that firms such as Microsoft, Intel, Cisco, and Hewlett-Packard enjoy. The gorilla advantage allows these market leaders to

- *Attract more customers* by enjoying better press coverage and shorter sales cycles just because information technology managers expect it to be the winner;

- *Keep more customers* because the cost of switching is high for customers and the cost of entry is high for competitors;

- *Drive costs down* by shifting some costly enhancements that customers demand to suppliers while retaining control of the critical components of value creation;

- *Keep profits up* because business partners place a priority on developing complementary products and applications that make the *whole product* of the market leader worth more to customers than competing products are worth (e.g., Apple's iPad).

The Internet presents an explosive area of growth in many sectors of the high-tech market as firms square off to gain a leadership position in mobile computing, wireless technologies, supply chain integration, and Web-focused security. The gorilla games are just beginning!

SOURCE: Geoffrey A. Moore, Paul Johnson, and Tom Kippola, *The Gorilla Game: An Investor's Guide to Picking Winners in High-Technology* (New York: HarperBusiness, 1998), pp. 43–70.

The Bowling Alley

In technology markets, each market segment is like a bowling pin, and the momentum from hitting one segment successfully carries over into surrounding segments. The bowling alley represents a stage in the adoption life cycle where a product gains acceptance from mainstream market segments but has yet to be adopted widely.

Consider the evolution of strategy for Lotus Notes.[51] When first introduced, Notes was offered as a new paradigm for corporate-wide communication. To cross into the mainstream market, the Lotus team shifted the product's focus from an enterprise-wide vision of corporate communication to specific solutions for particular business functions. The first niche served was the global account-management function of worldwide accounting and consulting firms. The solution was enhanced account activity coordination for highly visible products. This led to a second niche—global account management for sales teams, where enhanced coordination and information sharing spur productivity.

A Focused Strategy   A logical next step for Lotus was movement into the customer service function, where openly sharing information can support creative solutions to customer problems. Successful penetration of these segments created

---

[51]Moore, *Inside the Tornado*, pp. 35–37.

another opportunity—incorporating the customer into the Notes loop. Note the key lesson here: A customer-based, application-focused strategy provides leverage so that a victory in one market segment cascades into victories in adjacent market segments.

The Tornado

Although economic buyers who seek particular solutions are the key to success in the bowling alley, technical or infrastructure buyers in organizations can spawn a tornado. Information-technology (IT) managers are responsible for providing efficient and reliable infrastructures—the systems organizational members use to communicate and perform their jobs. They are pragmatists, and they prefer to buy from an established market leader.

IT professionals interact freely across company and industry boundaries and discuss the ramifications of the latest technology. IT managers watch each other closely—they do not want to be too early or too late. Often, they move together and create a tornado. Because a massive number of new customers are entering the market at the same time and because they all want the same product, demand dramatically outstrips supply and a large backlog of customers can appear overnight. At a critical stage, such market forces have surrounded Hewlett-Packard's laser and ink-jet printers, Microsoft's Windows products, Intel's Pentium microprocessors, and Apple's iPhones and iPads.

Tornado Strategy The central success factors for the tornado phase of the adoption life cycle differ from those that are appropriate for the bowling alley. Rather than emphasizing market segmentation, the central goal is to gear up production to capitalize on the opportunity the broad market presents. In its printer business, Hewlett-Packard demonstrated the three critical priorities during a tornado[52]:

1. "Just ship."

2. Extend distribution channels.

3. Drive to the next lower price point.

First, Hewlett-Packard's quality improvement process allowed it to significantly increase production—first with laser printers, and later with ink-jet printers—with few interruptions. Second, to extend market coverage, H-P began to sell its laser printers through PC dealer channels and extended its distribution channels for ink-jet printers to computer superstores, office superstores, mail order, and, more recently, to price clubs and other consumer outlets. Third, H-P drove down the price points for its printers—moving ink-jet printers below $1000, then below $500, and then well below that. As this example demonstrates, tornado strategy emphasizes product leadership and operational excellence in manufacturing and distribution.

---

[52]Ibid., p. 81. See also Stephen Kreider Yoder, "Shaving Back: How H-P Used Tactics of the Japanese to Beat Them at Their Game," *The Wall Street Journal*, September 8, 1994, pp. A1, A6.

Main Street

This stage of the technology adoption life cycle represents a period of aftermarket development. The frantic waves of mass-market adoption of the product begin to subside. Competitors in the industry have increased production, and supply now exceeds demand. Moore points out that "the defining characteristic of Main Street is that continued profitable market growth can no longer come from selling the basic commodity to new customers and must come instead from developing niche-specific extensions to the basic platform for existing customers."[53]

Main Street Strategy The goal here is to develop value-based strategies targeted to particular end-user segments. H-P, for example, matches its printers to the special needs of different segments of home-office users by offering:

- A compact portable printer for those users who are space-constrained;
- The OfficeJet printer-fax for those who do not yet own a fax;
- A high-performance color printer for those who create commercial flyers.

Main Street strategy emphasizes operational excellence in production and distribution as well as finely tuned market segmentation strategies. What signals the end of the technology adoption life cycle? A discontinuous innovation appears that incorporates breakthrough technology and promises new solutions for customers.

Summary

Some of the most valuable and enduring global brands belong to business-to-business firms. The power of a brand resides in the minds of customers through what they have experienced, seen, and heard about the brand over time. The customer-based brand equity model consists of four steps: establishing the right brand identity, defining the meaning of the brand through unique brand associations, developing responsive marketing programs to elicit a positive brand response from customers, and building brand relationships with customers, marked by loyalty and active engagement. Research vividly demonstrates that investments in building a strong brand yield a positive payoff in the financial performance of the firm.

Conceptualizing a product must go beyond mere physical description to include all the benefits and services that provide value to customers. The unifying goal for the business marketer is: *Provide superior market-perceived quality and value versus competitors*. To a business customer, value involves a trade-off between benefits and sacrifices. Business marketers can strengthen customer relationships by providing value-added services and helping customers reduce operations costs. A carefully coordinated product strategy recognizes the role of various functional areas in providing value to business customers. Special attention should be given to synchronizing the activities among the product-management, sales, and service units.

---

[53]Moore, *Inside the Tornado*, p. 111.

Industrial product lines can be broadly classified into: (1) proprietary or catalog items, (2) custom-built items, (3) custom-designed items, and (4) industrial services. Product management can best be described as the management of capability. In monitoring product performance and in formulating marketing strategy, the business marketer can profitably use product-positioning analysis. By isolating a product's competitive standing in a market, positioning analysis provides strategy insights to the planner. A product attribute is determinant if it is both important and differentiating.

Rapidly changing high-technology markets present special opportunities and challenges for the product strategist. The technology adoption life cycle includes five categories of customers: technology enthusiasts, visionaries, pragmatists, conservatives, and skeptics. New products gain acceptance from niches within the mainstream market, progress from segment to segment like one bowling pin knocking over another, and, if successful, experience the tornado of general, widespread adoption by pragmatists. Importantly, the technology adoption life cycle calls for different marketing strategies at different stages.

Discussion Questions

1. Bradley Gale, managing director of The Strategic Planning Institute, says: "People systematically knock out income statements and balance sheets, but they often don't monitor the nonfinancial factors that ultimately drive their financial performance. These nonfinancial factors include 'relative customer-perceived quality': how customers view the marketer's offering versus how they perceive competitive offerings." Explain.

2. Describe why a brand-positioning strategy should include points of difference and points of parity. Provide an illustration to support your case.

3. Distinguish among catalog items, custom-built items, custom-designed items, and services. Explain how marketing requirements vary across these classifications.

4. Regis McKenna notes that "no company in a technology-based industry is safe from unanticipated bumps in the night." In recent years, many industries have been jolted by technological change. In such an environment, what steps can a product strategist take?

5. A particular product strategy will stimulate a response from the market and a corresponding response from competitors. Which specific features of the competitive environment should the business marketing strategist evaluate?

6. Using the customer-based brand equity framework as a guide, describe the distinctive components of Apple's brand strategy.

7. Moving across the technology adoption life cycle, compare and contrast technology enthusiasts with pragmatists. Give special attention to the strategy guidelines that the marketing strategist should follow in reaching customers that fall into these two adoption categories.

8. Identify two business-to-business brands that you would deem to be strong and distinctive. Next, describe the characteristics of each brand that tend to set it apart from rival brands.

9. Firms such as Microsoft, Apple, Sony, and Intel have experienced a burst of demand for some of their products. During the "tornado" for a high-tech product, the guiding principle of operations for a market leader is "Just ship." Explain and discuss the changes in marketing strategy the firm must follow after the tornado.

10. Evaluate this statement: A brand is much more than a name, and branding is a strategy problem, not a naming problem.

Internet Exercise

1. United Technologies Corporation (UTC) provides a broad range of high-technology products and support services to the building systems and aerospace industries. Go to http://www.utc.com and identify UTC's major businesses (product lines).

CHAPTER

8

Managing Innovation and New Industrial Product Development

The long-term competitive position of most organizations is tied to their ability to innovate—to provide existing and new customers with a continuing stream of new products and services. Innovation is a high-risk and potentially rewarding process. After reading this chapter, you will understand:

1. The strategic processes, both formal and informal, through which product innovations take shape

2. The characteristics of innovation winners in high-technology markets

3. The factors that drive a firm's new product performance

4. The determinants of new product success and timeliness

With his American swagger and his hair bleached white, Tony Fadell stood out at button-down Philips Electronics, where he led an in-house operation designing … consumer electronics devices. It was there that he came up with the idea of marrying a Napster-like music store with a hard drive-based MP3 player. He shopped the concept around the Valley before Apple's Jon Rubenstein snapped it up and put Fadell in charge of the engineering team that built the first iPod.[1]

Once prototypes were developed, CEO Steve Jobs worked closely with the team and was instrumental in molding the shape, feel, and design of the device.[2] Through product innovations from the iPod to the iPhone and iPad and through strategic foresight and the careful management of its brand, Apple has transformed itself from a niche computer company to one of the most valuable enterprises in the world.[3]

Many firms derive much of their sales and profits from recently introduced products. Indeed, best-practice firms generate about 48 percent of sales and 45 percent of profits from products commercialized in the past five years.[4] But the risks of product innovation are high; significant investments are involved, and the likelihood of failure is high. With shortening product life cycles and accelerating technological change, speed and agility are central to success in the innovation battle.

This chapter examines product innovation in the business marketing environment. The first section provides a perspective on the firm's management of innovation. Second, product innovation is positioned within a firm's overall technological strategy. Third, key dimensions of the new-product-development process are examined. Attention centers on the forces that drive successful new product performance in the firm. The final section of the chapter explores the determinants of new product success and timeliness.

The Management of Innovation

Management practices in successful industrial firms reflect the realities of the innovation process itself. James Quinn asserts that "innovation tends to be individually motivated, opportunistic, customer responsive, tumultuous, nonlinear, and interactive in its development. Managers can plan overall directions and goals, but surprises are likely to abound."[5] Clearly, some new-product-development efforts are the outgrowth of deliberate strategies (intended strategies that become realized), whereas others result from emergent strategies (realized strategies that, at least initially, were never intended).[6] Bearing little resemblance to a rational, analytical process, many

---

[1]"After Steve Jobs: Apple's Next CEO—Tony Fadell (2)," June 26, 2008, accessed at http://money.cnn.com/galleries/2008/fortune/0806/gallery.apple_jobs_successors.fortune/2.html on July 16, 2008.

[2]Leander Kahney, "Inside Look at Birth of iPod," July 21, 2004, accessed at http://www.wired.com/gadgets/mac/news/2004/07/64286 on June 3, 2008.

[3]Joseph Beaulieu, "The Moat around Apple's iOS Platform Continues to Widen," April 20, 2011, Morningstar, Inc., p. 1, accessed at http://www.morningstar.com on May 25, 2011.

[4]John Hauser, Gerald J. Tellis, and Abbie Griffin, "Research on Innovation: A Review and Agenda for Marketing Science," *Marketing Science* 25 (November–December 2006): p. 707.

[5]James B. Quinn, "Managing Innovation: Controlled Chaos," *Harvard Business Review* 63 (May–June 1985): p. 83.

[6]Henry Mintzberg and James A. Walton, "Of Strategies, Deliberate and Emergent," *Strategic Management Journal* 6 (July–August 1985): pp. 257–272.

strategic decisions involving new products are rather messy, disorderly, and disjointed processes around which competing organizational factions contend. In studying successful innovative companies such as Sony, AT&T, and Hewlett-Packard, Quinn characterized the innovation process as controlled chaos:

> Many of the best concepts and solutions come from projects partly hidden or "bootlegged" by the organization. Most successful managers try to build some slack or buffers into their plans to hedge their bets.... They permit chaos and replications in early investigations, but insist on much more formal planning and controls as expensive development and scale-up proceed. But even at these later stages, these managers have learned to maintain flexibility and to avoid the tyranny of paper plans.[7]

Some new products result from a planned, deliberate process, but others follow a more circuitous and chaotic route.[8] Why? Research suggests that strategic activity within a large organization falls into two broad categories: induced and autonomous strategic behavior.[9]

Induced Strategic Behavior

Induced strategic behavior is consistent with the firm's traditional concept of strategy. It takes place in relationship to its familiar external environment (for example, its customary markets). By manipulating various administrative mechanisms, top management can influence the perceived interests of managers at the organization's middle and operational levels and keep strategic behavior in line with the current strategy course. For example, existing reward and measurement systems may direct managers' attention to some market opportunities and not to others. Examples of induced strategic behavior or deliberate strategies might emerge around product-development efforts for existing markets.

Autonomous Strategic Behavior

During any period, most strategic activity in large, complex firms is likely to fit into the induced behavior category. However, large, resource-rich firms are likely to possess a pool of entrepreneurial potential at operational levels, which expresses itself in autonomous strategic initiatives. The 3M Company encourages its technical employees to devote 15 percent of their work time to developing their own ideas. Through the personal efforts of individual employees, new products are born. For example,

- Gary Fadell is the engineering genius behind the iPod.

- Art Fry championed Post-it notes at 3M.

- P. D. Estridge promoted the personal computer at IBM.

- Stephanie L. Kwolek advanced the bulletproof material Kevlar at DuPont.

---

[7]Quinn, "Managing Innovation," p. 82.

[8]This section is based on Michael D. Hutt, Peter H. Reingen, and John R. Ronchetto Jr., "Tracing Emergent Processes in Marketing Strategy Formation," *Journal of Marketing* 52 (January 1988): pp. 4–19.

[9]Robert A. Burgelman, "A Process Model of Internal Corporate Venturing in the Diversified Major Firm," *Administrative Science Quarterly* 28 (April 1983): pp. 223–244.

- Michimosa Fujino championed the HondaJet that may shake up the small-jet business with the same value proposition—high fuel efficiency and sleek design—that the first-generation Honda Civic used to rattle U.S. auto manufacturers 30 years ago.[10]

"Civic of the Sky"   Senior executives at Honda and industry analysts alike believe that the HondaJet can quickly gain 10 percent of the small-jet market and turn a profit in three to four years. Compared to the popular Cessna Citation CJ1+ that seats four to six passengers, the HondaJet is priced at $3.65 million, $880,000 below the Cessna, uses about 22 percent less fuel, has 20 percent more passenger cabin space, and boasts the fit and finish of a luxury car.

Now in his mid-forties, Mr. Fujino has tirelessly promoted his idea for two decades. He succeeded in keeping the project alive by nurturing ties to senior executives and by tying his risk-taking to Honda's broader efforts to rekindle a spirit of innovation. Although formal reviews of the jet project have been intense and even "ugly" at times, he persevered because, behind the scenes, some senior executives enthusiastically supported his efforts. A crucial turning point for the project came at a critical board meeting where Mr. Fujino was presenting the idea. After an awkward start and what he describes as a "cold glaze" from some board members, "he was able to drive home the jet's potential when he analogized it to Honda's breakthrough car, calling the jet a 'Civic of the sky.'"[11]

Autonomous strategic behavior is conceptually equivalent to entrepreneurial activity and introduces new categories of opportunity into the firm's planning process. Managers at the product-market level conceive of market opportunities that depart from the current strategy course, then engage in product-championing activities to mobilize resources and create momentum for further development of the product. Emphasizing political rather than administrative channels, product champions question the firm's current concept of strategy and, states Robert Burgelman, "provide top management with the opportunity to rationalize, retroactively, successful autonomous strategic behavior."[12] Through these political mechanisms, successful autonomous strategic initiatives, or emergent strategies, can become integrated into the firm's concept of strategy.

Clayton M. Christensen and Michael E. Raynor observe:

> Emergent strategies result from managers' responses to problems or opportunities that were unforeseen in the analysis and planning stages of the deliberate strategy making process. When the efficacy of that strategy … is recognized, it is possible to formalize it, improve it, and exploit it, thus transforming an emergent strategy into a deliberate one.[13]

---

[10]This discussion is based on Norihiko Shirouzu, "Mr. Fujino's Bumpy Flight Lands Honda in the Jet Age," *The Wall Street Journal*, June 18, 2007, pp. B1 and B3.

[11]Ibid., p. B3.

[12]Robert A. Burgelman, "Corporate Entrepreneurship and Strategic Management: Insights from a Process Study," *Management Science* 29 (December 1983): p. 1352.

[13]Clayton M. Christensen and Michael E. Raynor, *The Innovator's Solution: Creating and Sustaining Successful Growth* (Boston: Harvard Business School Press, 2003), pp. 215–216.

TABLE 8.1	INDUCED VERSUS AUTONOMOUS STRATEGIC BEHAVIOR: SELECTED CHARACTERISTICS OF THE MARKETING STRATEGY FORMULATION PROCESS	
	Induced	**Autonomous**
Activation of the strategic decision process	An individual manager defines a market need that converges on the organization's concept of strategy.	An individual manager defines a market need that diverges from the organization's concept of strategy.
Nature of the screening process	A formal screening of technical and market merit is made using established administrative procedures.	An informal network assesses technical and market merit.
Type of innovation	Incremental (e.g., new product development for existing markets uses existing organizational resources).	Major (e.g., new product development projects require new combinations of organizational resources).
Nature of communication	Consistent with organizational work flow.	Departs from organizational work flow in early phase of decision process.
Major actors	Prescribed by the regular channel of hierarchical decision making.	An informal network emerges based on mobilization efforts of the product champion.
Decision roles	Roles and responsibilities for participants in the strategy formulation process are well defined.	Roles and responsibilities of participants are poorly defined in the initial phases but become more formalized as the strategy formulation process evolves.
Implications for strategy	Strategic alternatives are considered and commitment to a particular strategic course evolves.	Commitment to a particular strategic course emerges in the early phases through the sponsorship efforts of the product champion.

SOURCE: Adapted from Michael D. Hutt, Peter H. Reingen, and John R. Ronchetto Jr., "Tracing Emergent Processes in Marketing, Strategy Formation," *Journal of Marketing* 52 (January 1988): pp. 4–19. See also Clayton M. Christensen and Michael E. Raynor, *The Innovator's Solution: Creating and Sustaining Successful Growth* (Boston: Harvard Business School Press, 2003), pp. 213–231.

Product Championing and the Informal Network

Table 8.1 highlights several characteristics that may distinguish induced from autonomous strategic behavior. Autonomous strategic initiatives involve a set of actors and evoke strategic dialogue different from that found in induced initiatives. An individual manager, the product champion, assumes a central role in sensing an opportunity and in mobilizing an informal network to explore the idea's technical feasibility and market potential. A **product champion** is an organization member who creates, defines, or adopts an idea for an innovation and is willing to assume significant risk (for example, position or prestige) to successfully implement the innovation.[14]

Senior managers at 3M do not commit to a project unless a champion emerges and do not abandon the effort unless the champion "gets tired." Emphasizing a rich culture of innovation embraced by all employees, senior executives at 3M also encourage product-championing behavior and calculated risk-taking. Moreover, they tolerate what 3M employees call "well-intentioned" failures.[15]

---

[14]Modesto A. Maidique, "Entrepreneurs, Champions, and Technological Innovations," *Sloan Management Review* 21 (Spring 1980): pp. 59–70; see also Donna Kelly and Hyunsuk Lee, "Managing Innovation Champions: The Impact of Project Characteristics on the Direct Manager Role," *Journal of Product Innovation Management* 27 (December 2010): pp. 1007–1019.

[15]George S. Day, "Managing the Market Learning Process," *Journal of Business and Industrial Marketing* 17 (4, 2002): p. 246.

Compared with induced strategic behavior, autonomous or entrepreneurial initiatives are more likely to involve a communication process that departs from the regular work flow and the hierarchical decision-making channels. The decision roles and responsibilities of managers in this informal network are poorly defined in the early phases of the strategy-formulation process but become more formalized as the process evolves. Note in Table 8.1 that autonomous strategic behavior entails a creeping commitment toward a particular strategy course. By contrast, induced strategic initiatives are more likely to involve administrative mechanisms that encourage a more formal and comprehensive assessment of strategic alternatives at various levels in the firm's planning hierarchy.

Conditions Supporting Corporate Entrepreneurship[16]

Entrepreneurial initiatives cannot be precisely planned but they can be nurtured and encouraged. First, the availability of appropriate rewards can enhance a manager's willingness to assume the risks associated with entrepreneurial activity. Second, as 3M illustrates, senior management can assume an instrumental role in fostering innovation by promoting entrepreneurial initiatives and encouraging calculated risk-taking. Third, resource availability, including some slack time, is needed to provide entrepreneurs with some degrees of freedom to explore new possibilities. 3M encourages scientists to devote up to 15 percent of their time to particular projects that they find personally interesting. Fourth, an organizational structure supporting corporate entrepreneurship provides the administrative mechanisms that bring more voices to the innovation process across the firm and allow ideas to be evaluated, selected, and implemented.[17]

What Motivates Entrepreneurs?   Recent research identifies two additional dimensions that motivate corporate entrepreneurs: (1) intrinsic motivation (the drive originating within oneself) and (2) work design (for example, the availability of challenging projects; opportunities to interact directly with customers and other entrepreneurs). Matthew R. Marvel and his research colleagues describe what technical corporate entrepreneurs desire in their job:

> They want their innovative efforts to be connected to customer problems that need to be solved—and important customer problems at that. To understand these problems, they need contact with customers. To get breakthrough ideas on how to solve these problems, they also need contact with other world-class technologists.[18]

Managing Technology

Kodak, Lockheed, IBM, and the management teams of other corporations failed to recognize the major technological opportunity that xerographic copying presented. These firms were among the many that turned down the chance to participate with

---

[16]This section is based on Matthew R. Marvel, Abbie Griffin, John Hebda, and Bruce Vojak, "Examining the Technical Corporate Entrepreneurs' Motivation: Voices from the Field," *Entrepreneurship Theory and Practice*, 31 (September 2007): pp. 753–768.

[17]Gary Hamel, "The Why, What, and How of Management Innovation," *Harvard Business Review* 84 (February 2006): pp. 72–84.

[18]Marvel, Griffin, Hebda, and Vojak, "Examining the Technical Corporate Entrepreneurs' Motivation," p. 764.

the small and unknown Haloid Company in refining and commercializing this technology. In the end, Haloid pursued it alone and transformed this one technological opportunity into the Xerox Corporation. Among the "tales of high tech," this remains a classic.[19] Technological change, Michael Porter asserts, is "a great equalizer, eroding the competitive advantage of even well-entrenched firms and propelling others to the forefront. Many of today's great firms grew out of technological changes that they were able to exploit."[20] Clearly, the long-run competitive position of most business-to-business firms depends on their ability to manage, increase, and exploit their technology base. This section explores the nature of development projects, the disruptive innovation model, and the defining attributes of successful innovators in fast-changing high-technology markets.

Classifying Development Projects

A first step in exploring the technology portfolio of a firm is to understand the different forms that development projects can take. Some development projects center on improving the manufacturing process, some on improving products, and others on both process and product improvements. All of these represent commercial development projects. By contrast, research and development is the precursor to commercial development. A firm's portfolio can include four types of development projects.[21]

1. **Derivative projects** center on incremental product enhancements (for example, a new feature), incremental process improvements (for example, a lower-cost manufacturing process), or incremental changes on both dimensions.

   Illustration: A feature-enhanced or cost-reduced Canon color copier.

2. **Platform projects** create the design and components shared by a set of products. These projects often involve a number of changes in both the product and the manufacturing process.

   Illustrations: A common motor in all Black & Decker hand tools; multiple applications of Intel's microprocessor.

3. **Breakthrough projects** establish new core products and new core processes that differ fundamentally from previous generations.

   Illustrations: Computer disks and fiber-optic cable created new product categories.

4. **Research and development** is the creation of knowledge concerning new materials and technologies that eventually leads to commercial development.[22]

   Illustration: Cisco Systems' development of communications technology that underlies its networking systems used by diverse customers such as retailers, banks, and hotel chains.

---

[19]For a related discussion of Xerox's technology blunders, see Andrew Hargadon, *How Breakthroughs Happen: The Surprising Truth about How Companies Innovate* (Boston: Harvard Business School Press, 2003), pp. 168–182.

[20]Michael E. Porter, "Technology and Competitive Advantage," *Journal of Business Strategy* 6 (Winter 1985): p. 60; and Tamara J. Erickson, John F. Magee, Philip A. Roussel, and Komol N. Saad, "Managing Technology as Business Strategy," *Sloan Management Review* 31 (Spring 1990): pp. 73–83.

[21]This discussion is based on Steven C. Wheelwright and Kim B. Clark, "Creating Project Plans to Focus Product Development," *Harvard Business Review* 70 (March–April 1992): pp. 70–82.

[22]Ibid., p. 74.

A Product-Family Focus

A particular technology may provide the foundation or platform for several products. For example, Honda applies its multivalve cylinder technology to power-generation equipment, cars, business jets, motorcycles, and lawn mowers.[23] Products that share a common platform but have different specific features and enhancements required for different sets of consumers constitute a **product family**.[24] Each generation of a product family has a platform that provides the foundation for specific products targeted to different or complementary markets. By expanding on technical skills, market knowledge, and manufacturing competencies, entirely new product families may be formed, thereby creating new business opportunities.

Strategists argue that a firm should move away from planning that centers on single products and focus instead on families of products that can grow from a common platform. Consider Apple's stream of innovations—its operating system first helped it to gain market share in desktop and laptop computers.

> From there, new products and services appeared to just fall into place—the iTunes Store for purchasing music; new iPod models for different purposes; video playback on the iPod combined with the distribution of video content from the iTunes store; and finally, the iPhone ...[25]

The move toward a product-family perspective requires close interfunctional working relationships, a long-term view of technology strategy, and a multiple-year commitment of resources. Although this approach offers significant competitive leverage, Steven Wheelwright and Kim Clark note that companies often fail to invest adequately in platforms: "The reasons vary, but the most common is that management lacks an awareness of the strategic value of platforms and fails to create well-thought-out platform projects."[26]

The Disruptive Innovation Model[27]

Special insights into innovation management come from examining the rate at which products are improving and customers can use those improvements. For example, when personal computers were first introduced in the early 1980s, typists often had to pause for the Intel 286 chip to catch up. But today, only the most demanding customers can fully use the speed and performance of personal computers. For many products, from Excel spreadsheets to application-enriched handsets and information appliances, few customers absorb the performance features that innovating companies include as they introduce new and improved products.

---

[23]T. Michael Nevens, Gregory L. Summe, and Bro Uttal, "Commercializing Technology: What the Best Companies Do," *Harvard Business Review* 60 (May–June 1990): pp. 154–163; see also C. K. Prahalad, "Weak Signals versus Strong Paradigms," *Journal of Marketing Research* 32 (August 1995): pp. iii–vi.

[24]Marc H. Meyer and James M. Utterback, "The Product Family and the Dynamics of Core Capability," *Sloan Management Review* 34 (Spring 1993): pp. 29–47; see also Dwight L. Gertz and João P. A. Baptista, *Grow to Be Great: Breaking the Downsizing Cycle* (New York: The Free Press, 1995), pp. 92–103.

[25]Beaulieu, "The Moat around Apple's iOS Platform," pp. 1–2.

[26]Wheelwright and Clark, "Creating Project Plans," p. 74.

[27]This section is based on Christensen and Raynor, The Innovator's Solution, pp. 31–65. See also, Ashish Sood and Gerard J. Tellis, "Technological Evolution and Radical Innovation," *Journal of Marketing* 69 (July 2005): pp. 152–168.

FIGURE 8.1 | THE DISRUPTIVE INNOVATION MODEL

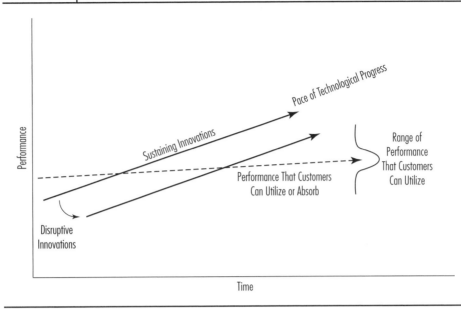

Overshooting   Figure 8.1 shows, first, a rate of improvement in a given product or technology that customers can use, represented by the dotted line, sloping slightly upward across the chart. Second, for a given product, innovating firms offer a trajectory of improvement as they develop new and improved versions over time. The pace of technological progress usually outstrips the ability of many, if not most, customers to keep up with it (see the steeply sloping solid lines in Figure 8.1). Therefore, as companies strive to make better products they can sell at higher profit margins to the most demanding customers, they overshoot and provide much more performance than mainstream customers are able to use.

Sustaining versus Disruptive Innovation   Third, from Figure 8.1, a distinction is made between a sustaining innovation and a disruptive innovation. According to Clayton M. Christensen and Michael E. Raynor, "A sustaining innovation targets demanding, high-end customers with better performance than what was previously available (for example, incremental product improvements or breakthrough products)."[28] A disruptive innovation represents a product or service that is not as good as currently available alternatives. "But disruptive technologies offer other benefits—typically, they are simpler, more convenient, and less expensive products that appeal to new or less-demanding customers."[29]

Disruptive Strategy Examples   Once a disruptive product or service gains a foothold, the improvement cycle begins and eventually it intersects with the needs

[28]Christensen and Raynor, *The Innovator's Solution*, p. 34.

[29]Ibid., p. 34.

INSIDE BUSINESS MARKETING

Disrupters Pull Different Innovation Levers

Before Intuit developed QuickBooks, the prevailing assumption was that software designed for small-business owners had to have accounting features. But by visiting customer prospects and watching them work, Intuit managers learned that small businesses did not care about, nor did they understand, most of those accounting features. Above all, they just wanted to make sure that they did not run out of cash. In recounting the story, Scott Cook, Intuit's founder observes:

> It was only by savoring the surprise and watching prospects work that we saw it. And that caused us to develop the first

accounting software with no accounting in it. And it became the market leader in a month … based on an entirely different mindset than the whole industry had.

Turning conventional wisdom on its head is what distributive innovations are all about. Disrupters redefine the notion of performance and use different innovation levers such as simplicity, convenience, accessibility, and affordability.

SOURCE: Scott D. Anthony, Mark W. Johnson, Joseph V. Sinfield, and Elizabeth J. Altman, *The Innovator's Guide to Growth* (Boston: Harvard Business School Press, 2008), p. 7.

of more demanding customers. For example, Xerox held a commanding position in the high-speed photocopier business until Canon's simple tabletop copier disrupted that strategy in the early 1980s. Likewise, Southwest Airlines disrupted established airlines; Amazon.com disrupted traditional bookstores; Staples disrupted small stationery stores and distributors of office supplies; and Google disrupted directories of all sorts, including Yellow Pages.

Types of Disruptive Strategies   Disruptive strategies can take two forms: low-end disruptions and new-market disruptions. Table 8.2 describes the characteristics of these strategies and contrasts them with a strategy geared to sustaining innovations. Note, for example, that the targeted customers for low-end disruption are *over-served customers*, whereas new-market disruptions target *nonconsumption*—customers who historically lacked the resources to buy and use the product.

Low-End Strategy Tests   For a low-end disruptive strategy to succeed, two requirements must be met:

1. There should be customers at the low end of the market who are eager to purchase a "good-enough" product if they could acquire it at a lower price.

2. The company must be able to create a business model that can yield attractive profits at the discount prices that are needed to attract customers at the low end of the market.

    Example: Southwest Airlines drew customers away from the major carriers.

New-Market Strategy Tests   For new-market disruptions, at least one and generally both of these requirements must be met:

1. A large population can be defined who have historically lacked the money, equipment, or skill to acquire this product or service for themselves.

TABLE 8.2 | **ALTERNATIVE APPROACHES TO CREATING NEW-GROWTH BUSINESSES**

Dimensions	Sustaining Innovations	Low-End Disruptions	New-Market Disruptions
Targeted performance of the product or service	Incremental or break-through improvement in attributes most valued by the industry's most demanding customers	Performance that is good enough to meet performance requirements at the low end of the mainstream market	Lower performance on key attributes but enhanced performance on new attributes, particularly simplicity and convenience
Targeted customers	Targets the most profitable customers in the mainstream markets who are willing to pay a premium for improved performance	Serves over-served customers in the low end of the mainstream market	Targets customers who historically lacked the money or skill to buy and use the product (i.e., nonconsumers)
Profitability of the business model	Improves or maintains profit margins by exploiting the existing processes, cost structure, and current competitive advantages	Uses a new operating or financial approach or both, that can earn attractive profits at the discount prices required to win business at the low end of the market	Business model must make money at lower price per unit sold and at unit production volumes that initially will be small

SOURCE: Reprinted by permission of the Harvard Business Review. From "Three Approaches to Creating New Growth Business" in The Innovator's Solution by Clayton Christensen, p. 51. Copyright © 2003 by the Harvard Business School Publishing Corporation; all rights reserved.

2. Present customers need to go to an inconvenient location to use the product or service.

   Examples: Canon desktop photocopiers were a new-market disruption in the 1980s because they enabled employees to make their own copies rather than taking their originals to the corporate high-speed copying center to get help from technical specialists. Also, Research in Motion Limited's BlackBerry was a new-market disruption relative to notebook computers.

A Final Litmus Test   Once an innovation passes the tests that apply to low-end or new-market disruptions, a final critical test remains: The innovation must be disruptive to all the significant competitive firms in the industry. If one or more of the significant industry players is pursuing the strategy, the odds will be stacked against the new entrant.

Illustration: A New-Market Disruption[30]

One principle for developing disruptive ideas is to "do what competitors won't." For instance, Salesforce.com has pursued a strategy that leaders in the customer relationship (CRM) software market—namely, SAP and Oracle—found unappealing. Before Salesforce.com entered the market, both of these formidable rivals sold relatively expensive solutions that required customization and installation to ensure proper

---

[30]Scott D. Anthony, Mark W. Johnson, Joseph V. Sinfield, and Elizabeth J. Altman, *The Innovator's Guide to Growth: Putting Disruptive Innovation to Work* (Boston: Harvard Business Press, 2008), pp. 125–126.

integration with the customer's other software packages. Customers also were charged an ongoing fee for maintenance of the installed software.

Adopting a Different Approach   Salesforce.com provides customers with access to programs that reside on centralized host computers. Users access these databases through the Web for a modest monthly fee. While customers often find these hosted solutions to be occasionally slower and somewhat more difficult to readily integrate with other applications, they are flexible, easy to use, and quite economical—all defining characteristics of a disruptive innovation.

Scott D. Anthony and his colleagues observe that "Salesforce.com used several tactics that made its competitors unwilling or uninterested in immediately responding:

- It started with nonconsumption (that is, selling to small customers purchasing their first CRM software).

- It targeted a customer its competitors considered undesirable (that is, small and medium-sized businesses that were the least profitable for rivals).

- It used a different distribution channel (that is, on the Web).

- It created a business model that did not depend on a revenue stream of vital importance to incumbents."[31] (By centering on installation and customization fees, SAP and Oracle did not find the fees related to a hosted model to be appealing.)

Innovation Winners in High-Technology Markets

In rapidly changing industries with short product life cycles and quickly shifting competitive landscapes, a firm must continually innovate to keep its offerings aligned with the market. A firm's ability to cope with change in a high-velocity industry is a key to competitive success. Shona Brown and Kathleen Eisenhardt provide an intriguing comparison of successful versus less successful product innovation in the computer industry.[32] Successful innovators were firms that were on schedule, on time to the market, and on target in addressing customer needs. The study found that firms with a successful record of product innovation use different organizational structures and processes than their competitors. In particular, four distinguishing characteristics marked the innovation approach of successful firms.

Limited Structure   Creating successful products to meet changing customer needs requires flexibility, but successful product innovators combine this flexibility with a few rules that are never broken. First, strict priorities for new products are established and tied directly to resource allocation. This allows managers to direct attention to the most promising opportunities, avoiding the temptation to pursue too many attractive opportunities. Second, managers set deadlines for a few key milestones and always meet them. Third, responsibility for a limited number of major outcomes is set. For example, at one firm, engineering managers were responsible

---

[31]Ibid., p. 126.

[32]This section is based on Shona L. Brown and Kathleen M. Eisenhardt, "The Art of Continuous Change: Linking Complexity Theory and Time-Paced Evolution in Relentlessly Shifting Organizations," *Administrative Science Quarterly* 42 (March 1997): pp. 1–34.

for product schedules while marketing managers were responsible for market defini-tion and product profitability. Although successful firms emphasized structure for a few areas (for example, priorities or deadlines), less successful innovators imposed more control—lockstep, checkpoint procedures for every facet of new product development—or virtually no structure at all. Successful firms strike a balance by using a structure that is neither so rigid as to stiffly control the process nor so chaotic that the process falls apart.

Real-Time Communication and Improvisation   Successful product innova-tors in the computer industry emphasize real-time communication within new-product-development teams *and* across product teams. Much of the communication occurs in formal meetings, but there is also extensive informal communication throughout the organization. Clear priorities and responsibilities, coupled with exten-sive communications, allow product developers to improvise. "In the context of jazz improvisation, this means creating music while adjusting to the changing musical interpretations of others. In the context of product innovation, it means creating a product while simultaneously adapting to changing markets and technologies."[33]

More formally, then, **improvisation** involves the design and execution of actions that approach convergence with each other in time.[34] The shorter the elapsed time between the design and implementation of an activity, the more that activity is improvisational. Successful firms expect constant change, and new product teams have the freedom to act. One manager noted: "We fiddle right up to the end" of the new-product-development process. Real-time communications among members of the product development team, coupled with limited structure, provide the founda-tion for such improvisation.

Experimentation: Probing into the Future   Some firms make a large bet on one version of the future, whereas others fail to update future plans in light of chang-ing competition. Creators of successful product portfolios did not invest in any one version of the future but, instead, used a variety of low-cost probes to create options. Examples of low-cost probes include developing experimental products for new mar-kets, entering into a strategic alliance with leading-edge customers to better under-stand future needs, or conducting regular planning sessions dedicated to the future. In turbulent industries, strategists cannot accurately predict which of many possible versions of the future will arrive. Probes create more possible responses for managers when the future does arrive while lowering the probability of being surprised by unanticipated futures.

Time Pacing   Successful product innovators carefully manage the transition between current and future projects, whereas less successful innovators let each proj-ect unfold according to its own schedule. Successful innovators, like Intel, practice time pacing—a strategy for competing in fast-changing markets by creating new products at predictable time intervals.[35] Organization members carefully

---

[33]Ibid., p. 15.

[34]Christine Moorman and Anne S. Miner, "The Convergence of Planning and Execution: Improvisation in New Product Development," *Journal of Marketing* 62 (July 1998): p. 3.

[35]Kathleen M. Eisenhardt and Shona L. Brown, "Time Pacing: Competing in Markets That Won't Stand Still," *Harvard Business Review* 76 (March-April 1998): pp. 59–69.

choreograph and understand transition processes. For example, marketing managers might begin work on the definition of the next product while engineering is completing work on the current product and moving it to manufacturing. Time pacing motivates managers to anticipate change and can have a strong psychological impact across the organization. "Time pacing creates a relentless sense of urgency around meeting deadlines and concentrates individual and team energy around common goals."[36]

The New-Product-Development Process

To sustain their competitive advantage, leading-edge firms such as Canon, Microsoft, and 3M make new product development a top management priority. They directly involve managers and employees from across the organization to speed actions and decisions. Because new product ventures can represent a significant risk as well as an important opportunity, new product development requires systematic thought. The high expectations for new products are often not fulfilled. Worse, many new industrial products fail. Although the definitions of failure are somewhat elusive, research suggests that 40 percent of industrial products fail to meet objectives.[37] Even though there may be some debate over the number of failures, there is no debate that a new product rejected by the market constitutes a substantial waste to the firm and to society.

This section explores: (1) the forces that drive a firm's new product performance, (2) the sources of new product ideas, (3) cross-functional barriers to successful innovation, and (4) team-based processes used in new product development. A promising method for bringing the "voice of the consumer" directly into the development process is also explored.

What Drives a Firm's New Product Performance?

A benchmarking study sought to uncover the critical success factors that drive a firm's new product performance.[38] It identified three factors (Figure 8.2): (1) the quality of a firm's new-product-development process, (2) the resource commitments made to new product development, and (3) the new product strategy.

Process Successful companies use a high-quality new-product-development process—they give careful attention to executing the activities and decision points that new products follow from the idea stage to launch and beyond. The benchmarking study identified the following characteristics among high-performing firms:

- The firms emphasized upfront market and technical assessments before projects moved into the development phase.

---

[36] Ibid., p. 60.

[37] Robert G. Cooper, Scott J. Edgett, and Elko J. Kleinschmidt, "Benchmarking Best NPD Practices–I," *Research Technology Management* 47 (January–February 2004): pp. 31–43; see also Robert G. Cooper and Scott J. Edgett, "Maximizing Productivity in Product Innovation," *Research Technology Management* 51 (March–April 2008): pp. 47–58.

[38] Robert G. Cooper and Elko J. Kleinschmidt, "Benchmarking Firms' New Product Performance and Practices," *Engineering Management Review* 23 (Fall 1995): pp. 112–120; see also Robert G. Cooper, Scott J. Edgett, and Elko J. Kleinschmidt, "Benchmarking Best NPD Practices–II," *Research Technology Management* 47 (May–June 2004): pp. 50–59.

FIGURE 8.2 | THE MAJOR DRIVERS OF A FIRM'S NEW PRODUCT PERFORMANCE

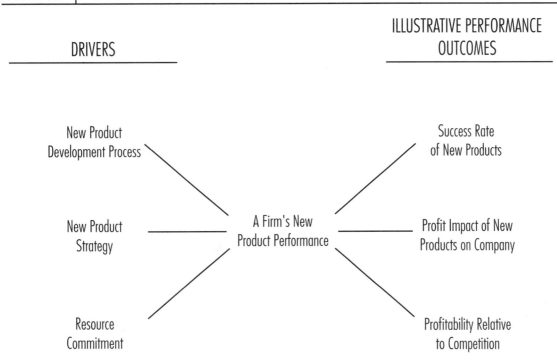

SOURCE: Adapted from Robert G. Cooper and Elko J. Kleinschmidt, "Benchmarking Firms' New Product Performance and Practices," *Engineering Management Review* 23 (Fall 1995): pp. 112–120.

- The process featured complete descriptions of the product concept, product benefits, positioning, and target markets before development work was initiated.

- Tough project go/kill decision points were included in the process, and the kill option was actually used.

- The new product process was flexible—certain stages could be skipped in line with the nature and risk of a particular project.

Detailed upfront homework on the product concept, the likely market response, and the product's technical feasibility, along with a thorough business and financial assessment, are important dimensions of the process successful product creators follow.

Resource Commitments   Adequate resources were invested in new product development in top-performing firms. Three ingredients were important here:

1. Top management committed the resources necessary to meet the firm's objectives for the total product effort.

2. R&D budgets were adequate and aligned with the stated new product objectives.

3. The necessary personnel were assigned and were relieved from other duties so that they could give full attention to new product development.

Research suggests that rather than being imposed by top management, the creative potential of new-product-development teams "is likely to be more fully realized when they are given the flexibility—within a broad strategic directive—to determine their own project controls and especially to pursue their own processes and procedures."[39]

New Product Strategy A clear and visible new product strategy was another driver of a firm's new product performance (see Figure 8.2). Successful firms like 3M set aggressive new product performance goals (for example, x percent of company sales and profit from new products) as a basic corporate goal and communicate it to all employees. In turn, Robert Cooper and Elko Kleinschmidt report that successful firms centered development efforts on clearly defined arenas—particular product, market, and technology domains—to direct the new product program:

> The new product strategy specifies "the arenas where we'll play the game," or perhaps more important, where we won't play … what's in bounds and out of bounds. Without arenas defined, the search for new product ideas or opportunities is unfocused.[40]

Anticipating Competitive Reactions[41]

Two-thirds of new product introductions trigger reactions by competitors. Consequently, business marketers can improve the odds of new-product-launch success by implementing a strong **competitor orientation** before and during the launch. Here the new product strategist develops detailed scenarios that provide a guide for countering different competitive responses. Competitors are strongly motivated to react when: (1) the new product represents a major threat to their market and (2) the market is experiencing a high rate of growth. Competitors are also more inclined to react when extensive marketing communications by the innovating firm enhance the visibility of the new product introduction.

Alternatively, if the new product introduction does not pose a direct challenge to the competitor's market, a reaction is less likely. Recent research suggests that radically new products or products that target niche markets are less likely to spawn competitive responses.

Sources of New Product Ideas

The business marketer should be alert to new product ideas and their sources, both inside and outside the company. Internally, new product ideas may flow from

---

[39]Joseph M. Bonner, Robert W. Ruekert, and Orville C. Walker Jr., "Upper Management Control of New Product Development Projects and Project Performance," *Journal of Product Innovation Management* 19 (May 2002): p. 243.

[40]Cooper and Kleinschmidt, "Benchmarking," p. 117; see also Robert G. Cooper and Scott J. Edgett, "Developing a Product Innovation and Technology Strategy for Your Business," *Research Technology Management* 53 (May–June 2010): pp. 33–40.

[41]Marion Debruyne, Rudy Moenaert, Abbie Griffin, Susan Hart, Erik Jan Hultink, and Henry Robben, "The Impact of New Product Launch Strategies on Competitive Reaction in Industrial Markets," *Journal of Product Innovation Management* 19 (March 2002): pp. 159–170; see also Beth A. Walker, Dimitri Kapelianis, and Michael D. Hutt, "Competitive Cognition," *MIT Sloan Management Review* 46 (Summer 2005): pp. 10–12.

B2B TOP PERFORMERS

Inviting New Product Suggestions

Leading-edge business marketing strategists gain valuable market insights by inviting their customers to post content on product Web sites. Salesforce.com, the leading provider of hosted customer relationship management software services, asked for and received thousands of customer suggestions for product upgrades. The company's marketing and development managers were overwhelmed by the number and diversity of the suggestions and could not agree on which features to add. Then, the firm launched its IdeaExchange, a Web site application that not only invites customers to suggest new product features but also to vote on them. The most popular ideas now float to the top of the list, while the less popular ones fade away. By defining customer priorities and setting clear new product goals, the company's development cycle has been dramatically reduced.

SOURCE: Dick Martin, *Secrets of the Marketing Masters* (New York: AMACOM, 2009), p. 155.

salespersons who are close to customer needs, from R&D specialists who are close to new technological developments, and from top management who know the company's strengths and weaknesses. Externally, ideas may come from channel members, such as distributors or customers, or from an assessment of competitive moves.

Eric von Hippel challenges the traditional view that marketers typically introduce new products to a passive market.[42] His research suggests that the customers in the business market often develop the idea for a new product and even select the supplier to make that product. The customer is responding to the perceived *capability* of the business marketer rather than to a specific physical product. This points up the need for involving customers in new product development and promoting corporate capability to consumers (idea generators).

Lead Users   Because many industrial product markets for high technology and, in particular, capital equipment consist of a small number of high-volume buying firms, special attention must be given to the needs of **lead users**. These include a small number of highly influential buying organizations that are consistent early adopters of new technologies.[43] Lead users face needs that are general in the marketplace, but they confront these needs months or years before most of that marketplace encounters them. In addition, they are positioned to benefit significantly by obtaining a solution that satisfies those needs. For example, if an automobile manufacturer wanted to design an innovative braking system, marketing managers might secure insights from auto racing teams, who have a strong need for better brakes. In turn, they might look to a related field like aerospace, where antilock braking systems were first developed so that military aircraft could land on short runways.[44]

---

[42]Eric von Hippel, "Get New Products from Customers," *Harvard Business Review* 60 (March–April 1982): pp. 117–122; see also Eric von Hippel, *The Sources of Innovation* (New York: Oxford University Press, 1988); Gerard A. Athaide and Rodney L. Stump, "A Taxonomy of Relationship Approaches during Technology Development in Technology-Based, Industrial Markets," *Journal of Product Innovation Management* 16 (September 1999): pp. 469–482.

[43]von Hippel, "Get New Products," pp. 120–121.

[44]Eric von Hippel, Stefan Thomke, and Mary Sonnack, "Creating Breakthroughs at 3M," *Harvard Business Review* 77 (September–October 1999): pp. 47–57.

FIGURE 8.3　|　**THE LEAD USER METHOD**

Phase	Central Focus	Description
Phase 1	Laying the Foundation	The team identifies target markets and secures support from internal stakeholders for the type and level of innovations desired.
Phase 2	Determining the Trends	The team talks to experts in the field who have a broad view of emerging technologies and pioneering applications in the particular area.
Phase 3	Identifying Lead Users	The team begins a networking process to identify lead users at the leading edge of the target market and to gather information that might contribute to breakthrough products.
Phase 4	Developing and Assessing Preliminary Product Ideas	The team begins to shape product ideas and to assess market potential and fit with company interests.
Phase 5	Developing the Breakthroughs	To design final concepts, the team hosts a workshop bringing together lead users with other in-house managers. After further refinement, the team presents its recommendations to senior management.

SOURCE: Adapted with modifications from Eric von Hippel, Stefan Thomke, and Mary Sonnack, "Creating Breakthroughs at 3M," *Harvard Business Review* 77 (September–October 1999), p. 52.

The Lead User Method　Lead user projects are conducted by a cross-functional team that includes four to six managers from marketing and technical departments; one member serves as project leader. Team members typically spend 12 to 15 hours per week on the projects, which are usually completed in four to six weeks. Lead user projects proceed through five phases (Figure 8.3). 3M has now successfully used the lead user method in eight different divisions, and support among project teams and divisional managers is strong. For example, the Medical-Surgical Markets Group at 3M used the lead user method to unearth new product ideas and to identify a revolutionary approach to infection control.[45] 3M reports that sales in year 5 for funded lead user project ideas were more than eight times greater than those generated by traditional approaches to idea generation.[46] Other firms adopting a lead user focus include Verizon, Nestle, Pitney Bowes, and Philips.

Customer Visits　A popular approach among business marketers for gaining new product insights is customer visits. Here a cross-functional team visits a customer organization to secure a firsthand account of customer needs. Based on a carefully crafted interview guide, in-depth interviews are conducted with key buying influentials to uncover user problems, needs, and desires. "The whole idea is to observe how

---

[45]Ibid., p. 56.

[46]"User Innovation: Changing Innovation Focus," *Strategic Direction* 23 (8, 2007): pp. 35–36.

customers use the product, to see firsthand how it fits into their business process, and to ask open-ended questions about their operations and business goals."[47]

Web-Based Methods for Improving Customer Inputs to Design Recognizing the ability of customers to innovate, many firms have developed tools that invite customers to design their own products. With these innovative toolkits, customers are given an array of features that can be configured, as desired, to create their own customized products. These toolkits often incorporate engineering and cost modules. To illustrate, if a customer wishes to change the length of a truck bed, the design tool automatically computes the additional cost and the associated changes that will be required in both the transmission and the engine. For aesthetic compatibility, the design tool might even modify the shape of the cab. Other examples: In its materials business, General Electric provides Web-based tools that customers use for designing better plastics products. Likewise, many software companies encourage users to add custom-designed modules to their standard products and then commercializes the best of those components.[48]

Determinants of New Product Performance and Timeliness

What factors are most important in determining the success or failure of the new product? Why are some firms faster than others in moving projects through the development process? Let's review the available evidence.

The Determinants of Success

Both strategic factors and a firm's proficiency in carrying out the new-product-development process determine new product success.[49] (See Figure 8.4.)

Strategic Factors Research suggests that four strategic factors appear to be crucial to new product success. The level of product advantage is the most important. **Product advantage** refers to customer perceptions of product superiority with respect to quality, cost–performance ratio, or function relative to competitors. Successful products offer clear benefits, such as reduced customer costs, and are of higher quality (for example, more durable) than competitors' products. A study of more than 100 new product projects in the chemical industry illustrates the point. Here, Robert Cooper and Elko Kleinschmidt assert, "The winners are new products that offer high relative product quality, have superior price/performance characteristics, provide good value for the money to the customer, are superior to competing

---

[47]Dick Martin, *Secrets of the Marketing Masters* (New York: AMACOM, 2009), p. 85; see also Edward F. McQuarrie, *Customer Visits: Building a Better Market Focus* (Armonk NY: M.E. Sharpe, 2008).

[48]Stephen Thomke and Eric von Hippel, "Customers as Innovators: A New Way to Create Value," *Harvard Business Review* 80 (April 2002): pp. 74–81.

[49]Mitzi M. Montoya-Weiss and Roger Calantone, "Determinants of New Product Performance: A Review and Meta- Analysis," *Journal of Product Innovation Management* 11 (November 1994): pp. 397–417; see also Robert G. Cooper, Scott J. Edgett, and Elko J. Kleinschmidt, "Benchmarking Best NPD Practices–III," *Research Technology Management* 47 (November–December 2004): pp. 43–55.

FIGURE 8.4 | **DETERMINANTS OF NEW BUSINESS PRODUCT SUCCESS**

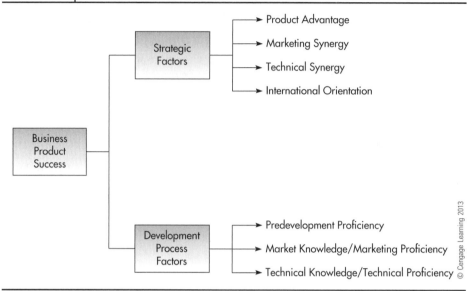

products in meeting customer needs, [and] have unique attributes and highly visible benefits that are easily seen by the customer."[50]

Marketing synergy and technical synergy are also pivotal in new product outcomes. **Marketing synergy** is the fit between the needs of the project and the firm's resources and skills in marketing (for example, personal selling or market research). By contrast, **technical synergy** concerns the fit between the needs of the project and the firm's R&D resources and competencies. New products that match the skills of the firm are likely to succeed.

In addition to the preceding three factors, an **international orientation** also contributes to the success of product innovation.[51] New products designed and developed to meet foreign requirements and targeted at world or nearest-neighbor export markets outperform domestic products on almost every measure, including success rate, profitability, and domestic and foreign market shares. Underlying this success is a strong international focus in market research, product testing with customers, trial selling, and launch efforts.

Development Process Factors   New product success is also associated with particular characteristics of the development process. **Predevelopment proficiency** provides the foundation for a successful product. Predevelopment involves several important tasks such as initial screening, preliminary market and technical

[50]Robert G. Cooper and Elko J. Kleinschmidt, "Major New Products: What Distinguishes the Winners in the Chemical Industry?" *Journal of Product Innovation Management* 10 (March 1993): p. 108; see also Roger Calantone, "Product Innovativeness Dimensions and Their Relationship with Product Advantage, Product Financial Performance, and Project Protocol," *Journal of Product Innovation Management* 27 (December 2010): pp. 991–1006.

[51]Elko J. Kleinschmidt and Robert G. Cooper, "The Performance Impact of an International Orientation on Product Innovation," *European Journal of Marketing* 22 (9, 1988): pp. 56–71; see also Ulrike de Brentani, Elko J. Kleinschmidt, and Soren Salomo, "Success in Global New Product Development: Impact of Strategy and the Behavioral Environment of the Firm," *Journal of Product Innovation Management* 27 (March 2010): pp. 143–160.

assessment, detailed market research study, and preliminary business/financial analysis. Firms that are skilled in completing these upfront tasks are likely to experience new product success.

Market knowledge and **marketing proficiency** are also pivotal in new product outcomes. As might be expected, business marketers with a solid understanding of market needs are likely to succeed. Robert Cooper describes the market planning for a successful product he examined: "Market information was very complete: there was a solid understanding of the customer's needs, wants, and preferences; of the customer's buying behavior and price sensitivity; of the size and trends of the market; and of the competitive situation. Finally, the market launch was well planned, well targeted, proficiently executed, and backed by appropriate resources."[52]

Technical knowledge and **technical proficiency** are other important dimensions of the new-product-development process. When technical developers have a strong base of knowledge about the technical aspects of a potential new product, and when they can proficiently pass through the stages of the new-product-development process (for example, product development, prototype testing, pilot production, and production start-up), these products succeed.

Fast-Paced Product Development

Rapid product development offers a number of competitive advantages. To illustrate, speed enables a firm to respond to rapidly changing markets and technologies. Moreover, fast product development is usually more efficient because lengthy development processes tend to waste resources on peripheral activities and changes.[53] Of course, although an overemphasis on speed may create other pitfalls, it is becoming an important strategic weapon, particularly in high-technology markets.

Matching the Process to the Development Task   How can a firm accelerate product development? A major study of the global computer industry provides some important benchmarks.[54] Researchers examined 72 product development projects of leading U.S., European, and Asian computer firms. The findings suggest that multiple approaches are used to increase speed in product development. Speed comes from properly matching the approach to the product development task at hand.

Compressed Strategy for Predictable Projects   For well-known markets and technologies, a **compression strategy** speeds development. This strategy views product development as a predictable series of steps that can be compressed. Speed comes from carefully planning these steps and shortening the time it takes to complete each one. This research indicates that the compressed strategy increased the speed of product development for products that had predictable designs and that were targeted for stable and mature markets. Mainframe computers fit into this category—they rely on proprietary hardware, have more predictable designs from project to project, and compete in a mature market.

---

[52]Robert G. Cooper, *Winning at New Products: Accelerating the Process from Idea to Launch* (Reading, MA: Addison-Wesley, 1993), p. 27; see also Robert G. Cooper, "Perspective: The Stage-Gate® Idea to Launch Process—Update, What's New, and NextGen Systems," *Journal of Product Innovation Management* 25 (May 2008): pp. 213–232.

[53]See, for example, Robert G. Cooper and Elko J. Kleinschmidt, "Determinants of Timeliness in Product Development," *Journal of Product Innovation Management* 11 (November 1994): pp. 381–417.

[54]Kathleen M. Eisenhardt and Behnam N. Tabrizi, "Accelerating Adaptive Processes: Product Innovation in the Global Computer Industry," *Administrative Science Quarterly* 40 (March 1995): pp. 84–110.

Experiential Strategy for Unpredictable Projects For uncertain markets and technologies, an **experiential strategy** accelerates product development. The underlying assumption of this strategy, explain Kathleen Eisenhardt and Behnam Tabrizi, is that "product development is a highly uncertain path through foggy and shifting markets and technologies. The key to fast product development is, then, rapidly building intuition and flexible options in order to learn quickly about and shift with uncertain environments."[55]

Under these conditions, speed comes from multiple design iterations, extensive testing, frequent milestones, and a powerful leader who can keep the product team focused. Here real-time interactions, experimentation, and flexibility are essential. The research found that the experiential strategy increased the speed of product development for unpredictable projects such as personal computers—a market characterized by rapidly evolving technology and unpredictable patterns of competition.

Summary

Product innovation is a high-risk and potentially rewarding process. Sustained growth depends on innovative products that respond to existing or emerging consumer needs. Effective managers of innovation channel and control its main directions but have learned to stay flexible and expect surprises. Within the firm, marketing managers pursue strategic activity that falls into two broad categories: induced and autonomous strategic behavior.

New-product-development efforts for existing businesses or market-development projects for the firm's present products are the outgrowth of induced strategic initiatives. In contrast, autonomous strategic efforts take shape outside the firm's current concept of strategy, depart from the current course, and center on new categories of business opportunity; middle managers initiate the project, champion its development, and, if successful, see the project integrated into the firm's concept of strategy. Corporate entrepreneurs thrive in a culture where senior managers promote and reward innovative behavior, encourage risk-taking, and provide the administrative mechanisms to screen, develop, and implement new product ideas.

The long-run competitive position of most business marketing firms depends on their ability to manage and increase their technological base. Core competencies provide the basis for products and product families. Each generation of a product family has a platform that serves as the foundation for specific products targeted at different or complementary market applications. Because companies keep working to make better products, they can sell at higher profit margins to the most demanding customers, and they often overshoot the needs of mainstream customers. A sustaining innovation provides demanding high-end customers with improved performance, whereas disruptive innovations target new or less-demanding customers with an easy-to-use, less expensive alternative that is "good enough." Disruptive strategies take two forms: low-end and new-market disruptions.

Firms that are successful innovators in turbulent markets combine limited structures (for example, priorities, deadlines) with extensive communication and the freedom to improvise on current projects. These successful product creators also explore

---

[55]Ibid., p. 91.

the future by experimenting with a variety of low-cost probes and build a relentless sense of urgency in the organization by creating new products at predictable time intervals (i.e., time pacing).

Effective new product development requires a thorough knowledge of customer needs and a clear grasp of the technological possibilities. Lead user analysis and customer visits often uncover valuable new product opportunities. Top-performing firms execute the new-product-development process proficiently, provide adequate resources to support new product objectives, and develop clear new product strategy. Both strategic factors and the firm's proficiency in executing the new-product-development process are critical to the success of industrial products. Fast-paced product development can provide an important source of competitive advantage. Speed comes from adapting the process to the new-product-development task at hand.

Discussion Questions

1. Rather than planning for and investing in just one version of the future, some firms use low-cost probes to experiment with many possible futures. Evaluate the wisdom of this approach.

2. In many markets, a new entrant might consider a strategy that provides potential customers with a product or technology that is "good enough" rather than "superior" to existing options. Describe the key tests that a disruptive strategy must pass in order to stack the odds for success in its favor.

3. Evaluate this statement: "To increase the speed of the new-product-development process, a firm might follow one strategy for unpredictable projects and an entirely different one for more predictable ones."

4. Compare and contrast induced and autonomous strategic behavior. Describe the role of the product champion in the new-product-development process.

5. Research by James Quinn suggests that few major innovations result from highly structured planning systems. What does this imply for the business marketer?

6. New industrial products that succeed provide clear-cut advantages to customers. Define product advantage and provide an example of a recent new product introduction that fits this definition.

7. Describe how Marriott might employ lead user analysis to better align its properties and services with the needs of the executive traveler.

8. In fast-changing high-tech industries, some firms have a better record in developing new products than others. Describe the critical factors that drive the new product performance of firms.

9. The breakthrough products for many companies did not emerge from the formal new-product-development process. Instead, they were championed by a few resourceful employees. What steps can organizations take to motivate and support corporate entrepreneurship?

10. Compare and contrast a low-end versus a new-market disruptive strategy.

Internet Exercise

1. Years ago, Corning sold dishes and glassware in the consumer market. Today, the firm might be characterized as a high-tech material science company that competes successfully in an array of business markets. Go to http://www.corning.com and identify its major product lines.

Managing Services for Business Markets

The important and growing market for business services poses special challenges and meaningful opportunities for the marketing manager. This chapter explores the unique aspects of business services and the special role they play in the business market environment. After reading this chapter, you will understand:

1. The value of systematically monitoring and managing the customer experience

2. The central role that business services assume in customer solutions

3. The roles that service quality, customer satisfaction, and loyalty assume in service market success

4. How offerings that combine products and services can be created to deliver innovative value propositions for customers

FedEx Corporation, the global package delivery service, mobilizes for trouble before it occurs: Each night, five empty FedEx jets roam over the United States.[1] Why? So the firm can respond on a moment's notice to unexpected events such as overbooking of packages in Atlanta or an equipment failure in Denver. FedEx excels by making promises to its customers and keeping them. The first major service organization to win the Malcolm Baldrige National Quality Award, FedEx makes specific promises about the timeliness and reliability of package delivery in its advertising and marketing communications. More importantly, FedEx aligns its personnel, facilities, information technology, and equipment to meet those promises. Says Scot Struminger, vice president of information technology at FedEx, "We know that customer loyalty comes from treating customers like you want to be treated."[2]

As this example demonstrates, *services* play a critical role in the marketing programs of many business-to-business firms, whether their primary focus is on a service (FedEx) or whether services provide a promising new path for growth. Indeed, high-tech brands, like IBM or Oracle, are built on a promise of value to customers, and service excellence is part of the value package customers demand. In fact, over 65 percent of IBM's massive revenue base now comes from services—not products. Clearly, many product manufacturers are now using integrated product and service solutions as a core marketing strategy for creating new growth opportunities. Moreover, a vast array of "pure service" firms exist to supply organizations with everything from office cleaning to management consulting and just-in-time delivery to key customers.[3]

This chapter examines the nature of business services, the role that services assume in customer solutions, the major strategic elements related to services marketing, and creative strategies for combining goods and services into hybrid offerings.

Understanding the Full Customer Experience

The traditional product-centric mindset rests on the assumption that companies win by creating superior products and continually enhancing the performance of existing products. But services are fundamental to the customer experience that every business-to-business firm provides. Customer experience encompasses every dimension of a company's offering—product and service features, advertising, ease of use, reliability, the process of becoming a customer, or the way problems are resolved—not to mention the ongoing sales relationship.[4]

The Customer Experience Life Cycle

Recent research highlights the importance of examining the customer's experience. A survey of the customers of 362 firms by Bain & Company revealed that only

---

[1]David Leonhardt, "The FedEx Economy," *The New York Times*, October 8, 2005, p. B1.

[2]Don Peppers and Martha Rogers, *Return on Customer: Creating Maximum Value from Your Scarcest Resource* (New York: Currency Doubleday, 2005), p. 144.

[3]Stephen W. Brown, Anders Gustafsson and Lars Witell, "Beyond Products," *The Wall Street Journal* (June 22, 2009), pp. R7–R8.

[4]Christopher Meyer and Andre Schwager, "Understanding Customer Experiences," *Harvard Business Review* 85 (February2007): pp. 116–127.

8 percent described their experience as "superior," yet 80 percent of the companies surveyed believed that the experience that they were delivering was indeed superior.[5] By focusing narrowly only on core-related product elements and overlooking the full customer experience, companies "can end up losing customers without understanding why. Moreover, such companies are missing out on some powerful opportunities to create value and cement their customers' loyalty," says David Rickard, Partner, The Boston Consulting Group.[6]

Customer experience represents the internal and subjective response a business customer has to any direct or indirect contact with a company. We will devote special attention to **touchpoints**—those instances in which the customer has direct contact with either the product or service itself or with representatives of it by a third party, such as a channel partner. A customer experience map provides a valuable tool for diagnosing key touchpoints or interactions between the company and the customer from the moment contact is made with a potential customer through the maintenance of an ongoing relationship (see Figure 9.1). Developed from interviews with customers, the map provides a foundation for defining what is most important in your customers' experience.

Applying the Customer Experience Map

The map was developed by the Boston Consulting Group for a large industrial-goods company that faced this dilemma: Traditional measures of product quality continued to indicate superb performance, but customer satisfaction remained stagnant and the company was losing market share.[7] Once the customer experience map is developed, the next step is to meet with customers and pare down the list to a smaller set of the most critical interactions and product and service characteristics. The ultimate goal of the analysis is to identify: (1) the value that customers place on different levels of performance (for example, high, average, low) for each element of their experience, (2) the customers' minimal expectations for each element, and (3) the customers' perception of the firm's performance versus that of key competitors.

Based on the analysis, strategists at the industrial-goods company were surprised to learn that only 40 percent of customers' most critical experiences were tied to the core product, whereas 60 percent were related to softer considerations (for example, the ease of making invoice corrections and resolving problems). This revelation proved crucial to understanding why the company was losing market share even though its customers' ratings of product quality were improving.

Customer Experience Management

Recall from Chapter 3 that customer relationship management captures what a company knows about a particular customer. Christopher Meyer and Andre Schwager persuasively argue that there is a corresponding need for well-developed **customer experience management** processes that capture customers' subjective thoughts about a particular company.[8] Such an approach requires surveys and targeted studies

---

[5]Ibid., p. 117.

[6]David Rickard, "Winning by Understanding the Full Customer Experience," The Boston Consulting Group, Inc., 2006, p. 1, accessed at http://www.bcg.com on May 15, 2008.

[7]This illustration is based on Rickard, "Winning," p. 5.

[8]Meyer and Schwager, "Understanding Customer Experiences."

FIGURE 9.1 | THE FIRST STEP IN UNDERSTANDING A CUSTOMER'S EXPERIENCE IS TO DEVELOP A LIFE CYCLE MAP

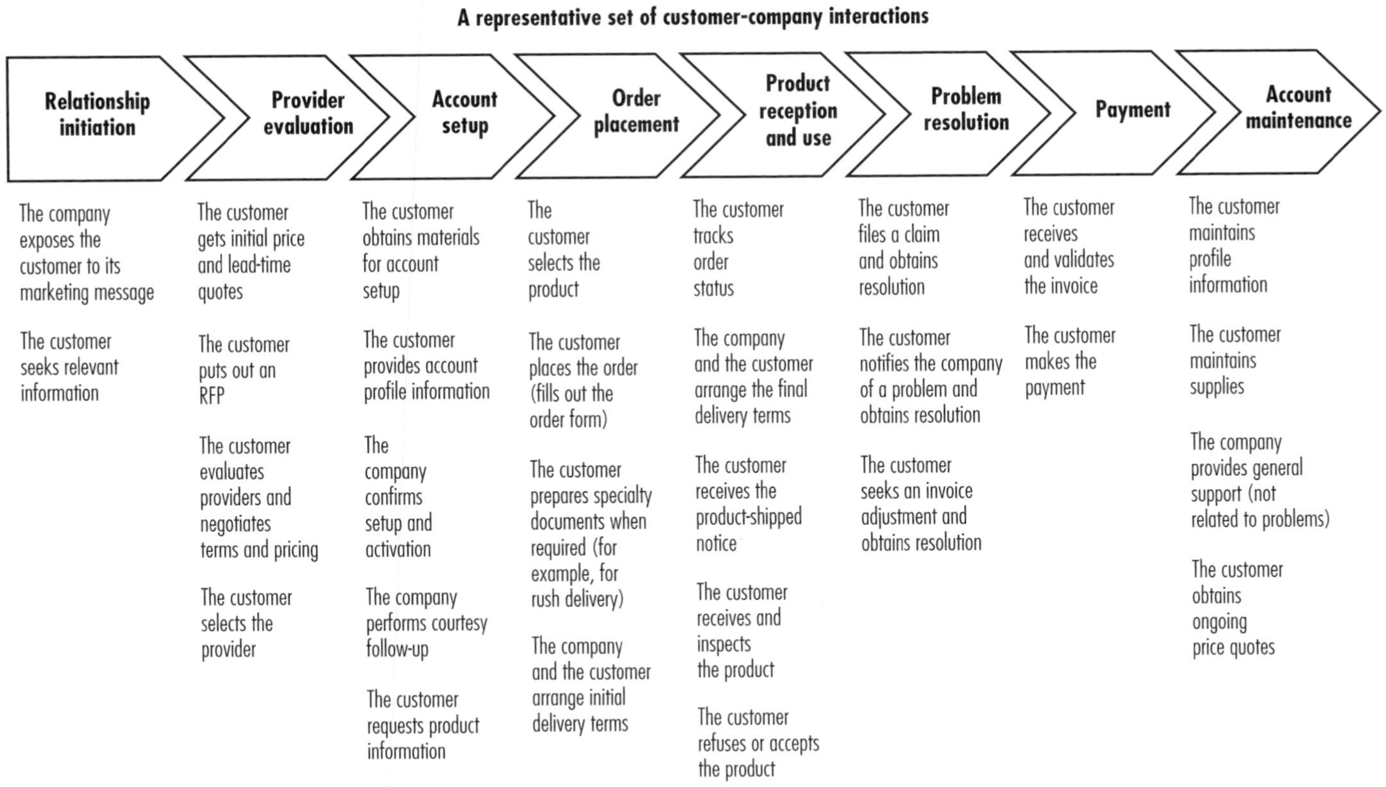

A representative set of customer-company interactions

Relationship initiation	Provider evaluation	Account setup	Order placement	Product reception and use	Problem resolution	Payment	Account maintenance
The company exposes the customer to its marketing message	The customer gets initial price and lead-time quotes	The customer obtains materials for account setup	The customer selects the product	The customer tracks order status	The customer files a claim and obtains resolution	The customer receives and validates the invoice	The customer maintains profile information
The customer seeks relevant information	The customer puts out an RFP	The customer provides account profile information	The customer places the order (fills out the order form)	The company and the customer arrange the final delivery terms	The customer notifies the company of a problem and obtains resolution	The customer makes the payment	The customer maintains supplies
	The customer evaluates providers and negotiates terms and pricing	The company confirms setup and activation	The customer prepares specialty documents when required (for example, for rush delivery)	The customer receives the product-shipped notice	The customer seeks an invoice adjustment and obtains resolution		The company provides general support (not related to problems)
	The customer selects the provider	The company performs courtesy follow-up	The company and the customer arrange initial delivery terms	The customer receives and inspects the product			The customer obtains ongoing price quotes
		The customer requests product information		The customer refuses or accepts the product			

TABLE 9.1 | **FROM A PRODUCT TO A SOLUTIONS PERSPECTIVE**

	Product Perspective	**Solutions Perspective**
Value Proposition	Win by creating innovative products and enriching features of existing products	Win by creating and delivering superior customer solutions
Value Creation	Value is created by the firm	Value is co-created by the customer and the firm
Designing Offerings	Start with the product or service, and then target customer segments	Start with the customer problem, and then assemble required products and services to solve the problem
Company-Customer Relationship	Transaction-based	Interaction-based and centered on the co-creation of solutions
Focus on Quality	Quality of internal processes and company offerings	Quality of customer–firm interactions

SOURCE: Adapted from Mohanbir Sawhney, "Going Beyond the Product: Defining, Designing, and Delivering Customer Solutions," Working Paper, Kellogg School of Management, Northwestern University, December 2004; and C. K. Prahalad and Venkat Ramaswamy, *The Future of Competition: Co-Creating Unique Value with Customers* (Boston: Harvard Business School Press, 2004).

at points of customer interaction that identify gaps between customer expectations and their actual experience. "Because a great many customer experiences aren't the direct consequence of the brand's message or the company's actual offerings ... the customers themselves ... must be monitored and probed."[9]

A Solution-Centered Perspective[10]

As global competition intensifies and product differentiation quickly fades, strategists at leading firms from General Electric and IBM to Staples and Home Depot are giving increased attention to services, particularly a solution-centric mindset. Rather than starting with the product, a solution-centered approach begins with an analysis of a customer problem and ends by identifying the products and services required to solve the problem. Rather than transaction based, the focus of the exchange process is interaction based, and value is co-created by the firm in concert with the customer (Table 9.1). So, customer offerings represent an "integrated combination of products and services designed to provide customized experiences for specific customer segments."[11] Services, as a critical feature of the solution, become a valuable basis for competitive advantage and an important driver of profitability.

UPS Solutions United Parcel Services of America began by mastering a narrow set of activities involved in the package delivery system—picking up, shipping,

---

[9]Ibid., p. 116.

[10]Except where noted, this section draws on Mohanbir Sawhney, "Going beyond the Product: Defining, Designing, and Delivering Customer Solutions," Working Paper, Kellogg School of Management, Northwestern University, December 2004, pp. 1–10.

[11]Ibid., p. 4.

tracking, and delivering packages. Adopting a solution-centered focus, UPS tapped new-market opportunities:[12]

- Designing transportation networks that reduced the time Ford needed to deliver vehicles from its plants to dealers by up to 40 percent;

- Managing the movement of National Semiconductor's products from its manufacturing plants to customers around the world and helping the customer reduce shipping and inventory costs by 15 percent;

- Partnering with Nike and managing all the back-office processes for direct selling from order management and delivery to customer support.

Determine Unique Capabilities   In developing solutions, business marketing firms must define their unique capabilities and determine how to use them to help customers reduce costs, increase responsiveness, or improve quality. In some cases, this may involve taking in some of the work or activities that customers now perform. To illustrate, DuPont first sold paint to Ford but now runs Ford's paint shops. "DuPont, which is paid on the basis of the number of painted vehicles, actually sells less paint than before because it has an incentive to paint cars with the least amount of waste. But the company makes more money as a result of the improved efficiency."[13] The DuPont example demonstrates a central point about solutions marketing: *Products provide the platform for the delivery of services.*[14]

Delivering Effective Customer Solutions

A recent research study suggests that companies can deliver more effective solutions at profitable prices if they adopt a stronger relationship focus.[15] The authors suggest that business marketers mistakenly view a solution as a customized and integrated combination of products and services for meeting a customer's business needs. In sharp contrast, customers view a solution as a set of customer–company relational processes that involve: "(1) customer requirements definition, (2) customization and integration of goods and/or services and (3) their deployment, and (4) postdeployment customer support, all of which are aimed at meeting customers' business needs."[16]

From Figure 9.2, observe how these relational processes took shape as a business marketing firm developed a software solution for the sales unit of a large pharmaceuticals customer.

---

[12]Mohanbir Sawhney, Sridhar Balasubramanian, and Vish V. Krishnan, "Creating Growth with Services," *MIT Sloan Management Review* 45 (Winter 2004): pp. 34–43.

[13]Ibid., p. 39.

[14]Stephen L. Vargo and Robert F. Lusch, "Evolving to a New Dominant Logic for Marketing," *Journal of Marketing* 68 (January 2004): pp. 1–18.

[15]Kapil R. Tuli, Ajay K. Kohli, and Sundar R. Bharadwaj, "Rethinking Customer Solutions for Product Bundles to Relational Process," *Journal of Marketing* 71 (July 2007): pp. 1–17.

[16]Ibid., p. 1.

FIGURE 9.2 | **RELATIONAL PROCESSES COMPRISING A CUSTOMER SOLUTION**

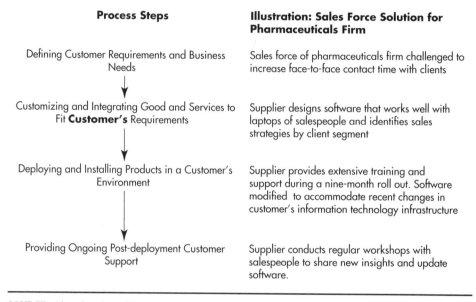

Process Steps	**Illustration: Sales Force Solution for Pharmaceuticals Firm**
Defining Customer Requirements and Business Needs	Sales force of pharmaceuticals firm challenged to increase face-to-face contact time with clients
Customizing and Integrating Good and Services to Fit **Customer's** Requirements	Supplier designs software that works well with laptops of salespeople and identifies sales strategies by client segment
Deploying and Installing Products in a Customer's Environment	Supplier provides extensive training and support during a nine-month roll out. Software modified to accommodate recent changes in customer's information technology infrastructure
Providing Ongoing Post-deployment Customer Support	Supplier conducts regular workshops with salespeople to share new insights and update software.

SOURCE: Adapted, with modifications, from Kapil R. Tuli, Ajay K. Kohli and Sundar G. Bharadwaj, "Rethinking Customer Solutions: From Product Bundles to Relational Processes," *Journal of Marketing* 71 (July 2007), pp. 5–8.

The Supplier's Role[17]

Detailing the four relational processes that comprise a solution brings into sharp focus the challenging coordination issues that a solution strategy presents for the business marketing strategist. Indeed, success hinges on developing appropriate mechanisms for coordinating the activities of different organizational units that contribute to particular stages of the customer solution development process.

First, the sales function typically performs requirements definition, whereas the customer service function provides postdeployment support. In fact, some solutions may require contributions from different business units. To deliver effective solutions, these different functional groups and business units have to be "on the same page." Solutions require employees to develop two types of skills that go beyond product-oriented selling: **multi-domain skills** (the ability to incorporate multiple products and services) and **boundary-spanning skills** (the ability to forge connections across internal units).[18]

Second, cross-unit coordination of a customer solution is promoted if employee incentives of the sales, development, operations, and support staff complement one another. For example, if the compensation of salespeople, beyond an initial commission, also depends on the customer's satisfaction with the solution, better postdeployment support is likely to result. For example, Cisco Systems uses a Web-based survey to determine the pre- and post-sale satisfaction of customers. Because all bonuses are

---

[17]Except, where noted, this section is based on Kapil Tuli, Ajay Kohli, and Sundar G. Bharadwaj, "Rethinking Customer Solutions: From Product Bundles to Relational Processes, *Journal of Marketing* 7 (July 2007): pp. 1–17.

[18]Ranjay Gulati, "Silo Busting: How to Execute on the Promise of Customer Focus," *Harvard Business Review* 85 (May 2007): pp. 98–108.

directly tied to these data, employees are encouraged to cooperate across organizational units.[19]

Third, solution effectiveness can be enhanced by documenting the history of effective and ineffective customer solution engagements.[20] **Document emphasis** refers to the extent to which employees of the business marketing firm are required to document the key milestones in the creation and deployment of a solution, including work performed, key functions involved, and outcomes. Documentation emphasis provides a tool for managing the complexity involved in creating solutions and for synchronizing work and sharing information across units.

Fourth, solution effectiveness can be facilitated by laying out a blueprint or process to guide employees in developing a specific solution. **Process articulation** refers to the extent to which a supplier firm clarifies the roles and responsibilities of organizational units and provides guidelines for sharing customer and product information in developing a solution.

The Customer's Role

Research also clearly reveals that solution effectiveness hinges on particular customer behaviors as well. First, a supplier can do a more effective job if the customer is willing to adapt to the supplier's needs or to unforeseen contingencies as they arise. **Customer adaptiveness** refers to the degree to which a customer is willing to adjust its routines and processes to accommodate a supplier's products.

Second, solution effectiveness is enhanced if the customer provides information and guidelines concerning the priorities and sensitivities of various stakeholders in the customer firm. **Political counseling** refers to the degree to which a customer provides a supplier with information regarding the political landscape in the customer organization. For example, the lack of political counseling created blunders for a supplier of an information-technology solution. While the sales team continued to center on the chief technology officer who had defined solution requirements, attention should have been directed to user groups in the customer organization who had been given total control of implementation.

Finally, solution effectiveness can be enhanced if the customer provides counseling to a supplier concerning the unique elements of its operations. **Operational counseling** refers to information provided to suppliers concerning the relevant technical systems, business processes, and company policies in the customer organization. Based on their research on solution selling, Kapil Tuli and his research colleagues observe:

> A supplier may want to avoid conducting business with a customer that is not adaptive or is unlikely to "educate" the supplier about its internal politics and operations. The solution that a supplier implements for such a customer is likely to be ineffective.[21]

---

[19]Ibid.

[20]Michelle D. Steward, Beth A. Walker, Michael D. Hutt, and Ajith Kumar, "The Coordination Strategies of High-Performing Salespeople: Internal Working Relationships that Drive Success," *Journal of the Academy of Marketing Science* 38 (October 2010): pp. 550–566.

[21]Tuli, Kohli, and Bharadwaj, "Rethinking Customer Solutions," p. 14.

B2B TOP PERFORMERS

Smart Customer Solutions from IBM

Developing and delivering complex customer solutions represent the cornerstone of IBM's Smarter Planet business initiative (see Chapter 7). For IBM, services account for over 65 percent of annual revenue. The Smarter Planet initiative seeks to highlight how forward-thinking leaders in business, government, education, and health care are capturing the potential of smarter systems to achieve sustainable development, advance growth, and improve the quality of life. Examples of smarter systems include smart grids, supply chains, transportation systems, water management systems, buildings, and even smart cities.

In developing its "smart city" model, IBM established a partnership with city planners in Dubuque, Iowa, to make the city of 60,000 residents a model for environmental sustainability. Initial attention centered on water conservation where 150 residents, who volunteered for a pilot test, were empowered with information, analysis, insights, and social computing around their water consumption. During the test period, water utilization was reduced by 6.6 percent for these households that had been equipped with smart meters. This represents annual water savings for the test

group of over 500,000 gallons per year and nearly 65 million gallons of potential water savings if all 23,000 households in the city were equipped with smart meters.

Milind Naphade, a program director for smarter cities services at IBM, notes, Our sustainability initiatives in Dubuque prove that, by using advanced analytics, community engagement, and cloud computing, government officials and citizens will have access to real-time data to alter their patterns of behavior, which will save them money. This water sustainability pilot case is a template for communities worldwide that seek to conserve various types of resources.

IBM plans to draw on the lessons it learns in Dubuque to create a template that it can apply in business engagements in cities across the United States.

SOURCE: "Dubuque, Iowa and IBM Combine Analytics, Cloud Computing and Community Engagement to Conserve Water," May 20, 2011, accessed at http://www.ibm.com on June 27, 2011.

Choose Customers Wisely

Some customers are better candidates for a solution offering than others. To illustrate, GE Healthcare developed a solution focus built around consulting services and a menu of products to address customer needs in a comprehensive fashion.[22] GE originally targeted solutions at large national accounts that turned out to be poor candidates for the solution offering because of their focus on price. The company then refined its target customer profile by centering on multihospital systems that: (1) generated at least $500 million in annual revenue and (2) demonstrated a willingness to provide GE with access to senior executives. Using this screening process, GE isolated 150 of the roughly 400 multihospital systems in the United States, directing particular attention to the 50 customer accounts that expressed a willingness to work with GE. The solutions group at GE secured over $500 million in new contracts.

---

[22]Gulati, "Silo Busting," p. 108.

Benefits of Solution Marketing

By shifting from a product to a solutions strategy, business-to-business firms gain two important benefits, namely, new avenues for growth and differentiation.

Creating Growth Opportunities Solutions create fresh opportunities for increasing the amount of business or share-of-wallet that a company receives from its customer base. An expanded portfolio of service-intensive offerings makes this possible. Often, services represent a far larger market opportunity than the core product market. To illustrate, Deere & Company, the agricultural equipment manufacturer, found that the proportion of each dollar farmers spend on equipment has been declining for years and that the bulk of that spending now goes for services. Moreover, by centering on that profit pool, Deere is tapping into a market opportunity that is 10 times larger than the equipment market. To that end, Deere provides a range of services for its customers (for example, health insurance and banking) and is employing innovative technologies to make the farmer's life easier and more productive. For example, Deere is experimenting with global positioning systems (GPS) and biosensors on its combines. C. K. Prahalad and Venkat Ramaswamy describe the initiative:

> Imagine driverless combines and tractors with onboard sensors that can measure the oil content of grain or distinguish between weeds and crops. The benefits are enormous. Farmers can ration herbicide according to soil conditions. GPS-guided steering ensures repeatable accuracy, eliminates overtreating of crops ... thereby reducing time, fuel, labor, and chemical costs.... Farmers can be more productive, minimizing the cost per acre.[23]

Sustaining Differentiation and Customer Loyalty As farmers view more and more products as commodities, business marketers who emphasize solutions can sustain differentiation more effectively than rivals who maintain a strict focus on the core product offering. Why? According to Mohanbir Sawhney, "Solutions offer many more avenues for differentiation than products because they include a variety of services that can be customized in many unique ways for individual customers."[24] Likewise, by developing a rich network of relationships with members of the customer organization, co-creating solutions with the customer, and becoming directly connected to the customer's operations, they enhance customer loyalty and throw up severe barriers to competing firms when they attempt to persuade the customer to switch suppliers.

Business Service Marketing: Special Challenges

The development of marketing programs for both products and services can be approached from a common perspective; yet the relative importance and form of various strategic elements differ between products and services. The underlying

---

[23]C. K. Prahalad and Venkat Ramaswamy, *The Future of Competition: Co-Creating Unique Value with Customers* (Boston: Harvard Business School Press, 2004), pp. 93–94.

[24]Mohanbir Sawhney, "Going beyond the Product," p. 6.

FIGURE 9.3 | **BUSINESS PRODUCT—SERVICE CLASSIFICATION BASED ON TANGIBILITY**

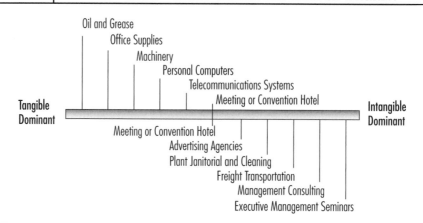

SOURCE: Adapted from G. Lynn Shostack, "Breaking Free from Product Marketing," *Journal of Marketing* 41 (April 1977): p. 77. Published by the American Marketing Association.

explanation for these strategic differences, asserts Henry Assael, lies in the distinctions between a product and a service:

> Services are intangible; products are tangible. Services are consumed at the time of production, but there is a time lag between the production and consumption of products. Services cannot be stored; products can. Services are highly variable; most products are highly standardized. These differences produce differences in strategic applications that often stand many product marketing principles on their head.[25]

Thus, success in the business service marketplace begins with understanding the meaning of *service*.

Services Are Different

There are inherent differences between goods and services, providing a unique set of marketing challenges for service businesses and for manufacturers that provide services as a core offering. Put simply, services are deeds, processes, and performances.[26] For example, a management consultant's core offerings are primarily deeds and actions performed for customers. The most basic, and universally recognized, difference between goods and services is *intangibility*. Services are more intangible than manufactured goods, and manufactured goods are more tangible than services. Because services are actions or performances, they cannot be seen or touched in the same way that consumers sense tangible goods.

---

[25]Henry Assael, *Marketing Management: Strategy and Action* (Boston: Kent Publishing, 1985), p. 693.

[26]Valarie A. Zeithaml, Mary Jo Bitner, and Dwayne D. Gremler, *Services Marketing: Integrating Customer Focus across the Firm*, 5th ed. (Boston: McGraw-Hill Irwin, 2009), p. 2.

Tangible or Intangible?

Figure 9.3 provides a useful tool for understanding the product-service definitional problem. The continuum suggests that there are very few *pure products* or *pure services*. For example, a personal computer is a physical object made up of tangible elements that facilitate the work of an individual and an organization. In addition to the computer's physical design and performance characteristics, the quality of technical service support is an important dimension of the marketing program. Thus, most market offerings comprise a combination of tangible and intangible elements.

Whether an offering is classified as a good or as a service depends on how the organizational buyer views it—whether the tangible or the intangible elements dominate. On one end of the spectrum, grease and oil are tangible-dominant; the essence of what is being bought is the physical product. Management seminars, on the other hand, are intangible-dominant because what is being bought— professional development, education, learning—has few, if any, tangible properties. A convention hotel is in the middle of the continuum because the buyer receives an array of both tangible elements (meals, beverages, notepads, and so on) and intangible benefits (courteous personnel, fast check-ins, meeting room ambiance, and so forth).

The concept of tangibility is especially useful to the business marketer because many business offerings are composed of product and service combinations. The key management task is to evaluate carefully (from the buyer's standpoint) which elements dominate. The more the market offering is characterized by intangible elements, the more difficult it is to apply the standard marketing tools that were developed for products. The business marketer must focus on specialized marketing approaches appropriate for services.

The concept of tangibility also helps the manager focus clearly on the firm's *total market offering*.[27] In addition, it helps the manager recognize that a change in one element of the market offering may completely change the offering in the customer's view. For example, a business marketer who decides to hold spare-parts inventory at a central location and use overnight delivery to meet customer requirements must refocus marketing strategy. The offering has moved toward the intangible end of the continuum because of the intangible benefits of reduced customer inventory and fast transportation. This new "service," which is less tangible, must be carefully explained, and the intangible results of lower inventory costs must be made more concrete to the buyer through an effective promotion program.

In summary, business services are market offerings that are predominantly intangible. However, few services are totally intangible—they often contain elements with tangible properties. In addition to tangibility, business services have other important distinguishing characteristics that influence how they are marketed. Table 9.2 summarizes the core characteristics that further delineate the nature of business services.

Simultaneous Production and Consumption

Because services are generally *consumed as they are produced*, a critical element in the buyer–seller relationship is the effectiveness of the individual who actually provides the service—the IBM technician, the UPS driver, the McKinsey consultant. From

---

[27]Arun Sharma, R. Krishnan, and Dhruv Grewal, "Value Creation in Markets: A Critical Area of Focus for Business-to-Business Markets," *Industrial Marketing Management* 30 (June 2001): pp. 391–402.

TABLE 9.2 | **UNIQUE SERVICE CHARACTERISTICS**

Characteristics	Examples	Marketing Implications
Simultaneous production and consumption	Telephone conference call; management seminar; equipment repair	Direct-seller interaction requires that service be done "right"; requires high-level training for personnel; requires effective screening and recruitment
Nonstandardized output	Management advice varies with the individual consultant; merchandise damages vary from shipment to shipment	Emphasizes strict quality control standards; develop systems that minimize deviation and human error; prepackage the service; look for ways to automate
Perishability: inability to store or stockpile	Unfilled airline seats; an idle computer technician; unrented warehouse space	Plan capacity around peak demand; use pricing and promotion to even out demand peaks and valleys; use overlapping shifts for personnel
Lack of ownership	Use of railroad car; use of consultant's know-how; use of mailing list	Focus promotion on the advantages of nonownership: reduced labor, overhead, and capital; emphasize flexibility

© Cengage Learning 2013

the service firm's perspective, the entire marketing strategy may rest on how effectively the individual service provider interacts with the customer. Here the actual service delivery takes place, and the promise to the customer is kept or broken. This critical point of contact with the customer is referred to as **interactive** or **real-time marketing**. Recruiting, hiring, and training personnel assume special importance in business service firms.

Service Variability

Observe in Table 9.2 that service is *nonstandardized*, meaning that the quality of the service output may vary each time it is provided.[28] Services vary in the amount of equipment and labor used to provide them. For example, a significant human element is involved in teaching an executive seminar compared with providing overnight airfreight service. Generally, the more labor involved in a service, the less uniform the output. In these labor-intensive cases, the user may also find it difficult to judge the quality before the service is provided. Because of uniformity problems, business service providers must focus on finely tuned quality-control programs, invest in "systems" to minimize human error, and seek approaches for automating the service.

Service Perishability

Generally, services *cannot be stored*; that is, if they are not provided at the time they are available, the lost revenue cannot be recaptured. Tied to this characteristic is the fact that demand for services is often unpredictable and widely fluctuating. The service marketer must carefully evaluate capacity—in a service business, **capacity** is a substitute for inventory. If capacity is set for peak demand, a "service inventory" must exist to supply the highest level of demand. As an example, some airlines that

[28]Valarie A. Zeithaml, A. Parasuraman, and Leonard R. Berry, "Problems and Strategies in Services Marketing," *Journal of Marketing* 49 (Spring 1985): p. 34; see also Valarie A. Zeithaml, Leonard R. Berry, and A. Parasuraman, "Communication and Control Processes in the Delivery of Service Quality," *Journal of Marketing* 52 (April 1988): pp. 35–48.

INSIDE BUSINESS MARKETING

Do Service Transition Strategies Pay Off?

To improve their competitive position in the era of intense global competition and the increasing commoditization that characterizes many product markets, a host of manufacturing firms have added services to their existing product offerings. If successful, such service transition strategies could make the firm's value proposition more unique, difficult for rivals to duplicate, and valuable to customers, thereby enhancing profitability and firm value. Do these service transition strategies pay off? A recent study by Eric Fang and his colleagues provides the answers.

- Before they can expect positive effects on firm value, business marketing firms should recognize that service transition strategies typically require achieving a critical mass in sales, estimated to be 20 to 30 percent of total sales.

- Transitioning to services is significantly more effective for companies that offer services related to their core product business. Sales of unrelated services demonstrate little impact on firm value.

- Adding services to a core product offering increases firm value for companies in slow growth and turbulent industries. However, "firms in high growth industries can destroy firm value by shifting their focus ... to service initiatives. In stable (low turbulence) industries, adding services has a negative effect on firm value. "

SOURCE: Eric (Er) Fang, Robert W. Palmatier, and Jan-Benedict E. M. Steenkamp, "Effect of Service Transition Strategies on Firm Value," *Journal of Marketing*, 72 (September 2008): pp. 1–14.

provide air shuttle service between New York, Washington, and Boston offer flights that leave every hour. If, on any flight, the plane is full, another plane is brought to the terminal—even for one passenger. An infinite capacity is set so that no single business traveler is dissatisfied. Obviously, setting high-capacity levels is costly, and the marketer must analyze the cost versus the lost revenue and customer goodwill that might result from maintaining lower capacity.

Nonownership

The final dimension of services shown in Table 9.2 is that the service buyer uses, but *does not own*, the service purchased. Essentially, payment for a service is a payment for the use of, access to, or hire of items. Renting or leasing is "a way for customers to enjoy use of physical goods and facilities that they cannot afford to buy, cannot justify purchasing, or prefer not to retain after use."[29] The service marketer must feature the advantages of nonownership in its communications to the marketplace. The key benefits to emphasize are reductions in staff, overhead, and capital from having a third party provide the service.

Although there may be exceptions, these characteristics provide a useful framework for understanding the nature of business services and isolating special marketing strategy requirements. The framework suggests that different types of

---

[29]Christopher Lovelock and Evert Gummesson, "Whither Services Marketing? In Search of a New Paradigm and Fresh Perspectives," *Journal of Services Research* 7 (August 2004): p. 36.

service providers should pursue different types of strategies because of the intangibility and heterogeneity of their services. In this case, providers of professional services (consulting, tax advising, accounting, and so on) should develop marketing strategies that emphasize word-of-mouth communication, provide tangible evidence, and employ value pricing to overcome the issues created by intangibility and heterogeneity.[30]

Service Quality

Quality standards are ultimately defined by the customer. Actual performance by the service provider or the provider's perception of quality are of little relevance compared with the customer's perception. "Good" service results when the service provider meets or exceeds the customer's expectations.[31] As a result, many management experts argue that service companies should carefully position themselves so that customers expect a little less than the firm can actually deliver. The strategy: underpromise and overdeliver.

Dimensions of Service Quality

Because business services are intangible and nonstandardized, buyers tend to have greater difficulty evaluating services than evaluating goods. Because they are unable to depend on consistent service performance and quality, service buyers may perceive more risk.[32] As a result, they use a variety of prepurchase information sources to reduce risk. Information from current users (word of mouth) is particularly important. In addition, the evaluation process for services tends to be more abstract, more random, and more heavily based on symbology rather than on concrete decision variables.[33]

Research provides some valuable insights into how customers evaluate service quality. From Table 9.3 note that customers focus on five dimensions in evaluating service quality: reliability, responsiveness, assurance, empathy, and tangibles. Among these dimensions, reliability—delivery on promises—is the most important to customers. High-quality service performance is also shaped by the way frontline service personnel provide it. To the customer, service quality represents a responsive employee, one who inspires confidence and one who adapts to the customer's unique needs or preferences and delivers the service in a professional manner. In fact, the performance of employees who are in contact with the customer may compensate for temporary service quality problems (for example, a problem reoccurs in a recently repaired photocopier).[34] By promptly acknowledging the error and responding quickly to the problem, the service employee may even strengthen the firm's relationship with the customer.

---

[30]Michael Clemes, Diane Mollenkopf, and Darryl Burn, "An Investigation of Marketing Problems across Service Typologies," *Journal of Services Marketing* 14 (no. 6–7, 2000): p. 568

[31]William H. Davidow and Bro Uttal, "Service Companies: Focus or Falter," *Harvard Business Review* 67 (July–August 1989): p. 84.

[32]Valarie A. Zeithaml, "How Consumer Evaluation Processes Differ between Goods and Services," in *Marketing of Services*, James H. Donnelly and William R. George, eds. (Chicago: American Marketing Association, 1981), pp. 200–204.

[33]Ibid.

[34]Christian Gronroos, "Relationship Marketing: Strategic and Tactical Implications," *Management Decision*, 34 (no. 3, 1996): pp. 5–14.

TABLE 9.3 | THE DIMENSIONS OF SERVICE QUALITY

Dimension	Description	Examples
Reliability	Delivering on promises	Promised delivery date met
Responsiveness	Being willing to help	Prompt reply to customers' requests
Assurance	Inspiring trust and confidence	Professional and knowledgeable staff
Empathy	Treating customers as individuals	Adapts to special needs of customer
Tangibles	Representing the service physically	Distinctive materials: brochures, documents

SOURCE: Adapted from Valarie A. Zeithaml, Mary Jo Bitner, and Dwayne D. Gremler, *Services Marketing: Integrating Customer Focus across the Firm*, 5th ed. (Boston: McGraw-Hill Irwin, 2009), pp. 116–120.

Customer Satisfaction and Loyalty

Four components of a firm's offering and its customer-linking processes affect customer satisfaction:

1. The basic elements of the product or service that customers expect all competitors to provide;

2. Basic support services, such as technical assistance or training, that make the product or service more effective or easier to use;

3. A recovery process for quickly fixing product or service problems;

4. Extraordinary services that so excel in solving customers' unique problems or in meeting their needs that they make the product or service seem customized.[35]

Leading service firms carefully measure and monitor customer satisfaction because it is linked to customer loyalty and, in turn, to long-term profitability.[36] Xerox, for example, regularly surveys more than 400,000 customers regarding product and service satisfaction using a 5-point scale from 5 (high) to 1 (low). In analyzing the data, Xerox executives made a remarkable discovery: Very satisfied customers (a 5 rating) were far more loyal than satisfied customers. Very satisfied customers, in fact, were *six times* more likely to repurchase Xerox products than satisfied customers.

Service Recovery

Business marketers cannot always provide flawless service. However, the way the firm responds to a client's service problems has a crucial bearing on customer retention and loyalty. **Service recovery** encompasses the procedures, policies, and processes a firm uses to resolve customer service problems promptly and effectively. For example, when IBM receives a customer complaint, a specialist who is an expert in the relevant product or service area is assigned as "resolution owner" of that complaint. On being assigned a customer complaint or problem, the IBM specialist must contact

---

[35]Thomas O. Jones and W. Earl Sasser Jr., "Why Satisfied Customers Defect," *Harvard Business Review* 73 (November–December 1995): p. 90.

[36]The Xerox illustration is based on James L. Heskett, Thomas O. Jones, Gary W. Loveman, W. Earl Sasser Jr., and Leonard A. Schlesinger, "Putting the Service-Profit Chain to Work," *Harvard Business Review* 72 (March–April 1994): pp. 164–174.

the customer within 48 hours (except in the case of severe problems, where the required response is made much faster). Larry Schiff, a marketing strategist at IBM, describes how the process works from there:

> They introduce themselves as owners of the customer's problem and ask: What's it going to take for you to be very satisfied with the resolution of this complaint? ... Together with the customer, we negotiate an action plan and then execute that plan until the customer problem is resolved. The problem only gets closed when the customer says it is closed, and we measure this [*that is, customer satisfaction with problem resolution*] as well.[37]

Service providers who satisfactorily resolve service failures often see that their customer's level of perceived service quality rises. One study in the ocean-freight-shipping industry found that clients who expressed higher satisfaction with claims handling, complaint handling, and problem resolution have a higher level of overall satisfaction with the shipping line.[38] Therefore, business marketers should develop thoughtful and highly responsive processes for dealing with service failures. Some studies have shown that customers who experienced a service failure and had it corrected to their satisfaction have greater loyalty to the supplier than those customers who did not experience a service failure!

Zero Defections

The quality of service provided to business customers has a major effect on customer "defections"—customers who do not come back. Service strategists point out that customer defections have a powerful effect on the bottom line.[39] As a company's relationship with a customer lengthens, profits rise—and generally rise considerably. For example, one service firm found that profit from a fourth-year customer is triple that from a first-year customer. Many additional benefits accrue to service companies that retain their customers: They can charge more, the cost of doing business is reduced, and the long-standing customer provides "free" advertising. The implications are clear: Service providers should carefully track customer defections and recognize that continuous improvement in service quality is not a cost but, say Frederick Reichheld and W. Earl Sasser, "an investment in a customer who generates more profit than the margin on a one-time sale."[40]

Return on Quality

A difficult decision for the business-services marketing manager is to determine how much to spend on improving service quality. Clearly, expenditures on quality have diminishing returns—at some point, additional expenditures do not increase profits. To make good decisions on the level of expenditures on quality, managers

---

[37]Larry Schiff, "How Customer Satisfaction Improvement Works to Fuel Business Recovery at IBM," *Journal of Organizational Excellence* 20 (Spring 2001): p. 12.

[38]Srinivas Durvasula, Steven Lysonski, and Subhash C. Mehta, "Business-to-Business Marketing: Service Recovery and Customer Satisfaction Issues with Ocean Shipping Lines," *European Journal of Marketing* 34 (no. 3–4, 2000): p. 441.

[39]Frederick F. Reichheld and W. Earl Sasser, "Zero Defections: Quality Comes to Services," *Harvard Business Review* 68 (September–October 1990): p. 105; see also Frederick F. Reichheld, *Loyalty Rules! How Today's Leaders Build Lasting Relationships* (Boston: Harvard Business School Press, 2001).

[40]Reichheld and Sasser, "Zero Defections," p. 107.

must justify quality efforts on a financial basis, knowing where to spend on quality improvement, how much to spend, and when to reduce or stop the expenditures. Roland Rust, Anthony Zahorik, and Timothy Keiningham have developed a technique for calculating the "return on investing in quality."[41] Under this approach, service quality benefits are successively linked to customer satisfaction, customer retention, market share, and, finally, to profitability. The relationship between expenditure level and customer-satisfaction change is first measured by managerial judgment and then through market testing. When the relationship has been estimated, the return on quality can be measured statistically. The significant conclusion is that quality improvements should be treated as investments: They must pay off, and spending should not be wasted on efforts that do not produce a return.

Service Packages

The **service package** can be thought of as the product dimension of service, including decisions about the essential concept of the service, the range of services provided, and the quality and level of service. In addition, the service package must consider some unique factors—the personnel who perform the service, the physical product that accompanies the service, and the process of providing the service.[42] A useful way to conceptualize the service product is shown in Figure 9.4.

Customer-Benefit Concept

Services are purchased because of the benefits they offer, and a first step in either creating a service or evaluating an existing one is to define the **customer-benefit concept**—that is, evaluate the core benefit the customer derives from the service. Understanding the customer-benefit concept focuses the business marketer's attention on those attributes—functional, effectual, and psychological—that must be not only offered but also tightly monitored from a quality-control standpoint. For example, a sales manager selecting a resort hotel for an annual sales meeting is purchasing a core benefit that could be stated as "a successful meeting." The hotel marketer must then assess the full range of service attributes and components necessary to provide a successful meeting. Obviously, a wide variety of service elements come into play: (1) meeting-room size, layout, environment, acoustics; (2) meals; (3) comfortable and quiet sleeping rooms; (4) audiovisual equipment; and (5) staff responsiveness.

Service Concept

Once the customer-benefit concept is understood, the next step is to articulate the **service concept**, which defines the general benefits the service company will provide through the bundle of goods and services it sells to the customer. The service concept translates the customer-benefit concept into the range of benefits the service

---

[41]Roland T. Rust, Anthony J. Zahorik, and Timothy L. Keiningham, "Return on Quality (ROQ): Making Service Quality Financially Accountable," *Journal of Marketing* 59 (April 1995): pp. 58–70; see also Roland T. Rust, Katherine N. Lemon, and Valarie A. Zeithaml, "Return on Marketing: Using Customer Equity to Focus Marketing Strategy," *Journal of Marketing* 68 (January 2004): pp. 109–127.

[42]Donald Cowell, *The Marketing of Services* (London: William Heinemann, 1984), p. 73.

FIGURE 9.4 | **Conceptualizing the Service Product**

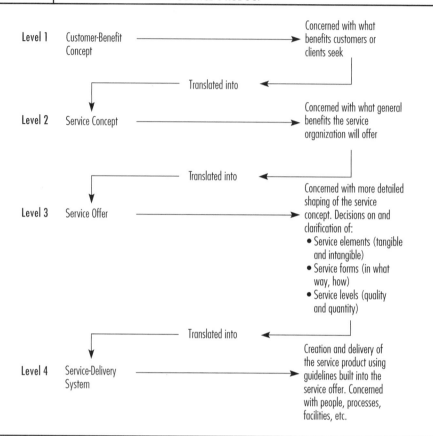

SOURCE: Adapted from Donald Cowell, *The Marketing of Services* (London: William Heinemann, Ltd., 1984), p. 100.

marketer will *provide*. For a hotel, the service concept might specify the benefits that it will develop: flexibility, responsiveness, and courteousness in providing meeting rooms; a full range of audiovisual equipment; flexible meal schedules; message services; professional personnel; and climate-controlled meeting rooms.

Service Offer

Intimately linked with the service concept is the **service offer**, which spells out in more detail those services to be offered; when, where, and to whom they will be provided; and how they will be presented. The service elements that make up the total service package, including both tangibles and intangibles, must be determined. The service offer of the hotel includes a multitude of tangible elements (soundproof meeting rooms, projection equipment, video players, slide projectors, flip charts, refreshments, heating and air-conditioning, meals) and intangible elements (attitude of meeting-room setup personnel, warmth of greetings from desk clerks and bellhops, response to unique requests, meeting-room ambiance). Generally, management finds it easier to manage the tangible (equipment and physical) elements of the service than to control the intangible elements.

Service Delivery System

The final dimension of the service product is the service delivery system—how the service is provided to the customer. The delivery system includes carefully conceived jobs for people; personnel with capabilities and attitudes necessary for successful performance; equipment, facilities, and layouts for effective customer work flow; and carefully developed procedures and processes aimed at a common set of objectives.[43] Thus, the service delivery system should provide a carefully designed blueprint that describes how the service is rendered for the customer.

For physical products, manufacturing and marketing are generally separate and distinct activities; for services, these two activities are often inseparable.[44] The service performance and the delivery system both create the product and deliver it to customers. This feature of services underscores the important role of people, particularly service providers, in the marketing process. Technicians, repair personnel, and maintenance engineers are intimately involved in customer contact, and they decidedly influence the customer's perception of service quality. The business service marketer must pay close attention to both people and physical evidence (tangible elements such as uniforms) when designing the service package.

Service Personnel

A first step in creating an effective service package is to ensure that all personnel know, understand, and accept the customer-benefit concept. As Donald Cowell states, "So important are people and their quality to organizations and … services that 'internal marketing' is considered to be an important management role to ensure that all staff are customer conscious."[45] In short, the attitudes, skills, knowledge, and behavior of service personnel have a critical effect on the customer's level of satisfaction with the service.

Hybrid Offerings[46]

To advance revenue and profit growth, many traditional manufacturers are creating hybrid offerings that combine products and services into innovative value propositions for customers. A **hybrid offering** represents a combination of one or more goods and one or more services that together offer more customer benefits than if the good and service were available separately.[47] For example, a manufacturer of ATM machines drew on its deep knowledge of consumer usage of its machines across its installed base and developed services for improving cash management and productivity in retail banking operations. While such offerings can provide a strong differential advantage, many manufacturing firms struggle when they venture into the services sphere. Recent research provides a valuable framework for

---

[43]James L. Heskett, *Managing in the Service Economy* (Boston: Harvard Business School Press, 1986), p. 20.

[44]Cowell, *The Marketing of Services*, p. 110.

[45]Cowell, *The Marketing of Services*, p. 110; see also, Francis X. Frei, "The Four Things a Service Business Must Get Right," *Harvard Business Review* 86 (April 2008): pp. 70–80.

[46]This section is based on Wolfgang Ulaga and Warren J. Reinartz, "Hybrid Offerings: How Manufacturing Firms Combine Goods and Services Successfully," *Journal of Marketing* 75 (November 2011), forthcoming.

[47]Venkatesh Shankar, Leonard L. Berry, and Thomas Detzel, "A Practical Guide to Combining Products and Services," *Harvard Business Review* 87 (November 2009): pp. 94–99.

identifying the unique resources that should be leveraged and for defining the distinctive capabilities that should be developed to create successful strategies for hybrid offerings (see Figure 9.5).

Unique Resources Manufacturing Firms Can Leverage

Compared to pure service firms, manufacturers possess four distinct resources that can be particularly valuable in developing hybrid offerings.

Installed Base Product Usage and Process Data   The installed base of products at customer organizations represents a unique asset for most manufacturing firms. For example, if a firm provides maintenance and repair services to its installed base, product usage data can be systematically gathered and used to tailor service offerings that advance customers' goals. Many goods, from elevators and earth-moving equipment to heating and air conditioning (HVAC) systems for buildings and

FIGURE 9.5 | **MANUFACTURER-SPECIFIC RESOURCES AND CAPABILITIES FOR SUCCESSFUL HYBRID OFFERINGS**

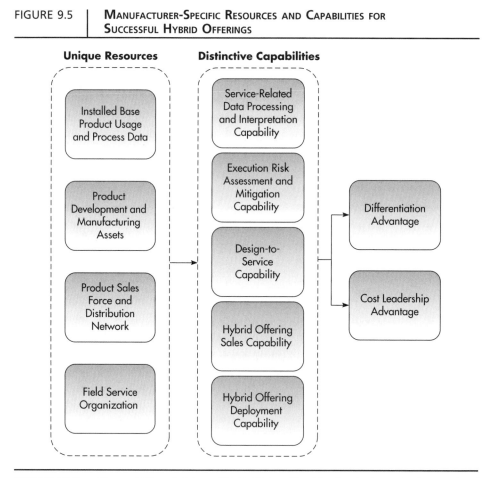

SOURCE: Wolfgang Ulaga and Werner J. Reinartz, Hybrid Offerings: How Manufacturing Firm's Combine Goods and Services Successfully *Journal of Marketing*, 75 (November 2011), forthcoming.

shopping malls, are equipped with smart technologies that can capture usage data and facilitate control from a remote location. An equipment manufacturer explains:

> Today, our forklift trucks are equipped with a multitude of data sensors. We remote-monitor operations on a real-time basis, 24/7, which allows us to collect data on how many hours the forklift truck runs per day, how many hours of downtime the equipment endures, etc. We consolidate all that data in an online database.[48]

Product Development and Manufacturing Assets   The stock of unique assets represented in a firm's R&D and manufacturing infrastructure can be leveraged to achieve a competitive advantage over direct competitors and pure service players in developing superior hybrid offerings. For example, a tire manufacturer developed a new tire casing that allowed it to regroove and retread its tires more frequently than those of its competitors. This innovation lowered the total cost of ownership for trucking company customers because the tires provided tens of thousands of miles more of wear than with any competitive offerings.

Product Sales Force and Distribution Network   Business-to-business firms generally rely on a direct sales force and/or work with channel partners to cover sales territories. By enabling access to a full range of buying influentials in customer organizations, the sales force provides a unique resource for developing and implementing strategies for hybrid offerings. Channel intermediaries can likewise represent a unique resource in the market but some manufacturers report difficulty in capturing the full potential of their dealer network for growing service revenue.

Field Service Organization   Most manufacturers have developed a field organization to deliver and install products as well as to provide service to customers. Research indicates that manufacturers typically earn 45 percent of gross profits from the aftermarket, though it accounts for only 24 percent of revenue.[49] The field service network provides a key resource for delivering after-sales services in a cost efficient manner but also provides an opportunity for pursuing new and more ambitious hybrid offerings.

These four resources represent the critical inputs that can be used to develop the distinctive capabilities that best-practice firms apply in developing profitable hybrid offerings (see Figure 9.5).

Distinctive Capabilities for Launching Hybrid Offerings

Superior resources and capabilities enable a firm to achieve competitive advantage through differentiated offerings or lower relative cost. Based on case studies and depth interviews with senior executives in manufacturing firms, Wolfgang Ulaga

---

[48]Ulaga and Reinartz, "Hybrid Offerings," p. 11.

[49]Morris A. Cohen, Narendra Agrawal, and Vipul Agraval, "Winning in the Aftermarket," *Harvard Business Review* 84 (May 2006): pp. 129–138. See also, Goutam Challagalla, R. Venkatesh, and Ajay K. Kohli, "Proactive Postsales Service: When and Why Does it Pay Off?" *Journal of Marketing* 73 (March 2009): pp. 70–87.

and Warren J. Reinartz identify five capabilities that are particularly critical to the successful launch of hybrid offerings:[50]

1. **Service-related data processing and interpretation capability** is the manufacturer's capacity to gather, analyze, and interpret installed base product usage and process data to help business customers reduce costs and/or increase productivity. For example, an industrial equipment manufacturer that installs electric motors in commercial buildings, used by customers to monitor energy consumption, drew on this rich data source to develop distinctive skills in facility management. Energy efficiency consulting services for business customers became a new source of revenue generation for the company.

2. **Execution risk assessment and mitigation capability** concerns the manufacturer's capacity to evaluate the likelihood that agreed-upon outcomes of hybrid offerings will be achieved and then to design and implement safeguarding mechanisms to meet performance commitments and to maintain internal profit targets. For example, a manufacturer of in-flight entertainment systems for commercial airlines thoroughly examined product usage and process data from the installed base of customers to develop reliable outcome expectations and performance guarantees.

3. **Design-to-service capability** is the manufacturer's capacity to integrate the product and service elements of the offering *early* in the development process to tap the full potential for revenue generation and/or cost reduction. To illustrate, by reengineering its offset printing presses, a manufacturer enabled its service technicians to perform first-level maintenance remotely, thereby reducing costs and increasing service responsiveness.

4. **Hybrid offering sales capability** is "the manufacturer's capacity to reach key decision makers in the customer organization, coordinate key contacts in the customer and vendor firms, sell hybrid offering value through specific documentation and communication tools, and align the sales force with both the field organization and channel partners to increase hybrid offering revenues."[51]

5. **Hybrid offering deployment capability** is the manufacturer's capacity to use flexible offering platforms that can standardize production and delivery processes while providing a menu of options to adapt to individual customers' needs. For example, a company offers six different maintenance packages for printers to cover the needs of retail banking customers. In describing the offerings, a manager observes: "we build 'service boxes.' "[52]

Classifying Services for Hybrid Offerings

From Table 9.4, observe that business services can be classified on two dimensions to identify four good-service combinations. The first dimension identifies whether the service is directed at the supplier's good or is targeted on the customer's

---

[50]Ulaga and Reinartz, "Hybrid Offerings," pp. 14–24.

[51]Ibid., p. 22.

[52]Ibid., p. 24

TABLE 9.4 | CLASSIFICATION SCHEME OF BUSINESS SERVICES FOR HYBRID OFFERINGS

		Service Recipient	
		Service Oriented Toward the Supplier's Good	**Service Oriented Toward the Customer's Process**
Nature of the Value Proposition	**Supplier's Promise to Perform a Deed (input-based)**	**1. Product Life Cycle Services (PLS)** **Definition:** Services to facilitate the customer's access to the supplier's good and ensure its proper functioning during all states of the life cycle. **Examples:** Delivery of industrial cables. Inspection of an ATM machine. Regrooving of an industrial tire. Recycling of a power transformer. **Primary Distinctive Capabilities:** Hybrid offering deployment capability. Design-to-service capability.	**3. Process Support Services (PSS)** **Definition:** Services to assist customers in improving their own business processes. **Examples:** Energy efficiency audit for a commercial building. Logistics consulting for material-handling processes in a warehouse. **Primary Distinctive Capabilities:** Service-related data processing and interpretation capability. Hybrid offering deployment capability. Hybrid offering sales capability.
	Supplier's Promise to Achieve Performance (output-based)	**2. Asset Efficiency Services (AES)** **Definition:** Services to achieve productivity gains from assets invested by customers. **Examples:** Remote monitoring of a jet engine. Welding robot software customization. **Primary Distinctive Capabilities:** Service-related data processing and interpretation capability. Execution risk assessment and mitigation capabilities. Hybrid offering sales capabilities.	**4. Process Delegation Services (PDS)** **Definition:** Services to perform processes on behalf of the customers. **Examples:** The fleet management on behalf of a trucking company. Gas and chemicals supply management for a semiconductor manufacturer. **Primary Distinctive Capabilities:** Service-related data processing and interpretation capability. Executive risk assessment and mitigation capabilities. Design-to-service capability. Hybrid offering sales capabilities. Hybrid offering deployment capability.

SOURCE: Adapted from Wolfgang Ulaga and Werner J. Reinartz, "Hybrid Offerings: How Manufacturing Firm's Combine Goods and Services Successfully," *Journal of Marketing*, 75 (November 2011), forthcoming.

process. A second dimension for classifying services for hybrid offerings concerns whether the supplier promises to perform a deed (input-based) or to achieve a performance outcome (output-based). Different resources and distinctive capabilities are needed to successfully deploy strategies for each of the resulting business service categories.

Product Life Cycle Services   **Product life cycle services (PLS)** refers to services that facilitate the customer's access to a manufacturer's product and ensure its desired functioning during all stages of its useful life from delivery, installation, and maintenance to recycling or disposal. Since these services are directly tied to the supplier's product, the value proposition represents a promise to perform a deed on behalf of the customer. While PLS, such as timely maintenance and repair, are expected by business customers, they can assume a valuable role in building the firm's reputation as a trusted service provider in the market.

Asset Efficiency Services   To achieve a differential advantage, some manufacturers create distinctive value-added services that are directly tied to their products. **Asset efficiency services (AES)** are services that are designed to provide customers with productivity gains on their asset investments. Rather than promising to perform a deed as with PLS, the value proposition for AES goes one step further and promises a level of performance related to asset productivity. For example, a manufacturer of in-flight entertainment systems makes this commitment: "We guarantee availability of 98.5 percent of video screens up and running in an aircraft."[53] To succeed with AES, manufacturers must possess distinctive capabilities for assessing and managing product failure risks.

Process Support Services   **Process support services (PSS)** are services provided by a manufacturer that assist customers in increasing the efficiency of their own business processes. Rather than focusing on the manufacturer's product, PSS centers on the customer's processes (for example, a manufacturer of material handling equipment offers warehouse optimization and logistics consulting to customers). To succeed with PSS, manufacturers report that fundamental changes are required in the sales approach and organization to reach a different set of buying influentials in the customer organization as well as to assist and train customer personnel in achieving process improvements. Often, there is a need to add specialized technicians to the field service organization and dedicated PSS salespersons to the sales force.

Process Delegation Services   **Process delegation services (PDS)** represent those services where a manufacturer performs specific processes on behalf of the customer (for example, DuPont not only supplies the paint but also manages Ford Paint shops). Other examples include fly-by-the-hour agreements for commercial jet engines or the fleet management of tires for a trucking enterprise. Unlike PSS where the supplier promises to perform a deed, the value proposition for PDS involves a promise to achieve a particular level of process performance (that is, output-based).

In contrast to outsourcing arrangements, PDS typically involves an integrated mix of product and service elements, a highly customized offering tailored to specific customer requirements, and often, a complex gain-sharing agreement. From Table 9.4, observe that manufacturers must master the full range of distinctive capabilities to succeed in the PDS category. For that reason, the availability of PDS are rather limited in many business market sectors and are only offered by the market leaders.

---

[53]Ibid., p. 28.

Summary

Customer satisfaction represents the culmination of a set of customer experiences with the business-to-business firm. A customer experience map provides a powerful platform for defining the most critical customer–company interactions, uncovering customer expectations, and spotting opportunities to create value and strengthen customer loyalty. Rather than selling individual products and services, leading-edge business-to-business firms focus on what customers really want—solutions. To design a solution, the business marketing manager begins by analyzing a customer problem and then identifies the products and services required to solve that problem. Because solutions can be more readily customized for individual customers, they provide more avenues for differentiation than products can offer.

Business customers view a solution as a set of customer-company relational processes that involve: (1) customer requirements definition, (2) customization and integration of goods and/or services, (3) their deployment, and (4) postdeployment customer support. To deliver effective solutions, the business marketer should develop appropriate mechanisms for coordinating the activities of different organizational units that contribute to different stages of the customer solution development process. Ultimately, solution effectiveness depends on supplier as well as customer behaviors.

Business services are distinguished by their intangibility, linked production and consumption, lack of standardization, perishability, and use as opposed to ownership. Together, these characteristics have profound effects on how services should be marketed. Buyers of business services focus on five dimensions of service quality: reliability, responsiveness, assurance, empathy, and tangibles. Because of intangibility and lack of uniformity, service buyers have significant difficulty in comparing and selecting service vendors. Service providers must deliver on promises, inspire trust and confidence, and provide tangible evidence (for example, documented savings) to create satisfied customers. A key first step in creating strategies for a service is to define the customer-benefit concept and develop the related service concept. Next, the service offer is detailed and a blueprint for the service delivery system is developed.

Many manufacturers are creating hybrid offerings to generate a new platform for revenue and profit growth. A hybrid offering represents a combination of one or more goods and one or more services that together offer more customer benefits than if the good and service were available separately. Building on unique resources, such as product usage and process data from the installed base of products, and building distinctive capabilities, such as the capability to integrate product and service elements early in the development process, manufacturers are developing four types of hybrid offerings: (1) product life cycle services, (2) asset efficiency services, (3) process support services, and (4) process delegation services.

Discussion Questions

1. What is the role of physical evidence in the marketing of a business service?

2. A new firm creates Web sites and electronic commerce strategies for small businesses. Describe the essential elements to be included in its service product.

3. Many firms have a recovery process in place for situations when their products or services fail to deliver what has been promised to the customer. Illustrate how such a process might work.

4. Hewlett-Packard (H-P) has an enormous installed base of its printers in customer organizations, large and small, all over the world. How could H-P capitalize on this installed base and develop some innovative hybrid offerings?

5. Compare and contrast product life cycle services to process delegation services.

6. Leading service companies such as American Express and FedEx measure customer satisfaction on a quarterly basis across the global market. Discuss the relationship between customer satisfaction and loyalty.

7. In selling solutions, a supplier may want to avoid conducting business with a customer that is not adaptive or is unlikely to "educate" the supplier about its internal politics and operations. Discuss.

8. When a company buys a high-end document processor from Xerox or Canon, it is buying a physical product with a bundle of associated services. Describe some of the services that might be associated with such a product. Develop a list of the elements or points of interaction that might be reflected in a customer experience map. How can buyers evaluate the quality or value of these services?

9. Local contractors who handle home remodeling and other building projects turn to Home Depot or Lowe's for many products, tools, and materials. Describe how these retailers could adopt a solutions marketing focus to serve those customers.

10. As a luxury resort hotel manager, what approaches might you utilize to manage business demand for hotel space?

Internet Exercise

1. Autodesk, Inc., a leading design software and digital content company, provides online collaborative services for the building industry that enables more effective management of all project information. Go to http://www.buzzsaw.com and describe the service solutions Autodesk provides for architects and engineers.

CHAPTER 10

Managing Business Marketing Channels

The channel of distribution is the marketing manager's bridge to the market. Channel innovation represents a source of competitive advantage that separates market winners from market losers. The business marketer must ensure that the firm's channel is properly aligned to the needs of important market segments. At the same time, the marketer must also satisfy the needs of channel members, whose support is crucial to the success of business marketing strategy. After reading this chapter, you will understand:

1. The alternative paths to business market customers

2. The critical role of industrial distributors and manufacturers' representatives in marketing channels

3. The central components of channel design

4. Requirements for successful channel strategy

Go to Market Strategy, an influential book by Lawrence G. Friedman, aptly describes the central focus of a channel strategy in the business market:

> The success of every go-to-market decision you make, indeed your ability to make smart go-to-market decisions at all, depends on how well you understand your customers.... You must build an accurate customer fact-base that clarifies who the customers are in your target market, what they buy, how they buy it, how they want to buy it, and what would motivate them to buy more of it from you.[1]

The channel component of business marketing strategy has two important and related dimensions. First, the channel structure must be designed to accomplish marketing objectives. However, selecting the best channel to accomplish objectives is challenging because: (1) the alternatives are numerous, (2) marketing goals differ, and (3) business market segments are so various that separate channels must often be used concurrently. The ever-changing business environment requires managers to periodically reevaluate the channel structure. Stiff competition, new customer requirements, and the rapid growth of online resources are among the forces that create new opportunities and signal the need for fresh channel strategies. Customers want simple and fast online transactions for some purchases but require highly complex solutions designed by an experienced sales team for others. Often, business-to-business firms need to develop a flexible multichannel approach that can seamlessly handle each transaction cost effectively.[2]

Second, once the channel structure has been specified, the business marketer must manage the channel to achieve prescribed goals. To do so, the manager must develop procedures for selecting intermediaries, motivating them to achieve desired performance, resolving conflict among channel members, and evaluating performance. This chapter provides a structure for designing and administering the business marketing channel.

The Business Marketing Channel

The link between manufacturers and customers is the **channel of distribution**. The channel accomplishes all the tasks necessary to effect a sale and deliver products to the customer. These tasks include making contact with potential buyers, negotiating, contracting, transferring title, communicating, arranging financing, servicing the product, and providing local inventory, transportation, and storage. These tasks may be performed entirely by the manufacturer or entirely by intermediaries, or they may be shared between them. The customer may even undertake some of these functions; for example, customers granted certain discounts might agree to accept larger inventories and the associated storage costs.

Fundamentally, channel management centers on these questions: Which channel tasks will be performed by the firm, and which tasks, if any, will be

---

[1]Lawrence G. Friedman, *Go to Market: Advanced Techniques and Tools for Selling More Products, to More Customers, More Profitably* (Boston: Butterworth-Heinemann, 2002), p. 116.

[2]Christopher Davie, Tom Stephenson, and Maria Valdivieso de Uster, "Three Trends in Business-to-Business Sales," *McKinsey Quarterly* (May 2010), pp. 1–4, accessed at http://www.mckinsey.com on May 20, 2011.

FIGURE 10.1 | **B2B Marketing Channels**

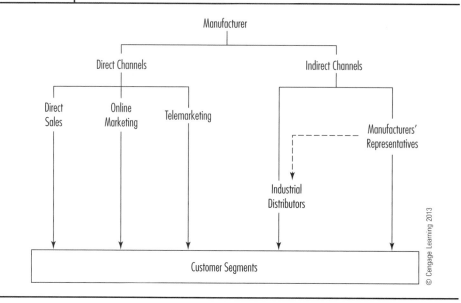

performed by channel members? Figure 10.1 shows various ways to structure business marketing channels. Some channels are **direct**—the manufacturer must perform all the marketing functions needed to make and deliver products. The manufacturer's direct sales force and online marketing channels are examples. Others are **indirect**; that is, some type of intermediary (such as a distributor or dealer) sells or handles the products.

A basic issue in channel management, then, is how to structure the channel so that the tasks are performed optimally. One alternative is for the manufacturer to do it all.

Direct Channels

Direct distribution, common in business marketing, is a channel strategy that does not use intermediaries. The manufacturer's own sales force deals directly with the customer, and the manufacturer has full responsibility for performing all the necessary channel tasks. Direct distribution is often required in business marketing because of the nature of the selling situation or the concentrated nature of industry demand. The direct sales approach is feasible when: (1) the customers are large and well defined, (2) the customers insist on direct sales, (3) sales involve extensive negotiations with upper management, and (4) selling has to be controlled to ensure that the total product package is properly implemented and to guarantee a quick response to market conditions.

A direct sales force is best used for the most complex sales opportunities: highly customized solutions, large customers, and complex products. Customized solutions and large customer accounts require professional account management, deep product knowledge, and a high degree of selling skill—all attributes a sales representative must possess. Also, when risk in a purchase decision is perceived as high and significant expertise is required in the sale, customers demand a high level of personal attention and relationship building from the direct sales force as a precondition for doing business. However, according to Lawrence Friedman and Timothy Furey, "in the broad middle market and small-customer market, where transactions are generally simpler, other channels can do a more cost-effective job—and can often reach more customers."[3]

Many business marketing firms, such as Xerox, Cisco, and Dell, emphasize e-commerce strategies. Surprisingly, many firms use their Web sites only for promotional purposes and not yet as a sales channel. Business marketing firms can use E-channels as: (1) information platforms, (2) transaction platforms, and (3) platforms for managing customer relationships. The effect on the business increases as a firm moves from level one to level three.

Indirect Channels

Indirect distribution uses at least one type of intermediary, if not more. Business marketing channels typically include fewer types of intermediaries than do consumer-goods channels. Indirect distribution accounts for a large share of sales in the United States. The Gartner Group reports that 60 percent of the U.S. gross domestic product (GDP) is sold through indirect channels.[4] Manufacturers' representatives and industrial distributors account for most of the transactions handled in this way. Indirect distribution is generally found where: (1) markets are fragmented and widely dispersed, (2) low transaction amounts prevail, and (3) buyers typically purchase a number of items, often different brands, in one transaction.[5] For example, IBM's massive sales organization concentrates on large corporate, government, and institutional customers. Industrial distributors effectively and efficiently serve literally thousands of other IBM customers—small to medium-sized organizations. These channel partners assume a vital role in IBM's strategy on a global scale. IBM offers a high level of support to its channel partners, including co-marketing opportunities, customer lead generation, extensive training, and technical assistance. (See a complete description of IBM's channel outreach program at http://www.ibm.com/partnerworld.)

Integrated Multichannel Models[6]

Leading business marketing firms use multiple sales channels to serve customers in a particular market. The goal of a multichannel model is to coordinate the activities of many channels, such as field sales representatives, channel partners, call centers, and the Web, in order to enhance the total customer experience and profitability. Consider a typical sales cycle that includes the following tasks: lead generation, lead qualification, negotiation and sales closure, fulfillment, and customer care and support (Figure 10.2). In a multichannel system, different channels can perform different tasks within a single sales transaction with a customer. For example, business marketing firms might use a call

---

[3]Lawrence G. Friedman and Timothy R. Furey, *The Channel Advantage* (Boston: Butterworth-Heinemann, 1999), p. 84.

[4]The Gartner Group, "Partnerware Reports, 'Top 10 Tips for Managing Indirect Sales Channels'," http://www.businesswire.com, June 18, 2002.

[5]E. Raymond Corey, Frank V. Cespedes, and V. Kasturi Rangan, *Going to Market: Distribution Systems for Industrial Products* (Boston: Harvard University Press, 1989), p. 26.

[6]This section is based on Friedman, *Go to Market*, pp. 229–257.

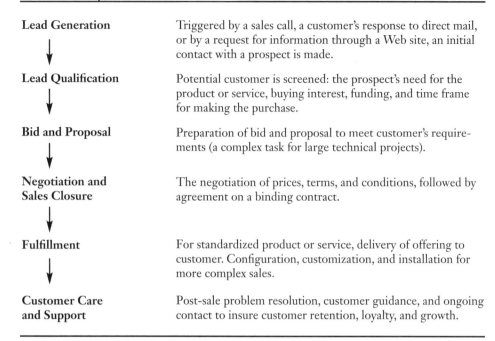

FIGURE 10.2 | TYPICAL SALES CYCLE: TASKS PERFORMED THROUGHOUT THE SALES PROCESS

Lead Generation
Triggered by a sales call, a customer's response to direct mail, or by a request for information through a Web site, an initial contact with a prospect is made.

Lead Qualification
Potential customer is screened: the prospect's need for the product or service, buying interest, funding, and time frame for making the purchase.

Bid and Proposal
Preparation of bid and proposal to meet customer's requirements (a complex task for large technical projects).

Negotiation and Sales Closure
The negotiation of prices, terms, and conditions, followed by agreement on a binding contract.

Fulfillment
For standardized product or service, delivery of offering to customer. Configuration, customization, and installation for more complex sales.

Customer Care and Support
Post-sale problem resolution, customer guidance, and ongoing contact to insure customer retention, loyalty, and growth.

SOURCE: Adapted from Lawrence G. Friedman, *Go to Market Strategy: Advanced Techniques and Tools for Selling More Products, to More Customers, More Profitably* (Boston: Butterworth-Heinemann, 2002), pp. 234–236.

center and direct mail to generate leads, field sales representatives to close sales, business partners (for example, industrial distributors) to provide fulfillment (that is, deliver or install product), and a Web site to provide post-sale support.

Managing Customer Contact Points   Figure 10.3 shows a particular multi-channel strategy that a number of leading firms like Oracle Corporation use to reach the vast middle market composed of many small and medium-sized businesses. First, the channels are arranged from top to bottom in terms of their *relative cost of sales* (that is, direct sales is the most expensive, whereas the Internet is the least). By shifting any selling tasks to lower-cost channels, the business marketer can boost profit margins and reach more customers, in more markets, more efficiently.

Business Partner's Key Role   Returning to Figure 10.3, observe the central role of business partners across the stages of the sales cycle. Low-cost, direct-to-customer channels—like the Internet—are used to generate sales leads, which are then given to channel partners. These partners are then expected to complete the sales cycle but can secure assistance from Oracle's sales representatives to provide guidance and support (when needed) in closing the sale. By emphasizing the partner channel for middle-market customers, Oracle can significantly increase market coverage and penetration while enjoying higher profit margins and lower selling costs. Moreover, this allows the sales force to concentrate on large enterprise customers.

This provides just one example of how a firm can coordinate and configure sales cycle tasks across various sales channels to create an integrated strategy for a

FIGURE 10.3 | MULTICHANNEL INTEGRATION MAP: SIMPLE EXAMPLE OF HIGH-COVERAGE PARTNERING MODEL

1. Consider the relative cost of alternative sales channels.

> Direct sales – most expensive
> Business partners
> Telechannels
> Direct mail
> Internet – least expensive

2. Employ business partners to cover SMB customers and perform the <u>primary</u> sales tasks.

3. Fully utilize other sales channels to lend direct <u>support</u> across the sales cycle.

> Lead generation from telechannels, direct mail and the internet
> Sales closure support from direct sales rep, as required
> Customer care from internet

SMB = small and medium-sized

SOURCE: Adapted with modifications from Lawrence G. Friedman, *Go to Market Strategy: Advanced Techniques and Tools for Selling More Products, to More Customers, More Profitably* (Boston: Butterworth-Heinemann, 2002), p. 243. Copyright 2002.

particular market. Any firm that serves a variety of markets requires distinctly different multichannel models to serve customers in those markets. To illustrate, a company might serve key corporate accounts through sales representatives and the middle market through channel partners, call centers, and the Internet.

Customer Relationship Management (CRM) Systems Many business marketing firms pursue very complex market coverage strategies and use *all* of the alternative paths to the market we have discussed. For example, Hewlett-Packard sells directly through a field sales organization to large enterprises; through channel partners and resellers to the government, education, and the midsize business market; and through retail stores to the small business and home market. According to Lawrence Friedman, a leading sales strategy consultant: "Add in its customer support channels, Web presence, and H-P has an army of channels that it deploys to provide sales, service, and support to its different market segments."[7] This multichannel mix features many points of contact that H-P must manage and coordinate to ensure a "singular" customer experience across channels. CRM systems provide a valuable tool for coordinating sales channel activities and managing crucial connections and handoffs between them (see Chapter 3). Friedman further notes:

> Channel coordination used to be a difficult, messy problem involving the tracking and frequent loss of hand-written memos, voice mails, paper lists of sales leads, and dog-eared customer history files. CRM has ushered in a new era of IT-driven channel coordination, enabling electronic transmission of leads and customer histories from one channel to another, with no loss of information or sales information falling through the cracks.[8]

[7]Ibid., p. 254.
[8]Ibid., p. 253.

Participants in the Business Marketing Channel

Channel members assume a central role in the marketing strategies of business-to-business firms, large and small. A channel management strategy begins with an understanding of the intermediaries that may be used. Primary attention is given to two: (1) industrial distributors and (2) manufacturers' representatives. They handle a sizable share of business-to-business sales made through intermediaries.

Distributors

Industrial distributors are the most pervasive and important single force in distribution channels. Distributors in the United States number more than 10,000, with sales exceeding $50 billion. Distributors are heavily used for MRO (maintenance, repair, and operations) supplies, with many industrial buyers reporting that they buy as much as 75 percent of their MRO supplies from distributors. Generally, about 75 percent of all business marketers sell *some* products through distributors. What accounts for the unparalleled position of the distributor in the industrial market? What role do distributors play in the industrial distribution process?

Distributors are generally small, independent businesses serving narrow geographic markets. Sales average almost $2 million, although some top $3 billion. Net profits are relatively low as a percentage of sales (4 percent); return on investment averages 11 percent. The typical order is small, and the distributors sell to a multitude of customers in many industries. The typical distributor is able to spread its costs over a sizable group of vendors—it stocks goods from between 200 and 300 manufacturers. A sales force of outside and inside salespersons generates orders. *Outside salespersons* make regular calls on customers and handle normal account servicing and technical assistance. *Inside salespersons* complement these efforts, processing orders and scheduling delivery; their primary duty is to take telephone orders. Most distributors operate from a single location, but some approach the "supermarket" status with as many as 400 branches. Among the largest industrial distributors are W. W. Grainger and Wesco International Inc. that each generate more than $5 billion in annual sales and are included in the *Fortune* 500.

Compared with their smaller rivals, large distributors seem to have significant advantages. Small distributors are typically unable to achieve the operating economies larger firms enjoy.[9] Large firms can automate much of their operations, enabling them to significantly reduce their sales and general administrative expenses, often to levels approaching 10 percent of sales.

Distributor Responsibilities Table 10.1 shows industrial distributors' primary responsibilities. The products they sell—cutting tools, abrasives, electronic components, ball bearings, handling equipment, pipe, maintenance equipment, and hundreds more—are generally those that buyers need quickly to avoid production disruptions. Thus, the critical elements of the distributor's function are to have these products readily available and to serve as the manufacturer's selling arm.

---

[9]Heidi Elliott, "Distributors, Make Way for the Little Guys," *Electronic Business Today* 22 (September 1996): p. 19.

TABLE 10.1 | KEY DISTRIBUTION RESPONSIBILITIES

Responsibility	Activity
Contact	Reach all customers in a defined territory through an outside sales force that calls on customers or through an inside group that receives telephone orders
Product availability	Provide a local inventory and include all supporting activities: credit, just-in-time delivery, order processing, and advice
Repair	Provide easy access to local repair facilities (unavailable from a distant manufacturer)
Assembly and light manufacturing	Purchase material in bulk, then shape, form, or assemble to user requirements

© Cengage Learning 2013

Distributors are full-service intermediaries; that is, they take title to the products they sell, and they perform the full range of marketing functions. Some of the more important functions are providing credit, offering wide product assortments, delivering goods, offering technical advice, and meeting emergency requirements. Not only are distributors valuable to their manufacturer-suppliers but their customers generally view them favorably. Some purchasing agents view the distributor as an extension of their "buying arms" because they provide service, technical advice, and product application suggestions.

INSIDE BUSINESS MARKETING

W. W. Grainger: Profile of a Leading-Edge Industrial Distributor

W. W. Grainger is one of the largest B2B distributors in the world. With nearly 600 branch locations throughout North America, over 2 million customers, 1900 customer service associates, and a robust line of 500,000 products (tools, pumps, motors, safety and material handling products, and lighting, ventilation, and cleaning items), Grainger is the leading industrial distributor of products that allow organizations of all types to keep their facilities and equipment running smoothly. Grainger's objective is to grow by capturing market share in the highly fragmented North American facilities maintenance market. With sales of $7.2 billion, Grainger is a *Fortune* 500 company and a perennial member on *Fortune's* list of Most Admired Companies.

Its large sales force and product line allow Grainger to meet customer needs in a highly responsive manner. For procuring maintenance and operating supplies, the company offers multiple channels:

- *Branch Network*—Customers can go directly to their local Grainger location to pick up their

order or have it shipped directly to them, often within hours.

- *The Grainger Catalog*—An icon in the industry and on the shelf of virtually every procurement manager in North America, the catalog includes over 300,000 facilities maintenance products.

- *Grainger.com*—Customers can access detailed descriptions and order from a massive collection of more than 700,000 products online. The products can be shipped directly to the customer's business or to the local branch for pickup by the customer. Grainger's annual e-commerce sales exceed $1.8 billion.

Grainger represents one of the strongest brands in industrial distribution because customers believe the firm can get them what they need, when they need it.

SOURCE: "Grainger at a Glance," W. W. Grainger Inc., pp. 1–2; accessed at http://www.grainger.com on May 20, 2011.

A Service Focus   To create more value for their customers, many large distributors have expanded their range of services. Value is delivered through various supply chain and inventory management services, including automatic replenishment, product assembly, in-plant stores, and design services. The most popular services involve helping customers design, construct, and, in some cases, operate a supply network. Other value-adding activities include partnerships in which the distributor's field application engineers work at a customer's site to help select components for new product designs. To reap the profits associated with these important services, many distributors now charge separate fees for each unique service.

Classification of Distributors   To select the best distributor for a particular channel, the marketing manager must understand the diversity of distributor operations. Industrial distributors vary according to product lines and user markets. Firms may be ultraspecialized (for example, selling only to municipal water works), or they may carry a broad line of generalized industrial products. However, three primary distributor classifications are usually recognized.

1. **General-line distributors** cater to a broad array of industrial needs. They stock an extensive variety of products and could be likened to the supermarket in consumer-goods markets. W.W. Grainger works with more than 3000 suppliers to provide customers with access to more than one million products from categories ranging from adhesives and electrical parts to motors, office furniture, and test equipment![10]

2. **Specialists** focus on one line or on a few related lines. Such a distributor may handle only power transmission equipment—belts, pulleys, and bearings. The most common specialty is fasteners, although specialization also occurs in cutting tools, power transmission equipment, pipes, valves, and fittings. There is a trend toward increased specialization as a result of increasing technical complexity of products and the need for higher levels of precision and quality control.

3. A **combination house** operates in two markets: industrial and consumer. Such a distributor might carry electric motors for industrial customers and hardware and automotive parts to be sold through retailers to final consumers.

Choosing a Distributor   The selection of a distributor depends on the manufacturer's requirements and the needs of target customer segments. The general-line distributor offers the advantage of one-stop purchasing. If customers do not need a high level of service and technical expertise, the general-line distributor is a good choice. The specialist, on the other hand, provides the manufacturer with a high level of technical capability and a well-developed understanding of complex customer requirements. Specialists handle fasteners, for instance, because of the strict quality-control standards that users impose.

Manufacturers and their distributors are finding the Internet to be a major catalyst for stimulating collaboration. A recent poll asked distributors which business strategies would have the largest effect on them in the future, and the top two were collaboration

---

[10]"Grainger at a Glance," p. 1, accessed at http://www.grainger.com on May 20, 2011.

with supply chain partners and new information technologies.[11] E-collaboration includes sales and services, ordering and billing, technical training and engineering, Internet meetings, auctions, and exchanges. These results suggest that Internet collaboration is a critical strategic force in managing channel relationships.

The Distributor as a Valuable Partner   The quality of a firm's distributors is often the difference between a highly successful marketing strategy and an ineffective one. Customers prize good distributors, making it all the more necessary to strive continually to engage the best in any given market. Distributors often provide the only economically feasible way of covering the entire market.

In summary, the industrial distributor is a full-service intermediary who takes title to the products sold; maintains inventories; provides credit, delivery, wide product assortment, and technical assistance; and may even do light assembly and manufacturing. Although the distributor is primarily responsible for contacting and supplying present customers, industrial distributors also solicit new accounts and work to expand the market. They generally handle established products—typically used in manufacturing operations, repair, and maintenance—with a broad and large demand.

Industrial distributors are a powerful force in business marketing channels, and all indications point to an expanded role for them. The manufacturer's representative is an equally viable force in the business marketing channel.

Manufacturers' Representatives

For many business marketers who need a strong selling job with a technically complex product, **manufacturers' representatives**, or reps, are the only cost-effective answer. In fact, Erin Anderson and Bob Trinkle note that the one area untouched by the outsourcing boom is field selling in the business-to-business area. They contend that many companies could benefit by using outsourced sales professionals, namely, manufacturers' reps, to augment or even replace the field sales force.[12] Reps are salespeople who work independently (or for a rep company), represent several companies in the same geographic area, and sell noncompeting but complementary products.

The Rep's Responsibilities   A rep neither takes title to nor holds inventory of the products handled. (Some reps do, however, keep a limited inventory of repair and maintenance parts.) The rep's forte is expert product knowledge coupled with a keen understanding of the markets and customer needs. Reps are usually limited to defined geographical areas; thus, a manufacturer seeking nationwide distribution usually works with several rep companies. Compared with a distributor channel, a rep generally gives the business marketer more control because the firm maintains title and possession of the goods.

The Rep-Customer Relationship   Reps are the manufacturers' selling arm, making contact with customers, writing and following up on orders, and linking the manufacturer with the industrial end users. Although paid by the manufacturer, the

---

[11]Al Tuttle, "E-Collaboration: Build Trust and Success," *Industrial Distribution* 92 (June 1, 2002): p. 59.

[12]Erin A. Anderson and Bob Trinkle, *Outsourcing the Sales Function: The Real Cost of Field Sales* (Mason, Ohio: Thomson Higher Education, 2005); see also Daniel H. McQuiston, "A Conceptual Model for Building and Maintaining Relationships between Manufacturers' Reps and Their Principals," *Industrial Marketing Management* 30 (February 2001): pp. 165–181.

B2B TOP PERFORMERS

Why Intel Uses Reps

Intel has a strong corporate brand, an experienced corporate sales force, and long-standing relationships with broad-line distributors such as Arrow Electronics. Intel also uses manufacturers' representatives. Why?

After purchasing a business unit from Digital Equipment Corporation in 1998, Intel realized that several product lines from the acquired unit provided promising market potential, particularly in networking and communications. Specifically, the product lines could spur profitable growth in embedded applications market segments, such as medical equipment and point-of-sale terminals, where the proper application function is based on microprocessors and network connections. At Intel, however, marketing managers argued that the go-to-market strategy that has proved so successful in the PC market would not be suitable for original equipment manufacturers (OEMs) in these sectors.

George Langer, Intel's worldwide representative program manager, explains:

There was no sales organization, few customer relationships, and more than a few OEMs who questioned Intel's renewed interest in the embedded segments. Intel did not have existing capability to get these product lines in front of appropriate customers. The customer base was large and diverse. (This was not the PC OEM customer base where Intel had nurtured strong relationships over time.) And, finally, the value of the Intel brand was not clearly associated with communications, embedded, and networking market segments. Intel turned to outsourced selling [that is, manufacturers' reps].

SOURCE: Erin Anderson and Bob Trinkle, *Outsourcing the Sales Function: The Real Cost of Field Sales* (Mason, Ohio: Thomson Higher Education, 2005), pp. 74–75.

rep is also important to customers. Often, a rep's efforts during a customer emergency (for example, an equipment failure) mean the difference between continuing or stopping production. Most reps are thoroughly experienced in the industries they serve—they can offer technical advice while enhancing the customer's leverage with suppliers in securing parts, repair, and delivery. The rep also provides customers with a continuing flow of information on innovations and trends in equipment, as well as on the industry as a whole.

Commission Basis Reps are paid a commission on sales; the commission varies by industry and by the nature of the selling job. Commissions typically range from a low of 2 percent to a high of 18 percent for selected products. The average commission rate is 5.3 percent.[13] Percentage commission compensation is attractive to manufacturers because they have few fixed sales costs. Reps are paid only when they generate orders, and commissions can be adjusted based on industry conditions. Because reps are paid on commission, they are motivated to generate high levels of sales—another fact the manufacturer appreciates.

Experience Reps possess sophisticated product knowledge and typically have extensive experience in the markets they serve. Most reps develop their field experience while working as salespersons for manufacturers. They are motivated to become

---

[13]Anderson and Trinkle, *Outsourcing the Sales Function*, p. 22.

reps by the desire to be independent and to reap the substantial monetary rewards possible on commission.

When Reps Are Used

- *Large and Small Firms*: Small and medium-sized firms generally have the greatest need for a rep, although many large firms—for example, Dow Chemical, Motorola, and Intel—use them. The reason is primarily economic: Smaller firms cannot justify the expense of maintaining their own sales forces. The rep provides an efficient way to obtain total market coverage, with costs incurred only as sales are made. The quality of the selling job is often very good as a result of the rep's prior experience and market knowledge.

- *Limited Market Potential*: The rep also plays a vital role when the manufacturer's market potential is limited. A manufacturer may use a direct sales force in heavily concentrated business markets, where the demand is sufficient to support the expense, and use reps to cover less-dense markets. Because the rep carries several lines, expenses can be allocated over a much larger sales volume.

- *Servicing Distributors*: Reps may also be employed by a firm that markets through distributors. When a manufacturer sells through hundreds of distributors across the United States, reps may sell to and service those distributors.

- *Reducing Overhead Costs*: Sometimes the commission rate paid to reps exceeds the cost of a direct sales force, yet the supplier continues to use reps. This policy is not as irrational as it appears. Assume, for example, that costs for a direct sales force approximate 8 percent of sales and that a rep's commission rate is 11 percent. Using reps in this case is often justified because of the hidden costs of a sales force. First, the manufacturer does not provide fringe benefits or a fixed salary to reps. Second, the costs of training a rep are usually limited to those required to provide product information. Thus, using reps eliminates significant overhead costs.

Multiple Paths to Market A wide array of factors influences the choice of intermediaries, with the tasks they perform being of prime importance.

Different Market Segments The primary reason for using more than one type of intermediary for the same product is that different market segments require different channel structures. Some firms use three distinct approaches. Large accounts are called on by the firm's own sales force, distributors handle small repeat orders, and manufacturers' reps develop the medium-sized firm market.

How Customers Buy Like size of accounts, differences in purchase behavior may also dictate using more than one type of intermediary. If a firm produces a wide line of industrial products, some may require high-caliber selling to numerous buying influences in a single buyer's firm. When this occurs, the firm's own sales force will focus on the more complex buying situations, whereas the distributors will sell standardized products from local stocks.

Channel Design

Channel design is the dynamic process of developing new channels where none existed and modifying existing channels. The business marketer usually deals with modification of existing channels, although new products and customer segments

FIGURE 10.4 | **THE CHANNEL DESIGN PROCESS**

Step 1   End-User Focus: Define Customer Segments
                              ↓
Step 2   Identify and Prioritize Customers' Channel Requirements by Segment
                              ↓
Step 3   Assess the Firm's Capabilities to Meet Customers' Requirements
                              ↓
Step 4   Benchmark Channel Offerings of Key Competitors
                              ↓
Step 5   Create Channel Solutions to Customers' Latent Needs
                              ↓
Step 6   Evaluate and Select Channel Options

SOURCE: Adapted from V. Kasturi Rangan, *Transforming Your Go-to-Market Strategy: The Three Disciplines of Channel Management* (Boston: Harvard Business Press, 2006), pp. 73–94.

may require entirely new channels. Regardless of whether the manager is dealing with a new channel or modifying an existing one, channel design is an active rather than a passive task. Effective distribution channels do not simply evolve; rather, they are developed by management, which takes action on the basis of a well-conceived plan that reflects overall marketing goals. Business firms formulate their marketing strategies to appeal to selected market segments, to earn targeted levels of profits, to maintain or increase sales and market share growth rates, and to achieve all this within specified resource constraints. Each element of the marketing strategy has a specific purpose.

Channel design is best conceptualized as a series of stages that the business marketing manager must complete to be sure that all important channel dimensions have been evaluated (Figure 10.4). The result of the process is to specify the structure that provides the highest probability of achieving the firm's objectives.[14] Note that the process focuses on channel structure and not on channel participants. **Channel structure** refers to the underlying framework: the number of channel levels, the number and types of intermediaries, and the linkages among channel members. Selection of individual intermediaries is indeed important—it is examined later in the chapter.

Step 1: Define Customer Segments

The primary goal of the distribution channel is to satisfy end-user needs, so the channel design process should begin there. Step 1 is about defining target market segments (see Chapter 4) and isolating the customer buying and usage behavior in each segment (what they buy, how they buy, and how they put their purchases to use).

Some business marketers err by considering their channel partners as "customers and rarely looking beyond them." To inform the channel design process, however,

---

[14]The discussion that follows is based on V. Kasturi Rangan, *Transforming Your Go-to-Market Strategy: The Three Disciplines of Channel Management* (Boston: Harvard Business Press, 2006), pp. 73–88.

TABLE 10.2 | **CHANNEL FUNCTIONS ALIGNED WITH CUSTOMER NEEDS**

Channel Function	**Customer Needs**
1. Product Information	Customers seek more information for new and/or technically complex products and those that are characterized by a rapidly changing market environment.
2. Product Customization	Some products must be technically modified or need to be adapted to meet the customer's unique requirements.
3. Product Quality Assurance	Because of its importance to the customer's operations, product integrity and reliability might be given special emphasis by customers.
4. Lot Size	For products that have a high unit value or those that are used extensively, the purchase represents a sizable dollar outlay and a significant financial decision for the customer.
5. Assortment	A customer may require a broad range of products, including complementary items, and assign special value to one-stop shopping.
6. Availability	Some customer environments require the channel to manage demand uncertainty and support a high level of product availability.
7. After-Sales Services	Customers require a range of services from installation and repair to maintenance and warranty.
8. Logistics	A customer organization may require special transportation and storage services to support its operations and strategy.

SOURCE: Adapted from V. Kasturi Rangan, Melvyn A. J. Menezes, and E. B. Maier, "Channel Selection for New Industrial Products: A Framework, Method, and Application," *Journal of Marketing* 56 (July 1992): pp. 72–74.

the marketing strategist should center on the importance of the product from the customer's perspective. V. Kasturi Rangan observes:

> Producers of agricultural channels, for example, should target farmers and not dealers. Producers of engineering plastics (pellets) for automobile bumpers, on the other hand, should focus on the auto manufacturer and not the consumer, because that is where the product has value in the eyes of the end user.... Other features of the automobile (not bumpers) are more salient [in the choice decision at the consumer level].[15]

Step 2: Identify Customers' Channel Needs by Segment

Identifying and prioritizing the channel function requirements for customers in each market segment is next. This information should be elicited directly from a sample of present or potential customers from each segment. Table 10.2 provides a representative list of channel functions that may be more or less important to customers in a particular segment. For example, large customers for information-technology products might rank product customization, product quality assurance, and after-sales service as their top three needs, whereas small customers may prioritize product information, assortment, and availability as their most important needs. The business

---

[15]Ibid., p. 76.

marketing manager should also probe customers on other issues that might provide strategy insights. For instance, how sensitive are customers to a two-hour versus six-hour service response time, or how much value do they perceive in a three-year versus one-year warranty?

Step 3: Assess the Firm's Channel Capabilities

Once customer requirements have been isolated and prioritized, an assessment is made of the strengths and weaknesses of the firm's channel. The central focus is on identifying the gaps between what customers in a segment desire and what the channel is now providing. Customers base their choice of a channel not on a single element, but on a complete bundle of benefits (that is, channel functions). To that end, the business-to-business firm should identify particular channel functions, like after-sales support or availability, where action could be taken to enhance the customer value proposition.

Step 4: Benchmark to Competitors

What go-to-market strategies are key competitors using? In designing a channel, cost considerations prevent the business marketer from closing all the gaps on channel capabilities that may appear. However, a clear direction for strategy is revealed by understanding the channel offerings of competitors. For example, an aggressive competitor that goes to market with its own team of account managers and dedicated service specialists might demonstrate special strength in serving large corporate customers. However, countless opportunities exist for smaller rivals to counter this strategy by developing special channel offerings tailored to small and medium-sized customers (for example, Intuit's success in retaining its market leadership position in small-business accounting software despite the aggressive challenge from Microsoft).

Step 5: Create Channel Solutions for Customers' Latent Needs

Sometimes, a review of competitor offerings can alert the marketer to opportunities for new offerings that may have special appeal to customers. "At other times, customers' needs may be latent and unarticulated, and it is the channel steward's responsibility to tap into and surface those requirements."[16] Based on such an assessment, a provider of information-technology equipment created an entirely new channel option for the small and medium-sized customer segment. Rather than selling equipment, this new channel takes responsibility for installing, upgrading, and maintaining the equipment at the customers' locations for an ongoing service fee.

Step 6: Evaluate and Select Channel Options

Channel decisions must ultimately consider the cost-benefit trade-offs and the estimated profitability that each of the viable channel options presents.[17] Some of the channel gaps that are uncovered in this assessment can be closed by the independent actions and investments of the business-to-business firm (for example, adding to the service support staff or the sales force). For the most part, however, the greatest progress will come from the channel partners (for example, distributors or reps)

---

[16]Ibid., p. 83.

[17]Arun Sharma and Anuj Mehrotra, "Choosing an Optimal Mix in Multichannel Environments," *Industrial Marketing Management* 36 (January 2007): pp. 21–28.

FIGURE 10.5 | CUSTOMERS DRIVE THE CHANNEL DESIGN PROCESS

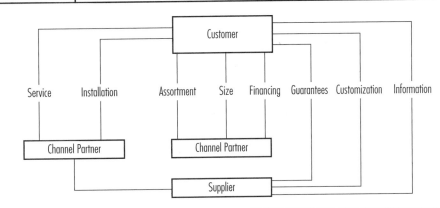

SOURCE: V. Kasturi Rangan, *Transforming Your Go-to-Market Strategy: The Three Disciplines of Channel Management* (Boston: Harvard Business Press, 2006), p. 91.

working together and discussing how channel capabilities can be aligned to customer needs. "The idea is to enhance the value delivered to customers through collaborative action among channel partners. If the partners can agree on how to pull it off and, indeed, accomplish their redefined tasks,"[18] they will squarely respond to customer needs and advance the performance of the channel. One important implication of the framework is that the design of the channel must change as customer and competitor behavior changes. Rather than a static structure, channel management is an ongoing process involving continuous adjustments and evolution.

Crucial Points in Channel Transformation

Marketing channels are often thought of as a series of product and information flows that originate with the business-to-business firm. In his rich and compelling perspective of the channel design process, V. Kasturi Rangan turns this notion on its head (see Figure 10.5):

> The starting point is the customer, and the customer's demand-chain requirements. The channel is constructed to meet this core need. Roles, responsibilities, and rewards are allocated as a consequence of this need, and not the other way around.[19]

Channel Administration

Once a particular business-to-business channel structure is chosen, channel participants must be selected, and arrangements must be made to ensure that all obligations are assigned. Next, channel members must be motivated to perform the tasks necessary to achieve channel objectives. Third, conflict within the channel must be properly controlled. Finally, performance must be controlled and evaluated.

---

[18]Rangan, *Transforming Your Go-to-Market Strategy*, p. 88.

[19]Ibid., p. 91.

Selection of Channel Members

Why is the selection of channel members (specific companies, rather than *type*, which is specified in the design process) part of channel management rather than an aspect of channel design? The primary reason is that intermediary selection is an ongoing process—some intermediaries choose to leave the channel, and the supplier terminates others. Thus, selection of intermediaries is more or less continuous. Performance of individual channel members must be evaluated continually. The manufacturer should be prepared to move quickly, replacing poor performers with potentially better ones. Including the selection process in ongoing channel management puts the process in its proper perspective.

Securing Good Intermediaries The marketer can identify prospective channel members through discussions with company salespeople and existing or potential customers, or through trade sources, such the Verified Directory of Manufacturers' Representatives. Once the list of potential intermediaries is reduced to a few names, the manufacturer uses the selection criteria to evaluate them. For example, the McGraw-Edison Company uses an intensive checklist to compare prospective channel members; important criteria are market coverage, product lines, personnel, growth, and financial standing.

The formation of the channel is not at all a one-way street. The manufacturer must now persuade the intermediaries to become part of the channel system. Some distributors evaluate potential suppliers just as rigorously as the manufacturers rate them—using many of the same considerations. Manufacturers must often demonstrate the sales and profit potential of their product and be willing to grant the intermediaries some territorial exclusivity. Special efforts are required to convince the very best rep in a market to represent a particular manufacturer's product. Those efforts must demonstrate that the manufacturer will treat the rep organization as a partner and support it.

Motivating Channel Members

Distributors and reps are independent and profit oriented. They are oriented toward their customers and toward whatever means are necessary to satisfy customer needs for industrial products and services. Their perceptions and outlook may differ substantially from those of the manufacturers they represent. As a consequence, marketing strategies can fail when managers do not tailor their programs to the capabilities and orientations of their intermediaries. To manage the business marketing channel effectively, the marketer must understand the intermediaries' perspective and devise ways to motivate them to perform in a way that enhances the manufacturer's long-term success. The manufacturer must continually seek support from intermediaries, and the quality of that support depends on the motivational techniques used.

A Partnership Channel member motivation begins with the understanding that the channel relationship is a *partnership*. Manufacturers and intermediaries are in business together; whatever expertise and assistance the manufacturer can provide to the intermediaries improves total channel effectiveness. One study of channel relationships suggested that manufacturers may be able to increase the level of resources directed to their products by developing a trusting relationship with their reps; by improving communication through recognition programs, product training, and consultation with the reps; and by informing the reps of plans, explicitly detailing objectives, and providing positive feedback.[20]

Another study of distributor-manufacturer working partnerships recommended similar approaches. It also suggested that manufacturers and their distributors engage in joint annual planning that focuses on specifying the cooperative efforts each firm requires of its partner to reach its objectives and that periodically reviews progress toward objectives.[21] The net result is trust and satisfaction with the partnership as the relationship leads to meeting performance goals.

Dealer Advisory Councils   One way to enhance the performance of all channel members is to facilitate the sharing of information among them. Distributors or reps may be brought together periodically with the manufacturer's management to review distribution policies, provide advice on marketing strategy, and supply industry intelligence.[22] Intermediaries can voice their opinions on policy matters and are brought directly into the decision-making process. Dayco Corporation uses a dealer council to keep abreast of distributors' changing needs.[23] One month after their meeting, council members receive a written report of suggestions they made and of the programs to be implemented as a result. Generally, Dayco enacts 75 percent of distributor proposals. For dealer councils to be effective, the input of channel members must have a meaningful effect on channel policy decisions.

Margins and Commission   In the final analysis, the primary motivating device is compensation. The surest way to lose intermediary support is compensation policies that do not meet industry and competitive standards. Reps or distributors who feel cheated on commissions or margins shift their attention to products generating a higher profit. The manufacturer must pay the prevailing compensation rates in the industry and must adjust the rates as conditions change.

Intermediaries' compensation should reflect the marketing tasks they perform. If the manufacturer seeks special attention for a new industrial product, most reps require higher commissions. As noted earlier in the chapter, many industrial distributors charge separate fees for the value-added services they provide. For this approach to work effectively, it is critical that the client understands the value it is receiving for the extra charges.

Building Trust   The very nature of a distribution channel—with each member dependent on another for success—can invite conflict. Conflict can be controlled in various ways, including channel-wide committees, joint goal setting, and cooperative programs involving a number of marketing strategy elements. To compete, business marketers need to be effective at cooperating within a network of organizations—the channel. For example, an IBM executive who led the team that developed the first IBM PC in 1981 also drove the decision to sell it through dealers and later through the channel. Soon after the introduction of the PC, an executive with American Express Travel Related Services approached the IBM executive with an idea to sell

[20]Erin Anderson, Leonard M. Lodish, and Barton A. Weitz, "Resource Allocation in Conventional Channels," *Journal of Marketing Research* 24 (February 1987): p. 95; see also McQuiston, "A Conceptual Model," pp. 165–181.

[21]James C. Anderson and James A. Narus, "A Model of Distribution Firm and Manufacturing Firm Working Partnerships," *Journal of Marketing* 54 (January 1990): p. 56.

[22]Doug Harper, "Councils Launch Sales Ammo," *Industrial Distribution* 80 (September 1990): pp. 27–30.

[23]James A. Narus and James C. Anderson, "Turn Your Distributors into Partners," *Harvard Business Review* 64 (March–April 1986): p. 68.

the PCs directly to American Express card members. The IBM executive refused—he wanted the *channel* to get the sale. As a result, IBM secured the commitment and trust of its channel partners, setting the stage for many other strategy initiatives.[24]

Successful cooperation results from relationships in which the parties have a strong sense of communication and trust. Robert M. Morgan and Shelby D. Hunt suggest that relationship commitment and trust develop when: (1) firms offer benefits and resources that are superior to what other partners could offer; (2) firms align themselves with other firms that have similar corporate values; (3) firms share valuable information on expectations, markets, and performance; and (4) firms avoid taking advantage of their partners.[25] By following these prescriptions, business marketers and their channel networks can enjoy sustainable competitive advantages over their rivals and their networks.

Summary

Channel strategy is an exciting and challenging aspect of business marketing. The challenge derives from the number of alternatives available to the manufacturer in distributing business products. The excitement results from the ever-changing nature of markets, user needs, and competitors.

Channel strategy involves two primary management tasks: designing the overall structure and managing the operation of the channel. Channel design includes evaluating distribution goals, activities, and potential intermediaries. Channel structure includes the number, types, and levels of intermediaries to be used. A central challenge is determining how to create a strategy that effectively blends e-commerce with traditional channels. Business marketing firms use multiple sales channels to serve customers in a particular market segment: company salespersons, channel partners, call centers, direct mail, and the Internet. The goal of a multichannel strategy is to coordinate activities across those channels to enhance the customer's experience while advancing the firm's performance.

The primary participants in business marketing channels are distributors and reps. Distributors provide the full range of marketing services for their suppliers, although customer contact and product availability are their most essential functions. Manufacturers' representatives specialize in selling, providing their suppliers with quality representation and with extensive product and market knowledge. The rep is not involved with physical distribution, leaving that burden to the manufacturers.

The central objective of channel management is to enhance the value delivered to customers through the carefully orchestrated activities of channel partners. The channel design process hinges on deep knowledge of customer needs, and the channel structure must be adjusted as customer or competitor behavior changes. Selection and motivation of channel partners are two management tasks vital to channel success. The business marketing manager may need to apply interorganizational management techniques to resolve channel conflict. Conflict can be controlled through a variety of means, including channel-wide committees, joint goal setting, and cooperative programs that demonstrate trust and commitment.

---

[24]Jeff O'Heir, "The Advocates: They Raised Their Voices to Legitimize the Channel," *Computer Reseller News*, June 17, 2002, p. 51.

[25]Robert M. Morgan and Shelby D. Hunt, "The Commitment-Trust Theory of Relationship Marketing," *Journal of Marketing* 58 (July 1994): pp. 20–38.

Discussion Questions

1. Compare and contrast the functions performed by industrial distributors and manufacturers' representatives.

2. What product/market factors lend themselves to the use of manufacturers' representatives?

3. Describe specific product, market, and competitive conditions that lend themselves to: (a) a direct channel of distribution and (b) an indirect channel of distribution.

4. Describe why it might be necessary for a business-to-business firm to serve some customers through reps, some through distributors, others exclusively online, and still others through a direct sales force.

5. Explain how a direct distribution channel may be the lowest-cost alternative for one business marketer and the highest-cost alternative for another in the same industry.

6. Explain how a change in segmentation policy (that is, entering new markets) may trigger the need for drastic changes in the industrial channel of distribution.

7. Using a multichannel integration map (see Figure 10.3), illustrate how a firm might cover small and medium-sized businesses versus large corporate customers.

8. For many years, critics have charged that intermediaries contribute strongly to the rising prices of goods in the American economy. Would business marketers improve the level of efficiency and effectiveness in the channel by reducing as far as possible the number of intermediate links in the channel? Support your position.

9. Describe the specific tasks in the typical sales cycle and discuss how different channels (for example, business partners versus the Internet) can perform different tasks within a single sales transaction.

10. Both business marketers and distributors are interested in achieving profit goals. Why, then, are manufacturer-distributor relationships characterized by conflict? What steps can the marketer take to reduce conflict and thus improve channel performance?

Internet Exercise

1. Sysco Corporation is a large distributor of food and food-related products to the food-service industry. The company provides its products and services to approximately 415,000 customers, including restaurants, health-care and educational facilities, lodging establishments, and other food-service customers. Although *Cisco Systems*, the leading supplier of data networking equipment supporting the Internet, is most visible in the business press, Sysco generates over $37 billion in sales annually and has more than 46,000 employees. Go to http://www.sysco.com and identify some of the services Sysco provides.

CHAPTER

11

Supply Chain Management

When suppliers fail to deliver products or services as promised, buyers search for a new supplier. Organizational buyers assign great importance to supply chain processes that eliminate the uncertainty of product delivery. Supply chain management assures that product, information, service, and financial resources all flow smoothly through the entire value-creation process. Business marketers invest considerable financial and human resources in creating supply chains to service the needs and special requirements of their customers. After reading this chapter, you will understand:

1. The role of supply chain management in business marketing strategy

2. The importance of integrating both firms and functions throughout the entire supply chain

3. The critical role of logistics activities in achieving supply chain management goals

4. The importance of achieving high levels of logistics service performance while simultaneously controlling the cost of logistics activities

Bill Copacino, a leading strategy consultant, puts the importance of supply chain management in focus:[1]

> In almost every industry, supply chain management has become a much more important strategic and competitive variable. It affects all of the shareholder value levers—cost, customer service, asset productivity, and revenue generation. Yet we are seeing a growing gap in performance between the leading and the average companies. The best are getting better faster than the average companies across almost every industry. The leading *supply chain* performers are applying new technology, new innovations, and new process thinking to great advantage. The average-performing companies and the laggards have a limited window of opportunity in which to catch up.

Who are the leading supply chain performers? Gartner, Inc., examines this question with its annual ranking of the top 25 chains.[2] Topping the most recent list are three mainstays—Apple, Dell, and Procter & Gamble. Apple has achieved the #1 ranking for four years in a row based on high inventory turns, stunning revenue growth, and a high return on assets (ROA). Both Apple and Dell operate with 40 to 50 inventory turns, more than two to three times that of their respective competitors.

Supply chain management (SCM) is a technique for linking a manufacturer's operations with those of all of its strategic suppliers and its key intermediaries and customers to enhance efficiency and effectiveness. Central to SCM are the coordination and collaboration activities performed with partners, which may include suppliers, intermediaries, third-party service providers, and customers.

SCM can advance a firm's financial performance in two fundamental ways: revenue enhancement and cost reduction.[3] First, by creating a more responsive supply chain to meet customer requirements and deliver on promises, successful SCM helps a company to win new customers and win more business (and increase revenue) from existing customers. Second, by integrating processes from procurement and manufacturing to logistics, successful SCM lowers costs across the entire enterprise, advancing profitability.

This chapter describes the nature of SCM, isolates the factors that lead to successful supply chain strategies, and demonstrates how logistics management is a key driver of supply chain success. Once the strategic role of SCM has been highlighted, the chapter examines how logistics processes form the core of the SCM strategy. The logistical elements are described in terms of their interface within the distribution channel and how they must be integrated to create desired customer service standards and responsive business marketing strategies.

---

[1]Bill Copacino, "Supply Chain Challenges: Building Relationships," *Harvard Business Review* 81 (July 2003): p. 69.

[2]Debra Hofman, Kevin O'Marah, and Carla Elvy, "The Gartner Supply Chain Top 25 for 2011," June 1, 2011, Gartner, Inc., accessed at http://www.gartner.com on July 2, 2011, pp. 1–21.

[3]Robert A. Rudzki, "Supply Chain Management Transformation: A Leader's Guide," *Supply Chain Management Review* 12 (March 2008): p. 14. See also Peter C. Brewer and Thomas W. Speh, "Using the Balanced Scorecard to Measure Supply Chain Performance," *Journal of Business Logistics* (Spring 2000): p. 75.

Supply Chain Management: A Tool for Competitive Advantage

The supply chain can be a powerful competitive weapon, as market leaders like Apple, Dell, and Cisco demonstrate. Based on their examination of top-performing supply chains, analysts at Gardner, Inc., observe:

> The old image of a supply chain organization limited to either inbound materials management or logistics, with procurement, planning, manufacturing, and customer service as totally separate functions, is fading. What's replacing it is a supply chain organization, often reporting at the board level, that includes the functions of plan, source, make, and deliver.[4]

In essence, this represents a shift from the notion of a "supply chain" to a "value chain" that is tightly connected to the overarching business strategy.

As a primary interface point with the customer, SCM can offer value in the form of competitively superior delivery and value-added services, as defined by customers. Best-in-class SCM practices provide advantages, including 10 to 30 percent higher on-time delivery performance, a 40 to 65 percent (or 1- to 2-month) advantage in cash-to-cash cycle time, and 50 to 80 percent less standing inventory, which all translates into 3 to 6 percent of a company's revenue. For a $100 million company, earnings improvements of up to $6 million are achievable by thoroughly adopting SCM practices.[5] However, SCM, as a source of competitive advantage, is not simply a way to reduce cost, but also a way to boost revenues.[6]

Supply Chain Management Goals

SCM is both a boundary- and function-spanning endeavor. The underlying premise of SCM is that waste reduction and enhanced supply chain performance come only with both intrafirm and interfirm functional integration, sharing, and cooperation. Therefore, each firm within the supply chain must tear down functional silos and foster true coordination and integration of marketing, production, procurement, sales, and logistics. Furthermore, actions, systems, and processes among *all* the supply chain participants must be integrated and coordinated. Firm-wide integration is a necessary, but not sufficient, condition for achieving the full potential benefits of SCM. Integration must be taken to a higher plane so that functions and processes are coordinated across all the organizations in the supply chain. SCM is undertaken to achieve four major goals: waste reduction, time compression, flexible response, and unit cost reduction.[7]

---

[4]Hofman, O'Marah, and Elvy, "The Gartner Supply Chain Top 25 for 2011," p. 7. See also Andreas Maurer, Sandra Wieland, Carl Marcus Wallenburg, and Martin Springinklee, "Achieving Supply Chain Advantage," November 2010, The Boston Consulting Group, pp. 1–9, accessed at http://www.bcg.com on June 25, 2011.

[5]Bill Faherenwald, "Supply Chain: Managing Logistics for the 21st Century," *Business Week*, December 28, 1998, Special Section, p. 3.

[6]Charles Batchelor, "Moving Up the Corporate Agenda," *The Financial Times*, December 1, 1998, p. 1.

[7]Brewer and Speh, "Using the Balanced Scorecard," p. 76.

Waste Reduction   Firms that practice SCM seek to reduce waste by minimizing duplication, harmonizing operations and systems, and enhancing quality. With respect to duplication, firms at all levels in the supply chain often maintain inventories. Efficiencies can be gained for the chain as a whole if the inventories can be centralized and maintained by just a few firms at critical points in the distribution process. With a joint goal of reducing waste, supply chain partners can work together to modify policies, procedures, and data-collection practices that produce or encourage waste.[8] Typically, waste across the supply chain manifests itself in excess inventory. Effective ways to address this issue are through postponement and customization strategies, which push the final assembly of a completed product to the last practical point in the chain. Dell provides an excellent illustration of how to reduce waste through effective "waste" management strategies. The company's build-to-order model produces a computer only when there is an actual customer order. Dell works with its suppliers to achieve a system where inventory turns are measured in hours rather than days. Because Dell does not maintain stocks of unsold finished goods, it has no need to conduct "fire sales." The result: Waste has been eliminated both on the component side and on the finished-goods side.

Time Compression   Another critical goal of SCM is to compress order-to-delivery cycle time. When production and logistics processes are accomplished in less time, everyone in the supply chain is able to operate more efficiently, and a primary result is reduced inventories throughout the system. Time compression also enables supply chain partners to more easily observe and understand the cumulative effect of problems that occur anywhere in the chain and respond quickly. Reduced cycle time also speeds the cash-to-cash cycle for all chain members, enhancing cash flow and financial performance throughout the system. Time compression means that information and products flow smoothly and quickly, thus permitting all parties to respond to customers in a timely manner while maintaining minimal inventory. Many industrial distributors, like W.W. Grainger, have designed supply chains that are able to respond to customer orders with "same-day" delivery, allowing customers to reduce inventories and to rest assured that timely delivery support is available to solve unexpected problems.

Flexible Response   The third goal of SCM is to develop flexible response throughout the supply chain. Flexible response in order handling, including how orders are handled, product variety, order configuration, order size, and several other dimensions, means that a customer's unique requirements can be met cost-effectively. To illustrate, a firm that responds flexibly can configure a shipment in almost any way (for example, different pallet patterns or different product assortments) and do it quickly without problems for the customer. Flexibility also may mean customizing products in the warehouse to correspond to a customer's need for unique packaging and unitization. The key to flexibility is to meet individual customer needs in a way that the customer views as cost-effective and the supply chain views as profitable.

---

[8]Kate Vitasek, Karl B. Manrodt, and Jeff Abbott, "What Makes a LEAN Supply Chain?" *Supply Chain Management Review* 9 (October 2005): pp. 39–45.

Unit Cost Reduction   The final goal of SCM is to operate logistics in a manner that reduces cost per unit for the end customer. Firms must determine the level of performance the customer desires and then minimize the costs of providing that service level. The business marketer should carefully assess the balance between level of cost and the degree of service provided. The goal is to provide an appropriate value equation for the customer, meaning that cost in some cases is higher for meaningful enhancements in service. Cost cutting is not an absolute, but the SCM approach is focused on driving costs to the lowest possible level for the level of service requested. For example, shipping product in full truckload quantities weekly is less expensive than shipping pallet quantities every day; however, when a customer like Honda wants daily deliveries to minimize inventories, the SCM goal is to offer daily shipments at the lowest possible cost. SCM principles drive down costs because they focus management attention on eliminating activities that unnecessarily add cost, such as duplicate inventories, double and triple handling of the product, unconsolidated shipments, and uncoordinated promotions, such as special sales.

Hau Lee, an internationally recognized expert, points out that supply chain efficiency is necessary, but it is not enough to ensure that firms do better than their rivals. Only companies that build agile, adaptable, and aligned supply chains get ahead of the competition.[9] Efficient supply chains often become uncompetitive because they do not adapt to changes in market structures: Supply chains need to keep adapting so that they can adjust to changing customer needs. In addition, low-cost supply chains are not always able to respond to sudden and unexpected changes in markets—like a shift in resource availability or the effect of a natural disaster. Finally, excellent supply chain companies align the interests of all the firms in their supply chain with their own—if any company's interests differ from those of the other organizations in the supply chain, its actions do not maximize the chain's performance.

Benefits to the Final Customer

A well-managed supply chain ultimately creates tangible benefits for customers throughout the supply chain. When the supply chain reduces waste, improves cycle time and flexible response, and minimizes costs, these benefits should flow through to ultimate customers. Thus, a key focus of the supply chain members is monitoring how much the customer is realizing these important benefits and assessing what may be preventing them from doing so. A supply chain's customer can be viewed on several dimensions, and it is important to focus on each. A producer of electronic radio parts views the radio manufacturer as an absolutely critical customer, but the auto manufacturer that installs the radio in a car is equally important, if not more so, and ultimately the final buyer of the automobile must be satisfied. So, different demands, desires, and idiosyncrasies of customers all along the supply chain must be understood and managed effectively.

---

[9]Hau L. Lee, "The Triple-A Supply Chain," *Harvard Business Review* 82 (October 2004): pp. 102–112.

INSIDE BUSINESS MARKETING

When the Supply Chain Gets Disrupted

Japan's devastating earthquake in May of 2011 wreaked havoc on global supply chains, particularly in the consumer electronics, auto, and medical device industries, and placed crisis management at the top of the corporate agenda. As global business expands, the odds of a major or minor disruption in supply chains dramatically increase.

Mark Freedman and his colleagues at the Boston Consulting Group propose specific steps companies should take—drawn from the tried-and-tested experience of those at the forefront of crisis management—to increase the flexibility of their supply chains:

1. *Analyze and monitor risk exposure.* Identify those products that generate the greatest share of company revenue and map the resource inputs for those products, flagging any single-source components.

2. *Diversify supply sources.* Develop a portfolio of supply sources and manufacturing sites in different regions to reduce risk.

3. *Reevaluate "make versus buy" decisions.* Prioritize critical inputs to key products and consider bringing some outsourced components "back in-house."

4. *Build stronger supplier relationships.* Identify the company's most valuable suppliers and develop a partnership by drawing on their expertise and providing them with a greater volume of business, longer-term contract, or gain-sharing arrangement where they share cost savings from ideas they provide.

5. *Share real-time information with supply chain partners.*

6. *Perform regular "stress tests" of the supply chain* to evaluate the likely impact of a disruption and correct vulnerabilities.

SOURCE: Mark Freedman, Satoshi Komiya, Joe Manget, Pierre Mercier, and Naoki Shigetake, "After Japan's Earthquake: Rethinking the Supply Chain," June 28, 2011, The Boston Consulting Group, Inc., accessed at http://www.bcg.com on July 7, 2011.

The Financial Benefits Perspective

Innovative supply chain strategies that couple physical goods movement with financial information sharing can open the door to greater end-to-end supply chain cost savings, better balance sheets, lower total costs, higher margins, and a more stable supply chain with everyone sharing the savings.[10] When supply chain partners are achieving their goals and the benefits are flowing through to customers, supply chain members should succeed financially. The most commonly reported benefits for firms that adopt SCM are lower costs, higher profit margins, enhanced cash flow, revenue growth, and a higher rate of return on assets. Because activities are harmonized and unduplicated, the cost of transportation, order processing, order selection, warehousing, and inventory is usually reduced. A study to validate the correlation between supply chain integration and business success shows that best-practice SCM companies have a 45 percent total supply chain cost advantage over their median supply chain competitors.[11] Cash flows are improved because the total

---

[10]Aura Drakšaite and Vytautas Snieška, "Advanced Cost Saving Strategies of Supply Chain Management in Global Markets," *Economics and Management* (2008): p. 113

[11]Brad Ferguson, "Implementing Supply Chain Management," *Production and Inventory Management Journal* (Second Quarter, 2000): p. 64.

cycle time from raw materials to finished product is reduced. The leading firms also enjoy greater cash flow—they have a cash-to-order cycle time exactly half that of the median company. On the other hand, recent evidence suggests that the stock market punishes firms that stumble in SCM. For example, one study showed that supply chain glitches can result in an 8.6 percent drop in stock price on the day the problem is announced and up to a 20 percent decline within 6 months.[12]

Information and Technology Drivers

Supply chains could not function at high levels of efficiency and effectiveness without powerful information systems. Many of the complex Internet supply chains maintained by companies like Hewlett-Packard and Cisco could not operate at high levels without sophisticated information networks and interactive software. The Internet—and Internet technology—is the major tool business marketers rely on to manage their lengthy and integrated systems. In addition, a host of software applications play a key role in helping a supply chain operate at peak efficiency.

Supply Chain Software   SCM software applications provide real-time analytical systems that manage the flow of products and information through the supply chain network.[13] Of course, many supply chain functions are coordinated, including procurement, manufacturing, transportation, warehousing, order entry, forecasting, and customer service. Much of the software is focused on each one of the different functional areas (for example, inventory planning or transportation scheduling). However, the trend is to move toward software solutions that integrate several or all of these functions. The result is that firms can work with a comprehensive "supply chain suite" of software that manages flow across the supply chain while including all of the key functional areas. Several firms producing Enterprise Resource Planning (ERP) software—such as SAP or Oracle—have developed applications that attempt to integrate functional areas and bridge gaps across the supply chain.

SCM software creates the ability to transmit data in real time and helps organizations *transform* supply chain processes into competitive advantages. Equipping employees with portable bar code scanners that feed a centralized database, FedEx is a *best-practices* leader at seamlessly integrating a variety of technologies to enhance all processes across an extended supply chain.[14] The company uses a real-time data transmission system (via the bar code scanners used for every package) to assist in routing, tracking, and delivering packages. The information recorded by the scanners is transmitted to a central database and is made available to *all* employees and customers. Each day FedEx's communications network processes nearly 400,000 customer service calls and tracks the location, pickup time, and delivery time of 2.5 million packages! FedEx is electronically linked so tightly with some customers that when the customer receives an order, FedEx's server is notified to print a shipping label, generate an internal request for pickup, and then download the label to the customer's server. The label, with all the needed customer information, is printed at the customer's warehouse and applied to the package just before FedEx picks it up.

---

[12]Robert J. Bowman, "Does Wall Street Really Care about the Supply Chain?" *Global Logistics and Supply Chain Strategies* (April 2001): pp. 31–35.

[13]Steven Kahl, "What's the 'Value' of Supply Chain Software?" *Supply Chain Management Review* 3 (Winter 1999): p. 61.

[14]Sandor Boyson and Thomas Corsi, "The Real-Time Supply Chain," *Supply Chain Management Review* 5 (January–February 2001): p. 48.

This tight electronic linkage adds significant efficiency to the customer's supply chain process and allows FedEx to deliver on its promises.[15]

Successfully Applying the Supply Chain Management Approach

The design of the firm's supply chain often depends on the nature of the demand for its products. Marshall Fisher suggests that products can be separated into two categories: "functional" items, like paper, maintenance supplies, and office furniture, for example; or "innovative" items, like smart phones, computer notepads, or other high-tech products. The importance of this distinction is that functional items require different supply chains than do innovative products.[16]

Functional products typically have predictable demand patterns, whereas innovative products do not. The goal for functional products is to design a supply chain with efficient physical distribution; that is, it minimizes logistics and inventory costs and assures low-cost manufacturing. Here, the key information sharing takes place within the supply chain so that all participants can effectively orchestrate manufacturing, ordering, and delivery to minimize production and inventory costs.

Innovative products, on the other hand, have less predictable demand, and the key concern is reacting to short life cycles, avoiding shortages or excess supplies, and taking advantage of high profits during peak demand periods. Rather than seeking to minimize inventory, supply chain decisions center on the questions of where to *position* inventory, along with production capacity, in order to hedge against uncertain demand. The critical task is to capture and distribute timely information on customer demand to the supply chain. When designing the supply chain, firms should concentrate on creating *efficient* processes for functional products and *responsive* processes for innovative products.

Successful Supply Chain Practices

Most successful supply chains have devised approaches for participants to work together in a partnering environment. Supply chains are not effective and, in reality, are *not* supply chains when the participants are adversaries. Supply chain partnerships form the foundation. Highly effective supply chains feature integrated operations across supply chain participants, timely information sharing, and delivering added value to the customer. As testimony to the importance of supply chain partnerships, the Malcolm Baldrige National Quality Award Committee recently made "key supplier and customer partnering and communication mechanisms" a separate category that it would use to recognize the best companies in the United States.[17] In considering the economic value created across *the supply chain*, one expert observes, "You should go for the best return on net assets for the supply chain, and trade off costs between income statements and balance sheets to see

[15]For a related discussion, see Pierre J. Richard and Timothy M. Devinney, "Modular Strategies: B2B Technology and Architectural Knowledge," *California Management Review* 47 (Summer 2005): pp. 86–113.

[16]Marshall Fisher, "What Is the Right Supply Chain for Your Product?" *Harvard Business Review* 75 (March–April 1997): p. 106.

[17]Jeffrey K. Liker and Thomas Y. Choi, "Building Deep Supplier Relationships," *Harvard Business Review* 82 (December 2004): p. 104.

B2B TOP PERFORMERS

Making Supplier Relationships Work

During the past decade, Toyota and Honda have struck remarkable partnerships with some of the same suppliers who describe their relationships with the Big Three U.S. automakers as adversarial. Of the 2.1 million Toyota/Lexuses and the 1.6 million Honda/Acuras sold in North America in 2003, Toyota manufactured 60 percent and Honda 80 percent in North America. Moreover, the two companies source about 70 to 80 percent of the costs of making each automobile from North American suppliers. Despite the odds, Toyota and Honda have managed to replicate in an alien Western culture the same kind of supplier webs they developed in Japan. Consequently, they enjoy the best supplier relations in the U.S. automobile industry, have the fastest product-development processes, and reduce costs and improve quality year after year. Toyota claims that over 60 percent of its innovations come from ideas provided by their suppliers! Hence, they understand the importance of maintaining excellent supplier relationships.

Both firms:

- Understand how their suppliers work and develop deep knowledge of the degree of efficiency and effectiveness that particular suppliers demonstrate.
- Turn supplier rivalry into an opportunity by rewarding quality, innovation, and cost-reduction initiatives.
- Actively supervise suppliers and help them improve their operational capabilities.
- Continuously and intensively share information with suppliers.
- Conduct joint improvement activities to advance mutual goals.

Rather than excelling on one dimension, Toyota and Honda win by applying all of them as a system for continuously improving supplier relationships.

SOURCE: Jeffrey K. Liker and Thomas Y. Choi, "Building Deep Supplier Relationships," *Harvard Business Review* 82 (December 2004): pp. 104–113.

that *everybody* shares in that gain."[18] For the supply chain partners to work as a unit, this enlightened perspective of collaboration is mandatory.

For the supply chain partnership to succeed, the partners need to clearly define their strategic objectives, understand where their objectives converge (and perhaps diverge), and resolve any differences.[19] Because the supply chain strategy drives all the important processes in each firm as well as those that connect the firms, managers in both organizations must participate in key decisions and support the chosen course. Once key participants specify and endorse supply chain strategies, performance metrics can be established to track how well the supply chain is meeting its common goals. The metrics used to measure performance are tied to the strategy and must be linked to the performance evaluation and reward systems for employees in each of the participating firms. Without this step, individual managers would not be motivated to accomplish the broad goals of the supply chain.

---

[18]Richard H. Gamble, "Financing Supply Chains," http://businessfinancemag.com (June 2002): p. 35.

[19]Peter C. Brewer and Thomas W. Speh, "Adapting the Balanced Scorecard to Supply Chain Management," *Supply Chain Management Review* 5 (March–April 2001): p. 49.

Logistics as the Critical Element in Supply Chain Management

Nowhere in business marketing strategy is SCM more important than in logistics.

> Logistics management is that part of supply chain management that plans, implements, and controls the efficient, effective forward and reverse flow and storage of goods, services, and related information between the point of origin and the point of consumption in order to meet customers' requirements. Logistics management is an integrating function that coordinates and optimizes all logistics activities, as well as integrates logistics activities with other functions including marketing, sales, manufacturing, finance, and information technology.[20]

Effective business marketing demands efficient, systematic delivery of finished products to channel members and customers. The importance of this ability has elevated the logistics function to a place of prominence in the marketing strategy of many business marketers.

Distinguishing Between Logistics and Supply Chain Management

Logistics is the critical element in SCM. In fact, there is considerable confusion over the difference between the discipline of SCM and logistics. As discussed, SCM is focused on the *integration of* all *business processes* that add value for customers.

The 1990s witnessed the rising importance of time-based competition, rapidly improving information technology, expanding globalization, increasing attention to quality, and the changing face of interfirm relationships. These trends combined to cause companies to expand their perspective on logistics to include all the firms involved in creating a finished product and delivering it to the buyer or user on time and in perfect condition. For example, the supply chain for electric motors would include raw material suppliers, steel fabricators, component parts manufacturers, transportation companies, the electric motor manufacturer, the distributor of electric motors, the warehouse companies that store and ship components and finished products, and the motor's ultimate buyer. Figure 11.1 graphically depicts such a supply chain. The SCM concept is an integrating philosophy for coordinating the total flow of a supply channel from supplier to ultimate user. Logistics is critical, however, to business marketers, because regardless of the orientation to the entire supply chain, the firm relies on its logistics system to deliver product in a timely, low-cost manner.

Managing Flows

The significance of the supply chain perspective in logistical management is that the business marketing manager focuses attention on the performance of *all participants* in the supply chain. The manager also coordinates their efforts to enhance the timely delivery of the finished product to the ultimate user at the lowest possible cost. Inherent in the supply chain approach is the need to form close *relationships* with

---

[20]CSCMP Definition of Logistics, accessed at http://cscmp.org/digital/glossary/glossary.asp accessed on September 22, 2011, p. 114.

FIGURE 11.1 | SUPPLY CHAIN FOR ELECTRIC MOTORS

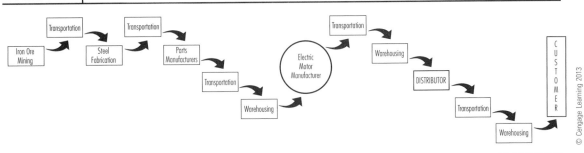

the supply chain participants, including vendors, transportation suppliers, warehousing companies, and distributors. The focus of logistics in the SCM for business marketers is the *flow of product* through the supply chain, with *timely information* driving the entire process.

Product flow in the reverse direction is also important in business supply chains. Many companies, like Xerox and Canon, routinely remanufacture products that are worn out or obsolete. Effective linkages and processes must be in place to return such products to a facility in order to remanufacture or retrofit them. If the reverse supply chains are operating effectively, companies can sometimes realize higher margins on the remanufactured products than they do on new items.[21]

The Strategic Role of Logistics

In the past, logistics was viewed simply as a cost of doing business but today, many companies view logistics as a critical strategic weapon that can add value to customer relationships. For many business marketers, logistics is their *primary* marketing tool for gaining and maintaining competitive superiority. These firms typically recognize that logistics performance is an important part of marketing strategy, and they exploit their logistics competencies. Companies that incorporate logistics planning and management into long-term business strategies can achieve significant benefits, which create real value for the company. To illustrate, Nucor Steel enjoys strong customer loyalty because it can deliver steel to a construction site within a 2- to 4-hour window and offload the truck in the sequence in which the steel beams will be used on the job! This advantage is significant because storage space is limited at most construction sites in urban areas. This strong value-added service allows Nucor to achieve higher levels of profitability than its competitors.

Sales-Marketing-Logistics Integration

The rising value of logistics as a strategic marketing weapon has fostered the integration of the sales, marketing, and logistics functions of many business marketers. In progressive firms, unified teams of sales, production, logistics, information

---

[21]James Stock, Thomas W. Speh, and Herbert Shear, "Many Happy (Product) Returns," *Harvard Business Review* 80 (July 2002): p. 14.

systems, and marketing personnel develop integrated logistics programs to offer to potential customers. Teams of specialists from each area make sales calls and tailor logistics solutions to customer problems. United Stationers, one of the largest U.S. office products distributors, brings operations and salespeople together to meet with the company's resellers in an effort to create customer-responsive logistics service. As a result of its efforts, United guarantees customers that orders placed by 7:00 p.m. will be received before noon on the following day. Customers can dial into United's mainframe computer and place orders electronically. The company considers all of its logistics personnel to be part of the sales function. Some firms have taken the integration even further. Baxter Healthcare warehouse workers team up with warehouse personnel at the hospitals that Baxter serves. During visits to the customer warehouse, the Baxter warehouser evaluates the operation, looking for ways to improve packing so that shipments are easier to unload and unpack. As a result, Baxter warehousers have become salespeople.

Just-in-Time Systems

To serve a customer, business marketers must be prepared to deliver their products frequently and with precise timing. The reason is the widespread adoption by manufacturing firms, like Honda of America, of the **just-in-time (JIT)** inventory principle. Under this principle, suppliers carefully coordinate deliveries with the manufacturer's production schedule—often delivering products just hours before they are used. The objective of a JIT system is to eliminate waste of all kinds from the production process by requiring the delivery of the specified product at the precise time and in the exact quantity needed. The quality must be perfect—there is no opportunity to inspect products in the JIT process. Because JIT attempts to relate purchases to production requirements, the typical order size shrinks, and more frequent deliveries are required. Increased delivery frequency presents a challenge to the business marketing production and logistics system. However, business marketers will have to meet this challenge, as many competitors now compete on the basis of inventory turns and speed to market.[22]

Just-in-Time Relationship A significant effect of JIT purchasing has been to drastically reduce the number of suppliers manufacturers use. Suppliers who are able to meet customers' JIT requirements find their share of business growing.[23] Meeting JIT requirements often represents a marketing edge and may mean survival for some suppliers. The relationship between JIT suppliers and manufacturers is unique and includes operational linkages that unite the buyer and seller. As a result, suppliers find that the relationships are longer lasting and usually formalized with a written contract that may span up to five years.

Elements of a Logistical System Table 11.1 presents the controllable variables of a logistical system. Almost no decision on a particular logistical activity can be made without evaluating its effect on other areas. The system of warehouse facilities, inventory commitments, order-processing methods, and transportation linkages determines the supplier's ability to provide timely product availability to customers. As a result of poor supplier performance, customers may have to bear the extra cost

---

[22]Andrew Tanzer, "Warehouses That Fly," *Forbes*, October 18, 1999, p. 121.

[23]Peter Bradley, "Just-in-Time Works, But...." *Purchasing* 118 (September 1995): p. 36.

TABLE 11.1 | CONTROLLABLE ELEMENTS IN A LOGISTICS SYSTEM

Elements	Key Aspects
Customer service	The "product" of logistics activities, *customer service* relates to the effectiveness in creating time and place utility. The level of customer service provided by the supplier has a direct impact on total cost, market share, and profitability.
Order processing	Order processing triggers the logistics process and directs activities necessary to deliver products to customers. Speed and accuracy of order processing affect costs and customer service levels.
Logistics communication	Information exchanged in the distribution process guides the activities of the system. It is the vital link between the firm's logistics system and its customers.
Transportation	The physical movement of products from source of supply through production to customers is the most significant cost area in logistics, and it involves selecting modes and specific carriers as well as routing.
Warehousing	Providing storage space serves as a buffer between production and use. Warehousing may be used to enhance service and to lower transportation costs.
Inventory control	Inventory is used to make products available to customers and to ensure the correct mix of products is at the proper location at the right time.
Packaging	The role of packaging is to provide protection to the product, to maintain product identity throughout the logistics process, and to create effective product density.
Materials handling	Materials handling increases the speed of, and reduces the cost of, picking orders in the warehouse and moving products between storage and the transportation carriers. It is a cost-generating activity that must be controlled.
Production planning	Utilized in conjunction with logistics planning, production planning ensures that products are available for inventory in the correct assortment and quantity.
Plant and warehouse location	Strategic placement of plants and warehouses increases customer service and reduces the cost of transportation.

SOURCE: Adapted from James R. Stock and Douglas M. Lambert, *Strategic Logistics Management*, 5th ed. (Homewood, IL: McGraw-Hill, 2000).

of higher inventories, institute expensive priority-order-expediting systems, develop secondary supply sources, or, worst of all, turn to another supplier.

Total-Cost Approach

In the management of logistical activities, two performance variables must be considered: (1) total distribution costs and (2) the level of logistical service provided to customers. The logistical system must be designed and administered to achieve that combination of cost and service levels that yields maximum profits. Logistical costs vary widely for business marketers, depending on the nature of the product and on the importance of logistical service to the buyer. Logistical costs can consume 16 to 36 percent of each sales dollar at the manufacturing level, and logistical activities can consume more than 40 percent of total assets. Thus, logistics can have a significant effect on corporate profitability. How, then, can the marketer manage logistical costs?

The **total-cost**, or trade-off, **approach** to logistical management guarantees to minimize total logistical costs in the firm and within the channel. The assumption is that costs of individual logistical activities are interactive; that is, a decision about one logistical variable affects all or some of the others. Management is thus concerned with the efficiency of the entire system rather than with minimizing the cost of any single logistical activity. The interactions among logistical activities (that is, transportation, inventory, warehousing) are described as cost trade-offs because a cost increase in one activity is traded for a large cost decrease in another activity, the net result being an overall cost reduction.

Calculating Logistics Costs

Activity-Based Costing

The activity-based costing (ABC) technique is used to precisely measure the costs of performing specific activities and then trace those costs to the products, customers, and channels that consumed the activities.[24] This is a powerful tool in managing the logistics operations of a supply chain. ABC provides a mechanism to trace the cost of performing logistics services for the customers that use these services, making it easier to assess the appropriate level of customer service to offer. Firms using ABC analysis can obtain more accurate information about how a particular customer or a specific product contributes to overall profitability.[25]

Total Cost of Ownership

Total cost of ownership (TCO) determines the total costs of acquiring and then using a given item from a particular supplier (see Chapter 2). The approach identifies costs—often buried in overhead or general expenses—that relate to the costs of holding inventory, poor quality, and delivery failure.[26] A buyer using TCO explicitly considers the costs that the supplier's logistics system either added to, or eliminated from, the purchase price and would take a long-term perspective in evaluating cost.[27] Thus, a supplier particularly efficient at logistics might be able to reduce the buyer's inventory costs and the buyer's expenses of inspecting inbound merchandise. As a result, the total cost of ownership from that supplier would be lower than the cost from other suppliers that were not able to rapidly deliver undamaged products. Increasing acceptance of the TCO approach will cause logistics efficiency to become an even more critical element of a business marketer's strategy.

---

[24]Bernard J. LaLonde and Terrance L. Pohlen, "Issues in Supply Chain Costing," *International Journal of Logistics Management* 7 (1, 1996): p. 3.

[25]Thomas A. Foster, "Time to Learn the ABCs of Logistics," *Logistics* (February 1999): p. 67.

[26]Lisa Ellram, "Activity-Based Costing and Total Cost of Ownership: A Critical Linkage," *Journal of Cost Management* 8 (Winter 1995): p. 22.

[27]Bruce Ferrin and Richard E. Plank, "Total Cost of Ownership Models: An Exploratory Study," *Journal of Supply Chain Management* 38 (Summer 2002): p. 18.

Business-to-Business Logistical Service

Many studies have shown that logistics service is often just as important as product quality as a measure of supplier performance. In many industries, a quality product at a competitive price is a given, so customer service is the key differentiator among competitors. In one industry, for example, purchasing managers begin the buying process by calling suppliers with the best delivery service to see whether they are willing to negotiate prices. Because it is so important to customers, reliable logistics service can lead to higher market share and higher profits. A study by Bain and Company showed that companies with superior logistics service grow 8 percent faster, collect a 7 percent price premium, and are 12 times as profitable as firms with inferior service levels.[28] These facts, together with the extensive spread of just-in-time manufacturing, make it clear that logistical service is important to organizational buyers.

Logistical service relates to the availability and delivery of products to the customer. It comprises the series of sales-satisfying activities that begin when the customer places the order and that end when the product is delivered. Responsive logistical service satisfies customers and creates the opportunity for closer and more profitable buyer-seller relationships.[29] Logistical service includes whatever aspects of performance are important to the business customer (Table 11.2). These service

TABLE 11.2 | COMMON ELEMENTS OF LOGISTICS SERVICE

Elements	Description
Delivery time	The time from the creation of an order to the fulfillment and delivery of that order encompasses both order-processing time and delivery or transportation time.
Delivery reliability	The most frequently used measure of logistics service, delivery reliability focuses on the capability of having products available to meet customer demand.
Order accuracy	The degree to which items received conform to the specification of the order. The key dimension is the incidence of orders shipped complete and without error.
Information access	The firm's ability to respond to inquiries about order status and product availability.
Damage	A measure of the physical conditions of the product when received by the buyer.
Ease of doing business	A range of factors, including the ease with which orders, returns, credits, billing, and adjustments are handled.
Value-added services	Such features as packaging, which facilitates customer handling, or other services such as prepricing and drop shipments.

SOURCE: Reprinted with permission from Jonathon L. S. Byrnes, William C. Copacino, and Peter Metz, "Forge Service into a Weapon with Logistics," *Transportation and Distribution*, Presidential Issue 28 (September 1987): p. 46.

---

[28]Mary Collins Holcomb, "Customer Service Measurement: A Methodology for Increasing Customer Value through Utilization of the Taguchi Strategy," *Journal of Business Logistics* 15 (1, 1994): p. 29.

[29]Arun Sharma, Dhruv Grewal, and Michael Levy, "The Customer Satisfaction/Logistics Interface," *Journal of Business Logistics* 16 (2, 1995): p. 1.

elements range from delivery time to value-added services, and each of these elements can affect production processes, final product output, costs, or all three.

Logistics Service Impacts on the Customer

Supplier logistical service translates into product availability. For a manufacturer to produce or for a distributor to resell, industrial products must be available at the right time, at the right place, and in usable condition. The longer the supplier's delivery time, the less available the product; the more inconsistent the delivery time, the less available the product. For example, a reduction in the supplier's delivery time permits a buyer to hold less inventory because needs can be met rapidly. The customer reduces the risk that the production process will be interrupted. Consistent delivery enables the buyer to program more effectively—or routinize—the purchasing process, thus lowering buyer costs. Consistent delivery-cycle performance allows buyers to cut their level of buffer or safety stock, thereby reducing inventory cost. However, for many business products, such as those that are low in unit value and relatively standardized, the overriding concern is not inventory cost but simply having the products. A malfunctioning $0.95 bearing could shut down a whole production line.

Determining the Level of Service

Buyers often rank logistics service right behind "quality" as a criterion for selecting a vendor. However, not all products or all customers require the same level of logistical service. Many made-to-order products—such as heavy machinery—have relatively low logistical service requirements. Others, such as replacement parts, components, and subassemblies, require extremely demanding logistical performance. Similarly, customers may be more or less responsive to varying levels of logistical service.

Profitable Levels of Service   In developing a logistical service strategy, business marketing strategists should assess the profit impact of the service options that they provide to customers. In nearly all industries, firms provide numerous supply chain services such as next-day delivery, customized handling, and specialized labeling. However, few companies actually trace the true costs of specialized services and the resulting effect on customer profitability (see Chapter 3).

To combat this unhealthy situation, some companies are now using *cost-to-serve* analytics to address the problem; among them are Dow Chemical, Eastman Chemical, and Georgia-Pacific (GP). GP used total-delivered-cost analysis to improve the performance of a major customer account.[30] By incorporating cost-to-serve data into the calculation of gross margin, GP's supply chain team determined that the costs to provide this customer with expedited transportation and distribution services were significantly reducing the account's profitability. In a top-to-top meeting with the customer, GP used the data to expose the root causes of the high costs and poor service, which included last-minute, uncoordinated promotional planning and purchasing across the customer's major business units and the customer's unwillingness to share inventory levels and positioning. Once confronted with the data, customers are often willing to collaborate on ways to improve service, reduce costs, and restore profitability.

---

[30]Remko Van Hoek, "When Good Customers Are Bad," *Harvard Business Review* 83 (September 2005): p. 19.

To recap, service levels are developed by assessing customer service requirements. The sales and cost of various service levels are analyzed to find the service level generating the highest profits. The needs of various customer segments dictate various logistical system configurations. For example, when logistical service is critical, industrial distributors can provide the vital product availability, whereas customers with less rigorous service demands can be served from factory inventories.

Logistics Impacts on Other Supply Chain Participants

A supplier's logistical system directly affects a distributor's ability to control cost and service to end users. Delivery time influences not only the customer's inventory requirements but also the operations of channel members. If a supplier provides erratic delivery service to distributors, the distributor is forced to carry higher inventory in order to provide a satisfactory level of product availability to end users.

Inefficient logistics service to the distributors either increases distributor costs (larger inventories) or creates shortages of the supplier's products at the distributor level. Neither result is good. In the first instance, distributor loyalty and marketing efforts will suffer; in the second, end users will eventually change suppliers. In some industries, distributors are expanding their role in the logistics process, which makes them even more valuable to their suppliers and customers. In the chemical industry, for example, the role of distributors is completely transforming as they offer logistics solutions—JIT delivery, repackaging, inventory management—to their customers.[31] The logistics expertise distributors provide enables their vendors (manufacturers) to focus on their own core competencies of production and marketing.

Business-to-Business Logistical Management

The elements of logistics strategy are part of a system, and as such, each affects every other element. The proper focus is the total-cost view. Although this section treats the decisions on facilities, transportation, and inventory separately, these areas are so intertwined that decisions in one area influence the others.

Logistical Facilities

The strategic development of a warehouse provides the business marketer with the opportunity to increase the level of delivery service to buyers, reduce transportation costs, or both. Business firms that distribute repair, maintenance, and operating supplies often find that the only way to achieve desired levels of delivery service is to locate warehouses in key markets. The warehouse circumvents the need for premium transportation (air freight) and costly order processing by keeping products readily available in local markets.

Serving Other Supply Chain Members The nature of the business-to-business (B2B) supply chain affects the warehousing requirements of a supplier. Manufacturers' representatives do not hold inventory, but distributors do. When manufacturers' reps are used, the supplier often requires a significant number of strategically located warehouses. On the other hand, a supply chain using distributors

---

[31]Daniel J. McConville, "More Work for Chemical Distributors," *Distribution* 95 (August 1996): p. 63.

offsets the need for warehousing. Obviously, local warehousing by the distributor is a real service to the supplier. A few well-located supplier warehouses may be all that is required to service the distributors effectively.

Outsourcing the Warehousing Function Operating costs, service levels, and investment requirements are essential considerations regarding the type of warehouse to use. The business firm may either operate its own warehouses or turn them over to a "third party"—a company that specializes in performing warehousing services. The advantages of third-party warehousing are flexibility, reduced assets, and professional management—the firm can increase or decrease its use of space in a given market, move into or out of any market quickly, and enjoy an operation managed by specialists. Third-party warehousing may sometimes supplement or replace distributors in a market.

Many third-party warehouses provide a variety of logistical services for their clients, including packaging, labeling, order processing, and some light assembly. Saddle Creek Corporation, a third-party warehouse company based in Lakeland, Florida, maintains warehouse facilities in a number of major markets. Clients can position inventories in all these markets while dealing with only one firm. Also, Saddle Creek can link its computer with the suppliers' computers to facilitate order processing and inventory updating. The Saddle Creek warehouse also repackages products to the end-user's order, labels, and arranges for local delivery. A business marketer can ship standard products in bulk to the Saddle Creek warehouse— gaining transportation economies—and still enjoy excellent customer delivery service. The public or contract warehouse is a feasible alternative to the distributor channel when the sales function can be economically executed either with a direct sales force or with reps.

Transportation

Transportation is usually the largest single logistical expense, and with continually rising fuel costs, its importance will probably increase. Typically, the transportation decision involves evaluating and selecting both a mode of transportation and the individual carrier(s) that will ensure the best performance at the lowest cost. Mode refers to the type of carrier—rail, truck, water, air, or some combination of the four. Individual carriers are evaluated on rates and delivery performance.[32] The supply chain view is important in selecting individual carriers. Carriers become an integral part of the supply chain, and close relationships are important. One study found evidence that carriers' operating performance improved when they were more involved in the relationship between buyer and seller.[33] By further integrating carriers into the supply chain, the entire supply chain can improve its competitive position. In this section we consider: (1) the role of transportation in industrial supply chains and (2) the criteria for evaluating transportation options.

Transportation and Logistical Service A business marketer must be able to effectively move finished inventory between facilities to channel intermediaries and

---

[32]For example, see James C. Johnson, Donald F. Wood, Danile L. Warlow, and Paul R. Murphy, *Contemporary Logistics*, 7th ed. (Upper Saddle River, NJ: Prentice Hall, 1998).

[33]Julie Gentry, "The Role of Carriers in Buyer-Supplier Strategic Partnerships: A Supply Chain Management Approach," *Journal of Business Logistics* 17 (2, 1996): p. 52.

to customers. The transportation system is the link that binds the logistical network together and ultimately results in timely delivery of products. Efficient warehousing does not enhance customer service levels if transportation is inconsistent or inadequate.

Effective transportation service may be used in combination with warehouse facilities and inventory levels to generate the required customer service level, or it may be used in place of them. Inventory maintained in a variety of market-positioned warehouses can be consigned to one centralized warehouse when rapid transportation services exist to deliver products from the central location to business customers. Xerox is one company that uses premium airfreight service to offset the need for high inventories and extensive warehouse locations. The decision on transportation modes and particular carriers depends on the cost trade-offs and service capabilities of each. It is interesting that in the age of next-day delivery and express airfreight services, barges that weave their way through a maze of rivers, lakes, and channels are thriving.[34] A barge trip that takes 17 hours would take a train 4 hours and a truck 90 minutes for a similar trip. Although very slow (averaging 15 miles per hour), the barge offers huge cost advantages compared with truck and rail. For products such as limestone, coal, farm products, and petroleum, the slow and unglamorous barge is an effective logistics tool.

Transportation Performance Criteria   **Cost of service** is the variable cost of moving products from origin to destination, including any terminal or accessory charges. The cost of service may range from as little as $0.01 per ton-mile via water to as high as $0.50 per ton-mile via airfreight. The important aspect of selecting the transportation mode is not cost per se but cost relative to the objective to be achieved. Bulk raw materials generally do not require prepaid delivery service, so the cost of anything other than rail or water transportation could not be justified. On the other hand, although airfreight may be almost 10 times more expensive than motor freight, the cost is inconsequential to a customer who needs an emergency shipment of spare parts. The cost of premium (faster) transportation modes may be justified by the resulting inventory reductions.

Speed of service refers to the elapsed time to move products from one facility (plant or warehouse) to another facility (warehouse or customer plant). Again, speed of service often overrides cost. Rail, a relatively slow mode used for bulk shipments, requires inventory buildups at the supplier's factory and at the destination warehouse. The longer the delivery time, the more inventory customers must maintain to service their needs while the shipment is in transit. The slower modes involve lower variable costs for product movement, yet they result in lower service levels and higher investments in inventory. The faster modes produce just the opposite effect. Not only must a comparison be made between modes in terms of service but various carriers within a mode must be evaluated on their "door-to-door" delivery time.

Service consistency is usually more important than average delivery time, and all modes of transportation are not equally consistent. Although air provides the lowest average delivery time, generally it has the highest variability in delivery time relative to the average. The wide variations in modal service consistency are particularly

[34]Anna Wilde Mathews, "Jet-Age Anomalies, Slowpoke Barges Do Brisk Business," *The Wall Street Journal*, May 15, 1998, p. B1.

critical in business marketing planning. The choice of transportation mode must be made on the basis of cost, average transit time, and consistency if effective customer service is to be achieved.

In summary, because business buyers often place a premium on effective and consistent delivery service, the choice of transportation mode is an important one—one where cost of service is often secondary. However, the best decision on transportation carriers results from a balancing of service, variable costs, and investment requirements. The manager must also consider the transportation requirements of ordinary, versus expedited (rush order), shipments.

Inventory Management

Inventory management is the buffer in the logistical system. Inventories are needed in business channels because:

1. Production and demand are not perfectly matched;

2. Operating deficiencies in the logistical system often result in product unavailability (for example, delayed shipments, inconsistent carrier performance);

3. Business customers cannot predict their product needs with certainty (for example, because a machine may break down or there may be a sudden need to expand production).

Inventory may be viewed in the same light as warehouse facilities and transportation: It is an alternative method for providing the level of service customers require, and the level of inventory is determined on the basis of cost, investment, service required, and anticipated revenue.

Quality Focus: Eliminate Inventories Today's prevalent total-quality-management techniques and just-in-time management principles emphasize the reduction or outright elimination of inventories. Current thinking suggests that inventories exist because of inefficiencies in the system: Erratic delivery, poor forecasting, and ineffective quality-control systems all force companies to hold excessive stocks to protect themselves from delivery, forecasting, and product failure. Instead, improved delivery, forecasting, and manufacturing processes should eliminate the need to buffer against failures and uncertainty. Information technology involving bar coding, scanner data, total quality processes, better transportation management, and more effective information flow among firms in the supply chain have made it possible to control inventories more carefully and reduce them to the lowest possible levels.

The Internet connectivity that unites the supply chain from an information standpoint has permitted substantial inventory reductions in several industries. One recent study showed that average inventory turnover for manufacturers has increased from 8 to more than 12 times per year.[35] Much of the credit for this improvement is attributed to more information sharing among the supply chain members, sophisticated inventory management software, and generally higher levels of supply chain

---

[35]Thomas W. Speh, *Changes in Warehouse Inventory Turnover* (Chicago: Warehousing Education and Research Council, 1999).

INSIDE BUSINESS MARKETING

The Profit Impact of Inventory Management

Deere & Company's core business is manufacturing equipment: agricultural, construction, commercial, and consumer equipment. For its supply chain practices, the firm enjoys an edge over its competitors in the industry, particularly in inventory management. The following illustration demonstrates the significance of this advantage.

On average, assume that Deere maintains 59 days' worth of sales in inventory and the worst firm in the industry maintains 137 days' worth of sales in inventory. Each 30 days' worth of inventory translates to a profit difference of 1.66 percent of sales in the industry. The difference between Deere and the worst competitor is 78 days' worth of inventory. To calculate the profit difference, the following calculations can be made:

Worst firm, inventories: 137 days

Deere & Company, inventories: 59 days

Difference: *78 days*

Each *30 days* is worth *1.66 percent of sales* in profits. The difference between Deere and its "worst" competitor is 78/30 = *2.6 times*.

The difference in profitability is: 2.6 X 1.66% = *4.3% of sales*.

The difference between the worst firm and the best firm as a result of effectively managing inventories is equal to 4.3 percent of sales. If each firm has $1 billion in sales, the best-managed firm will have *$43 million more profits*, all other things being equal!

© Cengage Learning 2013

coordination. Successful business marketing managers must develop quality processes that in themselves reduce or eliminate the need to carry large inventories, while coordinating and integrating a supply chain system that can function effectively with almost no inventory.

Third-Party Logistics

Using **third-party logistics firms** to perform logistics activities represents an important trend among business-to-business firms. These external firms perform a wide range of logistics functions traditionally performed within the organization. Most companies use some type of third-party firm, whether for transportation, warehousing, or information processing. The strategic decision to outsource logistics is often made by top management. The functions the third-party company performs can encompass the entire logistics process or selected activities within that process. Third parties can perform the warehousing; they may perform the transportation function (for example, a truck line like Schneider National); or they may perform the entire logistics process from production scheduling to delivery of finished products to the customer (for example, Ryder Dedicated Logistics). Third parties enable a manufacturer or distributor to concentrate on its core business while enjoying the expertise and specialization of a professional logistics company. The results are often lower costs, better service, improved asset utilization, increased flexibility, and access to leading-edge technology. Recently, some firms have advocated the use of "Fourth-Party Logistics"—firms that own no assets but serve to manage several third parties that are employed to perform various logistics functions.[36]

---

[36]"Fourth Party Logistics: An Analysis," *Logistics Focus* 1 (3, Summer 2002): p. 16.

Despite the advantages of third-party logistics firms, some firms are cautious because of reduced control over the logistics process, diminished direct contact with customers, and the problems of terminating internal operations. In analyzing the most effective and efficient way to accomplish logistics cost and service objectives, the business marketing manager should carefully consider the benefits and drawbacks of outsourcing part or all logistics functions to third-party providers. In an interesting application of third-party logistics, Caterpillar (the manufacturer of earthmoving equipment) formed a logistics services company to manage the parts distribution for other manufacturers.[37] The company applies the knowledge gained from its own experiences in distributing 300 families of products that require over 530,000 spare parts. Caterpillar transfers knowledge from the company's internal operations to customers and vice versa.

Future Focus: The Green Supply Chain   Many experts predict that we will see a major expansion in "green" supply chain initiatives whereby companies are committing to design, source, manufacture, and manage the end-of-life stage for all of their products in an environmentally and socially responsible manner.[38] Other initiatives include developing green packaging and refurbishing products to avoid or minimize landfill waste. One study showed that for many manufacturers, between 40 and 60 percent of a company's carbon footprint resides upstream in its supply chain—from raw materials, transport, and packaging to the energy consumed in manufacturing processes. Therefore, any significant carbon-abatement activities will require collaboration with supply chain partners, first to comprehensively understand the emissions associated with products and then to analyze abatement opportunities systematically.[39] A carefully orchestrated and cooperative approach among supply chain partners provides the foundation for tackling and solving these challenging environmental issues.

Summary

Leading business marketing firms demonstrate superior capabilities in supply chain management. SCM focuses on improving the flow of products, information, and services as they move from origin to destination. A key driver to SCM is coordination and integration among all the participants in the supply chain, primarily through sophisticated information systems and management software. Reducing waste, minimizing duplication, reducing cost, and enhancing service are the major objectives of SCM. Firms successful at managing the supply chain understand the nature of their products and the type of supply chain structure required to meet the needs of their customers. In particular, effective supply chains integrate operations, share information, and above all, provide added value to customers.

---

[37]Peter Marsh, "A Moving Story of Spare Parts," *The Financial Times*, August 29, 1997, p. 8.

[38]Hau Lee, "Don't Tweak Your Supply Chain—Rethink IT End to End," *Harvard Business Review* (October 2010).

[39]Chris Brickman and Drew Ungerman, "Climate Change and Supply Chain Management," McKinsey Quarterly, accessed at http://www.mckinseyquarterly.com/Operations/Supply_Chain_Logistics on August 5, 2008.

Logistics is the critical function in the firm's supply chain because logistics directs the flow and storage of products and information. Successful supply chains synchronize logistics with other functions such as production, procurement, forecasting, order management, and customer service. The systems perspective in logistical management cannot be stressed enough—it is the only way to assure management that the logistical function meets prescribed goals. Not only must each logistical variable be analyzed in terms of its effect on every other variable but the sum of the variables must be evaluated in light of the service level provided to customers. Logistics elements throughout the supply chain must be integrated to assure smooth product flow. Logistical service is critical in the buyer's evaluation of business marketing firms and generally ranks second only to product quality as a desired supplier characteristic.

Logistics decisions must be based on cost trade-offs among the logistical variables and on comparisons of the costs and revenues associated with alternative levels of service. The optimal system produces the highest profitability relative to the capital investment required. Three major variables—facilities, transportation, and inventory—form the basis of logistical decisions B2B logistics managers face. The business marketer must monitor the effect of logistics on all supply chain members and on overall supply chain performance. Finally, the strategic role of logistics should be carefully evaluated: Logistics can often provide a strong competitive advantage.

Discussion Questions

1. Describe a situation in which total logistical costs might be reduced by doubling transportation costs.

2. Explain how consistent delivery performance gives the organizational buyer the opportunity to cut the level of inventory maintained.

3. A key goal in logistical management is to find the optimum balance of logistical cost and customer service that yields optimal profits. Explain.

4. An increasing number of manufacturers are adopting more sophisticated purchasing practices and inventory control systems. What are the strategic implications of these developments for business marketers wishing to serve these customers?

5. Adopting the perspective of an organizational buyer, carefully illustrate how the most economical source of supply might be the firm that offers the highest price but also the fastest and most reliable delivery system.

6. Describe the role the Internet plays in enhancing supply chain management operations.

7. Explain the different elements of "waste" that exist in supply chains and how supply chain management focuses on eliminating the various elements of waste.

8. Explain why cooperation among supply chain participants determines whether the supply chain is effective.

9. Explain how an effective supply chain can create a strong competitive advantage for the firms involved in it.

10. What is supply chain management, and what are the types of functions and firms that make up the typical supply chain?

Internet Exercise

1. YRC Worldwide, Inc., is a *Fortune* 500 transportation company and one of the largest transportation firms in the world. Go to http://www.yrcw.com and examine the online tools available on the Web site. Discuss how the various tools would help a B2B marketer enhance the logistics services that they provide to customers.

CHAPTER

12

Pricing Strategies
for Business Markets

Understanding how customers define value is the essence of the pricing process. Pricing decisions complement the firm's overall marketing strategy. The diverse nature of the business market presents unique problems and opportunities for the price strategist. After reading this chapter, you will understand:

1. The central elements of the pricing process and a value-based strategy

2. How effective new-product prices are established and the need to periodically adjust the prices of existing products

3. How to respond to a price attack by an aggressive competitor

4. Strategic approaches to competitive bidding

Customer value represents the cornerstone of business-to-business (B2B) marketing in the twenty-first century.[1] Thus, business marketers must pursue this unifying strategic goal: Be better than your very best competitors in providing customer value.[2] According to Richard D'Aveni:

> While the average competitor fights for niches along a common ratio of price and value ("You get what you pay for"), innovative firms can enter the market by providing better value to the customer ("You can get more than what you pay for"). These companies offer lower cost and higher quality. This shift in value is like lowering the stick while dancing the limbo. All the competitors have to do the same dance with tighter constraints on both cost and quality.[3]

The business marketing manager must blend the various components of the marketing mix into a value proposition that responds to the customer's requirements and provides a return consistent with the firm's objectives. Price must be carefully meshed with the firm's product, distribution, and communication strategies. Thomas Nagle points out, "If effective product development, promotion, and distribution sow the seeds of business success, effective pricing is the harvest. Although effective pricing can never compensate for poor execution of the first three elements, ineffective pricing can surely prevent these efforts from resulting in financial success. Regrettably, this is a common occurrence."[4]

This chapter is divided into four parts. The first analyzes key determinants of the industrial pricing process and provides an operational approach to pricing decisions. The second examines pricing policies for new and existing products, emphasizing the need to actively manage a product throughout its life cycle. The third provides a framework to guide strategy when a competitor cuts prices. The final section examines an area of particular importance to the business marketer: competitive bidding.

The Pricing Process in Business Markets

There is no easy formula for pricing an industrial product or service. The decision is multidimensional: The interactive variables of demand, cost, competition, profit relationships, and customer usage patterns each assumes significance as the marketer formulates the role of price in the firm's marketing strategy. Pertinent considerations, illustrated in Figure 12.1, include: (1) pricing objectives, (2) demand determinants, (3) cost determinants, and (4) competition.

[1]Ajay Menon, Christian Homburg, and Nikolas Beutin, "Understanding Customer Value in Business-to-Business-Relationships," *Journal of Business-to-Business Marketing* 12 (2, 2005): pp. 1–33; see also James C. Anderson, Nirmalya Kumar, and James A. Narus, *Value Merchants: Demonstrating and Documenting Superior Value in Business Markets* (Boston: Harvard Business School Press, 2007).

[2]Bradley T. Gale, *Managing Customer Value: Creating Quality and Service That Customers Can See* (New York: The Free Press, 1994), pp. 73–75.

[3]Richard A. D'Aveni, *Hypercompetitive Rivalries* (New York: The Free Press, 1995), p. 27.

[4]Thomas T. Nagle, *The Strategy and Tactics of Pricing: A Guide to Profitable Decision Making* (Englewood Cliffs, NJ: Prentice-Hall, 1987), p. 1.

FIGURE 12.1 | KEY COMPONENTS OF THE PRICE-SETTING DECISION PROCESS

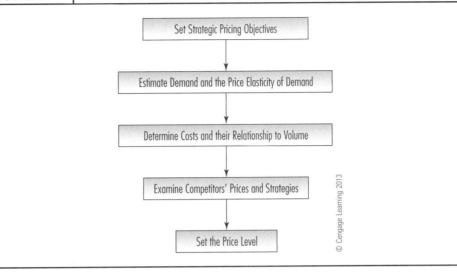

While more than one strategy path can be followed to achieve profitable results, all successful pricing strategies demonstrate three principles.[5] They are:

- *Value based* and reflect a clear understanding of how a firm's products or services create value for customers

- *Proactive* and anticipate disruptive events such as a competitive threat, negotiations with customers, or a technological change

- *Profit-driven* and judge success based on bottom-line performance, rather than the level of revenue generated

Price Objectives

The pricing decision must be based on objectives congruent with marketing and overall corporate objectives. The marketer starts with principal objectives and adds collateral pricing goals: (1) achieving a target return on investment, (2) achieving a market share goal, or (3) meeting competition. Many other potential pricing objectives extend beyond profit and market share goals, taking into account competition, channel relationships, and product-line considerations.

Because of their far-reaching effects, pricing objectives must be established with care. Each firm faces unique internal and external environmental forces. Contrasting the strategies of DuPont and Dow Chemical illustrates the importance of a unified corporate direction. Dow's strategy focuses first on pricing low-margin commodity goods *low* to build a dominant market share and then on maintaining that dominant share. DuPont's strategy, on the other hand, emphasizes higher-margin specialty products. Initially, these products are priced at a *high* level, and prices are reduced as the market expands and competition intensifies.

---

[5]Thomas T. Nagle, John E. Hogan, and Joseph Zale, *The Strategy and Tactics of Pricing: A Guide to Growing More Profitably*, Fifth Edition (Upper Saddle River, NJ: Prentice-Hall, 2011), p. 6.

Similarly, when Apple launched products, such as the iPhone or iPad, critics claimed that the price of each was far too high. However, the firm's strategists understood that a hard-core group of technology adopters would embrace the products and assign a high value to the unique differentiation of Apple's offerings. By meeting the needs of sophisticated technology adopters, Apple established a high benchmark for value for its products, providing latitude for planned price adjustments over time. Each firm requires explicit pricing objectives that are consistent with its corporate mission.

Demand Determinants

A strong market perspective is fundamental in pricing. The business market is diverse and complex. A single industrial product can be used in many ways; each market segment may represent a unique application for the product and a separate usage level. The importance of the industrial good in the buyer's end product also varies by market segment. Therefore, potential demand, sensitivity to price, and potential profitability can vary markedly across market segments. To establish an effective pricing policy, marketers should focus first on the value a customer places on a product or service. This reverses the typical process that gives immediate attention to the product cost and the desired markup.[6]

Differentiating through Value Creation Value-based strategies seek to move the selling proposition from one that centers on current prices and individual transactions to a longer-term relationship built around value and lower total cost in use. Importantly, recent research suggests that benefits have a greater effect on perceived value to business customers than sacrifices (price and costs). Ajay Menon, Christian Homburg, and Nikolas Beutin note: Contrary to the general belief in a cost-driven economy, "we encourage managers to emphasize benefits accruing from a relationship and not focus solely on lowering the price and related costs when managing customer value."[7] A better way is to provide unique add-on benefits by building trust, demonstrating commitment and flexibility, and initiating joint working relationships that enhance customer value and loyalty.

In support, recent research by Wolfgang Ulaga and Andreas Eggert indicates that relationship benefits display a stronger potential for differentiation in key supplier relationships than cost considerations.[8] Based on a best-practice profile for companies seeking key supplier status, the researchers identify service support and personal interaction as core differentiators, followed by a supplier's know-how and its ability to improve a customer's time to market. Product quality and delivery performance, along with acquisition cost and operation costs, display a moderate potential to help the awarding of key supplier status to a business-to-business firm by a customer. Interestingly, price shows the weakest potential for differentiation.

---

[6]Robert J. Dolan, "How Do You Know When the Price Is Right?" *Harvard Business Review* 73 (September–October 1995): pp. 174–183; see also Thomas T. Nagle and George E. Cressman Jr. "Don't Just Set Prices, Manage Them," *Marketing Management* 11 (November–December 2002): pp. 29–34.

[7]Menon, Homburg, and Beutin, "Understanding Customer Value," p. 25.

[8]Wolfgang Ulaga and Andreas Eggert, "Value-Based Differentiation in Business Relationships: Gaining and Sustaining Key Supplier Status," *Journal of Marketing* 70 (January 2006): pp. 119–136. See also Andreas Eggert and Wolfgang Ulaga, "Managing Customer Value in Key Supplier Relationships," *Industrial Marketing Management* 39 (November 2010): pp. 1346–1355.

A specific approach for designing value-based strategies is highlighted in the next section.

Capturing Value[9]   How organizational buyers evaluate the economic value of the total offering determines the appropriateness of a pricing strategy. Two competitors with similar products may ask different prices because buyers perceive their total offerings as unique. In the eyes of the organizational buyer, one firm may provide more value than another.

Economic value represents the cost savings and/or revenue gains that customers realize by purchasing the firm's product instead of the next-best alternative (the reference value). Some product or service features are quite similar across competitive offerings in a category (that is, points of parity) whereas others might be unique to a particular firm's brand (that is, points of differentiation). **Commodity value,** then, is the value that a customer assigns to product features that resemble those of competitors' offerings. By contrast, **differentiation value** is the value associated with product features that are unique and different from competitors'. Importantly, the price-per-unit of value that organizational buyers are willing to pay a firm for differentiating features is greater than the price-per-unit of value that they would pay for commodity features. "That's because refusal to pay a supplier's price for differentiating features means that the buyer must forgo those features. Refusal to pay a supplier's price for commodity features means simply that the customer must buy them elsewhere," says Gerald E. Smith and Thomas T. Nagle.[10] Recall that best-practice business-to-business firms create distinctive value propositions (see Chapter 3) that isolate those product and service features that matter the most to customers, demonstrate the value of their unique elements, and communicate that value in a manner that clearly conveys a deep understanding of the customer's business priorities.[11]

Isolating Value Drivers in Key Customer Segments   Exploratory methods such as depth interviews are required for identifying and measuring value. For example, depth interviews can be used to probe customer needs and problems and for learning how your products or services could address these problems. The goal here is to first identify the most significant drivers of value for customers in each market segment (see Figure 12.2). Economic value embodies both cost and revenue drivers. **Cost drivers** create value by providing economic savings while **revenue drivers** add incremental value by facilitating revenue or margin expansion.[12] For example, consider the value that Sonoco, a packaging supplier, provided for Lance, the snack food maker. One improvement involved the use of flexographic painted packaging film on some of Lance's key brands.[13] These efforts drastically reduced Lance's

---

[9]This section is based on Gerald E. Smith and Thomas T. Nagle, "A Question of Value," *Marketing Management* 14 (July/August 2005): pp. 38–43.

[10]Ibid., p. 40.

[11]James C. Anderson, James A. Narus, and Wouter van Rossum, "Customer Value Propositions in Business Markets," *Harvard Business Review* 86 (March 2006): p. 93.

[12]Gerald E. Smith and Thomas T. Nagle, "How Much Are Customers Willing to Pay?" *Marketing Research* 14 (Winter 2002): pp. 20–25.

[13]Maryanne Q. Hancock, Roland H. John, and Philip J. Wojcik, "Better B2B Selling," *The McKinsey Quarterly* (June 2005): pp. 1–8.

FIGURE 12.2 | **A VALUE-BASED APPROACH FOR PRICING**

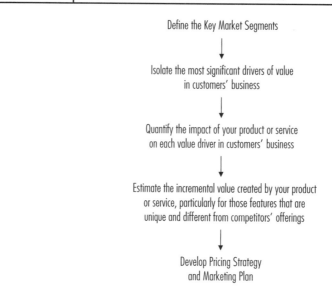

Define the Key Market Segments

Isolate the most significant drivers of value
in customers' business

Quantify the impact of your product or service
on each value driver in customers' business

Estimate the incremental value created by your product
or service, particularly for those features that are
unique and different from competitors' offerings

Develop Pricing Strategy
and Marketing Plan

SOURCE: Adapted from Gerald E. Smith and Thomas T. Nagle, "How Much Are Customers Willing to Pay," *Marketing Research* 14 (Winter 2002): pp. 20–25.

packaging costs (cost driver) and, by enhancing the appeal of the products, spawned a growth in sales (revenue driver).

Second, once the business marketing strategist has identified the most important value drivers for customers, attention then turns to quantifying the impact of the firm's product or service on the customer's business model. To illustrate, a medical equipment company developed a new surgical product. Based on depth interviews with surgical teams at key hospitals, value research found that this product could reduce the length of a particular surgical procedure from 55 minutes to 40 minutes, freeing up precious time in capacity-constrained operating rooms.[14] In addition to estimating the value of the product, the study also revealed ways in which surgical procedures could be more tightly scheduled to capture the full value potential of the new product.

Third, the strategist should compare the firm's product or service to the next-best alternative, isolating those features that are unique and different from competitors. Does the product provide favorable points of difference that provide value that a customer cannot access elsewhere? How much value does each of these features create for the customer? Finally, by understanding how customers actually use a product or service and realize value from its use, the business marketer is ideally equipped to set the price and develop a responsive marketing strategy. "Suppliers cannot expect a fair return on their supplier value if they cannot persuasively prove it to the customer's own satisfaction."[15]

---

[14]Smith and Nagle, "How Much Are Customers Willing to Pay?" p. 23.

[15]James C. Anderson, Marc Wouters, and Wouter van Rossum, "Why the Highest Price Isn't the Best Price," *MIT Sloan Management Review* 51 (Winter 2010): p. 72.

Value-Based Pricing Illustrated[16]

DataCare was planning to introduce a new data-based service targeting subacute hospitals where patients stay for longer recovery periods. Drawing on extensive operating data gathered from 300 hospitals throughout North America, DataCare developed software that enabled hospital administrators to make benchmarking comparisons with best-in-class institutions using the data. By subscribing to the service, customers could input their operating data into the firm's central operating database and, in return, would have access to the benchmarking capabilities and expert consultation from the nationally recognized physicians who founded the firm. Before introducing the service, the founders asked consultants at Strategic Pricing Research to examine this question: "Would the market be willing to pay a price of $2,000 per year?"

Value Research In addition to measuring willingness to pay, the consultants also calculated the value that DataCare's customers would receive from the new service. First, different market segments were identified, and a customer interview guide was developed: nonprofit hospitals, for-profit hospitals, and hospital chains. Second, several value drivers emerged from the customer interviews: nurse turnover, Health Care Financial Administration (HCFA) violations (that is, an oversight agency for Medicare and Medicaid), patient mix, and infection rates. Third, the potential impact of DataCare's new service on each of these value drivers was quantified. To illustrate, the database indicated that best-in-class institutions have nurse turnover rates of 30 percent. In turn, the analysis revealed that a hospital incurs a cost of $2200 to $2800 each time a nurse leaves. Assume that a hospital with a nursing staff of 50 has a turnover rate of 44 percent. A reduction in nurse turnover rate to the best-in-class level would be worth 14% X 50 X ($2200 to $2800), or $15,400 to $19,600. After providing this calculation, the customer was asked: Does this sound correct?

By repeating this process for each of the value drivers, the consultants concluded the interviews by summarizing the potential impact of the new service on each of the value drivers: $15,400 to $19,000 for nurse turnover; $9000 to $12,000 for lower infection rates; and $4000 for fewer HCFA violations.

In describing the study's conclusions, Gerald E. Smith and Thomas T. Nagle observe:

> The price DataCare originally proposed was well below the estimated value the customer would receive by adopting the new service, and well below the approximate price customers would be willing to pay if they were fully informed of the value of the new service. The study led to a substantial revision in pricing strategy and the marketing plan of DataCare's new service.[17]

As the DataCare case illustrates, the business marketing strategist can secure a competitive advantage by emphasizing a value-based approach and by developing

---

[16]This illustration is drawn from Smith and Nagle, "How Much Are Customers Willing to Pay?" p. 23.

[17]Ibid., p. 23.

the tools to document and communicate the unique value that its products and services create for customers in each market segment.[18]

Elasticity Varies by Market Segment   Price elasticity of demand measures the degree to which customers are sensitive to price changes. Specifically, **price elasticity of demand** refers to the rate of percentage change in quantity demanded attributable to a percentage change in price. Price elasticity of demand is not the same at all prices. A business marketer contemplating a change in price must understand the elasticity of demand. For example, total revenue (price times quantity) increases if price is decreased and demand is price elastic, whereas revenue falls if the price is decreased and demand is price inelastic. Many factors influence the price elasticity of demand—the ease with which customers can compare alternatives and switch suppliers, the importance of the product in the cost structure of the customer's product, and the value that the product represents to a customer.

Satisfied Customers Are Less Price Sensitive   Recent research demonstrates that highly satisfied customers are less sensitive to prices, compared with those who have a moderate level of customer satisfaction.[19] This relationship is particularly strong for purchase decisions that involve a high level of product/service complexity and a high degree of customization. Thus, reduced customer price sensitivity represents an important payoff to a business marketer for developing a customized solution for the customer.

Search Behavior and Switching Costs   The price sensitivity of buyers increases—and a firm's pricing latitude decreases—to the degree that:

- Organizational buyers can easily shop around and assess the relative performance and price of alternatives. Purchasing managers in many firms use information technology to track supplier prices on a global basis.

- The product is one for which it is easy to make price comparisons. For example, it is easier to compare alternative photocopiers than it is to compare specialized manufacturing equipment options.

- Buyers can switch from one supplier to another without incurring additional costs. As Chapter 3 highlights, low switching costs allow a buyer to focus on minimizing the cost of a particular transaction.[20]

End Use   Important insights can be secured by answering this question: How important is the business marketer's product as an input into the total cost of the end product? If the business marketer's product has an insignificant effect on cost, demand is likely inelastic. Consider this example:

> A manufacturer of precision electronic components was contemplating an across-the-board price decrease to increase sales. However, an item analysis

---

[18]Werner Reinartz and Wolfgang Ulaga, "How to Sell Services More Profitably," *Harvard Business Review* 86 (May 2008): pp. 91–96.

[19]Ruth Maria Stock, "Can Customer Satisfaction Decrease Price Sensitivity in Business-to-Business Marketing?" *Journal of Business-to-Business Marketing* 12 (3, 2005): pp. 59–85.

[20]Dolan, "How Do You Know When the Price Is Right?" pp. 178–179.

of the product line revealed that some of its low-volume components had exotic applications. A technical customer used the component in an ultrasonic testing apparatus that was sold for $8,000 a unit. This fact prompted the electronics manufacturer to raise the price of the item. Ironically, the firm then experienced a temporary surge of demand for the item as purchasing agents stocked up in anticipation of future price increases.[21]

Of course, the marketer must temper this estimate by analyzing the costs, availability, and suitability of substitutes. Generally, when the industrial product is an important but low-cost input into the end product, price is less important than quality and delivery reliability. When, however, the product input represents a larger part of the final product's total cost, changes in price may have an important effect on the demand for both the final product and the input. When demand in the final consumer market is price elastic, a reduction in the price of the end item (for example, a personal computer) that is caused by a price reduction of a component (for example, a microprocessor) generates an increase in demand for the final product (personal computer) and, in turn, for the industrial product (microprocessor).

End-Market Focus   Because the demand for many industrial products is derived from the demand for the product of which they are a part, a strong end-user focus is needed. The marketer can benefit by examining the trends and changing fortunes of important final consumer markets. Different sectors of the market grow at different rates, confront different levels of competition, and face different short-run and long-run challenges. A downturn in the economy does not fall equally on all sectors. Pricing decisions demand a two-tiered market focus—on organizational customers and on final-product customers. Thus, business marketers will have more success in raising prices to customers who are prospering than to customers who are hard pressed.

Value-Based Segmentation   The value customers assign to a firm's offering can vary by market segment because the same industrial product may serve different purposes for different customers. This underscores the important role of market segmentation in pricing strategies. Take Sealed Air Corporation, the innovative supplier of protective packaging, including coated air bubbles.[22] The company recognized that for some applications, substitutes were readily available. But for other applications, Sealed Air had an enormous advantage—for example, its packaging materials offered superior cushioning for heavy items with long shipping cycles. By identifying those applications where the firm had a clear advantage and understanding the unique value differential in each setting, marketing managers were ideally equipped to tackle product-line expansion and pricing decisions and to ignite Sealed Air's remarkable revenue growth for nearly two decades.

Cost Determinants

Business marketers often pursue a strong internal orientation; they base prices on their own costs, reaching the selling price by calculating unit costs and adding a

---

[21]Reed Moyer and Robert J. Boewadt, "The Pricing of Industrial Goods," *Business Horizons* 14 (June 1971): pp. 27–34; see also George Rostky, "Unveiling Market Segments with Technical Focus Research," *Business Marketing* 71 (October 1986): pp. 66–69.

[22]Dolan, "How Do You Know When the Price Is Right?" pp. 176–177.

percentage profit. A strict cost-plus pricing philosophy overlooks customer perceptions of value, competition, and the interaction of volume and profit. Many progressive firms, such as Canon, Toyota, and Hewlett-Packard (H-P), use target costing to capture a significant competitive advantage.

Target Costing[23]   **Target costing** features a design-to-cost philosophy that begins by examining market conditions: The firm identifies and targets the most attractive market segments. It then determines what level of quality and types of product attributes are required to succeed in each segment, given a predetermined target price and volume level. According to Robin Cooper and Regine Slagmulder, to set the target price, the business marketer has to understand the customer's perception of value: "A company can raise selling prices only if the perceived value of the new product exceeds not only that of the product's predecessor, but also that of competing products."[24]

Once the target selling price and target profit margins have been established, the firm calculates the allowable cost. The strategic cost-reduction challenge isolates the profit shortfall that occurs if the product designers are unable to achieve the allowable cost. The value of distinguishing the allowable cost from the target cost lies in the pressure that this exercise exerts on the product-development team and the company's suppliers. To transmit the competitive cost pressure it faces to its suppliers, the firm then breaks down the target price of a new product into a cascade of target costs for each component or function. For example, the major functions of an automobile include the engine, transmission, cooling system, and audio system.

A Profit-Management Tool   Toyota used target costing to reduce the price of its recently modified Camry model and did so while offering as standard equipment certain features that were expensive options on the model it replaced. Similarly, Canon used target costing to develop its breakthrough personal copier that transformed the photocopier industry.[25] Rather than a cost-control technique, Japanese managers who pioneered the approach view target costing as a profit-management tool. As Robin Cooper and W. Bruce Chew assert, "The task is to compute the costs that must not be exceeded if acceptable margins from specific products at specific price points are to be guaranteed."[26]

Classifying Costs[27]   The target costing approach stresses why the marketer must know which costs are relevant to the pricing decision and how these costs fluctuate with volume and over time; they must be considered in relation to demand, competition, and pricing objectives. Product costs are crucial in projecting the profitability of

---

[23]This section is based on Robin Cooper and Regine Slagmulder, "Develop Profitable New Products with Target Costing," *Sloan Management Review* 40 (Summer 1999): pp. 23–33.

[24]Ibid., p. 26.

[25]Jean-Phillippe Deschamps and P. Ranganath Nayak, *Product Juggernauts: How Companies Mobilize to Generate a Stream of Market Winners* (Boston: Harvard Business School Press, 1995), pp. 119–149.

[26]Robin Cooper and W. Bruce Chew, "Control Tomorrow's Costs through Today's Designs," *Harvard Business Review* 74 (January–February 1996): pp. 88–97.

[27]Kent B. Monroe, *Pricing: Making Profitable Decisions* (New York: McGraw-Hill, 1979), pp. 52–57; see also Nagle, *The Strategy and Tactics of Pricing*, pp. 14–43.

individual products as well as of the entire product line. Proper classification of costs is essential.

The goals of a cost-classification system are to: (1) properly classify cost data into their fixed and variable components and (2) properly link them to the activity causing them. The manager can then analyze the effects of volume and, more important, identify sources of profit. The following cost concepts are instrumental in the analysis:

1. **Direct traceable or attributable costs:** Costs, fixed or variable, are incurred by and solely for a particular product, customer, or sales territory (for example, raw materials).

2. **Indirect traceable costs:** Costs, fixed or variable, can be traced to a product, customer, or sales territory (for example, general plant overhead may be indirectly assigned to a product).

3. **General costs:** Costs support a number of activities that cannot be objectively assigned to a product on the basis of a direct physical relationship (for example, the administrative costs of a sales district).

General costs rarely change because an item is added or deleted from the product line. Marketing, production, and distribution costs must all be classified. When developing a new line or when deleting or adding an item to an existing line, the marketer must grasp the cost implications:

- What proportion of the product cost is accounted for by purchases of raw materials and components from suppliers?

- How do costs vary at differing levels of production?

- Based on the forecasted level of demand, can economies of scale be expected?

- Does our firm enjoy cost advantages over competitors?

- How does the "experience effect" impact our cost projections?

Competition

Competition establishes an upper limit on price. An individual industrial firm's degree of latitude in pricing depends heavily on how organizational buyers perceive the product's level of differentiation. Price is only one component of the cost/benefit equation; the marketer can gain a differential advantage over competitors on many dimensions other than physical product characteristics—reputation, technical expertise, delivery reliability, and related factors. Regis McKenna contends, "Even if a company manufactures commodity-like products, it can differentiate the products through the service and support it offers, or by target marketing. It can leave its commodity mentality in the factory, and bring a mentality of diversity to the marketplace."[28] In addition to assessing the product's degree of differentiation in various market segments, one must ask how competitors will respond to particular pricing decisions.

---

[28]Regis McKenna, *Relationship Marketing* (Reading, MA: Addison-Wesley, 1991), pp. 178–179.

Hypercompetitive Rivalries Some strategy experts emphasize that traditional patterns of competition in stable environments is being replaced by hypercompetitive rivalries in a rapidly changing environment.[29] In a stable environment, a company could create a fairly rigid strategy designed to accommodate long-term conditions. The firm's strategy focused on sustaining its own strategic advantage and establishing equilibrium where less-dominant firms accepted a secondary status.

In hypercompetitive environments, successful companies pursue strategies that create temporary advantage and destroy the advantages of rivals by constantly disrupting the market's equilibrium. For example, Intel continually disrupts the equilibrium of the microprocessor industry sector, and Apple stirs up the consumer electronics industry with its innovative products. Moreover, the Internet provides customers with real-time access to a wealth of information that drives the prices of many products lower. Leading firms in hypercompetitive environments constantly seek out new sources of advantage, further escalating competition and contributing to hypercompetition.

Consider the hypercompetitive rivalries in high-technology markets. Firms that sustain quality and that are the first to hit the next-lower strategic price point enjoy a burst of volume and an expansion of market share. For example, Hewlett-Packard has ruthlessly pursued the next-lower price point in its printer business, even as it cannibalized its own sales and margins.[30]

Gauging Competitive Response To predict the response of competitors, the marketer can first benefit by examining the cost structure and strategy of both direct competitors and producers of potential substitutes. The marketer can draw on public statements and records (for example, annual reports) to form rough estimates. Competitors that have ascended the learning curve may have lower costs than those just entering the industry and beginning the climb. An estimate of the cost structure is valuable when gauging how well competitors can respond to price reductions and when projecting the pattern of prices in the future.

Under certain conditions, however, followers into a market may confront lower initial costs than did the pioneer. Why? Some of the reasons are highlighted in Table 12.1. By failing to recognize potential cost advantages of late entrants, the business marketer can dramatically overstate cost differences.

The market strategy competing sellers use is also important here. Competitors are more sensitive to price reductions that threaten those market segments they deem important. They learn of price reductions earlier when their market segments overlap. Of course, competitors may choose not to follow a price decrease, especially if their products enjoy a differentiated position. Rather than matching competitors' price cuts, one successful steel company reacts to the competitive challenge by offering customized products and technical assistance to its customers.[31] Later in the chapter, special attention is given to this question: How should you respond to price attacks by competitors?

[29]D'Aveni, *Hypercompetitive Rivalries*, pp. 149–170.

[30]Geoffrey A. Moore, *Inside the Tornado: Marketing Strategies from Silicon Valley's Cutting Edge* (New York: HarperCollins, 1995), pp. 84–85.

[31]Arun Sharma, R. Krishnan, and Dhruv Grewal, "Value Creation in Markets: A Critical Area of Focus for Business-to-Business Markets," *Industrial Marketing Management* 30 (June 2001): pp. 397–398.

TABLE 12.1 | Selected Cost Comparison Issues: Followers versus the Pioneer

Technology/economies of scale	Followers may benefit by using more current production technology than the pioneer or by building a plant with a larger scale of operations.
Product/market knowledge	Followers may learn from the pioneer's mistakes by analyzing the competitor's product, hiring key personnel, or identifying through market research the problems and unfulfilled expectations of customers and channel members.
Shared experience	Compared with the pioneer, followers may be able to gain advantages on certain cost elements by sharing operations with other parts of the company.
Experience of suppliers	Followers, together with the pioneer, benefit from cost reductions achieved by outside suppliers of components or production equipment.

SOURCE: Adapted from George S. Day and David B. Montgomery, "Diagnosing the Experience Curve," *Journal of Marketing* 47 (Spring 1983): pp. 48–49.

The manager requires a grasp of objectives, demand, cost, competition, and legal factors (discussed later) to approach the multidimensional pricing decision. Price setting is not an act but an ongoing process.

Pricing across the Product Life Cycle

What price should be assigned to a distinctly new industrial product or service? When an item is added to an existing product line, how should it be priced in relation to products already in the line?

Pricing New Products

Establishing the correct launch price for a product or service can reset market price expectations and boost the profit trajectory across the remainder of that offering's life cycle.[32] The strategic decision of pricing new products can be best understood by examining the policies at the boundaries of the continuum—from **skimming** (high initial price) to **penetration** (low initial price). Consider again the pricing strategies of DuPont and Dow Chemical. Whereas DuPont assigns an initial high price to new products to generate immediate profits or to recover R&D expenditures, Dow follows a low-price strategy with the objective of gaining market share.

In evaluating the merits of skimming versus penetration, the marketer must again examine price from the buyer's perspective. This approach, asserts Joel Dean, "recognizes that the upper limit is the price that will produce the minimum acceptable rate of return on the investment of a sufficiently large number of prospects."[33] This is especially important in pricing new products because the potential profits to buyers

---

[32]Walter L. Baker, Michael V. Marn, and Craig C. Zowada, "Do You Have a Long-Term Pricing Strategy?" *McKinsey Quarterly* (October 2010), pp. 1–7, accessed at http://www.mckinsey.com on June 15, 2011.

[33]Joel Dean, "Pricing Policies for New Products," *Harvard Business Review* 54 (November–December 1976): p. 151.

of a new machine tool, for example, will vary by market segment, and these market segments may differ in the minimum rate of return that will induce them to invest in the machine tool.

Skimming   A skimming approach, appropriate for a distinctly new product, provides an opportunity to profitably reach market segments that are not sensitive to the high initial price. As a product ages, as competitors enter the market, and as organizational buyers become accustomed to evaluating and purchasing the product, demand becomes more price elastic. Joel Dean refers to the policy of skimming at the outset, followed by penetration pricing as the product matures, as **time segmentation**.[34] Skimming enables the marketer to capture early profits, then reduce the price to reach more price-sensitive segments. It also enables the innovator to recover high developmental costs more quickly.

Robert Dolan and Abel Jeuland demonstrate that during the innovative firm's monopoly period, skimming is optimal if the demand curve is stable over time (no diffusion) and if production costs decline with accumulated volume. A penetration policy is optimal if there is a relatively high repeat purchase rate for nondurable goods or if a durable good's demand is characterized by diffusion.[35]

Penetration   A penetration policy is appropriate when there is: (1) high price elasticity of demand, (2) strong threat of imminent competition, and (3) opportunity for a substantial reduction in production costs as volume expands. Drawing on the experience effect, a firm that can quickly capture substantial market share and experience can gain a strategic advantage over competitors. The feasibility of this strategy increases with the potential size of the future market. By taking a large share of new sales, a firm can gain experience when the growth rate of the market is large. Of course, the value of additional market share differs markedly between industries and often among products, markets, and competitors in an industry.[36] Factors to be assessed in determining the value of additional market share include the investment requirements, potential benefits of experience, expected market trends, likely competitive reaction, and short- and long-term profit implications.

Product-Line Considerations   The contemporary business-to-business firm with a long product line faces the complex problem of balancing prices in the product mix. Firms extend their product lines because the demands for various products are interdependent or because the costs of producing and marketing those items are interdependent, or both.[37] A firm may add to its product line—or even develop a new product line—to fit more precisely the needs of a particular market segment. If

[34]Ibid., p. 152.

[35]Robert J. Dolan and Abel P. Jeuland, "Experience Curves and Dynamic Demand Models: Implications for Optimal Pricing Strategies," *Journal of Marketing* 45 (Winter 1981): pp. 52–62; see also Paul Ingenbleek, Marion Debruyne, Rudd T. Frambach, and Theo M. Verhallen, "Successful New Product Pricing Practices: A Contingency Approach," *Marketing Letters* 14 (December 2004): pp. 289–304.

[36]Robert Jacobson and David A. Aaker, "Is Market Share All That It's Cracked Up to Be?" *Journal of Marketing* 49 (Fall 1985): pp. 11–22.

[37]Monroe, *Pricing*, p. 143; see also Robert J. Dolan, "The Same Make, Many Models Problem: Managing the Product Line," in *A Strategic Approach to Business Marketing*, Robert E. Spekman and David T. Wilson, eds. (Chicago: American Marketing Association, 1985), pp. 151–159.

INSIDE BUSINESS MARKETING

Understanding the Economic Value of New Products

Measuring the economic value that a product delivers to different customer segments is an essential ingredient in launching successful new products. Because customers will compare a new product offering to the next-best alternative, the marketing strategist must also understand the value delivered by competitors. Experts suggest that the most effective way to determine the value of a new product is through in-depth surveys. Here central attention is given to learning how a company's product affects the customer's business by

reducing costs and/or by increasing revenue. The results provide an important foundation for effective pricing and responsive sales strategies. For example, after uncovering the value of a new software product, the firm, which was planning on a $99 price, decided the correct price was $349. Sales results exceeded expectations.

SOURCE: John Hogan and Tom Lucke, "Driving Growth with New Products: Common Pricing Traps to Avoid," *Journal of Business Strategy* 27 (1, 2006): pp. 54–58.

both the demand and the costs of individual product-line items are interrelated, production and marketing decisions about one item inevitably influence both the revenues and costs of the others.

Are specific product-line items substitutes or complements? Will changing the price of one item enhance or retard the usage rate of this or other products in key market segments? Should a new product be priced high at the outset to protect other product-line items (for example, potential substitutes) and to give the firm time to revamp other items in the line? Such decisions require knowledge of demand, costs, competition, and strategic marketing objectives.

Legal Considerations

Because the business marketer deals with various classifications of customers and intermediaries as well as various types of discounts (for example, quantity discounts), an awareness of legal considerations in price administration is vital. The **Robinson-Patman Act** holds that it is unlawful to "discriminate in price between different purchasers of commodities of like grade and quality ... where the effect of such discrimination may be substantially to lessen competition or tend to create a monopoly, or to injure, destroy, or prevent competition...." Price differentials are permitted, but they must be based on cost differences or the need to "meet competition."[38] Cost differentials are difficult to justify, and clearly defined policies and procedures are needed in price administration. Such cost-justification guidelines are useful not only when making pricing decisions but also when providing a legal defense against price discrimination charges.

---

[38]For a comprehensive discussion of the Robinson-Patman Act, see Nagle, Hogan, and Zale, *The Strategy and Tactics of Pricing*, pp. 305–323.

Responding to Price Attacks by Competitors[39]

Rather than emphasizing the lowest price, most business marketers prefer to compete by providing superior value. However, across industries, marketing managers face constant pressure from competitors who are willing to use price concessions to gain market share or entry into a profitable market segment. When challenged by an aggressive competitor, many managers immediately want to fight back and match the price cut. However, because price wars can be quite costly, experts suggest a more systematic process that considers the long-run strategic consequences versus the short-term benefits of the pricing decision. Managers should never set the price simply to meet some immediate sales goal, but, instead, to enhance long-term project goals. George E. Cressman Jr. and Thomas T. Nagle, consultants from the Strategic Pricing Group, Inc., observe: "Pricing is like playing chess; players who fail to envision a few moves ahead will almost always be beaten by those who do."[40]

Evaluating a Competitive Threat

Figure 12.3 provides a systematic framework for developing a strategy when one or more competitors have announced price cuts or have introduced new products that offer more value to at least some of your customers. To determine whether to reduce price to meet a competitor's challenge, you should address four important questions:

1. *Is there a response that would cost you less than the preventable sales loss?* (See center of Figure 12.3.) Before responding to a competitor's price reduction, the marketing strategist should ask: Do the benefits justify the costs? If responding to a price change is less costly than losing sales, a price move may be the appropriate decision. On the other hand, if the competitor threatens only a small slice of expected sales, the revenue loss from ignoring the threat may be much lower than the costs of retaliation. Indeed, when the threat centers on a small segment of customers, the cost of reducing prices for all customers to prevent the small loss is likely to be prohibitively expensive.

   If a price response is required, the strategist should focus the firm's competitive retaliation on the most cost-effective actions. The cost of retaliating to a price threat can be reduced by incorporating one or more of the following elements into the pricing action:

   - Center reactive price cuts only on those customers likely to be attracted to the competitor's offer (for example, rather than cutting the price of its flagship Pentium chip, Intel offered the lower-priced Cerrus chip for the cost-conscious market segment).

   - Center reactive price cuts on a particular geographic region, distribution channel, or product line where the competitor has the most to lose from a price reduction.

---

[39]This section is based on George E. Cressman Jr. and Thomas T. Nagle, "How to Manage an Aggressive Competitor," *Business Horizons* 45 (March–April 2002), pp. 23–30.

[40]Ibid., p. 24.

FIGURE 12.3 | Evaluating a Competitive Threat

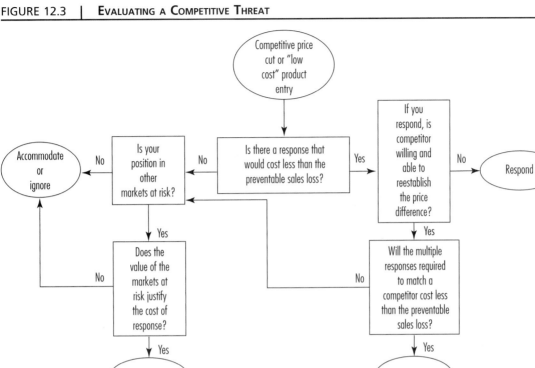

SOURCE: Reprinted from Business Horizons 45(2), George E. Cressman, Jr. and Thomas T. Nagle, "How to Manage an Aggressive Competitor," p. 25, copyright © 2002, with permission from Elsevier.

- Capitalize on any competitive advantages to increase the value of your offer as an alternative to matching the price (for example, a firm that has better-quality products can respond by offering a longer warranty period to customers).

- Raise the cost to the competitor related to its discounting. (For example, if the competitor's price reduction is limited only to new customers and not the firm's existing customers, "retaliate by educating the competitor's existing customers that they are being treated unfairly."[41]

2. *If you respond, is the competitor willing and able to merely reduce the price again to restore the price difference?* Matching a price cut will be ineffective if the competitor simply reestablishes the differential by a further price reduction. According to Cressman and Nagle, to determine the appropriate course, the strategist should attempt to understand why the competitor chose to compete on price in the first place: "If the competitor has little market share relative to the share that could be gained with a price advantage, and has no other way to

---

[41]Nagle, Hogan, and Zale, *The Strategy and Tactics of Pricing*, p. 254.

attract customers, then there is little to lose from bringing the price down as low as necessary to gain sales."[42] This is especially true when competitors have made huge investments in areas such as R&D that largely represent sunk costs. Under such conditions, accommodation—market share loss—is less costly than fighting a price war.

3. *Will the multiple responses that may be required to match the competitor's price still cost less than the avoidable sales loss?* A single response is rarely enough to stop price moves by competitors that are struggling to establish a market position. Price competition is particularly likely in industries where entry requires a significant investment in fixed manufacturing capacity. Rather than idling manufacturing capacity, a competitor may be willing to aggressively pursue sales that will make at least some contribution to covering fixed costs. If competitors are likely to continue to cut prices, the best strategy for the defender is to:

   - Allow the competitor to win where it is least damaging to profitability, such as in more price-sensitive, lower-margin customer segments (for example, government contracts).

   - Create barriers that make it more difficult for competitors to reach less price-sensitive, more profitable customer segments (for example, build switching costs by developing unique solutions for the most valued customers).

4. *Is your position in other markets (product or geographic) at risk if the competitor increases market share? Does the value of all the markets that are at risk justify the cost of the strategy response?* Before responding with a price reduction, the business marketer must clearly define the long-run strategic benefits as well as the risks of a particular strategy response. The benefits might include additional sales in a particular market in the future, or immediate sales gains of complementary products (such as software, peripherals, and services associated with the sale of a computer), or a lower cost of future sales resulting from increased volume. The risks are that a targeted price reduction will spread to other markets, creating a downward price spiral that undermines profitability.

Understanding the Rules of Competitive Strategy

Dealing effectively with an aggressive competitor requires more than a willingness to fight—it requires a competitive strategy and an understanding of when the appropriate response to a competitor's price cut is to ignore it, accommodate it, or retaliate. George E. Cressman and Thomas T. Nagle offer these guidelines for competitive strategy development:

   - Never participate in a competitive engagement you cannot win. Fight those battles where you have competitive strength, and avoid those where you are clearly at a disadvantage.

---

[42]Cressman and Nagle, "How to Manage an Aggressive Competitor," p. 27.

- Always participate in competitive engagements from a position of advantage. Don't fight by competitors' rules (which they select for their advantage); use what is advantageous for you.[43]

Competitive Bidding

A significant volume of business commerce is transacted through competitive bidding. Rather than relying on a specific list price, the business marketer must develop a price, or a bid, to meet a customer's particular product or service requirements.

Government and other public agencies buy almost exclusively through competitive bidding. Competitive bidding in private industry centers on two types of purchases. One type includes nonstandard materials, complex fabricated products where design and manufacturing methods vary, and products made to the buyer's specifications. This type has no generally established market level. Competitive bids enable the purchaser to evaluate the appropriateness of the prices.[44] The second type is the reverse auction, where many sellers bid for an order from a single buyer (see Chapter 2). GE, for example, uses reverse auctions to buy both direct (for example, standard component parts) and indirect materials (for example, maintenance items, office supplies), making roughly a third of its total purchasing expenditures in this fashion. Typically, reverse auctions are best suited for product categories that buyers view as commodities.[45] Competitive bidding may be either closed or open.

Closed Bidding

Closed bidding, often used by business and governmental buyers, involves a formal invitation to potential suppliers to submit written, sealed bids. All bids are opened and reviewed at the same time, and the contract is generally awarded to the lowest bidder who meets desired specifications. The low bidder is not guaranteed the contract—buyers often make awards to the lowest responsible bidder; the ability of alternative suppliers to perform remains part of the bidding process.

Online Sealed Bid Format   A sealed bid format is also used for online auctions. The term *sealed* means that only one supplier and the buyer have access to the details of the bid. According to Sandy Jap:

> The bid process is asynchronous in the sense that the buyer and supplier take turns viewing the bid. The buyer posts the RFP (request for purchase) electronically, the supplier submits a bid, and the buyer views the submitted bid. The buyer then either makes a decision after viewing all bids or, if multiple

---

[43]Ibid., p. 30.

[44]Stuart St. P. Slatter, "Strategic Marketing Variables under Conditions of Competitive Bidding," *Strategic Management Journal* 11 (May–June 1990): pp. 309–317; see also Arthur H. Mendel and Roger Poueymirou, "Pricing," in *The Purchasing Handbook*, Harold E. Fearon, Donald W. Dobler, and Kenneth H. Killen, eds. (New York: McGraw-Hill, 1993), pp. 201–227.

[45]See, for example, C. M. Sashi and Bay O'Leary, "The Role of Internet Auctions in the Expansion of B2B Markets," *Industrial Marketing Management* 31 (February 2002): pp. 103–110.

rounds of bidding are involved, may respond to the supplier, who then resubmits a new bid.[46]

Open Bidding

Open bidding is more informal and allows suppliers to make offers (oral and written) up to a certain date. The buyer may deliberate with several suppliers throughout the bidding process. Open bidding may be particularly appropriate when specific requirements are hard to define rigidly or when the products and services of competing suppliers vary substantially.

In some buying situations, prices may be negotiated. Complex technical requirements or uncertain product specifications may lead buying organizations first to evaluate the capabilities of competing firms and then to negotiate the price and the form of the product-service offering. Negotiated pricing is appropriate for procurement in both the commercial and the governmental sectors of the business market.

Online Open Bid Format   When conducted online, open bidding takes a different form. Here suppliers are invited to bid simultaneously during a designated time period for the contract. In contrast to the sealed-bid format, all suppliers and the buyer view the bids at the same time. The goal, of course, is to push the price down. Sandy Jap, who has conducted extensive research on reverse auctions, argues that the open-bid format, when used regularly, can damage buyer–supplier relationships:

> This harm occurs because open-bid formats reveal pricing information to competition, which erodes the supplier's bargaining power. Open-bid formats also place a more explicit focus on price, a short-term variable that is usually the focus of transaction-oriented exchanges rather than relational exchanges. When buyers use an open-bid format amid a context in which relational exchanges are emphasized, they send an inconsistent message to suppliers and may foster distrust.[47]

Recent research on the use of online reverse auctions suggests that the larger the number of bidders, the larger the economic stakes, and the less visible the price in an auction, the more positive is the impact on the buyer–seller relationship.[48] However, large price drops over the course of the event have a detrimental effect on the buyer–seller relationship (see Chapter 2).

Strategies for Competitive Bidding

Because making bids is costly and time consuming, firms should choose potential bid opportunities with care. Contracts offer differing levels of profitability according to the bidding firm's related technical expertise, past experience, and objectives.

---

[46]Sandy D. Jap, "Online Reverse Auctions: Issues, Themes, and Prospects for the Future," *Journal of the Academy of Marketing Science* 30 (Fall 2002): p. 507.

[47]Ibid., p. 514.

[48]Sandy Jap, "The Impact of Online Reverse Auction Design on Buyer-Seller Relationships," *Journal of Marketing* 71 (January 2007): pp. 146–159.

Therefore, careful screening is required to isolate contracts that offer the most promise.[49] Having isolated a project opportunity, the marketer must now estimate the probabilities of winning the contract at various prices. Assuming that the contract is awarded to the lowest bidder, the chances of the firm winning the contract decline as the bid price increases. How will competitors bid?

In many industries, business marketers confront situations in which the supplier that wins the initial contract has the advantage in securing long-term follow-up business. To illustrate, suppliers bidding on contracts to meet the worldwide information-technology service needs of American Express often submit attractive bids to form an initial relationship with the centralized purchasing unit.[50] Although they may sacrifice some immediate profit, they see the low bid as an investment that will lead to improved efficiencies and a continuing stream of profitable follow-up business.

In pursuing this type of bidding strategy, the business marketer must carefully assess how likely it is that the initial contract will lead to follow-up business opportunities. For example, the purchase of an office automation system may bond the buyer to a particular seller, thus providing the potential for future business. The costs of switching to another supplier are high because the buyer has made investments in employee training and new business procedures, as well as in the equipment itself.[51] Such investments create inertia against change. By contrast, for more standardized purchases, such bonding does not occur because the buyer's costs of switching to another supplier are quite low. In determining the initial bid strategy, the business marketer should examine the strength of the buyer–seller relationship, the probability of securing additional business, and the expected return from that business.

Summary

At the outset, the business marketer must assign pricing its role in the firm's overall marketing strategy. Giving a particular industrial product or service, an "incorrect" price can trigger a chain of events that undermines the firm's market position, channel relationships, and product and personal selling strategies. Successful pricing strategies are value-based, proactive, and profit-driven. Customer value represents a business customer's overall assessment of the utility of a relationship with a supplier based on benefits received and sacrifices made. Price is but one of the costs that buyers examine when considering the value of competing offerings. Thus, the marketer can profit by adopting a strong end-user focus that gives special attention to the way buyers trade off the costs and benefits of various products. Responsive pricing strategies can be developed by understanding the economic value that a product provides for a customer. Economic value represents the cost savings and/or revenue gains that customers realize by purchasing the firm's product instead of the

---

[49]For example, see Paul D. Boughton, "The Competitive Bidding Process: Beyond Probability Models," *Industrial Marketing Management* 16 (May 1987): pp. 87–94.

[50]Susan Avery, "American Express Charges Ahead," *Purchasing*, November 4, 2004, pp. 34–38.

[51]Barbara Bund Jackson, "Build Customer Relationships That Last," *Harvard Business Review* 63 (November–December 1985): pp. 120–128.

next-best alternative. By understanding how customers in a market segment actually use a product or service and realize value from its use, the business marketer is ideally equipped to set the price and develop a responsive strategy.

Price setting is a multidimensional decision. To establish a price, the manager must identify the firm's objectives and analyze the behavior of demand, costs, and competition. Hypercompetitive rivalries characterize the nature of competition in many high-technology industry sectors. Although this task is clouded with uncertainty, the industrial pricing decision must be approached actively rather than passively. For example, many business marketing firms use target costing to capture a competitive advantage. Likewise, by isolating demand, cost, or competitive patterns, the manager can gain insights into market behavior and neglected opportunities. Dealing effectively with an aggressive competitor requires more than a willingness to fight—it requires a competitive strategy and an understanding of when to ignore a price attack, when to accommodate it, and when to retaliate.

Competitive bidding, a unique feature of the business market, calls for a unique strategy. Again, carefully defined objectives are the cornerstone of strategy. These objectives, combined with a meticulous screening procedure, help the firm to identify projects that mesh with company capability.

Discussion Questions

1. Economic value embodies both cost and revenue drivers. Explain.

2. Many companies, including GE, Quaker Oats, and United Technologies, report millions of dollars of savings from using reverse auctions rather than traditional purchasing methods. Of course, business marketing strategists fear that these auctions will transform their products and services into commodities. Propose particular strategies that marketing managers might follow to deal with this challenging situation.

3. Describe an approach FedEx could use to demonstrate the value it provides to a small manufacturer of gourmet cooking supplies.

4. If a competitor's price cut threatens only a small portion of expected sales, the sales loss from ignoring the threat is probably much less than the cost of retaliation. Agree or disagree? Explain.

5. Explain why it is often necessary for the business marketer to develop a separate demand curve for various market segments. Would one total demand curve be better for making the industrial pricing decision? Explain.

6. Rather than time to market, Intel refers to the product development cycle for a new chip as "time to money." Andrew Grove, Intel's legendary leader, said, "Speed is the only weapon we have." What pricing advantages issue from a rapid product development process?

7. Evaluate this statement: To move away from the commodity mentality, companies must view their products as customer solutions, and then sell their offerings on that basis.

8. A business marketing manager often has great difficulty in arriving at the optimum price level for a product. First, describe the factors that complicate the pricing decision. Second, outline the approach you

would follow in pricing an industrial product. Be as specific as possible.

9. Compare and contrast *commodity value versus differentiation value*, highlighting the significance of each in setting a price.

10. The XYZ Manufacturing Corporation has experienced a rather large decline in sales for its component parts. Mary Vantage, vice president of marketing, believes that a 10 percent price cut may get things going again. What factors should Mary consider before reducing the price of the components?

Internet Exercise

1. Hill-Rom is a leading B2B firm that dominates a niche in the health-care industry. Go to http://www.hill-rom.com and, first, describe the products and services that Hill-Rom offers to hospitals. Next, describe how Hill-Rom products or solutions might reduce the total cost-in-use for a hospital.

CHAPTER

13

Business Marketing Communications: Advertising and Sales Promotion

Advertising supports and supplements personal selling efforts. The share of the marketing budget devoted to advertising is smaller in business than it is in consumer-goods marketing. A well-integrated business-to-business marketing communications program, however, can help make the overall marketing strategy more efficient and effective. After reading this chapter, you will understand:

1. The powerful role that social media can assume in business marketing strategy

2. The decisions that must be made when forming a business advertising program

3. The business media options, including the important role of online advertising

4. Ways to measure business advertising effectiveness

5. The role of trade shows in the business communications mix and how to measure trade show effectiveness

Let's consider the vital role that marketing communications can assume in business marketing strategy by exploring the stunning success of Bomgar Corporation.[1] While working as a network engineer for an information-technology integrator in Mississippi, Joel Bomgar grew tired of driving around the region, moving from client to client, and solving the same basic problem. So, Joel began to work on the original version of the Bomgar Box—a remote information-technology support system delivered on an appliance owned and controlled by the customer. Once the system was developed, he then recruited two college friends, created a Web site, and set out to launch the new product, targeting small and medium-sized businesses. Reflecting on this critical milestone for the business, Joel recalls his chief fears: "My entire advertising budget consisted of my personal debit card. How could I possibly compete with all the billion-dollar corporations out there?"[2]

Joel decided to use Google AdWords (that is, paid search engine advertising) to drive qualified customer prospects to the firm's new Web site. Joel and his team chose keywords and developed targeted messages that highlighted the important features that differentiate Bomgar's products from the competition, including ease of implementation and effective security controls. Patrick Norman, vice president of e-commerce for Bomgar, observes: "With Google, this guy in Mississippi who'd built this new technology was able to put it out there, and suddenly the world was open to him. That just doesn't happen with traditional media."[3] Once a foundation was established, Bomgar expanded the scope of its marketing strategy by running ads on the Google Content Network that reaches 75 percent of Internet users. Next the team used site targeting to display advertising on specific Web sites that are frequented by information-technology professionals. By 2011, 5000 corporate customers from all 50 states and 48 countries had chosen the Bomgar virtual support solution.[4] In addition to a wealth of mid-size enterprises, current customers include Humana, Ethan Allen, Nissan, and UnitedHealth Group.

Communication with existing and potential customers is vital to business marketing success. Experience has taught marketing managers that not even the best products sell themselves: The benefits, problem solutions, and cost efficiencies of those products must be effectively communicated to everyone who influences the purchase decision. As a result of the technical complexity of business products, the relatively small number of potential buyers, and the extensive negotiation process, the primary communication vehicle in business-to-business marketing is the salesperson. However, nonpersonal methods of communication, including advertising, catalogs, the Internet, and trade shows, have a unique and often crucial role in the communication process. To maximize the return on promotional spending, business-to-business firms are developing integrated marketing campaigns that align marketing communications strategies to strategic objectives.[5]

---

[1] This example is based on Google Content Network: Success Stories, "Remote Control," accessed on August 1, 2008 at http://www.adwords.google.com.

[2] Ibid., p. 1.

[3] Ibid., pp. 2–3.

[4] "About Bomgar," accessed on August 1, 2011 at http://www.bomgar.com.

[5] Don Schultz and Heidi Schultz, *IMC—The Next Generation* (New York: McGraw-Hill, 2004).

The focus of this chapter is fourfold: (1) to describe the influential role that social media assume in business marketing strategy; (2) to present a framework for structuring advertising decisions—a framework that integrates the decisions related to objectives, budgets, messages, media, and evaluation; (3) to develop an understanding of each business-to-business advertising decision area; and (4) to evaluate the valuable role of online advertising and trade shows in the promotional mix.

Business-to-Business (B2B) Social Media

B2B social media refers to the various channels of the social Web where customer prospects and businesses communicate across platforms as diverse as discussion forums, blogs, wikis, and social networks, engaging with each other through the exchange of content. Definitions for some key Web terms include the following:[6]

- **Discussion forum**—A Web site on which participants can contribute online discussions by posting opinions and questions related to particular subjects.

- **Blog**—An online journal maintained by an individual who uploads content intended to inform, express opinion, and/or encourage discussion.

- **Wiki**—A collaborative Web site on which users can develop and edit informative content through their Web browser.

- **Social Networks**—Web sites comprised of online profiles for individuals and groups that distribute content to others.

While considered by many to relate only to the consumer markets, "B2B companies are using social media to monitor what prospects are saying about their company, capture interest from prospects looking for their products and solutions, and coordinate the marketing and sales follow-ups to their social media interactions."[7] As organizational buyers spend more time on the Internet conducting independent research and obtaining information from their peers and third parties via social media, business marketers are increasing their marketing budgets for social media and are devoting dedicated resources to social media monitoring and analysis.[8]

Dell's Social Media Brand[9]

Consider the scope of Dell's social media efforts. Dell publishes several blogs in five languages, including blogs that center on specific topics such as enterprise IT

---

[6]Sunil Gupta, Kristen Armstrong, and Zachary Clayton, "Social Media," February 2011, Teaching Note #9-510-095 (Boston: Harvard Business School Publishing, 2011).

[7]"B2B Social Media," accessed at http://www.marketo.com on August 1, 2011.

[8]Jeff Zabin, "The Future of Online Communities: Leveraging Social Interaction to Drive Business Value," June 2009, Aberdeen Group, accessed at http://www.aberdeen.com on August 1, 2011.

[9]This discussion is based on David Aaker, "Beyond Communication to Changing the Marketplace," *Marketing News*, July 11, 2011, p. 14.

perspectives, health care, and education. Dell also sponsors a handful of online communities where customers can join discussions on issues ranging from small-business applications to gaming and the company's responsiveness. There are also several support forums that allow users to ask questions and find answers about laptop computers, servers, mobile devices, and other offerings. Likewise, Dell has more than 1.5 million followers on Twitter, 600,000 fans on Facebook, and 6000 subscribers to Dell's YouTube channel.

One of Dell's signature social media initiatives is its Idea Storm online community. Here consumers can post innovation ideas for Dell to consider, view their peers' ideas, and vote for or against ideas. To date, Dell has received over 15,000 ideas, from which 442 ideas have come to fruition. CEO Michael Dell considers the customer involvement essential to successful innovation:

> I'm sure there's a lot of things that I can't even imagine but our customers can imagine…. A company this size is not going to be about a couple of people coming up with ideas. It's going to be about millions of people and harnessing the power of those ideas.[10]

The Customer Decision Journey[11]

David Edelman, a strategy consultant at McKinsey and Company, asserts that marketers need to recognize how digital media channels have altered the customer decision process, or *customer decision journey* (CDJ). Based on a study of nearly 20,000 consumers across five industries, the research finds that the "single most important impetus to buy is someone else's advocacy. Yet many marketers focus on media spending (principally advertising) rather than on driving advocacy."[12] This demonstrates a mismatch between where marketing budgets are allocated and the touchpoints at which consumers are best influenced. Edelman describes how a lighting company, referred to as Global Light, radically altered its go-to-market approach, based on the study of the CDJ in its industry. Global Light serves a range of commercial markets, including public construction, retail, and hospitality.

Charting CDJ

The firm first conducted interviews with 40 customers (for example, architects and construction managers) to learn more about the process they followed in gathering information, evaluating alternatives, and buying lighting products. The company learned that customers were doing extensive research online before even making an initial contact with a manufacturer or distributor. Moreover, customers were engaging in discussions and giving advice to one another via trade associations or in threads tied to blogs. Other exchanges occurred on LinkedIn. In short, prospects

---

[10]Dick Martin, *Secrets of the Marketing Masters* (New York: AMACOM, 2009), p. 169.

[11]David C. Edelman, "Aligning with the Consumer Decision Journey," Idea in Practice, *Harvard Business Review* 89 (July 2011): pp. 1–4.

[12]David C. Edelman, "Branding in the Digital Age: You're Spending Your Money in All the Wrong Places," *Harvard Business Review* 88 (December 2010): p. 2, downloaded at http://www.hbr.org on July 25, 2011.

and customers invested more time on community and social sites than on those of the manufacturer or distributor.

Isolating Customer Touchpoints   From the study, company strategists realized that the CDJ included two critical steps that they had neglected:

1. **Inspiration,** where customers turn to online channels to find, create, and compare ideas.

2. **Sharing**, in which customers relate their experiences or post case studies using a variety of social media.

They also learned that customers expected to find tools (for example, calculators) that would allow them to make trade-offs, such as between lighting performance and total installed cost.

Transforming the Strategy   Drawing on these customer insights, Global Light refined its go-to-market strategy. First, once customer projects are completed, the marketing team encourages customers to post case studies on the company's Web site, detailing project highlights and recounting their experiences. These case studies and related images are then sent to relevant customer prospects and cross-posted to community sites. Second, the company created a team of marketing managers and salespeople who take turns monitoring community sites. The team answers questions, attaches links to favorable product reviews, and announces new product offerings.

Third, since most customers rely on the company Web site to gather data related to technical specifications, Global Light made that information much easier to access. Customer success stories are also linked directly to the product the site visitor is considering. Tools were also added to allow architects or lighting designers to make more informed product choices, such as the wattage required for different types of space or the total cost of ownership.

To implement these changes, Global Light hired a new vice president of digital strategy and made additional investments in social media and site design. The firm also created a new call center and developed programs to strengthen the capabilities of its distributors. Based on the market response to its refined strategy, the company predicts a five-fold return on investment.

Lessons Learned   The Global Light case illustrates that the customer experience includes everything from discussions in social media to face-to-face meetings with salespeople to continued interactions with the company and with other customers. Social media facilitate targeted, personalized contact across the customer experience landscape. "Rather than a tactical communication vehicle, social media can augment an offering to expand the value proposition, thereby changing what people buy and how they relate to a brand."[13]

---

[13] Aaker, "Beyond Communication," p. 14.

The Role of Advertising

B2B

Integrated Communication Programs

Advertising and sales promotion are rarely used alone in the business-to-business setting but are intertwined with the total communications strategy—particularly personal selling. Personal and nonpersonal forms of communication interact to inform key buying influentials. The challenge for the business marketer is to create an advertising and sales promotion strategy that effectively blends with personal selling in order to meet sales and profit objectives. In addition, the advertising, online media, and sales promotion tools must be integrated; that is, a comprehensive program of media and sales promotion methods must be coordinated to achieve the desired results.

Enhancing Sales Effectiveness

Effective advertising can make personal selling more productive. John Morrill examined nearly 100,000 interviews on 26 product lines at 30,000 buying locations in order to study the effect of business-to-business advertising on salesperson effectiveness.[14] He concluded that dollar sales per salesperson call were significantly higher when customers had been exposed to advertising. In addition to increasing company and product awareness, research indicates that buyers who had been exposed to a supplier's advertisement rated the supplier's salespeople substantially higher on product knowledge, service, and enthusiasm.[15] A primary role of business-to-business advertising is to enhance the reputation of the supplier.

Business-to-business advertising also increases sales efficiency. Increased spending on advertising leads to greater brand awareness for industrial products, which translates into larger market shares and higher profits.[16] One study used a tightly controlled experimental design to measure the effect of business-to-business advertising on sales and profits. For one product, sales, gross margin, and net profit were significantly higher with advertising, compared with the pretest period with no advertising.[17] In fact, gross margins ranged from four to six times higher with advertising than with no advertising.

Increased Sales Efficiency

The effect of advertising on the marketing program's overall efficiency is evidenced in two ways. First, business suppliers frequently need to remind actual and potential buyers of their products or make them aware of new products or services. Although these objectives could be partially accomplished through personal selling, the costs of reaching a vast group of buyers would be prohibitive. Carefully targeted advertising extends beyond the salesperson's reach to unidentified buying influentials. A properly placed advertisement can reach hundreds of buying influentials for only a few cents

---

[14]John E. Morrill, "Industrial Advertising Pays Off," *Harvard Business Review* 48 (March–April 1970): pp. 4–14.

[15]Ibid., p. 6. For a comprehensive study of the relationship between brand awareness and brand preference, see Eunsang Yoon and Valerie Kijewski, "The Brand Awareness-to-Preference Link in Business Markets: A Study of the Semiconductor Manufacturing Industry," *Journal of Business-to-Business Marketing* 2 (4, 1995): pp. 7–36.

[16]"New Proof of Industrial Ad Values," *Marketing and Media Decisions* (February 1981): p. 64.

[17]"ARF/ABP Release Final Study Findings," *Business Marketing* 72 (May 1987): p. 55.

each; the average cost of a business sales call is currently more than $200.[18] Sales call costs are determined by the salesperson's wages, travel and entertainment costs, and fringe benefits costs. If these costs total $800 per day and a salesperson can make four calls per day, then each call costs $200. Second, advertising appears to make all selling activities more effective. Advertising interacts effectively with all communication and selling activities, and it can boost efficiency for the entire marketing expenditure.

Creating Awareness

From a communications standpoint, the buying process takes potential buyers sequentially from unawareness of a product or supplier to awareness, to brand preference, to conviction that a particular purchase will fulfill their requirements, and, ultimately, to actual purchase. Business advertising often creates awareness of the supplier and the supplier's products. Sixty-one percent of the design engineers returning an inquiry card from a magazine ad indicated that they were unaware of the company that advertised before seeing the ad.[19] Business advertising may also make some contribution to creating preference for the product—all cost-effectively. In addition, advertising can create a corporate identity or image. Hewlett-Packard, Dell, IBM, and others use ads in general business publications such as *Business Week* and even television advertising to trumpet the value of their brand and to develop desired perceptions in a broad audience.[20]

What Business-to-Business Advertising Cannot Do

To develop an effective communications program, the business marketing manager must blend all communication tools (online and print formats) into an integrated program, using each tool where it is most effective. Business advertising quite obviously has limitations. Advertising cannot substitute for effective personal selling—it must supplement, support, and complement that effort. In the same way, personal selling is constrained by its costs and should not be used to create awareness or to disseminate information—tasks quite capably performed by advertising.

For many purchasing decisions, advertising alone cannot create product preference—this requires demonstration, explanation, and operational testing. Similarly, conviction and actual purchase can be ensured only by personal selling. Advertising has a supporting role in creating awareness, providing information, and uncovering important leads for salespeople; that is how the marketing manager must use it to be effective.

Managing Business-to-Business Advertising

The advertising decision model in Figure 13.1 shows the structural elements involved in managing business-to-business advertising. First, advertising is only one component of the entire marketing strategy and must be integrated with other components to achieve strategic goals. The advertising decision process begins with formulating

---

[18]Erin Anderson and Bob Trinkle, *Outsourcing the Sales Function: The Real Costs of Field Sales* (Mason, OH: Thomson Higher Education, 2005).

[19]Raymond E. Herzog, "How Design Engineering Activity Affects Supplies," *Business Marketing* 70 (November 1985): p. 143.

[20]David A. Aaker and Erich Joachimsthaler, "The Lure of Global Branding," *Harvard Business Review* 77 (November–December 1999): pp. 137–144.

FIGURE 13.1 | **THE DECISION STAGES FOR DEVELOPING THE BUSINESS-TO-BUSINESS ADVERTISING PROGRAM**

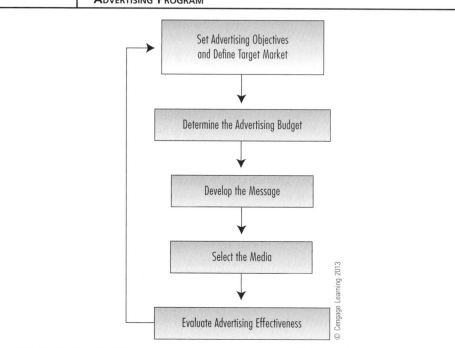

advertising objectives, which are derived from marketing goals. From this formulation the marketer can determine how much it has to spend to achieve those goals. Then, specific communication messages are formulated to achieve the market behavior specified by the objectives. Equally important is evaluating and selecting the media used to reach the desired audience. The result is an integrated advertising campaign aimed at eliciting a specific attitude or behavior from the target group. The final, and critical, step is to evaluate the campaign's effectiveness.

Defining Advertising Objectives

Knowing what advertising must accomplish enables the manager to determine an advertising budget more accurately and provides a yardstick for evaluating advertising. In specifying advertising goals, the marketing manager must realize that: (1) the advertising mission flows directly from the overall marketing strategy; advertising must fulfill a marketing strategy objective, and its goal must reflect the general aim and purpose of the entire strategy; and (2) the advertising program's objectives must respond to the roles for which advertising is suited: creating awareness, providing information, influencing attitudes, and reminding buyers of company and product existence.

Written Objectives

An advertising objective must be measurable and realistic, and must specify what is to be achieved and when. The objective must speak in unambiguous terms of a specific outcome. The purpose is to establish a single working direction for everyone involved in creating, coordinating, and evaluating the advertising program. Correctly conceived objectives set standards for evaluating the advertising effort. A specific objective might be "to increase from 15 percent (as measured in June 2012) to 30 percent (by June 2013) the proportion of general contractors associating 'energy efficiency' feature with our brand of commercial air conditioners." The objective directs the manager to create a message related to the major product benefit, using media that reaches general contractors. The objective also provides a way to measure accomplishment (awareness among 30 percent of the target audience).

Business advertising objectives frequently bear no direct relationship to specific dollar sales targets. Although dollar sales results would provide a "hard" measure of advertising accomplishment, it is often impossible to link advertising directly to sales. Personal selling, price, product performance, and competitive actions have a more direct relationship to sales levels, and it is almost impossible to sort out advertising's impact. Thus, advertising goals are typically stated in terms of *communication goals* such as brand awareness, recognition, and buyer attitudes. These goals can be measured; it is presumed that achieving them stimulates sales volume.

Target Audience   A significant task is specifying target audiences. Because a primary role of advertising is to reach buying influentials inaccessible to the salesperson, the business marketing manager must define the buying influential groups to be reached. Generally, each group of buying influentials is concerned with distinct product and service attributes and criteria, and the advertising must focus on these. Thus, the objectives must specify the intended audience and its relevant decision criteria.

Creative Strategy Statement   A final consideration is to specify the creative strategy statement. Once objectives and targets are established, the **creative strategy statement** provides guidelines for the company and advertising agency on how to position the product in the marketplace. Product position relates to how the target market perceives the product.

For example, if the commercial air conditioners cited earlier currently have an unfavorable product position with regard to energy efficiency but recent product development efforts have advanced performance, the firm might use the following creative strategy statement: "Our basic creative strategy is to reposition the product from that of a reliable air conditioner to a high-performance, energy-efficient air conditioner."

All creative efforts—copy, theme, color, and so forth—as well as media and tactics, should support the creative strategy statement. Planning an effective advertising campaign requires clearly defined objectives that provide a foundation for selecting media and measuring results.

Determining Advertising Expenditures

Collectively, business marketers spend billions of dollars on media advertising annually, and the Web is winning a growing share of these dollars. Included among the leading business-to-business advertisers are telecommunication firms such as Verizon and AT&T, high-tech firms (such as IBM, Hewlett-Packard, and Microsoft) and others such as General Electric and FedEx.[21] Typically, business marketers use a blend of intuition, judgment, experience, and, only occasionally, more advanced

---

[21]Kate Maddox, "Special Report: The Top 50 B2B Advertisers," *B to B*, September 13, 2010, accessed at http://www.btobonline.com on July 15, 2011.

decision-oriented techniques to determine advertising budgets. Some of the techniques business marketers most commonly use are rules of thumb (for example, percentage of past years' sales) and the objective-task method.

Rules of Thumb Often, because advertising is a relatively small part of the total marketing budget for business firms, the value of using sophisticated methods for advertising budgeting is not great. In these cases, managers tend to follow simple **rules of thumb** (for example, allocate 1 percent of sales to advertising or match competition spending). Unfortunately, percentage-of-sales rules are all too pervasive throughout business marketing, even where advertising is an important element.

The fundamental problem with percentage-of-sales rules is that they implicitly make advertising a consequence rather than a determinant of sales and profits and can easily give rise to dysfunctional policies. Percentage-of-sales rules suggest that the business advertiser reduce advertising when sales volume declines, just when increased advertising may be more appropriate. Nevertheless, simple rules of thumb continue to be applied in budget decisions because they are easy to use and familiar to management.

Objective-Task Method The task method for budgeting advertising expenditures relates advertising costs to the objective it is to accomplish. Because the sales dollar results of advertising are almost impossible to measure, the task method focuses on the communications effects of advertising, not on the sales effects.

The **objective-task method** is applied by evaluating the tasks advertising will perform, analyzing the costs of each task, and summing up the total costs to arrive at a final budget. The process can be divided into four steps:

1. Establish specific marketing objectives for the product in terms of such factors as sales volume, market share, profit contribution, and market segments.

2. Assess the communication functions that must be performed to realize the marketing objectives and then determine the role of advertising and other elements of the communications mix in performing these functions.

3. Define specific goals for advertising in terms of the measurable communication response required to achieve marketing objectives.

4. Estimate the budget needed to accomplish the advertising goals.

The task method addresses the major problem of the rule-of-thumb methods—funds are applied to accomplish a specific goal so that advertising is a *determinant* of those results, not a consequence. Using the task approach, managers allocate all the funds necessary to accomplish a specific objective rather than allocating some arbitrary percentage of sales. The most troubling problem with the method is that management must have some instinct for the proper relationship between expenditure level and communication response. It is difficult to know what produces a certain level of awareness among business marketing buying influentials. Will 12 two-page insertions in *Fortune* Magazine over the next six months create the desired recognition level, or will 24 insertions over one year be necessary?

Budgeting for advertising must not ignore the political and behavioral aspects of the process. Nigel Piercy's research suggests that firms pay insufficient attention to budgeting technique because they operate through structures and processes that are often political in nature.[22] Piercy suggests that what actually determines advertising budgets are the power "interests" in the company and the political behavior of various parties in the budgeting process. An implication of this research is that the manager may be well served by focusing on budgeting as a political activity, and not simply as a technique-driven process.

Passing the Threshold   Several communications are often needed to capture the attention of buyers, which complicates the budgeting decision. Research suggests that a brand must surpass a threshold level of awareness in the market before meaningful increases can be made to its brand preference share. A small advertising budget may not allow the marketer to move the firm's brand beyond a threshold level of awareness and on to preference. Eunsang Yoon and Valerie Kijewski warn that "the communications manager having limited marketing resources will then be in danger of making the mistake of stopping the program prematurely, thus wasting past investment, rather than pressing on to pass the threshold awareness level."[23]

Because budgeting is so important to advertising effectiveness, managers must not blindly follow rules of thumb. Instead, they should evaluate the tasks required and their costs against industry norms. With clear objectives and proper budgetary allocations, the next step is to design effective advertising messages.

Developing the Advertising Message

Message development is a complex, critical task in industrial advertising. Highlighting a product attribute that is unimportant to a particular buying group is not only a waste of advertising dollars but also a lost opportunity. Both the appeal and the way that appeal is conveyed are vital to successful communication. Thus, creating business-to-business advertising messages involves determining advertising objectives, evaluating the buying criteria of the target audience, and analyzing the most appropriate language, format, and style for presenting the message.

Perception   For an advertising message to be successful, an individual must first be exposed to it and pay attention to it. Thus, a business advertisement must catch the decision maker's attention. Once the individual has noticed the message, he or she must interpret it as the advertiser intended. Perceptual barriers often prevent a receiver from perceiving the intended message. Even though the individual is exposed to an advertisement, nothing guarantees that he or she processes the message. In fact, the industrial buyer may read every word of the copy and find a meaning in it opposite to the one the advertiser intended.

The business advertiser must therefore contend with two important elements of perception: attention and interpretation. Buyers tend to screen out messages that are inconsistent with their own attitudes, needs, and beliefs, and they tend to interpret information in the light of those beliefs (see Chapter 2). Unless advertising messages are carefully designed and targeted, they may be disregarded or interpreted improperly. Advertisers must put themselves in the position of the receivers to evaluate how the message appears to them.

---

[22]Nigel Piercy, "Advertising Budgeting: Process and Structure as Explanatory Variables," *Journal of Advertising* 16 (2, 1987): p. 34.

[23]Yoon and Kijewski, "The Brand Awareness-to-Preference Link," p. 32.

Whether an ad uses technical wording appears to have some effect on readers' perceptions of both the industrial product and the ad.[24] Technical ads were shown to create less desire in some readers to seek information because such ads suggest "more difficulty in operation." Therefore, it is important to remember that technical readers (engineers, architects, and so on) respond more favorably to the technical ads and nontechnical readers respond more favorably to nontechnical ads. From a message-development viewpoint, the business advertiser must carefully tailor the technical aspects of promotional messages to the appropriate audience.

Focus on Benefits   A business buyer purchases benefits—a better way to accomplish some task, a less expensive way to produce a final product, a solution to a problem, or a faster delivery time. Advertising messages need to focus on benefits that the target customer seeks and persuade the reader that the advertiser can deliver them.[25] Messages that have direct appeals or calls to action are viewed to be "stronger" than those with diffuse or indirect appeals to action. Robert Lamons, an advertising consultant, observes:

> A good call to action can actually start the selling process. Promise a test report; offer a product demonstration; direct them to a special section of your Web site…. Compare how your product stacks up to others in the field. Everyone is super-busy these days, and if you can offer something that helps them expedite or narrow their search, you're giving them something money can't buy: free time.[26]

Understanding Buyer Motivations   Which product benefits are important to each group of buying influentials? The business advertiser cannot assume that a standard set of "classical buying motives" applies in every purchase situation. Many business advertisers often do not understand the buying motives of important market segments. Developing effective advertising messages often requires extensive marketing research in order to fully delineate the key buying criteria of each buying influencer in each of the firm's different target markets.

Selecting Advertising Media for Business Markets

Although the message is vital to advertising success, equally important is the medium through which it is presented. An integrated marketing communications program might include a blend of online, print, and direct-mail advertisements that deliver a consistent story across formats. Business-to-business media are selected by the target audience—the particular purchase-decision participants to be reached. Selection of media also involves budgetary considerations: Where are dollars best spent to generate the customer contacts desired?

Online Advertising   As business marketing strategists seek more effective ways to communicate with customers and prospects, they continue to shift more of the

---

[24]Joseph A. Bellizzi and Jacqueline J. Mohr, "Technical versus Nontechnical Wording in Industrial Print Advertising," in *AMA Educators' Proceedings*, Russell W. Belk et al., eds. (Chicago: American Marketing Association, 1984), p. 174.

[25]Steve McKee, "Five Common B2B Advertising Myths," *Business Week*, April 2007, accessed at http://www.businessweek.com on July 29, 2008.

[26]Robert Lamons, "Tips for Distinguishing Your Ads from Bad Ads," *Marketing News* (November 19, 2001): p. 10.

advertising budget to digital formats. For example, during a recent global interactive campaign, more than 220,000 visitors clicked through to a Hewlett-Packard microsite designed for small and mid-sized businesses.[27] A **microsite** is a specialized Web page a visitor lands on after clicking an online ad or e-mail. Similarly, both IBM and GE make extensive use of online videos to show how their products and services are helping customers around the world to solve business problems.

A Shift to Digital   Online advertising spending by business-to-business firms exceeds $31 billion and will continue to grow at a rapid pace. Paid search engine advertising represents the prime format, accounting for over 45 percent of total online spending, followed by display ads.[28] Experiencing particularly rapid spending growth is the rich media/video format, particularly the online video category. "Video is a particularly compelling way to tell a brand or product story that can be very useful for b-to-b communications, as these businesses tend to be more complex and can require additional explanation," according to Andreas Combuechen, CEO–chief creative officer of Atmosphere BBDO.[29]

Motorola's Integrated Campaign   Like many other firms, Motorola Solutions is shifting its emphasis from traditional advertising to a more integrated focus. A recent integrated marketing campaign demonstrates Motorola's mission-critical public safety solutions.[30] The campaign features a microsite targeted at police chiefs, fire chiefs, and municipal chief information officers. The campaign includes print and online ads, direct mail, and e-mail, all of which are designed around a unifying goal: drive customer prospects to the microsite to observe Motorola's technology solutions at work in a virtual city environment.

Business Publications   More than 2700 business publications carry business-to-business advertising. For those specializing in the pharmaceutical industry, *Drug Discovery & Development*, *Pharmaceutical Executive*, and *Pharmaceutical Technology* are a few of the publications available. Business publications are either horizontal or vertical. **Horizontal publications** are directed at a specific task, technology, or function, whatever the industry. *Advertising Age*, *Purchasing*, and *Marketing News* are horizontal. **Vertical publications**, on the other hand, may be read by everyone from floor supervisor to president within a specific industry. Typical vertical publications are *Chemical Business* or *Computer Gaming World*.

If a business marketer's product has applications within only a few industries, vertical publications are a logical media choice. When many industries are potential users and well-defined functions are the principal buying influencers, a horizontal publication is effective.

Many trade publications are **requester publications,** which offer free subscriptions to selected readers. The publisher can select readers who are in a position to influence buying decisions and offer the free subscription in exchange for

---

[27]"B to B's Best Brands—Hewlett-Packard," B to B's Best: 2007, p. 26, accessed at http://www.btobonline.com on June 15, 2008.

[28]"eMarketer Projects U.S. Online Ad Spending Will Grow 20.2% This Year," *B to B*, June 8, 2011, accessed at http://www.btobonline.com on August, 2011.

[29]Ellis Booker, "Economic Slowdown Will Accelerate Online Shift," B to B's Interactive Guide: 2008, p. 3, accessed at http://www.btobonline.com on August 1, 2008.

[30]Kate Maddox, "Video in Play as Ad Vehicle," B to B's Interactive Marketing Guide: 2008, p. 26, accessed at http://www.btobonline.com on August 1, 2008.

B2B TOP PERFORMERS

Search Engine Marketing at Google: The Right Message, the Right Time

To reach customers through all stages of the buying cycle, from awareness to retention, business-to-business firms are devoting a greater share of their advertising budgets to e-marketing campaigns, including keyword advertising through leading Internet search engines such as Google or Yahoo. As marketing managers face increased pressure to demonstrate the return on investment of each advertising dollar spent, keyword advertising provides compelling value—it delivers qualified leads in the form of potential customers searching on terms specifically related to your products and services. You pay only when users click on your ads. Keyword advertising provides the lowest average cost-per-lead of any direct marketing method.[1] Says Eric Grates, business service manager at Dow Chemical, "With click through rates ranging from 2.5 to 7 percent, the Google advertising program continues to be a key component of our overall marketing efforts."[2]

Russ Cohn, who leads Google's business-to-business service operations, offers some useful guidelines for successful keyword advertising:

1. Ensure that your Web site is search-crawler friendly by providing a clear hierarchy, text links, and information-rich content.

2. Understand that relevance to the user is the goal: The most successful ads connect customers to the information or solution they are seeking.

3. Create a relevant, targeted keyword list by choosing specific words that accurately reflect your Web site and advertised products.

4. Write clear and compelling ads that use the keywords and that isolate your unique value proposition.

5. Track results and measure everything.

   • Monitor click-through rates to make adjustments to the campaign.

   • Test different keywords and ad copy.

   • Use free conversion tracking tools to analyze which keywords are providing the best returns.

   • Calculate the return on investment.

---

[1]Russ Cohn, "Unlocking Keyword Advertising," *B2B Magazine*, accessed at http://www.thefreelibrary.com/Google+Named+Top+5+Business-To-Business+Media+Property%3B+BtoB+Media...-a0101181530 on November 2, 2005.
[2]"Google Named Top 5 Business-to-Business Media Property," accessed at http://www.google.com on May 5, 2003.

information such as title, function, and buying responsibilities. Thus, the advertiser can tell whether each publication reaches the desired audience.

Obviously, publication choice is predicated on a complete understanding of the range of purchase-decision participants and of the industries where the product is used. Only then can the target audience be matched to the circulation statements of alternative business publications.

Characteristics of an Effective Print Ad   Recent research on the effectiveness of business-to-business print ads provides strong evidence that the marketing strategist should emphasize a "rational approach" and provide a clear description of the product and the benefits it offers to customers.[31] The effectiveness of ads is also

---

[31]Ritu Lohtia, Wesley J. Johnston, and Linda Rab, "Business-to-Business Advertising: What Are the Dimensions of an Effective Print Ad?" *Industrial Marketing Management* 24 (October 1995): pp. 369–378.

enhanced by detailing product quality and performance information in a concrete and logical manner.

Advertising Cost Circulation is an important criterion in the selection of publications, but circulation must be tempered by cost. First, the total advertising budget must be allocated among the various advertising tools, such as business publications, sales promotion, direct marketing (mail and e-mail), and online advertising. Of course, allocations to the various media options vary with company situation and advertising mission. The allocation of the business publication budget among various journals depends on their relative effectiveness and efficiency, usually measured in cost per thousand using the following formula:

$$\text{Cost per thousand} = \frac{\text{Cost per page}}{\text{Circulation in thousands}}$$

To compare two publications by their actual page rates would be misleading because the publication with the lower circulation is usually less expensive. The cost-per-thousand calculation should be based on circulation to the *target* audience, not the total audience. Although some publications may appear expensive on a cost-per-thousand basis, they may in fact be cost-effective, with little wasted circulation. Some publications also have popular Web sites that advertisers can use to create integrated marketing communications.

Frequency and Scheduling Even the most successful business publication advertisements are seen by only a small percentage of the people who read the magazine; therefore, one-time ads are generally ineffective. Because a number of exposures are required before a message "sinks in," and because the reading audience varies from month to month, a schedule of advertising insertions is required. To build continuity and repetitive value, at least 6 insertions per year may be required in a monthly publication, and 26 to 52 insertions (with a minimum of 13) in a weekly publication.[32]

Direct Marketing Tools

Direct mail and e-mail are among the direct marketing tools available to the business marketer. Direct mail delivers the advertising message firsthand to selected individuals. Possible mailing pieces range from a sales letter introducing a new product to a lengthy brochure or even a product sample. Direct mail can accomplish all of the major advertising functions, but its real contribution is in delivering the message to a precisely defined prospect. In turn, says marketing consultant Barry Silverstein, direct *e-mail* can have a substantial effect on creating and qualifying customer leads, *if* some important rules are strictly followed: "always seek permission to send e-mail" and "always provide the recipient with the ability to 'opt out.'"[33] Attention first centers on direct-mail advertising.

---

[32]See Stanton G. Cort, David R. Lambert, and Paula L. Garrett, "Effective Business-to-Business Frequency: New Management Perspectives from the Research Literature," *Advertising Research Foundation Literature Review* (October 1983).

[33]Barry Silverstein, *Business-to-Business Internet Marketing*, 3rd ed. (Gulf Breeze, FL.: MAXIMUM Press, 2001), p. 171. See also Carol Krol, "E-Mail: Integrating Channels Key," B to B's Interactive Marketing Guide: 2008, p. 8, accessed at http://www.btobonline.com on August 1, 2008.

Direct Mail   Direct mail is commonly used for corporate image promotion, product and service promotion, sales force support, distribution channel communication, and special marketing problems. In promoting corporate image, direct mail may help to establish a firm's reputation of technological leadership. On the other hand, product advertising by direct mail can put specific product information in the hands of buying influentials. For example, as part of a successful integrated marketing campaign to change perceptions of UPS from a ground shipping company to a supply chain leader, the firm used direct mail to target decision makers—from shipping managers to front-office administrators. The direct-mail strategy had strong results, achieving a 10.5 percent response rate, with 36 percent of those responders buying services.[34]

Direct E-Mail   Because marketers are devoting a larger share of their advertising budgets to online marketing, IBM's customer relationship program, called *Focusing on You*, rests on a simple but powerful idea—ask customers what information they want and give it to them.[35] By giving the customer the choice, IBM learns about the customer's unique preferences and is better equipped to tailor product and service information to that customer's specific needs. The program relies on e-mail marketing, which is far less costly than direct mail. IBM found that sending customers traditional printed materials by mail was 10 times more expensive than e-mail communications. Moreover, e-mail campaigns often yield higher responses than direct-mail campaigns, and the results are generated more quickly. For example, a third of all responses to a particular IBM e-mail campaign were generated in the first 24 hours!

Let the Customer Decide   Pamela Evans, director of worldwide teleweb marketing at IBM, describes the value of interactive marketing:

> In the IBM software business, for example, we have a long sales cycle, and the Web gives us the opportunity for our prospects and customers to go online where we establish a relationship that we can then continue to nurture electronically.… The challenge as marketers we all face is determining how the customer wants to interact with us, and really taking advantage of the Web and the power … there for self-service.[36]

Firms that plan to fully integrate direct e-mail into their marketing communications strategy should make a special effort to build their own e-mail list. Often such information is already available from the firm's customer relationship management (CRM) system. From Chapter 3, recall that a goal of the CRM system is to integrate customer records from all departments, including sales, marketing, and customer service. As a result, if a customer responds to an e-mail (or direct-mail) campaign, the CRM system captures that information in a centralized database for all contact employees (salespersons, call center employees, marketing managers) to retrieve.

---

[34]Kate Maddox and Beth Snyder Bulik, "Integrated Marketing Success Stories," *B2B* 89 (July 7, 2004): p. 23.

[35]Silverstein, *Business-to-Business Internet Marketing*, p. 226.

[36]Carol Krol, "The Internet Continues to Reshape Direct," *B to B*, accessed at http://www.b2bonline.com on October 10, 2005.

Other ways to create an e-mail list include offering an e-mail alert service or e-mail newsletter, asking for e-mail addresses in direct-mail campaigns, and collecting e-mail addresses at trade shows.[37] Business marketers must also realize that the response to an e-mail campaign can be immediate, so they must be prepared to acknowledge, process, and fulfill orders before the e-mail campaign is launched.

Measuring Advertising Effectiveness

The business advertiser rarely expects orders to result immediately from advertising. Advertising is designed to create awareness, stimulate loyalty to the company, or create a favorable attitude toward a product. Even though advertising may not directly precipitate a purchase decision, advertising programs must be held accountable, and marketing managers are facing increased pressure to demonstrate the actual returns on marketing expenditures.[38] Research suggests that firms that are adept at marketing performance measurement generate greater profitability and stock returns than their competitors.[39] Thus, the business advertiser must be able to measure the results of current advertising in order to improve future advertising and evaluate the effectiveness of advertising expenditures against expenditures on other elements of marketing strategy.

Measuring Impacts on the Purchase Decision

Measuring advertising effectiveness means assessing advertising's effect on what "intervenes" between the stimulus (advertising) and the resulting behavior (purchase decision). The theory is that advertising can affect awareness, knowledge, and other dimensions that more readily lend themselves to measurement. In essence, the advertiser attempts to gauge advertising's ability to move an individual through the purchase decision process. This approach assumes, correctly or not, that enhancement of any one phase of the process or movement from one step to the next increases the ultimate probability of purchase.

Research suggests that business marketers should also measure the **indirect communication effects of advertising**.[40] This study revealed that advertising affects word-of-mouth communications (indirect effect), and such communications play an important role in buyer decision making. Similarly, the study showed that advertising indirectly affects buyers on the basis of its effect on overall company reputation and on the sales force's belief that advertising aids selling. The study suggested that advertising effectiveness measurements include a procedure for tracking and measuring advertising's effect on the indirect communication effects.

In summary, advertising effectiveness is evaluated against objectives formulated in terms of the elements of the buyer's decision process as well as some of the

---

[37]Barry Silverstein, *Internet Marketing for Information Technology Companies*, 2d ed. (Gulf Breeze, FL: MAXIMUM Press, 2001), p. 107.

[38]Diane Brady and David Kiley, "Making Marketing Measure Up," *Business Week*, December 13, 2004, pp. 112–113.

[39]Dan O'Sullivan and Andrew V. Abela, "Marketing Performance Measurement Ability and Firm Performance," *Journal of Marketing* 71 (April 2007): pp. 79–93. See also Todd M. Powers and Anil Menon, "Practical Measurement of Advertising Impact: The IBM Experience" in Roger A. Kerin and Rob O'Regan (eds.), *Marketing Mix Decisions: New Perspectives and Practices* (Chicago: American Marketing Association 2008), pp. 77–109.

[40]C. Whan Park, Martin S. Roth, and Philip F. Jacques, "Evaluating the Effects of Advertising and Sales Promotion Campaigns," *Industrial Marketing Management* 17 (May 1988): p. 130.

indirect communication effects. Advertising efforts are also judged, in the final analysis, on cost per level of achievement (for example, dollars spent to achieve a certain level of awareness or recognition).

The Measurement Program

A sound measurement program entails substantial advanced planning. Figure 13.2 shows the basic areas of advertising evaluation. The advertising strategist must determine in advance what is to be measured, how, and in what sequence. A pre-evaluation phase is required to establish a benchmark for a new advertising campaign. For example, a pre-evaluation study would be conducted to capture the existing level of awareness a firm's product enjoys in a defined target market. After the advertising campaign, the evaluation study examines changes in awareness against this benchmark. Five primary areas for advertising evaluation include: (1) markets, (2) motives, (3) messages, (4) media, and (5) results.

Web Metrics   For online advertising, attention likewise centers on defined communication objectives. Was the ad designed to drive visitors to the Web site to view an online video or to download information on a new product?

FIGURE 13.2 | THE PRIMARY AREAS FOR ADVERTISING EVALUATION

AREA	FOCUS OF MEASUREMENT
Target Market Coverage	Degree to which advertising succeeded in reaching defined target markets
Key Buying Motives	Factors that triggered purchase decision
Effectiveness of Messages	Degree to which the message registered with key buying influentials in defined market segments
Media Effectiveness	Degree to which various media were successful in reaching defined target markets with message
Overall Results	Degree to which advertising accomplished its defined objectives

© Cengage Learning 2013

This event is the "desired action," and the business marketing manager wants to measure site traffic to this action and evaluate all of the components of the Web site that lead visitors to take this action. "Pulling in information from search marketing campaigns allows b-to-b marketers to better understand what visitors searched for to find their site and what text-based ads elicited the highest click-through and conversion (action) rates. In turn, these data can help marketers optimize their sites with language that resonates with their target audiences and customize their home pages with links that are most important to their visitors,"[41] says Jim Sterne, president, Target Media.

Evaluation Is Essential   The evaluation of business-to-business advertising is demanding and complex, but absolutely essential. Budgetary constraints are generally the limiting factors. However, professional research companies can be called on to develop field research studies. When determining the effect of advertising on moving a decision participant from an awareness of the product or company to a readiness to buy, the evaluations usually measure knowledge, recognition, recall, awareness, preference, and motivation. Measuring effects on actual sales are unfortunately seldom possible.

Managing Trade Show Strategy

Business advertising funds are designated primarily for online, print, and direct-mail formats, but these are reinforced by other promotional activities such as exhibits and trade shows, catalogs, and trade promotion. Special attention is given here to trade shows—an important promotional vehicle for business markets.

Trade Shows: Strategy Benefits

Most industries stage an annual business show or exhibition to display new advances and technological developments in the industry. The Center for Exhibition Industry Research indicates that some 1.5 million U.S. and Canadian firms place displays at trade shows each year and that 83 percent of trade-show visitors are classified as "buying influencers."[42] Exhibiting firms spend more than $21 billion annually on floor space at North American exhibitions, and the average company participates in more than 45 trade shows per year.[43] Generally, sellers present their products and services in booths visited by interested industry members. The typical exhibitor contacts four to five potential purchasers per hour on the show floor.

A trade-show exhibit offers a unique opportunity to publicize a significant contribution to technology or to demonstrate new and old products. According to Thomas Bonoma, "For many companies, trade-show expenditures are the major—and for

---

[41]Jim Sterne, "Must-have Web Metrics," *B to B*, March 10, 2008, accessed at http://www.btobonline.com on May 14, 2008.

[42]Douglas Ducante, "The Future of the United States Exhibition Industry—Flourish or Flounder," accessed at http://www.ceir.org on October 2002.

[43]Ruth P. Stevens, *Trade Show and Event Marketing* (Mason, OH: Thomson/South-Western, 2005), pp. 2–6. See also Sean Callahan, "Trade Shows Exhibit Enduring Appeal," *B to B*, March 14, 2011, accessed at http://www.btobonline.com on August 1, 2011.

more than a few, the only—form of organized marketing communication activity other than efforts by sales force and distributors."[44] Through the trade show:

- An effective selling message can be delivered to a relatively large and interested audience at one time (for example, more than 30,000 people attend the annual Plant Engineering Show).

- New products can be introduced to a mass audience.

- Customers can get hands-on experience with the product in a one-on-one selling situation.

- Potential customers can be identified, providing sales personnel with qualified leads.

- General goodwill can be enhanced.

- Free publicity is often generated for the company.

The cost of reaching a prospect at a trade show is approximately $250, much lower than the cost of making a personal sales call for many firms.[45] Furthermore, trade shows offer an excellent and cost-effective short-term method for introducing a product in new foreign markets.[46] An international trade fair enables a manufacturer to meet buyers directly, observe competition, and gather market research data. The entry time for exporting can easily be cut from six years to six months by attending foreign trade fairs.

Trade-Show Investment Returns

An insightful study evaluated the effect of a trade show on the sales and profitability of a new laboratory testing device.[47] In a controlled experiment where new product sales could be traced to customers both attending and not attending the show, sales levels were higher among attendees. In turn, the proportion of customers who bought the product was higher among those who had visited the booth during the show. Importantly, there was a positive return on trade-show investment (23 percent) based on incremental profits related to the cost of the trade show. This research is one of the first studies to show that the returns from trade-show investments can indeed be measured.

Improving Sales Efficiency   Another study demonstrated the powerful way personal selling and trade shows work together in an integrated marketing communications strategy.[48] The results demonstrate that follow-up sales efforts generate higher sales productivity when customers had already been exposed to the company's products at a trade show. The return-on-sales figures are higher among show attendees than

[44]Thomas V. Bonoma, "Get More Out of Your Trade Shows," *Harvard Business Review* 61 (January–February 1983): p. 76.

[45]Stevens, *Trade Show and Event Marketing*, p. 16.

[46]Brad O'Hara, Fred Palumbo, and Paul Herbig, "Industrial Trade Shows Abroad," *Industrial Marketing Maagement*n 22 (August 1993): p. 235.

[47]Srinath Gopalakrishna, Gary L. Lilien, Jerome D. Williams, and Ian K. Sequeira, "Do Trade Shows Pay Off?" *Journal of Marketing* 59 (July 1995): pp. 75–83.

[48]Timothy M. Smith, Srinath Gopalakrishna, and Paul M. Smith, "The Complementary Effect of Trade Shows on Personal Selling," *International Journal of Research in Marketing* 21 (March 2004): pp. 61–69.

nonattendees, illuminating the positive effects of trade shows on customer purchase intentions. Although dramatically enhancing performance, however, trade shows can be extremely costly and must be carefully planned.

Planning Trade-Show Strategy

To develop an effective trade-show communications strategy, managers must address four questions:

1. What functions should the trade show perform in the total marketing communications program?

2. To whom should the marketing effort at trade shows be directed?

3. What is the appropriate show mix for the company?

4. What should the trade-show investment-audit policy be? How should audits be carried out?[49]

Answering these questions helps managers crystallize their thinking about target audiences, about expected results, and about how funds should be allocated.

Trade-Show Objectives

The functions of trade shows in generating sales include identifying decision influencers; targeting potential customers; providing product, service, and company information; learning of potential application problems; creating actual sales; and handling current customer problems. In addition to these selling-related functions, the trade show can be valuable for building corporate image, gathering competitive intelligence, and enhancing sales force morale. Specific objectives are needed to guide the development of trade-show strategy and to specify the activities of company personnel while there. Once specific objectives are formulated, however, the exhibitor must evaluate alternative trade shows in light of the target market.

Selecting the Shows

The challenge is to decide which trade shows to attend and how much of the promotional budget to invest.[50] Clearly, the firm wants to attend those shows frequented by its most important customer segments, so it begins by soliciting ideas from salespeople and customers. A wealth of information can also be found in leading trade-show directories, like the *American Tradeshow Directory* (http://www.tradeshowbiz.net) or from the resources available at Exhibitor Online (http://www.exhibitoronline.com). Here information on each show is provided and exhibitors can promote their presence at the show on the site.

Some firms use the reports published by Exhibit Surveys, Inc., a company that surveys trade-show audiences. Two of the important measures Exhibit Surveys developed are the **net buying influences** and the **total buying plans**. The first measures the percentage of the show audience that has decision authority for the types of products being exhibited; the second measures the percentage of the audience planning to buy those products within the next 12 months. These measures are

---

[49]Bonoma, "Get More Out of Your Trade Shows," p. 79.

[50]Stevens, Trade Show and Event Marketing, pp. 58–62.

very useful to the business marketing manager when selecting the most effective shows to attend.

Many firms survey their target prospects before the trade show to learn which trade shows they will attend and what they hope to gain from attending. In this way the exhibitor can prepare its trade-show strategy to fit the needs of its potential customers. Others suggest that a firm rank-order various shows based on expected profitability.[51] The expected profitability is computed by calibrating a model of "lead efficiency" using the firm's historical sales lead and lead conversion-to-sale data, gross margin information, and total attendance at past shows. **Lead efficiency** is defined as the number of sales leads obtained at the show divided by the total number of show visitors with definite plans to buy the exhibitor's product or one similar to it.

Managing the Trade-Show Exhibit

To generate interest in an exhibit, business marketing firms run advertisements in business publications profiling new projects they will exhibit at the show. Trade-show strategies should also be linked to interactive marketing communications. This enables many exhibitors to schedule appointments with prospects and customers during the show.

Sales personnel must be trained to perform in the trade-show environment. The selling job differs from the typical sales call in that the salesperson may have only 5 to 10 minutes to make a presentation. On a typical sales call, salespersons usually sell themselves first, then the company, and finally the product. At the trade show, the process is reversed.

There must be a system for responding effectively to inquiries generated at the show. Some business marketers find it effective to use a laptop to transmit information to corporate headquarters electronically. Headquarters staff then generate a letter and send out the required information by mail or e-mail. When prospects return to their offices after a show, the material is immediately available.

Evaluating Trade-Show Performance

The measurement of trade-show performance is very important in assessing the success of a firm's trade-show strategy. Srinath Gopalakrishna and Gary Lilien present a useful framework to assess performance by considering traffic flow through the firm's booth as a sequence of three stages.[52] Figure 13.3 illustrates the process and three different indices of performance—attraction, contact, and conversion efficiency—for the three respective stages.

An important contribution of this framework is the link between performance indices and key decision variables the firm can control. Attraction efficiency is the proportion of *interested* visitors the booth is able to attract. Notice that the firm's target audience is the pool of visitors at the show who are interested in the firm's products, which is usually smaller than the total number of attendees at the show. The booth's attraction power is a function of space (square feet), show promotion, use of attention-getting techniques, and so on. Similarly, contact

[51]Srinath Gopalakrishna and Jerome D. Williams, "Planning and Performance Assessment of Industrial Trade Shows: An Exploratory Study," *International Journal of Research in Marketing* 9 (September 1992): pp. 207–224.

[52]Srinath Gopalakrishna and Gary L. Lilien, "A Three-Stage Model of Industrial Trade Show Performance," *Marketing Science* 14 (Winter 1995): pp. 22–42.

FIGURE 13.3 | **REPRESENTATION OF TRAFFIC FLOW MODEL AT TRADE SHOWS AS A SEQUENCE OF STAGES**

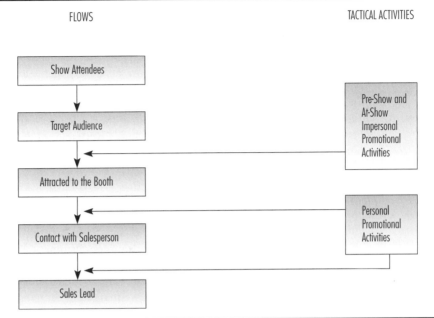

SOURCE: Srinath Gopalakrishna and Gary L. Lilien, "A Three-Stage Model of Industrial Trade Show Performance," Working paper #20-1992, Institute for the Study of Business Markets, Pennsylvania State University.

and conversion efficiencies are modeled as a function of the number of booth personnel and their level of training.

For an individual firm, trade-show expenditures should be tied to concrete marketing communication goals to secure an adequate return on investment. To this end, business marketing managers must carefully evaluate each trade show and its expenses in terms of the likely effect on sales, profit, and corporate image. As with all other promotional vehicles, the planning and budgeting for trade shows must focus on specific objectives. Once these objectives have been determined, the rational approach will then identify what has to be done and how much will have to be spent.

Summary

Business-to-business social media refers to various channels of the social Web where customers and businesses interact and exchange content across platforms as diverse as discussion forums, blogs, wikis, and social networks. As customers and prospects turn to social media channels to learn about a company's product and service offerings, business marketing strategists should facilitate targeted, personalized contact across the complete customer experience landscape. Social media can enhance the value proposition of an offering and change the way customers relate to a brand. Business-to-business marketers are developing integrated marketing communications strategies that align strategic business objectives with creative execution across a variety of media to achieve desired results.

Advertising supports personal selling by making the company and product known to potential buyers. The result is greater overall selling success and firm performance. Effective advertising makes the entire marketing strategy more efficient, often lowering total marketing and selling costs. Likewise, advertising can deliver information and build company or product awareness more efficiently than can personal selling.

Managing the advertising program begins by determining advertising objectives, which must be clearly defined and directed to a specific audience. Once objectives are specified, funds are allocated to advertising efforts. Rules of thumb, though common, are not the ideal methods for specifying advertising budgets. The objective-task method is far more effective. Advertising messages are created with the understanding that the potential buyer's perceptual process influences receptivity to the message. The most effective appeal is one that projects product benefits or the solution sought by the targeted buying influential.

Advertising media are selected on the basis of their circulation—how well their audience matches the desired audience of buying influentials. The Internet provides a powerful medium to communicate with target customers, and business-to-business firms are shifting a major share of the advertising budget to digital formats. Astute business marketers integrate the Web with other media and are using online videos to tell a brand or product story. Interactive marketing campaigns can be readily changed, personalized, and customized, making one-to-one marketing a reality.

Finally, advertising effectiveness must be evaluated against the advertising campaign's communication objectives. Readership, recognition, awareness, attitudes, and intention to buy are typical measures of business-to-business advertising performance. For online advertising, attention centers on the degree to which the ad moved potential customers to the desired action (for example, to download a new-product brochure).

Trade-show visitors tend to be buying influentials, and the cost of reaching a prospect here is far lower than through personal selling. A carefully planned and executed strategy is needed to secure promising returns on trade-show investments. Trade shows are an effective way to reach large audiences with a single presentation, but funds must be allocated carefully.

Discussion Questions

1. Given the rapid rise in the cost of making personal sales calls, should the business marketer attempt to substitute direct-mail advertising or online advertising for personal selling whenever possible? Support your position.

2. Outline how you would evaluate the effectiveness and efficiency of a business firm's advertising function. Focus on budgeting practices and performance results.

3. Explain how a message in a business-to-business advertisement in the *Wall Street Journal* may be favorably evaluated by the production manager, unfavorably evaluated by the purchasing manager, and fail even to trigger the attention of the quality-control engineer.

4. Although the bulk of the promotional budget of the business marketing firm is allocated to personal selling, advertising can play an important role in business marketing strategy. Explain.

5. Describe the role that online advertising might assume in the promotional mix of the business marketer. How can the business marketer use the Web to form close relationships with customers?

6. It is argued that business advertising is not expected to precipitate sales directly. If business advertising does not persuade organizational buyers to buy brand *A* versus brand *B*, what does it do, and how can we measure its effect against expenditures on other marketing strategy elements?

7. Breck Machine Tool would like you to develop a series of ads for a new industrial product. On request, Breck's marketing research department will provide you with any data they have about the new product and the market. Outline the approach you would follow in selecting media and developing messages for the campaign. Specify the types of data you would draw on to improve the quality of your decisions.

8. Evaluate this statement: "Social media channels have fundamentally changed the way in which many business customers compare alternatives and make buying decisions."

Internet Exercise

1. Intuit Inc., a leading provider of software for small and medium-sized enterprises, created a Web site to help these businesses develop their own customized Web sites. Go to http://blog.inuit.com/ and provide an assessment of this online initiative by Intuit.

CHAPTER

14

Business Marketing Communications: Managing the Personal Selling Function

Business marketing communications consist of advertising, sales promotion, and personal selling. As explored in Chapter 13, advertising and related sales promotion tools supplement and reinforce personal selling. Personal selling is the most important demand-stimulating force in the business marketer's promotional mix. Through the sales force, the marketer links the firm's total product and service offering to the needs of business customers. After reading this chapter, you will understand:

1. The methods for organizing the sales force

2. The skills and characteristics of high-performing account managers

3. The nature of the sales management function

4. Selected managerial tools that can be applied to sales force deployment decisions

By being entrusted with a firm's most valuable assets—its relationships with customers—the sales force assumes a central role in business-to-business marketing strategy. "Cisco, Microsoft, IBM, and Oracle each have over 11,000 salespeople in the United States. Pfizer, Johnson & Johnson, and GlaxoSmithKline each have more than 7,000. These seven companies spend a total of over $20 billion a year on their sales forces."[1]

In the marketing operations of the typical firm, selling has been a dominant component and a major determinant of overall company success, highlighting the importance of a strong structural linkage between marketing and sales.[2] U.S. businesses, alone, spend $800 billion annually on personal selling, roughly three times the amount spent on advertising.[3] Personal selling is dominant in business markets because, compared with consumer markets, the number of potential customers is relatively small and the dollar purchases are large. The importance of personal selling in the marketing mix depends on such factors as the nature and composition of the market, the product line, and the company's objectives and financial capabilities. Business marketers have many potential links to the market. Some rely on manufacturers' representatives and distributors; others rely exclusively on a direct sales force. Each firm must determine the relative importance of the promotional mix components—advertising versus sales promotion versus personal selling.

Across all industries, the average cost of an industrial sales call is more than $200.[4] Computer firms report much higher costs; chemical producers have much lower ones. Of course, these figures vary, depending on a host of company, product, and market conditions. They do indicate, however, that significant resources are invested in personal selling in the business market. In fact, Erin Anderson and Bob Trinkle persuasively argue that few firms have a clear understanding of the real costs of field sales.[5] To maximize effectiveness and efficiency, the personal selling function must be carefully managed and integrated into the firm's marketing mix. To enhance productivity and respond to intense competition, sales strategists are using a host of new approaches and technologies.

Regardless of how a firm implements its sales strategy, the salesperson is the initial link to the marketplace and specific customers. The task of the salesperson is both complex and challenging. To meet all their customers' expectations, salespeople must have broad knowledge that extends beyond their own products. They must be able to talk intelligently about competitors' products and about trends in the customer's industry. They must know not only their customer's business but also the business of their customer's customers. This chapter first considers methods for organizing the sales force and serving key customer accounts. Attention then turns to the characteristics of high-performing account managers and the central features of the sales management process.

---

[1]Andris A. Zoltners, Prabhakant Sinha, and Sally E. Lorimer, *Building a Winning Sales Force: Powerful Strategies for Driving High Performance* (Saranac Lake, NY: AMACOM Books, 2009), p. 3.

[2]Christian Homburg, Ore Jensen, and Harley Krohmer, "Configurations of Marketing and Sales: A Taxonomy," *Journal of Marketing* 72 (March 2008): pp. 133–154; see also James Cross, Steven W. Hartley, and William Rudelius, "Sales Force Activities and Marketing Strategies in Industrial Firms: Relationships and Implications," *Journal of Personal Selling and Sales Management* 21 (Summer 2001): pp. 199–206.

[3]Deborah Kreuze, "How Effective Is Personal Selling," *Insights from MSI* (Spring 2008): p. 3.

[4]"The Cost of Doing Business," *Sales and Marketing Management* 151 (September 1999): p. 56.

[5]Erin Anderson and Bob Trinkle, *Outsourcing the Sales Function: The Real Costs of Field Sales* (Mason, OH: Thomson Higher Education, 2005).

Managing the Sales Force

Effective management of the business-to-business sales force is fundamental to the firm's success. Sales management refers to planning, organizing, directing, and controlling personal selling efforts.[6] Sales force decisions are tempered by overall marketing objectives and must be integrated with the other elements of the marketing mix. Forecasts of the expected sales response guide the firm in determining the total selling effort required (sales force size) and in organizing and allocating the sales force (perhaps to sales territories). Techniques for estimating demand and forecasting sales (Chapter 4) are particularly valuable in sales planning. Sales management also involves the ongoing activities of selecting, training, deploying, supervising, and motivating sales personnel. Finally, sales operations must be monitored to identify problem areas and to assess the efficiency, effectiveness, and profitability of personal selling units.

This section considers strategic components of sales force management: (1) methods for organizing the sales force, (2) key account management, and (3) the distinctive characteristics of high-performing account managers.

Organizing the Personal Selling Effort

How should the sales force be organized? The appropriate form depends on such factors as the nature and length of the product line, the role of intermediaries in the marketing program, the diversity of the market segments served, the nature of buying behavior in each market segment, and the structure of competitive selling. The manufacturer's size and financial strength often dictate, to an important degree, the feasibility of particular organizational forms. The business marketer can organize the sales force by geography, product, or market. Large industrial enterprises that market diverse product lines may use all three.

Geographical Organization   The most common form of sales organization in business marketing is geographical. Each salesperson sells all the firm's products in a defined geographical area. By reducing travel distance and time between customers, this method usually minimizes costs. Likewise, sales personnel know exactly which customers and prospects fall within their area of responsibility.

The major disadvantage of the geographical sales organization is that each salesperson must be able to perform every selling task for all of the firm's products and for all customers in the territory. If the products have diverse applications, this can be difficult. A second disadvantage is that the salesperson has substantial leeway in choosing which products and customers to emphasize. Sales personnel may emphasize products and end-use applications they know best. Of course, this problem can be remedied through training and capable first-line supervision. Because the salesperson is crucial in implementing the firm's segmentation strategy, careful coordination and control are required to align personal selling effort with marketing objectives.

---

[6]A comprehensive treatment of all aspects of sales management is beyond the scope of this volume. For more extensive discussion, see Mark W. Johnston and Greg W. Marshall, *Sales Force Management* (New York: McGraw-Hill/Irwin, 2008).

Product Organization   In a product-oriented sales organization, salespersons specialize in relatively narrow components of the total product line. This is especially appropriate when the product line is large, diverse, or technically complex and when a salesperson needs a high degree of application knowledge to meet customer needs. Furthermore, various products often elicit various patterns of buying behavior. The salesperson concentrating on a particular product becomes more adept at identifying and communicating with members of buying centers.

A prime benefit of this approach is that the sales force can develop a level of product knowledge that enhances the value of the firm's total offering to customers. The product-oriented sales organization may also help identify new market segments.

One drawback is the cost of developing and deploying a specialized sales force. A product must have the potential to generate a level of sales and profit that justifies individual selling attention. Thus, a "critical mass" of demand is required to offset the costs. In turn, several salespersons may be required to meet the diverse product requirements of a single customer. To reduce selling costs and improve productivity, some firms have launched programs to convert product specialists into general-line specialists who know all the firm's products and account strategies. Often, as customers learn to use technology, they outgrow the need for product specialists and prefer working with a single salesperson for all products.

Market-Centered Organization   The business marketer may prefer to organize personal selling effort by customer type. Owens-Corning recently switched from a geographical sales structure to one organized by customer type. Similarly, Hewlett-Packard successfully used this structure to strengthen its market position in retailing, financial services, and oil and gas exploration.[7] Sales executives at *Fortune* 500 companies that use sales teams believe they are better able to secure customers and improve business results by adopting a more customer-focused sales structure.[8]

By learning the specific requirements of a particular industry or customer type, the salesperson is better prepared to identify and respond to buying influentials. Also, key market segments become more accessible, thus providing the opportunity for differentiated personal selling strategies. The market segments must, of course, be sufficiently large to warrant specialized treatment.

Key Account Management[9]

Many business marketing firms find that a small proportion of customers (for example, 20 percent) often account for a major share (for example, 80 percent) of its business. These customers possess enormous purchasing power by virtue of their size, and they are searching for ways to leverage their suppliers' capabilities to enhance the value they deliver to their own customers (see Chapter 2). In turn, many of these large buying firms have centralized procurement and expect suppliers to provide coordinated and uniform service support to organizational units that are geographically dispersed on a national or global scale. In exchange for a long-term

---

[7]Thayer C. Taylor, "Hewlett-Packard," *Sales and Marketing Management* 145 (January 1993): p. 59.

[8]Vincent Alonzo, "Selling Changes," *Incentive* 170 (September 1996): p. 46.

[9]This section is based on Joseph P. Cannon and Narakesari Narayandas, "Relationship Marketing and Key Account Management," in Jagdish N. Sheth and Atul Parvatiyar, eds., *Handbook of Relationship Marketing* (Thousand Oaks, CA: Sage Publications, 2000), pp. 407–429.

volume commitment, these customers expect the business marketing firm to provide additional value-added services (for example, new-product-development assistance) and support (for example, just-in-time delivery) that may not be available to other customers.

Unique Value Propositions   **Customer prioritization** represents the degree to which firms prioritize customers by developing different value propositions for its top-tier versus bottom-tier customers. A recent study reveals that customer prioritization leads to higher average customer profitability and a higher return on sales by: (1) positively affecting relationships with top-tier customers without affecting relationships with bottom-tier customers and (2) reducing marketing and sales costs.[10]

Key Accounts versus Regular Accounts   Given the importance of these large customers, firms are rethinking how they manage their most important customers and how they organize internal operations to meet these customers' complex needs. To that end, many firms—Hewlett-Packard, Xerox, 3M, IBM, and Dow Chemical, for example—are establishing key account managers and creating customer teams composed of individuals from sales, marketing, finance, logistics, and other functional groups. Key account managers are typically responsible for several important customers and report to a senior executive. For some customers, the key account manager may work directly in the customer's facilities. For example, an IBM key account team occupies offices at Boeing and works solely on that account.

A **key account** represents a customer who:

1. Purchases a significant volume as a percentage of a seller's total sales;

2. Involves several organizational members in the purchasing process;

3. Buys for an organization with geographically dispersed units;

4. Expects a carefully coordinated response and specialized services such as logistical support, inventory management, price discounts, and customized applications.[11]

Rather than calling them "key accounts," some companies describe such customers as strategic accounts or national accounts.

A Different Type of Relationship   Table 14.1 compares and contrasts the traditional selling paradigm with the key account selling paradigm. Key account customers purchase in very large volume, and the focus of exchange extends beyond a core product as the seller augments the offering through value-added services and support. For example, acting on behalf of Cisco, FedEx coordinates the delivery of Cisco components from geographically dispersed facilities to ensure a seamless installation in a customer's organization. Whereas traditional sales management objectives

---

[10]Christian Homburg, Mathias Droll, and Dirk Totzek, "Customer Prioritization: Does It Pay Off and How Should It Be Implemented?" *Journal of Marketing* 72 (September 2008): pp. 110–128.

[11]Frank V. Cespedes, *Concurrent Marketing: Integrating Products, Sales, and Service* (Boston: Harvard Business School Press, 1995), p. 187.

TABLE 14.1 | TRADITIONAL SELLING VERSUS KEY ACCOUNT SELLING

	Traditional Selling Focus	Key Account Selling Focus
Sales Volume	Varies	Large volume of purchases by the customer, often across multiple business units of the seller
Nature of Product/ Service Offering	Core product/service	Core product/service plus customized applications and value-added services
Time Horizon	Short-term	Long-term
Benefits to Customer	Lower prices and higher quality	Lower total costs Broader set of strategic benefits
Information Sharing	Limited: Narrow focus on price and product features	Extensive: Broader focus as firms share strategic goals
Sales Force Objectives	Maximize revenue Satisfied customers	Become preferred supplier Lower customer firm's total costs Enhance learning in the relationship
Structure of Selling Center	Individual salesperson is primary link to customer organization	Many individuals from multiple functional areas on the selling side interact with counterparts in the customer organization
Structure of Buying Center	Purchasing manager and a few other individuals are involved in buying decision	Many individuals within the customer organization interact in making decisions and evaluating the relationship

SOURCE: Adapted with modifications from Joseph P. Cannon and Narakesari Narayandas, "Relationship Marketing and Key Account Management," in *Handbook of Relationship Marketing*, Jagdish N. Sheth and Atul Parvatiyar, eds. (Thousand Oaks, CA: Sage Publications, 2000), p. 409; and Frank V. Cespedes, *Concurrent Marketing: Integrating Products, Sales, and Service* (Boston: Harvard Business School Press, 1995), pp. 186–202.

typically emphasize maximizing revenue, key account relationships involve multiple goals. To illustrate, firms may enter into a closer, long-term relationship to lower costs to both partnering firms by reducing the seller's marketing and logistics costs and reducing the buyer's acquisition and production costs.

Coordinated Action   To effectively deliver more value to an important customer, the interpersonal connections between the buying and selling firms must extend beyond the salesperson–purchasing manager relationship. A key account relationship involves frequent interactions between a team of functional experts from both organizations. The key account manager assumes a lead role in coordinating selling center activities and facilitating these cross-firm communications among functional experts. Nurturing these interpersonal connections creates an atmosphere in which these specialized personnel can cooperatively identify new solutions that lower costs or advance performance. When uncertainty is high or important product adaptations are required, the interorganizational team should feature the active participation of key personnel from the customer organization who join with members of the selling organization to create the desired solution.[12]

---

[12]Ruth Maria Stock, "Interorganizational Teams as Boundary Spanners between Supplier and Customer Companies," *Journal of the Academy of Marketing Science* 34 (October 2006): pp. 588–599.

Selecting Key Accounts[13] If the business marketing firm can have close and important relationships with a rather small set of customers, each requiring a large investment, the choice of the key accounts is critical. Because key accounts possess buying power, demand special services, and are generally more costly to serve, the account selection process must examine the sales and profit potential as well as the long-term resource commitments the relationship demands.

Frank V. Cespedes recommends a three-phase approach in selecting key accounts. To be chosen, a potential customer must meet the screening requirements of all three phases.

> Phase 1: Centers on: (a) the profit potential of a customer, measured in terms of incremental sales potential, and (b) the degree to which a customer values the firm's support services and is willing to pay a premium price for them. *(For example, if the product is critical to a customer's operations, support services are more valuable.)*
>
> Phase 2: Identifies customer accounts from Phase 1 that have unique support requirements that provide profitable organizational learning opportunities. *(For example, the goal here is to invest in support capabilities that are valued by multiple accounts.)*
>
> Phase 3: Considers the degree to which the transactions with the potential customer complement the economics of the seller's business. *(For example, some customers purchase higher-margin products than others or provide a better match to the firm's manufacturing capabilities.)*

Says Cespedes, "When there are clear criteria for determining the profit potential, learning benefits, and cost drivers associated with customers, the firm knows when (and when not) to incur the substantial commitments required for effective key-account relationships."[14]

National Account Success

Research suggests that successful national account units enjoy senior management support; have well-defined objectives, assignments, and implementation procedures; and are staffed by experienced individuals who have a solid grasp of their entire company's resources and capabilities and how to use them to create customer solutions.[15] Do key account management programs enhance profitability? Yes. A recent comprehensive study of U.S. and German firms demonstrates the clear performance advantages that firms with active key account management programs enjoy over peers without them. In turn, the research also indicates that successful programs provide the key account manager with ready access to resources and support across functional areas.[16] Successful national account programs also adopt a strong relationship

---

[13]This section is based on Cespedes, *Concurrent Marketing*, pp. 193–198; see also George S. Yip and Audrey J. M. Bink, "Managing Global Accounts," *Harvard Business Review* 84 (September 2007): pp. 103–111.

[14]Ibid., p. 197.

[15]John P. Workman Jr., Christian Homburg, and Ove Jensen, "Intraorganizational Determinants of Key Account Management Effectiveness," *Journal of the Academy of Marketing Science* 31 (Winter 2003): pp. 3–21; see also Homburg, Droll, and Totzek, "Customer Prioritization."

[16]Christian Homburg, John P. Workman Jr., and Ove Jensen, "A Configurational Perspective of Key Account Management," *Journal of Marketing* 66 (April 2002): pp. 38–60; see also Roberta J. Schultz and Kenneth R. Evans, "Strategic Collaborative Communication by Key Account Representatives," *Journal of Personal Selling and Sales Management* 22 (Winter 2002): pp. 23–32.

B2B TOP PERFORMERS

Using Customized Strategies to Outmaneuver Rivals

Competitive cognition refers to the framework a manager uses to organize and retain knowledge about competitors and to direct information acquisition and usage.[1] Research suggests that competitive cognition influences individual performance. For example, in an intriguing study in the sports literature, research demonstrates that elite athletes (for example, members of the U.S. Olympic wrestling team) use extensive competitive plans that involve customized strategies and tactics to beat individual competitors, whereas poorer performers do not develop customized plans but rely, instead, on a more generic approach to competition.[2]

Building on this line of inquiry, a study explored the role of competitive cognition in the competitive crafting that salespeople do.[3] **Competitive crafting** involves salespeople's use of information and knowledge about competitors to create a business proposition for the customer. Examples of crafting include speeding up the selling cycle to counter a slow rival or broadening the scope of the product and service offered to outmaneuver a niche rival. The results of the study indicate that each additional act of crafting increases the likelihood of the salesperson winning the customer's business by fivefold!

[1]Beth A. Walker, Dimitri Kapelianis, and Michael D. Hutt, "Competitive Cognition," *MIT Sloan Management Review* 46 (Summer 2005): pp. 10–12.

[2]Daniel Gould, Robert C. Eklund, and Susan A. Jackson, "1988 U.S. Olympic Wrestling Excellence: I. Mental Preparation, PreCompetitive Cognition, and Affect," *The Sports Psychologist* 6 (December 1992): pp. 358–382.

[3]Dimitri Kapelianis, Beth A. Walker, Michael D. Hutt, and Ajith Kumar, "Those Winning Ways: The Role of Competitive Crafting in Complex Sales," Working Paper (Tempe, AZ: Arizona State University, 2008).

marketing perspective and consistently demonstrate their ability to meet the customer's immediate and future needs.

To this point, we have examined the central role of personal selling in business marketing strategy and alternative ways to align the sales force to customer segments. Attention now turns to key milestones in managing an engagement with a particular customer.

Isolating the Account Management Process[17]

To explore the work that account managers perform, our focus is on complex sales situations in business markets, which are characterized by large dollar values, protracted sales cycles, customized solutions, and the involvement of many organizational members on both the buying and selling sides. Frequently, in these sales situations an account manager is assigned to a particular set of customers and then assembles an ad hoc team as customer requirements or opportunities dictate. For example, large information-technology firms, such as IBM, reserve key account

[17]This section draws on Michelle D. Steward, Beth A. Walker, Michael D. Hutt, and Ajith Kumar, "The Coordination Strategies of High-Performing Salespeople: Internal Working Relationships that Drive Success," *Journal of the Academy of Marketing Science* 38 (October 2010): pp. 550–566 and Michael D. Hutt and Beth A. Walker, "A Network Perspective of Account Manager Performance," *Journal of Business & Industrial Marketing* 21 (7, 2006): pp. 466–473.

teams for a carefully chosen set of customers but rely on an assigned account manager to cover the majority of large-enterprise customers.

Assuming a central role in a particular engagement is the account manager who diagnoses what the customer needs, identifies the appropriate set of internal experts, recruits them onto the ad hoc team, and then orchestrates the selling center's activities to deliver a solution that matches customer needs. Let's examine how high-performing account managers undertake these activities and highlight how they differ from their peers. Recent studies that explored the characteristics of high-performing account managers at two *Fortune* 500 firms provide some valuable insights.

Account Management Success

For complex sales situations, account manager performance is contingent on securing access to the right people and the right information to solve novel problems for the customer. Figure 14.1 highlights the key milestones in a customer engagement and emphasizes the crucial role of relationship-building activities in the firm and in the

FIGURE 14.1 | THE CYCLE OF ACCOUNT MANAGEMENT SUCCESS

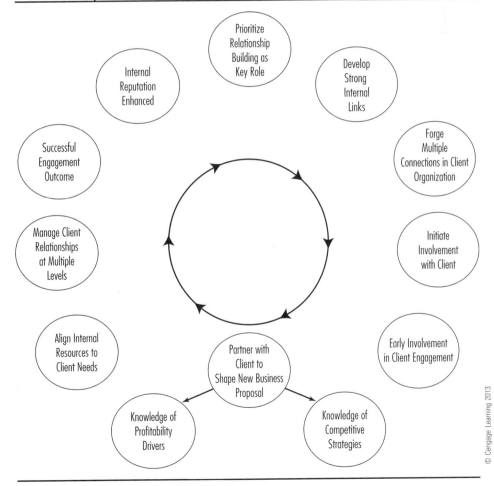

© Cengage Learning 2013

client organization. High performers excel at relationship building. Capitalizing on these relationship connections, the account manager is better equipped to design a business proposal that aligns the firm's capabilities to customer goals. Moreover, successful outcomes enhance the account manager's internal reputation, providing social capital the manager can invest in future customer engagements.

Building Internal Relationships　High-performing account managers form more cross-functional and cross-unit ties within the organization than their colleagues. A diverse social network provides a manager with access to unique skills and knowledge. Account managers with ties to a number of distinct knowledge pools in the organization can draw on a large array of skills, knowledge, and resources—thereby enhancing their customer responsiveness. Research suggests that top-performing salespeople are able to "navigate their own organization to discover personnel, resources, or capabilities that may benefit them in specific sales situations."[18]

Aligning Resources to Client Needs　In marshalling support and coordinating internal resources for a customer engagement, what sets high-performing salespeople apart? First, compared to lower performers, research indicates that high performers are more likely to consider relational as well as technical skills when identifying the set of internal experts who provide the best match for a particular customer engagement. This finding suggests that higher performers are more likely to recognize nuances of the customer relationship and identify team members who possess the interpersonal skills and technical orientation that best match the culture of the customer organization and the characteristics (for example, personality) of key decision makers.

Second, higher performers are more successful than their colleagues in recruiting desired ad hoc team members. In addition to understanding "who knows what," success may hinge on the salesperson's ability to persuade the targeted internal experts to join and actively participate on the team. This finding highlights the vital importance of the internal relationship-building skills of successful salespeople. Not only do high performers have ready access to the experts who may be needed to capitalize on a customer opportunity, they are also more successful than their colleagues in attracting these experts to the ad hoc selling team.

Forging Relationships within the Customer Organization　Being centrally involved in a customer organization's buying system improves an account manager's ability to understand the customer's requirements and business goals. Compared with their peers, high performers possess more cross-functional ties and a larger network of contacts within the customer organization. Because complex sales situations involve a buying center that includes participants from multiple levels of the organizational hierarchy and diverse units, an account manager's communication network must go beyond the focal purchasing unit.

Managing the Customer Engagement Process　By developing a network of relationships both within the firm and within the customer organization, an account manager is ideally equipped to manage the customer engagement process. Through

---

[18]Christopher R. Plouffe and Donald W. Barclay, "Salesperson Navigation: The Intraorganizational Dimension of the Sales Role," *Industrial Marketing Management* 36 (May 2007): p. 529.

these connections account managers receive vital information about emerging customer opportunities, customer requirements and solutions, and competitive challenges (see Figure 14.1).

Compared with low performers, high-performing account managers are more proactive in initiating involvement with the customer and tend to be involved in client engagements earlier in the purchasing process than their peers. Capitalizing on this early involvement, high performers are also more inclined to take an active role in shaping the client's request for proposals (RFP). Compared to peers, they are better able to choreograph the activities of the client management process by determining the most appropriate time and sequence to deploy key members of the ad hoc team during the sales cycle.

Aligning and Crafting   A successful client engagement hinges on both customer knowledge and competitive intelligence. High performers know more about client goals and the drivers of client profitability than low performers. When creating a customer solution, a salesperson must "act as a broker and assemble an ad hoc team of experts, coordinating the efforts of people who may not have met one another before."[19] Drawing on this knowledge allows them to align the capabilities of the firm to the goals of the customer. High-performing account managers develop sound competitive intelligence and use this knowledge to outmaneuver their rivals in a particular client engagement.

Enhanced Internal Reputation   By building a strong network of relationships within both the firm and the customer organization, high-performing account managers—compared with their peers—are better able to diagnose customer requirements, mobilize internal experts, and choreograph the activities that are required to outmaneuver rivals and create the desired customer solution. Successful outcomes enhance the reputation of an account manager in the organization, thereby strengthening internal working relationships and assuring ready access to the right people and right information for future engagements.

Best Practices   The coordination of expertise is fundamental to the salesperson's role in the business market, particularly for high-opportunity and complex customer engagements. **Expertise coordination** is the process that a salesperson follows in diagnosing customer requirements and subsequently identifying, assembling, and managing an ad hoc team of internal experts who possess the knowledge and skills to deliver a superior customer solution.

The best practices of high-performing salespeople can provide a template for improving the client management process for complex sales situations. For example, depth interviews with high performers indicate that they make a finer-grained assessment of customer requirements that includes customer-related dimensions such as the culture of the organization, the preferences and personalities of key decision makers with whom team members will interact, as well as key milestones in the buyer–seller relationship history. Such points could be accentuated in sales training and captured where possible in customer relationship management (CRM) systems.

High performers also attribute their success to carefully choreographing the activities of key members of the team across the sales cycle. For example, some

---

[19]Tuba Ustuner and David Godes, "Better Sales Networks," *Harvard Business Review* 84 (July–August 2006): p. 108.

specialists are best deployed early in the process when contract negotiations are underway. Others may be of use behind the scenes and are deployed to the customer organization as trouble shooters only if things go awry; still others may be best included from start to finish. Such best practices can be used to improve sales protocols and to refine sales training programs.

Sales Administration

Successful sales force administration involves recruiting and selecting salespersons, then training, motivating, supervising, evaluating, and controlling them. The industrial firm should foster an organizational climate that encourages the development of a successful sales force.

Recruitment and Selection of Salespersons

The recruiting process presents numerous trade-offs for the business marketer. Should the company seek experienced salespersons, or should it hire and train inexperienced individuals? The answer depends on the specific situation; it varies with the size of the firm, the nature of the selling task, the firm's training capability, and its market experience. Smaller firms often reduce training costs by hiring experienced and more expensive salespersons. In contrast, large organizations with a more complete training function can hire less experienced personnel and support them with a carefully developed training program.

A second trade-off is quantity versus quality. Often, sales managers screen as many recruits as possible when selecting new salespersons. However, this approach can overload the selection process, hampering the firm's ability to identify quality candidates. Recruiting, like selling, is an exchange process between two parties. Sales managers are realizing that, for prospective salespersons, they need to demonstrate the personal development and career opportunities that a career with the firm offers. A poorly organized recruiting effort that lacks closure leaves candidates with a negative impression. A well-organized recruiting effort ensures that qualified candidates get the proper level of attention in the screening process. Thus, procedures must be established to ensure that inappropriate candidates are screened out early so that the pool of candidates is reduced to a manageable size.[20]

Responsibility for recruiting and selecting salespersons may lie with the first-line supervisor (who often receives assistance from an immediate superior), with the human resources department, or with other executives at the headquarters level. The last-named group tends to be more involved when the sales force is viewed as the training ground for marketing or general managers.

Training

To prepare new salespersons adequately, the training program must be carefully designed. Periodic training is required to sharpen the skills of experienced salespersons, especially when the firm's environment is changing rapidly. Changes in business marketing strategy (for example, new products, new market segments) require corresponding changes in personal selling styles.

---

[20]Wesley J. Johnston and Martha C. Cooper, "Industrial Sales Force Selection: Current Knowledge and Needed Research," *Journal of Personal Selling and Sales Management* 1 (Spring/Summer 1981): pp. 49–53.

The salesperson needs a wealth of knowledge about the company, the product line, customer segments, competition, organizational buying behavior, and effective communication skills.[21] All of these elements must be part of sales training programs. Compared with their counterparts, top-performing sales organizations train new salespeople in a broader range of areas: market knowledge, communication skills, listening techniques, complaint-handling skills, and industry knowledge.[22]

With the expansion in global marketing, firms need to include a sales training module that examines how to approach and respond to customers of different cultures. Such training would focus on the role of intercultural communication in developing global buyer–seller relationships.[23] Effective training builds the salesperson's confidence and motivation, thereby increasing the probability of success. In turn, training helps the business marketer by keeping personal selling in line with marketing program objectives. A successful training effort can reduce the costs of recruiting; many business-to-business firms have found that salesperson turnover declines as training improves. Clearly, a salesperson who is inadequately prepared to meet the demands of selling can quickly become discouraged, frustrated, and envious of friends who chose other career options. Effective training and capable first-line supervision can alleviate much of this anxiety, which is especially prevalent in the early stages of many careers.

Supervision and Motivation

The sales force must be directed in a way that is consistent with the company's policies and marketing objectives. Critical supervisory tasks are continued training, counseling, assistance (for example, time management), and activities that help sales personnel plan and execute their work. Supervision also sets sales performance standards, fulfills company policy, and integrates the sales force with higher organizational levels.

Orville Walker, Gilbert Churchill, and Neil Ford define **motivation** as the amount of effort the salesperson "desires to expend on each of the activities or tasks associated with his (her) job, such as calling on potential new accounts, planning sales presentations, and filling out reports."[24] The model presented in Figure 14.2 hypothesizes that a salesperson's job performance is a function of three factors: (1) level of motivation, (2) aptitude or ability, and (3) perceptions about how to perform his or her role. Each factor is influenced by personal variables (for example, personality), organizational variables (for example, training programs), and environmental variables (for example, economic conditions). Sales managers can influence some of the personal and organizational variables through selection, training, and supervision.

---

[21]William L. Cron, Greg W. Marshall, Jagdip Singh, Rosann Spiro, and Harish Sujan, "Salesperson Selection, Training, and Development Trends: Implications, and Research Opportunities," *Journal of Personal Selling and Sales Management* 25 (Spring 2005): pp. 123–136.

[22]Adel I. El-Ansary, "Selling and Sales Management in Action: Sales Force Effectiveness Research Reveals New Insights and Reward-Penalty Patterns in Sales Force Training," *Journal of Personal Selling and Sales Management* 13 (Spring 1993): pp. 83–90.

[23]Victoria D. Bush and Thomas Ingram, "Adapting to Diverse Customers: A Training Matrix for International Marketers," *Industrial Marketing Management* 25 (September 1996): pp. 373–383.

[24]Orville C. Walker Jr., Gilbert A. Churchill Jr., and Neil M. Ford, "Motivation and Performance in Industrial Selling: Present Knowledge and Needed Research," *Journal of Marketing Research* 14 (May 1977): pp. 156–168; see also Steven P. Brown, William L. Cron, and Thomas W. Leigh, "Do Feelings of Success Mediate Sales Performance—Work Attitude Relationships?" *Journal of the Academy of Marketing Science* 21 (Spring 1993): pp. 91–100.

FIGURE 14.2 | DETERMINANTS OF A SALESPERSON'S PERFORMANCE

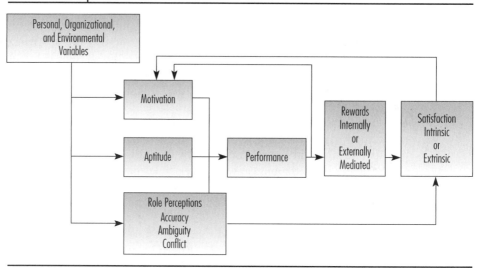

SOURCE: Orville C. Walker Jr., Gilbert A. Churchill Jr., and Neil M. Ford, "Motivation and Performance in Industrial Selling: Present Knowledge and Needed Research," *Journal of Marketing Research* 14 (May 1977): p. 158. Reprinted by permission of the American Marketing Association.

Motivation is related strongly to: (1) the individual's perceptions of the types and amounts of rewards from various degrees of job performance and (2) the value the salesperson places on these rewards. For a given level of performance, two types of rewards might be offered:

1. **Internally mediated rewards:** The salesperson attains rewards on a personal basis, such as feelings of accomplishment or self-worth.

2. **Externally mediated rewards:** Rewards are controlled and offered by managers or customers, such as financial incentives, pay, or recognition.

The rewards strongly influence salesperson satisfaction with the job and the work environment, which is also influenced by the individual's role perceptions. Job satisfaction declines when the salesperson's perception of the role is: (1) *inaccurate* in terms of the expectations of superiors, (2) characterized by *conflicting* demands among role partners (company and customer) that the salesperson cannot possibly resolve, or (3) surrounded by *uncertainty* because of a lack of information about the expectations and evaluation criteria of superiors and customers.

Business marketers often use formal incentive programs to achieve specified customer service, sales, and profit results. Typically, an incentive program offers rewards for achieving a well-defined goal during a specified time frame. The rewards must be well conceived, based on what salespeople value, tied to achieving desired behavior, and recognize both individual and team behavior.[25] Frequently, recognition is a key ingredient in sales incentive programs and may run the gamut from

---

[25]Katherine Morrall, "Motivating Sales Staff with Rewards," *Bank Marketing* 28 (July 1996): pp. 32–38.

Hewlett-Packard's quarterly award for a salesperson who was particularly astute in converting an objection into an order to the elaborate sales award presentations at IBM.

Incentive plans can also be linked directly to important marketing strategy initiatives. For example:

> When … FedEx wanted to encourage its salespeople to spend more time on three strategically important product lines, it gave salespeople goals for each of the three lines and provided them with weekly updates on their progress toward the goals. Salespeople earned certain bonuses and commissions if all three goals were achieved. The new incentive plan helped to ensure that the three key product lines got the majority of the sales force's attention.[26]

Organizational Climate and Job Satisfaction[27] Churchill, Ford, and Walker, who contributed the model in Figure 14.2, also provide empirical support for some propositions that flow from the model. In examining job satisfaction in a cross section of industrial salespersons, the authors found that role ambiguity and role conflict undermine job satisfaction. Salespersons are likely to be anxious and dissatisfied when they are uncertain about the expectations of role partners or feel that role partners (for example, customers, superiors) are making incompatible and impossible demands.

An effective approach for reducing role ambiguity among new salespeople is to provide training and socialization that offer sufficient information about role expectations and minimize potential confusion about performance requirements. Strategies that reduce role ambiguity are likely to boost sales performance and job satisfaction.[28] Moreover, a socialization program that gives newly hired salespersons a realistic picture of their job strengthens their commitment to the organization.[29]

Job Satisfaction Really Matters Salespersons tend to have a higher level of job satisfaction when: (1) they perceive that their first-line supervisor closely directs and monitors their activities, (2) management provides them with the assistance and support they need to solve unusual and nonroutine problems, and (3) they feel they have an active part in determining company policies and standards that affect them. Job satisfaction also appears to be related more to the substance of the contact between sales managers and salespersons than to its frequency. Also, satisfied salespersons appear to be able to accept direction from a number of departments in the organization without a significant negative effect on job satisfaction—unity of command does not appear to be a prerequisite for high morale.

---

[26]Zoltners, Sinha, and Lorimer, *Building a Winning Sales Force*, p. 388.

[27]This section is based on Gilbert A. Churchill Jr., Neil M. Ford, and Orville C. Walker Jr., "Organizational Climate and Job Satisfaction in the Salesforce," *Journal of Marketing Research* 13 (November 1976): pp. 323–332. For related discussions, see R. Kenneth Teas and James C. McElroy, "Causal Attributions and Expectancy Estimates: A Framework for Understanding the Dynamics of Salesforce Motivation," *Journal of Marketing* 50 (January 1986): pp. 75–86; William L. Cron, Alan J. Dubinsky, and Ronald E. Michaels, "The Influence of Career Stages on Components of Salesperson Motivation," *Journal of Marketing* 52 (January 1988): pp. 78–92; and Jeffrey K. Sager, Charles M. Futrell, and Rajan Varadarajan, "Exploring Salesperson Turnover: A Causal Model," *Journal of Business Research* 18 (June 1989): pp. 303–326.

[28]Steven P. Brown and Robert A. Peterson, "Antecedents and Consequences of Salesperson Job Satisfaction: Meta-Analysis and Assessment of Causal Effects," *Journal of Marketing Research* 30 (February 1993): pp. 63–77.

[29]Mark W. Johnston, A. Parasuraman, Charles M. Futrell, and William C. Black, "A Longitudinal Assessment of the Impact of Selected Organizational Influences on Salespeople's Organizational Commitment during Early Employment," *Journal of Marketing Research* 27 (August 1990): pp. 333–343.

Direct Link to Customer Satisfaction A recent study by Christian Homburg and Ruth M. Stock demonstrates a positive relationship between salespeople's job satisfaction and customer satisfaction.[30] Why? First, when they are exposed to a salesperson's positive emotions, customers experience a corresponding change in their own affective state. This phenomenon, rooted in the field of social psychology, is referred to as emotional contagion and has a positive influence on customer satisfaction. Second, the higher the salesperson's job satisfaction, the higher the quality of customer interaction, reflected by the salesperson's openness, flexibility, and customer orientation. The relationship between job satisfaction and customer satisfaction is particularly strong when customer interactions are frequent, customers assume a central role in the value-creation process, or innovative products or services are involved.

Turnover Performance and individual differences in motivation, self-esteem, and verbal intelligence may also affect job satisfaction. Richard Bagozzi notes:

> Salespeople tend to be more satisfied as they perform better, but the relationship is particularly sensitive to the level of motivation and positive self-image of the person. Although management may have no direct control over the performance achieved by salespeople, they can influence the level of motivation and self-esteem through effective incentive and sensitive supervisor-employee programs and thereby indirectly affect both performance and job satisfaction.[31]

Research suggests that sales manager leadership directly and indirectly influences salespersons' job satisfaction, which in turn affects sales force turnover.[32] In addition, another study indicates that salespeople who are managed by "high-performing" sales managers exhibit less role stress and are more satisfied than their colleagues.[33] Although some factors that influence job satisfaction and performance are beyond the control of sales managers, this line of research points up the importance of responsive training, supportive supervision, and clearly defined company policies that are congruent with the needs of the sales force.

Evaluation and Control

An ongoing sales management responsibility is to monitor and control the industrial sales force at all levels—national, regional, and district—in order to determine whether objectives are being attained and to identify problems, recommend

---

[30]Christian Homburg and Ruth M. Stock, "The Link between Salespeople's Job Satisfaction and Customer Satisfaction in a Business-to-Business Context: A Dyadic Analysis," *Journal of the Academy of Marketing Science* 32 (Spring 2004): pp. 144–158.

[31]Richard P. Bagozzi, "Performance and Satisfaction in an Industrial Sales Force: A Causal Modeling Approach," in *Sales Management: New Developments from Behavioral and Decision Model Research*, Richard P. Bagozzi, ed. (Cambridge, MA: Marketing Science Institute, 1979), pp. 70–91; see also Bagozzi, "Performance and Satisfaction in an Industrial Sales Force: An Examination of Their Antecedents and Simultaneity," *Journal of Marketing* 44 (Spring 1980): pp. 65–77.

[32]Eli Jones, "Leader Behavior, Work Attitudes, and Turnover of Salespeople: An Integrative Study," *Journal of Personal Selling and Sales Management* 16 (Spring 1996): pp. 13–23.

[33]Frederick A. Russ, Kevin M. McNeilly, and James M. Comer, "Leadership, Decision-Making, and Performance of Sales Managers," *Journal of Personal Selling and Sales Management* 16 (Summer 1996): pp. 1–15.

corrective action, and keep the sales organization in tune with changing competitive and market conditions.

Performance Measures[34]   Sales managers use both behavior-based and outcome measures of salesperson performance. When a sales force control system is more **behavior based**, the sales manager monitors and directs the activities of salespeople, uses subjective measures to evaluate performance, and emphasizes a compensation system with a large fixed component. Behavior-based selling measures include the salesperson's knowledge of product applications and the company's technology, as well as the salesperson's clarity of presentations to customers. Behavior-based control systems are a good match when salespeople lack experience, companies need to control how salespeople present their products and services, and when salespeople are asked to perform a number of non-sales activities (for example, assisting with new-product development).

By contrast, an **outcome-based** sales force control system involves less direct field supervision of salesperson activities and uses objective measures to evaluate performance and a compensation system with a large incentive component. Sales force outcome measures include sales results, market-share gains, new-product sales, and profit contributions. Outcome-based control fits when the skills and efforts of the sales force are the major determinants of sales results. "When sales reps make that big of a difference to the bottom line, it is worth it to give them autonomy and to pay them handsomely to do what they do," say Erin Anderson and Vincent Onyemah.[35]

Setting Performance Standards   The standards for evaluating salespersons offer ways to compare the performance of various salespersons or sales units (for example, districts), as well as for gauging the overall productivity of the sales organization. Managerial experience and judgment are important in developing appropriate standards. Importantly, the standards must relate to overall marketing objectives. They must also take into account differences in sales territories, which can vary markedly in number and aggressiveness of competitors, level of market potential, and workload.

Evidence suggests that a strict reliance on outcome measures and incentive compensation plans may not produce the desired sales or marketing performance results: "The alleged automatic supervisory power of incentive pay plans has lulled some sales executives into thinking that important sales outcomes could be reasonably accomplished without intense management reinforcement in noncompensation areas."[36] Often more effective is a more balanced approach that assigns a more prominent role to field sales managers and emphasizes behavior-based measures.[37]

Behavior-based measures also fit relationship selling—an important strategy in the business market. Relationship selling requires salespeople who have a team

---

[34]This section is based on Erin Anderson and Vincent Onyemah, "How Right Should the Customer Be?" *Harvard Business Review* 84 (July–August 2006): pp. 59–67.

[35]Ibid., p. 64.

[36]David W. Cravens, Thomas N. Ingram, Raymond W. LaForge, and Clifford E. Young, "Behavior-Based and Outcome-Based Salesforce Control Systems," *Journal of Marketing* 57 (October 1993): p. 56.

[37]Richard L. Oliver, "Behavior- and Outcome-Based Sales Control Systems: Evidence and Consequences of Price-Form and Hybrid Governance," *Journal of Personal Selling and Sales Management* 15 (Fall 1995): pp. 1–15.

orientation and can focus on activities such as sales planning and sales support, as well as on goals such as customer satisfaction.

Deployment Analysis: A Strategic Approach

To this point, our discussion has been concerned with: (1) recruiting and selection, (2) training, (3) motivating and supervising, and (4) evaluating and controlling. Poor decisions in one area can create a backlash in other areas. One critical sales management task remains: deploying the sales force. The objective is to form the most profitable sales territories, deploy salespersons to serve potential customers in those territories, and effectively allocate sales force time among those customers.

The size of the sales force establishes the level of selling effort that the business marketer can use. The selling effort is then organized by designating sales districts and sales territories. Allocation decisions determine how the selling effort is to be assigned to customers, prospects, and products. All these are illustrated in Table 14.2.

Proper deployment requires a multistage approach to find the most effective and efficient way to assign sales resources (for example, sales calls, number of salespersons, percentage of salesperson's time) across all of the **planning and control units (PCUs)** the firm serves (for example, prospects, customers, territories, districts, products).[38] Thus, effective deployment means understanding the factors that influence sales in a particular PCU, such as a territory.

Territory Sales Response

What influences the potential level of sales in a particular territory? Table 14.3 outlines eight classes of variables. This list shows the complexity of estimating sales response functions. Such estimates are needed, however, to make meaningful sales allocations.

Three territory traits deserve particular attention in sales response studies: potential, concentration, and dispersion.[39] **Potential** (as discussed in Chapter 5) is a measure of the total business opportunity for all sellers in a particular market. **Concentration** refers to how much potential lies with a few larger accounts in that territory. If potential is concentrated, the salesperson can cover with a few calls a large proportion of the potential. Finally, if the territory is geographically **dispersed**, sales are probably lower because of time wasted in travel. Past research often centered on **territory workload**—the number of accounts. However, Adrian Ryans and Charles Weinberg report that workload is of questionable value in estimating sales response: "From a managerial standpoint, the recurrent finding of an association between potential and sales results suggests that sales managers should stress territory potential when making sales force decisions."[40]

---

[38]David W. Cravens and Raymond W. LaForge, "Sales Force Deployment," in *Advances in Business Marketing*, vol. 1, Arch G. Woodside, ed. (Greenwich, CT: JAI Press, 1986), pp. 67–112; and LaForge and Cravens, "Steps in Selling Effort Deployment," *Industrial Marketing Management* 11 (July 1982): pp. 183–194.

[39]Adrian B. Ryans and Charles B. Weinberg, "Territory Sales Response," *Journal of Marketing Research* 16 (November 1979): pp. 453–465; see also Ryans and Weinberg, "Territory Sales Response Models: Stability over Time," *Journal of Marketing Research* 24 (May 1987): pp. 229–233.

[40]Ryans and Weinberg, "Territory Sales Response," p. 464.

TABLE 14.2 | DEPLOYMENT DECISIONS FACING SALES ORGANIZATIONS

Type of Decision	Specific Development Decisions
Set total level of selling effort	Determine sales force size
Organize selling effort	Design sales districts
	Design sales territories
Allocate selling effort	Allocate effort to trading areas
	Allocate sales calls to accounts
	Allocate sales calls to prospects
	Allocate sales call time to products
	Determine length of sales call

SOURCE: Reprinted from Industrial Marketing Management 11(3), Raymond LaForge and David W. Cravens, "Steps in Selling Effort Deployment," p. 184, copyright © 1982, with permission from Elsevier.

TABLE 14.3 | SELECTED DETERMINANTS OF TERRITORY SALES RESPONSE

1. Environmental factors (e.g., health of economy)

2. Competition (e.g., number of competitive salespersons)

3. Company marketing strategy and tactics

4. Sales force organization, policies, and procedures

5. Field sales manager characteristics

6. Salesperson characteristics

7. Territory characteristics (e.g., potential)

8. Individual customer factors

SOURCE: Adapted from Adrian B. Ryans and Charles B. Weinberg, "Territory Sales Response," *Journal of Marketing Research* 16 (November 1979): pp. 453–465.

Territory Alignment[41]

The territory alignment decision affects the workspace for each member of the sales force, defining the particular customers whom they will serve as well as their immediate supervisor. Leading business consultants report that many business-to-business firms have significant imbalances in the territory alignments of their sales personnel. When territories are out of balance, too much sales effort is devoted to low-potential customers and too little to high-potential customers. As a result, "companies often leave millions of dollars on the table."[42]

Sound territory alignment advances sales productivity and firm performance by:

- Promoting fair rewards (i.e., incentive pay) and boosting salesperson morale while balancing workload and opportunity (potential)

[41]Andris A. Zoltners and Prabhakant Sinha, "Sales Territory Design: Thirty Years of Modeling and Implementation," *Marketing Science* 24 (Summer 2005): pp. 313–331.

[42]Andris A. Zoltners and Sally E. Lorimer, "Sales Territory Alignment: An Overlooked Productivity Tool," *Journal of Personal Selling and Sales Management* 20 (Summer 2000): p. 139.

- Enhancing the coverage of customers and high-potential prospects

- Reducing travel time and costs (For example, after a sales territory realignment at industrial distributor W. W. Grainger, the company observed a 13.7 percent reduction in salesperson travel time that translated into a nearly $1 million reduction in travel expenses and an increase in selling time that contributed over $15 million in additional sales and $3 million in additional profits.)[43]

- Increasing company sales and profit

Developing the Customer Database

Alignment databases typically include a mix of internal and external information sources. Internal data sources may include customer purchasing activity, purchase frequency, cross-category buying, share-of-wallet, and marketing contacts by firm. External data sources center on the macrosegmentation characteristics of customers (Chapter 4) such as size of firm, industry, end market served as well as growth rate, credit rating, and office locations.

To develop initial workload measures, many companies first classify customers by segment and by historical sales volume. Next, the sales manager determines the frequency and desired length of each sales call for each account segment. By applying the frequency and sales call duration standards to each customer in the database, a customer account list can be converted into a workload database.

A number of territory alignment software programs, such as MAPS™ (ZS Associates), are available that combine a computerized map of territories with market, sales, and account workload data. A sales manager can use the software to evaluate the balance of workload and potential in the current alignment and experiment with possible changes to improve territory balance.

Sales Resource Opportunity Grid

Deployment analysis matches sales resources to market opportunities. Planning and control units such as sales territories or districts are part of an overall portfolio, with various units offering various levels of opportunity and requiring various levels of sales resources. A sales resource opportunity grid can be used to classify the business-to-business firm's portfolio of PCUs.[44] In Figure 14.3, each PCU is classified on the basis of PCU opportunity and sales organization strength.

PCU opportunity is the PCU's total potential for all sellers, whereas **sales organization strength** includes the firm's competitive advantages or distinctive competencies within the PCU. By positioning all PCUs on the grid, the sales manager can assign sales resources to those that have the greatest level of opportunity and capitalize on the particular strengths of the sales organization. For example, existing customers and prospects that are most appropriately positioned in the upper left cell of the grid represent the most attractive target, while those in the lower right cell represent the least attractive.

At various points in deployment decision making, the sales resource opportunity grid is important for screening the size of the sales force, the territory design, and the

---

[43]Zoltners and Sinha, "Sales Territory Design," p. 317.

[44]LaForge and Cravens, "Steps in Selling Effort Deployment," pp. 183–194.

FIGURE 14.3 | SALES RESOURCE OPPORTUNITY GRID

	High	**Low**
High	**Opportunity Analysis** PCU offers good opportunity because it has high potential and because sales organization has strong position **Sales Resource Assignment** High level of sales resources to take advantage of opportunity	**Opportunity Analysis** PCU may offer good opportunity if sales organization can strengthen its position **Sales Resource Assignment** Either direct a high level of sales resources to improve position and take advantage of opportunity or shift resources to other PCUs
Low	**Opportunity Analysis** PCU offers stable opportunity because sales organization has strong position **Sales Resource Assignment** Moderate level of sales resources to keep current position strength	**Opportunity Analysis** PCU offers little opportunity **Sales Resource Assignment** Minimal level of sales resources; selectively eliminate resource coverage; possible elimination of PCU

PCU Opportunity (vertical axis)

Sales Organization Strength (horizontal axis: High, Low)

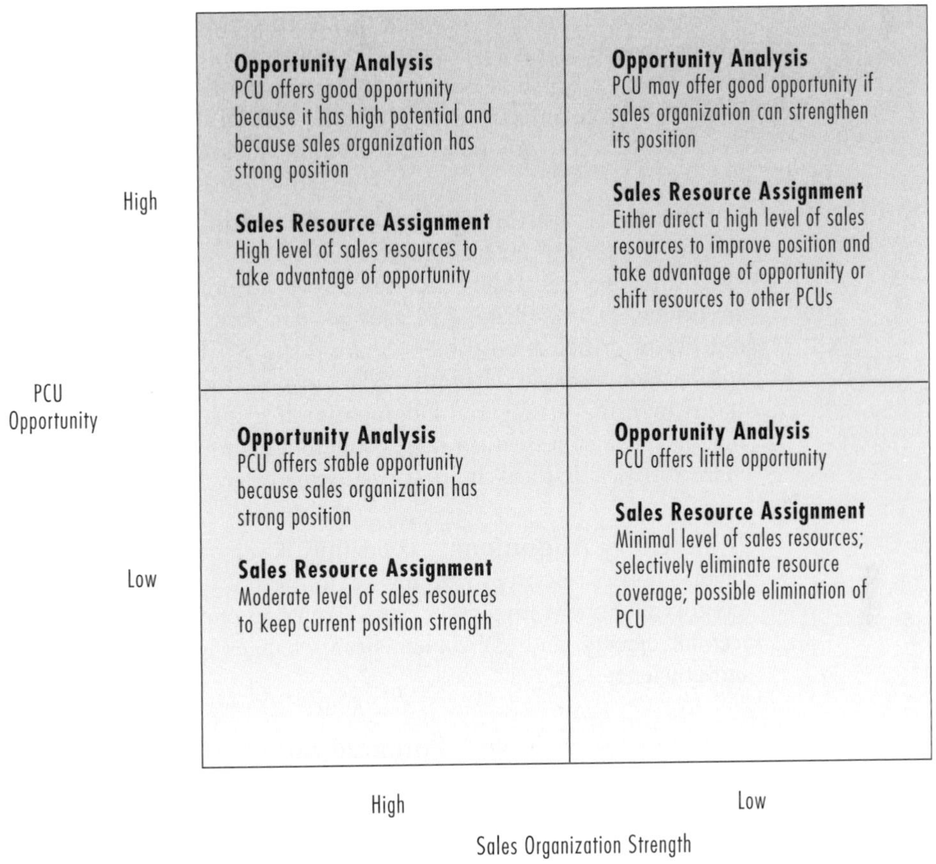

SOURCE: Reprinted by permission of the publisher from "Steps in Selling Effort Deployment," by Raymond LaForge and David W. Cravens, *Industrial Marketing Management* 11 (July 1982): p. 187. Copyright © 1982 by Elsevier Science Publishing Co., Inc.

allocation of sales calls to customer segments. This method can isolate deployment problems or deployment opportunities worthy of sales management attention and further data analysis.

Isolating High-Opportunity Customers

Many firms find that salespeople spend more time than they should with low-potential customer accounts. For example, a pharmaceutical firm found that the top 30 percent of physicians write 90 percent of the prescriptions for the classes of drugs that the company sells. These customers fall squarely in the top left quadrant of the sales resource opportunity grid. However, when the firm examined the actual sales calls being made by the sales force, they found that company salespersons were directing nearly half of their time to less profitable physician segments (for example, lower left and right quadrants).[45]

---

[45]Zoltners, Sinha, and Lorimer, *Building a Winning Sales Force*, p. 370.

GE's Sales Force Effectiveness Initiative[46]

Senior executives at GE surmised that, across the enterprise, the businesses that were driving organic growth were those that had been effective at utilizing data, processes, and tools to support sales force decision making. To that end, the firm established four sales force effectiveness priorities that illustrate best practices for any firm, large or small, that competes in the business market.

1. Customer Potential and Prioritization   Consistent with our discussion, defining customer and prospect potential represents a core requirement for sales force effectiveness. The GE framework for meeting this requirement includes three steps: (1) establishing a customer database, (2) calculating customer potential, and (3) prioritizing customers and prospects. The relationship between account profiles (for example, customer firm's size and industry) and potential can be estimated by using managerial judgment and/or quantitative methods (see Chapter 4). Several GE businesses use regression analysis to determine the particular customer characteristics that are the best predictors of account potential.

2. Territory Alignment   To identify coverage gaps across territories and to better match sales resources with market opportunity, the GE process for accomplishing territory alignment involves: (1) evaluating account quality (potential), (2) examining account density, and (3) implementing changes to enhance sales force effectiveness and efficiency.

3. Target Setting and Potentialization   The focus here is on setting sales targets based on best-performing salespeople in each market sector in which GE competes. "Territory targets should challenge all salespeople to improve their performance by moving toward the performance level achieved by the best performers in the company—those who are on the performance frontier."[47]

4. Variable Incentive Compensation   This priority involves designing compensation plans that motivate high levels of salesperson achievement by linking pay to performance, by using accelerators to reward peak performance, and by removing systemic caps on incentive compensation. The compensation plans at each of GE's businesses are also aligned with business goals and tied to profitability.

Implementation   To ensure that best practices for each of four sales force effectiveness initiatives become well engrained in the GE culture, company leaders developed a sales leader capability guide and a sales management training course. The guide identifies the core capabilities that a successful GE sales manager should possess, and the course describes the ways in which these capabilities can be applied to advance business performance. GE leaders have encouraged its 5800-plus sales managers to complete the course. The course has been widely praised by GE sales managers across businesses and geographic regions.

---

[46]This discussion is based on Zoltners, Sinha, and Lorimer, *Building a Winning Sales Force*, pp. 455–476.
[47]Ibid., p. 465.

Summary

Managing the sales force is a multifaceted task. First, the marketer must clearly define the role of personal selling in overall marketing strategy. Second, the sales organization must be appropriately structured—by geography, product, market, or some combination of all three. Regardless of the sales force organization, an increasing number of business-to-business firms are also establishing a key account sales force so that they can profitably serve large customers with complex purchasing requirements. Third, the ongoing process of sales force administration includes recruitment and selection, training, supervision and motivation, and evaluation and control.

To manage the complex web of influences that intersect in buyer–seller relationships, an account manager must initiate, develop, and sustain a network of relationships, within both the firm and the customer organization. Compared with their colleagues, high-performing account managers excel at building relationships and develop a richer base of customer and competitor knowledge that they use to create superior solutions for the customer. Compared with their peers, high-performing account managers are better able to diagnose customer requirements, mobilize internal experts, and choreograph the activities that are required to outmaneuver rivals and create the desired customer solution.

A particularly challenging sales management task is deploying sales effort across products, customer types, and territories. A properly aligned sales territory balances the workload and potential for salespersons. Good territory alignment enhances customer coverage, boosts salesperson morale by fostering an equitable reward system, reduces travel costs, and advances sales performance. A comprehensive customer database provides the foundation for territory alignment decisions. The sales resource opportunity grid is a useful framework for sales deployment decisions. Such tools can help the sales manager pinpoint high-potential customer accounts, deploy the selling effort, coordinate activities across multiple sales channels, and build customer loyalty. Leading-edge firms, such as GE, are giving heightened attention to sales force deployment analysis and to the fundamentals of sales management.

Discussion Questions

1. Describe how a sales manager might use the sales resource opportunity grid to evaluate the relative attractiveness of the firm's 400 existing customers in a particular territory. What information from company files might be useful for this assessment?

2. Explain how a successful sales training program can reduce the costs of recruiting.

3. Develop a list of skills and characteristics that distinguish between high performers and average performers in a sales organization. Next, describe the steps that a firm might take to improve the skill set of the average performers.

4. Research suggests that the greater the salesperson's satisfaction, the greater the customer satisfaction. Given the important relationship, what steps can a business-to-business firm take to nurture and sustain job satisfaction in the sales force?

5. To make effective and efficient sales force allocation decisions, the sales manager must analyze sales territories. Describe how the sales manager can profit by examining: (a) the potential, (b) the concentration, and (c) the dispersion of territories.

6. What steps can a sales manager take to enhance the job satisfaction of a salesperson?

7. Christine Lojacono started as a Xerox sales rep several years ago and is now a key account manager, directing activities for five key accounts. Compare the nature of the job and the nature of the selling task for a key account manager with those of a field sales representative.

8. Explain why poor territory alignment can lead to inequities in the sales force compensation plan.

9. When planning a sales call on a particular account in the business market, what information would you require about the buying center, the purchasing requirements, and the competition?

10. Some business marketers organize their sales force around products; others are market centered. What factors must be considered in selecting the most appropriate organizational arrangement for the sales force?

Internet Exercise

1. Oracle, Inc., designs, develops, markets, and supports a family of enterprise application software products for large and medium-sized organizations. For example, the company provides enterprise application software for customer relationship management (CRM). Go to http://www.oracle.com, click on "Products," then on "Customer Relationship Management" to locate case studies of customers that have purchased the Oracle CRM product. Identify one of these customers and describe the benefits that the CRM system provided.

EVALUATING BUSINESS MARKETING STRATEGY AND PERFORMANCE

Marketing Performance Measurement

Two business marketing managers facing identical market conditions and with equal resources to invest in marketing strategy could generate dramatically different results. Why? One manager might carefully monitor and control the performance of marketing strategy, whereas the other might not. The astute marketer evaluates the profitability of alternative segments and examines the effectiveness and efficiency of the marketing mix components to isolate problems and opportunities and alter the strategy as market or competitive conditions dictate. After reading this chapter, you will understand:

1. A system for converting a strategic vision into a concrete set of performance measures

2. The function and significance of marketing control in business marketing management

3. The components of the control process

4. The distinctive value of "dashboards" for evaluating marketing strategy performance

5. The importance of execution to the success of business marketing strategy

What keeps chief marketing officers (CMOs) up at night?[1]

> There's always too much to do, and you worry about addressing the right priorities; do you have the right dollar funding on the right bets?

> —*CMO, Software Company*

Why are robust measurement systems a critical priority for CMOs?[2]

> I'm not going to stand up in front of the CEO or our executive committee without being able to say, "We spent $10 million on marketing, and in return for that you got a $100 million worth of business opportunities, and $50 million that's closed."

> —*CMO, Consulting Company*

According to a study conducted by the Chief Marketing Officer (CMO) Council, chief marketing officers face intense pressure from bottom-line-focused CEOs and demanding corporate boards to improve the relevance, accountability, and performance of their organizations. Measuring marketing performance, quantifying and measuring marketing's worth, and improving marketing's efficiency and effectiveness continue to rank among the top challenges faced by marketers. The CMO Council study found that for today's marketers, proving marketing's value is the number-one challenge above other challenges, such as growing customer knowledge and extracting greater value and profitability from customers.[3] Thus, the critical importance of an effective control system that provides key measures of performance is highlighted for all business marketers, whether small or large.

Information generated by the marketing control system is essential for revising current marketing strategies, formulating new ones, and allocating funds. As Roland Rust and his colleagues note, "the effective dissemination of new methods of assessing marketing productivity to the business community will be a major step toward raising marketing's vitality in the firm and, more importantly, toward raising the performance of the firm itself."[4] While the effects of marketing investments play out over time, recent research provides evidence that brand equity, customer satisfaction, R&D, and product quality are all linked to firm value.[5] Thus, marketing control provides a critical foundation for diagnosing and advancing firm performance, and the assessment of marketing performance is as important as the formulation and execution of marketing strategy. Importantly, the requirements for an effective control system are strict—data must be gathered continuously on the appropriate performance measures. Thus, an effective marketing strategy is rooted in a carefully

---

[1]*The Evolved CMO*, a report produced by Forrester Research and Heidrick & Struggles, 2008, accessed at http://www.heidrick.com on July 1, 2011, p. 76.

[2]Ibid., p. 74.

[3]Laura Patterson, "Taking On the Metrics Challenge," *Journal of Targeting, Measurement and Analysis for Marketing* 15 (June 2007): p. 273. See also Pravin Nath and Vijay Mahajan, "Marketing in the C-Suite: A Study of Chief Marketing Officer Power in Firms' Top Management Teams," *Journal of Marketing* 75 (January 2010): pp. 60–77.

[4]Roland T. Rust, Tim Ambler, Gregory S. Carpenter, V. Kumar, and Rajendra K. Srivastava "Measuring Marketing Productivity: Current Knowledge and Future Directions," *Journal of Marketing* 68 (October, 2004): 76–90.

[5]Shuba Srinivasan and Dominique M. Hanssens, "Marketing and Firm Value: Metrics, Methods, Findings, and Future Directions," *Journal of Marketing Research* 46 (June 2009): pp. 293–312. See also Dominique M. Hanssens, Roland T. Rust, and Rajendra K. Srivastava, "Marketing Strategy and Wall Street: Nailing Down Marketing's Impact," *Journal of Marketing* 73 (November 2009): pp. 115–118.

designed and well-applied control system. Such a system must also monitor the quality of strategy implementation. Gary Hamel asserts that "implementation is often more difficult than it need be because only a handful of people have been involved in the creation of strategy and only a few key executives share a conviction about the way forward."[6]

This chapter presents the rudiments of a marketing control system, beginning with a framework that converts strategy goals into concrete performance measures. Next, it examines the components of the control process. Finally, it examines the implementation skills that ultimately shape successful business marketing strategies.

A Strategy Map: Portrait of an Integrated Plan[7]

A strategy map provides a visual representation of the cause-and-effect relationships among the components of a company's strategy. Recall that strategy maps were introduced in Chapter 5 to demonstrate how to align internal processes to support different marketing strategies. Figure 15.1 provides the strategy map for Boise Office Solutions—a $3.5 billion distributor of office and technology products, office furniture, and paper products that developed a distinctive customer relationship strategy, emphasizing customer solutions and personalized service. Leading firms widely use the strategy map concept, developed by Robert S. Kaplan and David P. Norton, because it isolates the interrelationships among four perspectives of a company that the authors refer to as a balanced scorecard[8] (see Chapter 5):

1. A **financial perspective** that describes the expected outcomes of the strategy, such as revenue growth, productivity improvements, or increased shareholder value

2. The **customer perspective** that defines how the firm proposes to deliver a competitively superior value proposition to targeted customers

3. The **internal perspective** that describes the business processes that have the greatest effect on the chosen strategy, such as customer relationship management (Chapter 3), innovation management (Chapter 8), or supply chain management (Chapter 11)

4. The **learning and growth perspective** that describes the human capital (personnel), information capital (information-technology systems), and organizational capital (climate) that must be aligned to the strategy to support value-creating internal processes

Using Boise Office Solutions as an illustrative case study, let's explore the six-step process that managers can use to build a tightly integrated strategy.[9]

---

[6]Gary Hamel, "Strategy as Revolution," *Harvard Business Review* 74 (July–August 1996): p. 82. See also Gary Hamel and Liisa Välikangas, "The Quest for Resilience," *Harvard Business Review* 81 (September 2003): pp. 52–63.

[7]This section is based on Robert S. Kaplan and David P. Norton, *Strategy Maps: Converting Intangible Assets into Tangible Outcomes* (Boston: Harvard Business School Publishing, 2004).

[8]Robert S. Kaplan and David P. Norton, "Using the Balanced Scorecard as a Strategic Management System," *Harvard Business Review* 74 (January–February 1996): pp. 75–85.

[9]Kaplan and Norton, *Strategy Maps*, pp. 355–360.

FIGURE 15.1 | CREATING BOISE OFFICE SOLUTIONS' STRATEGY MAP

Step 1: Define the Financial Objectives and Establish Growth and Productivity Goals

Increase Shareholder Value by:

- creating profitable customer revenue streams
- lowering operating costs

Step 2: Define the Customer Value Proposition for Target Segments

Boise created a new customer strategy defined by this strategic theme:
Create Distinctive Customer Value by Enhancing the Customer Relationship

- shift from commodity to customer solution focus
- provide personalized, customized service
- offer seamless access across sales channels

Step 3: Establish the Time Line for Results

Break down financial goals into targets for particular processes:

- operations management—reduce the cost of servicing customers
- customer management—increase the number of relationship customers
- innovation management—create new offerings

Step 4: Identify the Critical Strategic Themes and Internal Processes with the Greatest Impact on the Strategy

Critical internal process objectives:

- operational excellence—move more customers to e-channel to enhance customer convenience and lower cost
- customer management—deliver personalized, proactive service and improve customer experience
- innovation management—create new tools for customers to apply to control spending

Step 5: Identify the Human, Information, and Organizational Resources Required to Support the Strategy

Align organizational members with the strategy:

- training—a specialized course on the initiative
- information technology (a new CRM system)
- incentives tied to strategy goals

Step 6: Develop an Action Plan and Provide Required Funding for Each of the Separate Initiatives (Strategic Themes)

SOURCE: Adapted from Robert S. Kaplan and David P. Norton, *Strategy Maps: Converting Intangible Assets into Tangible Outcomes* (Boston: Harvard Business School Publishing, 2004), pp. 355–360.

Developing the Strategy: The Process

A strategy must provide a clear portrait that reveals how a firm will achieve its goals and deliver on its promises to customers, employees, and shareholders.[10] Boise Office Solutions sought a new strategy because the industry continued to consolidate and more and more of its customers viewed office products as a commodity. Without a fresh strategy, company executives believed that these challenging forces would continue to shrink profit margins and put increasing pressure on shareholder value. Likewise, in a service-driven, price-sensitive business, Boise managers were uncertain

---

[10]Robert S. Kaplan and David P. Norton, "Having Trouble with Your Strategy? Then Map It," *Harvard Business Review* 78 (September–October 2000): pp. 167–176.

which customers might contribute the most value over time and how to allocate marketing budgets among the diverse customers that it served—from small businesses to large corporate accounts.[11]

Step 1: Define the Financial Objectives and Establish Growth and Productivity Goals

Strategy maps start with financial objectives for creating shareholder value through two paths: long-term revenue and short-term productivity. The long-term goal often establishes a stretch target that creates a value gap—the difference between a desired future state and current reality. Kaplan and Norton note that the size of the value gap must be established with care: "Executives must balance the benefits from challenging the organization to achieve dramatic improvements in shareholder value with the realities of what can possibly be achieved."[12] So, specific targets for revenue growth and productivity improvements should be established along with a corresponding time line (for example, achieve revenue growth of 15 percent by year 1 and 30 percent by year 3).

Boise adopted a new customer strategy driven by this strategic theme: Create Distinctive Customer Value by Enhancing the Customer Relationship (see Figure 15.1). The financial objectives were to increase shareholder value by emphasizing market segmentation and measuring revenue, profit contribution, and cost-to-serve by individual customer segment.

Step 2: Define the Customer Value Proposition for Target Customer Segments

Achieving revenue growth goals requires explicit attention to generating revenue from new customers or increasing revenue from existing customers. Thus, the most important component of strategy is to develop and clarify the value proposition for customers in targeted segments. Recall that Chapter 5 presented four major value propositions and customer strategies: low total cost, product leadership, complete customer solutions, and system lock-in.

Boise adopted a customer solutions strategy that enhances value through one-to-one marketing, anticipates customers' needs to create customized service, and provides seamless access across sales channels (for example, sales force, Web, direct mail). A customer satisfaction survey assessed the core elements in the firm's new value proposition. The core objective, "to create distinctive value," was measured by:

- The number of customers retained in targeted segments;

- The number of new customers acquired;

- Estimates of the lifetime value of customers.

Step 3: Establish the Time Line for Results

To develop a coordinated plan, the high-level financial goals must be broken down into targets for particular functions or internal processes, like innovation management, so that organizational members unite behind the strategy and are comfortable with the overall target.

---

[11]Kaplan and Norton, *Strategy Maps*, pp. 355–360.

[12]Ibid., p. 353.

For Boise, operations management processes would reduce the costs of servicing customers, the customer management process would increase the number of relationship customers, and the innovation processes would create new offerings such as contract purchase plans. A time line for performance targets guided the efforts in each group.

Step 4: Identify the Critical Strategic Themes and Internal Processes with the Greatest Impact on the Strategy

This step identifies the key processes in delivering the customer value proposition and reaching the company's financial objectives.

Boise's internal process objectives emphasized three themes (see Figure 15.1):

- *Operational excellence*: Rationalize operations by moving more customers to an e-commerce channel to provide more convenient customer access and lower costs per customer contact.

- *Customer management*: Leverage customer service by personalizing the ordering process, making interactions easier for the customer, and meeting all the customer's needs in a single interaction.

- *Innovation management*: Redefine customer value expectations by creating new tools that customers can use to control spending on office supplies.

Once again, Boise developed measures—such as the percentage of customers in a target segment that used the e-commerce channel—for each of these themes. To illustrate, for operations, success at reaching cost reductions was measured by the percentage of business in targeted segments that came through e-channels; for innovation management, success was measured by the number of customers participating in new contract purchasing plans.

Step 5: Identify the Human, Information, and Organizational Resources Required to Support the Strategy

The learning and growth objectives assess how ready the organization is to support the internal processes that drive the strategy. This stage ensures that organizational members are aligned with the strategy and get with the training, information technology, and incentives to successfully implement it.

To introduce the strategy at Boise, every employee saw a video of the CEO describing the strategy, and more than 1000 employees attended a 6-hour course on the new customer management initiative. Moreover, the firm installed a comprehensive customer relationship management (CRM) system and provided 1500 customer service representatives and managers with 30 hours of training on it.[13] A video was likewise developed for customers to show them the benefits of the new strategy. Among the measures used were the percentage of employees trained for the new customer-centric strategy and the proportion of staff with incentives directly aligned to the strategy.

Step 6: Develop an Action Plan and Provide Required Funding for Each of the Separate Initiatives (Strategic Themes)

To reach financial targets and fulfill the strategic vision, several separate initiatives—involving different functions and processes in the company—must support the overall strategy in a

---

[13]Don Peppers and Martha Rogers, *Return on Customer: A Revolutionary Way to Measure and Strengthen Your Business* (New York: Currency/Doubleday, 2005), pp. 133–134.

coordinated fashion (see Figure 15.1). These initiatives create the performance results and form the foundation for successfully implementing the strategy. Rather than a series of stand-alone projects, these initiatives should be aligned to the overall strategy and managed as an integrated bundle of investments.

Strategy Results Boise's new strategy allowed the firm to reduce costs, boost growth, and offer even their most price-sensitive customers an integrated solution that delivered greater value than lower-priced competitors. In turn, customer retention improved dramatically, and sales from the firm's most valuable customers expanded. Don Peppers and Martha Rogers describe how the strategy achieves profit targets:

> The firm now has good customer profitability data, which is yielding steady benefits on a customer-by-customer basis. For instance, relying on this data, Boise chose to discontinue working with one of its largest customers, a hospital group that apparently cost Boise money with every sale. And a senior executive visited another customer's headquarters, shared data to show that the company was one of Boise's least profitable accounts, and won a price increase over two years.[14]

Maps: A Tool for Strategy Making

Because a firm's strategy is based on developing a differentiated customer value proposition, the business marketing manager assumes a lead role in both strategy development and implementation. Fundamental to this role is the challenging job of coordinating activities across functions to create and deliver a superior solution for customers.

Translating Objectives into Results The strategy map, coupled with the measures and targets from the balanced scorecard, provides a valuable framework for the strategist. First, the strategy map clearly describes the strategy, detailing objectives for the critical internal processes that create value and the organizational assets (for example, information technology, employee rewards) needed to support them. Second, the balanced scorecard translates objectives into specific measures and targets that guide critical components of the strategy. Third, to achieve financial or productivity goals, a set of well-integrated action plans must be designed that are carefully aligned to the overall strategy. Attention now turns to the central role of the control process in business marketing management.

Marketing Strategy: Allocating Resources

The purpose of any marketing strategy is to yield the best possible results. Resources are allocated to marketing in general and to individual strategy elements in particular to achieve prescribed objectives. Profit contribution, market share percentage, number of new customers, cost-to-serve customers, and level of expenses and sales

---

[14]Ibid., p. 135.

are typical performance criteria; but regardless of the criteria, four interrelated evaluations are required to design a marketing strategy:

1. How much should be spent on marketing in the planning period? (This is the budget for achieving marketing objectives.)

2. How are marketing dollars to be allocated? (For example, how much should be spent on advertising? On personal selling?)

3. Within each element of the marketing strategy, how should dollars be allocated to best achieve marketing objectives? (For example, which advertising media should be selected? How should sales personnel be deployed among customers and prospects?)

4. Which market segments, products, and geographic areas are most profitable? (Each market segment may require a different amount of effort because of competitive intensity or market potential.)

Guiding Strategy Formulation

Evaluation outcomes provide the foundation for integrating the market strategy formulation and the marketing control system. Results in the most recent operating period show how successful past marketing efforts were in meeting objectives. Performance below or above expectations then signals where funds should be reallocated. If the firm expected to reach 20 percent of the OEM market but reached only 12 percent, a change in strategy may be required. Performance information provided by the control system might demonstrate that sales personnel in the OEM market were reaching only 45 percent of potential buyers; additional funds could be allocated to expand either the sales force or the advertising budget. On the other hand, since performance was below targets, as pointed out by the control system, the problem may not be with the strategy, but with the way it is being implemented. Thus, additional funds may be allocated to marketing efforts, but it may be necessary to also carefully examine how effectively the sales force is executing the sales strategy or whether the advertising was implemented effectively—perhaps the message is wrong or the advertising media were not appropriate.

Managing Individual Customers for Profit[15]

As explored in Chapter 3, business marketers should also focus on revenues from individual customers and isolate the cost-to-serve them. For relationship customers, attention should be given to the share-of-wallet the firm is attracting. **Share-of-wallet** represents the portion of total purchases in a product and service category (for example, information technology) that a customer makes from the firm (for example, Hewlett-Packard).

For customers with a more transactional focus, the business marketer should:

- Develop a customer database that profiles the past purchasing patterns of customers;

- Determine the cost-to-serve each customer;

---

[15]Roland T. Rust, Katherine N. Lemon, and Das Narayandas, *Customer Equity Management* (Upper Saddle River, NJ: Prentice Hall, 2005), pp. 426–428.

- Set a revenue target and profit goal;

- Develop a customer contact plan that details the sales channel (for example, direct sales, telesales, Web-based contact) to be used;

- Monitor performance results and the relative effectiveness of different sales channels.

Marketing managers must weigh the interactions among the strategy elements and allocate resources to create effective and efficient strategies. To do so, a system for monitoring past performance is an absolute necessity. In effect, the control system enables management to keep abreast of all facets of performance.

The Marketing Control Process

Marketing control is a process management uses to generate information on marketing performance. Two major forms of control are: (1) control over efficient allocation of marketing effort and (2) comparison of planned and actual performance. In the first case, the business marketer may use past profitability data as a standard for evaluating future marketing expenditures. The second form of control alerts management to any differences between planned and actual performance and may also reveal reasons for performance discrepancies.

Control at Various Levels

The control process is universal in that it can be applied to any level of marketing analysis. For example, business marketers must frequently evaluate whether their general strategies are appropriate and effective. However, it is equally important to know whether the individual elements in the strategy are effectively integrated for a given market. Further, management must evaluate resource allocation within a particular element (for example, the effectiveness of direct selling versus that of industrial distributors). The control system should work in any of these situations. The four primary levels of marketing control are delineated in Table 15.1. In short, measures of marketing performance should be used both to assess the overall business success and to examine the health of particular products, markets, or distribution channels.[16]

Strategic Control

Strategic control is based on a comprehensive evaluation of whether the firm is headed in the right direction. Strategic control focuses on assessing whether the strategy is being implemented as planned and whether it produces the intended results.[17] Because the business marketing environment changes rapidly, existing product/market situations may lose their potential, and new-product/market match-ups provide important opportunities. Philip Kotler suggests that the firm periodically

---

[16]Bruce H. Clark, "A Summary of Thinking on Measuring the Value of Marketing," *Journal of Targeting, Measurement and Analysis for Marketing* 9 (June 2001): p. 361.

[17]Philip Kotler, "A Three-Part Plan for Upgrading Your Marketing Department for New Challenges," *Strategy and Leadership* 32 (May 2004): pp. 4–9.

TABLE 15.1 | **LEVELS OF MARKETING CONTROL**

Type of Control	Responsibility	Purpose of Control	Tools
Strategic control	Top management	To examine whether the company is pursuing its best opportunities with respect to markets, products, and channels	Marketing audit
Annual plan control	Top management, middle management	To examine whether the planned results are being achieved	Sales analysis; market-share analysis; expense-to-sales ratios; other ratios; attitude tracking
Efficiency and effectiveness control	Middle management	To examine how well resources have been utilized in each element of the marketing strategy to accomplish a specific goal	Expense ratios; advertising effectiveness measures; market potential; contribution margin analysis
Profitability control	Marketing controller	To examine where the company is making and losing money	Profitability by product territory, market segment, trade channel, order size

SOURCE: Adapted from Philip Kotler, *Marketing Management: The Millennium Edition* (Englewood Cliffs, NJ: Prentice-Hall, 2000), p. 698.

conduct a **marketing audit**—a comprehensive, periodic, and systematic evaluation of marketing operations that specifically analyzes the market environment and the firm's internal marketing activities.[18] An analysis of the environment assesses company image, customer characteristics, competitive activities, regulatory constraints, and economic trends. Evaluating this information may uncover threats the firm can counter and future opportunities it can exploit.

An internal evaluation of the marketing system scrutinizes marketing objectives, organization, and implementation. In this way, management may be able to spot where existing products could be adapted to new markets or new products could be developed for existing markets. The regular, systematic marketing audit is a valuable technique for evaluating the direction of marketing strategies.[19]

Marketing Performance Measurement (MPM) Strategies[20]   Many firms are now *strategically* developing performance measurement approaches to evaluate their marketing efforts: They have developed a marketing operations area that concentrates on maintaining a set of pragmatic *marketing performance* objectives and measures that become the marketing performance measurement (MPM) system. Very simply, **marketing performance measurement** is a business strategy that

---

[18]Philip Kotler, *Marketing Management: The Millennium Edition* (Englewood Cliffs, NJ: Prentice Hall, 2000), pp. 708–709; and Michael P. Mokwa, "The Strategic Marketing Audit: An Adoption/Utilization Perspective," *Journal of Business Strategy* 7 (Winter 1986): pp. 88–95.

[19]For example, see Philip Kotler, William T. Gregor, and William Rogers III, "SMR Classic Reprint: The Marketing Audit Comes of Age," *Sloan Management Review* 20 (Winter 1989): pp. 49–62; and Mokwa, "The Strategic Marketing Audit," pp. 88–95.

[20]This section is based on Michael Gerard, "The Best Technology Marketers Are Well Versed in MPM," *B to B* 93 (April 7, 2008): pp. 21–23.

provides performance feedback to the organization regarding the results of marketing efforts, and it is often viewed as a specific form of market information processing for the organization.[21]

For example, IBM maintains MPM from a central marketing operations function, providing its global marketing board with an integrated view across all business units. This process is part of marketing's strategic planning and resource management process, ensuring that the marketing measurement and specific metrics line up with the company's strategic and business objectives. IBM executives assert that MPM allows them to better align marketing priorities to business priorities and to connect marketing expenditures to business performance. Also, consistent use of common metrics under a common structure allows IBM to restructure programs, shift emphasis on particular offerings, and move investments to higher-growth opportunities—in other words, to drive actionable results.

In a different approach, Intel identifies four top-level broad strategies each year. Then it determines key business strategies, marketing metrics, and targets, and puts these on a "dashboard." These metrics are monitored quarterly or monthly and do not usually change radically throughout the year. Lastly, Intel drills down to the project level and identifies tasks and management by objectives (MBOs), which are measured by activity (completed or not) or results. Intel's dashboard increases visibility, reinforces accountability, and facilitates execution of key marketing strategies. Intel marketing managers believe that the dashboard has allowed them to sharpen marketing strategies and to more clearly understand how marketing programs can contribute to business success.

MPM Guidelines and Payoff   To effectively develop their MPM strategy, business marketing strategists should follow four important guidelines:

1. If the firm does not have an MPM process, it should begin slowly and should not aim for perfection.

2. The MPM should use relevant metrics that drive action.

3. All marketing groups and the sales department should be included in the MPM process.

4. The MPM process should become part of the weekly, monthly, quarterly, and annual reporting as well as a central component of the strategic planning process.

In a study conducted by Don O'Sullivan and Andrew V. Abela, MPM ability was shown to have a positive impact on firm performance in the high-tech sector.[22] The study found that firms with a strong MPM ability tend to outperform their competitors, as reported by senior marketers. The results also suggest that MPM ability has a positive influence on return on assets (ROA) and on stock returns. In addition, the research revealed that MPM ability has a significant, positive impact on CEO satisfaction with marketing. Development of MPM ability requires that marketers divert

---

[21]Bruce H. Clark, Andrew V. Abela, and Tim Ambler, "An Information Processing Model of Marketing Performance Measurement," *Journal of Marketing Theory and Practice* 14 (Summer 2006): p. 193.

[22]Don O'Sullivan and Andrew V. Abela, "Marketing Performance Measurement Ability and Firm Performance," *Journal of Marketing* 71 (April 2007): p. 79.

part of their budget and attention away from actual marketing programs and toward measurement efforts.

Annual Plan Control

In **annual plan control**, the objectives specified in the plan become the performance standards against which actual results are compared. Sales volume, profits, and market share are the typical performance standards for business marketers. **Sales analysis** is an attempt to determine why actual sales varied from planned sales. Expected sales may not be met because of price reductions, inadequate volume, or both. A sales analysis separates the effects of these variables so that corrective action can be taken.

Market share analysis assesses how the firm is doing relative to competition. A machine-tool manufacturer's 10 percent sales increase may, on the surface, appear favorable. However, if total machine-tool industry sales are up 25 percent, a market-share analysis would show that the firm has not fared well relative to competitors.

Finally, **expense-to-sales ratios** are analyses of the efficiency of marketing operations—whether the firm is overspending or underspending. Frequently, industry standards or past company ratios provide standards of comparison. Total marketing expenses and expenses of each strategic marketing element are evaluated in relation to sales. Recall the discussion in Chapter 13 on advertising expenditures, which provided a range of advertising expense-to-sales ratios for business-to-business firms. These figures provide management with a basis for evaluating the company's performance.

Marketing Control: The Marketing Performance Dashboard

Many business marketers have adopted the practice of creating "dashboards" of key metrics that provide information on the performance of the marketing function. Dashboards may be configured in many ways, but they typically present marketers with a highly graphical capsule view of key performance and operational metrics.[23] A **marketing dashboard** is "a relatively small collection of interconnected key performance metrics and underlying performance drivers that reflect both short and long-term interests," informing decision making throughout the organization.[24]

A marketing performance dashboard graphically depicts a company's marketing and operational performance through the use of simple gauges and scales. They represent graphical overlays on databases, providing managers with visual clues about what is happening in real time. Marketing dashboards are an appropriate visualization of critical underlying performance data.[25] Business marketers are increasingly using dashboards because of the high level of attention senior management is devoting to marketing return-on-investment. Importantly, dashboards help companies improve performance because dashboard metrics center on the key outcomes expected from

---

[23]Richard Karpinski, "Making the Most of a Marketing Dashboard," *B to B* 91 (March 13, 2006): p. 17.

[24]Koen Pauwels, Tim Ambler, Bruce Clark, Pat LaPointe, David Reibstein, Bernd Skiera, Berend Wierenga, and Thomas Wiesel, "Dashboards and Marketing: Why, What, How and What Research Is Needed," *MSI Report #08-203*, May 2008 (Boston: Marketing Science Institute), p. 7.

[25]Christopher Hosford, "Driving Business with Dashboards," *B to B* 91 (December 11, 2006): p. 18.

the marketing function. For example, Tektronix, a company that provides test and measurement equipment to high-tech firms, demonstrates the striking improvements that a performance dashboard can facilitate. Over the first 5 years of using the system, the company has achieved a 125 percent increase in responses to marketing programs and has seen a 90 percent increase in qualified sales leads. In addition, Tektronix has reduced its cost per lead by 70 percent. Moreover, the company's marketing forecast accuracy now has a variance of 3 percent, down from a variance of 50 percent before the dashboard was developed.[26]

Which Metrics Matter? The metrics to be included in a marketing dashboard will vary dramatically from one firm to the next, because each firm has different performance outcomes that are considered important.

> Marketers must accept that there's no one-size-fits-all dashboard they can use; they must customize the tool for themselves. After establishing what the company's true business drivers are, management must cull the myriad possibilities down to the three or four key ones that will be the most fruitful to follow. At least one of these drivers, such as share of wallet, should indicate performance relative to competitors. At least one, such as loyalty, should clearly measure the customers' experience. And one, such as customers' average annual expenditures or lifetime value, should measure the growth of retained customers' business. Finally, any driver on the dashboard must be one the company can manipulate. It might be informative for a supplier of hospital beds to track the number of elective surgeries in the US, but the company can't influence that number, so it's not a useful metric for them to follow—they cannot "manipulate" the number of elective surgeries.[27]

Isolating Performance Drivers There is both art and science in the creation of effective marketing dashboards. However, an effective dashboard maps out the relationships between business outcomes and marketing performance. One of the great challenges is determining where all the relevant data reside: The marketer has to define what the key performance metrics are and think about where to get the actual data to populate those metrics, according to one expert who designs marketing dashboards.[28] In addition, the information one really needs to make decisions almost always comes from multiple sources: internal sales and marketing data, as well as external partner or third-party data. A typical dashboard could include data from 6 to 10 sources, which presents a major challenge. Table 15.2 provides examples of the metrics used in the marketing dashboards by Cisco Systems, Cognos Corporation, and Adobe Systems. Note that each company employs a very different set of metrics. The dashboard elements for each firm reflect the importance that each particular element plays in the success of marketing strategy.

---

[26]Kate Maddox, "Tektronix Wins for Best Practices," *B to B* 90 (April 4, 2005): p. 33.

[27]Gail J. McGovern, David Court, John A. Quelch, and Blair Crawford, "Bringing Customers into the Boardroom," *Harvard Business Review* 82 (November 2004): pp. 70–80.

[28]Karpinski, "Making the Most of a Marketing Dashboard," p. 18.

TABLE 15.2 | MARKETING METRICS: SELECTED COMPANY EXAMPLES

Cognos Corp	Adobe Systems	Cisco Systems
Market share	Marketing activities: Ad reach; Web site hits	Image
Financial analyst firm rankings	Operational measures: Brand awareness	Brand perception
Average revenue per sales rep	Cost per sale; Program-to-people ratio	Lead generation
Penetration of top global companies	Outcome-based metrics: Market share; Number of leads	Employee retention
Number of customers using a company solution year-to-date	Leading indicators: Brand loyalty; Lifetime value of a customer	Customer satisfaction

SOURCE: Kelly Shermach, "Driving Performance," *Sales and Marketing Management* 157 (December 2005): p. 18; Kate Maddox, Sean Callahan, and Carol Krol, "Top Trends," *B to B* 90 (June 13, 2005): p. 24; and Sandra Swanson, "Marketers: James Richardson," *B to B* 90 (October 24, 2005): p. 10.

Desirable Dashboard Features   One expert in the development of marketing dashboards suggests that a good dashboard should accomplish several objectives. The dashboard should:

1. Foster decision making: the metrics should suggest a course of action to be followed;

2. Provide a unified view into marketing's value to the business;

3. Enable better alignment between marketing and the business;

4. Translate complex measures into a meaningful and coherent set of information.[29]

Finally, a dashboard should be focused on two levels: The dashboard should: (a) report operations metrics that are internally focused and (b) reflect execution metrics that mirror marketplace performance.[30]

> Operations metrics can include such measures as a marketing budget ratio, which tracks marketing investment as a percent of total revenue; a program-to-people ratio that determines the percent of a marketing dollar spent on programs versus staff; and an awareness-to-demand ratio that evaluates the percent of marketing investment focused on awareness-building versus demand-generation. Execution metrics, on the other hand, determine how effectively the marketing strategy is being executed. Here the measures include efficiency and effectiveness around implementation: Is awareness building? Are we developing preference? Is the company gaining consideration? Are leads being generated, opportunities identified and qualified? Are deals being closed?[31]

---

[29]Patterson, "Taking on the Metrics Challenge," p. 273.

[30]Michael Krauss, "Marketing Dashboards Drive Better Decisions," *Marketing News* 39 (October 1, 2005): p. 7.

[31]Ibid., p. 7.

B2B TOP PERFORMERS

CMO Profile

Martyn Etherington is Vice President, Worldwide Marketing for Tektronix, a subsidiary of Danaher Corporation. Tektronix manufactures test and measurement equipment including high-precision oscilloscopes used in telecommunications networking systems. As CMO, Etherington developed a sophisticated marketing measurement system, highlighted by a dashboard tool that has markedly improved forecasting accuracy, customer profitability, and marketing program effectiveness. For these efforts, he received a CMO Best Practices Award by International Data Corporation IDC. Beyond this recognition, he believes that the measurement system has enhanced the success of the marketing group by:

1. Establishing his credibility with key internal and external stakeholders;

2. Demonstrating that the marketing function executes its programs on-time and on-budget;

3. Shifting the focus of marketing from activity-centered to outcome-centered goals.

Etherington believes that the ultimate challenge for his marketing group is to prove that it is driving company growth. "We're proving our relevance to the customers. Now we need to lead growth, and be able to measure it. That is the holy grail." To build a more customer-centered and growth-oriented culture, he runs an annual Marketing University for his 115-member staff.

SOURCE: "Define and Align the CMO," CMO Council 2007, p. 23, accessed at http://cmocouncil.org on July 25, 2011.

Marketing performance dashboards are powerful control tools that provide management at all levels of the company with vital data concerning just how well marketing strategy is performing and how much value the marketing function is adding to the firm.

Efficiency and Effectiveness Control

Efficiency control examines how efficiently resources are being used in each element of marketing strategy (for example, sales force, advertising); **effectiveness control** evaluates whether the strategic component is accomplishing its objective. A good control system provides continuing data for evaluating the efficiency of resources used for a given element of marketing strategy to accomplish a given objective. Table 15.3 provides a representative sample of the types of data required. Performance measures and standards vary by company and situation, according to the goals and objectives in the marketing plan.

Profitability Control

The essence of **profitability control** is to describe where the firm is making or losing money in terms of the important segments of its business. A **segment** is the unit of analysis management uses for control purposes; it may be customer segments, product lines, territories, or channel structures. Suppose a business marketing firm focuses on three customer segments: health-care organizations, universities, and local government units. To allocate the marketing budget among the three segments, management must consider the profit contribution

TABLE 15.3 | ILLUSTRATIVE MEASURES FOR EFFICIENCY AND EFFECTIVENESS CONTROL

Product

Sales by market segments

Sales relative to potential

Sales growth rates

Market share

Contribution margin

Percentage of total profits

Return on investment

Distribution

Sales, expenses, and contribution by channel type

Sales and contribution margin by intermediary type and individual intermediaries

Sales relative to market potential by channel, intermediary type, and specific intermediaries

Expense-to-sales ratio by channel, etc.

Logistics cost by logistics activity by channel

Communication

Advertising effectiveness by type of media

Actual audience/target audience ratio

Cost per contact

Number of calls, inquiries, and information requests by type of media

Dollar sales per sales call

Sales per territory relative to potential

Selling expenses to sales ratios

New accounts per time period

Pricing

Price changes relative to sales volume

Discount structure related to sales volume

Bid strategy related to new contracts

Margin structure related to marketing expenses

General price policy related to sales volume

Margins related to channel member performance

of each segment and its expected potential. Profitability control, then, provides a methodology for linking marketing costs and revenues with specific segments of the business.

Profitability by Market Segment   Relating sales revenues and marketing costs to market segments improves decision making. More specifically, say Leland Beik and Stephen Buzby,

> For both strategic and tactical decisions, marketing managers may profit by knowing the effect of the marketing mix on the target segment at which

marketing efforts are aimed. If the programs are to be responsive to environmental change, a monitoring system is needed to locate problems and guide adjustments in marketing decisions. Tracing the profitability of segments permits improved pricing, selling, advertising, channel, and product management decisions. The success of marketing policies and programs may be appraised by a dollar-and-cents measure of profitability by segment.[32]

Profitability control, a prerequisite to strategy planning and implementation, has stringent information requirements. To be effective, the firm needs a marketing–accounting information system.

An Activity-Based Cost System   The accounting system must first be able to link costs with the various marketing activities and must then attach these "activity" costs to the important segments to be analyzed. The critical element in the process is to trace all costs to the activities (warehousing, advertising, and so on) for which the resources are used and then to the products or segments that consume them.[33] Such an **activity-based cost (ABC) system** reveals the links between performing particular activities and the demands those activities make on the organization's resources. As a result, it can give managers a clear picture of how products, brands, customers, facilities, regions, or distribution channels both generate revenues and consume resources.[34] An ABC analysis focuses attention on improving activities that have the greatest effect on profits.

Robin Cooper and Robert Kaplan capture the essence of ABC:

> ABC analysis enables managers to slice into the business many different ways—by product or group of similar products, by individual customer or client group, or by distribution channel—and gives them a close-up view of whatever slice they are considering. ABC analysis also illuminates exactly what activities are associated with that part of the business and how those activities are linked to the generation of revenues and the consumption of resources. By highlighting those relationships, ABC helps managers understand precisely where to take actions that drive profits. In contrast to traditional accounting, activity-based costing segregates the expenses of indirect and support resources by activities. It then assigns those expenses based on the drivers of the activities, rather than by some arbitrary percentage allocation.[35]

---

[32]Leland L. Beik and Stephen L. Buzby, "Profitability Analysis by Market Segments," *Journal of Marketing* 37 (July 1973): p. 49; see also Fred A. Jacobs, Wesley Johnston, and Natalia Kotchetova, "Customer Profitability: Prospective vs. Retrospective Approaches in a Business-to-Business Setting," *Industrial Marketing Management* 30 (June 2001): pp. 353–363.

[33]Robin Cooper and Robert S. Kaplan, "Measure Costs Right: Make the Right Decisions," *Harvard Business Review* 66 (September–October 1988): p. 96. For a related discussion, see Robin Cooper and W. Bruce Chew, "Control Tomorrow's Costs through Today's Designs," *Harvard Business Review* 74 (January–February 1996): pp. 88–97.

[34]Robin Cooper and Robert S. Kaplan, "Profit Priorities from Activity-Based Costing," *Harvard Business Review* 69 (May–June 1993): p. 130; see also Robin Cooper and Robert S. Kaplan, "The Promise—and Peril—of Integrated Cost Systems," *Harvard Business Review* 76 (July–August 1998): pp. 109–118.

[35]Cooper and Kaplan, "Profit Priorities from Activity-Based Costing," p. 131; see also Robert S. Kaplan and Steven R. Anderson, "Time-Driven Activity-Based Costing," *Harvard Business Review* 82 (November 2004): pp. 131–138.

ABC System Illustrated[36]   ABC analysis highlights for managers where their actions will likely have the greatest effect on profits. The ABC system at Kanthal Corporation led to a review of profitability by size of customer (see Chapter 3). Kanthal, a manufacturer of heating wire, used activity-based costing to analyze its customer profitability and discovered that the well-known 80/20 rule (80 percent of sales generated by 20 percent of customers) was in need of revision. A 20/225 rule was actually operating: 20 percent of customers were generating 225 percent of profits. The middle 70 percent of customers were hovering around the break-even point, and Kanthal was losing 125 percent of its profits on 10 percent of its customers.

The Kanthal customers generating the greatest losses were among those with the largest sales volume. Initially, this finding surprised managers, but it soon began to make sense. You cannot lose large amounts of money on a small customer. The large, unprofitable customers demanded lower prices, frequent deliveries of small lots, extensive sales and technical resources, and product changes. The newly revealed economics enabled management to change the way it did business with these customers—through price changes, minimum order sizes, and information technology—transforming the customers into strong profit contributors.

Using the ABC System   An ABC system requires the firm to break from traditional accounting concepts. Managers must refrain from allocating all expenses to individual units and instead separate the expenses and match them to the activity that consumes the resources.[37] Once resource expenditures are related to the activities they produce, management can explore different strategies for reducing the resource commitments. To enhance profitability, business marketing managers need to figure out how to reduce expenditures on those resources or increase the output they produce. For example, a sales manager would search for ways to reduce the number of sales calls on unprofitable customers or find ways to make the salesperson more effective with them. In summary, ABC systems enable the business marketing manager to focus on increasing profitability by understanding the sources of cost variability and developing strategies to reduce resource commitment or enhance resource productivity.

Implementation of Business Marketing Strategy

Many marketing plans fail because they are poorly implemented. Implementation is the critical link between strategy formulation and superior organizational performance.[38] **Marketing implementation** is the process that translates marketing plans into action assignments and ensures that such assignments are executed in a manner that accomplishes a plan's defined objectives.[39] Special implementation challenges

---

[36]This section is based on Cooper and Kaplan, "Profit Priorities from Activity-Based Costing," p. 130, and Cooper and Kaplan, "The Promise—and Peril—of Integrated Cost Systems," pp. 109–119.

[37]Cooper and Kaplan, "Profit Priorities from Activity-Based Costing," p. 130.

[38]Charles H. Noble and Michael P. Mokwa, "Implementing Marketing Strategies: Developing and Testing a Managerial Theory," *Journal of Marketing* 63 (October 1999): pp. 57–73.

[39]Kotler, *Marketing Management: The Millennium Edition*, p. 695.

emerge for the marketing manager because diverse functional areas participate in both developing and executing strategy.

The Strategy-Implementation Fit

Thomas Bonoma asserts that "marketing strategy and implementation affect each other. Although strategy obviously affects actions, execution also affects marketing strategies, especially over time."[40] Although the dividing line between strategy and execution is a bit fuzzy, it is often not difficult to diagnose implementation problems and distinguish them from strategy deficiencies. Bonoma presents the following scenario:

> A firm introduced a new portable microcomputer that incorporated a number of features that the target market valued. The new product appeared to be well positioned in a rapidly growing market, but initial sales results were miserable. Why? The 50-person sales force had little incentive to grapple with a new unfamiliar product and continued to emphasize the older models. Given the significant market potential, management had decided to set the sales incentive compensation level lower on the new machines than on the older ones. The older models had a selling cycle one-half as long as the new product and required no software knowledge or support. In this case, poor execution damaged good strategy.[41]

Marketing strategy and implementation affect each other. When both strategy and implementation are appropriate, the firm is likely to meet its objectives. Diagnosis becomes more difficult in other cases. For example, the cause of a marketing problem may be hard to detect when the strategy is on the mark but the implementation is poor. The business marketer may never become aware of the soundness of the strategy. Alternatively, excellent implementation of a poor strategy may give managers time to see the problem and correct it.

Implementation Skills

Thomas Bonoma identifies four important implementation skills for marketing managers: (1) interacting, (2) allocating, (3) monitoring, and (4) organizing.[42] Each assumes special significance in the business marketing environment.

Marketing managers are continually *interacting* with others both within and outside the corporation. Inside, a number of peers (for example, R&D personnel) over whom the marketer has little power often assume a crucial role in strategy development and implementation. Outside, the marketer deals with important customers, channel members, advertising agencies, and the like. The best implementers have good bargaining skills and the ability to understand how others feel.[43]

---

[40]Thomas V. Bonoma, "Making Your Marketing Strategy Work," *Harvard Business Review* 62 (March–April 1984): pp. 69–76. See also Robert S. Kaplan and David P. Norton, *The Execution Premium: Linking Strategy to Operations for Competitive Advantage* (Boston: Harvard Business Press, 2008), pp. 3–21.

[41]Ibid., p. 70.

[42]Ibid.

[43]Michael D. Hutt, "Cross-Functional Working Relationships in Marketing," *Journal of the Academy of Marketing Science* 23 (Fall 1995): pp. 351–357.

The implementer must also *allocate* time, assignments, people, dollars, and other resources among the marketing tasks at hand. Astute marketing managers, says Bonoma, are "tough and fair in putting people and dollars where they will be most effective. The less able ones routinely allocate too many dollars and people to mature programs and too few to richer ones."[44]

Bonoma asserts that marketing managers with good *monitoring* skills exhibit flexibility and intelligence in dealing with the firm's information and control systems: "Good implementers struggle and wrestle with their markets and businesses until they can simply and powerfully express the 'back of the envelope' ratios necessary to run the business, regardless of formal control system inadequacies."[45]

Finally, the best implementers are effective at *organizing*. Sound execution often hinges on the marketer's ability to work with both the formal and the informal organizational networks. The manager customizes an informal organization to solve problems and facilitate good execution.

The Marketing Strategy Center: An Implementation Guide[46]

Diverse functional areas participate to differing degrees in developing and implementing business marketing strategy. Research and development, manufacturing, technical service, physical distribution, and other functional areas play fundamental roles. Ronald McTavish points out that "marketing specialists understand markets, but know a good deal less about the nuts and bolts of the company's operations—its internal terrain. This is the domain of the operating specialist. We need to bring these different specialists together in a 'synergistic pooling' of knowledge and viewpoint to achieve the best fit of the company's skills with the market and the company's approach to it."[47] This suggests a challenging and pivotal interdisciplinary role for the marketing manager in the business-to-business firm.

The marketing strategy center provides a framework for highlighting this interdisciplinary role and for exploring key implementation requirements. Table 15.4 highlights important strategic topics examined throughout this textbook. In each case, nonmarketing personnel play active implementation roles. For example, product quality is directly or indirectly affected by several departments: manufacturing, research and development, technical service, and others. In turn, successful product innovation reflects the collective efforts of individuals from several functional areas. Clearly, effective strategy implementation requires well-defined decision roles, responsibilities, timetables, and coordination mechanisms.

On a global market scale, special coordination challenges emerge when selected activities such as R&D are concentrated in one country and other strategy activities such as manufacturing are dispersed across countries. Xerox, however, has been

---

[44]Bonoma, "Making Your Marketing Strategy Work," p. 75.

[45]Ibid.

[46]Michael D. Hutt and Thomas W. Speh, "The Marketing Strategy Center: Diagnosing the Industrial Marketer's Interdisciplinary Role," *Journal of Marketing* 48 (Fall 1984): pp. 53–61; and Michael D. Hutt, Beth A. Walker, and Gary L. Frankwick, "Hurdle the Cross-Functional Barriers to Strategic Change," *Sloan Management Review* 36 (Spring 1995): pp. 22–30.

[47]Ronald McTavish, "Implementing Marketing Strategy," *Industrial Marketing Management* 26 (November 5, 1988): p. 10; see also Deborah Dougherty and Edward H. Bowman, "The Effects of Organizational Downsizing on Product Innovation," *California Management Review* 37 (Summer 1995): pp. 28–44.

| TABLE 15.4 | INTERFUNCTIONAL INVOLVEMENT IN MARKETING STRATEGY IMPLEMENTATION: AN ILLUSTRATIVE RESPONSIBILITY CHART |

Decision Area	Marketing	Sales	Manufac- turing	R&D	Purcha- sing	Physical Distri- bution	Tech- nical Service	Strategic Business Unit	Corporate- Level Planner
Product/ service quality									
Technical service support									
Physical distribution service									
National accounts manage- ment									
Channel relations									
Sales support									
Product/ service innovation									

Use the following abbreviations to indicate decision roles: R = responsible; A = approval; C = consult; M = implement; I = inform; X = no role in decision.

successful in maintaining a high level of coordination across such dispersed activities. The Xerox brand, marketing approach, and servicing procedures are standardized worldwide.[48]

The Marketer's Role   To ensure maximum customer satisfaction and the desired market response, the business marketer must assume an active role in the strategy center by negotiating market-sensitive agreements and coordinating strategies with other members. While being influenced by other functional areas to varying degrees in the process, the marketer can potentially influence key areas such as the design of the logistical system, the selection of manufacturing technology, or the structure of a materials management system. Such negotiation with other functional areas is fundamental to the business marketer's strategic interdisciplinary role. Thus, the successful business marketing manager performs as an integrator by drawing on the collective strengths of the enterprise to satisfy customer needs profitably.

---

[48]Michael E. Porter, "Changing Patterns of International Competition," *California Management Review* 28 (Winter 1986): pp. 9–40.

Looking Back

Figure 15.2 synthesizes the central components of business marketing management and highlights the material presented in this textbook. Part I introduced the major classes of customers that constitute the business market: commercial enterprises, governmental units, and institutions. The timely themes of organizational buying behavior and customer relationship management provided the focus of Part II. Part III discussed the tools for assessing market opportunities; it explored techniques for identifying market segments and for forecasting sales. Functionally integrated marketing planning provides a framework for dealing with each component of the business marketing mix, as detailed in Part IV. Special attention was also given to the special challenges and unique opportunities that rapidly developing economies present for business-to-business firms.

FIGURE 15.2 | A FRAMEWORK FOR BUSINESS MARKETING MANAGEMENT

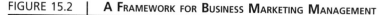

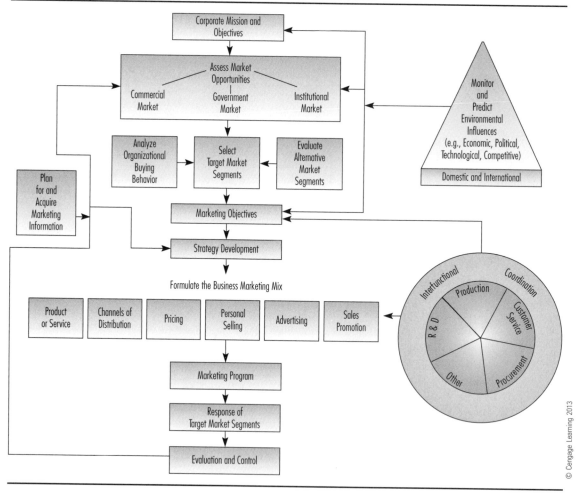

Once business marketing strategy is formulated, the manager must evaluate the response of target market segments to minimize any discrepancy between planned and actual results. This chapter, which constitutes Part V, explores the critical dimensions of the marketing control process, which is the final loop in the model presented in Figure 15.2: planning for and acquiring marketing information. Such information forms the core of the firm's management information system; it is derived internally through the marketing–accounting system and externally through the marketing research function. Evaluation and control enable the marketer to reassess business market opportunities and make adjustments as needed in business marketing strategy.

Summary

Central to market strategy is the allocation of resources to each strategy element and the application of marketing efforts to segments. The marketing control system is the process by which the business marketing firm generates information to make these decisions. Moreover, the marketing control system is the means by which current performance can be evaluated and steps can be taken to correct deficiencies. Used in conjunction with the balanced scorecard, the strategy map converts a strategy vision into concrete objectives and measures, organized into four different perspectives: financial, customer, internal business process, and learning and growth. The approach involves developing a customer strategy, identifying target market segments, isolating the critical internal processes the firm must develop to deliver value to customers in these segments, and selecting the organizational capabilities needed to achieve customer and financial objectives. A strategy map provides a visual representation of a firm's critical objectives and the cause-and-effect relationships among them that drive superior organizational performance.

An effective control system has four distinct components. Strategic control, which is operationalized through the marketing audit, provides valuable information on the present and future course of the firm's basic product/market mission. Annual plan control compares annual with planned results to provide input for future planning. Efficiency and effectiveness control evaluates whether marketing strategy elements achieve their goals in a cost-effective manner. Finally, profitability control seeks to evaluate profitability by segment. Marketing dashboards are effective tools for helping managers to isolate and monitor key performance metrics while providing top management with a compact profile concerning the impact of marketing strategies on overall company performance.

Many business marketing plans fail because they are poorly executed. Marketing implementation is the process that translates marketing plans into action assignments and ensures that such assignments are executed in a timely and effective manner. Four implementation skills are particularly important to the business marketing manager: (1) interacting, (2) allocating, (3) monitoring, and (4) organizing. Nonmarketing personnel play active roles in implementing business marketing strategy. This suggests a challenging and pivotal interdisciplinary role for the marketing manager.

Discussion Questions

1. Hamilton Tucker, president of Tucker Manufacturing Company, is concerned about the seat-of-the-pants approach managers use in allocating the marketing budget. He cites the Midwest and the East as examples. The firm increased its demand-stimulating expenditures (for example, advertising, personal selling) in the Midwest by 20 percent, but sales climbed only 6 percent last year. In contrast, demand-stimulating expenditures were cut by 17 percent in the East, and sales dropped by 22 percent. Hamilton would like you to assist the Midwestern and Eastern regional managers in allocating their funds next year. Carefully outline the approach you would follow.

2. Using the marketing strategy center concept as a guide, describe how a strategy that is entirely appropriate for a particular target market might fail because of poor implementation in the logistics and technical service areas.

3. Describe how the strategy implementation challenges for a marketing manager working at DuPont (an industrial firm) might be different from those for a marketing manager working at Pillsbury (a consumer-goods firm).

4. Susan Breck, president of Breck Chemical Corporation, added three new products to the firm's line 2 years ago to serve the needs of five NAICS groups. Each of the products has a separate advertising budget, although they are sold by the same salespersons. Susan requests your assistance in determining what type of information the firm should gather to monitor and control the performance of these products. Outline your reply.

5. Assume that the information you requested in question 4 has been gathered for you. How would you determine whether advertising and personal selling funds should be shifted from one product to another?

6. Discuss why a firm that plans to enter a new market segment may have to develop new internal business processes to serve customers in this segment.

7. Not all customer demands can be satisfied profitably. What steps should be taken by a marketing manager who learns that particular customer accounts—including some long-standing ones—are unprofitable?

8. Describe the relationships between and among the four central perspectives represented in the balanced scorecard and included in a strategy map: financial, customer, internal business process, and learning and growth.

9. Last December, Lisa Schmitt, vice president of marketing at Bock Machine Tool, identified four market segments her firm would attempt to penetrate this year. As this year comes to an end, Lisa would like to evaluate the firm's performance in each of these segments. Of course, Lisa turns to you for assistance. First, what information would you seek from the firm's marketing information system to perform the analysis? Second, how would you know whether the firm's performance in a particular market segment was good or bad?

10. Your company produces electric motors for use in appliances, machinery, and a variety of other industrial applications. The CEO of the company wants the chief marketing officer (CMO) to create a dashboard of marketing indicators that could be reviewed by top management to evaluate the contribution of marketing to overall firm performance. What advice would you give to the CMO in terms of criteria he or she should use in designing the dashboard? That is, what will be required to make the dashboard effective?

Internet Exercise

1. McKinsey & Company is a leading management consulting firm. The company publishes *McKinsey Quarterly*, an online journal that features the latest thinking on business strategy, finance, and management. Go to http://www.mckinsey.com, click on McKinsey Quarterly, and conduct a search for articles on "strategy implementation." Select a recent article on this topic and briefly outline the key insights that the article provides.

The Middleby Corporation

The Middleby Corporation manufactures cooking equipment for restaurants and institutional kitchens. Included in its product line are conveyor ovens, ranges, convection ovens, griddles, fryers, and food-warming equipment. Recognized by *Business Week* as one of the Top 100 Hot Growth Companies and by *Forbes* as one of the Best Small Companies, the firm enjoys particular strength among fast-food companies.[1] Among its customers are Subway, McDonalds, Papa John's, and Yum! Brands, the parent company of KFC, Pizza Hut, Taco Bell, and others. Commenting on the firm's rapid growth, one industry expert observed: "As these franchises go to China and Indonesia, Middleby ovens go there too."[2]

Middleby has developed a loyal customer base. For example, Middleby ovens are the only ovens used in Papa John's restaurants around the world. For its excellence in customer service, quality, value, and relationship management, the firm was named the Yum! Brands Supplier of the Year and received the 2010 "Slice of Appreciation" award from Papa John's International.[3]

Middleby leads the industry in energy-efficient food-preparation equipment. The company offers a broad array of Energy Star-approved products that cook food efficiently without sacrificing quality. For example, Middleby's WOW! Oven represents the most energy-efficient, fastest-cooking conveyor oven on the market—35 percent faster, yet 30 percent more efficient than the appliances offered by competitors.

To spur additional growth, Middleby is exploring the feasibility of adding casual dining chains to its targeted base.[4] Casual dining comprises a market segment between fast-food establishments and fine dining restaurants. By offering a complete suite of products to revamp their kitchens, Middleby strategists believe casual dining operators could cut labor and energy costs while increasing productivity. Such changes would represent a multimillion-dollar initiative in each restaurant. Middleby is currently conducting a test run with three casual dining chains to demonstrate the potential return on investment that its products could deliver. Middleby refuses to divulge the names of the dining chains involved in the test but reports that the results look very promising.

---

[1]"Middleby Corporation Named YUM! Brands Supplier of the Year," April 6, 2010, accessed at http://www.middleby.com on May 14, 2011.

[2]J. R. Brandstrader, "Food for Thought," *Barron's*, May 9, 2011, p. 56.

[3]"Middleby Marshall Receives 2010 'Slice of Appreciation' from Papa John's International," December 2010, accessed at http://www.middleby.com on May 14, 2011.

[4]Jim Royal, "The Hidden Play on Rising Energy Prices," The Motley Fool, March 22, 2011, accessed at http://www.fool.com on May 14, 2011.

Discussion Questions

1. Describe how the value proposition that Middleby offers to a casual dining chain, like Outback Steakhouse, might differ from one that is offered to a fast-food customer, like Papa John's International.

2. In planning marketing strategy, what adjustments might be needed in serving potential casual dining versus fast-food organizations?

Sealed Air Corporation: Delivering Packaging Solutions[1]

Sealed Air Corporation is a global leader in providing business customers with performance solutions for food, protective, and specialty packaging. Best known for its BubbleWrap® cushioning material, the firm has pioneered a number of packaging innovations that have sustained a remarkable pattern of sales growth for more than two decades. Using a consultative selling approach, field sales and technical support specialists at Sealed Air incorporate both packaging materials and specialized equipment to provide a complete packaging solution for customers, giving superior protection against shock, abrasion, and vibration, compared with other forms of packaging. Let's explore the packaging solution that Sealed Air developed for Davis Neon Inc., a wholesale neon sign manufacturer in Heath Springs, South Carolina.

Protecting custom-made neon signs that are shipped worldwide is a challenging problem for Dave Lytle, shipping manager at Davis Neon. "We were using preformed polyethylene foam sheets, which required a lot of storage space and time to unload from the trucks," noted Lytle. "We were keeping our eyes open for an alternative packaging method which would provide comparable protection, yet reduce costs and increase productivity."

After evaluating several alternatives, Dave Lytle chose a solution proposed by Sealed Air to package the neon signs—Instapak Continuous Foam Tubes made by Sealed Air's SpeedyPacker Insight system. Using the SpeedyPacker equipment, now installed in the shipping area at Davis Neon, an operator can create numerous variations of foam bags at the touch of a button. For each neon sign, Davis Neon employees create a custom-made wooden crate with dimensions just large enough to house the sign. The packager then puts a layer of foam tubes, made-to-order by the Speedy Packer equipment, on the bottom of the crate to form a pad. BubbleWrap cushioning is used on the back of the sign, between rows, and on the side to provide surface protection and prevent abrasion of the sign against the crate. Another layer of foam tubes is added on top before the lid is attached to the crate.

Before implementing the Sealed Air solution, packagers used preformed polyethylene foam sheets, each of which had to be cut by hand to fit the crate for the bottom pad and top layer, as well as to fit in between the letters on the neon sign. "The preformed polyethylene foam sheets took a long time to cut, were expensive, and produced significant material waste," stated Lytle. "After working with the new packaging system, the actual savings are 62 percent in material costs. We have also seen productivity increase by 20 percent." Employees at Davis are now able to pack more crates in less time.

---

[1]Case History, "Sealed Air Sheds Light on Davis Neon's Packaging," accessed at http://www.sealedair.com on June 6, 2008.

Discussion Questions

1. Given the significant value that Sealed Air can provide for a customer, like Davis Neon Inc., what approach should it follow in pricing a particular packaging solution for a customer?

2. Develop a list of other types of customers who face special packaging challenges and may represent promising customer prospects for Sealed Air to target.

IBM Challenge: How to Serve a Diverse Mix of Demanding Customers

IBM's offerings cover a wide spectrum of the technology industry, including hardware, software, and services. The company faces a different set of rivals in each sector, but maintains a leadership position in most areas through a combination of investments in R&D, worldwide distribution, and a respected brand.[1]

IBM serves a diverse set of customers in the business market and devotes special attention to the Global 1000—the 1000 largest enterprises in the world. Across these organizations, however, different perspectives and approaches are used in making information technology (IT) purchases. This diversity across customer groups presents a host of challenges for IBM.

- Customer Group A demands a wide variety of IT products, routine maintenance support, and customized services. These customers value the relationship with IBM and are willing to pay a premium for product and service quality.

- Customer Group B wants high-quality IT products (e.g., storage systems, servers), but, most of all, these customers want a rock-bottom price and choose suppliers on that basis.

- Customer Group C demands both quality products and extensive service support but wants all of this for a "rock-bottom" price. These customers will freely switch from one supplier to the next. As competition intensifies for IBM and others in the IT sector, more customers are moving into this group each month.

First, describe how IBM might develop a portfolio of relationship strategies to meet the needs of such diverse customer groups. Second, some customers in each group are more costly to serve than others. How should such cost differences be reflected in the particular relationship strategies that IBM follows? Third, what strategies can IBM follow to increase the switching costs of customers in Group B or Group C or increase the profits it derives from these customer groups?

© Cengage Learning 2013

---

[1]Sunit Gogia, "A Trusted Brand and an Unrivaled Product and Services Portfolio Hold IBM in Good Stead," Morningstar, Inc., April 26, 2011, pp. 1–2, accessed at http://www.morningstar.com on May 2, 2011.

Federated Insurance: Targeting Small Businesses[1]

Targeting customers, Federated Insurance offers clients and prospects a program of complete insurance protection, covering the spectrum from commercial property and casualty insurance and life and disability insurance to group health insurance. Since its founding over a century ago, the market plan for the company has centered on a clear-cut strategy: provide the highest quality, best-value service available to selected businesses.

Based in Owatonna, Minnesota, with regional offices in Atlanta and Phoenix, Federated has 2600 employees and operates in 48 states. Consistent with its heritage and original market plan, the company specializes in business insurance for selected industries:

- Auto dealers and auto parts wholesalers

- Building contractors (for example, electrical, plumbing-heating-cooling)

- Equipment dealers (for example, agricultural, lawn and garden)

- Funeral services

- Jewelers

- Machine shops

- Petroleum marketers and convenience stores

- Tire dealers

Cultivating Business Relationships

Marketing representatives at Federated can tailor insurance protection to meet virtually all of a business owner's insurance needs: property, casualty, health, retirement, and more. They also provide quality risk-management services that respond to the specific needs of business owners. The goal here is to help customers develop procedures and practices that can reduce losses and improve worksite safety conditions.

Federated enjoys a strong reputation among SMB customers, as the following testimonials demonstrate:

> One of the things Federated does very well is that they have focus. It's not about selling insurance, it's about taking care of your customers, and the businesses that do best are the ones that take care of their customers.

> [Tim Smith, President, Bob Smith BMW, Calabasas, California]

---

[1]"About Federated: Our History and Mission," accessed at http://www.federatedinsurance.com on July 10, 2008.

I've had friends who are in businesses that jump insurance companies all the time and they're price shopping. They don't realize the relationship that you have to build with an insurance company. It's such a close relationship, but yet so secure. With Federated, we don't worry—we don't have to.

[Greg Nesler, President, Rochester Plumbing and Heating, Rochester, Minnesota]

Discussion Questions

1. By directing attention to particular types of businesses (for example, convenience stores or auto dealers), Federated emphasizes macrosegmentation. To further sharpen strategy, suggest possible ways that particular macrosegments could be broken down further into meaningful microsegments.

2. In buying insurance, some SMB customers just want the lowest-priced option for each type of insurance, whereas others want value-added services (for example, risk-management guidance) and a complete, integrated insurance solution. How should Federated respond to customers who are strictly focused on price? In your view, what are the points of difference that Federated should illuminate in the customer value proposition?

Intuit's Solutions for Small and Medium-Sized Businesses[1]

Intuit's user-friendly accounting and tax software solutions have created a highly profitable business and a loyal customer base. QuickBooks, one of its flagship products, provides accounting and management solutions to small and medium-sized businesses (SMBs) and enjoys monopoly-like market leadership. The relatively low price points, high switching costs, and widespread adoption of the company's accounting solutions leave Intuit well-positioned for growth in this attractive market. There are roughly 300,000 new SMBs formed annually in the United States. Intuit also offers payroll and payment services to SMBs. According to the firm, further growth appears promising because only 40 percent of QuickBooks customers use the firm's payroll services and less than 10 percent of those users have adopted Intuit's payment services.

While enjoying a leadership position in the SMB market, Intuit may need to increase its R&D expenditures to keep Microsoft and Internet-based competitors at bay. While the firm currently benefits from a strong distribution channel, the advent of cloud computing could level the playing field. For example, multiple providers of accounting solutions already offer their solutions through Google's GOOG App Engine.

Discussion Questions

1. To sustain its leadership position in the SMB market, describe the differentiating value proposition that Intuit should offer to customers.

2. Drawing on the balanced scorecard, describe how Intuit's internal business processes (for example, operations, customer, innovation management) might be aligned to achieve targeted revenue and profit goals in the SMB market.

---

[1] Rafael Garcia, "Intuit Needs to Leverage the Strength of Its Products to Penetrate New International Markets," Morningstar Inc., March 18, 2011, pp. 1–2; accessed at http://www.morningstar.com on May 1, 2011.

Schwinn: Could the Story Have Been Different?[1]

At its peak, Schwinn had more than 2000 U.S. employees, produced hundreds of thousands of bicycles in five factories, and held 20 percent of the market. Today, however, Schwinn no longer exists as an operating company. The firm, founded in 1895, declared bankruptcy in 1992 and closed its last factory one year later. The Schwinn name is now owned by a Canada-based firm and all of the bikes are manufactured in Asia.

Harold L. Sirkin, a senior vice president at the Boston Consulting Group, argues that Schwinn's story could have been different. He outlines two alternative pathways that might have provided a happier ending to the Schwinn story.

Alternative Reality One: Aim High

Under this scenario, Schwinn decided to center on midrange and premium segments of the market, leaving low-end bicycles for competitors. However, the firm determined that it could substantially reduce costs by turning to low-cost partners in rapidly developing economies for labor-intensive parts. Schwinn interviewed hundreds of potential suppliers and locked the best ones into long-term contracts. Schwinn then reconfigured its operations to perform final assembly and quality inspection in the United States. Still, the changes forced Schwinn to make some painful choices—nearly 30 percent of the workforce was laid off. However, such moves allowed Schwinn to produce bikes at half the previous cost, maintain a significant position in the midrange bicycle market, and leverage its product design capabilities to build a strong position for its brand in the high-end market. As a result, Schwinn is extremely competitive in the U.S. market and is a major exporter of premium bikes to China and Europe. Because of this growth, Schwinn now employs twice as many people in the United States as it did before outsourcing began.

Alternative Reality Two: If You Can't Beat Them, Join Them

Schwinn went on the offensive and moved as quickly as possible to open its own factory in China. By bringing its own manufacturing techniques and by training employees in China, Schwinn was able to achieve high quality and a much lower cost. However, the decision meant that 70 percent of Schwinn's U.S. workers would lose their jobs. But Schwinn kept expanding its China operations and soon started selling bicycles in the Chinese market—not only at the low end but also to

---

[1]Harold L. Sirkin, "Don't Be a Schwinn," *BCG/Perspectives*, *The Boston Consulting Group, Inc.*, January 2005, accessed at http://www.bcg.com.

the high-end, luxury segment—leveraging its brand name. Schwinn then extended its global operations and reach by adding new facilities in eastern Europe and Brazil. The company has sold over 500,000 bikes in new markets and now has more employees in the United States than it did before deciding to expand into international markets.

Discussion Question

1. By facing fierce competition from low-cost rivals, many business-to-business firms in the United States and Europe face a situation today similar to Schwinn's. What lessons can they draw from the Schwinn story? How can they strengthen their competitive position?

Hidden Inside: International Flavors & Fragrances, Inc.

Founded in 1909 and based in New York City, International Flavors & Fragrances (IFF) manufactures flavors (46 percent of sales) and fragrances (54 percent of sales) for use in a wide array of consumer products.[1] The Flavors segment offers components for use in consumer products such as soft drinks, candies, pharmaceuticals, snack foods, and alcoholic beverages. The Fragrances segment provides functional fragrances for personal care and household products, including perfumes and colognes. The firm's customer base consists of large consumer product companies such as Pepsi, Procter & Gamble, Estee Lauder, and Unilever. IFF generates over 40 percent of its sales from rapidly developing economies.

Large consumer product firms are quite reluctant to put their brands at risk, so these customers favor trusted global suppliers, like IFF, that can meet their supply needs around the world, as well as ensure the safety and quality of their products. However, IFF competes with three other large market participants—Givaudan, Danisco, and Firmenich. When a consumer product company wants to launch a new flavor or fragrance, IFF, along with each of these rivals, has been offered the opportunity to develop a scent, making it difficult to lock in customer relationships. Since the value that IFF contributes to a consumer product is "hidden inside" and the IFF name is unfamiliar to end customers, some challenging questions emerge for managing the firm's brand:

Discussion Questions

1. What strategies could IFF follow to differentiate its offering from those of competitors and strengthen its position with its core base of consumer product companies?

2. Should IFF invest in a marketing communications strategy that seeks to establish its identity among end customers (i.e., its customers' customers)?

---

[1]This discussion is based on Erin Lash, "Analyst Note: International Flavors & Fragrances," Morningstar, Inc., May 10, 2011, accessed at http://www.morningstar.com on May 24, 2011.

Vscan: GE Healthcare's Pocket-Sized Imaging Device

"This could be the stethoscope of the 21st century," observed GE's CEO Jeffrey Immelt, as he demonstrated the device at a San Francisco technology conference.[1] Roughly the size of a smartphone, GE Healthcare's Vscan device incorporates powerful ultrasound technology to provide physicians with imaging capabilities at the point-of-care. "The device may be used by primary care doctors to more quickly diagnose ailments such as gallstones, by critical-care workers to quickly confirm symptoms such as fluid on the heart, and by cardiologists trying to determine how well a heart is pumping."[2] Vscan is portable and can be easily taken from room to room, facilitating its use in many clinical, hospital, emergency medicine, or primary care settings.

The innovative product was developed by GE Healthcare engineers from around the world, led by a new product development team in Norway. Vscan represents one of the first innovations to issue from a major strategic initiative at GE Healthcare, termed "healthymagination." Under this vision, GE plans to invest $6 billion by 2015 in the development of innovations focused on reducing costs, increasing access, and improving the quality and efficiency of health care around the world.[3]

The $8000 Vscan device, which offers image quality equivalent to that of a far more expensive midrange ultrasound console also produced by GE, has received approval from the U.S. Food and Drug Administration and from regulatory bodies in Canada and Europe.[4]

Discussion Questions

1. Does the Vscan represent a disruptive innovation? Will it cannibalize sales of GE Healthcare's more advanced and much higher-priced imaging equipment?

2. What marketing strategies should GE Healthcare follow to speed the adoption of Vscan in the United States and around the world?

[1]Rachel Layne, "GE Plans to Sell Phone-Size Ultrasound Device in 2010," October 2009, Bloomberg.com, p. 1, accessed at http://www.bloomberg.com on May 23, 2011.

[2]Ibid., p. 2.

[3]Ibid., p. 2.

[4]Stephanie Simon, "Medicine on the Move," March 28, 2011, *The Wall Street Journal*, p. 1, accessed at http://online.wsj.com on May 23, 2011.

Paychex, Inc.[1]

Paychex competes in the payroll outsourcing industry and focuses on providing this service to small and medium-sized businesses (SMB [50 to 100 employees]). From calculating payroll and filing tax payments to administering retirement plans and workers' compensation, Paychex gives its customers relief from administrative hassles so that they can focus on their core business and bottom line.

Switching from one payroll processing supplier to another is a very challenging task, and customers' reluctance to do so has allowed Paychex to build a relatively sticky customer base that now includes 540,000 clients. The firm's strong brand also fuels growth and promotes customer retention since customers are hesitant to entrust their critical human resource (HR) functions and payroll cash to an unproven competitor. "Strong scalability has also allowed the firm to be price competitive without feeling significant margin pressure."[2] Paychex can spread the costs associated with its servicing infrastructure across its large customer base. Collectively, these factors have allowed the firm to produce margins that have been well above 30 percent during the past decade.

Offering other HR-related services to its customers is a current strategy initiative at the firm. For example, Paychex is a leading provider of 401(K) record-keeping services for company retirement plans. Because of the relatively small incremental costs associated with these ancillary services, a meaningful portion of this additional revenue flows to the bottom line.

Discussion Questions

1. Describe the core service concept and benefits that Paychex provides to an SMB customer with its payroll outsourcing service.

2. Discuss how the selling process for a service, such as payroll outsourcing, differs from that of a product, such as photocopying equipment.

---

[1]Vishnu LeKraj, "Paychex's Unyielding Wide Moat Has Produced Steadfast Investment Returns," Morningstar, Inc., April 18, 2011, pp. 1–2, accessed at http://www.morningstar.com on June 25, 2011.

[2]Ibid., p. 1.

Snap-on, Inc.: A Unique Go-to-Market Strategy

Snap-on, Inc., a member company of the S&P 500, is a leading manufacturer and distributor of premium tools, equipment, and diagnostic systems primarily for independent auto repair centers but also for new vehicle dealerships.[1] Through its innovative products, strong brand, and services-focused distribution strategy, Snap-on captures a leading share of the automotive professional tool market against rivals such as Stanley Black & Decker and Danaher. Snap-on also serves technicians in the marine and aviation industries (i.e., aircraft repair) as well as government and industrial organizations. Among Snap-on's extensive product line are diagnostic tools that provide trouble-shooting information, including step-by-step instructions that technicians can follow in repairing a particular problem. Such solutions have made Snap-on particularly popular among independent repair shops—Snap-on's bread-and-butter market.

From its founding in 1920, the cornerstone of Snap-on's marketing strategy has been to take their tools directly to the customer's business and demonstrate their performance advantages.[2] Building on this concept, Snap-on has developed a national network of franchised dealers who make weekly visits to customers' workplaces in a tool-stocked walk-in van. "The company's United States van fleet consists of approximately 3,200 vans, more than twice that of its next largest competitor, allowing Snap-on dealers to serve smaller territories and focus on customer service."[3]

The franchised dealers receive extensive training and responsive service support in the field. For new dealers, after an introductory course, a trainer will accompany them on customer visits for 4 to 6 weeks to provide a smooth transition for the franchisee and for customers in the territory.

To capitalize on its strong product development capabilities and to spur future growth, Snap-on is working to expand its product offerings outside the vehicle service market to industries such as aerospace and power generation. Management believes the firm could garner strong margins from customers in these industries due to Snap-on's emphasis on high-performance, quality tools.

Discussion Questions

1. Channel design begins with an assessment of end-user customer needs. Assess the strength of Snap-on's dealer van channel in serving customer needs in the vehicle service market (for example, auto repair shops). Next, consider possible adjustments that might be required to serve customer needs in adjacent markets that the firm is exploring, such as aerospace companies and utilities.

2. Outline strategies that Snap-on might follow to capitalize on its strong brand in the vehicle service market and extend its reach into other industry sectors.

---

[1]Richard Hilgert, "Snap-on Should Benefit from an Aging U.S. Vehicle Fleet," April 28, 2011, Morningstar, Inc., accessed at http://www.morningstar.com on May 19, 2011. .

[2]"Snap-On, Incorporated," Wikipedia, accessed at http://en.wikipedia.org on May 20, 2011.

[3]Hilgert, "Snap-on Should Benefit," p. 2.

Supply Chain Issues at Optimal Medical Parts Company

Optimal Medical Parts (OMP) is a manufacturer of precision parts that are used to repair many types of medical equipment ranging from X-ray machines to oxygen pumps to laser-guided surgical devices. The company is headquartered in Peoria, Illinois where they also have a large manufacturing facility. Manufacturing facilities are also located in Scranton, Pennsylvania and Long Beach, California. The company makes over 200,000 different products that range in value from pennies per unit to over $1500 for a replacement scope on a CAT scan device. As with most companies making assemblies and parts, the company finds that a very large percentage of the volume is concentrated in about 20 percent of the products. Similarly, close to 85% of their sales are made to about 20% of their best customers. Total sales for OMP last year were over $6 billion.

OMP's market is primarily based in the US, but they are beginning to expand slowly to other parts of the world. With sales offices in eight major cities in the US, OMP recently opened offices in Frankfurt, Germany, Shanghai, China, and Sao Paulo, Brazil. Sales outside the US are relatively small at present, but the company expects to see their global sales grow by double digits over the next five years. The major customer segments for OMP are hospitals, both for-profit and not-for-profit, surgery centers, urgent care facilities, free-standing clinics, all branches of the U.S. military, large medical schools, and retirement facilities.

Currently the firm distributes its products through an extensive network of industrial distributors. Although OMP has its own sales force, distributors are used to call on many small and medium-sized customers, many of whom are also in remote locations. The very largest accounts are handled by OMP's sales force, and the remaining customers (about 85 percent of all customers) are called on by the distributor's sales force. Distributors are currently used exclusively to handle sales to non-U.S. customers. The major effort of the distributor network is to provide the logistics support to physically move product to customers. OMP does not manage any of the supply chain and logistics activities: these are all handled through the network of distributors in place throughout the US and selected locations outside the US. Hence, OMP manufactures the products in three factory locations, and from that point on the physical movement, inventory management, customer service activities, warehousing, order processing, and returns management are all handled by the distributors.

Top management is rather concerned about the firm's supply chain and logistics performance, as some of their key customers have been grumbling about late and short shipments, product damage issues, and the ability to track products and orders through the relatively complex logistics network. Currently one distributor is responsible for managing three "super warehouses" that accept truckload shipments of a variety of products from the three OMP factories. At these warehouses, the company's full line of products is maintained so that they are able to ship the full array of OMP items to satellite warehouses that are located closer to customers. Currently, OMP has agreements with four different distributor companies to manage the small satellite warehouses that actually ship to the final customer locations. At present, there are 12 satellite warehouses in the US. In Europe, final shipment to the customer is handled from one central warehouse in Frankfurt, Germany that is managed by the European distributor. Similar logistics/supply chain arrangements are in place in China and Brazil.

The issue with the current logistics and supply chain system is, as mentioned above, one of service level—delivering orders in a timely manner, in good condition to the right customer, along with a good data support system. In addition to service issues, the current distributor network appears to be a relatively high-cost network. The average cost of supply chain operations has hovered around 11% of sales for the past couple of years. Top management feels that something in the neighborhood of 8% would be a reasonable target. If this level were achieved, profits would be enhanced significantly, and if the service problem were eliminated, management feels that sales might grow significantly. So, at this juncture, the executive management team at OMP has asked the company's top internal supply chain manager to develop a bold, new strategy. The distributor supply chain network would be replaced by a centrally-controlled supply chain, with the company assuming all the logistics and supply chain operations, facilities, and activities.

Discussion Questions

1. Discuss the pros and cons of OMP assuming the total responsibility for owning and managing their supply chain operations, giving special attention to the problems OMP would face as well as the advantages that might be captured by such a strategy.

2. Based on your analysis, provide a recommendation to top management.

Free-Product Competitors Challenge Microsoft[1]

Since 2007, Microsoft's Office software, a highly profitable product that has long enjoyed a near monopoly position in the office applications business, has been under attack from free alternatives: Google Docs and Oracle's Open Office. Reluctantly, Microsoft responded in 2010 with Microsoft Live, a free "cloud" version of Office that, unlike Open Office, cannot be downloaded to and operated from an individual computer.

Based on high switching costs along with concerns about file incompatibility and the lack of functions in the competing free offerings, Microsoft has been able to retain the vast majority of its target corporate customers. However, the free offerings are being widely adopted by college students, small businesses, and some large educational institutions. To illustrate, a recent survey indicates that 20 percent of college students exclusively use free alternatives. Available evidence also suggests that Google Docs have been adopted by over 3 million small business users as well as some large educational institutions, including the University of Minnesota, the University of Virginia, the California State University System, and a host of others.

Discussion Questions

1. Adopting a cautious stance, Microsoft strategists have not aggressively promoted its free-product offering. Some experts argue that Microsoft should be taking the defection among price-sensitive customers more seriously. Agree or disagree? Support your position.

2. What steps should Microsoft take to retain its most valuable customers and prevent rivals from expanding their foothold in the market?

---

[1]David J. Bryce, Jeffrey H. Dyer, and Nile W. Hatch, "Competing Against Free," *Harvard Business Review* 89 (June 2011): pp. 26–30.

Johnson Controls, Inc.[1]

Johnson Controls, Inc., provides control and automotive systems worldwide. The Controls Division offers mechanical and electrical systems that control energy use, air-conditioning, lighting, security, and fire safety for buildings. The company also provides on-site management and technical services for customers in a range of settings, including manufacturing installations, commercial buildings, government buildings, hospitals, and major sports complexes.

While serving a full range of market sectors from manufacturers to educational institutions, Johnson Controls has developed a suite of products and services for large retail chains, including department stores, discount stores, grocers, and "big box" supercenters. Most major shopping malls in North America are customers. Johnson Controls' products include a variety of control panels that manage HVAC equipment, transportation, airflow, lighting levels, energy consumption, and air quality—and even determine how many customers enter and exit a store. Behind the control systems is a Remote Operations Center for 24-hour monitoring: Many problems can be diagnosed and corrected online.

Johnson Controls has recently developed a product and service solution that targets the convenience store industry. The convenience store controller smartly manages a store's lighting, refrigeration, and HVAC, alerting store personnel to malfunctions. Building on its deep experience in working with large grocery chains, Johnson Controls can demonstrate to a convenience store chain how the system reduces energy costs, prevents food spoilage, improves occupant comfort, and lowers the cost of maintenance.

Discussion Questions

1. Outline the advertising strategy Johnson Controls might follow to promote the convenience store controller. What benefits would you emphasize in the body of an ad?

2. Develop a list of keywords you would use in promoting the product through Google's Internet search advertising program.

---

[1]"Johnson Controls, Retail Industry Solutions," accessed at http://www.johnsoncontrols.com., November 5, 2005.

Account Management at YRC Worldwide: Choosing Customers Wisely

YRC Worldwide is a *Fortune* 500 company that provides a full range of transportation services for customers across all U.S. industry sectors. YRC's customers, which number more than 300,000, include industrial and consumer-goods manufacturers, large and small, as well as retailers, including those that operate on a regional or national scale. Whereas key account teams serve large corporate customers, YRC serves the majority of its customers through a network of local sales offices.

For example, in a metropolitan area, such as Seattle, Chicago, or Boston, account managers—working out of a fully staffed sales office and directed by a sales manager and area director—are assigned a particular section of the city and given responsibility for covering all of the customers within those boundaries. Depending on the concentration of business activity in an area, the number of potential customers that fall within an account manager's assigned territory might range from 300 to more than 1500. Of course, the transportation services each customer requires are unique— some need guaranteed, time-definite delivery service or expedited delivery, whereas others are looking for the lowest-cost route. Moreover, the products involved are equally diverse, ranging from appliances or heavy machinery to apparel, component parts, or specialty chemicals.

Given the large number of potential customers they cover, coupled with the unique shipping requirements that each can present, account managers must give special attention to the most promising prospects, reaching others only if time permits.

Discussion Question

1. Develop a list of criteria an account manager at YRC could use to evaluate the relative attractiveness of 600 potential customers and isolate the "top-100" prospects. Assume that you have full access to any company information, including past purchasing behavior, revenue and profit data, customer satisfaction reports, and a complete demographic profile of each customer organization.

Danaher Corporation[1]

Danaher Corporation, together with its subsidiaries, is a diversified manufacturer, housing more than 40 industrial brands. The portfolio of brands covers three segments. The professional instrumentation segment produces electronic, medical, and water test equipment. The industrial technology segment produces precision motors and controls as well as product-identification equipment. The tool and component division makes Sears' Craftsman line of hand tools, Matco tools for professional mechanics, as well as other store-branded tools.

Danaher's path to success rests on two fundamental building blocks: acquiring companies that succeed in attractive niche markets and then effectively integrating them into the larger organization to maximize potential efficiencies. Included among its stable of brands is Fluke, the leader in handheld electronic test equipment; Leica Microsystems, a producer of high-end microscopes; Tektronix, the leader for high-precision oscilloscopes used in telecom networking; and Sybron Dental, a producer of light equipment for the professional dental market.

By executing the principles of the Danaher Business System (DBS), Danaher consistently delivers higher operating margins and stronger cash flows than industry peers. DBS basically centers on the lean manufacturing methods and quality improvement that manufacturers have used for years. However, Danaher was one of the earliest U.S. companies to embrace the philosophy and has been devoted to making it pay off for over 25 years.

The following description puts the DBS into focus:

> In a typical Danaher factory, floors are covered with strips of tape indicating where everything should be, from the biggest machine to the humblest trash can. Managers determine the most efficient place for everything so a worker won't have to walk an extra few yards to pick up a tool, for instance. The lean attitude permeates the culture of Danaher—only 40 people work in the Washington, D.C. corporate headquarters, at a company of 40,000.[2]

Discussion Question

1. In line with DBS, can Danaher apply a common set of marketing performance metrics across its diverse businesses, or does each business and niche market (for example, dentists versus health scientists or mechanics) require a more carefully tailored set of metrics? Explain.

---

[1]Daniel Holland, "The Beckman Acquisition Provides an Opportunity for Danaher Business System to Shine," Morningstar, Inc., July 21, 2011, pp. 1–2, accessed at http://www.morningstar.com on July 26, 2011.

[2]Brian Hindo, "A Dynamo Called Danaher," *Business Week*, February 19, 2007, p. 2, accessed at http://www.businessweek.com on July 26, 2011.

NAME INDEX

SUBJECT INDEX